CONSUMER GUIDE®

1995 CARS

CONTENTS

CONSUMER GUIDE®

INTRODUCTION

1995 Cars covers more than 150 passenger cars, minivans, and sport-utility vehicles. Major changes for 1995, key features, and latest available prices are included for each model, along with ratings for the specific model tested by the auto editors of Consumer Guide®.

To help readers compare direct competitors, vehicles are divided into 10 model groups based on their size, price, and market position. A complete list of model groups, including vehicles not covered in this issue, follows the Shopping Tips. Each report lists the model group to which the vehicle belongs and mentions similar vehicles built from the same design.

How Cars Are Rated

The Rating Guide with each report has numerical ratings in 16 categories. These ratings apply only to the vehicle as it was tested by the editors. For example, the ratings for the Ford Contour apply only to the SE model, which has a standard V-6 engine and was tested with the optional anti-lock brakes (ABS). A Contour without ABS or the V-6 engine may not score as highly in braking or acceleration. The chart below the Rating Guide lists major specifications for the vehicle that was tested.

In addition to the ratings, the editors have selected Best Buys in each of the 10 model groups as the best overall choices. In some groups, there are models labeled Recommended and Budget Buy that also are worthy of attention. Road test results play a major role in the editors' decisions. Other factors include price, cost of ownership, reputation for reliability and durability, warranties, and safety features.

Price Information

The latest available prices are provided for all models (and optional equipment) in this issue. In most cases, this includes dealer invoice prices and our estimated fair price. In some cases, only suggested retail prices were available. With some models that hadn't yet gone on sale when this book was printed (such as the Nissan Sentra), no prices were available.

Two federal taxes affect car prices. First, a gas-guzzler tax is levied on cars that attain less than 22.5 mpg in combined city/highway mileage based on EPA estimates. Some manufacturers include the gas-guzzler tax in the base prices; others list it separately. Guzzler taxes range from $1000 to more than $5000, so they can have a substantial impact on the purchase price.

Second, a 10 percent "luxury tax" is levied on cars selling for more than $32,000. The tax applies only to the amount over $32,000, so a car that sells for $38,000 will carry a tax of $600 and one that sells for $50,000 will be hit with an $1800 tax. The tax applies to the *transaction* or sale price of the vehicle, not the suggested retail price. In addition, the tax is figured on the full purchase price before any trade-in value is deducted.

The dealer invoice prices are what the dealer pays the manufacturer for the car, including its factory- or port-installed options. The dealer's cost of preparing a car for delivery to the consumer is included in the invoice price of all domestic cars. On some imported vehicles, this cost may not be included in the dealer invoice. In most cases, the destination charge is not included in either the suggested retail or dealer invoice prices, so it must be added to the total cost of the vehicle.

The fair prices listed in this book are estimates based on national market conditions for each model. Since market conditions can vary greatly in different parts of the country, the fair prices should only be used as a guide. If possible, it's best to price the same car at three or more dealers to get a better idea of the fair price in your area.

Fair prices aren't listed for some models because of insufficient information about market conditions for that particular vehicle.

While we have done all we can to see that the prices in this issue are accurate, car companies are free to change their prices at any time. Most car companies have raised their prices more than once during recent model years.

However, many dealers routinely tell our readers that the prices we publish are incorrect so they can eliminate dealer-invoice price from consideration. Once they accomplish that, then they're back in the driver's seat on price negotiations.

If a dealer claims our prices are incorrect or the information in this issue doesn't match what you see in showrooms, contact us and we'll do our best to help you out.

Advertising fees are not included in the price lists because they vary greatly in different parts of the country and not all dealers try to charge their customers for advertising. We think it's unfair for consumers to reimburse dealers for their advertising expenses, so we strongly suggest you argue against paying such a fee. It's their cost of doing business, not yours.

The editors invite your questions and comments. Address them to:

Consumer Guide®
7373 N. Cicero Ave.
Lincolnwood, IL 60646

KEY TO SPECIFICATIONS

Dimensions and capacities are supplied by the manufacturers. **Body types: notchback** = coupe or sedan with a separate trunk; **hatchback** = coupe or sedan with a rear liftgate. **Wheelbase** = distance between the front and rear wheels. **Curb weight** = weight of base models, not including optional equipment. **Engine types: ohv** = overhead valve; **ohc** = overhead camshaft; **dohc** = dual overhead camshafts; **I** = inline cylinders; **V** = cylinders in V configuration; **flat** = horizontally opposed cylinders. **Engine size, (l/cu. in.)** = liters/cubic inches. **Rpm** = revolutions per minute. **Brakes: ABS** = anti-lock braking system. **NA** = not available.

SHOPPING TIPS

Before you venture out to test drive and compare some of the new models, here are some suggestions to get you started on the right road:

● Determine how much you are willing to pay—or can afford to pay. If you plan on buying a car (instead of leasing) you should shop for a loan at a bank or other lending institution before you shop for a car. It's better to figure out how much you can afford at a bank than in a dealer's showroom, where they can juggle numbers faster than you can count.

● Decide which vehicle or type of vehicle best suits your needs and pocketbook. If you're single and seldom carry more than one passenger, a small car or even a 2-seater can be perfect. If you're married and have three children, you should be looking at larger cars or minivans.

● If you have an old car you intend to sell, you'll almost always get more money by selling it yourself instead of trading it in. Dealers want to make money on your old car, so they'll only give you wholesale value or less. You might be able to sell it for close to its retail value, which can easily put hundreds of dollars into your pocket.

Showroom Strategies

If you intend to buy a new vehicle instead of leasing one, here are some suggestions for planning your shopping strategy:

● There are no formulas for calculating a "good deal." You can't just "knock 10 percent off the sticker." It all depends on supply and demand for a particular model in your area and how much competition there is among dealers.

● Don't tell a car salesman how much you're willing to pay. Your price might be higher than what others are paying. Even if it's right on target, a salesman might reject it by saying, "We couldn't possibly sell it for that." It's their job to price the products they sell. It's your privilege to accept or reject their price.

● Once you've settled on a car, shop at least three dealers—more if you can—to compare prices on the same model with the same equipment. Let them know you're comparison shopping and that you'll buy from the dealer who gives you the lowest price and the best treatment.

● Get written price quotes that are good next week, not just today. If a dealer won't give you a price in writing, take your business elsewhere. They're not being straight with you if they offer you a verbal quote that's "good for today only."

Take your time and think about it at home. Don't be pressured into making a snap decision in the showroom.

● Don't put a deposit on a car just to get a price quote or a test drive. Dealers want to get a deposit because then you've made a commitment to them and you're less likely to keep shopping. Go to another dealer instead.

● Don't shop for a monthly payment. Dealers will try to convince you to buy a car you can't afford by stretching the payments from 48 months to 60 months. That lowers your monthly payment, but it means you'll pay more interest and be in hock longer.

For example, if you borrow $15,000 for 48 months at eight percent interest, you'll pay $366 per month, or $17,568 in total.

If you borrow $15,000 for 60 months you'll likely pay a higher interest rate, say, 8.5 percent. Your monthly payment drops to $308.25, but you'll pay $18,495 over the 5-year life of the loan. That's $927 more in interest than you'll pay on a 4-year loan.

● Keep your trade-in out of the new-car price. If you're thinking about trading in your old vehicle, get a written trade-in value *after* you settle on a price for the new car.

When the dealer asks if you're trading in your old car, tell him "Maybe. We can talk about that later." Some dealers will try to lure you with the offer of a high trade-in allowance and then inflate the price of the new vehicle.

"One-Price" Models

If you're uneasy—or terrified—about negotiating a price from a dealer, then shop for a "one-price" model, such as a Ford Escort or a Saturn, or go to dealers that advertise "no-dicker" sales practices. "One-price" isn't necessarily the lowest price for a particular car, but it can reduce the stress and let you concentrate on finding the model that best meets your needs.

In addition to Ford and Saturn, Oldsmobile, Buick, Chevrolet, Mercury, and others this year offer one-price and so-called "value-priced" models that typically have more standard features for less money than a base model.

For example, the Buick LeSabre Custom, the base model, has a list price of $21,735 and a destination charge of $585. The value-priced LeSabre Custom Select Series comes with a rear defogger, cassette player, cruise control, alloy wheels and other features that would cost $1161 as a regular option package, and it includes the destination charge for a total price of $20,995, or $2486 less than a comparable Custom model.

Lease Instead of Buy?

Leasing has become a popular alternative to buying as tax laws have changed, eliminating deductions for interest on car loans. Also, prices of new cars have soared to where many people can no longer afford to buy.

Recent estimates indicate that leases account for about 25 percent of new car sales overall and well over 50 percent of luxury models that cost $30,000 or more.

Is leasing right for you? It depends on your particular financial situation, so sit down with an accountant or tax adviser for a heart-to-heart talk on whether leasing is the best way to go. Some people still buy simply because they're more comfortable with "owning" a vehicle than "renting" one. However, some financial advisers argue that most advantages to owning a car have disappeared, making leasing more attractive.

Here are some guidelines to help you decide whether you should lease or buy:

● One of leasing's major advantages is that a large down payment isn't needed, though some leases require a substantial initial payment (often called a "capital cost reduction"). Also, monthly lease payments are generally lower than the monthly loan payment for an equivalent car.

When you buy a car, lenders typically want a down payment of at least 20 percent. With the average price of a new car around $18,000, that requires $4500 in cash or trade-in value on a used car. If you don't have that much, then leasing might be a better bet.

● The major disadvantage to leasing is that unless you eventually buy a car, you'll always be making a monthly payment. At the end of a lease you have the option of giving it back to the leasing company or buying it. Either way, you're going to have to dig into your pocket again to keep a car in your driveway.

Think ahead two or three years. Will your financial situation allow you to lease another new car or take out a loan to buy one?

● While the monthly payments may be lower on a lease, in the long run it is usually cheaper to buy if you keep cars five years or longer. For example, if you pay off a car loan in four years and keep the car another three years, your only expenses once the car is paid for will be for maintenance and repairs.

If your car needs few repairs—and that can be a big "if"—then you'll be thousands of dollars ahead because you make a monthly payment.

● On the other hand, would you rather drive a 7-year-old car or a much newer one? A 2- or 3-year lease gives you the option of having a new car more often. The car you drive will always be under warranty and you don't have the hassle of selling or trading in an old car. After two or three years, you simply turn it in to the leasing agent.

● Leasing used to be cheaper than buying for those who claimed their car as a business expense because of tax advantages. Tax laws have changed so the advantages may be greatly reduced for some people.

How do you find out? Talk to your accountant or financial adviser—not the guy next door. Because everyone has a different situation, leasing can be a great deal for your next-door neighbor but of no real benefit to you.

Read the Fine Print

If you're enticed by leasing ads that tout "No money down, $299 a month" for a $25,000 car, read the fine print. It should explain some of the following:

● Most leases allow 15,000 miles a year. Over 15,000 miles, you'll pay a penalty of 10 to 15 cents a mile.

● On most leases, you have to pay up front the first month's payment and a refundable security deposit.

● Many states require that the lessee—that's you—pay sales tax on the full suggested retail price of the car. If the sales tax is eight percent in your area and you're leasing a $30,000 car, that's $2400 you have to pay. You usually have the option of rolling the sales tax into your monthly payment.

In addition, if you purchase the car at the end of the lease, you'll probably have to pay sales tax on that amount. Check your local tax laws.

● Early termination and purchase options: Before signing, learn whether you can terminate the lease early and how much of a penalty you must pay. It might cost thousands of dollars to terminate a lease.

● End-of-lease costs: You'll be liable for "excessive wear" or may be charged for having the car prepped for resale. It pays to take good care of a leased car so it passes inspection when you turn it in.

MODEL GROUPS

Subcompact Cars
Chevrolet Cavalier
Dodge Neon
Eagle Summit
Ford Aspire
Ford Escort
Geo Metro
Geo Prizm
Honda Civic
Hyundai Accent
Hyundai Elantra
Kia Sephia
Mazda Protege
Mercury Tracer
Mitsubishi Mirage
Nissan Sentra
Plymouth Neon
Pontiac Sunfire
Saturn Sedan/Wagon
Subaru Impreza
Suzuki Swift
Toyota Corolla
Toyota Tercel
Volkswagen Golf/Jetta

Compact Cars
Buick Skylark
Chevrolet Corsica
Dodge Spirit
Ford Contour
Mazda 626
Mercury Mystique
Mitsubishi Galant
Nissan Altima
Oldsmobile Achieva
Plymouth Acclaim
Pontiac Grand Am
Subaru Legacy
Toyota Camry
Volkswagen Passat

Mid-size Cars
Buick Century
Buick Regal
Chrysler Cirrus
Chevrolet Lumina/Monte Carlo
Dodge Stratus

Ford Taurus
Ford Thunderbird
Honda Accord
Hyundai Sonata
Mercury Cougar
Mercury Sable
Oldsmobile Cutlass Ciera
Oldsmobile Cutlass Supreme
Pontiac Grand Prix

Full-size Cars
Buick LeSabre
Buick Roadmaster
Chevrolet Caprice/Impala SS
Chrysler Concorde
Dodge Intrepid
Eagle Vision
Ford Crown Victoria
Mercury Grand Marquis
Oldsmobile Eighty Eight
Pontiac Bonneville
Toyota Avalon

Premium Coupes
Acura Legend
Audi Cabriolet
BMW 8-Series
Buick Riviera
Cadillac Eldorado
Jaguar XJS
Lexus SC 300/400
Lincoln Mark VIII
Mercedes-Benz E320
Mercedes-Benz SL-Class
Mercedes-Benz S500/600

Premium Sedans
Acura Legend
Audi A6/S6
Audi 90
BMW 3-Series
BMW 5-Series
BMW 7-Series
Buick Park Avenue
Cadillac De Ville/Concours
Cadillac Fleetwood
Cadillac Seville

Chrysler New Yorker/LHS
Infiniti G20
Infiniti J30
Infiniti Q45
Jaguar XJ Sedan
Lexus ES 300
Lexus GS 300
Lexus LS 400
Lincoln Continental
Lincoln Town Car
Mazda Millenia
Mazda 929
Mercedes-Benz C-Class
Mercedes-Benz E-Class
Mercedes-Benz S-Class
Mitsubishi Diamante
Nissan Maxima
Oldsmobile Aurora
Oldsmobile Ninety Eight
Saab 900
Saab 9000
Volvo 850
Volvo 940/960

Sports Coupes
Acura Integra
Chevrolet Beretta
Chrysler LeBaron
Chrysler Sebring
Dodge Avenger
Eagle Talon
Ford Probe
Honda del Sol
Honda Prelude
Hyundai Scoupe
Mazda MX-3
Mazda MX-6
Mitsubishi Eclipse
Nissan 200SX
Nissan 240SX
Saturn SC1/SC2
Toyota Celica
Toyota Paseo
Volkswagen Cabrio

Sports and GT Cars
Acura NSX
Chevrolet Camaro
Chevrolet Corvette
Dodge Stealth
Dodge Viper

Ford Mustang
Mazda Miata
Mazda RX-7
Mitsubishi 3000GT
Nissan 300ZX
Pontiac Firebird
Subaru SVX
Toyota MR2
Toyota Supra

Sport-Utility Vehicles
Chevrolet Blazer
Ford Explorer
Geo Tracker
GMC Jimmy
Honda Passport
Isuzu Rodeo
Isuzu Trooper
Jeep Cherokee
Jeep Grand Cherokee
Jeep Wrangler
Kia Sportage
Land Rover Defender 90
Land Rover Discovery
Mitsubishi Montero
Nissan Pathfinder
Range Rover County LWB
Range Rover 4.0 SE
Suzuki Samurai
Suzuki Sidekick
Toyota Land Cruiser
Toyota 4Runner

Minivans
Chevrolet Astro
Chevrolet Lumina Minivan
Chrysler Town & Country
Dodge Caravan
Ford Aerostar
Ford Windstar
GMC Safari
Honda Odyssey
Mazda MPV
Mercury Villager
Nissan Quest
Oldsmobile Silhouette
Plymouth Voyager
Pontiac Trans Sport
Toyota Previa
Volkswagen EuroVan

ACURA INTEGRA — `RECOMMENDED`

Built in Japan.

Acura Integra LS 3-door

SPORTS COUPE

The main news for the entry-level Acura line is the addition of luxury-oriented Special Edition versions of the LS 3-door hatchback coupe and 4-door notchback sedan. Other changes include a standard power moonroof for the LS sedan and optional leather interior trim for the sporty GS-R coupe and sedan. Returning to complete Integra's lineup are an LS coupe and base RS coupe and sedan. The new Special Edition models include standard leather, body-color side moldings, and 195/55R15 tires. In addition, the coupe gets a rear spoiler like the GS-R's. The front-drive Integra is based on the Honda Civic platform. GS-R models have a 1.8-liter 4-cylinder engine with dual overhead camshafts and 170 horsepower. Other models use a different 1.8-liter engine rated at 142 horsepower. A 5-speed transmission is standard on all models and a 4-speed automatic is optional on all but the GS-R. Dual air bags are standard across the board and anti-lock brakes are standard on all models except the RS (where they're not available). Both Integra engines rev like crazy but lack enough low-speed torque to perform with much gusto with the automatic transmission. We timed a GS-R at 7.6 seconds to 60 mph and an LS with the 5-speed at 8.3 seconds. Fuel economy also is commendable with the 5-speed. Expect slower progress and lower fuel economy with the automatic, which also shifts harshly in hard acceleration. All models have commendable cornering ability and sharp steering, but the ride is bouncy on 3-door versions. The hatchback has plenty of room for medium-size people in the front seats, but only pre-teens fit in the cramped back seat.

Acura Integra prices are on page 240.

ACURA INTEGRA LS

Rating Guide	1	2	3	4	5
Performance					
Acceleration	▓▓▓▓▓▓▓▓▓▓▓▓▓▓▓▓				
Economy	▓▓▓▓▓▓▓▓▓▓▓▓				
Driveability	▓▓▓▓▓▓▓▓▓▓▓▓				
Ride	▓▓▓▓▓▓▓▓▓▓▓▓				
Steering/handling	▓▓▓▓▓▓▓▓▓▓▓▓				
Braking	▓▓▓▓▓▓▓▓▓▓▓▓▓▓▓▓▓▓▓▓				
Noise	▓▓▓▓▓▓▓▓▓▓▓▓				
Accommodations					
Driver seating	▓▓▓▓▓▓▓▓▓▓▓▓				
Instruments/controls	▓▓▓▓▓▓▓▓▓▓▓▓▓				
Visibility	▓▓▓▓▓▓▓▓▓▓▓▓				
Room/comfort	▓▓▓▓▓▓▓▓▓▓				
Entry/exit	▓▓▓▓▓▓▓▓▓▓				
Cargo room	▓▓▓▓▓▓▓▓▓▓▓▓				
Workmanship					
Exterior	▓▓▓▓▓▓▓▓▓▓▓▓▓				
Interior	▓▓▓▓▓▓▓▓▓▓▓▓▓				
Value	▓▓▓▓▓▓▓▓▓▓▓▓▓				

Total Points...**58**

Specifications

Body type	3-door hatchback	Engine type	dohc I-4
Wheelbase (in.)	101.2	Engine size (l/cu. in.)	1.8/112
Overall length (in.)	172.4	Horsepower @ rpm	142 @ 6300
Overall width (in.)	67.5	Torque @ rpm	127 @ 5200
Overall height (in.)	52.6	Transmission	manual/5-sp.
Curb weight (lbs.)	2529	Drive wheels	front
Seating capacity	4	Brakes, F/R	disc/disc (ABS)
Front head room (in.)	38.5	Tire size	195/60HR14
Max. front leg room (in.)	42.7	Fuel tank capacity (gal.)	13.2
Rear head room (in.)	35.0	EPA city/highway mpg	25/31
Min. rear leg room (in.)	28.1	Test mileage (mpg)	24.8
Cargo volume (cu. ft.)	13.3		

Warranties The entire car is covered for 4 years/50,000 miles. Body perforation rust is covered for 5 years/unlimited miles.

Rating scale 5=Exceptional; 4=Above average; 3=Average; 2=Below average; 1=Poor

ACURA LEGEND ———

Built in Japan.

Acura Legend Sedan GS

PREMIUM SEDAN/COUPE

Acura's flagship line is a carryover for 1995. Last redesigned for 1991, the front-drive Legend is scheduled to be redesigned next year. Models comprise L, LS, and GS 4-door sedans and L and LS 2-door coupes. All have a 3.2-liter V-6 engine. In the L and LS sedans it packs 200 horsepower and in the GS sedan and both coupes it has 230 horsepower. A 4-speed automatic transmission is standard on the LS sedan and optional on other models. The L sedan has a standard 5-speed manual; both coupes and the GS sedan have a standard 6-speed transmission. Traction control is standard on the LS coupe and GS sedan, and not available on the others. All models have dual air bags and anti-lock brakes. As its prices have escalated and the competition has intensified, Legend sales have declined. Legend also has been hampered by its lack of a V-8 engine, which is available in the BMW 5-Series and other rivals. Even so, performance is lively in all models; 0-60 mph takes eight seconds or less. Fuel economy in our tests has ranged from 16-18 mpg in urban driving to low 20s on the highway; premium gas is required. Legend handles and rides like a sports car. The suspension provides a stable ride, but it can be harsh and abrupt on rough surfaces. The sedan provides decent room for five adults, though four is the practical limit on long trips. The coupes have a tight rear seat and, thus, are more "2+2s" than full 4-seaters. Both body styles have an attractive dashboard with convenient controls. Legend isn't the outstanding dollar value it once was, but dealers are discounting to spark sales, so you should be able to get one for well below retail. In addition, Acura is heavily subsidizing leases.

Acura Legend prices are on page 241.

ACURA LEGEND SEDAN GS

Rating Guide	1	2	3	4	5
Performance					
Acceleration					▮
Economy	▮				
Driveability				▮	
Ride				▮	
Steering/handling				▮	
Braking					▮
Noise				▮	
Accommodations					
Driver seating				▮	
Instruments/controls				▮	
Visibility				▮	
Room/comfort				▮	
Entry/exit				▮	
Cargo room				▮	
Workmanship					
Exterior					▮
Interior				▮	
Value				▮	

Total Points..**62**

Specifications

Body type ....4-door notchback
Wheelbase (in.) 114.6
Overall length (in.) 194.9
Overall width (in.) 71.3
Overall height (in.) 55.1
Curb weight (lbs.) 3516
Seating capacity 5
Front head room (in.) 38.5
Max. front leg room (in.) 42.7
Rear head room (in.) 36.5
Min. rear leg room (in.) 33.5
Cargo volume (cu. ft.).............14.8

Engine type ....ohc V-6
Engine size (l/cu. in.)........3.2/196
Horsepower @ rpm ...230 @ 6200
Torque @ rpm ....206 @ 5000
Transmission...................auto/4-sp.
Drive wheels ....front
Brakes, F/R...........disc/disc (ABS)
Tire size....................215/55VR16
Fuel tank capacity (gal.) 18.0
EPA city/highway mpg 18/23
Test mileage (mpg) 17.6

Warranties The entire car is covered for 4 years/50,000 miles. Body perforation rust is covered for 5 years/unlimited miles.

Rating scale 5=Exceptional; 4=Above average; 3=Average; 2=Below average; 1=Poor

AUDI A6/S6

Built in Germany.

Audi A6 Quattro 4-door

PREMIUM SEDAN

The A6 is last year's Audi 100 with a mild restyling and a new name, while the S6 is last year's S4, also with revised styling. The A6 is available as a 4-door sedan and a 5-door wagon with either front-wheel drive or permanent all-wheel drive (called Quattro). The sportier S6 comes only as a sedan with AWD. All models have new front and rear fascias, a new hood, and new ellipsoidal headlights. The S6 also has new wheelwell flares and twin exhaust pipes. The only engine for the A6 is a 172-horsepower 2.8-liter V-6 that mates to either a 5-speed manual or 4-speed automatic on the sedan. The wagon comes only with the automatic. The S6 has a turbocharged 227-horsepower 2.2-liter 5-cylinder engine and comes only with a 5-speed manual. Anti-lock brakes and dual air bags are standard on all models. Audi aims the A6 at the Acura Legend, and though it beats its target in interior room and cargo capacity, it doesn't match the Legend in acceleration or overall value. Other Japanese competitors such as the Infiniti J30 and Lexus GS 300 also rate higher in some key areas, such as acceleration. The A6's 2.8-liter V-6 doesn't produce much torque at low speeds, so it requires a heavy throttle foot for lively pickup. Handling and roadholding are commendable, but the A6 has a stiff, busy ride that transmits nearly every bump to the passenger compartment. The S6 is quick, has an even harder ride, and costs as much as rival sedans that boast V-8 engines. Prices have been cut nearly $5000 on the A6 and nearly $4000 on the S6 this year. In addition, Audi throws in free maintenance for the first 3 years/50,000 miles.

Audi A6/S6 prices are on page 242.

AUDI A6 QUATTRO

Rating Guide	1	2	3	4	5
Performance					
Acceleration	▓▓▓▓▓▓				
Economy	▓▓▓▓				
Driveability	▓▓▓▓▓▓▓▓				
Ride	▓▓▓▓▓▓				
Steering/handling	▓▓▓▓▓▓				
Braking	▓▓▓▓▓▓▓▓				
Noise	▓▓▓▓▓▓				
Accommodations					
Driver seating	▓▓▓▓▓▓▓▓				
Instruments/controls	▓▓▓▓▓▓▓▓				
Visibility	▓▓▓▓▓▓▓				
Room/comfort	▓▓▓▓▓▓▓				
Entry/exit	▓▓▓▓▓▓▓				
Cargo room	▓▓▓▓▓▓				
Workmanship					
Exterior	▓▓▓▓▓▓▓▓				
Interior	▓▓▓▓▓▓▓▓▓▓				
Value	▓▓▓▓▓▓				

Total Points **60**

Specifications

Body type ....4-door notchback	Engine type ....ohc V-6
Wheelbase (in.) 105.8	Engine size (l/cu. in.) 2.8/169
Overall length (in.) 192.6	Horsepower @ rpm ...172 @ 5500
Overall width (in.) 70.0	Torque @ rpm ....184 @ 3000
Overall height (in.) 56.3	Transmission ....auto/4-sp.
Curb weight (lbs.) 3363	Drive wheels ....all
Seating capacity 5	Brakes, F/R ....disc/disc (ABS)
Front head room (in.) 38.4	Tire size 195/65HR15
Max. front leg room (in.) 42.2	Fuel tank capacity (gal.) 21.1
Rear head room (in.) 37.6	EPA city/highway mpg 19/24
Min. rear leg room (in.) 34.8	Test mileage (mpg) ....NA
Cargo volume (cu. ft.) 16.8	

Warranties The entire car is covered for 3 years/50,000 miles. Body perforation rust is covered for 10 years/unlimited miles.

Rating scale 5=Exceptional; 4=Above average; 3=Average; 2=Below average; 1=Poor

AUDI 90/CABRIOLET

Built in Germany.

Audi Cabriolet

PREMIUM SEDAN/COUPE

The biggest change this fall is the addition of a Sport90 model with a lowered suspension, sport seats, a cloth interior, and 5-spoke alloy wheels. Both the new Sport90 and returning 90 models are available only as 4-door notchback sedans. The Audi Cabriolet is a 2-door convertible based on a shortened version of the 90 platform. By next fall, Audi plans to replace the 90 with a new sedan called the A4 that will be built from a different design. The Cabriolet, however, will continue in its present configuration. Both 90 models and the Cabriolet are powered by a 172-horsepower 2.8-liter V-6 engine. The standard transmission on the 90 and Sport90 is a 5-speed manual; a 4-speed automatic is optional. The Cabriolet comes only with the 4-speed automatic. Dual air bags and anti-lock brakes are standard across the line. All models have standard front-wheel drive. Audi's permanently engaged all-wheel-drive system, called Quattro, is optional on the 90 and Sport90. Though these cars have some attractive features, they haven't been big sellers in the "near-luxury" market, which is dominated by Japanese brands such as Acura and Lexus. Audi is trying to remedy this by cutting prices $2000 to $3000 this year below comparable 1994 models. The V-6 engine runs smoothly, but the automatic transmission drains its ability to quickly deliver bursts of speed in urban driving. Also, the ride is too firm for pock-marked urban roads and there's lots of tire and suspension noise. The Cabriolet looks great but suffers from too much body shake and flex on bumpy roads for a convertible that's priced in the $40,000 range. Audi dealers should be discounting and offering cut-rate leases.

Audi 90/Cabriolet prices are on page 243.

AUDI CABRIOLET

Rating Guide	1	2	3	4	5
Performance					
Acceleration	▭▭▭▭▭▭▭▭				
Economy	▭▭▭▭▭				
Driveability	▭▭▭▭▭▭▭▭▭				
Ride	▭▭▭▭▭▭				
Steering/handling	▭▭▭▭▭▭▭				
Braking	▭▭▭▭▭▭▭▭▭▭				
Noise	▭▭▭▭▭▭				
Accommodations					
Driver seating	▭▭▭▭▭▭▭▭				
Instruments/controls	▭▭▭▭▭▭▭▭				
Visibility	▭▭▭▭▭▭				
Room/comfort	▭▭▭▭▭▭				
Entry/exit	▭▭▭▭▭▭▭				
Cargo room	▭▭▭▭				
Workmanship					
Exterior	▭▭▭▭▭▭▭▭				
Interior	▭▭▭▭▭▭				
Value	▭▭▭▭▭▭				

Total Points...**53**

Specifications

Body type ....2-door convertible		Engine type ....ohc V-6
Wheelbase (in.) 100.6		Engine size (l/cu. in.)........2.8/169
Overall length (in.)................176.0		Horsepower @ rpm ...172 @ 5500
Overall width (in.) 67.6		Torque @ rpm ....184 @ 3000
Overall height (in.).................54.3		Transmission.................auto/4-sp.
Curb weight (lbs.) 3494		Drive wheels ....front
Seating capacity.........................4		Brakes, F/R..........disc/disc (ABS)
Front head room (in.) 38.3		Tire size 195/65HR15
Max. front leg room (in.) 40.7		Fuel tank capacity (gal.).........17.4
Rear head room (in.) 36.4		EPA city/highway mpg 18/26
Min. rear leg room (in.)..........26.5		Test mileage (mpg) 20.3
Cargo volume (cu. ft.)..............6.6		

Warranties The entire car is covered for 3 years/50,000 miles. Body perforation rust is covered for 10 years/unlimited miles.

Rating scale 5=Exceptional; 4=Above average; 3=Average; 2=Below average; 1=Poor

BMW 3-SERIES

Built in Germany and Greer, S.C.

BMW 325i

PREMIUM SEDAN

New Premium and Sports option packages are the main additions this year on BMW's smallest model. A small number of 3-Series sedans sold in the U.S. this year will be built at BMW's new plant in South Carolina. A high-performance M3 coupe bowed last spring with a 240-horsepower 3.0-liter 6-cylinder engine. The M3 comes only with a 5-speed manual transmission. The other 3-Series models are basically unchanged. The 318i sedan, 318is coupe, and 318i convertible use a 1.8-liter 4-cylinder with 138 horsepower; the 325i, 325is, and 325i convertible use a 2.5-liter 6-cylinder with 189 horses. All come with a standard 5-speed manual transmission or optional 4-speed automatic. New for 1995 are Premium Package option groups that for the first time make leather upholstery, heated seats, and a tilt steering wheel available on 4-cylinder models and wood interior trim on the 325 models. The Sports Package is now available on the 318 as well as the 325 models. It has a firmer suspension, alloy wheels, and a limited-slip differential. All models have standard anti-lock brakes and dual air bags. BMW's 325 models have outstanding overall performance, while the less-expensive 4-cylinder 318 models are geared toward driving enthusiasts who prefer a manual transmission. Where all 3-Series cars shine is in their sporty handling. They devour twisting roads with aplomb and have fluid, precise steering. Though the suspension is firm, ride quality is better than on many cars with softer suspensions. Without the optional traction control, however, these rear-drive cars demand caution in rain and snow because they can't match the traction of front-drive rivals.

BMW 3-Series prices are on page 244.

BMW 325i

Rating Guide	1	2	3	4	5
Performance					
Acceleration	▓▓▓▓▓▓▓▓ (≈4)				
Economy	▓▓▓▓ (≈2.5)				
Driveability	▓▓▓▓▓▓▓▓ (≈4)				
Ride	▓▓▓▓▓▓▓ (≈3.5)				
Steering/handling	▓▓▓▓▓▓▓▓ (≈4)				
Braking	▓▓▓▓▓▓▓▓▓▓ (≈5)				
Noise	▓▓▓▓▓▓ (≈3)				
Accommodations					
Driver seating	▓▓▓▓▓▓▓ (≈3.5)				
Instruments/controls	▓▓▓▓▓▓▓▓ (≈4)				
Visibility	▓▓▓▓▓▓▓ (≈3.5)				
Room/comfort	▓▓▓▓▓▓▓ (≈3.5)				
Entry/exit	▓▓▓▓▓▓▓ (≈3.5)				
Cargo room	▓▓▓▓▓▓▓ (≈3.5)				
Workmanship					
Exterior	▓▓▓▓▓▓▓▓ (≈4)				
Interior	▓▓▓▓▓▓▓▓ (≈4)				
Value	▓▓▓▓ (≈2.5)				

Total Points...60

Specifications

Body type ....4-door notchback	Engine type ....dohc I-6
Wheelbase (in.) 106.3	Engine size (l/cu. in.).........2.5/162
Overall length (in.)................174.5	Horsepower @ rpm ...189 @ 5900
Overall width (in.) 66.8	Torque @ rpm ....181 @ 4200
Overall height (in.) 54.8	Transmission ....manual/5-sp.
Curb weight (lbs.) 2866	Drive wheels ....rear
Seating capacity.........................5	Brakes, F/R ....disc/disc (ABS)
Front head room (in.) 37.8	Tire size 205/60HR15
Max. front leg room (in.) 40.9	Fuel tank capacity (gal.) 17.2
Rear head room (in.) 37.3	EPA city/highway mpg 19/28
Min. rear leg room (in.)...........34.1	Test mileage (mpg) 20.5
Cargo volume (cu. ft.).............15.4	

Warranties The entire car is covered for 4 years/50,000 miles. Body perforation rust is covered for 6 years/unlimited miles.

Rating scale 5=Exceptional; 4=Above average; 3=Average; 2=Below average; 1=Poor

BMW 5-SERIES

Built in Germany.

BMW 540i

PREMIUM SEDAN

A new 6-speed manual transmission for the top-line 540i sedan is the big change for BMW's mid-size model. The rear-drive 5-Series returns in 4-door sedan and 5-door Touring (station wagon) body styles. The 525i sedan and Touring come with a 189-horsepower 2.5-liter 6-cylinder engine. The sedan has a standard 5-speed manual transmission and an optional 4-speed automatic; the Touring comes only with the automatic. There are three V-8 models. The 530i sedan and Touring have a 3.0-liter V-8 with 215 horsepower. The 540i sedan has a 4.0-liter version with 282 horsepower. The 530i comes with a standard 5-speed manual and an optional 5-speed automatic. The 5-speed automatic is standard on the 530i Touring. The 6-speed manual is an extra-cost alternative to the standard 5-speed automatic on the 540i. With the 6-speed manual, the 540i adds 12-way power sport seats and a sport suspension. All models switch from V-rated tires (speeds up to 149 mph) to H-rated tires (speeds up to 129 mph) for higher EPA mileage. BMW sales suffered for a few years at the hands of Japanese and American rivals, but the German company has fought back with V-8s that move these cars back into the fast lane. The 525i and 525i Touring have the same enthusiast-oriented road manners as the V-8 models. However, their 6-cylinder engine trades somewhat higher mileage for a noticeable loss of acceleration, especially with the automatic transmission. The 5-Series models cover a broad price range of more than $10,000, and none is bargain-priced. Even so, BMW's current value-oriented strategy makes them much more competitive with rivals such as the Lexus LS 400 and Mercedes-Benz E-Class.

BMW 5-Series prices are on page 246.

BMW 540i

Rating Guide	1	2	3	4	5
Performance					
Acceleration					
Economy					
Driveability					
Ride					
Steering/handling					
Braking					
Noise					
Accommodations					
Driver seating					
Instruments/controls					
Visibility					
Room/comfort					
Entry/exit					
Cargo room					
Workmanship					
Exterior					
Interior					
Value					

Total Points...**61**

Specifications

Body type ....4-door notchback	Engine type......................dohc V-8
Wheelbase (in.) 108.7	Engine size (l/cu. in.)........4.0/243
Overall length (in.).................185.8	Horsepower @ rpm ...282 @ 5800
Overall width (in.) 68.9	Torque @ rpm ....295 @ 4500
Overall height (in.)...................55.6	Transmission.................auto/5-sp.
Curb weight (lbs.) 3804	Drive wheels ....rear
Seating capacity.........................5	Brakes, F/R...........disc/disc (ABS)
Front head room (in.) 36.9	Tire size 225/60HR15
Max. front leg room (in.) 41.6	Fuel tank capacity (gal.) 21.1
Rear head room (in.) 36.4	EPA city/highway mpg 17/25
Min. rear leg room (in.)...........37.0	Test mileage (mpg) 15.7
Cargo volume (cu. ft.).............16.2	

Warranties The entire car is covered for 4 years/50,000 miles. Body perforation rust is covered for 6 years/unlimited miles.

Rating scale 5=Exceptional; 4=Above average; 3=Average; 2=Below average; 1=Poor

BMW 7-SERIES

Built in Germany.

BMW 740i

PREMIUM SEDAN

BMW's flagship sedan is redesigned for 1995, with evolutionary styling that the company decribes as "dynamic elegance." A new 740i went on sale first in the fall and long-wheelbase 740iL and 750iL models are to arrive in early spring. Against the previous generation, the 1995 models are three to four inches longer in wheelbase and overall length, slightly wider and lower, and around 150 pounds heavier. The 740i and 740iL retain last year's 282-horsepower 4.0-liter V-8 engine and a 5-speed automatic transmission. The transmission has new electronic adaptive shift controls, which change shift points based on how the car is driven. The 750iL trades a 4-speed automatic for the 5-speed and exchanges a 5.0-liter V-12 for a more potent 5.4-liter version with 323 horsepower (up from 296). Besides standard anti-lock brakes and dual air bags, the new 7-Series has a "door-anchoring system" that BMW says "hooks" the trailing edges of the doors into the main body structure for more rigidity in a crash. After a crash, the doors are released so they can open. The new 740i is quieter, more comfortable, and even more enjoyable to drive than the old one. There's more passenger room and the seats are supportive and comfortable on long drives. The 740i has more exhaust and road noise than the Lexus LS 400, but is still quieter than most rivals at highway speeds. Though there's ample passing power on the highway, a heavy right foot is required to overcome stiff throttle resistance to induce the transmission to downshift. Overall, though, the new 740i is a formidable opponent for the LS 400. At $57,900 to start, it's also more reasonably priced than the rival Mercedes-Benz S-Class.

BMW 7-Series prices are on page 247.

BMW 740i (Preliminary)

Rating Guide	1	2	3	4	5
Performance					
Acceleration	||||||||||||||||||||||||||||||||||||		
Economy	|||||||||||||||				
Driveability	|||||||||||||||||||||||||||||||||||		
Ride	|||||||||||||||||||||||||||||||||		
Steering/handling	||||||||||||||||||||||||||||||||		
Braking	||||||||||||||||||||||||||||||||||||||		
Noise	||||||||||||||||||||||||||||||||||		
Accommodations					
Driver seating	|||||||||||||||||||||||||||||||||||||		
Instruments/controls	|||||||||||||||||||||||||||||||||||||||		
Visibility	||||||||||||||||||||||||||||||||||		
Room/comfort	|||||||||||||||||||||||||||||||||		
Entry/exit	|||||||||||||||||||||||||||||||||||		
Cargo room	||||||||||||||||||||||||||||||		
Workmanship					
Exterior	||||||||||||||||||||||||||||||||||||||||		
Interior	||||||||||||||||||||||||||||||||||||||||		
Value					
Total Points **64**					

Specifications

Body type ....4-door notchback	Engine type.....................dohc V-8
Wheelbase (in.) 115.4	Engine size (l/cu. in.).........4.0/243
Overall length (in.)...............196.2	Horsepower @ rpm ...282 @ 5800
Overall width (in.) 73.3	Torque @ rpm ....295 @ 4500
Overall height (in.) 56.5	Transmission..................auto/5-sp.
Curb weight (lbs.) 4145	Drive wheels ....rear
Seating capacity...........................5	Brakes, F/R...........disc/disc (ABS)
Front head room (in.) 37.7	Tire size 235/60HR16
Max. front leg room (in.) 41.9	Fuel tank capacity (gal.) 22.5
Rear head room (in.) 37.9	EPA city/highway mpg 16/24
Min. rear leg room (in.) 36.7	Test mileage (mpg) ....NA
Cargo volume (cu. ft.).............13.0	

Warranties The entire car is covered for 4 years/50,000 miles. Body perforation rust is covered for 6 years/unlimited miles.

Rating scale 5=Exceptional; 4=Above average; 3=Average; 2=Below average; 1=Poor

BUICK LE SABRE/ OLDSMOBILE EIGHTY EIGHT/ PONTIAC BONNEVILLE

✓ BEST BUY

Built in Flint and Orion, Mich.

Buick LeSabre Limited

FULL-SIZE

LeSabre, Buick's full-size, front-drive sedan, has new climate controls, a new family of radios, and optional steering-wheel controls for the stereo and climate system as its major changes this year. The similar Eighty Eight and Bonneville get a new standard engine and the Eighty Eight gains a supercharged V-6 as a new option. The new standard engine for the Eighty Eight and Bonneville is the Series II 3800 V-6, a 3.8-liter engine that produces 205 horsepower, 35 more than last year's version. A 225-horsepower supercharged 3.8-liter is a new option for the sporty Eighty Eight LSS. The supercharged engine already was optional on the Bonneville. The LeSabre retains a 170-horsepower version of the 3.8-liter V-6. All engines team with an electronic 4-speed automatic transmission that has new transmission fluid that doesn't need to be changed for 100,000 miles. Dual air bags and anti-lock brakes are standard on all models. These front-drive sedans are excellent choices among full-size cars. All three have ample passenger space and roomy trunks, plus acceleration that rivals V-8-powered cars. LeSabre and Eighty Eight are available as fully equipped "value-priced" models that come with additional standard features at hefty discounts that make them less expensive than some Japanese compacts. Though Pontiac has a more traditional pricing policy and more optional features, the Bonneville also is reasonably priced. The Chrysler LH sedans are roomier and have more daring styling, but the GM rivals are high-quality cars that can be equipped to suit a variety of driving needs.

Buick LeSabre prices are on page 251.
Oldsmobile Eighty Eight prices are on page 402.
Pontiac Bonneville prices are on page 412.

BUICK LE SABRE

Rating Guide	1	2	3	4	5
Performance					
Acceleration				▓	
Economy			▓		
Driveability					▓
Ride				▓	
Steering/handling			▓		
Braking					▓
Noise				▓	
Accommodations					
Driver seating				▓	
Instruments/controls				▓	
Visibility				▓	
Room/comfort				▓	
Entry/exit				▓	
Cargo room				▓	
Workmanship					
Exterior					▓
Interior				▓	
Value				▓	

Total Points...63

Specifications

Body type ....4-door notchback	Engine type ....ohv V-6
Wheelbase (in.) 110.8	Engine size (l/cu. in.)..........3.8/231
Overall length (in.) 200.0	Horsepower @ rpm ...170 @ 4800
Overall width (in.) 74.9	Torque @ rpm ....225 @ 3200
Overall height (in.) 55.7	Transmission.................auto/4-sp.
Curb weight (lbs.) 3449	Drive wheels ....front
Seating capacity 6	Brakes, F/R ....disc/drum (ABS)
Front head room (in.) 38.8	Tire size 205/70R15
Max. front leg room (in.) 42.5	Fuel tank capacity (gal.) 18.0
Rear head room (in.) 37.8	EPA city/highway mpg 19/29
Min. rear leg room (in.)...........40.4	Test mileage (mpg) 19.3
Cargo volume (cu. ft.).............17.1	

Warranties The entire car is covered for 3 years/36,000 miles. Body perforation rust is covered for 6 years/100,000 miles.

Rating scale 5=Exceptional; 4=Above average; 3=Average; 2=Below average; 1=Poor

BUICK PARK AVENUE/ ——— OLDSMOBILE NINETY EIGHT

Built in Wentzville, Mo., and Orion, Mich.

Buick Park Avenue

PREMIUM SEDAN

The Park Avenue and similar Ninety Eight have a more powerful base engine this year, the 3800 Series II. This is a 3.8-liter V-6 with 205 horsepower, 35 more than last year's version. A 225-horsepower supercharged 3.8-liter V-6 remains standard on Buick's top-of-the-line Park Avenue Ultra and optional on the Ninety Eight. Both engines team with an electronic 4-speed automatic transmission that has new transmission fluid that doesn't need to be changed for 100,000 miles under normal operating conditions. Park Avenue and Ninety Eight are built from the same design but have different styling. Oldsmobile is trimming models across its lineup this year, so the axe has fallen on last year's base Regency model. That leaves only the Regency Elite, but this year it comes in Series I and Series II equipment levels with a limited number of options for both. Dual air bags and anti-lock brakes are standard on all versions of these front-drive luxury sedans. Though the supercharged engine delivers decidedly stronger acceleration, the base 3800 Series II engine has ample power for most situations and returns better fuel economy. The supercharged engine also requires expensive premium gas. Both engines have seamless power delivery through General Motors' smooth 4-speed automatic transmission. Both Park Avenue and Ninety Eight have roomy interiors and spacious trunks, plus loads of comfort and convenience features. However, you can get the same amount of room and similar features for less money on the Buick LeSabre and Olds Eighty Eight.

Buick Park Avenue prices are on page 253.
Oldsmobile Ninety Eight prices are on page 403.

BUICK PARK AVENUE

Rating Guide	1	2	3	4	5
Performance					
Acceleration				▮	
Economy		▮			
Driveability					▮
Ride				▮	
Steering/handling			▮		
Braking				▮	
Noise				▮	
Accommodations					
Driver seating			▮		
Instruments/controls				▮	
Visibility			▮		
Room/comfort				▮	
Entry/exit				▮	
Cargo room				▮	
Workmanship					
Exterior					▮
Interior				▮	
Value			▮		

Total Points...62

Specifications

Body type ....4-door notchback	Engine ....ohv V-6
Wheelbase (in.) 110.8	Engine size (l/cu. in.)........3.8/231
Overall length (in.) 205.9	Horsepower @ rpm ...205 @ 5200
Overall width (in.) 74.1	Torque @ rpm ....230 @ 4000
Overall height (in.) 55.1	Transmission ....auto/4-sp.
Curb weight (lbs.) 3536	Drive wheels ....front
Seating capacity 6	Brakes, F/R ....disc/drum (ABS)
Front head room (in.) 38.8	Tire size 205/70R15
Max. front leg room (in.) 42.7	Fuel tank capacity (gal.) 18.0
Rear head room (in.) 37.8	EPA city/highway mpg 19/29
Min. rear leg room (in.)...........40.7	Test mileage (mpg) ....NA
Cargo volume (cu. ft.).............20.3	

Warranties The entire car is covered for 3 years/36,000 miles. Body perforation rust is covered for 6 years/100,000 miles.

Rating scale 5=Exceptional; 4=Above average; 3=Average; 2=Below average; 1=Poor

BUICK REGAL

Built in Canada.

Buick Regal Custom 4-door

MID-SIZE

Regal gets its most extensive interior revisions since it was redesigned for the 1988 model year, including a new dashboard with a passenger-side air bag and new seats. Regal gained a standard driver-side air bag last year. The new dashboard has larger analog gauges, a standard tachometer, and redesigned climate controls stacked on top of the radio in the center. The front-drive Regal comes in two body styles. The 4-door sedan comes in Custom, Gran Sport and Limited price levels, and the 2-door coupe comes in Custom and Gran Sport price levels. All models wear new grilles, taillamps, and front and rear fascias. A 160-horsepower 3.1-liter V-6 is standard on the Custom. A 170-horsepower 3.8-liter V-6 is standard on the Gran Sport and Limited and optional on the Custom. Both engines come with an electronic 4-speed automatic transmission that doesn't require a fluid change for 100,000 miles under normal conditions. A new brake/transmission shift interlock requires applying the brake pedal before a drive gear can be engaged. Regal is built from the same design as the Chevrolet Lumina/Monte Carlo, Oldsmobile Cutlass Supreme, and Pontiac Grand Prix. Each has its own exterior styling and interior design, and Regal is the only one to offer the 3.8-liter V-6. The new dashboard is more attractive and has gauges and controls that are easier to see and operate while driving. The base 3.1-liter V-6 provides adequate acceleration and is smooth and generally quiet. We prefer the 3.8-liter V-6, which delivers stronger acceleration and swift, safe passing. The 3.8-liter engine gives Regal a performance edge over the similar General Motors mid-size cars.

Buick Regal prices are on page 256.

BUICK REGAL CUSTOM

Rating Guide	1	2	3	4	5
Performance					
Acceleration					
Economy					
Driveability					
Ride					
Steering/handling					
Braking					
Noise					
Accommodations					
Driver seating					
Instruments/controls					
Visibility					
Room/comfort					
Entry/exit					
Cargo room					
Workmanship					
Exterior					
Interior					
Value					

Total Points...61

Specifications

Body type ....4-door notchback
Wheelbase (in.) 107.5
Overall length (in.) 193.7
Overall width (in.) 72.5
Overall height (in.) 54.5
Curb weight (lbs.) 3340
Seating capacity..........................5
Front head room (in.) 38.5
Max. front leg room (in.) 42.4
Rear head room (in.) 37.8
Min. rear leg room (in.)...........36.2
Cargo volume (cu. ft.).............15.9

Engine type......................ohv V-6
Engine size (l/cu. in.).........3.8/231
Horsepower @ rpm ...170 @ 4800
Torque @ rpm ....225 @ 3200
Transmission................auto/4-sp.
Drive wheels ....front
Brakes, F/R..........disc/disc (ABS)
Tire size 225/60R16
Fuel tank capacity (gal.) 16.5
EPA city/highway mpg 19/29
Test mileage (mpg) 17.3

Warranties The entire car is covered for 3 years/36,000 miles. Body perforation rust is covered for 6 years/100,000 miles.

Rating scale 5=Exceptional; 4=Above average; 3=Average; 2=Below average; 1=Poor

BUICK RIVIERA — RECOMMENDED

Built in Orion, Mich.

Buick Riviera

PREMIUM COUPE

A redesigned Riviera went on sale last spring as an early 1995 model. The new model is nine inches longer, 1.9 inches wider, 238 pounds heavier, and more powerful than its predecessor. It comes with a standard front bench seat for 6-passenger capacity. Front buckets are optional. Riviera is built on the same front-drive platform as the Oldsmobile Aurora sedan, though the two cars don't share styling or major mechanical features. Two 3.8-liter V-6s are available in Riviera. The standard engine has 205 horsepower and the optional supercharged version has 225 horsepower. Both engines mate with an electronic 4-speed automatic transmission. Dual air bags and anti-lock brakes are standard and traction control is optional. Acceleration, handling, and ride quality are vastly improved compared to the old Riviera, giving the 1995 model performance to rival premium coupes that cost thousands more. Despite its size, the new Riv feels balanced and nimble in turns, with little body lean and good grip. We've had more experience with the supercharged engine, which is smooth, refined, and potent. The base engine, by contrast, struggles with the Riviera's 3748-pound curb weight at low speeds and is a couple of steps slower in highway passing. The dashboard layout is one of the weakest areas. The speedometer and tachometer are spaced too far apart and the steering wheel blocks the headlamp and cruise control switches, which are on the dashboard. The long, heavy doors are cumbersome in tight parking spaces and you have to duck around the front seatbelts to get into the rear seat. The base price is a reasonable $27,632 and a Riviera with the supercharged V-6 lists for less than $30,000.

Buick Riviera prices are on page 259.

CONSUMER GUIDE®

BUICK RIVIERA

Rating Guide	1	2	3	4	5
Performance					
Acceleration	▓▓▓▓▓▓▓▓▓▓▓▓▓▓▓▓▓▓▓▓				
Economy	▓▓▓▓▓▓▓				
Driveability	▓▓▓▓▓▓▓▓▓▓▓▓▓▓▓▓▓▓▓▓				
Ride	▓▓▓▓▓▓▓▓▓▓▓▓▓				
Steering/handling	▓▓▓▓▓▓▓▓▓▓▓▓▓				
Braking	▓▓▓▓▓▓▓▓▓▓▓▓▓▓▓▓				
Noise	▓▓▓▓▓▓▓▓▓▓▓▓▓				
Accommodations					
Driver seating	▓▓▓▓▓▓▓▓▓▓▓▓▓				
Instruments/controls	▓▓▓▓▓▓▓▓▓▓▓				
Visibility	▓▓▓▓▓▓▓▓▓▓▓▓				
Room/comfort	▓▓▓▓▓▓▓▓▓▓▓▓▓				
Entry/exit	▓▓▓▓▓▓▓▓▓▓▓▓				
Cargo room	▓▓▓▓▓▓▓▓▓▓▓▓▓▓▓▓				
Workmanship					
Exterior	▓▓▓▓▓▓▓▓▓▓▓▓▓▓				
Interior	▓▓▓▓▓▓▓▓▓▓▓▓▓▓				
Value	▓▓▓▓▓▓▓▓▓▓▓▓▓▓▓				

Total Points...59

Specifications

Body type ....2-door notchback	Engine ....Supercharged ohv V-6
Wheelbase (in.) 113.8	Engine size (l/cu. in.).........3.8/231
Overall length (in.)................207.2	Horsepower @ rpm ...225 @ 5000
Overall width (in.) 75.0	Torque @ rpm ....275 @ 3200
Overall height (in.).................55.2	Transmission ....auto/4 sp.
Curb weight (lbs.) 3748	Drive wheels ....front
Seating capacity...........................5	Brakes, F/R...........disc/disc (ABS)
Front head room (in.) 38.2	Tire size 225/60R16
Max. front leg room (in.) 42.6	Fuel tank capacity (gal.) 20.0
Rear head room (in.) 36.2	EPA city/highway mpg 17/27
Min. rear leg room (in.)...........37.3	Test mileage (mpg) 17.7
Cargo volume (cu. ft.).............17.4	

Warranties The entire car is covered for 3 years/36,000 miles. Body perforation rust is covered for 6 years/100,000 miles.

Rating scale 5=Exceptional; 4=Above average; 3=Average; 2=Below average; 1=Poor

CADILLAC DE VILLE/ CONCOURS

Built in Hamtramck, Mich.

Cadillac De Ville Concours

PREMIUM SEDAN

The De Ville and Concours, which were redesigned last year, get several new features for 1995. Key changes include making traction control standard instead of optional on the Sedan De Ville (it already was standard on the Concours) and new transmission fluid that doesn't need changing for 100,000 miles. On both models, the traction control system can be turned off, a new feature. These front-drive luxury sedans share styling and major features except their engines. The De Ville, the base model in this line, has a 200-horsepower 4.9-liter overhead-valve V-8 engine. The higher-priced Concours uses Cadillac's 4.6-liter V-8, which has dual overhead camshafts and 275 horsepower (five more than last year). Both engines come with an electronic 4-speed automatic transmission. Headlamps that automatically turn on when the windshield wipers are activated are a new standard feature for both models. The Concours also gets a new 3-channel garage door opener (it's optional on the De Ville). The Concours has the more impressive performance, but the De Ville is a bargain in the luxury sedan field with a base price of $34,900, less than some 6-cylinder imported rivals. The De Ville's 4.9-liter V-8 produces strong acceleration and brisk passing response. The 4.6-liter engine in the Concours is smoother and furnishes stronger acceleration than some rivals that purport to be sports sedans. Unfortunately, both engines use expensive premium gas— and lots of it. There's ample space for six adults in the roomy interior and the trunk has a wide, flat floor that can hold lots of luggage. Don't judge the De Ville and Concours only by their conservative styling. They offer good performance and good value.

Cadillac De Ville/Concours prices are on page 265.

CADILLAC DE VILLE CONCOURS

Rating Guide	1	2	3	4	5
Performance					
Acceleration	▓▓▓▓▓▓▓▓▓▓▓▓▓▓▓▓▓				
Economy	▓▓▓▓▓				
Driveability	▓▓▓▓▓▓▓▓▓▓▓▓▓▓▓▓▓				
Ride	▓▓▓▓▓▓▓▓▓▓▓▓▓				
Steering/handling	▓▓▓▓▓▓▓▓▓				
Braking	▓▓▓▓▓▓▓▓▓▓▓▓▓▓▓▓				
Noise	▓▓▓▓▓▓▓▓▓▓▓▓▓				
Accommodations					
Driver seating	▓▓▓▓▓▓▓▓▓▓▓▓▓				
Instruments/controls	▓▓▓▓▓▓▓▓▓▓▓▓▓				
Visibility	▓▓▓▓▓▓▓▓▓▓▓				
Room/comfort	▓▓▓▓▓▓▓▓▓▓▓▓▓▓▓▓				
Entry/exit	▓▓▓▓▓▓▓▓▓▓▓▓▓▓▓▓				
Cargo room	▓▓▓▓▓▓▓▓▓▓▓▓▓				
Workmanship					
Exterior	▓▓▓▓▓▓▓▓▓▓▓▓▓▓				
Interior	▓▓▓▓▓▓▓▓▓▓▓▓▓▓				
Value	▓▓▓▓▓▓▓▓▓▓▓▓▓▓				

Total Points...63

Specifications

Body type	4-door notchback	Engine type	dohc V-8
Wheelbase (in.)	113.8	Engine size (l/cu. in.)	4.6/279
Overall length (in.)	209.2	Horsepower @ rpm	275 @ 5600
Overall width (in.)	76.6	Torque @ rpm	300 @ 4000
Overall height (in.)	56.3	Transmission	auto/4-sp.
Curb weight (lbs.)	3758	Drive wheels	front
Seating capacity	6	Brakes, F/R	disc/disc (ABS)
Front head room (in.)	38.5	Tire size	225/60HR16
Max. front leg room (in.)	42.6	Fuel tank capacity (gal.)	20.0
Rear head room (in.)	38.4	EPA city/highway mpg	16/25
Min. rear leg room (in.)	43.3	Test mileage (mpg)	15.8
Cargo volume (cu. ft.)	20.0		

Warranties The entire car is covered for 4 years/50,000 miles. Body perforation rust is covered for 6 years/100,000 miles.

Rating scale 5=Exceptional; 4=Above average; 3=Average; 2=Below average; 1=Poor

CADILLAC FLEETWOOD

Built in Arlington, Tex.

Cadillac Fleetwood

PREMIUM SEDAN

Cadillac's rear-drive sedan gains more standard features and an on/off switch for its standard traction control system this year. Fleetwood, the longest production car built in the U.S., comes in a single price series, but there also is a Brougham equipment package with additional amenities. The only powertrain is a 260-horsepower 5.7-liter V-8, derived from the Chevrolet Corvette's LT1 engine, and an electronic 4-speed automatic transmission. The engine has new platinum-tipped spark plugs and the transmission has new fluid; neither have to be changed for 100,000 miles under normal conditions. Dual air bags and anti-lock brakes also are standard. A new anti-lockout feature disables the door locks if the key is left in the ignition. Other new standard features include remote keyless entry, central unlocking, automatic door locks, and an automatic dim feature for the inside rearview mirror. With its considerable size and weight, the Fleetwood wasn't much of a sprinter until the Corvette engine was installed last year. Now, it has quick takeoffs and strong passing power; Cadillac estimates 60 mph can be reached in 8.5 seconds. Fuel economy, however, is no bargain: 14.8 mpg in our last test. At nearly 4500 pounds, this car isn't designed for zipping around winding roads. There's too much body lean and the soft suspension allows lots of bouncing on wavy roads. There's room for adults to stretch their legs at the four outboard seating positions and the trunk can hold several suitcases or a foursome's golf bags. Though the Fleetwood is clearly aimed at older buyers, Cadillac has updated its rear-drive sedan considerably the past few years and it's now a better choice than the rival Lincoln Town Car.

Cadillac Fleetwood prices are on page 267.

CADILLAC FLEETWOOD

Rating Guide	1	2	3	4	5
Performance					
Acceleration	▓▓▓▓▓▓▓▓▓▓▓▓▓▓▓▓▓▓▓▓▓▓▓▓▓ (≈5)				
Economy	▓▓▓▓▓ (≈2)				
Driveability	▓▓▓▓▓▓▓▓▓▓▓▓▓▓▓▓▓▓▓ (≈4)				
Ride	▓▓▓▓▓▓▓▓▓▓▓▓▓▓ (≈3)				
Steering/handling	▓▓▓▓▓▓▓▓▓▓▓▓▓ (≈3)				
Braking	▓▓▓▓▓▓▓▓▓▓▓▓▓▓▓▓▓ (≈4)				
Noise	▓▓▓▓▓▓▓▓▓▓▓▓▓▓▓▓ (≈4)				
Accommodations					
Driver seating	▓▓▓▓▓▓▓▓▓▓▓▓▓ (≈3)				
Instruments/controls	▓▓▓▓▓▓▓▓▓▓▓▓▓ (≈3)				
Visibility	▓▓▓▓▓▓▓▓▓▓▓▓▓ (≈3)				
Room/comfort	▓▓▓▓▓▓▓▓▓▓▓▓▓▓▓▓▓ (≈4)				
Entry/exit	▓▓▓▓▓▓▓▓▓▓▓▓▓▓▓▓▓ (≈4)				
Cargo room	▓▓▓▓▓▓▓▓▓▓▓▓▓▓▓▓▓ (≈4)				
Workmanship					
Exterior	▓▓▓▓▓▓▓▓▓▓▓▓▓▓▓▓▓ (≈4)				
Interior	▓▓▓▓▓▓▓▓▓▓▓▓▓▓▓▓▓ (≈4)				
Value	▓▓▓▓▓▓▓▓▓▓▓▓▓▓▓▓▓ (≈4)				

Total Points 59

Specifications

Body type ....4-door notchback	Engine type ....ohv V-8
Wheelbase (in.) 121.5	Engine size (l/cu. in.).........5.7/350
Overall length (in.) 225.0	Horsepower @ rpm ...260 @ 5000
Overall width (in.) 78.0	Torque @ rpm ....335 @ 2400
Overall height (in.) 57.1	Transmission ....auto/4-sp.
Curb weight (lbs.) 4477	Drive wheels ....rear
Seating capacity..........................6	Brakes, F/R ....disc/drum (ABS)
Front head room (in.) 38.7	Tire size 235/70R15
Max. front leg room (in.) 42.5	Fuel tank capacity (gal.) 23.0
Rear head room (in.) 39.1	EPA city/highway mpg 17/25
Min. rear leg room (in.) 43.9	Test mileage (mpg) 14.8
Cargo volume (cu. ft.)..............21.1	

Warranties The entire car is covered for 4 years/50,000 miles. Body perforation rust is covered for 6 years/100,000 miles.

Rating scale 5=Exceptional; 4=Above average; 3=Average; 2=Below average; 1=Poor

CADILLAC SEVILLE/ ELDORADO

Built in Hamtramck, Mich.

Cadillac Seville SLS

PREMIUM SEDAN/COUPE

Both versions of the Northstar engine offered in the Seville and Eldorado have more power this year and both models have new electronic chassis controls designed to improve braking, handling, and operation of the traction control system. All models use Cadillac's Northstar V-8, a 4.6-liter engine with dual overhead camshafts. On the Seville SLS and base Eldorado, the V-8 has 275 horsepower and on the Seville STS and Eldorado Touring Coupe it has 300, five more than last year for both versions. All models have front-wheel drive and an electronic 4-speed automatic transmission. The Seville sedan and Eldorado coupe are built from the same design but have different styling. In addition, the Seville has a longer wheelbase (111 inches versus 108). The 300-horsepower engine in the Seville STS and Eldorado Touring Coupe provides a performance advantage only at higher speeds where most drivers seldom venture. The 275-horsepower version produces more power at low speeds, making it more usable in urban driving, when you often need a quick burst of power to merge with traffic or pass. Both engines require premium gas and neither is an economy champ. The firmer suspension and more aggressive tires (rated for speeds over 149 mph) on the STS and Touring Coupe ride harshly and thump loudly over bumps. By contrast, the softer suspension and tires on the SLS and base Eldo easily absorb rough pavement. With base prices well below rivals such as the Lexus LS 400 and Mercedes E420, Seville is a worthy alternative to Japanese and European premium sedans, while the Eldorado is competitive with premium coupe rivals.

Cadillac Seville prices are on page 268.
Cadillac Eldorado prices are on page 266.

CADILLAC SEVILLE SLS

Rating Guide	1	2	3	4	5
Performance					
Acceleration	|||||||||||||||||||||||||||||||||||||||||||||||||||||
Economy	||||||||||||||
Driveability	||||||||||||||||||||||||||||||||||||||||
Ride	|||||||||||||||||||||||||||||||||||
Steering/handling	||||||||||||||||||||||||||||||||||||||||
Braking	|||||||||||||||||||||||||||||||||||||||||||||||||||
Noise	|||||||||||||||||||||||||||||||||||
Accommodations					
Driver seating	||||||||||||||||||||||||||||||||||||||||
Instruments/controls	||||||||||||||||||||||||||||||||||||||||
Visibility	||||||||||||||||||||||||||||||||||||||||
Room/comfort	||||||||||||||||||||||||||||||||||||||||
Entry/exit	||||||||||||||||||||||||||||||||||||||||
Cargo room	||||||||||||||||||||||||||||||||||||||||
Workmanship					
Exterior	|||||||||||||||||||||||||||||||||||||||||||||||||||
Interior	||||||||||||||||||||||||||||||||||||||||
Value	||||||||||||||||||||||||||||||||||||||||

Total Points...61

Specifications

Body type ....4-door notchback	Engine type ....dchc V-8
Wheelbase (in.) 111.0	Engine size (l/cu. in.)..........4.6/279
Overall length (in.)...............204.4	Horsepower @ rpm ...275 @ 5600
Overall width (in.) 74.2	Torque @ rpm ....300 @ 4000
Overall height (in.) 54.5	Transmission.................auto/4-sp.
Curb weight (lbs.) 3892	Drive wheels ....front
Seating capacity..........................5	Brakes, F/R..........disc/disc (ABS)
Front head room (in.) 38.0	Tire size 225/60R16
Max. front leg room (in.) 43.0	Fuel tank capacity (gal.) 20.0
Rear head room (in.) 38.3	EPA city/highway mpg 16/25
Min. rear leg room (in.)...........39.1	Test mileage (mpg) 15.9
Cargo volume (cu. ft.)............14.4	

Warranties The entire car is covered for 4 years/50,000 miles. Body perforation rust is covered for 6 years/100,000 miles.

Rating scale 5=Exceptional; 4=Above average; 3=Average; 2=Below average; 1=Poor

CHEVROLET BLAZER/ GMC JIMMY

Built in Moraine, Ohio, and Linden, N.J.

Chevrolet Blazer LS 5-door

SPORT-UTILITY VEHICLE

General Motors has redesigned its compact sport-utility vehicle for 1995, giving it new sheetmetal and a revamped interior with a driver-side air bag. Instead of S10 Blazer, Chevy's version is now called Blazer. GMC's version is still called Jimmy. Oldsmobile will use this same design for a luxury 4x4 but not until the 1996 model year. Blazer and Jimmy come in 3- and 5-door wagon body styles on 100.5- and 107-inch wheelbases, respectively. Overall length increases 4.3 inches on the 3-door and 4.4 inches on the 5-door. Both body styles are available with rear-wheel drive or on-demand, part-time 4-wheel drive that's for use only on slippery surfaces. A permanently engaged 4WD system is supposed to be available later this model year. A 195-horsepower 4.3-liter V-6, which was optional last year, is the sole engine this year. An electronic 4-speed automatic transmission is standard. Four-wheel anti-lock brakes that work in 2WD and 4WD are standard on all models. Five suspension packages tailored to specific driving needs from daily commuting to serious off-roading are available. The redesigned Blazer/Jimmy make their biggest advances in interior design, ride comfort, and noise levels. The modern-looking dashboard has clear gauges and simple, easy-to-use controls. There's less engine noise this year and road and wind noise are well muffled. Ride quality is more car-like than most vehicles in this class. GM missed the boat by not including a passenger-side air bag in the new interior, but the Blazer and Jimmy are competitive in most other areas.

Chevrolet Blazer prices are on page 271.
GMC Jimmy prices are on page 334.

CHEVROLET BLAZER (Preliminary)

Rating Guide	1	2	3	4	5
Performance					
Acceleration	||||||||||||||||||||||||||||||||||||||||		
Economy	|||||||||||||||||||||||||			
Driveability	||||||||||||||||||||||||||||||			
Ride	||||||||||||||||||||||||||||||||||			
Steering/handling	||||||||||||||||||||||||||||||			
Braking	||||||||||||||||||||||||||||||||||||||||		
Noise	||||||||||||||||||||||||||||||||||||		
Accommodations					
Driver seating	||||||||||||||||||||||||||||||			
Instruments/controls	||||||||||||||||||||||||||||||||			
Visibility	||||||||||||||||||||||||||||||			
Room/comfort	||||||||||||||||||||||||||||||			
Entry/exit	||||||||||||||||||||||||||||||			
Cargo room	||||||||||||||||||||||||||||||||||			
Workmanship					
Exterior	||||||||||||||||||||||||||||||||||			
Interior	||||||||||||||||||||||||||||||||			
Value	||||||||||||||||||||||||||||||||||			

Total Points...59

Specifications

Body type ....5-door wagon
Wheelbase (in.) 107.0
Overall length (in.)................181.2
Overall width (in.) 67.8
Overall height (in.).................67.0
Curb weight (lbs.) 4071
Seating capacity..........................5
Front head room (in.) 39.6
Max. front leg room (in.) 42.5
Rear head room (in.) 38.2
Min. rear leg room (in.)...........36.2
Cargo volume (cu. ft.).............74.1

Engine type ....ohv V-6
Engine size (l/cu. in.).........4.3/262
Horsepower @ rpm ...195 @ 4500
Torque @ rpm ....260 @ 3400
Transmission.................auto/4-sp.
Drive wheels....................rear/all
Brakes, F/R ....disc/drum (ABS)
Tire size 205/75R15
Fuel tank capacity (gal.).........19.0
EPA city/highway mpg 16/21
Test mileage (mpg) ....NA

Warranties The entire vehicle is covered for 3 years/36,000 miles. Body perforation rust is covered for 6 years/100,000 miles.

Rating scale 5=Exceptional; 4=Above average; 3=Average; 2=Below average; 1=Poor

CHEVROLET CAMARO/
PONTIAC FIREBIRD `RECOMMENDED`

Built in Canada.

Chevrolet Camaro Z28 3-door

SPORTS AND GT

Optional traction control is the big news for these rear-drive sporty cars, though it won't be available until spring. Both Camaro and Firebird come as 3-door hatchbacks and 2-door convertibles with a power top and glass rear window. Both are built from the same design but have different styling. Camaro is available in base and high-performance Z28 trim, while Firebird comes in base, Formula, and Trans Am models. Dual air bags and anti-lock brakes are standard on all. The base Camaro and Firebird use a 160-horsepower 3.4-liter V-6. The Z28, Formula, and Trans Am have a 275-horsepower 5.7-liter V-8 derived from the Corvette's LT1 engine. Later this model year, a 200-horsepower 3.8-liter V-6 is supposed to become optional on the base models. Traction control was to be added last year, but Chevy and Pontiac say it will finally appear later this season as an option on V-8 models. The current generation is the most solid and comfortable version of the Camaro and Firebird, though you'll never mistake either for a family car. The racy styling still dictates many compromises. Climbing in or out is a chore because of the low seats, and wide rear roof pillars block the driver's view to the rear. The tiny rear seat suits only children and cargo space is minimal. V-8 models have outstanding acceleration with either transmission, but they consume lots of gas. The 3.4-liter V-6 is more economical and provides adequate performance.

Chevrolet Camaro prices are on page 274.
Pontiac Firebird prices are on page 415.

CHEVROLET CAMARO Z28

Rating Guide	1	2	3	4	5
Performance					
Acceleration					▇
Economy		▇			
Driveability			▇		
Ride		▇			
Steering/handling			▇		
Braking				▇	
Noise		▇			
Accommodations					
Driver seating			▇		
Instruments/controls			▇		
Visibility		▇			
Room/comfort		▇			
Entry/exit		▇			
Cargo room			▇		
Workmanship					
Exterior				▇	
Interior				▇	
Value			▇		
Total Points					53

Specifications

Body type	3-door hatchback	Engine type	ohv V-8
Wheelbase (in.)	101.1	Engine size (l/cu. in.)	5.7/350
Overall length (in.)	193.2	Horsepower @ rpm	275 @ 5000
Overall width (in.)	74.1	Torque @ rpm	325 @ 2000
Overall height (in.)	51.3	Transmission	auto/4-sp.
Curb weight (lbs.)	3373	Drive wheels	rear
Seating capacity	4	Brakes, F/R	disc/disc (ABS)
Front head room (in.)	37.2	Tire size	245/50ZR16
Max. front leg room (in.)	43.0	Fuel tank capacity (gal.)	15.5
Rear head room (in.)	35.3	EPA city/highway mpg	17/25
Min. rear leg room (in.)	26.8	Test mileage (mpg)	17.4
Cargo volume (cu. ft.)	12.9		

Warranties The entire car is covered for 3 years/36,000 miles. Body perforation rust is covered for 6 years/100,000 miles.

Rating scale 5=Exceptional; 4=Above average; 3=Average; 2=Below average; 1=Poor

CHEVROLET CAPRICE AND IMPALA SS/ BUICK ROADMASTER

Built in Arlington, Tex.

Chevrolet Impala SS

FULL-SIZE

The Caprice sedan gets the "dog-leg" rear roof pillar treatment introduced last year on Chevy's sporty Impala SS model, and all these full-size rear-drive cars have new radios and seats. The basic body-on-frame design used for the rear-drive Caprice is also used for the Roadmaster, though styling and equipment differ. The Caprice 4-door sedan and 5-door wagon come in a Classic price level and as "value-priced" Special Value models that include additional equipment and the destination charge. The Impala SS bowed during 1994 as a high-performance sedan available only in black. Dark cherry and green-gray exterior colors are added for '95. Roadmaster comes as a 4-door sedan in base and Limited price levels and as the Estate 5-door wagon. All versions have standard dual air bags and anti-lock brakes. The sedans have seats for six and the wagon, with its standard 2-place rear-facing seat, holds eight. Caprice's base engine is a 200-horsepower 4.3-liter V-8. A 260-horsepower 5.7-liter V-8, derived from the LT1 engine used in the Corvette and Camaro, is standard on the Impala SS and Roadmaster and optional on the Caprice. A 4-speed automatic is the sole transmission. Though we prefer GM's front-drive full-size cars, such as the Buick LeSabre, because they handle better and use less gas, none matches the towing ability of the Caprice or Roadmaster (5000 pounds) or comes as a wagon. Both V-8s are smooth, strong performers that run on regular rather than premium gas. However, don't expect to average more than 20 mpg except in straight highway driving.

Chevrolet Caprice and Impala SS prices are on page 276.
Buick Roadmaster prices are on page 260.

CHEVROLET IMPALA SS

Rating Guide	1	2	3	4	5
Performance					
Acceleration	▓▓▓▓▓▓▓▓				
Economy	▓▓▓▓▓				
Driveability	▓▓▓▓▓▓▓▓				
Ride	▓▓▓▓▓▓▓▓				
Steering/handling	▓▓▓▓▓▓				
Braking	▓▓▓▓▓▓▓▓▓				
Noise	▓▓▓▓▓▓▓				
Accommodations					
Driver seating	▓▓▓▓▓▓				
Instruments/controls	▓▓▓▓▓▓				
Visibility	▓▓▓▓▓▓				
Room/comfort	▓▓▓▓▓▓▓▓				
Entry/exit	▓▓▓▓▓▓				
Cargo room	▓▓▓▓▓▓				
Workmanship					
Exterior	▓▓▓▓▓▓▓▓				
Interior	▓▓▓▓▓▓▓▓				
Value	▓▓▓▓▓▓				

Total Points 61

Specifications

Body type	4-door notchback	Engine type	ohv V-8
Wheelbase (in.)	115.9	Engine size (l/cu. in.)	5.7/350
Overall length (in.)	214.1	Horsepower @ rpm	260 @ 4800
Overall width (in.)	77.0	Torque @ rpm	330 @ 3200
Overall height (in.)	55.7	Transmission	auto/4-sp.
Curb weight (lbs.)	4061	Drive wheels	rear
Seating capacity	6	Brakes, F/R	disc/disc (ABS)
Front head room (in.)	39.2	Tire size	255/50ZR17
Max. front leg room (in.)	42.2	Fuel tank capacity (gal.)	23.0
Rear head room (in.)	39.7	EPA city/highway mpg	17/25
Min. rear leg room (in.)	39.5	Test mileage (mpg)	17.0
Cargo volume (cu. ft.)	20.4		

Warranties The entire car is covered for 3 years/36,000 miles. Body perforation rust is covered for 6 years/100,000 miles.

Rating scale 5=Exceptional; 4=Above average; 3=Average; 2=Below average; 1=Poor

CHEVROLET CAVALIER ———

Built in Lansing, Mich., and Lordstown, Ohio.

Chevrolet Cavalier 4-door

SUBCOMPACT

Chevrolet has redesigned its best-selling car for the first time in 13 years, giving it a longer wheelbase, fresh styling, and a new interior with standard dual air bags. Pontiac's version of this front-drive subcompact also is redesigned (see Sunfire report). Cavalier comes as a 2-door coupe and 4-door sedan, which arrived in the fall, and a 2-door convertible, which is due in the spring. All models have a 104.1-inch wheelbase, 2.8-inches longer than last year, and more rear leg room. The current lineup includes base versions of the coupe and sedan and an LS sedan. A Z24 coupe and an LS convertible are due in the spring. Base models and the LS sedan use a 120-horsepower 2.2-liter overhead-valve 4-cylinder. A 5-speed manual transmission is standard on the base models and a 3-speed automatic is optional. The automatic is standard on the LS. Coming in the spring as standard on the Z24 and optional on the convertible and LS is a dual-camshaft 2.3-liter 4-cylinder with 150 horsepower. Anti-lock brakes are standard on all models. The new Cavalier is more refined and rides more comfortably than the old one. The base and LS models are well isolated from road and wind noise, a welcome departure from their predecessors. Acceleration is adequate with either transmission. We haven't had a chance to measure fuel economy but expect around 25 mpg in urban driving and over 30 mpg on the highway. Compared to its natural rivals, the sporty Dodge and Plymouth Neon, the new Cavalier puts comfort and utility ahead of performance and style. Base prices are slightly higher than the comparable 1994 versions, making Cavalier a good value.

Chevrolet Cavalier prices are on page 279.

CHEVROLET CAVALIER (Preliminary)

Rating Guide	1	2	3	4	5
Performance					
Acceleration	▮▮▮▮▮▮▮▮▮▮▮▮				
Economy	▮▮▮▮▮▮▮▮▮▮▮▮▮▮▮▮▮				
Driveability	▮▮▮▮▮▮▮▮▮▮▮▮				
Ride	▮▮▮▮▮▮▮▮▮▮▮▮▮▮▮				
Steering/handling	▮▮▮▮▮▮▮▮▮				
Braking	▮▮▮▮▮▮▮▮▮▮▮▮▮▮▮▮▮				
Noise	▮▮▮▮▮▮▮▮▮▮				
Accommodations					
Driver seating	▮▮▮▮▮▮▮▮▮				
Instruments/controls	▮▮▮▮▮▮▮▮▮▮▮▮				
Visibility	▮▮▮▮▮▮▮▮▮▮▮▮				
Room/comfort	▮▮▮▮▮▮▮▮▮				
Entry/exit	▮▮▮▮▮▮▮▮▮				
Cargo room	▮▮▮▮▮▮▮▮▮				
Workmanship					
Exterior	▮▮▮▮▮▮▮▮▮▮▮▮▮▮▮▮				
Interior	▮▮▮▮▮▮▮▮▮▮▮▮▮▮▮▮				
Value	▮▮▮▮▮▮▮▮▮▮▮▮▮▮▮▮				

Total Points..**58**

Specifications

Body type ....4-door notchback	Engine type ....ohv I-4
Wheelbase (in.) 104.1	Engine size (l/cu. in.).........2.2/132
Overall length (in.)................180.3	Horsepower @ rpm ...120 @ 5200
Overall width (in.) 67.1	Torque @ rpm ....130 @ 4000
Overall height (in.)..................54.8	Transmission................auto/3-sp.
Curb weight (lbs.) 2601	Drive wheels ....front
Seating capacity..........................5	Brakes, F/R ....disc/drum (ABS)
Front head room (in.) 39.0	Tire size 195/70R14
Max. front leg room (in.) 42.3	Fuel tank capacity (gal.) 15.2
Rear head room (in.) 37.2	EPA city/highway mpg 25/32
Min. rear leg room (in.)...........34.6	Test mileage (mpg) ....NA
Cargo volume (cu. ft.).............13.2	

Warranties The entire car is covered for 3 years/36,000 miles. Body perforation rust is covered for 6 years/100,000 miles.

Rating scale 5=Exceptional; 4=Above average; 3=Average; 2=Below average; 1=Poor

CHEVROLET CORSICA/ BERETTA

Built in Wilmington, Del.

Chevrolet Corsica

COMPACT/SPORTS COUPE

Corsica, Chevy's front-drive compact sedan, has new daytime running lights and a revised rear suspension. Corsica is built from the same design as the Beretta coupe (which gets the same changes) but has different styling. Corsica comes as a 4-door notchback sedan and Beretta as a 2-door coupe, both with a standard driver-side air bag and anti-lock brakes. Corsica comes in a base price level and as Special Value models that include additional equipment and the destination charge. A 120-horsepower 2.2-liter 4-cylinder engine is standard and a 155-horsepower 3.1-liter V-6 is optional. Beretta comes in base and Z26 price levels, as well as Special Value versions of both. The 4-cylinder engine is standard on the base Beretta and the V-6 is standard on the Z26 and optional on the base model. Revisions to the rear suspension include relocating the coil springs from ahead of the rear axle to in line with the rear wheel hubs. Chevy says this improves ride quality. If you're interested in a Corsica or Beretta, we recommend you get the V-6 because the noisy 4-cylinder engine barely delivers adequate acceleration. You'll lose some fuel economy with the V-6 but gain much better performance. There's ample room in front in both models, but rear leg room is marginal for tall passengers. The dashboard controls for the lights and wiper/washer functions can't be operated without taking your hands off the steering wheel and the climate controls are too low to easily reach while driving. Corsica and Beretta are priced well below comparably equipped imports, though they don't match the assembly quality or refined

Chevrolet Beretta prices are on page 269.
Chevrolet Corsica prices are on page 280.

CHEVROLET CORSICA

Rating Guide	1	2	3	4	5
Performance					
Acceleration	▓▓▓▓▓▓▓▓				
Economy	▓▓▓▓				
Driveability	▓▓▓▓▓▓				
Ride	▓▓▓▓▓				
Steering/handling	▓▓▓▓▓▓				
Braking	▓▓▓▓▓▓▓▓▓				
Noise	▓▓▓▓▓				
Accommodations					
Driver seating	▓▓▓▓▓▓				
Instruments/controls	▓▓▓▓▓				
Visibility	▓▓▓▓▓				
Room/comfort	▓▓▓▓▓				
Entry/exit	▓▓▓▓▓				
Cargo room	▓▓▓▓▓				
Workmanship					
Exterior	▓▓▓▓▓▓				
Interior	▓▓▓▓▓				
Value	▓▓▓▓▓				

Total Points..**54**

Specifications

Body type ....4-door notchback
Wheelbase (in.) 103.4
Overall length (in.) 183.4
Overall width (in.) 68.5
Overall height (in.) 54.2
Curb weight (lbs.) 2745
Seating capacity..........................5
Front head room (in.) 38.1
Max. front leg room (in.) 43.4
Rear head room (in.) 37.4
Min. rear leg room (in.) 35.0
Cargo volume (cu. ft.).............13.4

Engine type......................ohv V-6
Engine size (l/cu. in.).........3.1/191
Horsepower @ rpm ...155 @ 5200
Torque @ rpm ....185 @ 4000
Transmission................auto/4-sp.
Drive wheels ....front
Brakes, F/R ....disc/drum (ABS)
Tire size 195/70R14
Fuel tank capacity (gal.) 15.2
EPA city/highway mpg 21/29
Test mileage (mpg) 19.6

Warranties The entire car is covered for 3 years/36,000 miles. Body perforation rust is covered for 6 years/100,000 miles.

Rating scale 5=Exceptional; 4=Above average; 3=Average; 2=Below average; 1=Poor

CHEVROLET CORVETTE ⸺

Built in Bowling Green, Ky.

Chevrolet Corvette ZR-1

SPORTS AND GT

Base coupe and convertible versions of this 2-seat sports car get the heavy-duty brakes previously standard on the high-performance ZR-1 model, automatic-transmission models gain a transmission-fluid temperature gauge, and all versions get new "gill" panels on the fenders behind the front wheels. The rear-drive Corvette continues as a 3-door hatchback coupe and a 2-door convertible with a manual top. Standard on both is the LT1 V-8, a 300-horsepower 5.7-liter with overhead valves. It comes with a choice of a 4-speed automatic transmission or a 6-speed manual. Optional on the hatchback is the ZR-1 package, which includes the LT5, a 405-horsepower 5.7-liter V-8 with dual overhead camshafts. It comes only with the 6-speed manual. The ZR-1 option was introduced for 1990 and will be discontinued after a final 448 copies are built for 1995. Dual air bags, anti-lock brakes, and Acceleration Slip Regulation, a traction control system, are standard on all models. This is a car for those who enjoy life in the fast lane and have money to burn. Corvette has become more civilized in recent years and improved assembly quality has greatly reduced squeaks and rattles. The suspension no longer jars your teeth over bumps, though it's still quite firm. Wide tires, a firm suspension, and a low center of gravity allow Corvette to handle like a race car, and acceleration is magnificent. Both engines deliver a seamless rush of power from virtually any speed. There's a definite performance advantage with the ZR-1 package but not enough to justify its astronomical tariff over the standard engine. However, if you're a collector, this is your last chance for a new ZR-1.

Chevrolet Corvette prices are on page 281.

CHEVROLET CORVETTE ZR-1

Rating Guide	1	2	3	4	5
Performance					
Acceleration	‖‖‖‖‖‖‖‖‖‖‖‖‖‖‖‖‖‖‖‖‖‖‖‖‖‖‖‖‖‖‖‖				
Economy	‖‖‖‖‖‖‖‖‖				
Driveability	‖‖‖‖‖‖‖‖‖‖‖‖‖‖‖‖‖‖‖‖‖‖				
Ride	‖‖‖‖‖‖‖‖‖‖‖‖‖‖				
Steering/handling	‖‖‖‖‖‖‖‖‖‖‖‖‖‖‖‖‖‖‖‖‖‖‖‖‖‖‖‖				
Braking	‖‖‖‖‖‖‖‖‖‖‖‖‖‖‖‖‖‖‖‖‖‖‖‖‖‖‖‖				
Noise	‖‖‖‖‖‖‖‖‖‖‖‖‖‖				
Accommodations					
Driver seating	‖‖‖‖‖‖‖‖‖‖‖‖‖‖‖‖‖‖‖‖‖				
Instruments/controls	‖‖‖‖‖‖‖‖‖‖‖‖‖‖‖‖‖‖‖‖‖				
Visibility	‖‖‖‖‖‖‖‖‖‖‖‖‖‖‖				
Room/comfort	‖‖‖‖‖‖‖‖‖‖‖‖‖‖‖‖‖‖‖‖‖				
Entry/exit	‖‖‖‖‖‖‖‖‖				
Cargo room	‖‖‖‖‖‖‖‖‖				
Workmanship					
Exterior	‖‖‖‖‖‖‖‖‖‖‖‖‖‖‖‖‖‖‖‖‖‖‖‖‖‖‖‖				
Interior	‖‖‖‖‖‖‖‖‖‖‖‖‖‖‖‖‖‖‖‖‖‖‖‖‖‖‖‖				
Value	‖‖‖‖‖‖‖‖‖‖‖‖‖‖‖				

Total Points...48

Specifications

Body type	3-door hatchback	Engine type	dohc V-8
Wheelbase (in.)	96.2	Engine size (l/cu. in.)	5.7/350
Overall length (in.)	178.5	Horsepower @ rpm	405 @ 5800
Overall width (in.)	73.1	Torque @ rpm	385 @ 5200
Overall height (in.)	46.3	Transmission	manual/6-sp.
Curb weight (lbs.)	3383	Drive wheels	rear
Seating capacity	2	Brakes, F/R	disc/disc (ABS)
Front head room (in.)	36.5	Tire size	315/35ZR17
Max. front leg room (in.)	42.0	Fuel tank capacity (gal.)	20.0
Rear head room (in.)	—	EPA city/highway mpg	17/25
Min. rear leg room (in.)	—	Test mileage (mpg)	NA
Cargo volume (cu. ft.)	12.6		

Warranties The entire car is covered for 3 years/36,000 miles. Body perforation rust is covered for 6 years/100,000 miles.

Rating scale 5=Exceptional; 4=Above average; 3=Average; 2=Below average; 1=Poor

CHEVROLET LUMINA MINIVAN/OLDSMOBILE SILHOUETTE/PONTIAC TRANS SPORT

Built in Tarrytown, N.Y.

Chevrolet Lumina Minivan

MINIVAN

General Motors's front-drive minivans get only minor revisions this year after getting a driver-side air bag last year. All three are built from the same design and have plastic body panels. Each has its own styling. All three are scheduled to be redesigned for 1996, when they will get steel body panels. The Lumina Minivan and Trans Sport come with a standard 120-horsepower 3.1-liter V-6 engine and 3-speed automatic transmission. A 170-horsepower 3.8-liter V-6 and 4-speed automatic are optional at Chevy and Pontiac and standard on the Silhouette. Both transmissions gain an interlock that prevents shifting out of park unless the brake pedal is applied. Anti-lock brakes are standard and traction control is optional. Other options include two integrated child safety seats and a power sliding side door that opens and closes at the push of a button. Lumina and its Pontiac and Oldsmobile counterparts are competitively priced and worth considering. Among key rivals, the Dodge Caravan, Plymouth Voyager, and Ford Windstar come with dual air bags. The 3.8-liter V-6 and 4-speed automatic give these minivans performance that matches or exceeds their rivals. The 3.1-liter engine, by contrast, feels weak with even a light load. One of the big reasons these vehicles haven't sold better is that forward visibility is severely compromised by the sloped nose, front roof pillars, and expansive shelf on top of the dashboard.

Chevrolet Lumina Minivan prices are on page 283.
Oldsmobile Silhouette prices are on page 404.
Pontiac Trans Sport prices are on page 423.

CHEVROLET LUMINA MINIVAN

Rating Guide	1	2	3	4	5

Performance

	Rating
Acceleration	3
Economy	3
Driveability	3
Ride	3
Steering/handling	3
Braking	5
Noise	3

Accommodations

	Rating
Driver seating	4
Instruments/controls	3
Visibility	3
Room/comfort	5
Entry/exit	4
Cargo room	5

Workmanship

	Rating
Exterior	4
Interior	3

	Rating
Value	3

Total Points **59**

Specifications

Body type	4-door van	Engine type	ohv V-6
Wheelbase (in.)	109.8	Engine size (l/cu. in.)	3.8/231
Overall length (in.)	191.5	Horsepower @ rpm	170 @ 4800
Overall width (in.)	73.9	Torque @ rpm	225 @ 3200
Overall height (in.)	65.7	Transmission	auto/4-sp.
Curb weight (lbs.)	3554	Drive wheels	front
Seating capacity	7	Brakes, F/R	disc/drum (ABS)
Front head room (in.)	39.2	Tire size	205/70R15
Max. front leg room (in.)	40.1	Fuel tank capacity (gal.)	20.0
Rear head room (in.)	39.0	EPA city/highway mpg	17/25
Min. rear leg room (in.)	36.1	Test mileage (mpg)	19.0
Cargo volume (cu. ft.)	112.6		

Warranties The entire vehicle is covered for 3 years/36,000 miles. Body perforation rust is covered for 6 years/100,000 miles.

Rating scale 5=Exceptional; 4=Above average; 3=Average; 2=Below average; 1=Poor

CHEVROLET LUMINA/ MONTE CARLO

RECOMMENDED

Built in Canada.

Chevrolet Lumina LS

MID-SIZE

Redesigned versions of Chevrolet's front-drive mid-size car went on sale last summer. The 4-door sedan is again called Lumina, but the 2-door coupe is called Monte Carlo, a name last used by Chevrolet on a rear-drive 1988 model. Among new standard features on both are dual air bags. The 1995 models also have new exterior styling and redesigned interiors. As before, the front-drive platform is similar to the one used for the Buick Regal, Oldsmobile Cutlass Supreme, and Pontiac Grand Prix. Each model has its own exterior styling and interior design. Lumina comes in base and LS price levels, both with a standard 160-horsepower 3.1-liter V-6 engine. A 210-horsepower 3.4-liter V-6 is optional on the LS. The base Monte Carlo LS comes with the 3.1-liter V-6 and the sportier Z34 comes with the 3.4-liter V-6. A 4-speed electronic automatic transmission is standard on all models. Anti-lock brakes are standard on all models except the base Lumina, where they're optional. The new Lumina is a pleasant, competent family sedan that deserves a close look among mid-size cars. While it isn't head and shoulders above the rival Ford Taurus, it's more refined overall. The 3.1-liter engine feels a little slow initially but delivers adequate acceleration. The 4-speed automatic changes gears smoothly and downshifts promptly for passing power. The 3.4-liter V-6 has a more potent passing punch. However, it isn't much stronger at low speeds and is louder in hard acceleration. The new dashboard has a clean, contemporary design with simple controls that are easy to see and reach. Lumina is a clear winner over Taurus on price, undercutting its rival by more than $2000.

Chevrolet Lumina/Monte Carlo prices are on page 284.

CHEVROLET LUMINA LS

Rating Guide	1	2	3	4	5
Performance					
Acceleration	▓▓▓▓▓▓▓▓▓▓▓▓				
Economy	▓▓▓▓▓▓▓▓				
Driveability	▓▓▓▓▓▓▓▓▓▓▓▓				
Ride	▓▓▓▓▓▓▓▓▓▓▓▓				
Steering/handling	▓▓▓▓▓▓▓▓▓▓				
Braking	▓▓▓▓▓▓▓▓▓▓▓▓▓▓▓▓▓▓▓▓				
Noise	▓▓▓▓▓▓▓▓▓▓▓▓				
Accommodations					
Driver seating	▓▓▓▓▓▓▓▓▓▓▓▓				
Instruments/controls	▓▓▓▓▓▓▓▓▓▓▓▓				
Visibility	▓▓▓▓▓▓▓▓▓▓▓▓				
Room/comfort	▓▓▓▓▓▓▓▓▓▓▓▓				
Entry/exit	▓▓▓▓▓▓▓▓▓▓▓▓				
Cargo room	▓▓▓▓▓▓▓▓▓▓▓▓				
Workmanship					
Exterior	▓▓▓▓▓▓▓▓▓▓▓▓				
Interior	▓▓▓▓▓▓▓▓▓▓▓▓				
Value	▓▓▓▓▓▓▓▓▓▓▓▓				

Total Points...61

Specifications

Body type ....4-door notchback	Engine type.......................ohv V-6
Wheelbase (in.) 107.5	Engine size (l/cu. in.).........3.1/191
Overall length (in.)................200.7	Horsepower @ rpm ...160 @ 5200
Overall width (in.) 71.9	Torque @ rpm ....185 @ 4000
Overall height (in.) 53.8	Transmission................auto/4-sp.
Curb weight (lbs.) 3451	Drive wheels ....front
Seating capacity..........................6	Brakes, F/R ....disc/drum (ABS)
Front head room (in.) 37.9	Tire size 205/70R15
Max. front leg room (in.) 42.4	Fuel tank capacity (gal.) 17.1
Rear head room (in.) 36.9	EPA city/highway mpg 17/26
Min. rear leg room (in.)...........34.9	Test mileage (mpg) 20.1
Cargo volume (cu. ft.).............15.7	

Warranties The entire car is covered for 3 years/36,000 miles. Body perforation rust is covered for 6 years/100,000 miles.

Rating scale 5=Exceptional; 4=Above average; 3=Average; 2=Below average; 1=Poor

CHRYSLER CIRRUS/————
DODGE STRATUS

Built in Sterling Heights, Mich.

Chrysler Cirrus LXi

MID-SIZE

The Cirrus bowed in the fall as the first of Chrysler's new front-drive sedans. The similar Stratus is set to go on sale in early 1995 and an unnamed Plymouth version is to follow next fall. Cirrus comes in LX and LXi trim levels, with prices starting at $17,435. Dodge hadn't yet announced prices, but the base Stratus should be around $15,500, with the sportier ES about $1500 higher. In both cases, dual air bags and anti-lock brakes are standard. Standard on the base Stratus are a 132-horsepower 2.0-liter 4-cylinder and 5-speed manual transmission. Optional is a new 140-horsepower 2.4-liter 4-cylinder that comes with a 4-speed electronic automatic transmission. Standard on the sporty ES and optional on the base Stratus is a 164-horsepower 2.5-liter V-6, again teamed only with the automatic. This is the sole powertrain available on the Cirrus. The 2.0-liter 4-cylinder and 5-speed manual are a credit option on the Stratus ES. Standard features on all include air conditioning, a height-adjustable driver's seat, folding rear seat, and an AM/FM/cassette stereo. An integrated rear child safety seat and in-dash CD changer are optional. There's a great deal to like about these cars, starting with a spacious interior with ample rear leg room. However, rear head room is tight for taller folks and rear visibility suffers from a high package shelf. We've only driven V-6 versions and they have adequate acceleration and fairly strong passing power. Overall, these new sedans impress us as highly capable 4-doors that soundly beat most competitors in passenger and cargo space.

Chrysler Cirrus prices are on page 286.
Dodge Stratus standard equipment is on page 305.

CHRYSLER CIRRUS LXi (Preliminary)

Rating Guide	1	2	3	4	5
Performance					
Acceleration	||||||||||||||||||||||||||||||||||			
Economy	||||||||||||||||||||				
Driveability	|||||||||||||||||||||||||||			
Ride	||||||||||||||||||||||||||			
Steering/handling	||||||||||||||||||||||||||			
Braking	||||||||||||||||||||||||||||||||||||			
Noise	||||||||||||||||||				
Accommodations					
Driver seating	||||||||||||||||||||||||||			
Instruments/controls	|||||||||||||||||||||||||||			
Visibility	||||||||||||||||||||||||||			
Room/comfort	||||||||||||||||||||||||||			
Entry/exit	||||||||||||||||||||||||||			
Cargo room	||||||||||||||||||||||||||			
Workmanship					
Exterior	||||||||||||||||||||||||||||||			
Interior	||||||||||||||||||||||||||||||			
Value	||||||||||||||||||||||||||||||			

Total Points...61

Specifications

Body type ....4-door notchback	Engine type......................ohc V-6
Wheelbase (in.) 108.0	Engine size (l/cu. in.).........2.5/152
Overall length (in.) 186.0	Horsepower @ rpm ...164 @ 5900
Overall width (in.) 71.0	Torque @ rpm ....163 @ 4350
Overall height (in.)..................54.1	Transmission ....auto/4-sp.
Curb weight (lbs.) 3150	Drive wheels ....front
Seating capacity..........................5	Brakes, F/R ....disc/drum (ABS)
Front head room (in.) 38.1	Tire size 195/65HR15
Max. front leg room (in.) 42.3	Fuel tank capacity (gal.) 16.0
Rear head room (in.) 36.8	EPA city/highway mpg 20/29
Min. rear leg room (in.)...........37.8	Test mileage (mpg) ....NA
Cargo volume (cu. ft.).............15.7	

Warranties The entire car is covered for 3 years/36,000 miles. Body perforation rust is covered for 7 years/100,000 miles.

Rating scale 5=Exceptional; 4=Above average; 3=Average; 2=Below average; 1=Poor

CHRYSLER LE BARON ———

Built in Newark, Del.

Chrysler LeBaron GTC

SPORTS COUPE

The LeBaron 4-door sedan has been replaced by the new Chrysler Cirrus (see separate report), leaving the convertible as the lone LeBaron model for 1995 (a coupe variant was dropped after 1993). A new convertible based on the Cirrus is due during 1996. The front-drive LeBaron convertible comes only as a well-equipped GTC model that includes a 141-horsepower Mitsubishi 3.0-liter V-6, 4-speed automatic transmission, dual air bags, air conditioning, power top with an electric rear-window defroster, AM/FM/cassette stereo, and power windows among its standard features. Chrysler has basically gone to a one-price version of the LeBaron convertible, loading it up with features while keeping the base price at a modest—for a ragtop—$17,469. With all that's standard, LeBaron is a good value in a convertible. Our last test netted an average 22.9 mpg from a mix of city and highway driving. The engine provided spirited acceleration and brisk passing response. On the down side, the engine had a coarse, loud growl in hard acceleration and an abundance of road noise made it hard to talk in normal tones at highway speeds. In addition, even minor bumps in the road made the body twist and flex more than most convertibles. There's room for 6-footers in front, but the rear seat is no place for adults on long trips, and the trunk is small. Spy shots of the LeBaron convertible's replacement indicate that it will carry the "cab-forward" design philosophy favored by Chrysler of late. The new convertible is expected to debut in mid-1996, which means the current model may return for an abbreviated appearance next year.

Chrysler LeBaron prices are on page 288.

CONSUMER GUIDE®

CHRYSLER LE BARON GTC

Rating Guide	1	2	3	4	5
Performance					
Acceleration	▓▓▓▓▓▓▓▓▓▓▓▓▓▓▓▓▓▓▓▓				
Economy	▓▓▓▓▓▓▓				
Driveability	▓▓▓▓▓▓▓▓▓▓▓▓				
Ride	▓▓▓▓▓▓▓▓▓▓▓▓				
Steering/handling	▓▓▓▓▓▓▓▓▓▓▓▓▓▓▓				
Braking	▓▓▓▓▓▓▓▓▓▓▓▓▓▓▓▓▓▓▓▓				
Noise	▓▓▓▓▓▓▓▓▓				
Accommodations					
Driver seating	▓▓▓▓▓▓▓▓▓▓▓▓				
Instruments/controls	▓▓▓▓▓▓▓▓▓▓▓▓				
Visibility	▓▓▓▓▓▓▓▓▓▓▓▓				
Room/comfort	▓▓▓▓▓▓▓▓▓▓▓▓				
Entry/exit	▓▓▓▓▓▓▓▓▓▓▓▓				
Cargo room	▓▓▓▓▓▓▓▓▓				
Workmanship					
Exterior	▓▓▓▓▓▓▓▓▓▓▓▓▓▓▓				
Interior	▓▓▓▓▓▓▓▓▓▓▓▓				
Value	▓▓▓▓▓▓▓▓▓▓▓▓▓▓▓				

Total Points 52

Specifications

Body type ....2-door convertible	Engine type ....ohc V-6
Wheelbase (in.) 100.6	Engine size (l/cu. in.).........3.0/181
Overall length (in.)................184.8	Horsepower @ rpm ...141 @ 5000
Overall width (in.) 69.2	Torque @ rpm ....171 @ 2400
Overall height (in.).................52.4	Transmission.................auto/4-sp.
Curb weight (lbs.)..................3122	Drive wheels ....front
Seating capacity 4	Brakes, F/R..........disc/disc (ABS)
Front head room (in.) 38.3	Tire size 205/60R15
Max. front leg room (in.) 42.5	Fuel tank capacity (gal.) 14.0
Rear head room (in.) 37.0	EPA city/highway mpg 20/29
Min. rear leg room (in.)...........33.0	Test mileage (mpg) 22.9
Cargo volume (cu. ft.)..............9.2	

Warranties The entire car is covered for 3 years/36,000 miles. Body perforation rust is covered for 7 years/100,000 miles.

Rating scale 5=Exceptional; 4=Above average; 3=Average; 2=Below average; 1=Poor

CHRYSLER NEW YORKER/LHS

Built in Canada.

Chrysler LHS

PREMIUM SEDAN

Chrysler's front-drive luxury sedans return with few changes. The remote keyless entry system now requires that the "trunk" button be pressed twice within five seconds before the trunk will unlock to prevent accidental opening. Also, the standard cruise control has a new cancel feature. On the outside, the only difference for 1995 is the new corporate hood badge, which resembles the one used by Chrysler in the 1920s. Like last year, the only powertrain is a 214-horsepower 3.5-liter overhead-camshaft V-6 and a 4-speed automatic transmission. Dual air bags and anti-lock brakes are standard on both models. The New Yorker and LHS are based on the LH sedans (Chrysler Concorde, Dodge Intrepid, and Eagle Vision) but have different styling and are about six inches longer. The more-expensive LHS has front bucket seats and comes virtually loaded, with a CD player its only major option. The New Yorker comes with a 50/50 split bench front seat (giving it 6-passenger capacity) and fewer standard features. Almost everything standard on the LHS is available as an option on the New Yorker. New Yorker's base price has increased just $55 to $25,596, while the LHS's has dropped $688 to $29,595, a clear indication Chrysler had trouble selling these cars last year without incentives. We're generally impressed with these luxury versions of the LH sedans. Acceleration is brisk and handling agile, though the suspension could be more compliant. Both have a lot of road noise, restricted rear visibility due to a small rear window, and interiors that are trimmed with too much cheap-feeling plastic. However, they have all the positives of the "regular" LH sedans, plus rear leg room that would do a limousine proud.

Chrysler New Yorker/LHS prices are on page 290.

CHRYSLER LHS

Rating Guide	1	2	3	4	5
Performance					
Acceleration	▓▓▓▓▓▓▓▓				
Economy	▓▓▓				
Driveability	▓▓▓▓▓▓▓▓				
Ride	▓▓▓▓▓▓▓				
Steering/handling	▓▓▓▓▓▓▓				
Braking	▓▓▓▓▓▓▓▓				
Noise	▓▓▓▓▓▓▓				
Accommodations					
Driver seating	▓▓▓▓▓▓▓▓				
Instruments/controls	▓▓▓▓▓▓▓▓				
Visibility	▓▓▓▓▓▓▓				
Room/comfort	▓▓▓▓▓▓▓▓▓				
Entry/exit	▓▓▓▓▓▓▓				
Cargo room	▓▓▓▓▓▓▓▓				
Workmanship					
Exterior	▓▓▓▓▓▓▓▓▓				
Interior	▓▓▓▓▓▓▓▓▓				
Value	▓▓▓▓▓▓▓▓▓				

Total Points...61

Specifications

Body type ....4-door notchback
Wheelbase (in.) 113.0
Overall length (in.) 207.4
Overall width (in.) 74.4
Overall height (in.) 56.3
Curb weight (lbs.) 3592
Seating capacity...........................5
Front head room (in.) 39.3
Max. front leg room (in.) 42.3
Rear head room (in.) 37.8
Min. rear leg room (in.)...........40.6
Cargo volume (cu. ft.).............17.9

Engine type ....ohc V-6
Engine size (l/cu. in.).........3.5/215
Horsepower @ rpm ...214 @ 5800
Torque @ rpm ....221 @ 3100
Transmission.................auto/4-sp.
Drive wheels ....front
Brakes, F/R...........disc/disc (ABS)
Tire size 225/60R16
Fuel tank capacity (gal.) 18.0
EPA city/highway mpg 18/26
Test mileage (mpg) 18.4

Warranties The entire car is covered for 3 years/36,000 miles. Body perforation rust is covered for 7 years/100,000 miles.

Rating scale 5=Exceptional; 4=Above average; 3=Average; 2=Below average; 1=Poor

DODGE AVENGER/ CHRYSLER SEBRING

Built in Normal, Ill.

Dodge Avenger ES

SPORTS COUPE

Avenger, a front-drive coupe aimed at the Honda Accord and Toyota Camry coupes, joins the Dodge lineup for 1995. Riding a 103.7-inch wheelbase and stretching 187.2 inches overall, the 2-door Avenger is close to the Camry in both dimensions. Inside, the Avenger has about one inch less headroom in the rear seat but two inches more leg room. Both Avenger and its corporate cousin, the Chrysler Sebring, were designed by Chrysler but are built by Mitsubishi at its Diamond-Star Motors plant in Illinois. Avenger leans toward the sporty side, while Sebring is aimed at more luxury-oriented buyers. Avenger went on sale in late fall; Sebring isn't scheduled to go on sale until early 1995. Avenger comes in base and ES models, the Sebring in LX and upscale LXi versions. Base engine is a 2.0-liter 4-cylinder with dual camshafts and 140 horsepower. A 5-speed manual transmission is standard and a 4-speed automatic is optional. The ES and LXi have a 155-horsepower 2.5-liter single-camshaft V-6 that comes only with the automatic. Dual air bags are standard on all models; anti-lock brakes are standard on the Avenger ES and optional on the base. Sebring standard equipment hadn't been released at time of publication. On a brief test drive, an Avenger ES suffered quite a bit of road noise. It was no hot rod either, though it had more than adequate acceleration, and the engine wasn't as smooth or quiet as some V-6s. Suspension settings were aimed more at handling than comfort, but the ride was never harsh over bumps. Rear seat room was impressive, allowing adults to ride comfortably in back.

Dodge Avenger prices are on page 292.
Chrysler Sebring standard equipment is on page 291.

DODGE AVENGER ES (Preliminary)

Rating Guide	1	2	3	4	5
Performance					
Acceleration					
Economy					
Driveability					
Ride					
Steering/handling					
Braking					
Noise					
Accommodations					
Driver seating					
Instruments/controls					
Visibility					
Room/comfort					
Entry/exit					
Cargo room					
Workmanship					
Exterior					
Interior					
Value					

Total Points..**57**

Specifications

Body type ....2-door notchback	Engine type......................ohc V-6
Wheelbase (in.) 103.7	Engine size (l/cu. in.)..........2.5/152
Overall length (in.)................187.2	Horsepower @ rpm ...155 @ 5500
Overall width (in.)..................68.5	Torque @ rpm ....161 @ 4400
Overall height (in.)..................53.0	Transmission................auto/4-sp.
Curb weight (lbs.) 2822	Drive wheels ....front
Seating capacity..........................5	Brakes, F/R...........disc/disc (ABS)
Front head room (in.) 39.1	Tire size 205/55HR16
Max. front leg room (in.) 43.3	Fuel tank capacity (gal.) 16.0
Rear head room (in.) 36.5	EPA city/highway mpg 20/29
Min. rear leg room (in.)...........35.0	Test mileage (mpg) ....NA
Cargo volume (cu. ft.).............13.1	

Warranties The entire car is covered for 3 years/36,000 miles. Body perforation rust is covered for 7 years/100,000 miles.

Rating scale 5=Exceptional; 4=Above average; 3=Average; 2=Below average; 1=Poor

DODGE CARAVAN/ CHRYSLER TOWN & COUNTRY/PLYMOUTH VOYAGER

✓ BEST BUY

Built in St. Louis, Mo., and Canada.

Dodge Grand Caravan ES

MINIVAN

Chrysler's front-drive minivans receive a surprising number of changes considering that redesigned versions are due next spring as early 1996 models. The optional remote keyless entry system (standard on Town & Country) now requires pressing the "liftgate" button twice within five seconds to unlatch the liftgate. New for the Caravan are Sport and SE Decor option packages, while the Voyager offers a new Rallye Group decor package for SE versions. Base engine for Caravan and Voyager remains a 100-horsepower 2.5-liter 4-cylinder, but it now comes only with a 3-speed automatic transmission. Three V-6s are available: a 3.0-liter with 142 horsepower and 3.3- and 3.8-liter engines, both with 162 horsepower. The 3.8-liter engine is standard on the Town & Country, the most luxurious and most expensive of this trio. Caravan and Voyager come in regular and extended lengths (called "Grand") while Town & Country comes only in the extended length. Dual air bags are standard on all models. Anti-lock brakes are standard on the more-expensive models, optional on the others. Permanently engaged all-wheel drive is optional on extended versions. These minivans set the standard for this class, combining car-like road manners and efficient use of interior space with an impressive list of available features. With Caravan and Voyager, we recommend the V-6 engines because the 4-cylinder doesn't have enough power.

Dodge Caravan prices are on page 293; Chrysler Town & Country prices are on page 291; Plymouth Voyager prices are on page 408.

DODGE GRAND CARAVAN ES

Rating Guide	1	2	3	4	5
Performance					
Acceleration				|||||||||||	
Economy		||||		
Driveability				|||||||||||	
Ride				|||||||||||	
Steering/handling				|||||||||||	
Braking					|||||||||||||
Noise			||||||		
Accommodations					
Driver seating				|||||||||||	
Instruments/controls				|||||||||||	
Visibility			|||||||		
Room/comfort				|||||||||||	
Entry/exit				|||||||||||	
Cargo room					|||||||||||||
Workmanship					
Exterior				|||||||||||	
Interior				|||||||||||	
Value				|||||||||||	
Total Points **62**					

Specifications

Body type	4-door van	Engine type	ohv V-6
Wheelbase (in.)	119.3	Engine size (l/cu. in.)	3.3/201
Overall length (in.)	192.8	Horsepower @ rpm	162 @ 4800
Overall width (in.)	72.0	Torque @ rpm	194 @ 3600
Overall height (in.)	66.7	Transmission	auto/4-sp.
Curb weight (lbs.)	3602	Drive wheels	front
Seating capacity	7	Brakes, F/R	disc/disc (ABS)
Front head room (in.)	39.1	Tire size	205/70R15
Max. front leg room (in.)	38.3	Fuel tank capacity (gal.)	20.0
Rear head room (in.)	38.7	EPA city/highway mpg	18/23
Min. rear leg room (in.)	37.7	Test mileage (mpg)	18.5
Cargo volume (cu. ft.)	141.3		

Warranties The entire vehicle is covered for 3 years/36,000 miles. Body perforation rust is covered for 7 years/100,000 miles.

Rating scale 5=Exceptional; 4=Above average; 3=Average; 2=Below average; 1=Poor

DODGE INTREPID/ RECOMMENDED
CHRYSLER CONCORDE/
EAGLE VISION

Built in Newark, Del., and Canada.

Dodge Intrepid ES

FULL-SIZE

Chrysler's full-size, front-drive LH cars return for 1995 with few changes. Intrepid is offered in base and sportier ES models, the Vision in ESi and upscale TSi versions, and the Concorde in a single price level. All have standard dual air bags. Anti-lock brakes are optional on the base Intrepid and Vision ESi and standard on the Intrepid ES, Vision TSi, and Concorde, which also offer optional traction control. The available remote keyless entry system now requires that the "trunk" button be pressed twice within five seconds to release the latch to prevent accidental opening, and the cruise control system now includes a cancel feature. Standard powertrain for Intrepid, Concorde, and the Vision ESi is a 161-horsepower 3.3-liter V-6 and a 4-speed automatic transmission. A 214-horsepower overhead-camshaft 3.5-liter V-6 is optional on all models except the Vision TSi, where it's standard. Acceleration is adequate with the 3.3-liter engine and quite zippy with the 3.5. All three models have abundant interior space, even for rear-seat occupants. They also feel more nimble than most cars this large and can corner as well as some sport sedans. However, all versions have too much road noise at highway speeds. We're also put off by the abundance of flimsy plastic interior trim and though most controls are conveniently placed, reaching the climate controls is a stretch for most drivers. Overall, though, the LH cars are among the best choices in a large sedan.

Dodge Intrepid prices are on page 299; Chrysler Concorde prices are on page 287; Eagle Vision prices are on page 309.

DODGE INTREPID ES

Rating Guide	1	2	3	4	5
Performance					
Acceleration					
Economy					
Driveability					
Ride					
Steering/handling					
Braking					
Noise					
Accommodations					
Driver seating					
Instruments/controls					
Visibility					
Room/comfort					
Entry/exit					
Cargo room					
Workmanship					
Exterior					
Interior					
Value					

Total Points...60

Specifications

Body type ....4-door notchback	Engine type ....ohc V-6
Wheelbase (in.) 113.0	Engine size (l/cu. in.).........3.5/215
Overall length (in.)................201.7	Horsepower @ rpm ...214 @ 5800
Overall width (in.) 74.4	Torque @ rpm ....221 @ 2800
Overall height (in.).................56.3	Transmission.................auto/4-sp.
Curb weight (lbs.) 3310	Drive wheels ....front
Seating capacity..........................5	Brakes, F/R..........disc/disc (ABS)
Front head room (in.) 38.4	Tire size 225/60R16
Max. front leg room (in.) 42.3	Fuel tank capacity (gal.) 18.0
Rear head room (in.) 37.2	EPA city/highway mpg 18/26
Min. rear leg room (in.) 38.7	Test mileage (mpg) 19.3
Cargo volume (cu. ft.).............16.7	

Warranties The entire car is covered for 3 years/36,000 miles. Body perforation rust is covered for 7 years/100,000 miles.

Rating scale 5=Exceptional; 4=Above average; 3=Average; 2=Below average; 1=Poor

DODGE/ PLYMOUTH NEON

Built in Belvidere, Ill.

Dodge Neon Sport 4-door

SUBCOMPACT

The front-drive Neon was introduced as an early 1995 model, available in identical form though Dodge and Plymouth dealers. At first offered only as a 4-door sedan, Neon gained a 2-door coupe running mate in the fall. While the sedan is offered in base, Highline, and Sport price levels, the coupe comes only in Highline and Sport versions. All but the 2-door Sport come with a 132-horsepower 2.0-liter 4-cylinder engine with a single overhead camshaft. The 2-door Sport gets a dual-cam version of this engine that produces 150 horsepower. The 2-door Sport also has a domed hood, rear spoiler, stiffer suspension, and specific 14-inch cast-aluminum wheels. On all Neons, a 5-speed manual transmission is standard and a 3-speed automatic is optional. Dual air bags are standard across the board and anti-lock brakes are standard on Sport models, optional on the others. Also optional is an integrated child safety seat that folds out of the rear seatback. Power windows weren't available initially; they are now optional on the 4-door Sport. Neon is solid, roomy, fun to drive, and priced below most Japanese rivals. The base engine is quick off the line with either transmission, though it growls loudly under hard throttle. The suspension soaks up bumps with little harshness and neither floats nor bottoms out. Interior space is impressive, with enough head and leg room to seat four 6-footers without squeezing. Where Neon falls short is in its interior materials and assembly quality, neither of which are up to the same level as rival Toyota or Honda cars. Nevertheless, Neon is a "must see" for anyone shopping for a compact or subcompact.

Dodge Neon prices are on page 301.
Plymouth Neon prices are on page 405.

DODGE NEON SPORT

Rating Guide	1	2	3	4	5
Performance					
Acceleration	▓▓▓▓▓▓▓▓▓				
Economy	▓▓▓▓▓▓▓▓▓▓				
Driveability	▓▓▓▓▓▓				
Ride	▓▓▓▓▓▓▓▓				
Steering/handling	▓▓▓▓▓▓▓▓				
Braking	▓▓▓▓▓▓▓▓▓▓				
Noise	▓▓▓▓▓▓				
Accommodations					
Driver seating	▓▓▓▓▓▓▓				
Instruments/controls	▓▓▓▓▓▓▓▓				
Visibility	▓▓▓▓▓▓				
Room/comfort	▓▓▓▓▓▓▓▓				
Entry/exit	▓▓▓▓▓▓▓				
Cargo room	▓▓▓▓▓▓				
Workmanship					
Exterior	▓▓▓▓▓▓▓▓				
Interior	▓▓▓▓▓▓▓				
Value	▓▓▓▓▓▓▓				

Total Points...59

Specifications

Body type	4-door notchback	Engine type	ohc I-4
Wheelbase (in.)	104.0	Engine size (l/cu. in.)	2.0/122
Overall length (in.)	171.8	Horsepower @ rpm	132 @ 6000
Overall width (in.)	67.4	Torque @ rpm	129 @ 5000
Overall height (in.)	54.8	Transmission	manual/5-sp.
Curb weight (lbs.)	2338	Drive wheels	front
Seating capacity	5	Brakes, F/R	disc/drum (ABS)
Front head room (in.)	39.6	Tire size	185/65R14
Max. front leg room (in.)	42.5	Fuel tank capacity (gal.)	11.2
Rear head room (in.)	36.5	EPA city/highway mpg	29/38
Min. rear leg room (in.)	35.1	Test mileage (mpg)	31.2
Cargo volume (cu. ft.)	11.8		

Warranties The entire car is covered for 3 years/36,000 miles. Body perforation rust is covered for 7 years/100,000 miles.

Rating scale 5=Exceptional; 4=Above average; 3=Average; 2=Below average; 1=Poor

FORD ASPIRE

Built in South Korea.

Ford Aspire SE

SUBCOMPACT

Ford's smallest car, the Aspire, comes in 3- and 5-door hatchback styling. Introduced in January 1994, the front-drive Aspire enters its second model year with few changes. A base model is available in both body styles and a sportier SE is available only as a 3-door. Dual air bags are standard and anti-lock brakes are optional on both the 3- and 5-door. The only option package on the Aspire is the Interior Decor and Convenience Group, available on the base models. It adds intermittent wipers, a cargo cover, manual remote mirrors, front door map pockets, split rear seatbacks, and upgraded interior trim. All of this equipment is now standard on the SE. The only available engine is a 1.3-liter 4-cylinder with 63 horsepower, mated to a standard 5-speed manual transmission. A 3-speed automatic is optional on the base models. Power steering is optional on the base 5-door with the automatic transmission. Though the 1.3-liter engine is adequate around town, on the highway there isn't enough power for safe passing. Fuel economy is exceptional with the 5-speed, but the automatic isn't as stingy with gas since it lacks a fuel-saving overdrive gear. The manual transmission has vague and rubbery shift linkage, while the automatic shifts harshly in hard acceleration. The engine is loud under throttle and tolerably quiet when cruising. There's enough room for 6-footers in front, though the thinly padded seat grows uncomfortable after about an hour. The dashboard has a modern, convenient design and visibility is good in all directions. Aspire is worth a look if low price and high fuel economy are of prime importance.

Ford Aspire prices are on page 310.

FORD ASPIRE SE

Rating Guide	1	2	3	4	5
Performance					
Acceleration					
Economy					
Driveability					
Ride					
Steering/handling					
Braking					
Noise					
Accommodations					
Driver seating					
Instruments/controls					
Visibility					
Room/comfort					
Entry/exit					
Cargo room					
Workmanship					
Exterior					
Interior					
Value					

Total Points **52**

Specifications

Body type ....3-door hatchback	Engine type ....ohc I-4
Wheelbase (in.) 90.7	Engine size (l/cu. in.)...........1.3/81
Overall length (in.)................152.8	Horsepower @ rpm .....63 @ 5000
Overall width (in.) 65.7	Torque @ rpm ....74 @ 3000
Overall height (in.)..................55.6	Transmission ....manual/5-sp.
Curb weight (lbs.) 2004	Drive wheels ....front
Seating capacity 4	Brakes, F/R....................disc/drum
Front head room (in.) 37.8	Tire size 165/70R13
Max. front leg room (in.) 41.6	Fuel tank capacity (gal.).........10.0
Rear head room (in.) 35.5	EPA city/highway mpg 36/42
Min. rear leg room (in.)...........33.6	Test mileage (mpg) ....NA
Cargo volume (cu. ft.).............37.7	

Warranties The entire car is covered for 3 years/36,000 miles. Body perforation rust is covered for 5 years/unlimited miles.

Rating scale 5=Exceptional; 4=Above average; 3=Average; 2=Below average; 1=Poor

FORD CONTOUR

Built in Kansas City, Mo., and Mexico

Ford Contour SE

COMPACT

Contour went on sale in the fall as Ford's new rival for the Honda Accord, Nissan Altima, Mazda 626, and other compact and mid-size sedans. Contour, a front-drive 4-door sedan, replaces the Tempo in Ford's lineup. Mercury has a similar model called Mystique (see separate report). The 106.5-inch wheelbase on Contour is half an inch longer than the mid-size Taurus's, but the overall length of 183.9 inches is eight inches shorter. Contour comes in GL, LX, and sporty SE price levels. Dual air bags are standard on all versions and anti-lock brakes and traction control are optional. Base engine is a 125-horsepower 2.0-liter 4-cylinder with dual overhead camshafts. Standard on the SE and optional on the others is a 170-horsepower 2.5-liter V-6, also with dual camshafts. Both engines are available with a standard 5-speed manual or optional electronic 4-speed automatic transmission. The V-6 is smooth, responsive, and delivers lively acceleration. By contrast, the 4-cylinder feels sluggish going uphill and requires a heavy throttle foot for brisk acceleration even on flat roads. With either engine the automatic shifts smoothly and downshifts promptly for passing. Though Contour has a firm suspension, it doesn't ride harshly over bumps or tar strips. Road noise is prominent on all models. Contour's interior has ample leg room for the front seats and adequate leg room for adults in the rear. Head room is generous in front and adequate in back. Entry/exit is easy to all seats. The modern, attractive dashboard is well designed, though the stereo has too many small buttons. Our early conclusion is that Contour is a formidable new entry in the compact class.

Ford Contour prices are on page 311.

FORD CONTOUR SE

Rating Guide	1	2	3	4	5
Performance					
Acceleration	▓▓▓▓▓▓▓▓▓▓▓▓▓▓▓▓ (≈4)				
Economy	▓▓▓▓▓▓▓▓▓▓▓ (≈3)				
Driveability	▓▓▓▓▓▓▓▓▓▓▓ (≈3)				
Ride	▓▓▓▓▓▓▓▓▓▓▓▓▓▓ (≈4)				
Steering/handling	▓▓▓▓▓▓▓▓▓▓▓▓▓▓ (≈4)				
Braking	▓▓▓▓▓▓▓▓▓▓▓▓▓▓▓▓▓▓▓ (≈5)				
Noise	▓▓▓▓▓▓▓▓▓▓▓ (≈3)				
Accommodations					
Driver seating	▓▓▓▓▓▓▓▓▓▓▓▓▓▓ (≈4)				
Instruments/controls	▓▓▓▓▓▓▓▓▓▓▓▓▓▓ (≈4)				
Visibility	▓▓▓▓▓▓▓▓▓▓▓ (≈3)				
Room/comfort	▓▓▓▓▓▓▓▓▓▓▓ (≈3)				
Entry/exit	▓▓▓▓▓▓▓▓▓▓▓ (≈3)				
Cargo room	▓▓▓▓▓▓▓▓▓▓▓▓▓▓ (≈4)				
Workmanship					
Exterior	▓▓▓▓▓▓▓▓▓▓▓▓▓▓ (≈4)				
Interior	▓▓▓▓▓▓▓▓▓▓▓▓▓▓ (≈4)				
Value	▓▓▓▓▓▓▓▓▓▓▓▓▓▓ (≈4)				

Total Points...60

Specifications

Body type	4-door notchback	Engine type	dohc V-6
Wheelbase (in.)	106.5	Engine size (l/cu. in.)	2.5/155
Overall length (in.)	183.9	Horsepower @ rpm	170 @ 6250
Overall width (in.)	69.1	Torque @ rpm	165 @ 4250
Overall height (in.)	54.5	Transmission	manual/5-sp.
Curb weight (lbs.)	2769	Drive wheels	front
Seating capacity	5	Brakes, F/R	disc/disc (ABS)
Front head room (in.)	39.0	Tire size	205/60R15
Max. front leg room (in.)	42.4	Fuel tank capacity (gal.)	14.5
Rear head room (in.)	36.7	EPA city/highway mpg	21/29
Min. rear leg room (in.)	34.3	Test mileage (mpg)	22.8
Cargo volume (cu. ft.)	14.1		

Warranties The entire car is covered for 3 years/36,000 miles. Body perforation rust is covered for 5 years/unlimited miles.

Rating scale 5=Exceptional; 4=Above average; 3=Average; 2=Below average; 1=Poor

FORD CROWN VICTORIA/ ——
MERCURY GRAND MARQUIS

Built in Canada.

Ford Crown Victoria

FULL-SIZE

Ford's rear-drive Crown Victoria and the similar Mercury Grand Marquis receive their first major changes since being redesigned for 1992. Both are full-size 6-passenger sedans. Crown Victoria comes in base and plusher LX models, while the Grand Marquis comes in GS and LS versions. Outside, both have new grilles, bumper fascias, and taillamps. Inside, they get a new instrument panel with woodgrain trim. Dual air bags return as standard. A rear defroster and heated outside mirrors, optional last year, are now standard, as is a battery saver function. The battery saver automatically shuts off the headlights if they are accidentally left on. Both the Crown Vic and Grand Marquis use Ford's 4.6-liter overhead-camshaft V-8. It produces 190 horsepower in base form and 210 horsepower with the optional dual exhaust. The only transmission available is an electronic 4-speed automatic. Anti-lock brakes and traction control are optional. The V-8 engine is quiet and enables these cars to accelerate swiftly and smoothly. However, it lacks enough low-speed torque to respond quickly to the throttle in the 20-to-45-mph range. The base suspension provides a stable ride without wallowing or floating, but the optional suspension included in the Handling and Performance Package makes the ride harsh and jittery. It also makes the power steering, which is already too light and numb, feel nervous. Both cars hold six adults and have ample trunk space. Overall, we favor front-drive rivals such as the Buick LeSabre and Dodge Intrepid, though they can't tow as much.

Ford Crown Victoria prices are on page 313.
Mercury Grand Marquis prices are on page 376.

FORD CROWN VICTORIA

Rating Guide	1	2	3	4	5
Performance					
Acceleration	‖‖‖‖‖‖‖‖‖‖‖‖‖‖‖‖‖‖‖‖‖‖‖‖‖				
Economy	‖‖‖‖‖‖				
Driveability	‖‖‖‖‖‖‖‖‖‖‖‖‖‖‖‖‖‖				
Ride	‖‖‖‖‖‖‖‖‖‖‖‖‖‖‖‖‖‖				
Steering/handling	‖‖‖‖‖‖‖‖‖‖‖‖‖‖‖‖‖‖				
Braking	‖‖‖‖‖‖‖‖‖‖‖‖‖‖‖‖‖‖‖‖‖‖‖‖‖				
Noise	‖‖‖‖‖‖‖‖‖‖‖‖‖‖‖‖‖‖‖‖‖				
Accommodations					
Driver seating	‖‖‖‖‖‖‖‖‖‖‖‖‖‖‖‖‖‖‖‖‖				
Instruments/controls	‖‖‖‖‖‖‖‖‖‖‖‖‖‖‖‖‖‖‖‖‖				
Visibility	‖‖‖‖‖‖‖‖‖‖‖‖‖				
Room/comfort	‖‖‖‖‖‖‖‖‖‖‖‖‖‖‖‖‖‖‖‖‖‖‖‖‖				
Entry/exit	‖‖‖‖‖‖‖‖‖‖‖‖‖‖‖‖‖‖‖‖‖‖‖‖‖				
Cargo room	‖‖‖‖‖‖‖‖‖‖‖‖‖‖‖‖‖‖‖‖‖				
Workmanship					
Exterior	‖‖‖‖‖‖‖‖‖‖‖‖‖‖‖‖‖‖‖‖‖				
Interior	‖‖‖‖‖‖‖‖‖‖‖‖‖‖‖‖‖‖‖‖‖				
Value	‖‖‖‖‖‖‖‖‖‖‖‖‖				
Total Points..60					

Specifications

Body type	4-door notchback	Engine	ohc V-8
Wheelbase (in.)	114.4	Engine size (l/cu. in.)	4.6/281
Overall length (in.)	212.0	Horsepower @ rpm	210 @ 4600
Overall width (in.)	77.8	Torque @ rpm	270 @ 3400
Overall height (in.)	56.8	Transmission	auto/4-sp.
Curb weight (lbs.)	3776	Drive wheels	rear
Seating capacity	6	Brakes, F/R	disc/disc (ABS)
Front head room (in.)	39.4	Tire size	225/60R15
Max. front leg room (in.)	42.5	Fuel tank capacity (gal.)	20.0
Rear head room (in.)	38.0	EPA city/highway mpg	17/25
Min. rear leg room (in.)	39.7	Test mileage (mpg)	15.3
Cargo volume (cu. ft.)	20.6		

Warranties The entire car is covered for 3 years/36,000 miles. Body perforation rust is covered for 5 years/unlimited miles.

Rating scale 5=Exceptional; 4=Above average; 3=Average; 2=Below average; 1=Poor

FORD ESCORT/ MERCURY TRACER

Built in Wayne, Mich., and Mexico.

Ford Escort LX 4-door

SUBCOMPACT

The front-drive Escort and similar Mercury Tracer gain a passenger-side air bag in a redesigned dashboard for 1995. Even with dual air bags now standard, both front seats retain motorized shoulder belts with manual lap belts. Escort comes in four body styles: 3-door hatchback, 4-door sedan, 5-door hatchback, and 5-door wagon. There are three price levels: Standard, LX, and GT. The Standard and GT are available only as 3-door models; the LX is available in all body styles. Tracer comes as a 4-door sedan and a 5-door wagon in a base price level, and as a sedan in a sportier LTS version. An integrated child seat that folds out of the rear backrest is scheduled to become optional later this year. When the child seat is folded away, the rear seat can be used normally. Powertrain choices carry over from last year. The base engine is a Ford 1.9-liter 4-cylinder that produces 88 horsepower. The Escort GT and Tracer LTS come with a Mazda 1.8-liter 4-cylinder with 127 horsepower and dual overhead camshafts. A 5-speed manual transmission is standard with both engines and a 4-speed automatic is optional. Anti-lock brakes are optional only on the GT and LTS. The Escort LX models are the most popular and nearly all are sold as well-equipped "one-price" models. In refinement and performance, Escort and Tracer trail such competitors as the Geo Prizm, the similar Toyota Corolla, and the Honda Civic. In addition, the Dodge and Plymouth Neon are roomier and sportier. Escort's advantage is that it costs thousands less than most small cars when similarly equipped.

Ford Escort prices are on page 315.
Mercury Tracer prices are on page 381.

FORD ESCORT LX

Rating Guide	1	2	3	4	5
Performance					
Acceleration	▮▮▮				
Economy	▮▮▮▮				
Driveability	▮▮▮				
Ride	▮▮▮▮				
Steering/handling	▮▮▮				
Braking	▮▮▮				
Noise	▮▮▮▮				
Accommodations					
Driver seating	▮▮▮				
Instruments/controls	▮▮▮				
Visibility	▮▮▮▮				
Room/comfort	▮▮▮				
Entry/exit	▮▮▮				
Cargo room	▮▮▮				
Workmanship					
Exterior	▮▮▮				
Interior	▮▮▮				
Value	▮▮▮▮				

Total Points..**55**

Specifications

Body type ....4-door notchback	Engine type ....ohc I-4
Wheelbase (in.) 98.4	Engine size (l/cu. in.).........1.9/114
Overall length (in.)................170.9	Horsepower @ rpm .....88 @ 4400
Overall width (in.) 66.7	Torque @ rpm ....108 @ 3800
Overall height (in.)..................52.7	Transmission ....auto/4-sp.
Curb weight (lbs.) 2404	Drive wheels ....front
Seating capacity..........................5	Brakes, F/R....................disc/drum
Front head room (in.) 38.4	Tire size 175/65R14
Max. front leg room (in.) 41.7	Fuel tank capacity (gal.) 11.9
Rear head room (in.) 37.4	EPA city/highway mpg 26/34
Min. rear leg room (in.)...........34.6	Test mileage (mpg) 26.8
Cargo volume (cu. ft.).............12.1	

Warranties The entire car is covered for 3 years/36,000 miles. Body perforation rust is covered for 5 years/unlimited miles.

Rating scale 5=Exceptional; 4=Above average; 3=Average; 2=Below average; 1=Poor

FORD EXPLORER

Built in Louisville, Ky.

Ford Explorer Eddie Bauer

SPORT-UTILITY VEHICLE

America's best-selling sport-utility vehicle gets its first redesign since it was introduced as a 1991 model. For 1995, Ford has restyled the front end with a sloping hood and grille, added dual air bags in a redesigned dashboard, and adopted a new automatic 4-wheel-drive system. Later in the model year, Explorer is scheduled to gain an optional child safety seat. The 3-door Explorer returns in XL and Sport models, and a new Expedition model has been added. The 5-door repeats in XL, XLT, Eddie Bauer, and Limited models. The standard 4.0-liter V-6 engine is unchanged at 160 horsepower. A 5-speed manual transmission is standard and a 4-speed automatic is optional. Both body styles come with rear-wheel drive or Ford's new Control Trac 4WD, in which power automatically is sent to the front wheels when rear-wheel slip is detected. Control Trac can be used on dry pavement. Previously, Explorer's 4WD system could be used only on slippery surfaces. Anti-lock brakes are standard and rear disc brakes are a new feature for 1995. Explorer earned its way to the top of the sport-utility field with its ability to double as a roomy 4WD vehicle and an upscale family wagon. Though it has less power than its domestic rivals, acceleration is more than adequate. The 5-door model rides more comfortably than the 3-door and has a much roomier rear seat. Ford has plenty of competition from the redesigned Chevrolet Blazer/GMC Jimmy and the Jeep Grand Cherokee, but the improvements to Explorer this year keep it at the front of the herd among sport-utility vehicles. The 1995 prices weren't announced in time for this issue.

1994 Ford Explorer prices are on page 317.

FORD EXPLORER EDDIE BAUER

Rating Guide	1	2	3	4	5
Performance					
Acceleration	▓▓▓▓▓▓▓▓▓▓				
Economy	▓▓▓▓				
Driveability	▓▓▓▓▓▓▓				
Ride	▓▓▓▓▓▓▓▓				
Steering/handling	▓▓▓▓▓▓▓				
Braking	▓▓▓▓▓▓▓▓▓▓▓				
Noise	▓▓▓▓▓▓▓				
Accommodations					
Driver seating	▓▓▓▓▓▓▓				
Instruments/controls	▓▓▓▓▓▓▓				
Visibility	▓▓▓▓▓▓▓				
Room/comfort	▓▓▓▓▓▓▓				
Entry/exit	▓▓▓▓▓▓▓				
Cargo room	▓▓▓▓▓▓▓▓▓▓▓				
Workmanship					
Exterior	▓▓▓▓▓▓▓				
Interior	▓▓▓▓▓▓▓				
Value	▓▓▓▓▓▓▓				
Total Points					**61**

Specifications

Body type ....5-door wagon
Wheelbase (in.) 111.5
Overall length (in.)................188.5
Overall width (in.) 70.2
Overall height (in.)................67.3
Curb weight (lbs.) 4189
Seating capacity..........................5
Front head room (in.) 39.9
Max. front leg room (in.) 42.4
Rear head room (in.) 39.3
Min. rear leg room (in.) 37.7
Cargo volume (cu. ft.).............81.6

Engine type......................ohv V-6
Engine size (l/cu. in.)........4.0/245
Horsepower @ rpm ...160 @ 4400
Torque @ rpm ....225 @ 2800
Transmission.................auto/4-sp.
Drive wheels......................rear/all
Brakes, F/R..........disc/disc (ABS)
Tire size 235/75R15
Fuel tank capacity (gal.) 21.0
EPA city/highway mpg 15/20
Test mileage (mpg) ....NA

Warranties The entire vehicle is covered for 3 years/36,000 miles. Body perforation rust is covered for 5 years/unlimited miles.

Rating scale 5=Exceptional; 4=Above average; 3=Average; 2=Below average; 1=Poor

FORD MUSTANG— RECOMMENDED

Built in Dearborn, Mich.

Ford Mustang GT 2-door

SPORTS AND GT

Ford unveiled a new Mustang for 1994 and it carries over for 1995 with no major changes. Available in 2-door coupe and 2-door convertible styling, the rear-drive Mustang comes in base and GT price levels. The convertible has a power top with a glass rear window. The GT adds a more powerful engine, bigger tires, firmer suspension, fog lights, and other features. A 3.8-liter V-6 engine with 145 horsepower is standard on the base model and a 5.0-liter V-8 with 215 horsepower is standard on the GT. Both engines come with a standard 5-speed manual transmission or optional 4-speed automatic. A high-performance Cobra version of the GT coupe is due to be added in the spring. The 1994 Cobra had a 240-horsepower version of the V-8 and came only with a 5-speed manual transmission. The Cobra also had a firmer suspension, anti-lock disc brakes, and unique exterior treatment. On the other models, 4-wheel disc brakes are standard and an anti-lock system is optional. All Mustangs come with standard dual air bags. The current Mustang feels much more solid than pre-1994 models, with the biggest gains in the convertible, which flexes and twists far less than previous models on rough pavement. The V-6 gives the base Mustang adequate acceleration. Though the GT's V-8 delivers brisk acceleration, it doesn't pin you back in your seat like the more-powerful engine in the rival Chevrolet Camaro Z28. Ford has softened the suspension so that bumps don't jar occupants like they used to, though the GT is still quite firm over broken surfaces. Mustang has a more upright design than Camaro, so the interior feels airier, though the rear seat is still best suited to those under 5-foot-6.

Ford Mustang prices are on page 320.

FORD MUSTANG GT

Rating Guide	1	2	3	4	5
Performance					
Acceleration	▐▐▐▐▐▐▐▐▐▐▐▐▐▐▐▐▐▐▐▐				
Economy	▐▐▐▐▐▐▐▐				
Driveability	▐▐▐▐▐▐▐▐▐▐▐▐▐▐				
Ride	▐▐▐▐▐▐▐▐▐▐				
Steering/handling	▐▐▐▐▐▐▐▐▐▐▐▐▐▐▐▐▐				
Braking	▐▐▐▐▐▐▐▐▐▐▐▐▐▐▐▐▐				
Noise	▐▐▐▐▐▐▐▐				
Accommodations					
Driver seating	▐▐▐▐▐▐▐▐▐▐▐▐▐▐▐▐▐				
Instruments/controls	▐▐▐▐▐▐▐▐▐▐▐▐▐▐				
Visibility	▐▐▐▐▐▐▐▐▐▐▐▐				
Room/comfort	▐▐▐▐▐▐▐▐				
Entry/exit	▐▐▐▐▐▐▐▐				
Cargo room	▐▐▐▐▐▐▐▐				
Workmanship					
Exterior	▐▐▐▐▐▐▐▐▐▐▐▐▐▐				
Interior	▐▐▐▐▐▐▐▐▐▐▐▐				
Value	▐▐▐▐▐▐▐▐				

Total Points...53

Specifications

Body type ....2-door notchback	Engine type.......................ohv V-8
Wheelbase (in.) 101.3	Engine size (l/cu. in.).........5.0/302
Overall length (in.)...............181.5	Horsepower @ rpm ...215 @ 4200
Overall width (in.) 71.8	Torque @ rpm ....285 @ 3400
Overall height (in.)..................52.9	Transmission............auto/4-sp.
Curb weight (lbs.) 3341	Drive wheels ....rear
Seating capacity........................4	Brakes, F/R..........disc/disc (ABS)
Front head room (in.) 38.1	Tire size......................225/55ZR16
Max. front leg room (in.) 42.6	Fuel tank capacity (gal.) 15.4
Rear head room (in.) 35.9	EPA city/highway mpg 17/25
Min. rear leg room (in.)...........30.3	Test mileage (mpg) 16.5
Cargo volume (cu. ft.)..............10.8	

Warranties The entire car is covered for 3 years/36,000 miles. Body perforation rust is covered for 5 years/unlimited miles.

Rating scale 5=Exceptional; 4=Above average; 3=Average; 2=Below average; 1=Poor

FORD PROBE/
MAZDA MX-6

Built in Flat Rock, Mich.

Ford Probe GT

SPORTS COUPE

The Probe and MX-6 have different styling but share their front-drive platform and major mechanical features. Probe is a 3-door hatchback that comes in base and GT models. There also is an SE package for the base Probe, which adds some of the GT's appearance items. MX-6 comes in only one model this year, with most options grouped in packages. Neither car receives any major changes, though the Probe GT has new 16-inch wheels and Ford has deleted some options. Gone are the rear wiper/washer and the 4-way seat height adjustment for the base model. The MX-6 and base Probe are powered by a 2.0-liter 4-cylinder engine with dual camshafts and 118 horsepower. The Probe GT has a dual-cam 2.5-liter V-6 with 164 horsepower. The V-6 is available on the MX-6 as part of the new $3075 LS Equipment Group. A 5-speed manual transmission is standard and a 4-speed automatic is optional with both engines, which are made by Mazda. Dual air bags are standard and anti-lock brakes are optional on both cars. While the V-6 versions are strong performers, the 4-cylinder models are satisfying as well. However, the optional automatic transmission saps the verve of both engines. Base models offer secure, sporty handling. The Probe GT's larger tires and stiffer suspension make it more agile but also much stiffer, which makes it pound over broken pavement. Front-seat room is good in both cars, but only children will be comfortable in the cramped rear seats. Though interior designs differ between the two, both have a convenient dashboard layout. Probe and the MX-6 are the best choices in the competitive sports coupe class, and you should consider both.

Ford Probe prices are on page 322.
Mazda MX-6 prices are on page 367.

FORD PROBE GT

Rating Guide	1	2	3	4	5
Performance					
Acceleration	▓	▓	▓	▓	
Economy	▓	▓	▓		
Driveability	▓	▓	▓		
Ride	▓	▓			
Steering/handling	▓	▓	▓	▓	
Braking	▓	▓	▓	▓	▓
Noise	▓	▓	▓		
Accommodations					
Driver seating	▓	▓	▓	▓	
Instruments/controls	▓	▓	▓	▓	
Visibility	▓	▓	▓		
Room/comfort	▓	▓			
Entry/exit	▓	▓			
Cargo room	▓	▓	▓		
Workmanship					
Exterior	▓	▓	▓	▓	
Interior	▓	▓	▓	▓	
Value	▓	▓	▓	▓	

Total Points...55

Specifications

Body type	3-door hatchback	Engine type	dohc V-6
Wheelbase (in.)	102.8	Engine size (l/cu. in.)	2.5/153
Overall length (in.)	178.9	Horsepower @ rpm	164 @ 5600
Overall width (in.)	69.8	Torque @ rpm	160 @ 4800
Overall height (in.)	51.6	Transmission	auto/4-sp.
Curb weight (lbs.)	2690	Drive wheels	front
Seating capacity	4	Brakes, F/R	disc/disc (ABS)
Front head room (in.)	37.8	Tire size	225/50VR16
Max. front leg room (in.)	43.1	Fuel tank capacity (gal.)	15.5
Rear head room (in.)	34.8	EPA city/highway mpg	20/26
Min. rear leg room (in.)	28.5	Test mileage (mpg)	22.2
Cargo volume (cu. ft.)	18.0		

Warranties The entire car is covered for 3 years/36,000 miles. Body perforation rust is covered for 5 years/unlimited miles.

Rating scale 5=Exceptional; 4=Above average; 3=Average; 2=Below average; 1=Poor

FORD TAURUS/ MERCURY SABLE

Built in Atlanta, Ga., and Chicago, Ill.

Ford Taurus SE

MID-SIZE

Taurus and Sable each gain a new model for 1995, the last year for the current design. This year, Taurus gains an SE (Sport Edition) model that joins GL, LX, and SHO models. The GL and LX are available as 4-door sedans and 5-door wagons, and the new SE and high-performance SHO only as sedans. Sable has GS and LS sedans and wagons, and the new LTS sedan. All have front-wheel drive and dual air bags. Anti-lock brakes are standard on the Sable LS and LTS and Taurus SHO. They're optional on other models. The new Taurus SE gets standard aluminum wheels and sport bucket seats; the Sable LTS gets the same plus leather upholstery. Air conditioning is now standard on all models. The standard engine on all but the Taurus LX wagon and Taurus SHO is a 140-horsepower 3.0-liter V-6. Standard on the LX wagon and optional on other models except the SHO is a 3.8-liter V-6 that also produces 140 horsepower but has more torque: 215 pounds/feet versus 165. On the SHO, the standard powertrain is a 3.0-liter V-6 with dual overhead camshafts and a 5-speed manual transmission. A 3.2-liter dual-cam V-6 comes with the optional 4-speed automatic. Both SHO engines produce 220 horsepower. A 4-speed automatic is standard on all other models. These cars offer an impressive combination of utility, style, safety features, and performance. They are still among the best choices in the mid-size class. However, the Honda Accord now offers a V-6 engine and the new Chevrolet Lumina has a substantial price advantage over Taurus, so the competition has intensified.

Ford Taurus prices are on page 323.
Mercury Sable prices are on page 379.

FORD TAURUS SE

Rating Guide	1	2	3	4	5
Performance					
Acceleration				▓	
Economy		▓			
Driveability				▓	
Ride			▓		
Steering/handling			▓		
Braking					▓
Noise			▓		
Accommodations					
Driver seating			▓		
Instruments/controls			▓		
Visibility			▓		
Room/comfort				▓	
Entry/exit				▓	
Cargo room				▓	
Workmanship					
Exterior				▓	
Interior				▓	
Value			▓		
Total Points					**60**

Specifications

Body type ....4-door notchback	Engine type ....ohv V-6
Wheelbase (in.) 106.0	Engine size (l/cu. in.) 3.8/232
Overall length (in.) 192.0	Horsepower @ rpm ...140 @ 3800
Overall width (in.) 70.7	Torque @ rpm ....215 @ 2200
Overall height (in.) 54.1	Transmission ....auto/4-sp.
Curb weight (lbs.) 3118	Drive wheels ....front
Seating capacity 6	Brakes, F/R ....disc/disc (ABS)
Front head room (in.) 38.3	Tire size 205/65R15
Max. front leg room (in.) 41.7	Fuel tank capacity (gal.) 16.0
Rear head room (in.) 37.6	EPA city/highway mpg 19/28
Min. rear leg room (in.) 37.5	Test mileage (mpg) 17.9
Cargo volume (cu. ft.).............18.0	

Warranties The entire car is covered for 3 years/36,000 miles. Body perforation rust is covered for 5 years/unlimited miles.

Rating scale 5=Exceptional; 4=Above average; 3=Average; 2=Below average; 1=Poor

FORD THUNDERBIRD/——
MERCURY COUGAR

Built in Lorain, Ohio.

Ford Thunderbird LX

MID-SIZE

The rear-drive Thunderbird and similar Cougar 2-door coupes return for 1995 with no major changes. Thunderbird comes in two models, the luxury LX and high-performance Super Coupe (SC), while Cougar comes in a single XR7 trim level. Base engine for the Thunderbird LX and Cougar is a 3.8-liter V-6 that makes 140 horsepower. Optional on those two is an overhead-camshaft 4.6-liter V-8 with 205 horsepower. Both engines mate to a 4-speed automatic transmission. The Thunderbird SC is powered by a 230-horsepower supercharged 3.8-liter V-6. This engine comes with a standard 5-speed manual transmission; a 4-speed automatic is optional. Anti-lock brakes are standard on the Thunderbird SC and optional on the others. Dual air bags are standard on all and traction control is optional. The Thunderbird LX and Cougar are impressive values, with dual air bags, air conditioning, and several other standard features for less than $18,000. Their biggest shortfall is the standard V-6, which can't move these 3600-pound coupes with any verve. We recommend the optional V-8, which is quieter and much stronger, though response in the 20-to-45 mph range is unimpressive. However, the V-8 has good acceleration off the line and strong highway passing power. The Thunderbird SC is the speedster of this bunch, though the supercharged V-6 is noisier and rougher than the V-8. In addition, the SC has a stiffer ride than the LX, which puts comfort ahead of handling prowess. Snow-belt residents should note that we tested a V-8 LX last winter that got stuck in snow a couple of times despite having the optional traction control.

Ford Thunderbird prices are on page 326.
Mercury Cougar prices are on page 374.

FORD THUNDERBIRD LX

Rating Guide	1	2	3	4	5
Performance					
Acceleration					
Economy					
Driveability					
Ride					
Steering/handling					
Braking					
Noise					
Accommodations					
Driver seating					
Instruments/controls					
Visibility					
Room/comfort					
Entry/exit					
Cargo room					
Workmanship					
Exterior					
Interior					
Value					

Total Points...57

Specifications

Body type ....2-door notchback	Engine type ....ohc V-8
Wheelbase (in.) 113.0	Engine size (l/cu. in.).........4.6/281
Overall length (in.)................200.3	Horsepower @ rpm ...205 @ 4500
Overall width (in.) 72.7	Torque @ rpm ....265 @ 3200
Overall height (in.)..................52.5	Transmission.................auto/4-sp.
Curb weight (lbs.) 3575	Drive wheels ....rear
Seating capacity 5	Brakes, F/R...........disc/disc (ABS)
Front head room (in.) 38.1	Tire size 215/70R15
Max. front leg room (in.) 42.5	Fuel tank capacity (gal.) 18.0
Rear head room (in.) 37.5	EPA city/highway mpg 17/25
Min. rear leg room (in.)...........35.8	Test mileage (mpg) 18.2
Cargo volume (cu. ft.).............15.1	

Warranties The entire car is covered for 3 years/36,000 miles. Body perforation rust is covered for 5 years/unlimited miles.

Rating scale 5=Exceptional; 4=Above average; 3=Average; 2=Below average; 1=Poor

FORD WINDSTAR — RECOMMENDED

Built in Canada.

Ford Windstar LX

MINIVAN

Windstar, Ford's first front-drive minivan, was introduced as an early 1995 model and aimed directly at the Dodge Grand Caravan and Plymouth Grand Voyager. Standard equipment includes dual air bags and seats for seven. Currently, both the GL and upscale LX models come with a 155-horsepower 3.8-liter V-6 engine. Later this year, a 147-horsepower 3.0-liter V-6 will become standard on the GL. The only transmission available with either engine is a 4-speed electronic automatic. Anti-lock brakes are standard on both models. Windstar comes in one size with a sliding right rear door and a one-piece liftgate. The 120.7-inch wheelbase is the longest of any minivan. At 201 inches overall, Windstar is 8.2 inches longer than the Grand Caravan. It comes with two bucket seats in front and two removable bench seats. New seating options include four bucket seats and integrated child seats for the middle bench. Ford said it designed Windstar to be quieter and more car-like than any minivan rival—and we think it hits the mark on both counts. The step-in height is low, and Windstar has less road and engine noise than its major rivals. It also has an absorbent suspension that delivers a comfortable, stable ride. Body lean is moderate and the tires grip well in spirited cornering, though the steering feels loose and imprecise. Acceleration is adequate from a standing start, but the transmission usually pauses a moment or two before downshifting for passing, and it often shifts roughly in first and second gears. Windstar offers good value in a competent package, and it is the biggest threat yet to Chrysler's minivans.

Ford Windstar prices are on page 328.

CONSUMER GUIDE®

FORD WINDSTAR LX

Rating Guide	1	2	3	4	5
Performance					
Acceleration	▓▓▓▓▓▓				
Economy	▓▓▓▓▓				
Driveability	▓▓▓▓▓▓				
Ride	▓▓▓▓▓▓▓				
Steering/handling	▓▓▓▓▓▓▓				
Braking	▓▓▓▓▓▓▓▓				
Noise	▓▓▓▓▓▓▓				
Accommodations					
Driver seating	▓▓▓▓▓▓▓				
Instruments/controls	▓▓▓▓▓▓▓				
Visibility	▓▓▓▓▓▓▓				
Room/comfort	▓▓▓▓▓▓▓▓				
Entry/exit	▓▓▓▓▓▓▓				
Cargo room	▓▓▓▓▓▓▓▓				
Workmanship					
Exterior	▓▓▓▓▓▓				
Interior	▓▓▓▓▓▓				
Value	▓▓▓▓▓▓				

Total Points...61

Specifications

Body type	4-door van	Engine type	ohv V-6
Wheelbase (in.)	120.7	Engine size (l/cu. in.)	3.8/232
Overall length (in.)	201.0	Horsepower @ rpm	155 @ 4000
Overall width (in.)	75.0	Torque @ rpm	220 @ 3000
Overall height (in.)	68.0	Transmission	auto/4-sp.
Curb weight (lbs.)	3800	Drive wheels	front
Seating capacity	7	Brakes, F/R	disc/drum (ABS)
Front head room (in.)	39.3	Tire size	215/70R15
Max. front leg room (in.)	40.7	Fuel tank capacity (gal.)	20.0
Rear head room (in.)	38.9	EPA city/highway mpg	17/24
Min. rear leg room (in.)	39.2	Test mileage (mpg)	15.9
Cargo volume (cu. ft.)	144.3		

Warranties The entire vehicle is covered for 3 years/36,000 miles. Body perforation rust is covered for 5 years/unlimited miles.

Rating scale 5=Exceptional; 4=Above average; 3=Average; 2=Below average; 1=Poor

GEO METRO/
SUZUKI SWIFT

Built in Canada.

Geo Metro 4-door

SUBCOMPACT

The front-drive Metro and Swift have been redesigned for 1995 and dual air bags are a new standard feature on all models and anti-lock brakes are a new option. Both are assembled at a plant in Canada jointly owned by General Motors and Suzuki. The Metro, which is sold by Chevrolet dealers with Geo franchises, comes in 3-door hatchback and new 4-door notchback body styles. Both ride a 93.1-inch wheelbase, 3.9 inches longer than last year. Last year's 5-door hatchback body style and the gas-miser XFi 3-door are gone. A 55-horsepower 1.0-liter 3-cylinder, last year's only engine, returns as standard on the 3-door. New to the Metro line is a 70-horsepower 1.3-liter 4-cylinder. It's standard on the sedan and optional on the LSi hatchback. A 5-speed manual transmission is standard with both engines and a 3-speed automatic is optional with the 4-cylinder. For now, Swift comes only as a 3-door hatchback with the 4-cylinder engine. Suzuki says a 4-door notchback sedan will be added next spring as an early 1996 model, and it will be substantially different than the 4-door Metro. We've driven the new Metro only at Geo's press preview and found it far more substantial than its predecessor. The light weight is still evident, however. Bumps jar the suspension and create kickback through the steering wheel. Only the 4-cylinder engine/5-speed manual transmission combination provides suitable acceleration for both city and highway work. Fuel economy will be high with any powertrain. Our initial review puts Metro ahead of the Ford Aspire in the minicar field, but a larger car may be a better choice in the long run.

Geo Metro prices are on page 330.
Suzuki Swift prices are on page 432.

GEO METRO (Preliminary)

Rating Guide	1	2	3	4	5
Performance					
Acceleration					
Economy					
Driveability					
Ride					
Steering/handling					
Braking					
Noise					
Accommodations					
Driver seating					
Instruments/controls					
Visibility					
Room/comfort					
Entry/exit					
Cargo room					
Workmanship					
Exterior					
Interior					
Value					

Total Points **50**

Specifications

Body type ....4-door notchback	Engine type ....ohc I-4
Wheelbase (in.) 93.1	Engine size (l/cu. in.) 1.3/79
Overall length (in.) 164.0	Horsepower @ rpm .....70 @ 6000
Overall width (in.) 62.8	Torque @ rpm ....74 @ 3500
Overall height (in.) 55.7	Transmission ....manual/5-sp.
Curb weight (lbs.) 1940	Drive wheels ....front
Seating capacity 4	Brakes, F/R...................disc/drum
Front head room (in.) 39.3	Tire size 155/80R13
Max. front leg room (in.) 42.5	Fuel tank capacity (gal.) 10.6
Rear head room (in.) 37.3	EPA city/highway mpg 39/43
Min. rear leg room (in.) 32.8	Test mileage (mpg) ....NA
Cargo volume (cu. ft.).............10.3	

Warranties The entire car is covered for 3 years/36,000 miles. Body perforation rust is covered for 6 years/100,000 miles.

Rating scale 5=Exceptional; 4=Above average; 3=Average; 2=Below average; 1=Poor

GEO TRACKER/
SUZUKI SIDEKICK

Built in Canada.

Geo Tracker LSi convertible

SPORT-UTILITY VEHICLE

All 4-wheel-drive versions of these pint-sized sport-utility vehicles get a more powerful engine and convertibles have a new manual top designed for easier operation. Tracker comes as a 2-door convertible and a 2-door hardtop wagon. The similar Sidekick also comes as a 2-door convertible but adds a longer 5-door wagon body style. Both brands are built in Canada at a plant jointly owned by General Motors and Suzuki (GM owns a stake in Suzuki). The base engine for 2-door 2-wheel drive models is an 80-horsepower 1.6-liter 4-cylinder with two valves per cylinder. For 1995, all 5-door Sidekicks and 2-door 4WD models have a 95-horsepower version of this engine with four valves per cylinder. The 4-valve engine also is used in all models sold in California and Massachusetts to meet stricter emissions requirements in those states. Rear anti-lock brakes that function only in 2WD are standard. The new convertible top can still be folded halfway back like a sunroof, but design revisions are intended to make it easier to fully lower. Compared to the paramilitary Jeep Wrangler, the 2-door Tracker/Sidekick is more modern and refined. Even so, it has excessive noise levels, a choppy ride, a tiny back seat, and minuscule cargo space behind the rear seat. The roomier Sidekick 5-door is more practical for daily use, though not enough to get us interested. We have a hard time recommending any of these vehicles as everyday transportation because of their small size, lightweight construction, and absence of air bags. They also lack the comfort and performance of cars in the same price range.

Geo Tracker prices are on page 333.
Suzuki Sidekick prices are on page 431.

GEO TRACKER LSi

Rating Guide	1	2	3	4	5
Performance					
Acceleration	▓▓▓▓▓▓▓▓▓▓▓▓▓				
Economy	▓▓▓▓▓▓▓▓▓▓▓▓▓				
Driveability	▓▓▓▓▓▓▓▓▓▓▓▓▓				
Ride	▓▓▓▓▓▓▓▓▓▓▓				
Steering/handling	▓▓▓▓▓▓▓▓▓▓▓▓▓				
Braking	▓▓▓▓▓▓▓▓▓▓▓▓▓▓▓▓				
Noise	▓▓▓▓▓▓▓▓				
Accommodations					
Driver seating	▓▓▓▓▓▓▓▓▓▓▓▓▓				
Instruments/controls	▓▓▓▓▓▓▓▓▓▓▓▓▓▓				
Visibility	▓▓▓▓▓▓▓▓▓▓▓▓▓				
Room/comfort	▓▓▓▓▓▓▓▓▓▓▓▓▓				
Entry/exit	▓▓▓▓▓▓▓▓▓▓▓▓▓				
Cargo room	▓▓▓▓▓▓▓▓▓▓▓▓▓				
Workmanship					
Exterior	▓▓▓▓▓▓▓▓▓▓▓▓▓▓				
Interior	▓▓▓▓▓▓▓▓▓▓▓▓▓				
Value	▓▓▓▓▓▓▓▓▓▓▓▓▓				
Total Points **45**					

Specifications

Body type	2-door convertible	Engine type	ohc I-4
Wheelbase (in.)	86.6	Engine size (l/cu. in.)	1.6/97
Overall length (in.)	142.5	Horsepower @ rpm	95 @ 5600
Overall width (in.)	64.2	Torque @ rpm	98 @ 4000
Overall height (in.)	64.3	Transmission	manual/5-sp.
Curb weight (lbs.)	2246	Drive wheels	rear/all
Seating capacity	4	Brakes, F/R	disc/drum (ABS)
Front head room (in.)	39.5	Tire size	205/75R15
Max. front leg room (in.)	42.1	Fuel tank capacity (gal.)	11.1
Rear head room (in.)	39.0	EPA city/highway mpg	23/26
Min. rear leg room (in.)	31.6	Test mileage (mpg)	24.0
Cargo volume (cu. ft.)	32.9		

Warranties The entire vehicle is covered for 3 years/36,000 miles. Body perforation rust is covered for 6 years/100,000 miles.

Rating scale 5=Exceptional; 4=Above average; 3=Average; 2=Below average; 1=Poor

HONDA ACCORD

Built in Marysville, Ohio, and Japan.

Honda Accord EX V-6

MID-SIZE

The front-drive Accord finally pulls abreast of mid-size competitors in 1995 with its first V-6 engine, a 2.7-liter with 170 horsepower. Because the V-6 is larger than Accord's 4-cylinder, V-6 models have a longer nose and different grille. The V-6 teams only with a 4-speed automatic transmission in the Accord sedan. There are two V-6 models, the LX and EX, both with standard anti-lock brakes. Other standard equipment parallels the 4-cylinder LX and EX sedans, except for 205/60VR15 tires on both V-6 models and leather upholstery and an 8-way power driver's seat on the EX. The V-6 won't be available in the Accord coupe or wagon for 1995. Because Accord was redesigned last year, the 4-cylinder lineup sees few changes. Offerings consist of DX, LX, and EX sedans, and LX and EX 2-door coupes and 5-door wagons. All 4-cylinder models have a 2.2-liter engine. In the EX, horsepower is 145 and in the others it's 130. The EX wagon is now offered only with a 4-speed automatic. A 5-speed manual remains standard on other 4-cylinder models and the automatic is optional. The V-6 engine is quiet, smooth, and potent. We clocked a V-6 Accord at 8.9 seconds to 60 mph, versus 9.6 seconds for a 4-cylinder EX. The 4-cylinder Accords are solid family cars with refined, sporty manners. All Accords have poised handling and ride quality that is on the firm side yet stable and comfortable. There's plenty of room for four adults and the dashboard has clear gauges and simple, smooth-working controls. Our main criticism of the Accord last year was that it needed a V-6 to compete with the front runners in the mid-size class. The V-6 is here, and Accord again runs with the leaders.

Honda Accord prices are on page 338.

HONDA ACCORD EX V-6

Rating Guide	1	2	3	4	5
Performance					
Acceleration	▐▐▐▐▐▐▐▐▐▐▐▐▐▐				
Economy	▐▐▐▐▐▐▐▐▐▐				
Driveability	▐▐▐▐▐▐▐▐▐▐▐▐▐▐				
Ride	▐▐▐▐▐▐▐▐▐▐▐▐▐▐				
Steering/handling	▐▐▐▐▐▐▐▐▐▐▐▐▐▐				
Braking	▐▐▐▐▐▐▐▐▐▐▐▐▐▐▐▐▐▐▐▐▐▐				
Noise	▐▐▐▐▐▐▐▐▐▐				
Accommodations					
Driver seating	▐▐▐▐▐▐▐▐▐▐▐▐▐▐				
Instruments/controls	▐▐▐▐▐▐▐▐▐▐▐▐▐▐				
Visibility	▐▐▐▐▐▐▐▐▐▐▐▐▐▐				
Room/comfort	▐▐▐▐▐▐▐▐▐▐▐▐▐▐				
Entry/exit	▐▐▐▐▐▐▐▐▐▐▐▐▐▐				
Cargo room	▐▐▐▐▐▐▐▐▐▐▐▐▐▐				
Workmanship					
Exterior	▐▐▐▐▐▐▐▐▐▐▐▐▐▐				
Interior	▐▐▐▐▐▐▐▐▐▐▐▐▐▐				
Value	▐▐▐▐▐▐▐▐▐▐				

Total Points...63

Specifications

Body type ....4-door notchback		Engine type ....ohc V-6
Wheelbase (in.) 106.9		Engine size (l/cu. in.)..........2.7/163
Overall length (in.)...............184.0		Horsepower @ rpm ...170 @ 5600
Overall width (in.) 70.1		Torque @ rpm ....165 @ 4500
Overall height (in.) 55.1		Transmission.................auto/4-sp.
Curb weight (lbs.) 3285		Drive wheels ....front
Seating capacity...........................5		Brakes, F/R ....disc/disc (ABS)
Front head room (in.) 38.4		Tire size....................205/60VR15
Max. front leg room (in.) 42.7		Fuel tank capacity (gal.) 17.0
Rear head room (in.) 36.7		EPA city/highway mpg 19/25
Min. rear leg room (in.)...........34.3		Test mileage (mpg) 21.0
Cargo volume (cu. ft.).............13.0		

Warranties The entire car is covered for 3 years/36,000 miles. Body perforation rust is covered for 3 years/unlimited miles.

Rating scale 5=Exceptional; 4=Above average; 3=Average; 2=Below average; 1=Poor

HONDA CIVIC

Built in East Liberty, Ohio; Canada; and Japan.

✓ BEST BUY

Honda Civic EX 4-door

SUBCOMPACT

The front-drive Civic is unchanged for 1995, which should be the last for the current design if Honda sticks to its usual 4-year product cycle. The lineup comprises 2-door coupes and 4-door sedans in DX and EX price levels, a mid-range LX sedan, and 3-door hatchbacks in CX, VX, DX, and sporty Si trim. All Civics have a 4-cylinder engine and a standard 5-speed manual transmission. The entry-level CX hatchback has a 70-horsepower 1.5-liter engine and the VX a high-mileage 92-horsepower version. The DX and LX models, Civic's mainstay sellers, use a 102-horsepower 1.5-liter. The EX models and Si hatchback have a 1.6-liter engine with 125 horsepower. A 4-speed automatic transmission is optional on all models except the CX and VX hatchbacks. Anti-lock brakes are standard on the EX sedan and optional on the EX coupe, LX sedan, and Si hatchback. All models have standard dual air bags. Civic is no longer the design and value leader, but it remains an excellent choice among subcompacts because of its nimble handling, smooth engines, and good mileage. The Toyota Corolla and similar Geo Prizm and the Dodge and Plymouth Neon are Civic's most formidable rivals. Try some of those rivals before you buy—and don't be surprised to find Honda dealers readily discounting their prices. The sedan, the best-selling Civic body style, has ride quality that rivals bigger cars and more interior space than some compacts. However, an EX 4-door can cost as much as a low-end Accord when similarly equipped. A DX sedan will be cheaper, though it isn't available with anti-lock brakes, a feature we highly recommend. An LX with the anti-lock feature is the best choice.

Honda Civic prices are on page 339.

CONSUMER GUIDE®

HONDA CIVIC EX

Rating Guide	1	2	3	4	5
Performance					
Acceleration	▓	▓	▓	▓	
Economy	▓	▓	▓	▓	
Driveability	▓	▓	▓		
Ride	▓	▓	▓		
Steering/handling	▓	▓	▓	▓	
Braking	▓	▓	▓	▓	▓
Noise	▓	▓	▓		
Accommodations					
Driver seating	▓	▓	▓		
Instruments/controls	▓	▓	▓	▓	
Visibility	▓	▓	▓		
Room/comfort	▓	▓	▓		
Entry/exit	▓	▓	▓		
Cargo room	▓	▓	▓		
Workmanship					
Exterior	▓	▓	▓	▓	
Interior	▓	▓	▓	▓	
Value	▓	▓	▓		

Total Points..**59**

Specifications

Body type	4-door notchback	Engine type	ohc I-4
Wheelbase (in.)	103.2	Engine size (l/cu. in.)	1.6/97
Overall length (in.)	173.0	Horsepower @ rpm	125 @ 6600
Overall width (in.)	67.0	Torque @ rpm	106 @ 55200
Overall height (in.)	51.7	Transmission	manual/5-sp.
Curb weight (lbs.)	2522	Drive wheels	front
Seating capacity	5	Brakes, F/R	disc/disc (ABS)
Front head room (in.)	39.1	Tire size	175/65R14
Max. front leg room (in.)	42.5	Fuel tank capacity (gal.)	11.9
Rear head room (in.)	37.2	EPA city/highway mpg	29/35
Min. rear leg room (in.)	32.8	Test mileage (mpg)	30.7
Cargo volume (cu. ft.)	12.4		

Warranties The entire car is covered for 3 years/36,000 miles. Body perforation rust is covered for 3 years/unlimited miles.

Rating scale 5=Exceptional; 4=Above average; 3=Average; 2=Below average; 1=Poor

HONDA DEL SOL

Built in Japan.

Honda del Sol Si

SPORTS COUPE

This 2-seat semi-convertible was launched two years ago in S and sportier Si trim as a derivative of the front-drive Civic sub-compact. An even sportier VTEC version with Honda's variable-valve-timing technology was added last year. The most noteworthy addition for 1995 is standard anti-lock brakes for the VTEC, which, along with the Si, adds power door locks as well. The anti-lock brakes aren't available on the other models. Dual air bags return as standard across the board. All del Sols add a low-fuel warning light and a remote trunk release. The base del Sol S has a 102 horse-power 1.5-liter 4-cylinder engine, also used in the Civic DX and LX models. The Si uses a 125-horsepower 1.6-liter 4-cylinder also found in the Civic EX and Si models. The VTEC engine is a dual-camshaft 1.6-liter with 160 horsepower, and it mates solely with a 5-speed manual transmission. On the S and Si, a 5-speed manual is standard and a 4-speed automatic is optional. All del Sols have a removable aluminum roof panel that weighs 24 pounds and stores on a hinged frame in the trunk. A power roll-down rear window with a defroster also is standard. The del Sol is attractively styled, cleverly designed, and fun to drive. It's not a true sports car in the mold of the similarly priced Mazda Miata. Rather, its main appeal is its ability to provide open-air motoring or fully enclosed security. With the roof panel off, the del Sol is remarkably free of the cockpit buffeting typical of convertibles. Unfortunately, it's also prone to body flex and twisting—flaws that diminish with the roof panel in place. Acceleration is good in the S model, enthusiastic in the Si, and inspiring in the VTEC.

Honda del Sol prices are on page 340.

HONDA DEL SOL Si

Rating Guide	1	2	3	4	5
Performance					
Acceleration	▓▓▓▓▓▓▓▓				
Economy	▓▓▓▓▓▓▓▓				
Driveability	▓▓▓▓▓▓▓▓				
Ride	▓▓▓▓▓▓▓				
Steering/handling	▓▓▓▓▓▓▓▓				
Braking	▓▓▓▓▓▓▓▓				
Noise	▓▓▓▓▓				
Accommodations					
Driver seating	▓▓▓▓▓▓▓▓				
Instruments/controls	▓▓▓▓▓▓▓▓				
Visibility	▓▓▓▓▓▓▓				
Room/comfort	▓▓▓▓▓▓				
Entry/exit	▓▓▓▓▓▓▓				
Cargo room	▓▓▓▓▓				
Workmanship					
Exterior	▓▓▓▓▓▓▓▓				
Interior	▓▓▓▓▓▓▓▓				
Value	▓▓▓▓▓▓▓▓				
Total Points					**56**

Specifications

Body type	2-door notchback	Engine type	ohc I-4
Wheelbase (in.)	93.3	Engine size (l/cu. in.)	1.6/97
Overall length (in.)	157.3	Horsepower @ rpm	125 @ 6600
Overall width (in.)	66.7	Torque @ rpm	106 @ 5200
Overall height (in.)	49.4	Transmission	manual/5-sp.
Curb weight (lbs.)	2414	Drive wheels	front
Seating capacity	2	Brakes, F/R	disc/disc
Front head room (in.)	37.5	Tire size	185/60HR14
Max. front leg room (in.)	40.3	Fuel tank capacity (gal.)	11.9
Rear head room (in.)	—	EPA city/highway mpg	29/35
Min. rear leg room (in.)	—	Test mileage (mpg)	33.4
Cargo volume (cu. ft.)	10.5		

Warranties The entire car is covered for 3 years/36,000 miles. Body perforation rust is covered for 3 years/unlimited miles.

Rating scale 5=Exceptional; 4=Above average; 3=Average; 2=Below average; 1=Poor

HONDA ODYSSEY

Built in Japan.

Honda Odyssey EX

MINIVAN

Honda becomes the last major automaker to field a minivan with the front-drive Odyssey, which is nearly a foot longer than the standard-size Chrysler minivans and about six inches shorter than Chrysler's extended-length "Grand" models. Prices weren't announced in time for this issue, but Honda says the base price will be around $24,000, near the top of the minivan field. Odyssey departs from most other minivans in having four swing-open side doors (instead of two front doors and a sliding right-rear door). Odyssey also has a one-piece rear liftgate, making it a 5-door van. It is built on a stretched version of Accord's front-drive platform but has unique exterior styling and interior features. The only engine this year is a 140-horsepower 2.2-liter 4-cylinder borrowed from the Accord. The sole transmission is Accord's 4-speed automatic, but with the shift lever on the steering column instead of the floor. LX and upscale EX versions are offered, both with standard dual air bags and anti-lock brakes. The standard 6-passenger seating includes a pair of removable center "captain's chairs" that weigh 38 pounds each. The LX offers a no-cost 7-passenger option with a 3-place middle bench. Both models have a novel 2-place third seat that folds flush into the floor but is not removable. Odyssey is visibly narrower than most other minivans: from two to five inches by Honda's own tape measure. That limits cargo width and makes for cramped 3-abreast seating with the optional middle bench. However, it's pleasant to drive, well-equipped, and accommodates six people nicely. We think it needs a V-6 engine and a more reasonable starting price.

Honda Odyssey standard equipment is on page 340.

HONDA ODYSSEY EX (Preliminary)

Rating Guide	1	2	3	4	5
Performance					
Acceleration	▓▓▓▓▓▓▓▓▓▓▓▓▓▓▓				
Economy	▓▓▓▓▓▓▓▓▓				
Driveability	▓▓▓▓▓▓▓▓▓▓▓				
Ride	▓▓▓▓▓▓▓▓▓▓▓▓▓▓				
Steering/handling •	▓▓▓▓▓▓▓▓▓▓▓▓				
Braking	▓▓▓▓▓▓▓▓▓▓▓▓▓▓▓▓				
Noise	▓▓▓▓▓▓▓▓▓▓▓▓				
Accommodations					
Driver seating	▓▓▓▓▓▓▓▓▓▓▓				
Instruments/controls	▓▓▓▓▓▓▓▓▓▓▓				
Visibility	▓▓▓▓▓▓▓▓▓▓				
Room/comfort	▓▓▓▓▓▓▓▓▓▓▓				
Entry/exit	▓▓▓▓▓▓▓▓▓▓				
Cargo room	▓▓▓▓▓▓▓▓▓▓▓▓▓				
Workmanship					
Exterior	▓▓▓▓▓▓▓▓▓▓▓▓▓▓▓				
Interior	▓▓▓▓▓▓▓▓▓▓▓▓▓▓▓▓				
Value	▓▓▓▓▓▓▓▓▓▓▓				
Total Points					**60**

Specifications

Body type ....5-door van
Wheelbase (in.) 111.4
Overall length (in.) 186.7
Overall width (in.) 70.5
Overall height (in.) 64.7
Curb weight (lbs.) 3468
Seating capacity 6
Front head room (in.) 36.7
Max. front leg room (in.) 40.7
Rear head room (in.) 39.3
Min. rear leg room (in.) 34.1
Cargo volume (cu. ft.)...............NA

Engine type ....ohc I-4
Engine size (l/cu. in.) 2.2/132
Horsepower @ rpm ...140 @ 5600
Torque @ rpm ....145 @ 4600
Transmission ....auto/4-sp.
Drive wheels ....front
Brakes, F/R...........disc/disc (ABS)
Tire size 205/65R15
Fuel tank capacity (gal.) 17.2
EPA city/highway mpg 19/23
Test mileage (mpg) ....NA

Warranties The entire vehicle is covered for 3 years/36,000 miles. Body perforation rust is covered for 3 years/unlimited miles.

Rating scale 5=Exceptional; 4=Above average; 3=Average; 2=Below average; 1=Poor

HONDA PRELUDE

Built in Japan.

Honda Prelude Si

SPORTS COUPE

Prelude is unchanged for 1995 except that the base S now comes with air conditioning, which already was standard on the Si and VTEC models, and the slow-selling Si model with 4-wheel steering has been dropped. Honda's front-drive sports coupe continues with 4-cylinder power and a standard 5-speed manual transmission. The S has a 2.2-liter engine with a single camshaft and 135 horsepower. The Si has a dual-cam 2.3-liter with 160 horsepower. The VTEC has a 2.2-liter dual-cam engine with Honda's variable-valve-timing system and 190 horsepower. A 4-speed automatic is optional on the S and Si. The Si and VTEC come with anti-lock brakes, wider V-rated tires (for speeds up to 149 mph), alloy wheels, and power door locks, features that aren't available on the S. Dual air bags are standard on all models. Prelude, one of the most expensive cars in the crowded sports-coupe class, isn't selling well, so dealers should be cutting their prices to move their merchandise. All Prelude engines run turbine-smooth and the Si's 2.3-liter is quick and fairly frugal (8.4 seconds to 60 mph and 25.5 mpg with manual transmission in our test). The VTEC packs bundles of horsepower and provides outstanding performance at higher speeds. However, like most other multi-valve engines, it doesn't produce much torque at low speeds, so you have to work it hard for good results. Dashboard controls are conveniently placed, but warning lights run across the dashboard too far to the right for the driver to quickly check while underway and the gauges don't stand out enough in daylight when the headlights are on. The tiny rear seat is best left to toddlers or small pets, and trunk space is meager.

Honda Prelude prices are on page 342.

HONDA PRELUDE Si

Rating Guide	1	2	3	4	5
Performance					
Acceleration	▓▓▓▓▓▓▓▓▓▓				
Economy	▓▓▓▓▓▓				
Driveability	▓▓▓▓▓▓▓				
Ride	▓▓▓▓▓▓				
Steering/handling	▓▓▓▓▓▓▓				
Braking	▓▓▓▓▓▓▓▓▓▓				
Noise	▓▓▓▓▓▓				
Accommodations					
Driver seating	▓▓▓▓▓▓				
Instruments/controls	▓▓▓▓▓▓				
Visibility	▓▓▓▓▓				
Room/comfort	▓▓▓▓				
Entry/exit	▓▓▓▓				
Cargo room	▓▓▓▓				
Workmanship					
Exterior	▓▓▓▓▓▓▓▓▓▓				
Interior	▓▓▓▓▓▓▓▓▓▓				
Value	▓▓▓▓▓▓				

Total Points...54

Specifications

Body type	2-door notchback	Engine type	dohc I-4
Wheelbase (in.)	100.4	Engine size (l/cu. in.)	2.3/138
Overall length (in.)	174.8	Horsepower @ rpm	160 @ 5800
Overall width (in.)	69.5	Torque @ rpm	156 @ 4500
Overall height (in.)	50.8	Transmission	manual/5-sp.
Curb weight (lbs.)	2866	Drive wheels	front
Seating capacity	4	Brakes, F/R	disc/disc (ABS)
Front head room (in.)	38.0	Tire size	205/55VR15
Max. front leg room (in.)	44.2	Fuel tank capacity (gal.)	15.9
Rear head room (in.)	35.1	EPA city/highway mpg	22/26
Min. rear leg room (in.)	28.1	Test mileage (mpg)	25.5
Cargo volume (cu. ft.)	7.9		

Warranties The entire car is covered for 3 years/36,000 miles. Body perforation rust is covered for 3 years/unlimited miles.

Rating scale 5=Exceptional; 4=Above average; 3=Average; 2=Below average; 1=Poor

HYUNDAI ACCENT

Built in South Korea.

Hyundai Accent 4-door

SUBCOMPACT

Scheduled to go on sale in February, the Accent replaces the Excel as Hyundai's entry-level model. Like the Excel, the front-drive Accent comes as a 3-door hatchback and 4-door notchback sedan. Dimensions are about the same as before, except the 4-door shrinks by about six inches in length. The 4-door comes only in a base price level. The 3-door comes in base trim and lower-level L trim. Accent is powered by Hyundai's "Alpha" 1.5-liter 4-cylinder engine with 92 horsepower. A 5-speed manual transmission is standard and a 4-speed automatic is optional on all but the L 3-door. Dual air bags and height-adjustable manual front seatbelts are standard on all. Hyundai says Accent meets 1997 federal side impact standards. Anti-lock brakes are optional on the base 3-door and 4-door. Noise appears to be the Accent's biggest problem. There's lots of road noise at highway speeds and even moderate acceleration produces a loud moan from the engine, though it isn't altogether unpleasant. Acceleration is adequate around town with either transmission, but highway passing requires a long, open stretch of road. The automatic transmission struggles with hills, frequently shifting in and out of the overdrive gear. The suspension is a pleasant surprise. It absorbs most bumps well and feels stable at higher speeds. Front head and leg room are ample for 6-footers. The rear seat on both body styles has adequate space for people up to about 5-foot-10, though it's hard to squeeze through the narrow rear door openings of the sedan. Overall, Accent is much more satisfying to drive than the Excel. Prices weren't announced in time for this issue, but Accent is expected to be the lowest-priced car in the U.S.

Hyundai Accent standard equipment is on page 342.

HYUNDAI ACCENT (Preliminary)

Rating Guide	1	2	3	4	5
Performance					
Acceleration	||||||||||||||||||||||||||||||||		
Economy	||||||||||||||||||||||||||||||||||||||||		
Driveability	||||||||||||||||||||||||||||||||		
Ride	|||||||||||||||||||||||||||||||||||		
Steering/handling	||||||||||||||||||||||||||||||||		
Braking	||||||||||||||||||||||||||||||||		
Noise	|||||||||||||||||||||||||			
Accommodations					
Driver seating	||||||||||||||||||||||||||||||||		
Instruments/controls	||||||||||||||||||||||||||||||||		
Visibility	||||||||||||||||||||||||||||||||		
Room/comfort	||||||||||||||||||||||||||||||||		
Entry/exit	||||||||||||||||||||||||||||||||		
Cargo room	||||||||||||||||||||||||||||||||		
Workmanship					
Exterior	|||||||||||||||||||||||||||||||||||		
Interior	|||||||||||||||||||||||||||||||||||		
Value	||||||||||||||||||||||||||||||||||||||||		

Total Points...55

Specifications

Body type	4-door notchback	Engine type	ohc I-4
Wheelbase (in.)	94.5	Engine size (l/cu. in.)	1.5/91
Overall length (in.)	162.1	Horsepower @ rpm	92 @ 5500
Overall width (in.)	63.8	Torque @ rpm	96 @ 3000
Overall height (in.)	54.9	Transmission	auto/4-sp.
Curb weight (lbs.)	2167	Drive wheels	front
Seating capacity	5	Brakes, F/R	disc/drum
Front head room (in.)	38.7	Tire size	175/70R13
Max. front leg room (in.)	42.6	Fuel tank capacity (gal.)	11.9
Rear head room (in.)	38.0	EPA city/highway mpg	28/36
Min. rear leg room (in.)	32.7	Test mileage (mpg)	NA
Cargo volume (cu. ft.)	10.7		

Warranties The entire car is covered for 3 years/36,000 miles. Major powertrain components are covered for 5 years/60,000 miles. Body perforation rust is covered for 5 years/100,000 miles.

Rating scale 5=Exceptional; 4=Above average; 3=Average; 2=Below average; 1=Poor

HYUNDAI ELANTRA

Built in South Korea.

Hyundai Elantra GLS

SUBCOMPACT

The front-drive Elantra is in a holding pattern because it is scheduled to be replaced next year. It returns for 1995 as a 4-door
notchback sedan available in base and plusher GLS price levels. A
driver-side air bag is standard on both and anti-lock brakes are
optional on the GLS. A 113-horsepower 1.6-liter 4-cylinder is standard on base models with the 5-speed manual transmission. Base
models with the optional 4-speed automatic come with a 124-
horsepower 1.8-liter 4-cylinder. The GLS has the 1.8-liter engine
with either transmission. Both engines are built by Hyundai under
license from Mitsubishi, which owns an equity interest in Hyundai,
South Korea's largest automaker. Elantra is sized and priced
between the mid-size Hyundai Sonata and entry-level Accent subcompact. Last year, Elantra gained the standard air bag and
optional anti-lock brakes, and Hyundai made several changes to
the structure, powertrain, and sound insulation to reduce noise. As
Hyundai claims, the current models are quieter than earlier
Elantras. However, there's still too much wind noise at highway
speeds and excessive engine noise during acceleration. The GLS
has adequate acceleration with the 5-speed manual transmission,
but with the automatic you have to use a heavy throttle foot to keep
pace with traffic. Fuel economy is mediocre with the automatic.
Elantra has more passenger and cargo space than most subcompacts, a good driving position with a clear view all around, and
functional instruments and controls. Elantra isn't as well-built or
refined as cars like the Dodge and Plymouth Neon, Honda Civic,
Geo Prizm, and Toyota Corolla but is competitively priced.

Hyundai Elantra prices are on page 343.

HYUNDAI ELANTRA GLS

Rating Guide	1	2	3	4	5
Performance					
Acceleration	‖‖‖‖‖‖‖‖‖‖‖‖‖‖‖‖‖‖‖‖‖‖‖‖				
Economy	‖‖‖‖‖‖‖‖‖‖‖‖‖‖‖‖‖‖‖‖				
Driveability	‖‖‖‖‖‖‖‖‖‖‖‖‖‖‖‖‖‖‖‖				
Ride	‖‖‖‖‖‖‖‖‖‖‖‖‖‖‖				
Steering/handling	‖‖‖‖‖‖‖‖‖‖‖‖‖‖‖‖‖‖‖‖				
Braking	‖‖‖‖‖‖‖‖‖‖‖‖‖‖‖‖‖‖‖‖				
Noise	‖‖‖‖‖‖‖‖‖‖‖‖‖‖‖				
Accommodations					
Driver seating	‖‖‖‖‖‖‖‖‖‖‖‖‖‖‖‖‖‖‖‖				
Instruments/controls	‖‖‖‖‖‖‖‖‖‖‖‖‖‖‖‖‖‖‖‖‖‖‖‖‖‖				
Visibility	‖‖‖‖‖‖‖‖‖‖‖‖‖‖‖‖‖‖‖‖‖‖‖‖‖‖				
Room/comfort	‖‖‖‖‖‖‖‖‖‖‖‖‖‖‖‖‖‖‖‖				
Entry/exit	‖‖‖‖‖‖‖‖‖‖‖‖‖‖‖‖‖‖‖‖				
Cargo room	‖‖‖‖‖‖‖‖‖‖‖‖‖‖‖‖‖‖‖‖				
Workmanship					
Exterior	‖‖‖‖‖‖‖‖‖‖‖‖‖‖‖‖‖‖‖‖				
Interior	‖‖‖‖‖‖‖‖‖‖‖‖‖‖‖‖‖‖‖‖				
Value	‖‖‖‖‖‖‖‖‖‖‖‖‖‖‖‖‖‖‖‖‖‖‖‖				
Total Points..**51**					

Specifications

Body type ....4-door notchback	Engine type ....dohc I-4
Wheelbase (in.) 98.4	Engine size (l/cu. in.).........1.8/110
Overall length (in.)...............172.8	Horsepower @ rpm ...124 @ 6000
Overall width (in.) 66.1	Torque @ rpm ....116 @ 4500
Overall height (in.)..................52.0	Transmission.................auto/4-sp.
Curb weight (lbs.) 2500	Drive wheels ....front
Seating capacity.........................5	Brakes, F/R....................disc/drum
Front head room (in.) 38.4	Tire size 185/60R14
Max. front leg room (in.) 42.6	Fuel tank capacity (gal.) 13.7
Rear head room (in.) 37.6	EPA city/highway mpg 22/29
Min. rear leg room (in.)...........33.4	Test mileage (mpg) 22.5
Cargo volume (cu. ft.).............11.8	

Warranties The entire car is covered for 3 years/36,000 miles. Major powertrain components are covered for 5 years/60,000 miles. Body perforation rust is covered for 5 years/100,000 miles.

Rating scale 5=Exceptional; 4=Above average; 3=Average; 2=Below average; 1=Poor

HYUNDAI SONATA —————

Built in South Korea.

Hyundai Sonata GL

MID-SIZE

The front-drive Sonata went on sale last spring as an early 1995 model. While the previous generation was built in both South Korea and Canada, the new one is built only in Korea. At 185 inches overall, the 1995 model is less than an inch longer than the original Sonata. Wheelbase, however, has grown two inches to 106.3, with most of the additional space used to increase rear leg room. Base engine is a 2.0-liter 4-cylinder that has been substantially revised for 1995 to produce 137 horsepower, nine more than previously. The 4-cylinder is standard on the base model and the GL. On the base model, it's available with a standard 5-speed manual or optional 4-speed automatic; on the GL it comes only with the automatic. A 142-horsepower 3.0-liter V-6 is standard on the GLS and optional on the GL and comes only with the 4-speed automatic. Dual air bags are standard on all models and anti-lock brakes are optional on models with the V-6. The new Sonata is more refined than the original but doesn't match mid-size class leaders such as the Ford Taurus and Honda Accord in overall quality. Even so, because it is priced well below those rivals, it's worth considering by value-conscious shoppers. The 4-cylinder engine feels sluggish with the automatic transmission in standing-start acceleration but provides adequate passing power. The V-6 engine furnishes more than adequate acceleration (9.2 seconds in our test) and even better passing response. While the previous Sonata was roomy, the new one is noticeably roomier. The longer wheelbase makes the rear seat look huge compared to some rivals'. A trunk that opens at bumper level and has a wide, flat floor gives the Sonata generous cargo space.

Hyundai Sonata prices are on page 344.

HYUNDAI SONATA GL

Rating Guide	1	2	3	4	5
Performance					
Acceleration	▓▓▓▓▓▓▓▓▓▓▓▓▓▓▓				
Economy	▓▓▓▓▓▓▓				
Driveability	▓▓▓▓▓▓▓▓▓▓▓▓				
Ride	▓▓▓▓▓▓▓▓▓▓▓▓▓▓				
Steering/handling	▓▓▓▓▓▓▓▓▓▓				
Braking	▓▓▓▓▓▓▓▓▓▓▓▓▓▓▓				
Noise	▓▓▓▓▓▓▓▓▓▓				
Accommodations					
Driver seating	▓▓▓▓▓▓▓▓▓▓▓▓				
Instruments/controls	▓▓▓▓▓▓▓▓▓▓▓▓				
Visibility	▓▓▓▓▓▓▓▓▓▓				
Room/comfort	▓▓▓▓▓▓▓▓▓▓				
Entry/exit	▓▓▓▓▓▓▓▓▓▓▓▓				
Cargo room	▓▓▓▓▓▓▓▓▓▓				
Workmanship					
Exterior	▓▓▓▓▓▓▓▓▓▓▓▓▓▓				
Interior	▓▓▓▓▓▓▓▓▓▓▓▓				
Value	▓▓▓▓▓▓▓▓▓▓▓▓				

Total Points..58

Specifications

Body type	4-door notchback	Engine type	ohc V-6
Wheelbase (in.)	106.3	Engine size (l/cu. in.)	3.0/181
Overall length (in.)	185.0	Horsepower @ rpm	142 @ 5000
Overall width (in.)	69.7	Torque @ rpm	168 @ 2500
Overall height (in.)	55.3	Transmission	auto/4-sp.
Curb weight (lbs.)	3025	Drive wheels	front
Seating capacity	5	Brakes, F/R	disc/drum (ABS)
Front head room (in.)	38.5	Tire size	205/60R15
Max. front leg room (in.)	43.3	Fuel tank capacity (gal.)	16.9
Rear head room (in.)	NA	EPA city/highway mpg	18/24
Min. rear leg room (in.)	NA	Test mileage (mpg)	17.8
Cargo volume (cu. ft.)	13.2		

Warranties The entire car is covered for 3 years/36,000 miles. Major powertrain components are covered for 5 years/60,000 miles. Body perforation rust is covered for 5 years/100,000 miles.

Rating scale 5=Exceptional; 4=Above average; 3=Average; 2=Below average; 1=Poor

INFINITI G20

Built in Japan.

Infiniti G20

PREMIUM SEDAN

The entry-level model in Nissan's luxury division sees only two changes for 1995: a switch from black to body-color rocker panels (the area below the doors and between the front and rear wheels) and all-season tires for the Touring model, which is badged G20t. The previously standard performance tires are now a no-cost option on the Touring model. Now in its sixth year in the U.S., the G20 is a compact sedan with front-wheel drive and a 2.0-liter 4-cylinder engine with 140 horsepower. A 5-speed manual transmission is standard and a 4-speed automatic is optional. Anti-lock disc brakes and dual air bags also are standard. The G20 is sold in Japan and Europe as the Nissan Primera, a less-luxurious car that's about to be redesigned. That indicates a new G20 should arrive in the U.S. for the 1996 model year. This spring, Infiniti will introduce a new V-6 sedan, called the I30, that is based on the Nissan Maxima and will fit between the G20 and the J30 in size and price. Though the G20 comes with a long list of standard features, there are larger, more refined cars in the same price range, such as the Honda Accord and Toyota Camry (which are available with a V-6 engine). However, the G20 comes with a longer warranty, roadside assistance, and other benefits that have helped Infiniti score at the top of customer satisfaction ratings. The G20's engine is smooth and quiet in low-speed driving but growls loudly during hard acceleration. There's plenty of room for four adults and ample cargo space. Slow sales mean Infiniti dealers are offering budget leases and big discounts on the G20. It's not a great car, but Infiniti has a reputation for great customer service.

Infiniti G20 prices are on page 345.

INFINITI G20

Rating Guide	1	2	3	4	5
Performance					
Acceleration	▓▓▓▓▓▓▓▓▓▓▓				
Economy	▓▓▓▓▓▓▓▓▓▓▓				
Driveability	▓▓▓▓▓▓▓▓▓▓▓				
Ride	▓▓▓▓▓▓▓▓▓▓▓				
Steering/handling	▓▓▓▓▓▓▓▓▓▓▓▓▓▓				
Braking	▓▓▓▓▓▓▓▓▓▓▓▓▓▓▓▓▓				
Noise	▓▓▓▓▓▓▓▓▓▓▓				
Accommodations					
Driver seating	▓▓▓▓▓▓▓▓▓▓▓▓				
Instruments/controls	▓▓▓▓▓▓▓▓▓▓▓▓				
Visibility	▓▓▓▓▓▓▓▓▓▓▓▓				
Room/comfort	▓▓▓▓▓▓▓▓▓▓▓▓				
Entry/exit	▓▓▓▓▓▓▓▓▓▓▓▓				
Cargo room	▓▓▓▓▓▓▓▓▓▓▓▓				
Workmanship					
Exterior	▓▓▓▓▓▓▓▓▓▓▓▓				
Interior	▓▓▓▓▓▓▓▓▓▓▓▓				
Value	▓▓▓▓▓▓▓▓▓▓▓▓				

Total Points...**58**

Specifications

Body type ....4-door notchback
Wheelbase (in.) 100.4
Overall length (in.)................174.8
Overall width (in.) 66.7
Overall height (in.) 54.9
Curb weight (lbs.) 2877
Seating capacity.........................5
Front head room (in.) 38.8
Max. front leg room (in.) 42.0
Rear head room (in.) 37.3
Min. rear leg room (in.).........32.2
Cargo volume (cu. ft.).............14.2

Engine type ....dohc I-4
Engine size (l/cu. in.)........2.0/122
Horsepower @ rpm ...140 @ 6400
Torque @ rpm ....132 @ 4800
Transmission..................auto/4-sp.
Drive wheels ....front
Brakes, F/R..........disc/disc (ABS)
Tire size 195/65HR14
Fuel tank capacity (gal.) 15.9
EPA city/highway mpg 22/28
Test mileage (mpg) 21.7

Warranties The entire car is covered for 4 years/60,000 miles. Major powertrain components are covered for 6 years/70,000 miles. Body perforation rust is covered for 7 years/unlimited miles.

Rating scale 5=Exceptional; 4=Above average; 3=Average; 2=Below average; 1=Poor

INFINITI J30

Built in Japan.

Infiniti J30t

PREMIUM SEDAN

Infiniti's mid-level sedan has a new full-width taillight cluster with subtle vertical ribbing behind the lens—so subtle, in fact, that you may need a second look to spot it. The only other changes are an automatic-dimming inside rearview mirror and a power lumbar adjustment for the driver's seat as additions to an already lengthy list of standard features. The J30 is a mid-size, rear-drive 4-door that competes in the premium sedan market against the likes of the BMW 5-Series, Cadillac Seville, Lexus ES 300 and GS 300, Mercedes E320, and Volvo 960. The J30 comes only with 4-speed automatic transmission and a 210-horsepower 3.0-liter V-6 engine. Standard features include dual air bags and anti-lock brakes. Two models are available, the base J30 and the J30t, which has a Touring Package that includes performance tires, a firmer suspension, and a rear spoiler. The Super-HICAS rear-wheel steering feature has been dropped from the J30t as a cost-saving measure. The J30 comes with a full load of safety and convenience features but lacks the polish and refinement of rivals such as the less-expensive Lexus ES 300. With a 0-60 mph time of under nine seconds, it's competitive among luxury sedans in this price range, but in hard acceleration the engine is surprisingly loud and even a little coarse. The J30 is nearly as long as an Acura Legend but has less passenger and cargo room than the ES 300, which is shorter in wheelbase and overall length. With just 10.1 cubic feet of cargo space, the J30 has one of the smallest trunks among luxury sedans. Several good cars can be found in the $35,000 to $40,000 range, so check out some competitors before deciding on a J30.

Infiniti J30 prices are on page 345.

INFINITI J30t

Rating Guide	1	2	3	4	5
Performance					
Acceleration	▮▮▮▮▮▮▮▮▮▮▮▮▮▮▮▮▮▮▮▮▮▮▮				
Economy	▮▮▮▮▮▮▮▮▮				
Driveability	▮▮▮▮▮▮▮▮▮▮▮▮▮▮				
Ride	▮▮▮▮▮▮▮▮▮▮▮▮▮▮				
Steering/handling	▮▮▮▮▮▮▮▮▮▮▮▮▮▮				
Braking	▮▮▮▮▮▮▮▮▮▮▮▮▮▮▮▮▮▮▮▮▮▮▮				
Noise	▮▮▮▮▮▮▮▮▮▮▮				
Accommodations					
Driver seating	▮▮▮▮▮▮▮▮▮▮▮				
Instruments/controls	▮▮▮▮▮▮▮▮▮▮▮				
Visibility	▮▮▮▮▮▮▮▮				
Room/comfort	▮▮▮▮▮▮▮▮▮▮▮				
Entry/exit	▮▮▮▮▮▮▮▮▮▮▮				
Cargo room	▮▮▮▮▮▮▮▮				
Workmanship					
Exterior	▮▮▮▮▮▮▮▮▮▮▮▮▮▮▮▮▮▮▮▮▮▮▮				
Interior	▮▮▮▮▮▮▮▮▮▮▮▮▮▮▮▮▮▮▮▮▮▮▮				
Value	▮▮▮▮▮▮▮▮▮▮▮				

Total Points...59

Specifications

Body type	4-door notchback	Engine type	dohc V-6
Wheelbase (in.)	108.7	Engine size (l/cu. in.)	3.0/181
Overall length (in.)	191.3	Horsepower @ rpm	210 @ 6400
Overall width (in.)	69.7	Torque @ rpm	193 @ 4800
Overall height (in.)	54.7	Transmission	auto/4-sp.
Curb weight (lbs.)	3527	Drive wheels	rear
Seating capacity	5	Brakes, F/R	disc/disc (ABS)
Front head room (in.)	37.7	Tire size	215/60HR15
Max. front leg room (in.)	41.3	Fuel tank capacity (gal.)	19.0
Rear head room (in.)	36.7	EPA city/highway mpg	18/23
Min. rear leg room (in.)	30.5	Test mileage (mpg)	18.3
Cargo volume (cu. ft.)	10.1		

Warranties The entire car is covered for 4 years/60,000 miles. Major powertrain components are covered for 6 years/70,000 miles. Body perforation rust is covered for 7 years/unlimited miles.

Rating scale 5=Exceptional; 4=Above average; 3=Average; 2=Below average; 1=Poor

INFINITI Q45 ───
Built in Japan.

Infiniti Q45

PREMIUM SEDAN

After getting a facelift and more standard equipment last year, the flagship of Nissan's luxury division stands pat for 1995 except for new alloy wheels for the base model. The Q45 is a rear-drive 4-door sedan with a 4.5-liter V-8 that has dual overhead camshafts and 278 horsepower. It teams with a 4-speed automatic transmission. Anti-lock disc brakes and dual air bags are standard. The only major factory option is traction control, available on the base model and the mid-level Q45t, whose Touring Package comprises a rear spoiler, heated front seats, forged alloy wheels, performance tires, and stiffer stabilizer bars. Nissan's Super-HICAS rear-wheel steering system has been dropped from the Q45t. The top-of-the-line Q45a includes traction control and Full-Active Suspension, which uses electronic actuators in place of shock absorbers to control body lean, roll, pitch, and dive. Though arch-rival Lexus is introducing a new LS 400 this fall, the Q45 should continue in its present form for another year or so. The Q45 has the athletic feel of a European luxury sedan, while the LS 400 provides more luxurious isolation. Though the Q45's suspension is firmer than the LS 400's, it doesn't ride harshly. There's more road noise in the Q45 than in the LS 400, but it's not objectionable or even inappropriate. The interior has ample rear leg room, though the transmission hump makes the middle position uncomfortable, discouraging 3-across seating. Cargo room is unimpressive for a sedan this large. The Q45 is still a good car, but try the new LS 400 before deciding to spend $50,000 or more. We also recommend the Cadillac Seville, Mercedes-Benz E420, and Oldsmobile Aurora as alternatives.

Infiniti Q45 prices are on page 346.

INFINITI Q45

Rating Guide	1	2	3	4	5
Performance					
Acceleration	▒	▒	▒	▒	▒
Economy	▒	▒			
Driveability	▒	▒	▒	▒	
Ride	▒	▒	▒	▒	
Steering/handling	▒	▒	▒	▒	
Braking	▒	▒	▒	▒	▒
Noise	▒	▒	▒	▒	
Accommodations					
Driver seating	▒	▒	▒	▒	
Instruments/controls	▒	▒	▒	▒	
Visibility	▒	▒	▒	▒	
Room/comfort	▒	▒	▒	▒	
Entry/exit	▒	▒	▒	▒	
Cargo room	▒	▒	▒		
Workmanship					
Exterior	▒	▒	▒	▒	▒
Interior	▒	▒	▒	▒	▒
Value	▒	▒	▒	▒	

Total Points...65

Specifications

Body type ....4-door notchback
Wheelbase (in.) 113.2
Overall length (in.) 199.8
Overall width (in.) 71.9
Overall height (in.) 56.5
Curb weight (lbs.) 4039
Seating capacity.........................5
Front head room (in.) 38.2
Max. front leg room (in.) 43.9
Rear head room (in.) 36.3
Min. rear leg room (in.) 32.0
Cargo volume (cu. ft.).............14.8

Engine type....................dohc V-8
Engine size (l/cu. in.).........4.5/274
Horsepower @ rpm ...278 @ 6000
Torque @ rpm ....292 @ 4000
Transmission..................auto/4-sp.
Drive wheels ....rear
Brakes, F/R..........disc/disc (ABS)
Tire size.....................215/65VR15
Fuel tank capacity (gal.) 22.5
EPA city/highway mpg 17/22
Test mileage (mpg) 16.6

Warranties The entire car is covered for 4 years/60,000 miles. Major powertrain components are covered for 6 years/70,000 miles. Body perforation rust is covered for 7 years/unlimited miles.

Rating scale 5=Exceptional; 4=Above average; 3=Average; 2=Below average; 1=Poor

ISUZU RODEO/ HONDA PASSPORT

Built in Lafayette, Ind.

Isuzu Rodeo S

SPORT-UTILITY VEHICLE

These similar sport-utility wagons return for 1995 with the same lineups as last year and few changes. Isuzu builds both at its plant in Indiana. The Passport is identical to the Rodeo except for cosmetic details. At Isuzu, the base Rodeo S model is available with either 2- or 4-wheel drive and either a 120-horsepower 2.6-liter 4-cylinder or a 175-horsepower 3.2-liter V-6. The LS comes with the V-6 and is available with both 2WD and 4WD. New for 1995 on the Rodeo is an optional Bright Package with chrome exterior trim. Honda's version has the same engine choices and a similar lineup. Passport is unchanged from its 1994 debut except that a 16-inch wheel/tire package is now standard instead of optional on the top-line EX model. All models come in 5-door wagon styling with standard anti-lock rear brakes. The 4WD system is the part-time type—not for use on dry pavement. Isuzu says 4WD High can be engaged at speeds up to 5 mph, but the vehicle must be stopped and reversed to fully disengage 4WD. Though Rodeo and Passport have some good points, a well-equipped 4WD model from either brand is in the same price range as a Ford Explorer, Jeep Grand Cherokee, or a Chevy Blazer/GMC Jimmy, all of which are roomier and have full shift-on-the-fly 4WD systems and 4-wheel anti-lock brakes that operate in both 2WD and 4WD. The others also have a driver-side air bag and the Explorer has a passenger-side air bag as well.

Isuzu Rodeo prices are on page 346.
Honda Passport prices are on page 341.

ISUZU RODEO S

Rating Guide	1	2	3	4	5
Performance					
Acceleration	▐▐▐▐▐▐▐▐▐▐▐▐▐▐▐▐▐▐▐				
Economy	▐▐▐▐▐▐▐▐				
Driveability	▐▐▐▐▐▐▐▐▐▐▐▐▐▐▐▐▐▐▐				
Ride	▐▐▐▐▐▐▐▐▐▐▐▐▐▐▐▐▐				
Steering/handling	▐▐▐▐▐▐▐▐▐▐▐▐▐				
Braking	▐▐▐▐▐▐▐▐▐▐▐▐▐▐▐▐▐▐▐				
Noise	▐▐▐▐▐▐▐▐▐▐▐▐▐▐▐▐▐				
Accommodations					
Driver seating	▐▐▐▐▐▐▐▐▐▐▐▐▐▐▐▐▐				
Instruments/controls	▐▐▐▐▐▐▐▐▐▐▐▐▐▐▐▐▐				
Visibility	▐▐▐▐▐▐▐▐▐▐▐▐▐				
Room/comfort	▐▐▐▐▐▐▐▐▐▐▐▐▐▐▐▐▐				
Entry/exit	▐▐▐▐▐▐▐▐▐▐▐▐▐				
Cargo room	▐▐▐▐▐▐▐▐▐▐▐▐▐▐▐▐▐▐▐				
Workmanship					
Exterior	▐▐▐▐▐▐▐▐▐▐▐▐▐▐▐▐▐				
Interior	▐▐▐▐▐▐▐▐▐▐▐▐▐▐▐▐▐				
Value	▐▐▐▐▐▐▐▐▐▐▐▐▐▐▐▐▐				
Total Points					**54**

Specifications

Body type	5-door wagon	Engine type	ohc V-6
Wheelbase (in.)	108.7	Engine size (l/cu. in.)	3.2/193
Overall length (in.)	183.9	Horsepower @ rpm	175 @ 5200
Overall width (in.)	66.5	Torque @ rpm	188 @ 4000
Overall height (in.)	65.4	Transmission	auto/4-sp.
Curb weight (lbs.)	3545	Drive wheels	rear/all
Seating capacity	5	Brakes, F/R	disc/disc (ABS)
Front head room (in.)	38.2	Tire size	225/75R15
Max. front leg room (in.)	42.5	Fuel tank capacity (gal.)	21.9
Rear head room (in.)	37.8	EPA city/highway mpg	15/18
Min. rear leg room (in.)	36.1	Test mileage (mpg)	14.6
Cargo volume (cu. ft.)	74.9		

Warranties The entire vehicle is covered for 3 years/50,000 miles. Major powertrain components are covered for 5 years/60,000 miles. Body perforation rust is covered for 6 years/100,000 miles.

Rating scale 5=Exceptional; 4=Above average; 3=Average; 2=Below average; 1=Poor

ISUZU TROOPER

Built in Japan.

Isuzu Trooper LS

SPORT-UTILITY VEHICLE

Big changes are in store for the 1995 Trooper, which is scheduled to go on sale in January. Dual air bags in a redesigned instrument panel are new standard features and the RS 2-door wagon has been dropped. All models now come in a 4-door body style with 70/30 split rear doors. Returning models include the base S and luxury-oriented LS. Later this year, Isuzu will add a top-of-the-line Limited model with features such as leather upholstery and a sunroof. In addition to the new air bags, standard equipment on all models includes anti-lock brakes, part-time 4-wheel drive, and power steering. On the LS and Limited, the anti-lock system covers all four wheels; on the S, it covers only the rear wheels. The 4WD system allows shifting into 4WD High at speeds up to five mph. Returning to 2WD requires stopping and backing up a few feet to fully disengage the front hubs. All Troopers use a 3.2-liter V-6 engine. The S model has a single overhead camshaft and 175 horsepower. The LS and Limited have a dual-camshaft version that develops 190 horsepower. A 5-speed manual transmission is standard with both engines and a 4-speed overdrive automatic is optional. The addition of standard dual air bags is welcome on the Trooper, which is roomy, comfortable, and competitive in all but one key area—the 4WD system. All of Trooper's domestic rivals and most imported rivals have full shift-on-the-fly or permanently engaged 4WD. Trooper's prices are pretty steep, but dealers should be giving big discounts to remain competitive in the crowded sport-utility field.

1994 Isuzu Trooper prices are on page 348.

ISUZU TROOPER LS

Rating Guide	1	2	3	4	5
Performance					
Acceleration	▓▓▓▓▓▓▓				
Economy	▓▓▓▓				
Driveability	▓▓▓▓▓▓▓▓				
Ride	▓▓▓▓▓▓▓▓				
Steering/handling	▓▓▓▓▓▓▓▓				
Braking	▓▓▓▓▓▓▓▓▓▓▓				
Noise	▓▓▓▓▓▓▓				
Accommodations					
Driver seating	▓▓▓▓▓▓▓				
Instruments/controls	▓▓▓▓▓▓▓				
Visibility	▓▓▓▓▓▓▓				
Room/comfort	▓▓▓▓▓▓▓▓				
Entry/exit	▓▓▓▓▓▓▓				
Cargo room	▓▓▓▓▓▓▓▓▓▓▓▓				
Workmanship					
Exterior	▓▓▓▓▓▓▓▓				
Interior	▓▓▓▓▓▓▓▓				
Value	▓▓▓▓▓▓▓▓				

Total Points..58

Specifications

Body type	4-door wagon	Engine type	dohc V-6
Wheelbase (in.)	108.7	Engine size (l/cu. in.)	3.2/193
Overall length (in.)	183.5	Horsepower @ rpm	190 @ 5600
Overall width (in.)	68.7	Torque @ rpm	195 @ 3800
Overall height (in.)	72.8	Transmission	auto/4-sp.
Curb weight (lbs.)	4210	Drive wheels	rear/all
Seating capacity	5	Brakes, F/R	disc/disc (ABS)
Front head room (in.)	39.8	Tire size	245/70R16
Max. front leg room (in.)	40.8	Fuel tank capacity (gal.)	22.5
Rear head room (in.)	39.8	EPA city/highway mpg	14/17
Min. rear leg room (in.)	39.1	Test mileage (mpg)	15.8
Cargo volume (cu. ft.)	90.0		

Warranties The entire vehicle is covered for 3 years/50,000 miles. Major powertrain components are covered for 5 years/60,000 miles. Body perforation rust is covered for 6 years/100,000 miles.

Rating scale 5=Exceptional; 4=Above average; 3=Average; 2=Below average; 1=Poor

JAGUAR XJ SEDAN

Built in England.

Jaguar Vanden Plas

PREMIUM SEDAN

A redesigned Jaguar sedan went on sale in the fall with new styling that bears strong resemblance to sedans from this British company's past. Among this year's four models is a new XJR with a 322-horsepower supercharged 4.0-liter 6-cylinder, the first engine in Jaguar's 72-year history that isn't naturally aspirated. The base XJ6 model has a heavily revised version of last year's 4.0-liter 6-cylinder. It produces 245 horsepower, 22 more than in 1994. The plusher Vanden Plas model has the same engine but more standard features. The flagship XJ12 has a 6.0-liter V-12 engine with 313 horsepower, 12 more than last year. All exterior body panels are new and the styling recalls pre-1988 Jaguars with a sloping, contoured hood accented by four round headlamps. Jaguar's traditional "leaping cat" hood ornament is a $200 option. The rear-drive XJ sedans ride the same 113-inch wheelbase as the 1988-94 generation, but overall length is 1.4 inches greater. All models have dual air bags, anti-lock brakes, and new electronic variable-assist power steering. We drove all four new sedans at Jaguar's press preview and were impressed with their performance, better ergonomics, and apparent improvements in overall quality. The base 6-cylinder engine is smoother and quieter than before and provides brisk acceleration from a standing start and strong passing power. The V-12 doesn't offer a big enough gain in acceleration to justify its higher price. By contrast, the supercharged 6-cylinder gives the XJR a big performance boost. The new XJ sedan clearly moves Jaguar closer to the leaders in the luxury field. We'll reserve final judgment until we can give them full road tests.

Jaguar XJ Sedan prices are on page 349.

CONSUMER GUIDE®

JAGUAR VANDEN PLAS (Preliminary)

Rating Guide	1	2	3	4	5
Performance					
Acceleration					
Economy					
Driveability					
Ride					
Steering/handling					
Braking					
Noise					
Accommodations					
Driver seating					
Instruments/controls					
Visibility					
Room/comfort					
Entry/exit					
Cargo room					
Workmanship					
Exterior					
Interior					
Value					

Total Points..**59**

Specifications

Body type	4-door notchback	Engine type	dohc I-6
Wheelbase (in.)	113.0	Engine size (l/cu. in.)	4.0/243
Overall length (in.)	197.8	Horsepower @ rpm	245 @ 4700
Overall width (in.)	70.8	Torque @ rpm	289 @ 4000
Overall height (in.)	53.1	Transmission	auto/4-sp.
Curb weight (lbs.)	4080	Drive wheels	rear
Seating capacity	5	Brakes, F/R	disc/disc (ABS)
Front head room (in.)	37.2	Tire size	225/60ZR16
Max. front leg room (in.)	41.2	Fuel tank capacity (gal.)	23.1
Rear head room (in.)	NA	EPA city/highway mpg	17/23
Min. rear leg room (in.)	NA	Test mileage (mpg)	NA
Cargo volume (cu. ft.)	11.1		

Warranties The entire car is covered for 4 years/50,000 miles. Body perforation rust is covered for 6 years/unlimited miles.

Rating scale 5=Exceptional; 4=Above average; 3=Average; 2=Below average; 1=Poor

JEEP CHEROKEE

BUDGET BUY

Built in Toledo, Ohio.

Jeep Cherokee Sport 5-door

SPORT-UTILITY VEHICLE

Cherokee gains a standard driver-side air bag and the base SE model also gets reclining front bucket seats as the main changes for its 12th model year. Cherokee comes in 3- and 5-door wagon body styles, both available with rear- or 4-wheel-drive. Three price levels are offered: SE, Sport, and Country, the latter only as a 5-door model. Base engine on the SE is a 130-horsepower 2.5-liter 4-cylinder. Standard on the Sport and Country and optional on the SE is a 190-horsepower 4.0-liter inline 6-cylinder. A 5-speed manual transmission is standard on all models. A 4-speed automatic is optional with the 6-cylinder engine. There has been no optional automatic for the 4-cylinder engine in recent years, but Jeep says a 3-speed automatic should be available later this year. Four-wheel anti-lock brakes that work in both 2- and 4-wheel drive are optional with the 6-cylinder engine. Cherokee offers two 4-wheel drive systems. Command-Trac, a part-time system for use only on slick surfaces, is available on all models. Sport and Country models with the automatic are available with Selec-Trac, a full-time system that can be left engaged on smooth, dry surfaces. Cherokee shows its age, though it's still a good choice among compact sport-utilities. It has convenient 4WD systems, commendable off-road capabilities, and civilized on-road manners. It isn't as roomy as a Grand Cherokee or Ford Explorer but can carry four adults. Jeep's 4-cylinder is hard-pressed to provide even adequate performance with the 5-speed manual. It's likely to be even slower with the automatic. Most Cherokees are sold with the strong 6-cylinder engine, which allows you to scoot off the line and pass other vehicles quickly.

Jeep Cherokee prices are on page 350.

JEEP CHEROKEE SPORT

Rating Guide	1	2	3	4	5
Performance					
Acceleration				▮	
Economy			▮		
Driveability				▮	
Ride				▮	
Steering/handling				▮	
Braking					▮
Noise			▮		
Accommodations					
Driver seating			▮		
Instruments/controls			▮		
Visibility				▮	
Room/comfort				▮	
Entry/exit				▮	
Cargo room					▮
Workmanship					
Exterior				▮	
Interior				▮	
Value				▮	

Total Points **57**

Specifications

Body type ....5-door wagon	Engine type ....ohv I-6
Wheelbase (in.) 101.4	Engine size (l/cu. in.).........4.0/242
Overall length (in.)...............166.9	Horsepower @ rpm ...190 @ 4750
Overall width (in.) 67.7	Torque @ rpm ....225 @ 4000
Overall height (in.)..................63.9	Transmission.................auto/4-sp.
Curb weight (lbs.) 3090	Drive wheels.......................rear/all
Seating capacity..........................5	Brakes, F/R..........disc/disc (ABS)
Front head room (in.) 38.3	Tire size 225/70R15
Max. front leg room (in.) 41.0	Fuel tank capacity (gal.) 20.2
Rear head room (in.) 38.0	EPA city/highway mpg 14/19
Min. rear leg room (in.)............35.3	Test mileage (mpg) 16.4
Cargo volume (cu. ft.)............71.8	

Warranties The entire vehicle is covered for 3 years/36,000 miles. Body perforation rust is covered for 7 years/100,000 miles.

Rating scale 5=Exceptional; 4=Above average; 3=Average; 2=Below average; 1=Poor

JEEP GRAND CHEROKEE

Built in Detroit, Mich.

Jeep Grand Cherokee Limited

SPORT-UTILITY VEHICLE

Four-wheel disc brakes, which were previously standard only on the top-line Limited model, now are standard on the base Grand Cherokee SE as well. There also are Laredo option packages for the SE. All models come with a driver-side air bag and anti-lock brakes. All are available with either rear-wheel drive or 4-wheel drive, and come standard with a 190-horsepower 4.0-liter inline 6-cylinder engine. A 220-horsepower 5.2-liter V-8 is optional. Both engines come with a 4-speed automatic transmission; last year's 5-speed manual has been dropped. A child safety seat that folds out of the rear seatback is a new option, but it isn't available with the new Orvis trim package. A flip-up liftgate window also is a new option. The SE and Laredo 4x4s come standard with Command-Trac, a part-time (not for use on dry pavement) 4WD system. Optional are Selec-Trac, a full-time 4WD system that can be used on dry pavement, and Quadra-Trac, a permanently engaged 4WD system. Quadra-Trac is standard on the Limited and required with the V-8 engine. Though the Ford Explorer is the best-selling sport-utility vehicle and our Best Buy in this class, the Grand Cherokee also deserves consideration, along with the new Chevrolet Blazer and GMC Jimmy. The optional V-8 engine gives the Grand Cherokee a noticeable boost in low-speed acceleration, but Jeep's 6-cylinder is all most people will need. The Grand Cherokee has impressive performance on-road and off-road, plus a broad range of choices in engines and 4WD systems. It's smaller inside than the Explorer but larger than many other rivals. Jeep dealers should be discounting because of the strong competition from Ford and General Motors.

Jeep Grand Cherokee prices are on page 354.

JEEP GRAND CHEROKEE

Rating Guide	1	2	3	4	5
Performance					
Acceleration	▓▓▓▓▓▓▓▓▓				
Economy	▓▓▓▓▓				
Driveability	▓▓▓▓▓▓▓▓▓				
Ride	▓▓▓▓▓▓▓				
Steering/handling	▓▓▓▓▓▓▓▓▓				
Braking	▓▓▓▓▓▓▓▓▓▓▓				
Noise	▓▓▓▓▓▓▓				
Accommodations					
Driver seating	▓▓▓▓▓▓▓▓				
Instruments/controls	▓▓▓▓▓▓▓▓				
Visibility	▓▓▓▓▓▓▓				
Room/comfort	▓▓▓▓▓▓▓▓				
Entry/exit	▓▓▓▓▓▓▓▓				
Cargo room	▓▓▓▓▓▓▓▓▓				
Workmanship					
Exterior	▓▓▓▓▓▓▓▓				
Interior	▓▓▓▓▓▓▓▓				
Value	▓▓▓▓▓▓▓▓				

Total Points..**60**

Specifications

Body type ....5-door wagon
Wheelbase (in.) 105.9
Overall length (in.)................179.0
Overall width (in.) 70.9
Overall height (in.).................64.9
Curb weight (lbs.) 3674
Seating capacity.........................5
Front head room (in.) 39.0
Max. front leg room (in.) 40.8
Rear head room (in.) 39.0
Min. rear leg room (in.)..........35.7
Cargo volume (cu. ft.).............81.0

Engine type ....:...ohv I-6
Engine size (l/cu. in.).........4.0/242
Horsepower @ rpm ...190 @ 4750
Torque @ rpm ....225 @ 4000
Transmission.................auto/4-sp.
Drive wheels.......................rear/all
Brakes, F/R...........disc/disc (ABS)
Tire size 225/70R15
Fuel tank capacity (gal.) 23.0
EPA city/highway mpg 15/20
Test mileage (mpg) 16.5

Warranties The entire vehicle is covered for 3 years/36,000 miles. Body perforation rust is covered for 7 years/100,000 miles.

Rating scale 5=Exceptional; 4=Above average; 3=Average; 2=Below average; 1=Poor

JEEP WRANGLER

Built in Canada.

Jeep Wrangler Rio Grande

SPORT-UTILITY VEHICLE

Wrangler returns in two price levels, S and SE, both with a part-time (not for use on dry pavement) 4-wheel-drive system. The base S model gets a new optional appearance package called the Rio Grande Edition Group. It includes "bright mango" paint, cloth reclining front seats, and 5-spoke steel wheels. A Sahara appearance package, optional on the SE, returns from last year, but the Renegade Package is gone. The S model has a 123-horsepower 2.5-liter 4-cylinder engine. The SE comes with a 180-horsepower 4.0-liter 6-cylinder engine. A 5-speed manual transmission is standard with both engines and a 3-speed automatic is optional. The 4-cylinder used to come only with a 5-speed manual, but the 3-speed automatic was added late last year. Wrangler doesn't have air bags and the optional anti-lock brakes are available only on the SE and Sahara. Air conditioning, the Off-Road Group, and Trac-Lok limited-slip differential are also optional only on the SE and Sahara. A removable hard-top is optional on the convertible Wrangler. Among Wrangler's key rivals are the Geo Tracker and Suzuki Sidekick, which are more modern, more refined, and have friendlier ergonomics. Neither, however, has 4-wheel anti-lock brakes. Instead, they have rear-wheel anti-lock systems that work only in 2WD. They're also limited to 4-cylinder engines that can't match Jeep's muscular 6-cylinder. Wrangler, however, has a stiff ride, little rear leg room, and a high step-up that hinders entry/exit. You'll also be assaulted by road noise and wind buffeting—top up or down. Because of these negatives, we don't recommend Wrangler or any small 4x4 as daily transportation instead of a passenger car.

Jeep Wrangler prices are on page 356.

JEEP WRANGLER

Rating Guide	1	2	3	4	5
Performance					
Acceleration	▓▓▓▓▓▓▓░				
Economy	▓▓▓▓				
Driveability	▓▓▓▓▓				
Ride	▓▓▓▓				
Steering/handling	▓▓▓▓▓				
Braking	▓▓▓▓▓				
Noise	▓▓▓▓				
Accommodations					
Driver seating	▓▓▓▓▓				
Instruments/controls	▓▓▓▓▓				
Visibility	▓▓▓▓▓▓				
Room/comfort	▓▓▓▓				
Entry/exit	▓▓▓▓▓				
Cargo room	▓▓▓▓▓				
Workmanship					
Exterior	▓▓▓▓▓				
Interior	▓▓▓▓▓				
Value	▓▓▓▓▓				

Total Points 45

Specifications

Body type	2-door convertible	Engine type	ohv I-6
Wheelbase (in.)	93.4	Engine size (l/cu. in.)	4.0/242
Overall length (in.)	151.9	Horsepower @ rpm	180 @ 4750
Overall width (in.)	66.0	Torque @ rpm	220 @ 4000
Overall height (in.)	71.9	Transmission	manual/5-sp.
Curb weight (lbs.)	2934	Drive wheels	rear/all
Seating capacity	4	Brakes, F/R	disc/drum
Front head room (in.)	41.4	Tire size	215/75R15
Max. front leg room (in.)	39.4	Fuel tank capacity (gal.)	15.0
Rear head room (in.)	40.3	EPA city/highway mpg	15/18
Min. rear leg room (in.)	35.0	Test mileage (mpg)	NA
Cargo volume (cu. ft.)	22.1		

Warranties The entire vehicle is covered for 3 years/36,000 miles. Body perforation rust is covered for 7 years/unlimited miles.

Rating scale 5=Exceptional; 4=Above average; 3=Average; 2=Below average; 1=Poor

LEXUS ES 300

Built in Japan.

Lexus ES 300

PREMIUM SEDAN

The ES 300, the least expensive and most popular model in the Lexus line, has minor styling changes at both the front and rear. Among the changes are a new front air intake and standard fog lamps. At the rear, the brake/turn signal lights are new and the model badge has been moved up to the trunk lid. In addition, chrome wheels are a new option and a trunk-mounted Pioneer CD changer is now available as a dealer-installed option. Lexus is the luxury division of Toyota and the ES 300 is positioned as a "near-luxury" sedan that competes with cars such as the Acura Legend, BMW 3-Series, and Mazda Millenia. The front-drive ES 300 is built from the same design as the Toyota Camry but has different styling and more standard features. The ES 300 comes with a 3.0-liter V-6 engine with 188 horsepower and an electronic 4-speed automatic transmission. Dual air bags and anti-lock brakes are standard. The ES 300 is the best-selling Lexus model because it has many of the attributes of the larger LS 400 sedan at a much lower price. The ES 300 accelerates swiftly, smoothly, and quietly, and has more than adequate passing power at highway speeds. On twisting roads the ES 300 doesn't feel as sporty as a BMW 325i or a Mazda Millenia, but the supple suspension absorbs bumps well and remains stable on wavy highways. The ES 300 has more passenger space than its exterior dimensions imply. Four adults fit easily. Despite sharing its basic design and most mechanical features with the Toyota Camry, the ES 300 is different enough to justify its higher price. It also has a more comprehensive warranty than the Camry and the promise of better customer service that comes with buying a Lexus.

Lexus ES 300 prices are on page 359.

LEXUS ES 300

Rating Guide	1	2	3	4	5
Performance					
Acceleration	▓	▓	▓	▓	
Economy	▓	▓	▓		
Driveability	▓	▓	▓	▓	
Ride	▓	▓	▓	▓	
Steering/handling	▓	▓	▓	▓	
Braking	▓	▓	▓	▓	▓
Noise	▓	▓	▓	▓	
Accommodations					
Driver seating	▓	▓	▓		
Instruments/controls	▓	▓	▓		
Visibility	▓	▓	▓		
Room/comfort	▓	▓	▓		
Entry/exit	▓	▓	▓		
Cargo room	▓	▓	▓		
Workmanship					
Exterior	▓	▓	▓	▓	▓
Interior	▓	▓	▓	▓	▓
Value	▓	▓	▓	▓	

Total Points...64

Specifications

Body type	4-door notchback	Engine type	dohc V-6
Wheelbase (in.)	103.1	Engine size (l/cu. in.)	3.0/181
Overall length (in.)	187.8	Horsepower @ rpm	188 @ 5200
Overall width (in.)	70.0	Torque @ rpm	203 @ 4400
Overall height (in.)	53.9	Transmission	auto/4-sp.
Curb weight (lbs.)	3374	Drive wheels	front
Seating capacity	5	Brakes, F/R	disc/disc (ABS)
Front head room (in.)	37.8	Tire size	205/65VR15
Max. front leg room (in.)	43.5	Fuel tank capacity (gal.)	18.5
Rear head room (in.)	36.6	EPA city/highway mpg	20/28
Min. rear leg room (in.)	33.1	Test mileage (mpg)	19.4
Cargo volume (cu. ft.)	14.3		

Warranties The entire car is covered for 4 years/50,000 miles. Major powertrain components are covered for 6 years/70,000 miles. Body perforation rust is covered for 6 years/unlimited miles.

Rating scale 5=Exceptional; 4=Above average; 3=Average; 2=Below average; 1=Poor

LEXUS GS 300

Built in Japan.

Lexus GS 300

PREMIUM SEDAN

The GS 300 is carried over unchanged for 1995. In size and price, this rear-drive 4-door sedan fits between the flagship LS 400 and entry-level ES 300 sedans at Lexus, the luxury division of Toyota. The GS 300 has the same 3.0-liter inline 6-cylinder engine as the Lexus SC 300 coupe. In the GS 300, it makes 220 horsepower and teams with an electronic 4-speed automatic transmission. Among the competitors for the GS 300 are the BMW 3-Series and 5-Series sedans, the Mercedes-Benz C-Class and E-Class, the Infiniti J30, and the Cadillac Seville. Standard equipment includes driver- and passenger-side air bags, anti-lock brakes, a power tilt and telescopic steering column, automatic temperature control, and walnut interior trim. The GS 300 is a step up from the ES 300 in performance and features, and virtually all the amenities found on the LS 400 are offered on the GS 300 at a starting price that's nearly $9000 less. Despite that, the GS 300 is the least popular of the three Lexus sedans. It isn't as swift or quiet as the LS 400 and doesn't ride as comfortably, either. The GS 300 handles deftly and has a firmer ride than the LS 400, though it's never harsh. It also lacks the library-quiet highway ride of the LS 400. The suspension and tires make prominent "thumps" over bumps and ruts, though road noise isn't objectionable. There's plenty of leg room all around but not much head room in the rear seat with the optional power moonroof. If you're shopping in this price range, check out some of the rivals. Lexus dealers should be discounting and offering heavily subsidized leases.

Lexus GS 300 prices are on page 359.

LEXUS GS 300

Rating Guide	1	2	3	4	5
Performance					
Acceleration	▮▮▮▮▮▮▮▮▮▮▮▮▮▮▮▮▮▮				
Economy	▮▮▮▮▮▮▮▮▮▮▮				
Driveability	▮▮▮▮▮▮▮▮▮▮▮▮▮▮▮▮▮▮				
Ride	▮▮▮▮▮▮▮▮▮▮▮▮▮▮▮▮▮▮				
Steering/handling	▮▮▮▮▮▮▮▮▮▮▮▮▮▮▮▮▮▮				
Braking	▮▮▮▮▮▮▮▮▮▮▮▮▮▮▮▮▮▮▮▮▮				
Noise	▮▮▮▮▮▮▮▮▮▮▮				
Accommodations					
Driver seating	▮▮▮▮▮▮▮▮▮▮▮▮▮▮▮▮▮▮				
Instruments/controls	▮▮▮▮▮▮▮▮▮▮▮▮▮▮▮▮▮▮				
Visibility	▮▮▮▮▮▮▮▮▮▮▮▮				
Room/comfort	▮▮▮▮▮▮▮▮▮▮▮▮▮▮▮▮▮▮				
Entry/exit	▮▮▮▮▮▮▮▮▮▮▮▮▮▮▮▮▮▮				
Cargo room	▮▮▮▮▮▮▮▮▮▮▮				
Workmanship					
Exterior	▮▮▮▮▮▮▮▮▮▮▮▮▮▮▮▮▮▮▮▮▮				
Interior	▮▮▮▮▮▮▮▮▮▮▮▮▮▮▮▮▮▮▮▮▮				
Value	▮▮▮▮▮▮▮▮▮▮▮				
Total Points					**61**

Specifications

Body type	4-door notchback	Engine type	dohc I-6
Wheelbase (in.)	109.4	Engine size (l/cu. in.)	3.0/183
Overall length (in.)	194.9	Horsepower @ rpm	220 @ 5800
Overall width (in.)	70.7	Torque @ rpm	210 @ 4800
Overall height (in.)	55.1	Transmission	auto/4-sp.
Curb weight (lbs.)	3660	Drive wheels	rear
Seating capacity	5	Brakes, F/R	disc/disc (ABS)
Front head room (in.)	36.9	Tire size	215/60VR16
Max. front leg room (in.)	44.0	Fuel tank capacity (gal.)	21.1
Rear head room (in.)	35.6	EPA city/highway mpg	18/23
Min. rear leg room (in.)	33.8	Test mileage (mpg)	17.3
Cargo volume (cu. ft.)	13.0		

Warranties The entire car is covered for 4 years/50,000 miles. Major powertrain components are covered for 6 years/70,000 miles. Body perforation rust is covered for 6 years/unlimited miles.

Rating scale 5=Exceptional; 4=Above average; 3=Average; 2=Below average; 1=Poor

LEXUS LS 400

Built in Japan.

Lexus LS 400

PREMIUM SEDAN

The second-generation LS 400 went on sale in November with new styling, more power, and a roomier interior. Overall length is unchanged at 196.7 inches, but the wheelbase has been stretched 1.4 inches to 112.2. The rear seat has 2.6 inches more leg room than the original LS 400, which spanned the 1990-94 model years. The rear-drive LS 400 retains a 4.0-liter V-8, but horsepower increases from 250 to 260. Lexus says the additional horsepower and a 209-pound weight reduction have lowered the 0-60 mph time to 6.9 seconds, about a second faster than the previous model. Lexus retained major styling cues from the previous generation while giving the new one sharper edges and creases. The nose has a larger grille, new headlamps, and more prominent character lines in the hood. The dashboard layout is similar to the previous model's with the biggest changes to the stereo and climate controls. There are fewer buttons and they're larger. A 6-disc CD changer is optional, though now it fits in the right side of the dashboard instead of the trunk. Dual air bags and anti-lock brakes are standard. The new LS 400 feels more agile and has less body lean in turns. The suspension is slightly firmer, yet still absorbent, and the steering feels much crisper. The old LS 400 was one of the quietest cars, and the new one is quieter still. There's less road noise and the V-8 is even more hushed in full throttle acceleration. With the longer wheelbase, there is now ample room for adults to stretch their legs in the back seat. Even though the LS 400 has been redesigned, the base price of $51,200 is unchanged from last year. That's a lot, but the new LS 400 is even better than the original.

Lexus LS 400 prices are on page 360.

LEXUS LS 400

Rating Guide	1	2	3	4	5
Performance					
Acceleration					
Economy					
Driveability					
Ride					
Steering/handling					
Braking					
Noise					
Accommodations					
Driver seating					
Instruments/controls					
Visibility					
Room/comfort					
Entry/exit					
Cargo room					
Workmanship					
Exterior					
Interior					
Value					

Total Points 68

Specifications

Body type	4-door notchback	Engine type	dohc V-8
Wheelbase (in.)	112.2	Engine size (l/cu. in.)	4.0/242
Overall length (in.)	196.7	Horsepower @ rpm	260 @ 5300
Overall width (in.)	72.0	Torque @ rpm	270 @ 4500
Overall height (in.)	55.7	Transmission	auto/4-sp.
Curb weight (lbs.)	3650	Drive wheels	rear
Seating capacity	5	Brakes, F/R	disc/disc (ABS)
Front head room (in.)	38.9	Tire size	225/60VR16
Max. front leg room (in.)	43.8	Fuel tank capacity (gal.)	22.5
Rear head room (in.)	36.8	EPA city/highway mpg	19/25
Min. rear leg room (in.)	36.9	Test mileage (mpg)	NA
Cargo volume (cu. ft.)	14.9		

Warranties The entire car is covered for 4 years/50,000 miles. Major powertrain components are covered for 6 years/70,000 miles. Body perforation rust is covered for 6 years/unlimited miles.

Rating scale 5=Exceptional; 4=Above average; 3=Average; 2=Below average; 1=Poor

LEXUS SC 300/400

Built in Japan.

Lexus SC 400

PREMIUM COUPE

The 1995 versions of the Lexus coupes went on sale last spring with several appearance and equipment changes. Lexus, Toyota's luxury-car division, offers two coupe models, the SC 300 and SC 400. Both have new grilles, taillamps, and alloy wheels. The SC 300 trades 15-inch diameter wheels and tires for 16-inchers, matching the SC 400. Both versions also get structural reinforcements to meet the stricter 1997 federal side impact standards and additional sound insulation. Interior changes include a cup holder for the front passenger, a headlamps-on indicator, outside temperature indicator, and a confirmation tone for the remote entry system. The SC 300 uses the same 3.0-liter inline 6-cylinder engine as the Lexus GS 300 sedan, though in the coupe it's rated at 225 horsepower, five more than in the sedan. The SC 400 has a 250-horsepower 4.0-liter V-8. A 5-speed manual transmission is standard on the SC 300 and an electronic 4-speed automatic is optional. The SC 400 comes only with the automatic. Both models have rear-wheel drive, dual air bags, and anti-lock brakes. The SC coupes have a more distinctive, sportier personality than the Lexus sedans. Though they have a much firmer ride than the Lexus sedans, they're never harsh. Both models are quick. We timed an SC 400 at 7.3 seconds to 60 mph and an SC 300 with automatic at 8.1 seconds to 60. Lexus accurately describes its coupes as "2+2s." Rear head room is skimpy and rear leg room vanishes if the front seats are pushed back more than halfway. Though there are good alternatives available for less, the Lexus coupes rank at the top in quality and customer satisfaction.

Lexus SC 300/400 prices are on page 361.

LEXUS SC 400

Rating Guide	1	2	3	4	5
Performance					
Acceleration	▐▐▐▐▐▐▐▐▐▐				
Economy	▐▐▐▐▐				
Driveability	▐▐▐▐▐▐▐▐▐▐				
Ride	▐▐▐▐▐▐▐				
Steering/handling	▐▐▐▐▐▐▐▐				
Braking	▐▐▐▐▐▐▐▐▐				
Noise	▐▐▐▐▐▐▐▐				
Accommodations					
Driver seating	▐▐▐▐▐▐▐				
Instruments/controls	▐▐▐▐▐▐▐				
Visibility	▐▐▐▐▐▐▐				
Room/comfort	▐▐▐▐▐▐				
Entry/exit	▐▐▐▐▐▐				
Cargo room	▐▐▐▐▐▐				
Workmanship					
Exterior	▐▐▐▐▐▐▐▐▐▐				
Interior	▐▐▐▐▐▐▐▐▐▐				
Value	▐▐▐▐▐▐▐▐▐				

Total Points...60

Specifications

Body type	2-door notchback	Engine type	dohc V-8
Wheelbase (in.)	105.9	Engine size (l/cu. in.)	4.0/242
Overall length (in.)	191.1	Horsepower @ rpm	250 @ 5600
Overall width (in.)	70.5	Torque @ rpm	260 @ 4400
Overall height (in.)	52.4	Transmission	auto/4-sp.
Curb weight (lbs.)	3575	Drive wheels	rear
Seating capacity	4	Brakes, F/R	disc/disc (ABS)
Front head room (in.)	38.3	Tire size	225/55VR16
Max. front leg room (in.)	44.1	Fuel tank capacity (gal.)	20.6
Rear head room (in.)	36.1	EPA city/highway mpg	18/22
Min. rear leg room (in.)	27.2	Test mileage (mpg)	17.2
Cargo volume (cu. ft.)	9.3		

Warranties The entire car is covered for 4 years/50,000 miles. Major powertrain components are covered for 6 years/70,000 miles. Body perforation rust is covered for 6 years/unlimited miles.

Rating scale 5=Exceptional; 4=Above average; 3=Average; 2=Below average; 1=Poor

LINCOLN CONTINENTAL

Built in Wixom, Mich.

Lincoln Continental

PREMIUM SEDAN

A redesigned Continental sedan was scheduled to go on sale in late December with new styling, a V-8 engine with dual overhead camshafts, a redesigned instrument panel with virtual-image graphics, and adjustable electronic ride control. Prices weren't announced in time for this issue. Base prices on the 1994 models ranged from $33,750 to $35,600. Wheelbase on the front-drive Continental is unchanged at 109 inches, but the 1995 model is longer and wider by about an inch. The hood, trunklid, and fenders are made of fiberglass; other body panels are made of steel. The styling is much more rounded than the previous model's and resembles that of the Lincoln Mark VIII, a 2-door coupe. A new suspension system has electronic controls that automatically stiffen or soften the shock absorbers to match driving conditions. In addition, the suspension can be manually set to Firm, Normal, or Plush settings and the variable-assist power steering can be set to Low, Medium, or High steering effort. The new Continental comes only as a 4-door sedan with a 260-horsepower 4.6-liter V-8 engine, based on the one in the rear-drive Mark VIII, and a new electronic 4-speed automatic transmission. This is the first front-drive application for Ford Motor Company's overhead-camshaft V-8. The previous Continental, which spanned the 1988-1994 model years, had a 165-horsepower 3.8-liter V-6 engine. It was the first Lincoln with front-wheel drive and fewer than eight cylinders. Standard equipment on the 1995 Continental includes dual air bags and anti-lock brakes. We haven't driven the new Continental so we can't provide ratings.

Lincoln Continental standard equipment is on page 362.

LINCOLN CONTINENTAL (Ratings Not Available)

Rating Guide	1	2	3	4	5
Performance					
Acceleration					
Economy					
Driveability					
Ride					
Steering/handling					
Braking					
Noise					
Accommodations					
Driver seating					
Instruments/controls					
Visibility					
Room/comfort					
Entry/exit					
Cargo room					
Workmanship					
Exterior					
Interior					
Value					
Total Points..					

Specifications

Body type	.........4-door notchback	Engine type	....................dohc V-8
Wheelbase (in.)	....................109.0	Engine size (l/cu. in.)	........4.6/281
Overall length (in.)	................206.3	Horsepower @ rpm	...260 @ 5750
Overall width (in.)	...................73.3	Torque @ rpm	...........265 @ 4750
Overall height (in.)	..................55.9	Transmission	.................auto/4-sp.
Curb weight (lbs.)	3969	Drive wheels	...........................front
Seating capacity	6	Brakes, F/R	..........disc/disc (ABS)
Front head room (in.)	.............39.1	Tire size	......................225/60R16
Max. front leg room (in.)	........41.8	Fuel tank capacity (gal.)	.........18.0
Rear head room (in.)	..............38.0	EPA city/highway mpg	.............NA
Min. rear leg room (in.)	...........39.2	Test mileage (mpg)	.................NA
Cargo volume (cu. ft.)	.............18.1		

Warranties The entire car is covered for 4 years/50,000 miles. Body perforation rust is covered for 5 years/unlimited miles.

Rating scale 5=Exceptional; 4=Above average; 3=Average; 2=Below average; 1=Poor

LINCOLN MARK VIII

Built in Wixom, Mich.

Lincoln Mark VIII

PREMIUM COUPE

Lincoln's rear-drive premium coupe goes into its third model year with several changes, including a redesigned instrument panel with a new stereo. At mid-year, Lincoln plans to introduce a sportier version of the Mark VIII without exterior chrome and new features such as a firmer suspension, high-intensity discharge headlamps, and perforated leather upholstery. The special edition will use the same dual-camshaft 4.6-liter V-8 as the base model. However, it will have a full dual exhaust system that will increase horsepower an unspecified amount above the base model's 280. On the base model, there's a new center console and the climate and audio systems have been more fully integrated with the walnut dashboard trim. The new stereo has larger buttons that Lincoln says are easier to use. Most of the interior switches have been color-keyed for easier recognition. Standard equipment includes dual air bags, anti-lock brakes, a 4-speed electronic automatic transmission, and automatic air conditioning. The Mark VIII provides a pleasant balance of performance and luxury. It's quick off the line and once above 15 mph it really flies. We tested this car on snow and ice and were disappointed with the performance of the optional traction control system. The rear wheels spun readily in snow, making takeoffs slow and laborious. Interior space isn't a strong point either. Tall passengers don't have much head room, even without the optional moonroof. Rear leg room is limited and two adults is the comfortable maximum in back. Though the Mark VIII is a good car, don't buy one without first testing a Cadillac Eldorado, Lexus SC 400, or Acura Legend Coupe, rivals that we rate higher overall.

Lincoln Mark VIII prices are on page 362.

LINCOLN MARK VIII

Rating Guide	1	2	3	4	5
Performance					
Acceleration	▓▓▓▓▓▓▓▓▓▓▓▓▓▓▓▓▓▓▓▓▓▓▓▓▓				
Economy	▓▓▓▓▓				
Driveability	▓▓▓▓▓▓▓▓▓▓▓▓▓▓▓				
Ride	▓▓▓▓▓▓▓▓▓▓▓▓▓▓▓				
Steering/handling	▓▓▓▓▓▓▓▓▓▓▓▓▓▓▓				
Braking	▓▓▓▓▓▓▓▓▓▓▓▓▓▓▓▓▓▓▓▓				
Noise	▓▓▓▓▓▓▓▓▓▓▓▓▓▓▓				
Accommodations					
Driver seating	▓▓▓▓▓▓▓▓▓▓▓▓▓▓▓				
Instruments/controls	▓▓▓▓▓▓▓▓▓▓▓▓▓▓▓				
Visibility	▓▓▓▓▓▓▓▓▓▓▓▓▓▓▓▓▓				
Room/comfort	▓▓▓▓▓▓▓▓▓▓▓▓▓▓▓				
Entry/exit	▓▓▓▓▓▓▓▓▓▓▓▓▓▓▓				
Cargo room	▓▓▓▓▓▓▓▓▓▓▓▓▓▓▓▓▓▓▓▓▓▓▓▓▓				
Workmanship					
Exterior	▓▓▓▓▓▓▓▓▓▓▓▓▓▓▓▓▓▓▓▓▓▓▓▓▓				
Interior	▓▓▓▓▓▓▓▓▓▓▓▓▓▓▓▓▓▓▓▓▓▓				
Value	▓▓▓▓▓▓▓▓▓▓▓▓▓▓▓				
Total Points					**59**

Specifications

Body type	2-door notchback	Engine type	dohc V-8
Wheelbase (in.)	113.0	Engine size (l/cu. in.)	4.6/281
Overall length (in.)	207.3	Horsepower @ rpm	280 @ 5500
Overall width (in.)	74.8	Torque @ rpm	285 @ 4500
Overall height (in.)	53.6	Transmission	auto/4-sp.
Curb weight (lbs.)	3768	Drive wheels	rear
Seating capacity	5	Brakes, F/R	disc/disc (ABS)
Front head room (in.)	38.1	Tire size	225/60VR16
Max. front leg room (in.)	42.6	Fuel tank capacity (gal.)	18.0
Rear head room (in.)	37.5	EPA city/highway mpg	18/25
Min. rear leg room (in.)	32.5	Test mileage (mpg)	14.9
Cargo volume (cu. ft.)	14.4		

Warranties The entire car is covered for 4 years/50,000 miles. Body perforation rust is covered for 5 years/unlimited miles.

Rating scale 5=Exceptional; 4=Above average; 3=Average; 2=Below average; 1=Poor

LINCOLN TOWN CAR

Built in Wixom, Mich.

Lincoln Town Car Signature Series

PREMIUM SEDAN

The Town Car returns for 1995 with several significant exterior and functional changes. This full-size, rear-drive luxury sedan continues in Executive, Signature, and Cartier Designer Series models, all with standard dual air bags and anti-lock brakes. A new electronic adjustable steering effort feature is standard. A dashboard switch lets the driver choose heavy, medium, or light steering effort. Exterior changes include new headlamps, taillamps, grille, front and rear bumper fascias, color-keyed side moldings, and larger outside mirrors that have been moved forward to improve visibility. Inside, the Town Car has new seats with more travel, a redesigned instrument panel, and a 2-spoke steering wheel. New stereos have larger, simpler controls and, on the Signature and Cartier models, there are new climate and audio controls mounted in the steering wheel. Also standard on the Signature and Cartier models is a new garage door opener integrated with the driver's sun visor. It can be programmed to three different frequencies. The only powertrain consists of a 210-horsepower 4.6-liter V-8 and an electronic 4-speed automatic transmission. Traction control is optional on all models. With its pillowy ride, isolation from mechanical noise, and expansive interior, Town Car delivers all the indulgences a car of this type should. However, the rival Cadillac Fleetwood matches Town Car in spaciousness and luxury and has a 260-horsepower V-8. In addition, Fleetwood comes with standard traction control—all for a lower base price. That's not to say those who prefer a full-size, rear-drive luxury car would be disappointed with the Town Car. However, the Fleetwood is the better choice overall.

Lincoln Town Car prices are on page 363.

LINCOLN TOWN CAR

Rating Guide	1	2	3	4	5
Performance					
Acceleration				▓	
Economy		▓			
Driveability				▓	
Ride				▓	
Steering/handling			▓		
Braking					▓
Noise					▓
Accommodations					
Driver seating			▓		
Instruments/controls			▓		
Visibility			▓		
Room/comfort				▓	
Entry/exit				▓	
Cargo room			▓		
Workmanship					
Exterior			▓		
Interior			▓		
Value			▓		

Total Points...59

Specifications

Body type ....4-door notchback	Engine type ....ohc V-8
Wheelbase (in.) 117.4	Engine size (l/cu. in.)........4.6/281
Overall length (in.)................218.9	Horsepower @ rpm ...210 @ 4600
Overall width (in.) 76.9	Torque @ rpm ....270 @ 3400
Overall height (in.)..................56.9	Transmission .... auto/4-sp.
Curb weight (lbs.) 4050	Drive wheels .... rear
Seating capacity 6	Brakes, F/R .... disc/disc (ABS)
Front head room (in.) 39.0	Tire size 215/70R15
Max. front leg room (in.) 42.6	Fuel tank capacity (gal.) 20.0
Rear head room (in.) 38.0	EPA city/highway mpg 17/25
Min. rear leg room (in.)...........41.1	Test mileage (mpg) 17.0
Cargo volume (cu. ft.).............22.3	

Warranties The entire car is covered for 4 years/50,000 miles. Body perforation rust is covered for 5 years/unlimited miles.

Rating scale 5=Exceptional; 4=Above average; 3=Average; 2=Below average; 1=Poor

MAZDA MIATA

Built in Japan.

Mazda Miata

SPORTS AND GT

Miata, Mazda's 2-seat, rear-drive roadster, returns with minor revisions for 1995. Last year, a 116-horsepower 1.6-liter 4-cylinder engine was replaced by a 1.8-liter with 128 horsepower. The dual-camshaft 1.8-liter engine continues with a standard 5-speed manual transmission or optional 4-speed automatic. Also new last year was a passenger-side air bag, which joined a driver-side air bag that had been standard since Miata's debut in 1990. Anti-lock brakes are optional. For 1995, option packages have been regrouped. The former A and B Packages are combined in a new Popular Equipment Group. Included are alloy wheels, power steering, leather-wrapped steering wheel, power mirrors, headrest speakers, a limited-slip differential, power windows, cruise control, and a power antenna. The new Leather Package replaces the previous C Package and includes all the above items plus tan leather upholstery and a tan vinyl top. Lively, agile, and fun, Miata has all the requisites for a sports car. The 1.8-liter engine doesn't have much kick at low speed, especially with the automatic transmission, but the free-revving 4-cylinder quickly gets into its power band for brisk acceleration. We clocked a 5-speed model at 8.3 seconds to 60 mph. You feel nearly every bump in the firmly sprung Miata, but the suspension absorbs enough of the impact. Though the prominent exhaust note is appropriate, there is also lots of wind and road noise at highway speeds. The cozy cockpit has well-placed gauges and controls and enough space to give tall people adequate working room. With a base price of $17,500, Miata remains an affordable sports car.

Mazda Miata prices are on page 364.

MAZDA MIATA

Rating Guide	1	2	3	4	5
Performance					
Acceleration	████████████████████				
Economy	████████████████				
Driveability	████████████████				
Ride	███████████████				
Steering/handling	████████████████████				
Braking	██████████████████████████				
Noise	███████████				
Accommodations					
Driver seating	████████████████				
Instruments/controls	████████████████				
Visibility	████████████████				
Room/comfort	██████████████				
Entry/exit	████████████████				
Cargo room	███████				
Workmanship					
Exterior	████████████████				
Interior	████████████████				
Value	████████████████				

Total Points..**56**

Specifications

Body type ....2-door convertible	Engine type .... dohc I-4
Wheelbase (in.) 89.2	Engine size (l/cu. in.).........1.8/112
Overall length (in.).................155.4	Horsepower @ rpm ...128 @ 6500
Overall width (in.).....................65.9	Torque @ rpm ....110 @ 5000
Overall height (in.)..................48.2	Transmission .... manual/5-sp.
Curb weight (lbs.) 2293	Drive wheels .... rear
Seating capacity...........................2	Brakes, F/R...........disc/disc (ABS)
Front head room (in.) 37.1	Tire size 185/60HR14
Max. front leg room (in.) 42.7	Fuel tank capacity (gal.) 12.7
Rear head room (in.) .... —	EPA city/highway mpg 23/29
Min. rear leg room (in.) .... —	Test mileage (mpg) 26.7
Cargo volume (cu. ft.).............. 3.6	

Warranties The entire car is covered for 3 years/50,000 miles. Body perforation rust is covered for 5 years/unlimited miles.

Rating scale 5=Exceptional; 4=Above average; 3=Average; 2=Below average; 1=Poor

MAZDA MILLENIA

Built in Japan.

Mazda Millenia S

PREMIUM SEDAN

Millenia went on sale in the spring as a new front-drive luxury sedan positioned against the Lexus ES 300, BMW 3-Series, Infiniti J30, and others. Millenia originally was intended to be the entry-level model for Amati, a luxury division planned by Mazda that was scrapped last year. It is sized and priced between the Mazda 626 family sedan and the 929 luxury sedan and comes in three versions: base, base with a leather interior package, and top-line S. The base models have a 170-horsepower 2.5-liter V-6 engine (also used in the 626). The S comes with a 210-horsepower 2.3-liter V-6 with Miller-cycle technology, which works like a supercharger to produce more power. All versions come only with a 4-speed electronic automatic transmission. Standard on all models are dual air bags, anti-lock brakes, and automatic climate control. The S model also has traction control and 16-inch wheels and tires (the others have 15-inch). The Millenia feels solid over rough roads and has top-notch refinement, with little wind noise or engine noise, and only a touch more tire noise than a luxury car should have. The base Millenia always feels rather "sleepy," and proved it by reaching 60 mph in 9.4 seconds. By contrast, an S model took just 7.8 seconds and felt much stronger. Though the automatic transmission in both models is generally smooth and responsive, flooring the throttle can result in harsh, abrupt downshifts. The interior has adequate space for four adults and the dashboard is attractive and convenient. The base Millenia delivers lots of luxury for a few thousand less than most rivals but can't match their performance. The S packs plenty of performance but charges an extra $5000 or so for it.

Mazda Millenia prices are on page 365.

MAZDA MILLENIA S

Rating Guide	1	2	3	4	5
Performance					
Acceleration	▐▐▐▐▐▐▐▐▐▐▐▐▐▐▐▐▐▐				
Economy	▐▐▐▐▐▐▐▐				
Driveability	▐▐▐▐▐▐▐▐▐▐▐▐				
Ride	▐▐▐▐▐▐▐▐▐▐▐▐▐▐▐				
Steering/handling	▐▐▐▐▐▐▐▐▐▐▐▐▐				
Braking	▐▐▐▐▐▐▐▐▐▐▐▐▐▐▐▐▐▐▐▐				
Noise	▐▐▐▐▐▐▐▐▐▐▐▐▐				
Accommodations					
Driver seating	▐▐▐▐▐▐▐▐▐▐▐▐▐▐▐				
Instruments/controls	▐▐▐▐▐▐▐▐▐▐▐▐▐				
Visibility	▐▐▐▐▐▐▐▐▐▐▐				
Room/comfort	▐▐▐▐▐▐▐▐▐▐▐▐▐▐▐				
Entry/exit	▐▐▐▐▐▐▐▐▐▐▐▐▐▐▐				
Cargo room	▐▐▐▐▐▐▐▐▐▐▐				
Workmanship					
Exterior	▐▐▐▐▐▐▐▐▐▐▐▐▐▐▐▐				
Interior	▐▐▐▐▐▐▐▐▐▐▐▐▐▐▐				
Value	▐▐▐▐▐▐▐▐▐▐▐				

Total Points...**59**

Specifications

Body type ....4-door notchback	Engine type.....................dohc V-6
Wheelbase (in.) 108.3	Engine size (l/cu. in.)........2.3/138
Overall length (in.)...............189.8	Horsepower @ rpm ...210 @ 4800
Overall width (in.) 69.7	Torque @ rpm ....210 @ 3500
Overall height (in.)................54.9	Transmission................auto/4-sp.
Curb weight (lbs.) 3216	Drive wheels ....front
Seating capacity.........................5	Brakes, F/R..........disc/disc (ABS)
Front head room (in.) 39.3	Tire size.....................215/55VR16
Max. front leg room (in.) 43.3	Fuel tank capacity (gal.) 18.0
Rear head room (in.) 37.0	EPA city/highway mpg 20/28
Min. rear leg room (in.)..........34.1	Test mileage (mpg) 21.8
Cargo volume (cu. ft.).............13.3	

Warranties The entire car is covered for 3 years/50,000 miles. Body perforation rust is covered for 5 years/unlimited miles.

Rating scale 5=Exceptional; 4=Above average; 3=Average; 2=Below average; 1=Poor

MAZDA MPV

Built in Japan.

Mazda MPV LX

MINIVAN

Mazda's MPV minivan changes from a single model with several stand-alone options and option packages to three models with fewer options packaged into groups. The new lineup consists of L, LX, and LXE models, all with 7-passenger seating. Last year, seats for five were standard and seats for seven and eight were optional. The optional Touring Package that included the 8-passenger seating has been dropped. Rear-wheel drive is standard and on-demand 4-wheel drive is optional. All models now come with a 155-horsepower 3.0-liter V-6 and a 4-speed automatic transmission. Last year's base engine, a 121-horsepower 2.6-liter 4-cylinder, is gone. The MPV (multi-purpose vehicle) has two front doors, a conventional swing-open right rear door, and a rear liftgate. A driver-side air bag and rear-wheel anti-lock brakes are standard on all models. The MPV lacks the room and some of the features of class leaders like the Dodge Caravan/Plymouth Voyager and Ford Windstar, yet costs about as much. The 3.0-liter V-6 provides adequate pickup, but falls far short of the performance of 3.8-liter V-6s available in the Chrysler vans and the Pontiac Trans Sport, Chevrolet Lumina Minivan, and Oldsmobile Silhouette. In addition, the standard rear-wheel drive is a poor choice in areas that get lots of snow. The 4WD models have great traction but sluggish acceleration because they weigh nearly 300 pounds more. The heavier 4WD models also guzzle more gas (14.2 mpg in our last test) and have a rather truck-like ride. The MPV has modest cargo space at the back and a rear seat that's bolted in so it can't be easily removed.

Mazda MPV prices are on page 366.

MAZDA MPV LX

Rating Guide	1	2	3	4	5
Performance					
Acceleration			||||||||||||		
Economy		|||			
Driveability				||||||||	
Ride			|||||||		
Steering/handling				||||||||	
Braking				||||||||	
Noise			||||||||		
Accommodations						
Driver seating				||||||	
Instruments/controls				||||||	
Visibility				||||||	
Room/comfort				||||||	
Entry/exit				||||||	
Cargo room				||||||||||	
Workmanship						
Exterior				||||||||	
Interior				||||||||	
Value				||||||	
Total Points					**57**

Specifications

Body type	4-door van	Engine type	ohc V-6
Wheelbase (in.)	110.4	Engine size (l/cu. in.)	3.0/180
Overall length (in.)	175.8	Horsepower @ rpm	155 @ 5000
Overall width (in.)	71.9	Torque @ rpm	169 @ 4000
Overall height (in.)	68.1	Transmission	auto/4-sp.
Curb weight (lbs.)	3745	Drive wheels	rear
Seating capacity	7	Brakes, F/R	disc/disc (ABS)
Front head room (in.)	40.0	Tire size	195/75R15
Max. front leg room (in.)	40.6	Fuel tank capacity (gal.)	19.6
Rear head room (in.)	39.0	EPA city/highway mpg	16/22
Min. rear leg room (in.)	34.8	Test mileage (mpg)	NA
Cargo volume (cu. ft.)	37.5		

Warranties The entire vehicle is covered for 3 years/50,000 miles. Body perforation rust is covered for 5 years/unlimited miles.

Rating scale 5=Exceptional; 4=Above average; 3=Average; 2=Below average; 1=Poor

MAZDA PROTEGE

Built in Japan.

Mazda Protege LX

SUBCOMPACT

Mazda's front-drive subcompact sedan is redesigned, growing more than four inches in wheelbase (to 102.6 inches) and three inches in overall length (to 174.8). Dual air bags are a new standard feature. Protege's companion in the previous generation, the 323 3-door hatchback, has been dropped due to slow sales. The new Protege comes as a 4-door sedan in three price levels. The base DX and mid-level LX are powered by a new 1.5-liter 4-cylinder engine with 92 horsepower. The top-line ES gets a 1.8-liter 4-cylinder with 122 horsepower. Both engines come with a standard 5-speed manual transmission or an optional 4-speed automatic. The ES also has standard air conditioning, 14-inch wheels (in place of 13s), and anti-lock brakes. The anti-lock feature is optional on the LX and not available on the DX. Mazda is stressing the interior room of this new sedan and claims the Protege has the largest interior volume in the subcompact class: 95 cubic feet, 10 more than a Honda Civic. Though there's ample space for four adults in Protege's roomy interior, the rear doors are narrow at the bottom, making it awkward to get in or out of the back. The dashboard is generally well laid out. However, the radio is mounted too low on the dashboard and has small buttons that require a long look away from the road to adjust. The 1.5-liter engine is one of the smallest and least powerful in this class, but it manages to deliver adequate acceleration with either transmission. The 1.8-liter engine in the ES is noticeably stronger for highway merging and passing. The new Protege deserves a look if you're shopping for a small sedan.

Mazda Protege prices are on page 368.

MAZDA PROTEGE LX

Rating Guide	1	2	3	4	5
Performance					
Acceleration	▓▓▓▓▓▓▓▓▓▓▓▓				
Economy	▓▓▓▓▓▓▓▓▓▓▓▓▓▓▓▓				
Driveability	▓▓▓▓▓▓▓▓▓▓▓▓				
Ride	▓▓▓▓▓▓▓▓▓▓▓▓				
Steering/handling	▓▓▓▓▓▓▓▓▓▓▓▓				
Braking	▓▓▓▓▓▓▓▓▓▓▓▓				
Noise	▓▓▓▓▓▓▓▓▓▓▓▓				
Accommodations					
Driver seating	▓▓▓▓▓▓▓▓▓▓▓▓▓▓▓▓				
Instruments/controls	▓▓▓▓▓▓▓▓▓▓▓▓▓▓▓▓				
Visibility	▓▓▓▓▓▓▓▓▓▓▓▓▓▓▓▓				
Room/comfort	▓▓▓▓▓▓▓▓▓▓▓▓▓▓▓▓				
Entry/exit	▓▓▓▓▓▓▓▓▓▓▓▓				
Cargo room	▓▓▓▓▓▓▓▓▓▓▓▓				
Workmanship					
Exterior	▓▓▓▓▓▓▓▓▓▓▓▓▓▓▓▓				
Interior	▓▓▓▓▓▓▓▓▓▓▓▓▓▓▓▓				
Value	▓▓▓▓▓▓▓▓▓▓▓▓				

Total Points...57

Specifications

Body type	4-door notchback	Engine type	dohc I-4
Wheelbase (in.)	102.6	Engine size (l/cu. in.)	1.5/91
Overall length (in.)	174.8	Horsepower @ rpm	92 @ 5500
Overall width (in.)	67.3	Torque @ rpm	96 @ 4000
Overall height (in.)	55.9	Transmission	manual/5-sp.
Curb weight (lbs.)	2385	Drive wheels	front
Seating capacity	5	Brakes, F/R	disc/drum
Front head room (in.)	39.2	Tire size	175/70R13
Max. front leg room (in.)	42.2	Fuel tank capacity (gal.)	14.5
Rear head room (in.)	37.4	EPA city/highway mpg	31/39
Min. rear leg room (in.)	35.6	Test mileage (mpg)	28.4
Cargo volume (cu. ft.)	13.1		

Warranties The entire car is covered for 3 years/50,000 miles. Body perforation rust is covered for 5 years/unlimited miles.

Rating scale 5=Exceptional; 4=Above average; 3=Average; 2=Below average; 1=Poor

MAZDA 626

Built in Flat Rock, Mich.

Mazda 626 LX

COMPACT

Mazda's front-drive compact sedan returns with a handful of new features for 1995. The 626 comes in DX, LX, LX V-6, and ES versions. DX and LX models have a 118-horsepower 2.0-liter 4-cylinder engine. The LX V-6 and ES have a 164-horsepower 2.5-liter V-6. All come with a standard 5-speed manual transmission or an optional 4-speed automatic. A new remote keyless entry system is standard on the ES and included with the LX Luxury Package and LX V-6 Premium Package. For the DX, a new Convenience Package includes air conditioning, a stereo with cassette player, and carpeted floor mats. Dual air bags are standard across the board and anti-lock brakes are standard on the ES, optional on the LX and LX V-6. All 626s sold in the U.S. are built at a plant in Flat Rock, Michigan, that is jointly owned by Mazda and Ford Motor Co. The Mazda MX-6 and Ford Probe sports coupes also are built there. The 626 is a highly competitive entry in the compact sedan segment. One of the principal rivals is the Toyota Camry, which is quieter and more luxurious. The 626 though, has sportier handling, more personality, and lower prices. There's adequate head room for tall people in the 626 even with the power sunroof and ample leg room for all seats. Though the V-6 engine is clearly the performance leader in the 626 line, the 4-cylinder engine is no slouch. We timed one at 9.5 seconds to 60 mph with the 5-speed manual, which is more than adequate for most situations. We clocked a V-6 model, also with the 5-speed manual, at a quick 7.8 seconds. A 626 with automatic transmission will be slower. In addition, the automatic is slow to downshift for passing and often shifts harshly.

Mazda 626 prices are on page 369.

MAZDA 626 LX

Rating Guide	1	2	3	4	5
Performance					
Acceleration			▓		
Economy			▓		
Driveability			▓		
Ride			▓		
Steering/handling			▓		
Braking					▓
Noise			▓		
Accommodations					
Driver seating			▓		
Instruments/controls			▓		
Visibility			▓		
Room/comfort			▓		
Entry/exit			▓		
Cargo room			▓		
Workmanship					
Exterior			▓		
Interior			▓		
Value			▓		

Total Points..61

Specifications

Body type ....4-door notchback
Wheelbase (in.) 102.8
Overall length (in.)................184.4
Overall width (in.) 68.9
Overall height (in.) 55.1
Curb weight (lbs.) 2743
Seating capacity 5
Front head room (in.) 39.2
Max. front leg room (in.) 43.5
Rear head room (in.) 37.8
Min. rear leg room (in.) 35.8
Cargo volume (cu. ft.).............13.8

Engine type ....dohc I-4
Engine size (l/cu. in.).........2.0/122
Horsepower @ rpm ...118 @ 5500
Torque @ rpm ....127 @ 4500
Transmission ....manual/5-sp.
Drive wheels ....front
Brakes, F/R..........disc/disc (ABS)
Tire size 195/65R14
Fuel tank capacity (gal.) 15.9
EPA city/highway mpg 26/34
Test mileage (mpg) 25.1

Warranties The entire car is covered for 3 years/50,000 miles. Body perforation rust is covered for 5 years/unlimited miles.

Rating scale 5=Exceptional; 4=Above average; 3=Average; 2=Below average; 1=Poor

MAZDA 929

Built in Japan.

Mazda 929

PREMIUM SEDAN

Mazda's rear-drive luxury sedan was trimmed to one model last year, and this year it gains more standard equipment. Leather upholstery and wood console trim used to be part of the 929's optional Premium Package, which also included an upgraded audio system with a multi-disc CD changer. This year, the leather and wood and remote keyless entry are standard. An in-dash single-disc CD changer and trunk-mounted 6-disc changer are new dealer-installed options. The Four Seasons Package (not available in California) contains heated front seats, all-season tires, a limited-slip differential, heavy-duty wiper motor, a larger windshield-washer fluid reservoir, and a heavy-duty battery. The sole powertrain is a 193-horsepower 3.0-liter V-6 with dual-overhead camshafts. It mates with a 4-speed automatic transmission. Standard equipment includes dual air bags, anti-lock brakes, and height-adjustable front seatbelts. The 929 is attractively styled and has a full complement of safety and convenience features. However, it's short of interior and trunk space and lags in refinement compared to rivals such as the Acura Legend and Lexus ES 300. The 929's V-6 engine delivers more than adequate acceleration (9.4 seconds to 60 mph in our test) but sounds harsh when it's cold and feels a little rough in hard acceleration. Despite a long 112.2-inch wheelbase, the front seats aren't that spacious. In addition, the steering wheel is fixed, so it doesn't suit everyone. The trunk floor is so short it's hard to fit more than a couple of suitcases. The 929 comes up short in too many areas to be a prime choice among cars in the $35,000 to $40,000 range.

Mazda 929 prices are on page 370.

MAZDA 929

Rating Guide	1	2	3	4	5
Performance					
Acceleration	▓▓▓▓▓▓▓▓				
Economy	▓▓▓▓				
Driveability	▓▓▓▓▓▓▓▓				
Ride	▓▓▓▓▓▓▓▓				
Steering/handling	▓▓▓▓▓▓▓▓				
Braking	▓▓▓▓▓▓▓▓▓▓				
Noise	▓▓▓▓▓▓▓▓				
Accommodations					
Driver seating	▓▓▓▓▓▓▓▓				
Instruments/controls	▓▓▓▓▓▓▓▓				
Visibility	▓▓▓▓▓▓				
Room/comfort	▓▓▓▓▓▓▓				
Entry/exit	▓▓▓▓▓▓▓				
Cargo room	▓▓▓▓▓▓				
Workmanship					
Exterior	▓▓▓▓▓▓▓▓				
Interior	▓▓▓▓▓▓▓▓				
Value	▓▓▓▓▓▓				

Total Points 59

Specifications

Body type ....4-door notchback	Engine type.....................dohc V-6
Wheelbase (in.) 112.2	Engine size (l/cu. in.)........3.0/180
Overall length (in.)...............193.7	Horsepower @ rpm ...193 @ 5750
Overall width (in.) 70.7	Torque @ rpm ....200 @ 3500
Overall height (in.).................54.9	Transmission.................auto/4-sp.
Curb weight (lbs.) 3627	Drive wheels ....rear
Seating capacity..........................5	Brakes, F/R..........disc/disc (ABS)
Front head room (in.) 37.4	Tire size 205/65R15
Max. front leg room (in.).........43.4	Fuel tank capacity (gal.).........18.5
Rear head room (in.) 37.4	EPA city/highway mpg 19/24
Min. rear leg room (in.)...........37.0	Test mileage (mpg) 19.0
Cargo volume (cu. ft.).............12.4	

Warranties The entire car is covered for 3 years/50,000 miles. Body perforation rust is covered for 5 years/unlimited miles.

Rating scale 5=Exceptional; 4=Above average; 3=Average; 2=Below average; 1=Poor

MERCEDES-BENZ C-CLASS —

Built in Germany.

Mercedes-Benz C280

PREMIUM SEDAN

The C-Class, Mercedes's entry-level line, was introduced last year. This fall, it gets a new optional traction control system for the base C220 and standard all-season tires for both the C220 and the top-line C280. This spring, Mercedes plans to introduce a high-performance version of this rear-drive compact sedan. Called the C36, it will have a 3.6-liter 6-cylinder engine with "270 horsepower plus," according to the German automaker. The other C-Class cars return for 1995 with the same engines as last year. The C220 has a 147-horsepower 2.2-liter 4-cylinder and the C280 a 194-horsepower 2.8-liter 6-cylinder. Both come only with a 4-speed automatic transmission. Anti-lock brakes and dual air bags are standard. Optional on the C220 this year is Electronic Traction System (ETS)—traction control that applies the brakes to either drive wheel if there is slip and transfers more power to the other wheel. Acceleration Slip Control, a more advanced system that also has throttle control to reduce power when there is wheel slip, remains optional on the C280. This year, it gains a dashboard switch that allows turning off the throttle-control portion. The C-Class sedans are rock-solid and well-engineered. Their engines are quiet and refined, even under hard acceleration. Both cars suffer leisurely pickup off the line but gather steam quickly and have strong passing power. Tall drivers may not have enough leg room or head room in the compact C-Class. Moving the driver's seat all the way back drastically cuts into rear leg room, which is only adequate at best. Overall, the C-Class deserves a look among sedans in the $30,000 to $40,000 range.

Mercedes-Benz C-Class prices are on page 371.

MERCEDES-BENZ C280

Rating Guide	1	2	3	4	5
Performance					
Acceleration	▐▐▐▐▐▐▐▐▐▐▐▐▐▐▐▐▐ (4)				
Economy	▐▐▐▐▐▐▐ (2)				
Driveability	▐▐▐▐▐▐▐▐▐▐▐▐▐▐▐ (4)				
Ride	▐▐▐▐▐▐▐▐▐▐▐▐▐▐▐ (4)				
Steering/handling	▐▐▐▐▐▐▐▐▐▐▐▐▐▐▐ (4)				
Braking	▐▐▐▐▐▐▐▐▐▐▐▐▐▐▐▐▐▐▐ (5)				
Noise	▐▐▐▐▐▐▐▐▐ (3)				
Accommodations					
Driver seating	▐▐▐▐▐▐▐▐▐▐▐▐▐▐ (4)				
Instruments/controls	▐▐▐▐▐▐▐▐▐▐▐▐▐▐ (4)				
Visibility	▐▐▐▐▐▐▐▐▐▐▐▐▐▐ (4)				
Room/comfort	▐▐▐▐▐▐▐▐ (3)				
Entry/exit	▐▐▐▐▐▐▐▐ (3)				
Cargo room	▐▐▐▐▐▐▐▐ (3)				
Workmanship					
Exterior	▐▐▐▐▐▐▐▐▐▐▐▐▐▐▐▐▐▐▐ (5)				
Interior	▐▐▐▐▐▐▐▐▐▐▐▐▐▐▐▐▐▐▐ (5)				
Value	▐▐▐▐▐▐▐▐ (3)				

Total Points..60

Specifications

Body type ....4-door notchback	Engine type ....dohc I-6
Wheelbase (in.) 105.9	Engine size (l/cu. in.)..........2.8/173
Overall length (in.) 177.4	Horsepower @ rpm ...194 @ 5500
Overall width (in.) 67.7	Torque @ rpm ....199 @ 3750
Overall height (in.) 56.1	Transmission.................auto/4-sp.
Curb weight (lbs.) 3173	Drive wheels ....rear
Seating capacity..........................5	Brakes, F/R...........disc/disc (ABS)
Front head room (in.) 37.2	Tire size 195/65HR15
Max. front leg room (in.) 41.5	Fuel tank capacity (gal.) 16.4
Rear head room (in.) 37.0	EPA city/highway mpg 20/26
Min. rear leg room (in.)...........32.8	Test mileage (mpg) 19.2
Cargo volume (cu. ft.)..............13.7	

Warranties The entire car (including body perforation rust) is covered for 4 years/50,000 miles.

Rating scale 5=Exceptional; 4=Above average; 3=Average; 2=Below average; 1=Poor

MERCEDES-BENZ E-CLASS —

Built in Germany.

Mercedes-Benz E320

PREMIUM SEDAN/COUPE

Mercedes's mid-range line is scheduled to be redesigned for 1996, so it gets only a handful of equipment changes for its 10th and final season. The E300 Diesel arrived last spring as an early 1995 model with a new 134-horsepower 3.0-liter diesel 6-cylinder. Other than the engine, it has the same equipment as the E320 sedan, which uses a 217-horsepower 3.2-liter gas 6-cylinder. The E300 Diesel comes only as a 4-door sedan. The E320 comes as a sedan, 2-door coupe, and a convertible (called Cabriolet). Topping the line is the E420 sedan with a 275-horsepower 4.2-liter V-8. All models have rear-wheel drive, a 4-speed automatic transmission, anti-lock brakes, and dual air bags. Electronic Traction System (ETS) replaces a locking rear differential on the options list this fall for the E300 Diesel. ETS applies the brakes to either drive wheel if there is slip and transfers more power to the other wheel. A more advanced traction control system that also governs the throttle remains optional on other E-Class models. All models gain standard all-season tires and new alloy wheels. Mercedes is back in the hunt after lowering prices on many of its 1994 models. The biggest seller is the E320 sedan, which starts at $43,500. The 3.2-liter 6-cylinder engine provides strong acceleration and the automatic transmission generally shifts smoothly and downshifts quickly for passing. The E-Class sedan isn't very space-efficient for its 110.2-inch wheelbase. There's generous leg room in front but only adequate leg room in the back. However, the E-Class sedan has the same high quality as Mercedes' larger S-Class cars and is much more reasonably priced.

Mercedes-Benz E-Class prices are on page 372.

MERCEDES-BENZ E320

Rating Guide	1	2	3	4	5
Performance					
Acceleration	▪▪▪▪▪▪▪▪▪▪▪▪▪▪▪▪▪▪▪▪▪▪▪▪▪				
Economy	▪▪▪▪▪▪▪▪▪▪▪				
Driveability	▪▪▪▪▪▪▪▪▪▪▪▪▪▪▪▪▪▪▪				
Ride	▪▪▪▪▪▪▪▪▪▪▪▪▪▪▪▪▪▪▪				
Steering/handling	▪▪▪▪▪▪▪▪▪▪▪▪▪▪▪▪▪▪▪				
Braking	▪▪▪▪▪▪▪▪▪▪▪▪▪▪▪▪▪▪▪▪				
Noise	▪▪▪▪▪▪▪▪▪▪▪▪▪▪				
Accommodations					
Driver seating	▪▪▪▪▪▪▪▪▪▪▪▪▪▪▪▪▪▪▪				
Instruments/controls	▪▪▪▪▪▪▪▪▪▪▪▪▪▪▪▪▪▪▪				
Visibility	▪▪▪▪▪▪▪▪▪▪▪▪▪▪▪▪▪▪▪				
Room/comfort	▪▪▪▪▪▪▪▪▪▪▪▪▪▪▪▪				
Entry/exit	▪▪▪▪▪▪▪▪▪▪▪▪▪▪▪▪▪▪▪				
Cargo room	▪▪▪▪▪▪▪▪▪▪▪▪				
Workmanship					
Exterior	▪▪▪▪▪▪▪▪▪▪▪▪▪▪▪▪▪▪▪▪				
Interior	▪▪▪▪▪▪▪▪▪▪▪▪▪▪▪▪▪▪▪▪				
Value	▪▪▪▪▪▪▪▪▪▪▪▪▪▪▪▪▪▪				

Total Points...63

Specifications

Body type	4-door notchback	Engine type	dohc I-6
Wheelbase (in.)	110.2	Engine size (l/cu. in.)	3.2/195
Overall length (in.)	187.2	Horsepower @ rpm	217 @ 5500
Overall width (in.)	68.5	Torque @ rpm	229 @ 3750
Overall height (in.)	56.3	Transmission	auto/4-sp.
Curb weight (lbs.)	3525	Drive wheels	rear
Seating capacity	5	Brakes, F/R	disc/disc (ABS)
Front head room (in.)	36.9	Tire size	195/65R15
Max. front leg room (in.)	41.7	Fuel tank capacity (gal.)	18.5
Rear head room (in.)	36.9	EPA city/highway mpg	20/26
Min. rear leg room (in.)	33.5	Test mileage (mpg)	18.8
Cargo volume (cu. ft.)	14.6		

Warranties The entire car (including body perforation rust) is covered for 4 years/50,000 miles.

Rating scale 5=Exceptional; 4=Above average; 3=Average; 2=Below average; 1=Poor

MERCEDES-BENZ S-CLASS —

Built in Germany.

Mercedes-Benz S420

PREMIUM SEDAN/COUPE

The flagship line from Mercedes-Benz has fresh styling for its sedans and lower base prices for most models. The S-Class roster starts with the S350 Turbodiesel sedan, which retains a 119.7-inch wheelbase. The S320 moves up a size this year to join the S420, S500, and S600 sedans on a 123.6-inch wheelbase. The S500 and S600 2-door coupes continue on a 115.9-inch wheelbase. Styling changes encompass the front and rear bumpers and lights, the grille, trunk lid, and lower body-side panels for what Mercedes calls a "softer, lower look." There are bigger changes to the window stickers, which show price cuts ranging from $4700 on the S350 and S320 sedans (now $65,900) up to $7900 on the S500 coupe, which is now $91,900. Powertrains are unchanged. The S320 has a 228-horsepower 3.2-liter 6-cylinder. The S350 Turbodiesel has a 148-horsepower 3.5-liter turbocharged diesel 6-cylinder. The S420 has a 275-horsepower 4.2-liter V-8 and the S500 a 315-horsepower 5.0-liter V-8. S600s have a 389-horsepower 6.0-liter V-12. All S-Class models have rear-wheel drive, dual air bags, and anti-lock brakes. Acceleration runs from tepid on the diesel S350 (Mercedes estimates 12.5 seconds to 60 mph) and S320 to terrific on the S600 (6.3 seconds according to Mercedes). All models have commendable ride and handling ability, roomy interiors that are isolated from the outside world by double-pane side windows, and solid structures. The brakes, steering, and driving position inspire confidence and make long-distance travel more enjoyable. The S-Class cars are among the world's best, but even with this year's price cuts there are excellent alternatives that offer plenty of luxury and performance for thousands less.

Mercedes-Benz S-Class prices are on page 373.

MERCEDES-BENZ S420

Rating Guide	1	2	3	4	5
Performance					
Acceleration	▓	▓	▓	▓	▓
Economy	▓				
Driveability	▓	▓	▓	▓	
Ride	▓	▓	▓	▓	▓
Steering/handling	▓	▓	▓	▓	
Braking	▓	▓	▓	▓	▓
Noise	▓	▓	▓	▓	▓
Accommodations					
Driver seating	▓	▓	▓	▓	
Instruments/controls	▓	▓	▓		
Visibility	▓	▓	▓		
Room/comfort	▓	▓	▓	▓	
Entry/exit	▓	▓	▓	▓	
Cargo room	▓	▓	▓		
Workmanship					
Exterior	▓	▓	▓	▓	▓
Interior	▓	▓	▓	▓	▓
Value	▓	▓			

Total Points...65

Specifications

Body type	4-door notchback	Engine type	dohc V-8
Wheelbase (in.)	123.6	Engine size (l/cu. in.)	4.2/256
Overall length (in.)	205.2	Horsepower @ rpm	275 @ 5700
Overall width (in.)	74.3	Torque @ rpm	295 @ 3900
Overall height (in.)	58.9	Transmission	auto/4-sp.
Curb weight (lbs.)	4760	Drive wheels	rear
Seating capacity	5	Brakes, F/R	disc/disc (ABS)
Front head room (in.)	38.0	Tire size	235/60HR16
Max. front leg room (in.)	41.3	Fuel tank capacity (gal.)	26.4
Rear head room (in.)	38.5	EPA city/highway mpg	15/20
Min. rear leg room (in.)	39.6	Test mileage (mpg)	NA
Cargo volume (cu. ft.)	15.6		

Warranties The entire car (including body perforation rust) is covered for 4 years/50,000 miles.

Rating scale 5=Exceptional; 4=Above average; 3=Average; 2=Below average; 1=Poor

MERCURY MYSTIQUE

Built in Kansas City, Mo., and Mexico.

Mercury Mystique LS

COMPACT

Mystique is Mercury's version of the Ford Motor Company "world car," which also debuted in the U.S. this year as the Ford Contour (see separate report). Both are based on the Ford Mondeo, which has been sold in Europe since 1993. The U.S. models use the same front-drive platform, engines, transmissions, and other key components as the European models. Mystique and Contour, which come only as 4-door sedans, have different styling. The 106.5-inch wheelbase exceeds the mid-size Sable's by half an inch. The overall length of 183.5 inches, however, is nearly nine inches shorter than Sable's. Mystique, which replaces the Topaz (a compact), comes in two models, the base GS and plusher LS. A 125-horsepower 2.0-liter 4-cylinder engine is standard and a 170-horsepower 2.5-liter V-6 is optional on both. A 5-speed manual transmission is standard with both engines and an electronic 4-speed automatic is optional. Dual air bags are standard. Anti-lock brakes and traction control that works at all speeds are optional. Mystique's best powertrain combination is the V-6/4-speed automatic. The V-6 has plenty of power and the new automatic transmission shifts crisply and smoothly. Though the automatic works just as well with the 4-cylinder, the base engine is noisier and has trouble mustering enough power to conquer hills. There's adequate room for four adults in the Mystique, which has a functional, modern-looking dashboard. Our main gripe: the stereo has small, poorly marked controls. Based on our first impressions, Mystique and Contour are competitive alternatives to Japanese compact sedans and the new Chrysler Cirrus and Dodge Stratus.

Mercury Mystique prices are on page 378.

MERCURY MYSTIQUE LS (Preliminary)

Rating Guide	1	2	3	4	5
Performance					
Acceleration	▐▐▐▐▐▐▐▐▐▐▐▐▐▐				
Economy	▐▐▐▐▐▐▐▐▐▐▐▐▐▐				
Driveability	▐▐▐▐▐▐▐▐▐▐▐▐▐▐▐▐				
Ride	▐▐▐▐▐▐▐▐▐▐▐▐▐▐				
Steering/handling	▐▐▐▐▐▐▐▐▐▐▐▐▐▐				
Braking	▐▐▐▐▐▐▐▐▐▐▐▐▐▐▐▐▐▐▐▐				
Noise	▐▐▐▐▐▐▐▐▐▐▐▐▐				
Accommodations					
Driver seating	▐▐▐▐▐▐▐▐▐▐▐▐▐▐▐▐▐▐▐▐				
Instruments/controls	▐▐▐▐▐▐▐▐▐▐▐▐▐▐▐▐▐				
Visibility	▐▐▐▐▐▐▐▐▐▐▐▐▐▐▐▐				
Room/comfort	▐▐▐▐▐▐▐▐▐▐▐▐▐				
Entry/exit	▐▐▐▐▐▐▐▐▐▐▐▐▐▐▐				
Cargo room	▐▐▐▐▐▐▐▐▐▐▐▐▐▐▐				
Workmanship					
Exterior	▐▐▐▐▐▐▐▐▐▐▐▐▐▐▐▐▐				
Interior	▐▐▐▐▐▐▐▐▐▐▐▐▐▐▐▐▐				
Value	▐▐▐▐▐▐▐▐▐▐▐▐▐▐▐				

Total Points...**59**

Specifications

Body type	4-door notchback	Engine type	dohc I-4
Wheelbase (in.)	106.5	Engine size (l/cu. in.)	2.0/121
Overall length (in.)	183.5	Horsepower @ rpm	125 @ 5500
Overall width (in.)	69.1	Torque @ rpm	130 @ 4000
Overall height (in.)	54.5	Transmission	auto/4-sp.
Curb weight (lbs.)	2824	Drive wheels	front
Seating capacity	5	Brakes, F/R	disc/drum (ABS)
Front head room (in.)	39.0	Tire size	205/60R15
Max. front leg room (in.)	42.4	Fuel tank capacity (gal.)	14.5
Rear head room (in.)	36.7	EPA city/highway mpg	24/32
Min. rear leg room (in.)	34.3	Test mileage (mpg)	NA
Cargo volume (cu. ft.)	14.1		

Warranties The entire car is covered for 3 years/36,000 miles. Body perforation rust is covered for 5 years/unlimited miles.

Rating scale 5=Exceptional; 4=Above average; 3=Average; 2=Below average; 1=Poor

MERCURY VILLAGER/
NISSAN QUEST

Built in Avon Lake, Ohio.

Mercury Villager LS

MINIVAN

These similar front-drive minivans continue for 1995 with no significant changes. Villager and Quest were introduced in the 1993 model year. Last year a driver-side air bag was added. Both front seats also have motorized front shoulder belts. Villager returns in three trim levels: GS, LS, and Nautica. Quest comes in two, base XE and upscale GXE. All models come with a Nissan 3.0-liter V-6 engine and 4-speed automatic transmission. The engine is rated at 151 horsepower. Anti-lock brakes are standard on all Villagers and the Quest GXE; they're optional on the XE. Quest and Villager were designed by Nissan but are built at a plant owned by Ford. In performance and driving feel, Villager and Quest rank among the most car-like minivans. These are luxury-oriented people movers that stress comfort over towing and heavy-duty work. The 3.0-liter engine can't match the muscle of the 3.8-liter V-6s in front-drive minivans from General Motors and Chrysler Corporation. Though acceleration is adequate, there's not enough power to easily merge into highway traffic with a full load of passengers and cargo. Head room and leg room are ample for the front seats, and adequate for the middle and rear seats. With all seats in their regular positions, there's only a small cargo area at the rear. It's a chore to remove the cumbersome middle seats. Once done, you can slide the rear seat forward for ample cargo room. Villager and Quest lack some of the features available on Chrysler's minivans, and they aren't as roomy as the new Ford Windstar, which is even more car-like to drive. They're still worth a close look.

Mercury Villager prices are on page 383.
Nissan Quest prices are on page 395.

MERCURY VILLAGER LS

Rating Guide	1	2	3	4	5
Performance					
Acceleration	▓▓▓▓▓▓▓▓▓				
Economy	▓▓▓▓▓▓▓				
Driveability	▓▓▓▓▓▓▓▓▓				
Ride	▓▓▓▓▓▓▓▓▓				
Steering/handling	▓▓▓▓▓▓▓▓▓				
Braking	▓▓▓▓▓▓▓▓▓▓▓▓▓▓▓				
Noise	▓▓▓▓▓▓▓▓▓				
Accommodations					
Driver seating	▓▓▓▓▓▓▓▓▓				
Instruments/controls	▓▓▓▓▓▓▓▓▓				
Visibility	▓▓▓▓▓▓▓▓▓				
Room/comfort	▓▓▓▓▓▓▓▓▓				
Entry/exit	▓▓▓▓▓▓▓▓▓				
Cargo room	▓▓▓▓▓▓▓▓▓▓▓▓▓▓▓				
Workmanship					
Exterior	▓▓▓▓▓▓▓▓▓				
Interior	▓▓▓▓▓▓▓▓▓				
Value	▓▓▓▓▓▓▓▓▓				

Total Points **59**

Specifications

Body type	4-door van	Engine type	ohc V-6
Wheelbase (in.)	112.2	Engine size (l/cu. in.)	3.0/181
Overall length (in.)	189.9	Horsepower @ rpm	151 @ 4800
Overall width (in.)	73.7	Torque @ rpm	174 @ 4400
Overall height (in.)	67.6	Transmission	auto/4-sp.
Curb weight (lbs.)	4015	Drive wheels	front
Seating capacity	7	Brakes, F/R	disc/disc (ABS)
Front head room (in.)	39.4	Tire size	205/75R15
Max. front leg room (in.)	39.9	Fuel tank capacity (gal.)	20.0
Rear head room (in.)	39.7	EPA city/highway mpg	17/23
Min. rear leg room (in.)	34.8	Test mileage (mpg)	19.7
Cargo volume (cu. ft.)	114.8		

Warranties The entire vehicle is covered for 3 years/36,000 miles. Body perforation rust is covered for 5 years/unlimited miles.

Rating scale 5=Exceptional; 4=Above average; 3=Average; 2=Below average; 1=Poor

MITSUBISHI DIAMANTE

Built in Japan and Australia.

Mitsubishi Diamante LS

PREMIUM SEDAN

Mitsubishi designates the slow-selling base Diamante sedan for fleet sales this year, while the surviving sedan and wagon get minor trim and appearance changes. Diamante returns as a 4-door sedan built in Japan and as a 5-door wagon built in Australia. Both have front-wheel drive. Last year's base ES sedan is now available only to fleet buyers, such as rental-car companies. The wagon returns in a base trim level and the sedan is back only in upscale LS guise. The wagon uses a 175-horsepower 3.0-liter V-6 engine. The sedan has a 202-horsepower dual-camshaft version of the V-6. A 4-speed automatic is the only transmission. Dual air bags are standard on both models. Four-wheel disc brakes also are standard, with anti-lock control standard on the sedan and optional on the wagon. Traction control is optional on the sedan. Diamante competes in the "near-luxury" class, where there are several good cars in the $25,000-35,000 range. We timed the LS sedan at a respectable 9.2 seconds 0-60 mph and the wagon at a less lively 10.5. Noise levels are generally low, though the sedan's exhaust is loud and coarse in hard acceleration. The suspension provides a supple ride and good cornering grip with only modest body roll. Diamante has decent space for four adults. The dashboard is nicely done except for the stereo, which sits too low for easy operation on the move, making the standard duplicate audio controls on the steering wheel all the more useful. Interested in a Diamante? Look at rivals such as the BMW 3-Series, Lexus ES 300, and Mazda Millenia, and then price them against the Diamante, which is being heavily discounted.

Mitsubishi Diamante prices are on page 385.

MITSUBISHI DIAMANTE LS

Rating Guide	1	2	3	4	5
Performance					
Acceleration	||||||||||||||||||||||||||||||			
Economy	|||||||||||||||||				
Driveability	||||||||||||||||||||||||||||||			
Ride	|||||||||||||||||||||||				
Steering/handling	||||||||||||||||||||||||||||||			
Braking	||||||||||||||||||||||||||||||||||||||||		
Noise	|||||||||||||||||||||||				
Accommodations					
Driver seating	||||||||||||||||||||||||||||||			
Instruments/controls	||||||||||||||||||||||||||||||			
Visibility	||||||||||||||||||||||||||||||			
Room/comfort	||||||||||||||||||||||||||||||			
Entry/exit	||||||||||||||||||||||||||||||			
Cargo room	||||||||||||||||||||||||||||||			
Workmanship					
Exterior	||||||||||||||||||||||||||||||			
Interior	||||||||||||||||||||||||||||||			
Value	|||||||||||||||||||||||				

Total Points...59

Specifications

Body type ....4-door notchback	Engine type.....................dohc V-6
Wheelbase (in.) 107.1	Engine size (l/cu. in.).........3.0/182
Overall length (in.)...............190.2	Horsepower @ rpm ...202 @ 6000
Overall width (in.) 69.9	Torque @ rpm ....201 @ 3500
Overall height (in.) 52.6	Transmission.................auto/4-sp.
Curb weight (lbs.) 3605	Drive wheels ....front
Seating capacity.........................5	Brakes, F/R..........disc/disc (ABS)
Front head room (in.) 38.6	Tire size....................205/65VR15
Max. front leg room (in.) 43.9	Fuel tank capacity (gal.) 19.0
Rear head room (in.) 36.9	EPA city/highway mpg 18/25
Min. rear leg room (in.)...........34.2	Test mileage (mpg) 19.0
Cargo volume (cu. ft.)..............13.6	

Warranties The entire car is covered for 3 years/36,000 miles. Major powertrain components are covered for 5 years/60,000 miles. Body perforation rust is covered for 7 years/100,000 miles.

Rating scale 5=Exceptional; 4=Above average; 3=Average; 2=Below average; 1=Poor

MITSUBISHI ECLIPSE/ EAGLE TALON

Built in Normal, Ill.

Mitsubishi Eclipse GSX

SPORTS COUPE

The Eclipse and Talon sports coupes are redesigned for 1995 and come with standard dual air bags, more rounded styling, a larger interior, and a new base engine. Like the 1990-94 models, both are built in Illinois by Diamond-Star Motors, a Mitsubishi plant where the Galant and Dodge Avenger and Chrysler Sebring are produced. Eclipse comes in four models. The base RS, the GS, and the GS-T have front-wheel drive; the top-line GSX has permanent all-wheel drive. The Talon lineup has base ESi and mid-level TSi models with front-wheel drive and a top-line TSi AWD version. All come with a standard 5-speed manual transmission or an optional 4-speed automatic. The Eclipse RS and GS and Talon ESi use a new Chrysler 2.0-liter 4-cylinder engine with 140 horsepower. Eclipse GS-T and GSX models and the Talon TSi and TSi AWD use a turbocharged Mitsubishi 2.0-liter 4-cylinder with 210 horsepower. Anti-lock brakes are optional across the board. The Chrysler-built base engine is no powerhouse below 3500 rpm, so pickup with the automatic transmission is marginal for freeway merging and passing sprints. Progress is livelier with the 5-speed manual. We timed a GS with the manual at 9.2 seconds to 60 mph. Turbo models are much faster (6.9 seconds to 60 mph in our test). All models have nimble handling, but the ride turns choppy on freeways and rough secondary roads, especially on the turbocharged models, and there is lots of road noise. The front seats have adequate room, but the back seat is tiny. Though the 1995 versions are better in most areas, except for the AWD models there's nothing here you can't get in other sports coupes.

Mitsubishi Eclipse prices are on page 386.
Eagle Talon prices are on page 307.

MITSUBISHI ECLIPSE GSX

Rating Guide	1	2	3	4	5
Performance					
Acceleration	‖‖‖‖‖‖‖‖‖‖‖‖‖‖‖‖‖‖‖‖‖‖‖‖
Economy	‖‖‖‖‖‖‖‖‖‖‖‖‖
Driveability	‖‖‖‖‖‖‖‖‖‖‖‖‖‖‖‖‖
Ride	‖‖‖‖‖‖‖‖‖‖‖‖‖‖‖‖
Steering/handling	‖‖‖‖‖‖‖‖‖‖‖‖‖‖‖‖‖‖‖‖‖‖‖‖
Braking	‖‖‖‖‖‖‖‖‖‖‖‖‖‖‖‖‖‖‖‖‖‖‖‖
Noise	‖‖‖‖‖‖‖‖‖‖‖‖‖
Accommodations					
Driver seating	‖‖‖‖‖‖‖‖‖‖‖‖‖‖‖‖‖
Instruments/controls	‖‖‖‖‖‖‖‖‖‖‖‖‖‖‖‖‖
Visibility	‖‖‖‖‖‖‖‖‖‖‖‖‖
Room/comfort	‖‖‖‖‖‖‖‖‖‖‖‖‖
Entry/exit	‖‖‖‖‖‖‖‖‖‖‖‖‖
Cargo room	‖‖‖‖‖‖‖‖‖‖‖‖‖
Workmanship					
Exterior	‖‖‖‖‖‖‖‖‖‖‖‖‖‖‖‖‖
Interior	‖‖‖‖‖‖‖‖‖‖‖‖‖‖
Value	‖‖‖‖‖‖‖‖‖‖‖‖‖‖

Total Points...50

Specifications

Body type ....3-door hatchback
Wheelbase (in.) 98.8
Overall length (in.)................172.2
Overall width (in.) 68.3
Overall height (in.)..................51.0
Curb weight (lbs.) 2723
Seating capacity..........................4
Front head room (in.) 37.9
Max. front leg room (in.) 43.3
Rear head room (in.) 34.1
Min. rear leg room (in.) 28.4
Cargo volume (cu. ft.).............16.6

Engine type............Turbo dohc I-4
Engine size (l/cu. in.)........2.0/122
Horsepower @ rpm ...210 @ 6000
Torque @ rpm ....214 @ 3000
Transmission ....manual/5-sp.
Drive wheels ....all
Brakes, F/R...........disc/disc (ABS)
Tire size....................215/55VR16
Fuel tank capacity (gal.).........15.9
EPA city/highway mpg 20/27
Test mileage (mpg) 19.7

Warranties The entire car is covered for 3 years/36,000 miles. Major powertrain components are covered for 5 years/60,000 miles. Body perforation rust is covered for 7 years/100,000 miles.

Rating scale 5=Exceptional; 4=Above average; 3=Average; 2=Below average; 1=Poor

MITSUBISHI GALANT ———

Built in Normal, Ill.

Mitsubishi Galant ES

COMPACT

Mitsubishi's front-drive compact sedan gains a V-6 model next spring as its big change for 1995. The current Galant was introduced as a 1994 model and comes with standard dual air bags. While previous Galants were imported from Japan, the current model is built only at Diamond-Star Motors, Mitsubishi's plant in Illinois. Four price levels are available: base S, ES, luxury-oriented LS, and the new LS V-6. All but the LS V-6 have a 141-horsepower 2.4-liter 4-cylinder engine. The LS V-6 uses a 155-horsepower 2.5-liter V-6. A 5-speed manual transmission is standard on the Galant S. A 4-speed automatic is optional on the S and standard on all other models. The LS V-6 has 4-wheel disc brakes, while other Galants use rear drum brakes. Anti-lock brakes are optional on all models except the base S. Among other changes for 1995, all Galants get a new hood that eliminates the bulge of the previous design. The Galant is roomy, comfortable, competent, and competitively priced against other 4-cylinder compact sedans. We timed a 4-cylinder/automatic at 9.4 seconds to 60 mph, a little quicker than a 4-cylinder Honda Accord. Mitsubishi's automatic transmission shifts smoothly and downshifts promptly for passing. We haven't driven the new V-6 yet, so we can't comment on its performance. The interior has ample space for four adults, with a rear seat that has generous head and leg room. The roomy trunk has a wide, flat floor and a low liftover for easier loading. The dashboard has an attractive 4-dial gauge cluster and an accessible control layout. Mitsubishi should be subsidizing lease programs and giving dealers incentives to discount their prices on Galant.

Mitsubishi Galant prices are on page 387.

MITSUBISHI GALANT ES

Rating Guide	1	2	3	4	5
Performance					
Acceleration	▓▓▓▓▓▓▓▓▓▓				
Economy	▓▓▓▓▓▓				
Driveability	▓▓▓▓▓▓▓▓				
Ride	▓▓▓▓▓▓▓▓				
Steering/handling	▓▓▓▓▓▓▓▓				
Braking	▓▓▓▓▓▓▓▓▓▓▓▓				
Noise	▓▓▓▓▓▓				
Accommodations					
Driver seating	▓▓▓▓▓▓▓▓				
Instruments/controls	▓▓▓▓▓▓▓▓				
Visibility	▓▓▓▓▓▓				
Room/comfort	▓▓▓▓▓▓				
Entry/exit	▓▓▓▓▓▓▓▓				
Cargo room	▓▓▓▓▓▓▓▓				
Workmanship					
Exterior	▓▓▓▓▓▓▓▓				
Interior	▓▓▓▓▓▓▓▓				
Value	▓▓▓▓▓▓				

Total Points..**59**

Specifications

Body type	4-door notchback	Engine type	ohc I-4
Wheelbase (in.)	103.7	Engine size (l/cu. in.)	2.4/144
Overall length (in.)	187.0	Horsepower @ rpm	141 @ 5500
Overall width (in.)	68.1	Torque @ rpm	148 @ 3000
Overall height (in.)	53.1	Transmission	auto/4-sp.
Curb weight (lbs.)	2755	Drive wheels	front
Seating capacity	5	Brakes, F/R	disc/disc (ABS)
Front head room (in.)	39.4	Tire size	185/70R14
Max. front leg room (in.)	43.3	Fuel tank capacity (gal.)	16.9
Rear head room (in.)	37.5	EPA city/highway mpg	22/28
Min. rear leg room (in.)	35.0	Test mileage (mpg)	19.5
Cargo volume (cu. ft.)	12.5		

Warranties The entire car is covered for 3 years/36,000 miles. Major powertrain components are covered for 5 years/60,000 miles. Body perforation rust is covered for 7 years/100,000 miles.

Rating scale 5=Exceptional; 4=Above average; 3=Average; 2=Below average; 1=Poor

MITSUBISHI MIRAGE/ EAGLE SUMMIT

Built in Japan.

Mitsubishi Mirage LS

SUBCOMPACT

Mitsubishi relegates 4-door Mirage models to rental-car duty and adds a passenger-side air bag to the surviving coupe, which comes in base S and upscale LS trim for 1995. The similar Summit returns in both body styles, also with the passenger-side air bag. A driver-side air bag was added for 1994. Anti-lock brakes are optional on the Summit ESi 4-door but aren't available on Mirage. Engine choices are unchanged. The Mirage S and Summit coupe have a 92-horsepower 1.5-liter 4-cylinder engine. The Mirage LS and the 4-door Summit have a 113-horsepower 1.8-liter 4-cylinder. Mitsubishi has dropped the Expo wagon this year, but this "mini-minivan" continues to be available as the Eagle Summit Wagon with either front-wheel drive or permanent all-wheel drive. Standard dual air bags are a plus, but anti-lock brakes are available only on the most-expensive Summit model. Acceleration is lackluster with the 1.5-liter engine and more than adequate with the 1.8-liter and 5-speed manual. The automatic transmission saps a lot of verve from the 1.8-liter engine. However, fuel economy is good with all powertrain combinations. Noise levels are high in all models, with engine and road noise the main culprits. Seating arrangements clearly favor those in front; the rear seat is too crowded for adults to be comfortable. Mirage and Summit prices climb quickly as popular options are added, but stiff competition means you won't have to pay full retail. Dodge and Plymouth have dropped their version of this car, which was called Colt, and replaced it with the Neon.

Mitsubishi Mirage prices are on page 388.
Eagle Summit prices are on page 306.

170   CONSUMER GUIDE®

MITSUBISHI MIRAGE LS

Rating Guide	1	2	3	4	5
Performance					
Acceleration	▓▓▓▓▓▓▓▓▓▓▓▓				
Economy	▓▓▓▓▓▓▓▓▓▓▓▓▓▓▓▓				
Driveability	▓▓▓▓▓▓▓▓▓▓▓▓				
Ride	▓▓▓▓▓▓▓▓▓▓▓▓				
Steering/handling	▓▓▓▓▓▓▓▓▓▓▓▓				
Braking	▓▓▓▓▓▓▓▓▓▓▓▓				
Noise	▓▓▓▓▓▓▓▓▓▓▓▓				
Accommodations					
Driver seating	▓▓▓▓▓▓▓▓▓▓▓▓				
Instruments/controls	▓▓▓▓▓▓▓▓▓▓▓▓				
Visibility	▓▓▓▓▓▓▓▓▓▓▓▓				
Room/comfort	▓▓▓▓▓▓▓▓▓▓▓▓				
Entry/exit	▓▓▓▓▓▓▓▓▓▓▓▓				
Cargo room	▓▓▓▓▓▓▓▓▓▓▓▓				
Workmanship					
Exterior	▓▓▓▓▓▓▓▓▓▓▓▓▓▓				
Interior	▓▓▓▓▓▓▓▓▓▓▓▓▓▓				
Value	▓▓▓▓▓▓▓▓▓▓▓▓				

Total Points...54

Specifications

Body type	2-door notchback	Engine type	ohc I-4
Wheelbase (in.)	96.1	Engine size (l/cu. in.)	1.8/112
Overall length (in.)	171.1	Horsepower @ rpm	113 @ 6000
Overall width (in.)	66.5	Torque @ rpm	116 @ 4500
Overall height (in.)	51.6	Transmission	auto/4-sp.
Curb weight (lbs.)	2085	Drive wheels	front
Seating capacity	5	Brakes, F/R	disc/drum
Front head room (in.)	38.6	Tire size	185/65R14
Max. front leg room (in.)	42.9	Fuel tank capacity (gal.)	13.2
Rear head room (in.)	36.4	EPA city/highway mpg	26/33
Min. rear leg room (in.)	31.1	Test mileage (mpg)	28.4
Cargo volume (cu. ft.)	10.7		

Warranties The entire car is covered for 3 years/36,000 miles. Major powertrain components are covered for 5 years/60,000 miles. Body perforation rust is covered for 7 years/100,000 miles.

Rating scale 5=Exceptional; 4=Above average; 3=Average; 2=Below average; 1=Poor

MITSUBISHI MONTERO ———

Built in Japan.

Mitsubishi Montero LS

SPORT-UTILITY VEHICLE

Amore-powerful 3.0-liter V-6 engine for the base Montero heads the news for 1995. Montero has 5-door styling with a side-hinged rear door and standard 4-wheel drive that can be used on dry pavement. Base LS and premium SR models are offered, both with a standard driver-side air bag and 7-passenger seating. The LS model's new 3.0-liter V-6 engine has four valves per cylinder instead of two and 177 horsepower instead of 151. The SR returns with a 3.5-liter V-6 with 215 horsepower. A 5-speed manual transmission is standard on the LS and a 4-speed automatic is standard on the SR, optional on the LS. On both models, towing capacity is 5000 pounds, 1000 pounds more than last year. Anti-lock brakes are standard on the SR and optional on the LS. New standard equipment includes alloy wheels for the LS model and a power sunroof for the SR. Montero is a roomy, versatile 4x4, but against domestic rivals like the Ford Explorer, Jeep Grand Cherokee, and Chevrolet Blazer/GMC Jimmy, it's no bargain. Like other Japanese sport-utility models, it trails the domestic leaders in dollar value. However, Mitsubishi's Active-Trac 4WD equals Jeep's Selec-Trac system and Ford's new Control Trac system for shift-on-the-fly convenience and being able to operate as a permanently engaged system. This year's stronger engine gives the LS a much-needed improvement in acceleration. The SR is still quicker; we timed one at a brisk 10.2 seconds to 60 mph, which is faster than nearly all rivals. Passenger room and cargo space are abundant, but the Montero sits high off the ground, making it hard to get in or out. Despite its good points, Montero isn't at the top of our sport-utility list.

Mitsubishi Montero prices are on page 389.

MITSUBISHI MONTERO LS

Rating Guide	1	2	3	4	5
Performance					
Acceleration	▮▮▮▮▮▮▮▮				
Economy	▮▮▮▮▮				
Driveability	▮▮▮▮▮▮▮▮				
Ride	▮▮▮▮▮▮				
Steering/handling	▮▮▮▮▮▮				
Braking	▮▮▮▮▮▮▮▮▮▮				
Noise	▮▮▮▮▮▮▮▮				
Accommodations					
Driver seating	▮▮▮▮▮▮▮▮				
Instruments/controls	▮▮▮▮▮▮				
Visibility	▮▮▮▮▮▮				
Room/comfort	▮▮▮▮▮▮▮▮▮▮				
Entry/exit	▮▮▮▮▮▮				
Cargo room	▮▮▮▮▮▮▮▮▮▮				
Workmanship					
Exterior	▮▮▮▮▮▮▮▮				
Interior	▮▮▮▮▮▮▮▮				
Value	▮▮▮▮▮▮				

Total Points...57

Specifications

Body type	5-door wagon	Engine type	ohc V-6
Wheelbase (in.)	107.3	Engine size (l/cu. in.)	3.0/181
Overall length (in.)	185.2	Horsepower @ rpm	177 @ 5500
Overall width (in.)	66.7	Torque @ rpm	188 @ 4500
Overall height (in.)	73.4	Transmission	auto/4-sp.
Curb weight (lbs.)	4285	Drive wheels	rear/all
Seating capacity	7	Brakes, F/R	disc/disc (ABS)
Front head room (in.)	40.9	Tire size	235/75R15
Max. front leg room (in.)	40.3	Fuel tank capacity (gal.)	24.3
Rear head room (in.)	40.0	EPA city/highway mpg	15/18
Min. rear leg room (in.)	37.6	Test mileage (mpg)	16.0
Cargo volume (cu. ft.)	72.7		

Warranties The entire vehicle is covered for 3 years/36,000 miles. Major powertrain components are covered for 5 years/60,000 miles. Body perforation rust is covered for 7 years/100,000 miles.

MITSUBISHI 3000GT/ ——————
DODGE STEALTH

Built in Japan.

Mitsubishi 3000GT VR-4

SPORTS AND GT

A hardtop-convertible model is scheduled to join Mitsubishi's line of sports cars in January. Mitsubishi builds the 3000GT and Stealth in Japan, but there won't be a Stealth convertible. Called the 3000GT Spyder, the new convertible is available in SL and VR-4 trim. A single button activates an electro-hydraulic system that in 35 seconds opens the trunklid and lowers or raises the articulated top, which is made of plastic composites. Spyder prices weren't announced, but the VR-4 version is expected to be more than $60,000. All 3000GT and Stealth models have a 3.0-liter V-6 engine. The base Stealth comes with a 164-horsepower version with a single camshaft. The Stealth R/T and base 3000GT use a dual-camshaft version with 222 horsepower. All have front-wheel drive and a standard 5-speed manual transmission. A 4-speed automatic is optional. The 3000GT VR-4 and Stealth R/T Turbo models have a twin turbocharged version of the 3.0-liter with 320 horsepower, plus all-wheel drive (AWD) and 4-wheel steering. The AWD models come only with a 6-speed manual. Dual air bags are standard on all models. Anti-lock brakes are standard on the 3000GT SL and VR-4 and the Stealth R/T Turbo and optional on the base Stealth and R/T. Despite the outstanding performance and AWD traction of the VR-4 and R/T Turbo, we're turned off by their stiff ride and high prices. The front-drive models have a more livable demeanor that makes them better choices as everyday transportation. Slow sales mean dealers should be discounting, whether you're shopping the Mitsubishi or Dodge versions.

Mitsubishi 3000GT prices are on page 390.
Dodge Stealth prices are on page 304.

MITSUBISHI 3000GT VR-4

Rating Guide	1	2	3	4	5
Performance					
Acceleration	▓▓▓▓▓▓▓▓▓▓▓▓▓▓▓▓▓▓▓▓▓▓▓▓▓▓				
Economy	▓▓▓▓▓▓				
Driveability	▓▓▓▓▓▓▓▓▓▓▓▓▓▓▓▓▓▓▓▓				
Ride	▓▓▓▓▓▓▓▓▓▓▓▓▓				
Steering/handling	▓▓▓▓▓▓▓▓▓▓▓▓▓▓▓▓▓▓▓▓▓▓▓▓▓▓				
Braking	▓▓▓▓▓▓▓▓▓▓▓▓▓▓▓▓▓▓▓▓▓▓				
Noise	▓▓▓▓▓▓▓▓▓▓▓▓▓				
Accommodations					
Driver seating	▓▓▓▓▓▓▓▓▓▓▓▓▓▓▓▓▓▓▓▓▓▓▓				
Instruments/controls	▓▓▓▓▓▓▓▓▓▓▓▓▓▓▓▓▓▓▓▓				
Visibility	▓▓▓▓▓▓▓▓▓▓▓▓▓				
Room/comfort	▓▓▓▓▓▓▓▓▓▓▓▓▓				
Entry/exit	▓▓▓▓▓▓▓▓▓▓▓▓▓				
Cargo room	▓▓▓▓▓▓▓▓▓▓▓▓▓				
Workmanship					
Exterior	▓▓▓▓▓▓▓▓▓▓▓▓▓▓▓▓▓▓▓▓▓▓				
Interior	▓▓▓▓▓▓▓▓▓▓▓▓▓▓▓▓▓▓▓▓▓▓				
Value	▓▓▓▓▓▓▓▓▓▓▓▓▓▓▓▓				

Total Points...**49**

Specifications

Body type ....3-door hatchback	Engine type ....Turbo dohc V-6
Wheelbase (in.) 97.2	Engine size (l/cu. in.).........3.0/181
Overall length (in.)................179.7	Horsepower @ rpm ...320 @ 6000
Overall width (in.) 72.4	Torque @ rpm ....315 @ 2500
Overall height (in.)..................49.1	Transmission ....manual/6-sp.
Curb weight (lbs.) 3803	Drive wheels ....all
Seating capacity 4	Brakes, F/R...........disc/disc (ABS)
Front head room (in.) 37.1	Tire size...................245/405ZR18
Max. front leg room (in.) 44.2	Fuel tank capacity (gal.) 19.8
Rear head room (in.) 34.1	EPA city/highway mpg 18/24
Min. rear leg room (in.)...........28.5	Test mileage (mpg) 14.8
Cargo volume (cu. ft.)..............11.1	

Warranties The entire car is covered for 3 years/36,000 miles. Major powertrain components are covered for 5 years/60,000 miles. Body perforation rust is covered for 7 years/100,000 miles.

Rating scale 5=Exceptional; 4=Above average; 3=Average; 2=Below average; 1=Poor

NISSAN ALTIMA —

Built in Smyrna, Tenn.

Nissan Altima GXE

COMPACT

The front-drive Altima sees only minor changes for 1995, all of them cosmetic. The grille insert switches from a honeycomb pattern to slim horizontal bars; taillamps are subtly altered; and wheels and wheel covers are redesigned. Last year's lineup returns unchanged: There are base XE, volume-selling GXE, sporty SE, and luxury-oriented GLE models. All have 4-door notchback styling, standard dual air bags, and a 2.4-liter 4-cylinder engine with dual overhead camshafts and 150 horsepower. The GLE comes with a 4-speed automatic transmission. On other models, a 5-speed manual is standard and the automatic is optional. Anti-lock brakes are optional across the board. All Altimas are built at Nissan's Smyrna, Tennessee, plant, where the Sentra, 200SX, and the Nissan pickup also are built. Though it's not the roomiest or most refined compact sedan, Altima has above-average acceleration and handling ability, and it comes well-equipped at competitive prices. The engine is loud and rather rough at higher speeds and the automatic transmission tends to shift sluggishly. Altima's firm steering and suspension make it feel more like a sports sedan than a family sedan. Though you feel most bumps, there is little harshness because the suspension and rigid body absorb most of the impact. The interior has ample room in front and adequate space for two adults in the rear seat. The trunk has a wide, flat floor that gives Altima adequate cargo room. However, the rear seatback doesn't fold down. Overall, we rate Nissan's compact sedan highly and encourage you to give it a close look.

Nissan Altima prices are on page 391.

NISSAN ALTIMA GXE

Rating Guide	1	2	3	4	5
Performance					
Acceleration	▓	▓	▓	▓	
Economy	▓	▓	▓		
Driveability	▓	▓	▓		
Ride	▓	▓	▓		
Steering/handling	▓	▓	▓	▓	
Braking	▓	▓	▓	▓	▓
Noise	▓	▓	▓		
Accommodations					
Driver seating	▓	▓	▓	▓	
Instruments/controls	▓	▓	▓	▓	
Visibility	▓	▓	▓		
Room/comfort	▓	▓	▓	▓	
Entry/exit	▓	▓	▓	▓	
Cargo room	▓	▓	▓	▓	
Workmanship					
Exterior	▓	▓	▓	▓	▓
Interior	▓	▓	▓	▓	▓
Value	▓	▓	▓	▓	
Total Points					**59**

Specifications

Body type	4-door notchback	Engine type	dohc I-4
Wheelbase (in.)	103.1	Engine size (l/cu. in.)	2.4/146
Overall length (in.)	180.5	Horsepower @ rpm	150 @ 5600
Overall width (in.)	67.1	Torque @ rpm	154 @ 4400
Overall height (in.)	55.9	Transmission	auto/4-sp.
Curb weight (lbs.)	2829	Drive wheels	front
Seating capacity	5	Brakes, F/R	disc/disc (ABS)
Front head room (in.)	39.3	Tire size	205/60R15
Max. front leg room (in.)	42.6	Fuel tank capacity (gal.)	15.9
Rear head room (in.)	37.6	EPA city/highway mpg	21/29
Min. rear leg room (in.)	34.7	Test mileage (mpg)	20.2
Cargo volume (cu. ft.)	14.0		

Warranties The entire car is covered for 3 years/36,000 miles. Major powertrain components are covered for 5 years/ 60,000 miles. Body perforation rust is covered for 5 years/unlimited miles.

Rating scale 5=Exceptional; 4=Above average; 3=Average; 2=Below average; 1=Poor

NISSAN MAXIMA —

Built in Japan.

Nissan Maxima GXE

PREMIUM SEDAN

Nissan introduced a redesigned Maxima in the spring as an early 1995 model. Front-wheel drive, V-6 power, and 4-door sedan styling continue from the 1989-94 series. However, the new styling is more rounded and there's two more inches of wheelbase (distance between front and rear wheels). Models include a new luxury GLE model, a base GXE, and a sporty SE. All share a new aluminum 3.0-liter V-6 with dual overhead camshafts and 190 horsepower. The GXE and SE come with a standard 5-speed manual transmission. An electronic 4-speed automatic is optional on those models and standard on the GLE. Anti-lock brakes are optional on all Maximas except the 5-speed GXE. Maxima's basic design will be used for the I30, a new "near-luxury" sedan scheduled to be added next spring to the lineup at Infiniti, Nissan's luxury division. We timed a Maxima GXE with the automatic transmission at 7.9 seconds to 60 mph, an impressive showing. Passing power also is impressive. The automatic is slow to downshift for passing at times and occasionally shifts harshly. Maxima has a comfortable, stable ride, precise steering, and crisp handling. With a little more head room and an additional inch of rear leg room, the new Maxima is more accommodating for tall passengers. However, some of the rear head room seems to be gained by lowering the rear cushion, so tall people "fall" into the rear seat and ride with their knees up. Though we classify the Maxima as a premium sedan, its closest rival might actually be the top-line XLE V-6 version of the Toyota Camry, which we classify as a compact. Maxima and Camry are close in size, performance, and features.

Nissan Maxima prices are on page 392.

NISSAN MAXIMA GXE

Rating Guide	1	2	3	4	5
Performance					
Acceleration	▓▓▓▓▓▓▓▓▓				
Economy	▓▓▓▓▓▓				
Driveability	▓▓▓▓▓▓▓▓▓				
Ride	▓▓▓▓▓▓▓▓▓				
Steering/handling	▓▓▓▓▓▓▓▓▓				
Braking	▓▓▓▓▓▓▓▓▓▓▓▓				
Noise	▓▓▓▓▓▓▓▓▓				
Accommodations					
Driver seating	▓▓▓▓▓▓▓▓▓				
Instruments/controls	▓▓▓▓▓▓▓▓▓				
Visibility	▓▓▓▓▓▓▓▓▓				
Room/comfort	▓▓▓▓▓▓▓▓▓				
Entry/exit	▓▓▓▓▓▓▓▓▓				
Cargo room	▓▓▓▓▓▓▓▓▓				
Workmanship					
Exterior	▓▓▓▓▓▓▓▓▓				
Interior	▓▓▓▓▓▓▓▓▓				
Value	▓▓▓▓▓▓▓▓▓				

Total Points..**63**

Specifications

Body type ....4-door notchback	Engine type ....dohc V-6
Wheelbase (in.) 106.3	Engine size (l/cu. in.).........3.0/181
Overall length (in.)................187.7	Horsepower @ rpm ...190 @ 5600
Overall width (in.) 69.7	Torque @ rpm ....205 @ 4000
Overall height (in.)..................55.7	Transmission.................auto/4-sp.
Curb weight (lbs.) 3001	Drive wheels ....front
Seating capacity...........................5	Brakes, F/R..........disc/disc (ABS)
Front head room (in.) 40.1	Tire size 205/65R15
Max. front leg room (in.) 43.9	Fuel tank capacity (gal.) 18.5
Rear head room (in.)...............37.4	EPA city/highway mpg 22/27
Min. rear leg room (in.)...........34.3	Test mileage (mpg) 18.2
Cargo volume (cu. ft.).............14.5	

Warranties The entire car is covered for 3 years/36,000 miles. Major powertrain components are covered for 5 years/60,000 miles. Body perforation rust is covered for 5 years/unlimited miles.

Rating scale 5=Exceptional; 4=Above average; 3=Average; 2=Below average; 1=Poor

NISSAN PATHFINDER

Built in Japan.

Nissan Pathfinder LE

SPORT-UTILITY VEHICLE

The main news for Pathfinder this year is the addition of a 2-wheel-drive version of the luxury LE model, which was added last year only with 4-wheel drive. Pathfinder comes as a 5-door wagon with a 153-horsepower 3.0-liter V-6. The base XE model continues in 2WD and 4WD versions, both with a standard 5-speed manual transmission and an optional 4-speed automatic. The mid-level SE model also come with the manual or automatic but only with 4WD. Both LE models come only with the automatic transmission. Pathfinder's 4-wheel drive system is the part-time type that is not for use on dry pavement. Its allows shifting into 4WD High at speeds up to 25 mph, but the vehicle must be stopped and reversed to disengage 4WD. Anti-lock rear brakes are standard across the line. Pathfinder is higher-priced and has a more truck-like demeanor than rivals like the Ford Explorer, Jeep Grand Cherokee, and Chevy Blazer/GMC Jimmy, the class leaders. Pathfinder also lacks an air bag and 4-wheel anti-lock brakes. Even so, Pathfinder sales have continue to grow with the booming sport-utility market. Though off-the-line acceleration is decent, Pathfinder is shy of low-end torque for strong pull up steep hills, especially with heavy loads. Fuel economy was dismal in our last test: 14.7 mpg with automatic. The 4WD is another minus. Without full shift-on-the-fly, it's far less convenient than most competitors'. To its credit, Pathfinder has ample cargo room and it's as rugged and versatile as a Swiss Army knife. However, Pathfinder's domestic rivals are just as rugged and versatile and more car-like to boot.

Nissan Pathfinder prices are on page 394.

NISSAN PATHFINDER LE

Rating Guide	1	2	3	4	5
Performance					
Acceleration					
Economy					
Driveability					
Ride					
Steering/handling					
Braking					
Noise					
Accommodations					
Driver seating					
Instruments/controls					
Visibility					
Room/comfort					
Entry/exit					
Cargo room					
Workmanship					
Exterior					
Interior					
Value					

Total Points..53

Specifications

Body type	5-door wagon	Engine type	ohc V-6
Wheelbase (in.)	104.3	Engine size (l/cu. in.)	3.0/181
Overall length (in.)	171.9	Horsepower @ rpm	153 @ 4800
Overall width (in.)	66.5	Torque @ rpm	180 @ 4000
Overall height (in.)	65.7	Transmission	auto/4-sp.
Curb weight (lbs.)	3890	Drive wheels	rear/all
Seating capacity	5	Brakes, F/R	disc/disc (ABS)
Front head room (in.)	39.3	Tire size	31×10.5
Max. front leg room (in.)	42.6	Fuel tank capacity (gal.)	20.4
Rear head room (in.)	36.8	EPA city/highway mpg	15/18
Min. rear leg room (in.)	33.1	Test mileage (mpg)	14.7
Cargo volume (cu. ft.)	80.2		

Warranties The entire vehicle is covered for 3 years/36,000 miles. Major powertrain components are covered for 5 years/60,000 miles. Body perforation rust is covered for 5 years/unlimited miles.

Rating scale 5=Exceptional; 4=Above average; 3=Average; 2=Below average; 1=Poor

NISSAN SENTRA/200SX

Built in Smyrna, Tenn.

Nissan Sentra XE

SUBCOMPACT/SPORTS COUPE

Nissan plans to unwrap a redesigned Sentra subcompact in January that comes only in 4-door notchback sedan styling. The new Sentra retains front-wheel drive and comes in base, XE, GXE, and new luxury GLE price levels. All models have dual air bags and side door guard beams that meet 1997 federal side-impact standards. The 2-door Sentra is effectively being replaced by the new 200SX sports coupe that goes on sale at about the same time. The 200SX shares the Sentra's 99.8-inch wheelbase, front styling, and dashboard but has a different semi-fastback 2-door body design. Besides more rounded styling, the 1995 Sentra has more interior space than the previous design. Overall length is virtually the same as last year, but the wheelbase (distance between the front and rear wheels) is 4.1 inches longer. All Sentras use a dual-camshaft 1.6-liter 4-cylinder engine with 115 horsepower. All models have a standard 5-speed manual transmission and an optional 4-speed automatic. Anti-lock brakes are optional on the GXE and GLE. The 200SX SE shares Sentra's 115-horsepower 1.6-liter 4-cylinder engine, while the 200SX SE-R comes with a 140-horsepower 2.0-liter 4-cylinder. Our first impression of the new Sentra is that it's near the front of the subcompact class for quietness and solidity. Even over the roughest roads, Sentra feels far more substantial than most small cars, with a supple, well-controlled ride. The 1.6-liter engine needs lots of throttle for good pickup, and with the automatic transmission it still doesn't have enough muscle for merging onto freeways. Prices weren't announced in time for this issue, but the new Sentra appears to be a solid, refined subcompact.

Nissan Sentra standard equipment is on page 396.

NISSAN SENTRA XE (Preliminary)

Rating Guide	1	2	3	4	5
Performance					
Acceleration	▓▓▓▓▓▓				
Economy	▓▓▓▓▓▓				
Driveability	▓▓▓▓▓▓				
Ride	▓▓▓▓▓▓				
Steering/handling	▓▓▓▓▓▓				
Braking	▓▓▓▓▓▓				
Noise	▓▓▓▓▓▓				
Accommodations					
Driver seating	▓▓▓▓▓▓				
Instruments/controls	▓▓▓▓▓▓				
Visibility	▓▓▓▓▓▓▓▓▓▓				
Room/comfort	▓▓▓▓▓▓				
Entry/exit	▓▓▓▓▓▓▓▓				
Cargo room	▓▓▓▓▓▓				
Workmanship					
Exterior	▓▓▓▓▓▓▓▓				
Interior	▓▓▓▓▓▓				
Value	▓▓▓▓▓▓				

Total Points...58

Specifications

Body type	4-door notchback	Engine type	dohc I-4
Wheelbase (in.)	99.8	Engine size (l/cu. in.)	1.6/97
Overall length (in.)	170.1	Horsepower @ rpm	115 @ 6000
Overall width (in.)	66.6	Torque @ rpm	108 @ 4000
Overall height (in.)	54.5	Transmission	auto/4-sp.
Curb weight (lbs.)	2410	Drive wheels	front
Seating capacity	5	Brakes, F/R	disc/drum
Front head room (in.)	39.1	Tire size	175/70R13
Max. front leg room (in.)	42.3	Fuel tank capacity (gal.)	13.2
Rear head room (in.)	36.5	EPA city/highway mpg	28/37
Min. rear leg room (in.)	32.4	Test mileage (mpg)	NA
Cargo volume (cu. ft.)	10.7		

Warranties The entire car is covered for 3 years/36,000 miles. Major powertrain components are covered for 5 years/60,000. Body perforation rust is covered for 5 years/unlimited miles.

Rating scale 5=Exceptional; 4=Above average; 3=Average; 2=Below average; 1=Poor

NISSAN 240SX

Built in Japan.

Nissan 240SX SE

SPORTS COUPE

The 1995 240SX arrived in the spring with a new design that retains rear-wheel drive but comes only as a 2-door notchback coupe. The 3-door hatchback body style is gone, as is the convertible that was the sole 240SX offering for 1994. A convertible based on the current design apparently isn't in Nissan's current plans. Wheelbase (distance between front and rear wheels) is two inches longer, but overall length is about half an inch shorter. Dual air bags are standard and the 240SX meets the more stringent 1997 federal side-impact standards. Inherited from the previous 240SX is a dual-camshaft 2.4-liter 4-cylinder engine with 155 horsepower. It teams with a standard 5-speed manual or optional 4-speed automatic transmission. Anti-lock brakes combined with a limited-slip differential are optional on both the base and SE models. The 240SX may have a short future in the U.S. Nissan executives say the front-drive 200SX sports coupe, scheduled to go on sale early in 1995, has much greater sales potential than the rear-drive 240SX, which is hard to sell in Snow Belt states. In addition, the 200SX is based on the new Sentra and built in the U.S., which should give it a price advantage over the 240SX. Sharp steering and agile handling are the hallmarks of the 240SX's rear-drive chassis, but poor traction in slippery conditions remains a sore spot. The firmer suspension on the SE rides more harshly than the base suspension, which does a better job of absorbing bumps and tar strips. Despite the longer wheelbase and wider body, the interior is still snug, especially in back. We're not overwhelmed by the performance or styling of the new 240SX.

Nissan 240SX prices are on page 396.

NISSAN 240SX SE

Rating Guide	1	2	3	4	5
Performance					
Acceleration	████████████████				
Economy	████████████████				
Driveability	████████████████				
Ride	███████████				
Steering/handling	███████████████████				
Braking	██████████████████████				
Noise	██████████████				
Accommodations					
Driver seating	███████████████████				
Instruments/controls	████████████████				
Visibility	████████████████				
Room/comfort	█████████████				
Entry/exit	█████████████				
Cargo room	█████████████				
Workmanship					
Exterior	███████████████████				
Interior	███████████████████				
Value	████████████████				
Total Points					**50**

Specifications

Body type	2-door notchback
Wheelbase (in.)	99.4
Overall length (in.)	177.2
Overall width (in.)	68.1
Overall height (in.)	50.8
Curb weight (lbs.)	2753
Seating capacity	4
Front head room (in.)	38.3
Max. front leg room (in.)	42.6
Rear head room (in.)	34.3
Min. rear leg room (in.)	20.8
Cargo volume (cu. ft.)	8.6
Engine type	dohc I-4
Engine size (l/cu. in.)	2.4/146
Horsepower @ rpm	155 @ 5600
Torque @ rpm	160 @ 4400
Transmission	auto/4-sp.
Drive wheels	rear
Brakes, F/R	disc/disc (ABS)
Tire size	205/55VR16
Fuel tank capacity (gal.)	17.2
EPA city/highway mpg	21/26
Test mileage (mpg)	20.8

Warranties The entire car is covered for 3 years/36,000 miles. Major powertrain components are covered for 5 years/60,000 miles. Body perforation rust is covered for 5 years/unlimited miles.

Rating scale 5=Exceptional; 4=Above average; 3=Average; 2=Below average; 1=Poor

NISSAN 300ZX

Built in Japan.

Nissan 300ZX Turbo

SPORTS AND GT

Nissan's high-performance sports car returns for 1995 unchanged. Now in its sixth year, the 300ZX is scheduled to be replaced in about a year. The 300ZX carries on in five models, all with rear-wheel drive and 3.0-liter V-6 power. A 2-seat hatchback coupe is available with and without removable T-tops, using a 222-horsepower version of the V-6. The 2-seat Turbo model comes only with the T-roof and 300 horsepower from a pair of turbochargers. Also back are a 2-seat convertible and a longer-wheelbase 2+2 T-roof coupe, both with the 222-horsepower engine. All but the base hardtop coupe offer an optional 4-speed automatic transmission in lieu of the standard 5-speed manual. Dual air bags and anti-lock 4-wheel disc brakes are standard across the board. The Turbo adds Nissan's rear-wheel steering system (called "Super-HICAS"), plus Z-rated tires (for speeds over 149 mph) instead of V-rated (up to 149 mph). The convertible has a manual folding top and an integral hoop over the interior designed to improve structural rigidity. The base engine can hit 60 mph in eight seconds or less, while the turbo version does it in about 6.2 seconds. The price you'll pay is low fuel economy (less than 20 mpg except in straight highway cruising). All models zip around tight corners with virtually no body lean and commendable grip—as long as the pavement is dry. Traction diminishes greatly on wet roads in the rear-drive 300ZX. The sports-car handling also comes at a price—ride comfort. The stiff suspension and wide tires don't absorb bumps well. The least-expensive 300ZX is now $35,009—out of reach for most buyers. Nissan dealers, however, should be willing to bargain on price.

Nissan 300ZX prices are on page 397.

NISSAN 300ZX TURBO

Rating Guide	1	2	3	4	5
Performance					
Acceleration					▮
Economy	▮				
Driveability			▮		
Ride	▮				
Steering/handling					▮
Braking				▮	
Noise	▮				
Accommodations					
Driver seating			▮		
Instruments/controls			▮		
Visibility		▮			
Room/comfort		▮			
Entry/exit		▮			
Cargo room			▮		
Workmanship					
Exterior				▮	
Interior				▮	
Value			▮		
Total Points					**51**

Specifications

Body type ....3-door hatchback	Engine type ....Turbo dohc V-6
Wheelbase (in.) 96.5	Engine size (l/cu. in.).........3.0/181
Overall length (in.) 169.5	Horsepower @ rpm ...300 @ 6400
Overall width (in.) 70.5	Torque @ rpm ....283 @ 3600
Overall height (in.) 48.3	Transmission ....auto/4-sp.
Curb weight (lbs.) 3453	Drive wheels ....rear
Seating capacity..........................2	Brakes, F/R...........disc/disc (ABS)
Front head room (in.) 36.8	Tire size 245/45ZR16
Max. front leg room (in.) 43.0	Fuel tank capacity (gal.) 18.7
Rear head room (in.) ....—	EPA city/highway mpg 18/23
Min. rear leg room (in.) ....—	Test mileage (mpg) ....NA
Cargo volume (cu. ft.).............23.7	

Warranties The entire car is covered for 3 years/36,000 miles. Major powertrain components are covered for 5 years/60,000 miles. Body perforation rust is covered for 5 years/unlimited miles.

Rating scale 5=Exceptional; 4=Above average; 3=Average; 2=Below average; 1=Poor

OLDSMOBILE ACHIEVA/ BUICK SKYLARK

Built in Lansing, Mich.

Oldsmobile Achieva S 4-door

COMPACT

Both the Achieva and similar Skylark have a new base engine, a 2.3-liter 4-cylinder with dual camshafts, 150 horsepower, and new balance shafts that are designed to provide quieter, smoother operation. A 155-horsepower 3.1-liter V-6 is available in both lines. At Olds, a 5-speed manual transmission is standard with the 4-cylinder and a 4-speed electronic automatic is optional. At Buick, a 3-speed automatic is standard and the 4-speed automatic is optional. At both brands, the V-6 comes only with the automatic, which has new transmission fluid that doesn't need to be changed for 100,000 miles under normal operating conditions. The Achieva S is available as a coupe and sedan in Series I and II equipment levels. Skylark comes in both body styles in Custom, Limited, and Gran Sport price levels, with "value-priced" Select Series versions of all three. A driver-side air bag and anti-lock brakes are standard on all. Achieva, Skylark, and the Pontiac Grand Am are built from the same design but have different exterior styling and interior features. The 4-cylinder engines in these cars have always been potent and economical, but until now they've also been noisy and rough. This year's version is much quieter and smoother and just as potent and economical as before, so we no longer find it necessary to recommend the V-6 engine. General Motors's value-pricing strategy means a fully equipped Achieva or Skylark is thousands of dollars less than comparable Japanese rivals such as the Toyota Camry and Mazda 626. However, the GM cars feel crude by comparison, banging and clunking over bumps that the Japanese rivals easily absorb.

Oldsmobile Achieva prices are on page 398.
Buick Skylark prices are on page 263.

OLDSMOBILE ACHIEVA S

Rating Guide	1	2	3	4	5
Performance					
Acceleration	▓▓▓▓▓▓▓▓▓▓▓▓▓▓▓▓▓▓▓▓▓▓				
Economy	▓▓▓▓▓▓▓▓▓▓▓▓▓				
Driveability	▓▓▓▓▓▓▓▓▓▓▓▓▓				
Ride	▓▓▓▓▓▓▓▓▓▓▓▓▓				
Steering/handling	▓▓▓▓▓▓▓▓▓▓▓▓▓				
Braking	▓▓▓▓▓▓▓▓▓▓▓▓▓▓▓▓▓▓▓▓▓▓▓▓				
Noise	▓▓▓▓▓▓▓▓▓▓▓▓▓				
Accommodations					
Driver seating	▓▓▓▓▓▓▓▓▓▓▓▓▓▓▓▓▓				
Instruments/controls	▓▓▓▓▓▓▓▓▓▓▓▓▓▓▓▓▓				
Visibility	▓▓▓▓▓▓▓▓▓▓▓▓▓▓▓▓▓				
Room/comfort	▓▓▓▓▓▓▓▓▓▓▓▓▓▓				
Entry/exit	▓▓▓▓▓▓▓▓▓▓▓▓▓▓				
Cargo room	▓▓▓▓▓▓▓▓▓▓▓▓▓▓				
Workmanship					
Exterior	▓▓▓▓▓▓▓▓▓▓▓▓▓▓				
Interior	▓▓▓▓▓▓▓▓▓▓▓▓▓▓				
Value	▓▓▓▓▓▓▓▓▓▓▓▓▓▓▓▓▓				

Total Points...56

Specifications

Body type	4-door notchback	Engine type	dohc I-4
Wheelbase (in.)	103.4	Engine size (l/cu. in.)	2.3/138
Overall length (in.)	187.9	Horsepower @ rpm	150 @ 6000
Overall width (in.)	67.5	Torque @ rpm	145 @ 4800
Overall height (in.)	53.4	Transmission	auto/4-sp.
Curb weight (lbs.)	2779	Drive wheels	front
Seating capacity	5	Brakes, F/R	disc/drum (ABS)
Front head room (in.)	37.8	Tire size	195/70R14
Max. front leg room (in.)	43.3	Fuel tank capacity (gal.)	15.2
Rear head room (in.)	37.0	EPA city/highway mpg	21/31
Min. rear leg room (in.)	33.5	Test mileage (mpg)	NA
Cargo volume (cu. ft.)	14.0		

Warranties The entire car is covered for 3 years/36,000 miles. Body perforation rust is covered for 6 years/100,000 miles.

Rating scale 5=Exceptional; 4=Above average; 3=Average; 2=Below average; 1=Poor

OLDSMOBILE AURORA

Built in Orion, Mich.

Oldsmobile Aurora

PREMIUM SEDAN

Aurora went on sale last spring as a new luxury sedan aimed at owners of Japanese brands such as Acura, Infiniti, and Lexus. In designing the Aurora, Oldsmobile started from scratch. The audio systems are the only components shared with other Olds cars. Aurora is built on a new front-drive chassis shared with the 1995 Buick Riviera coupe and comes only as a 4-door sedan with seats for five. Though Aurora and Riviera are built from the same basic design, they share no major mechanical features or styling cues. Aurora has a 250-horsepower 4.0-liter V-8 engine that is derived from the Cadillac 4.6-liter Northstar V-8 and teams with an electronic 4-speed automatic transmission. Standard equipment includes dual air bags, anti-lock brakes, and traction control that can be turned off by an interior switch. Aurora has gotten off to a fast start, with demand exceeding supply in most areas. Oldsmobile has announced it plans to increase the base price $1000 to $1500 in the near future above the present $31,370. This new sedan combines luxury amenities with sporty performance and distinctive styling. Though the engine doesn't snap your head back in hard acceleration, it delivers brisk acceleration and ample passing power. The transmission shifts so smoothly you seldom notice it. Aurora has commendable ride control at high speeds and though the ride is firmer than the LS 400's, it's not harsh or stiff with the standard tires. The optional V-rated tires (for speeds up to 149 mph) make the ride noticeably stiffer. The roomy interior has ample space for four adults and the dashboard has controls that are easy to reach. Aurora is a competitive entry in the premium sedan field.

Oldsmobile Aurora prices are on page 399.

OLDSMOBILE AURORA

Rating Guide	1	2	3	4	5
Performance					
Acceleration	▮▮▮▮▮▮▮▮				
Economy	▮▮▮				
Driveability	▮▮▮▮▮▮▮▮▮▮				
Ride	▮▮▮▮▮				
Steering/handling	▮▮▮▮▮▮▮▮▮▮				
Braking	▮▮▮▮▮▮▮▮				
Noise	▮▮▮▮▮				
Accommodations					
Driver seating	▮▮▮▮▮▮▮▮▮▮				
Instruments/controls	▮▮▮▮▮▮▮▮▮▮				
Visibility	▮▮▮▮▮				
Room/comfort	▮▮▮▮▮▮▮▮▮▮				
Entry/exit	▮▮▮▮▮▮▮▮▮▮				
Cargo room	▮▮▮▮▮▮▮▮▮▮				
Workmanship					
Exterior	▮▮▮▮▮▮▮▮▮▮				
Interior	▮▮▮▮▮▮▮▮▮▮				
Value					
	▮▮▮▮▮▮▮▮▮▮				

Total Points..60

Specifications

Body type	4-door notchback	Engine type	dohc V-8
Wheelbase (in.)	113.8	Engine size (l/cu. in.)	4.0/244
Overall length (in.)	205.4	Horsepower @ rpm	250 @ 5600
Overall width (in.)	74.4	Torque @ rpm	260 @ 4400
Overall height (in.)	55.4	Transmission	auto/4-sp.
Curb weight (lbs.)	3967	Drive wheels	front
Seating capacity	5	Brakes, F/R	disc/disc (ABS)
Front head room (in.)	38.4	Tire size	235/60VR16
Max. front leg room (in.)	42.6	Fuel tank capacity (gal.)	20.0
Rear head room (in.)	36.9	EPA city/highway mpg	17/24
Min. rear leg room (in.)	38.4	Test mileage (mpg)	16.6
Cargo volume (cu. ft.)	16.1		

Warranties The entire car is covered for 4 years/50,000 miles. Body perforation rust is covered for 6 years/100,000 miles.

Rating scale 5=Exceptional; 4=Above average; 3=Average; 2=Below average; 1=Poor

OLDSMOBILE CUTLASS CIERA/BUICK CENTURY

Built in Oklahoma City, Okla.

BUDGET BUY

Oldsmobile Cutlass Ciera SL 4-door

MID-SIZE

Oldsmobile has consolidated its older line of front-drive mid-size cars into a single SL model available with two levels of equipment. Both the wagon and the 4-door sedan are sold as "value-priced" models, which have more standard features and fewer options than traditional domestic cars. The similar Century comes as a 4-door sedan in Special and Custom price series and as a 5-door wagon in the Special series. In addition, there are value-priced Select Series Centurys. A driver-side air bag and anti-lock brakes are standard on all models. The Cutlass Series I sedan and Century Special have a 120-horsepower 2.2-liter 4-cylinder engine and a 3-speed automatic transmission. The Cutlass Series II sedan and wagon and Century Custom come with a 160-horsepower 3.1-liter V-6 and a 4-speed electronic automatic. The V-6 and 4-speed automatic are optional on the Century Special. The 4-speed automatic has new transmission fluid that doesn't need to be changed for 100,000 miles under normal conditions. In addition, with both transmissions the brake pedal now has to be applied before a drive gear can be engaged. Both of these cars debuted for the 1982 model year, yet they continue to outsell newer, more modern cars such as the Olds Cutlass Supreme because they offer good utility as either a sedan or wagon and come fully equipped at reasonable cost. The 4-cylinder engine doesn't have enough power for cars this big, so we strongly recommend the V-6. Though these are aged, conservatively styled cars, they have been highly rated in recent customer-satisfaction surveys.

Oldsmobile Cutlass Ciera prices are on page 400.
Buick Century prices are on page 248.

OLDSMOBILE CUTLASS CIERA SL

Rating Guide	1	2	3	4	5
Performance					
Acceleration	‖‖‖‖‖‖‖‖‖‖‖‖‖‖‖‖‖‖‖‖				
Economy	‖‖‖‖‖‖‖‖‖‖‖‖‖				
Driveability	‖‖‖‖‖‖‖‖‖‖‖‖‖‖‖‖‖‖				
Ride	‖‖‖‖‖‖‖‖‖‖‖‖‖‖‖‖‖				
Steering/handling	‖‖‖‖‖‖‖‖‖‖‖‖‖‖‖				
Braking	‖‖‖‖‖‖‖‖‖‖‖‖‖‖‖‖‖‖‖‖				
Noise	‖‖‖‖‖‖‖‖‖‖‖‖‖‖‖‖				
Accommodations					
Driver seating	‖‖‖‖‖‖‖‖‖‖‖‖				
Instruments/controls	‖‖‖‖‖‖‖‖‖‖‖‖				
Visibility	‖‖‖‖‖‖‖‖‖‖‖‖				
Room/comfort	‖‖‖‖‖‖‖‖‖‖‖‖‖‖				
Entry/exit	‖‖‖‖‖‖‖‖‖‖‖‖‖‖				
Cargo room	‖‖‖‖‖‖‖‖‖‖‖‖‖‖				
Workmanship					
Exterior	‖‖‖‖‖‖‖‖‖‖‖‖‖‖‖‖‖				
Interior	‖‖‖‖‖‖‖‖‖‖‖‖‖‖				
Value	‖‖‖‖‖‖‖‖‖‖‖‖‖‖‖‖‖				
Total Points					**58**

Specifications

Body type	4-door notchback
Wheelbase (in.)	104.9
Overall length (in.)	190.3
Overall width (in.)	69.4
Overall height (in.)	54.2
Curb weight (lbs.)	2974
Seating capacity	6
Front head room (in.)	38.6
Max. front leg room (in.)	42.1
Rear head room (in.)	38.3
Min. rear leg room (in.)	35.9
Cargo volume (cu. ft.)	15.8
Engine type	ohv V-6
Engine size (l/cu. in.)	3.1/191
Horsepower @ rpm	160 @ 5200
Torque @ rpm	185 @ 4000
Transmission	auto/4-sp.
Drive wheels	front
Brakes, F/R	disc/drum (ABS)
Tire size	195/75R14
Fuel tank capacity (gal.)	16.5
EPA city/highway mpg	19/29
Test mileage (mpg)	NA

Warranties The entire car is covered for 3 years/36,000 miles. Body perforation rust is covered for 6 years/100,000 miles.

Rating scale 5=Exceptional; 4=Above average; 3=Average; 2=Below average; 1=Poor

OLDSMOBILE CUTLASS SUPREME

Built in Doraville, Ga.

Oldsmobile Cutlass Supreme SL 4-door

MID-SIZE

The Cutlass Supreme gets a passenger-side air bag in a redesigned dashboard and a condensed lineup with fewer options. A driver-side air bag became standard last year. The front-drive Cutlass Supreme sedan and coupe now come only as SL models, but both are available in Series I and Series II equipment levels. The convertible comes in a single unnamed equipment level. Only a handful of options are available on all versions. A front bench seat is no longer available, so all models have front buckets and a center console with integral cup holders. A 160-horsepower 3.1-liter V-6 and an electronic 4-speed automatic transmission are standard on all models. A 210-horsepower 3.4-liter V-6 with dual overhead camshafts is optional across the board. All models have standard anti-lock brakes. The Cutlass Supreme is built from the same design as the Buick Regal, Chevrolet Lumina/Monte Carlo, and Pontiac Grand Prix, but each has its own styling and interior features. The old Cutlass Supreme dashboard had too many small buttons and small gauges squeezed into a narrow band. The new one has simple controls that are easy to find and use, and large gauges that can be read at a glance. With dual air bags now standard, the Cutlass supreme is a much more serious contender among mid-size cars. However, there's still stiff competition from the Ford Taurus and Honda Accord. While the Cutlass Supreme isn't the best choice, it's a much better one this year. Oldsmobile's pricing strategy is designed to eliminate the traditional haggling between the dealer and consumer. If that appeals to you, this car belongs on your shopping list.

Oldsmobile Cutlass Supreme prices are on page 401.

OLDSMOBILE CUTLASS SUPREME SL

Rating Guide	1	2	3	4	5
Performance					
Acceleration	▓▓▓▓▓▓▓▓▓▓				
Economy	▓▓▓▓				
Driveability	▓▓▓▓▓▓▓▓▓▓				
Ride	▓▓▓▓▓▓				
Steering/handling	▓▓▓▓▓▓▓				
Braking	▓▓▓▓▓▓▓▓▓▓				
Noise	▓▓▓▓▓				
Accommodations					
Driver seating	▓▓▓▓▓▓▓▓				
Instruments/controls	▓▓▓▓▓▓▓				
Visibility	▓▓▓▓▓▓▓				
Room/comfort	▓▓▓▓▓▓▓				
Entry/exit	▓▓▓▓▓▓▓				
Cargo room	▓▓▓▓▓▓▓				
Workmanship					
Exterior	▓▓▓▓▓▓▓▓				
Interior	▓▓▓▓▓▓▓				
Value	▓▓▓▓▓▓▓				

Total Points...59

Specifications

Body type ....4-door notchback	Engine type.....................dohc V-6
Wheelbase (in.) 107.5	Engine size (l/cu. in.).........3.4/207
Overall length (in.)................193.7	Horsepower @ rpm ...210 @ 5200
Overall width (in.) 71.0	Torque @ rpm ....215 @ 4000
Overall height (in.) 54.8	Transmission................auto/4-sp.
Curb weight (lbs.) 3369	Drive wheels ....front
Seating capacity..........................5	Brakes, F/R...........disc/disc (ABS)
Front head room (in.) 38.7	Tire size 215/60R16
Max. front leg room (in.) 42.4	Fuel tank capacity (gal.) 16.5
Rear head room (in.) 38.3	EPA city/highway mpg 17/26
Min. rear leg room (in.)...........36.2	Test mileage (mpg) 17.2
Cargo volume (cu. ft.)..............15.5	

Warranties The entire car is covered for 3 years/36,000 miles. Body perforation rust is covered for 6 years/100,000 miles.

Rating scale 5=Exceptional; 4=Above average; 3=Average; 2=Below average; 1=Poor

PLYMOUTH ACCLAIM/
DODGE SPIRIT

Built in Newark, Del.

Plymouth Acclaim

COMPACT

These identical front-drive sedans return with few changes for their seventh—and probably last—season. Spirit will be replaced next spring by the new Stratus sedan, while Acclaim is scheduled to be replaced by a similar car next fall. A name hasn't been announced for Plymouth's version. Acclaim and Spirit continue in a single price level with a standard driver-side air bag. Standard powertrain is a 100-horsepower 2.5-liter 4-cylinder Chrysler engine and a 3-speed automatic transmission. A 142-horsepower 3.0-liter Mitsubishi V-6 is the only powertrain option. Cut from last year's options list are anti-lock brakes, a flexible-fuel version of the 4-cylinder that could run on gasoline or a mix of 85-percent methanol and 15-percent gasoline, and a 4-speed automatic transmission. These cars are low on excitement, high on value, and available at big discounts. With the 4-cylinder and 3-speed automatic, they have adequate performance, though the base engine is too loud even when cruising. Road noise also is prominent at highway speeds. Acceleration is quicker with the smoother, quieter V-6 engine. The suspension doesn't absorb bumps well, so it bangs and bounces over rough pavement. Four adults can spread out in the roomy interior. A flat floor and low liftover make it easy to load the large trunk, and an optional split folding rear seat is available to increase cargo room. Japanese-brand rivals such as the Toyota Camry and Mazda 626 are more modern and refined than Acclaim and spirit but also far more expensive. Plymouth and Dodge were offering $1500 rebates earlier this year.

Plymouth Acclaim prices are on page 405.
Dodge Spirit prices are on page 303.

PLYMOUTH ACCLAIM

Rating Guide	1	2	3	4	5
Performance					
Acceleration	▓▓▓▓▓▓▓▓▓▓▓▓				
Economy	▓▓▓▓▓▓▓▓▓▓▓▓				
Driveability	▓▓▓▓▓▓▓▓▓▓▓▓				
Ride	▓▓▓▓▓▓▓▓▓▓▓▓				
Steering/handling	▓▓▓▓▓▓▓▓▓▓▓▓				
Braking	▓▓▓▓▓▓▓▓▓▓▓▓				
Noise	▓▓▓▓▓▓▓▓▓▓				
Accommodations					
Driver seating	▓▓▓▓▓▓▓▓▓▓▓▓▓▓▓▓				
Instruments/controls	▓▓▓▓▓▓▓▓▓▓▓▓▓▓▓▓				
Visibility	▓▓▓▓▓▓▓▓▓▓▓▓▓▓▓▓				
Room/comfort	▓▓▓▓▓▓▓▓▓▓▓▓▓▓▓▓				
Entry/exit	▓▓▓▓▓▓▓▓▓▓▓▓▓▓▓▓				
Cargo room	▓▓▓▓▓▓▓▓▓▓▓▓▓▓▓▓				
Workmanship					
Exterior	▓▓▓▓▓▓▓▓▓▓▓▓▓▓				
Interior	▓▓▓▓▓▓▓▓▓▓▓▓▓▓				
Value	▓▓▓▓▓▓▓▓▓▓▓▓▓▓▓▓				

Total Points..**55**

Specifications

Body type ....4-door notchback	Engine type ....ohc I-4
Wheelbase (in.) 103.5	Engine size (l/cu. in.)..........2.5/153
Overall length (in.)...............181.2	Horsepower @ rpm ...100 @ 4800
Overall width (in.) 68.1	Torque @ rpm ....135 @ 2800
Overall height (in.)..................53.5	Transmission..................auto/3-sp.
Curb weight (lbs.) 2862	Drive wheels ....front
Seating capacity...........................6	Brakes, F/R......................disc/drum
Front head room (in.) 38.4	Tire size 185/70R14
Max. front leg room (in.) 41.9	Fuel tank capacity (gal.) 16.0
Rear head room (in.) 37.9	EPA city/highway mpg 22/28
Min. rear leg room (in.)..........38.3	Test mileage (mpg) 22.3
Cargo volume (cu. ft.).............14.4	

Warranties The entire car is covered for 3 years/36,000 miles. Body perforation rust is covered for 7 years/100,000 miles.

Rating scale 5=Exceptional; 4=Above average; 3=Average; 2=Below average; 1=Poor

PONTIAC GRAND AM

Built in Lansing, Mich.

Pontiac Grand Am GT 2-door

COMPACT

Pontiac's best-selling car has a new base engine for 1995. The front-drive Grand Am returns as a 2-door coupe and 4-door sedan, both available in base SE and sporty GT trim. A driver-side air bag and anti-lock brakes are standard. Standard on both models is a 150-horsepower 2.3-liter 4-cylinder engine called the Quad 4. It has new internal balance shafts designed to make it run smoother. The only optional engine on both models is a 155-horsepower 3.1-liter V-6. A 5-speed manual transmission is standard with the Quad 4 engine. The Quad 4 can be ordered with an optional 3-speed automatic on SE models and with a 4-speed automatic on both models. The V-6 comes only with the 4-speed automatic. The automatics now have transmission fluid that lasts 100,000 miles under normal conditions. Grand Am is built from the same design as the Buick Skylark and Oldsmobile Achieva but has different styling and interior features. Grand Am has been far more successful than its cousins at Buick and Oldsmobile because Pontiac provides the right blend of image and price. Previously, we recommended the V-6 engine over the noisy 4-cylinder engines. This year, however, the Quad 4 engine is quieter and smoother, so test drive one before you insist on the V-6, a $350 option. We also recommend that you try an SE with the 14- or 15-inch wheels and tires before you sign a contract for a GT, which has standard 16-inch wheels and tires. The GT has a stiffer ride that makes long drives more tiring. With a standard driver-side air bag and anti-lock brakes, sporty looks, and reasonable prices, Grand Am has some attractions. However, the new Pontiac Sunfire makes the Grand Am feel old and unrefined.

Pontiac Grand Am prices are on page 418.

CONSUMER GUIDE®

PONTIAC GRAND AM GT

Rating Guide	1	2	3	4	5
Performance					
Acceleration				▊	
Economy			▊		
Driveability				▊	
Ride			▊		
Steering/handling				▊	
Braking					▊
Noise			▊		
Accommodations					
Driver seating				▊	
Instruments/controls				▊	
Visibility			▊		
Room/comfort			▊		
Entry/exit			▊		
Cargo room			▊		
Workmanship					
Exterior			▊		
Interior			▊		
Value			▊		

Total Points...57

Specifications

Body type	2-door notchback	Engine type	dohc I-4
Wheelbase (in.)	103.4	Engine size (l/cu. in.)	2.3/138
Overall length (in.)	186.9	Horsepower @ rpm	150 @ 6000
Overall width (in.)	68.7	Torque @ rpm	145 @ 4800
Overall height (in.)	53.2	Transmission	auto/4-sp.
Curb weight (lbs.)	2824	Drive wheels	front
Seating capacity	5	Brakes, F/R	disc/drum (ABS)
Front head room (in.)	37.8	Tire size	205/55R16
Max. front leg room (in.)	43.3	Fuel tank capacity (gal.)	15.2
Rear head room (in.)	36.5	EPA city/highway mpg	21/31
Min. rear leg room (in.)	33.9	Test mileage (mpg)	NA
Cargo volume (cu. ft.)	13.2		

Warranties The entire car is covered for 3 years/36,000 miles. Body perforation rust is covered for 6 years/100,000 miles.

Rating scale 5=Exceptional; 4=Above average; 3=Average; 2=Below average; 1=Poor

PONTIAC GRAND PRIX

Built in Kansas City, Kan.

Pontiac Grand Prix SE 2-door

MID-SIZE

This front-drive mid-size car gains a standard brake/transmission shift interlock and optional variable-effort power steering. Grand Prix returns as a 2-door coupe and 4-door sedan in a single SE price series with a standard 160-horsepower 3.1-liter V-6 engine. Option packages, labeled GTP on the coupe and GT on the sedan, include aero body trim, a dual-camshaft 3.4-liter V-6 rated at 210 horsepower, and the new variable-effort steering, which decreases power assist as vehicle speed increases. All Grand Prixs have dual air bags. Anti-lock brakes are optional (and included in the GT and GTP packages). A 4-speed electronic automatic is the only transmission and this year has fluid that lasts 100,000 miles. The new shift interlock prevents shifting the transmission out of park unless the brake pedal is depressed. Grand Prix shares its basic design with the Buick Regal, Oldsmobile Cutlass Supreme, and Chevrolet Lumina and Monte Carlo, though styling and features differ. Coupe or sedan, Grand Prix's cabin has ample room for four adults, though the rear seat is too low and uncomfortable. The interior was redesigned last year, when dual air bags became standard. Though the dashboard has convenient controls that are easy to reach and use, it also has a lot of flimsy plastic that looks and feels cheap. The standard 3.1-liter engine is smooth and delivers enough acceleration to satisfy most needs. The 3.4-liter V-6 is quicker—though not by that much—but also louder. Considering all that's standard, the Grand Prix is priced competitively against mid-size rivals such as the Ford Taurus and Thunderbird. The new Lumina and Monte Carlo have the same engines as the Grand Prix—and lower prices.

Pontiac Grand Prix prices are on page 420.

PONTIAC GRAND PRIX SE

Rating Guide

	1	2	3	4	5
Performance					
Acceleration	▓▓▓▓▓▓				
Economy	▓▓▓▓▓				
Driveability	▓▓▓▓▓▓▓▓				
Ride	▓▓▓▓▓▓				
Steering/handling	▓▓▓▓▓▓▓				
Braking	▓▓▓▓▓▓▓▓▓▓				
Noise	▓▓▓▓▓▓▓▓				
Accommodations					
Driver seating	▓▓▓▓▓▓▓▓				
Instruments/controls	▓▓▓▓▓▓▓▓				
Visibility	▓▓▓▓▓▓▓				
Room/comfort	▓▓▓▓▓▓▓▓				
Entry/exit	▓▓▓▓▓▓				
Cargo room	▓▓▓▓▓▓▓▓				
Workmanship					
Exterior	▓▓▓▓▓▓▓				
Interior	▓▓▓▓▓▓▓				
Value	▓▓▓▓▓▓				

Total Points...57

Specifications

Body type	2-door notchback	Engine type	ohv V-6
Wheelbase (in.)	107.5	Engine size (l/cu. in.)	3.1/191
Overall length (in.)	194.8	Horsepower @ rpm	160 @ 5200
Overall width (in.)	71.9	Torque @ rpm	185 @ 4000
Overall height (in.)	52.8	Transmission	auto/4-sp.
Curb weight (lbs.)	3275	Drive wheels	front
Seating capacity	5	Brakes, F/R	disc/disc (ABS)
Front head room (in.)	37.8	Tire size	215/60R16
Max. front leg room (in.)	42.3	Fuel tank capacity (gal.)	17.1
Rear head room (in.)	36.6	EPA city/highway mpg	19/29
Min. rear leg room (in.)	34.8	Test mileage (mpg)	NA
Cargo volume (cu. ft.)	14.9		

Warranties The entire car is covered for 3 years/36,000 miles. Body perforation rust is covered for 6 years/100,000 miles.

Rating scale 5=Exceptional; 4=Above average; 3=Average; 2=Below average; 1=Poor

PONTIAC SUNFIRE

Built in Lordstown, Ohio.

Pontiac Sunfire SE 2-door

SUBCOMPACT

Pontiac shelves its Sunbird subcompact after 13 years and replaces it with a new model, Sunfire, which shares its front-drive chassis and mechanical components with the redesigned Chevrolet Cavalier but is styled more aggressively. Sunbird didn't have an air bag, but Sunfire's new interior has dual air bags. Anti-lock brakes also are standard. Sunfire's 104.1-inch wheelbase is 2.8 inches longer than Sunbird's and overall length has grown 1.2 inches to 181.9. A 4-door sedan and 2-door coupe arrived in the fall in base SE trim. Due later in the model year are an SE convertible and a GT coupe. The convertible has a power top and, like all Sunfires, a rear seat that folds for more cargo room. Last year's V-6 engine is gone, leaving two 4-cylinder choices. SE models have a 2.2-liter with 120 horsepower. The Quad 4, a 150-horsepower 2.3-liter 4-cylinder with dual overhead camshafts, is standard on the GT and optional on the SE. A 5-speed manual transmission is standard with both engines. A 3-speed automatic is optional with the 2.2-liter and a 4-speed automatic is optional with the Quad 4. Traction control is a new option on the GT with automatic trans-mission. The newest Pontiac shapes up as a strong entry in the subcompact field, taking a sportier route than the similar Cavalier. The base engine is somewhat coarse under hard throttle, but acceleration is adequate with the manual transmission and there's enough power at low speeds so that the 3-speed automatic isn't always downshifting. Interior space is adequate for four adults. However, Sunfire's low rear seat cushion forces those with long legs into an uncomfortable knees-up position.

Pontiac Sunfire prices are on page 421.

PONTIAC SUNFIRE SE (Preliminary)

Rating Guide	1	2	3	4	5
Performance					
Acceleration	▬▬▬				
Economy	▬▬▬▬				
Driveability	▬▬▬				
Ride	▬▬▬				
Steering/handling	▬▬▬				
Braking	▬▬▬▬▬				
Noise	▬▬				
Accommodations					
Driver seating	▬▬				
Instruments/controls	▬▬				
Visibility	▬▬▬▬				
Room/comfort	▬▬▬				
Entry/exit	▬▬				
Cargo room	▬▬▬				
Workmanship					
Exterior	▬▬▬				
Interior	▬▬▬				
Value	▬▬▬				
Total Points					**58**

Specifications

Body type	2-door notchback	Engine type	ohv I-4
Wheelbase (in.)	104.1	Engine size (l/cu. in.)	2.2/133
Overall length (in.)	181.9	Horsepower @ rpm	120 @ 5200
Overall width (in.)	67.4	Torque @ rpm	130 @ 4000
Overall height (in.)	53.2	Transmission	auto/3-sp.
Curb weight (lbs.)	2679	Drive wheels	front
Seating capacity	5	Brakes, F/R	disc/drum (ABS)
Front head room (in.)	37.6	Tire size	195/70R14
Max. front leg room (in.)	42.4	Fuel tank capacity (gal.)	15.2
Rear head room (in.)	36.6	EPA city/highway mpg	25/32
Min. rear leg room (in.)	32.0	Test mileage (mpg)	NA
Cargo volume (cu. ft.)	13.1		

Warranties The entire car is covered for 3 years/36,000 miles. Body perforation rust is covered for 6 years/100,000 miles.

Rating scale 5=Exceptional; 4=Above average; 3=Average; 2=Below average; 1=Poor

SAAB 900

Built in Sweden and Finland.

Saab 900 S 3-door

PREMIUM SEDAN

Saab introduced the first redesigned 900 model in 15 years in fall 1993 when it unveiled a new 5-door hatchback. It was followed last spring by a new 3-door hatchback and in the summer by a 2-door convertible. These are the first Saabs built with help from General Motors, which owns 50 percent of Saab's car business. The 900 models retain front-wheel drive and gain 3.3 inches in wheelbase but lose two inches in overall length compared to the previous generation. All three body styles come in S and SE trim levels. Dual air bags and anti-lock brakes are standard. A 150-horsepower 2.3-liter 4-cylinder engine is standard on S models and a 185-horsepower turbocharged 2.0-liter 4-cylinder is standard on the SE 3-door and convertible. A 170-horsepower V-6 is standard on the SE 5-door and optional on the SE convertible. The V-6 is built by GM, which uses it in some of its European cars. A 5-speed manual transmission is standard with all three engines. A 4-speed automatic is optional with the 2.3-liter 4-cylinder and the V-6. The new 900 has generous head and leg room and enormous cargo space for a compact-sized car, but the traditional Saab styling probably won't appeal to mainstream buyers. The base 4-cylinder has adequate power with the manual transmission but feels weak with automatic. The V-6 is strong and smooth and works well with the automatic, while the turbocharged SE models have excellent acceleration. The base price on the 900 S has climbed nearly $2500 in the past year, so it's not as attractive from a cost stand-point. Even so, the new 900 models deserve a look by those who value function over form.

Saab 900 prices are on page 425.

SAAB 900 S

Rating Guide	1	2	3	4	5
Performance					
Acceleration	▓▓▓▓▓▓▓▓▓				
Economy	▓▓▓▓▓▓				
Driveability	▓▓▓▓▓▓				
Ride	▓▓▓▓▓▓				
Steering/handling	▓▓▓▓▓▓▓				
Braking	▓▓▓▓▓▓▓▓▓▓				
Noise	▓▓▓▓▓▓				
Accommodations					
Driver seating	▓▓▓▓▓▓▓				
Instruments/controls	▓▓▓▓▓▓▓				
Visibility	▓▓▓▓▓▓▓				
Room/comfort	▓▓▓▓▓▓				
Entry/exit	▓▓▓▓▓▓				
Cargo room	▓▓▓▓▓▓▓				
Workmanship					
Exterior	▓▓▓▓▓▓▓				
Interior	▓▓▓▓▓▓▓				
Value	▓▓▓▓▓▓▓				

Total Points...**58**

Specifications

Body type	3-door hatchback	Engine type	dohc I-4
Wheelbase (in.)	102.4	Engine size (l/cu. in.)	2.3/140
Overall length (in.)	182.6	Horsepower @ rpm	150 @ 5700
Overall width (in.)	67.4	Torque @ rpm	155 @ 4300
Overall height (in.)	56.5	Transmission	manual/5-sp.
Curb weight (lbs.)	2940	Drive wheels	front
Seating capacity	5	Brakes, F/R	disc/disc (ABS)
Front head room (in.)	39.3	Tire size	195/60VR15
Max. front leg room (in.)	42.3	Fuel tank capacity (gal.)	18.0
Rear head room (in.)	37.8	EPA city/highway mpg	20/29
Min. rear leg room (in.)	36.0	Test mileage (mpg)	24.4
Cargo volume (cu. ft.)	49.8		

Warranties The entire car is covered for 4 years/50,000 miles. Body perforation rust is covered for 6 years/unlimited miles.

Rating scale 5=Exceptional; 4=Above average; 3=Average; 2=Below average; 1=Poor

SAAB 9000

Built in Sweden.

Saab 9000 CDE

PREMIUM SEDAN

Saab's larger car gets two new engines for 1995—its first V-6 and a "light pressure" turbocharged 4-cylinder. All versions of this car have front-wheel drive, dual air bags, and anti-lock brakes. Two body styles are offered, a 5-door hatchback and a 4-door notchback sedan. The hatchback line starts with the CS model, which has a 2.3-liter 4-cylinder engine with a "light-pressure" turbocharger and 170 horsepower. Saab says this turbo furnishes boost at lower engine manifold pressure and for longer duration than traditional turbochargers. The CSE hatchback comes with either a 200-horsepower 2.3-liter turbocharged 4-cylinder or a new 210-horsepower 3.0-liter V-6. The performance-oriented 9000 Aero hatchback returns with a 225-horsepower 2.3-liter turbo 4-cylinder. The lone 4-door notchback model is the CDE with the V-6 engine. It gets new front end styling similar to the CS model's. A 5-speed manual transmission is standard on 4-cylinder models and a 4-speed automatic is optional. V-6 models come only with the automatic. A 6-cylinder engine is the price of admission these days for luxury cars in the $30,000 to $40,000 range, and some, such as the Oldsmobile Aurora, even have V-8s. Saab executives feel their turbocharged 4-cylinder engines have more than enough power and are appropriate for U.S. driving conditions. Sluggish sales of the 9000 indicate otherwise, however, and we think the new V-6 is the way to go in a 9000. It's quiet, smooth, and strong. All 9000 models have capable handling, generous cargo space, and huge, comfortable interiors. Even with the new V-6 engine Saab dealers should be discounting prices on the 9000.

Saab 9000 prices are on page 426.

SAAB 9000 CDE

Rating Guide	1	2	3	4	5
Performance					
Acceleration	▓▓▓▓▓▓▓▓▓▓▓▓▓▓▓▓▓▓▓				
Economy	▓▓▓▓▓▓▓▓▓				
Driveability	▓▓▓▓▓▓▓▓▓▓▓▓▓▓▓				
Ride	▓▓▓▓▓▓▓▓▓▓▓▓				
Steering/handling	▓▓▓▓▓▓▓▓▓▓▓▓▓▓▓				
Braking	▓▓▓▓▓▓▓▓▓▓▓▓▓▓▓▓▓▓▓▓				
Noise	▓▓▓▓▓▓▓▓▓▓▓▓▓▓▓				
Accommodations					
Driver seating	▓▓▓▓▓▓▓▓▓				
Instruments/controls	▓▓▓▓▓▓▓▓▓				
Visibility	▓▓▓▓▓▓▓▓▓				
Room/comfort	▓▓▓▓▓▓▓▓▓▓▓				
Entry/exit	▓▓▓▓▓▓▓▓▓▓▓				
Cargo room	▓▓▓▓▓▓▓▓▓▓▓▓▓▓▓▓▓				
Workmanship					
Exterior	▓▓▓▓▓▓▓▓▓▓▓▓▓▓▓▓▓				
Interior	▓▓▓▓▓▓▓▓▓▓▓▓▓▓▓▓▓				
Value	▓▓▓▓▓▓▓▓▓				

Total Points...59

Specifications

Body type	4-door notchback	Engine type	dohc V-6
Wheelbase (in.)	105.2	Engine size (l/cu. in.)	3.0/182
Overall length (in.)	188.7	Horsepower @ rpm	210 @ 6100
Overall width (in.)	69.4	Torque @ rpm	200 @ 3300
Overall height (in.)	55.9	Transmission	auto/4-sp.
Curb weight (lbs.)	3260	Drive wheels	front
Seating capacity	5	Brakes, F/R	disc/disc (ABS)
Front head room (in.)	38.5	Tire size	205/60ZR15
Max. front leg room (in.)	41.5	Fuel tank capacity (gal.)	17.4
Rear head room (in.)	37.4	EPA city/highway mpg	18/27
Min. rear leg room (in.)	38.7	Test mileage (mpg)	NA
Cargo volume (cu. ft.)	17.8		

Warranties The entire car is covered for 4 years/50,000 miles. Body perforation rust is covered for 6 years/unlimited miles.

Rating scale 5=Exceptional; 4=Above average; 3=Average; 2=Below average; 1=Poor

SATURN SC1/SC2 — BUDGET BUY

Built in Spring Hill, Tenn.

Saturn SC2

SPORTS COUPE

A standard passenger-side air bag and a redesigned interior are the highlights for 1995 on Saturn's front-drive sports coupe. In addition, the base engine has 15 more horsepower and both models have minor styling changes. A driver-side air bag already was standard on both the SC1 and SC2. With the addition of the passenger-side air bag, the motorized front shoulder belts have been replaced by height-adjustable manual 3-point seatbelts. The redesigned interior includes a new instrument panel, new bucket seats for the SC1, a new 2-spoke steering wheel for all models, cup holders, and new steering column stalks for the headlights and windshield wiper/washer. The SC1's 1.9-liter 4-cylinder engine switches from single-point to multi-point fuel injection this year, boosting horsepower from 85 to 100. The SC2's dual-camshaft version of the 1.9-liter engine, which already had multi-point injection, is unchanged at 124 horsepower. Both engines come with a standard 5-speed manual transmission or optional 4-speed automatic. Anti-lock brakes (ABS) are optional on all models. With the automatic transmission, traction control is included with the ABS. Though the SC1 and SC2 are noisy and unrefined compared to most rivals, they have impressive records for customer satisfaction. Saturn's no-haggle price policy means that the buying experience is relatively painless—and even enjoyable. The SC1 offers most of the virtues of the SC2 at lower cost. This year's more-powerful single-cam engine performs well with the 5-speed manual transmission, but acceleration is still tepid with the automatic. The more powerful dual-cam engine in the SC2 performs well with either transmission.

Saturn SC1/SC2 prices are on page 427.

SATURN SC2

Rating Guide	1	2	3	4	5
Performance					
Acceleration	‖‖‖‖‖‖‖‖‖‖‖‖‖‖‖‖‖‖‖‖‖‖‖				
Economy	‖‖‖‖‖‖‖‖‖‖‖‖‖‖‖‖‖‖‖‖‖‖‖				
Driveability	‖‖‖‖‖‖‖‖‖‖‖‖‖‖‖‖‖‖				
Ride	‖‖‖‖‖‖‖‖‖‖‖‖‖‖‖‖‖‖				
Steering/handling	‖‖‖‖‖‖‖‖‖‖‖‖‖‖‖‖‖‖‖‖‖				
Braking	‖‖‖‖‖‖‖‖‖‖‖‖‖‖‖‖‖‖‖‖‖‖‖‖‖‖‖‖				
Noise	‖‖‖‖‖‖‖‖‖‖‖‖‖‖				
Accommodations					
Driver seating	‖‖‖‖‖‖‖‖‖‖‖‖‖‖‖‖‖‖‖‖‖				
Instruments/controls	‖‖‖‖‖‖‖‖‖‖‖‖‖‖‖‖‖‖‖‖‖				
Visibility	‖‖‖‖‖‖‖‖‖‖‖‖‖‖‖‖‖‖				
Room/comfort	‖‖‖‖‖‖‖‖‖‖‖‖				
Entry/exit	‖‖‖‖‖‖‖‖‖‖‖‖				
Cargo room	‖‖‖‖‖‖‖‖‖‖‖‖‖‖‖‖‖‖				
Workmanship					
Exterior	‖‖‖‖‖‖‖‖‖‖‖‖‖‖‖‖‖‖				
Interior	‖‖‖‖‖‖‖‖‖‖‖‖‖‖‖‖‖‖				
Value	‖‖‖‖‖‖‖‖‖‖‖‖‖‖‖‖‖‖				

Total Points..56

Specifications

Body type ....2-door notchback	Engine type ....dohc I-4
Wheelbase (in.) 99.2	Engine size (l/cu. in.)........1.9/116
Overall length (in.) 173.2	Horsepower @ rpm ...124 @ 5600
Overall width (in.) 67.5	Torque @ rpm ....122 @ 4800
Overall height (in.) 50.6	Transmission.................auto/4-sp.
Curb weight (lbs.) 2280	Drive wheels ....front
Seating capacity..........................4	Brakes, F/R...........disc/disc (ABS)
Front head room (in.) 37.6	Tire size 195/60R15
Max. front leg room (in.) 42.6	Fuel tank capacity (gal.) 12.8
Rear head room (in.) 35.0	EPA city/highway mpg 24/34
Min. rear leg room (in.)...........26.4	Test mileage (mpg) 25.2
Cargo volume (cu. ft.).............10.9	

Warranties The entire car is covered for 3 years/36,000 miles. Body perforation rust is covered for 6 years/100,000 miles.

Rating scale 5=Exceptional; 4=Above average; 3=Average; 2=Below average; 1=Poor

SATURN SEDAN/ WAGON

RECOMMENDED

Built in Spring Hill, Tenn.

Saturn SL1

SUBCOMPACT

Saturn's front-drive sedan and wagon get a passenger-side air bag in a redesigned interior and a more powerful base engine for 1995, the last year for the current design. The sedan and wagon are scheduled to be restyled for 1996, the first major appearance change for these cars since they debuted for 1990. The similar SC1 and SC2 coupes won't be restyled until 1997. All versions add a standard passenger-side air bag this year. A driver-side air bag has been standard since 1993. With the second air bag and redesigned interior, manual 3-point seatbelts replace motorized shoulder belts for the front seats. The sedan comes in SL, SL1, and SL2 price levels, while the wagon comes in SW1 and SW2 price levels. Horsepower on the base engine (used in the SL, SL1, and SW1) jumps from 85 to 100 with the addition of multi-point fuel injection. Previously, the base 1.9-liter 4-cylinder had single-point injection. The dual-camshaft 1.9-liter engine used in the SL2 and SW2 is unchanged at 124 horsepower. Both engines come with a standard 5-speed manual or optional 4-speed automatic transmission. Anti-lock brakes (ABS) are optional on all models. With the automatic transmission, traction control is included with the ABS. The single-cam engine gives these cars decent acceleration with the manual transmission, but with the automatic you often have to floor the throttle to keep up with traffic. The dual-cam engine provides lively acceleration and decent passing power with either transmission. Both engines are loud and harsh at higher speeds. Despite some flaws, good assembly quality, competent performance, and reasonable prices make these cars well worth considering.

Saturn Sedan/Wagon prices are on page 428.

SATURN SL1

Rating Guide	1	2	3	4	5
Performance					
Acceleration	▓▓▓▓▓▓▓▓▓▓▓▓				
Economy	▓▓▓▓▓▓▓▓▓▓▓▓▓				
Driveability	▓▓▓▓▓▓▓▓▓▓▓▓				
Ride	▓▓▓▓▓▓▓▓▓▓				
Steering/handling	▓▓▓▓▓▓▓▓▓▓▓				
Braking	▓▓▓▓▓▓▓▓▓▓▓▓▓▓				
Noise	▓▓▓▓▓▓▓				
Accommodations					
Driver seating	▓▓▓▓▓▓▓▓▓▓▓				
Instruments/controls	▓▓▓▓▓▓▓▓▓▓▓				
Visibility	▓▓▓▓▓▓▓▓▓▓▓				
Room/comfort	▓▓▓▓▓▓▓▓▓▓▓				
Entry/exit	▓▓▓▓▓▓▓▓▓▓▓				
Cargo room	▓▓▓▓▓▓▓▓▓▓				
Workmanship					
Exterior	▓▓▓▓▓▓▓▓▓▓▓				
Interior	▓▓▓▓▓▓▓▓▓▓▓				
Value	▓▓▓▓▓▓▓▓▓▓▓				

Total Points..57

Specifications

Body type	4-door notchback	Engine type	ohc I-4
Wheelbase (in.)	102.4	Engine size (l/cu. in.)	1.9/116
Overall length (in.)	176.3	Horsepower @ rpm	100 @ 5000
Overall width (in.)	67.6	Torque @ rpm	115 @ 2400
Overall height (in.)	52.5	Transmission	manual/5-sp.
Curb weight (lbs.)	2325	Drive wheels	front
Seating capacity	5	Brakes, F/R	disc/disc (ABS)
Front head room (in.)	38.5	Tire size	175/70R14
Max. front leg room (in.)	42.5	Fuel tank capacity (gal.)	12.8
Rear head room (in.)	36.3	EPA city/highway mpg	28/40
Min. rear leg room (in.)	32.6	Test mileage (mpg)	NA
Cargo volume (cu. ft.)	11.9		

Warranties The entire car is covered for 3 years/36,000 miles. Body perforation rust is covered for 6 years/100,000 miles.

Rating scale 5=Exceptional; 4=Above average; 3=Average; 2=Below average; 1=Poor

SUBARU IMPREZA

Built in Japan.

Subaru Impreza LX 2-door

SUBCOMPACT

Impreza, introduced for 1993 in sedan and wagon versions, this year adds a 2-door coupe to the lineup. All have standard dual air bags and all but the wagon come with standard front-wheel drive or optional permanently engaged all-wheel drive (AWD). The wagon now comes only with AWD. Previously, the only engine offered was a 110-horsepower 1.8-liter 4-cylinder with "flat," or horizontally opposed, cylinders. That engine continues as standard, but this year the 135-horsepower 2.2-liter engine from the larger Legacy is available. The 1.8-liter comes with a standard 5-speed manual transmission or optional 4-speed automatic. The 2.2-liter comes only with the automatic. The coupe and sedan are available in three price levels: Base, L, and LX (formerly called LS). The wagon comes in L, LX, and a new Outback version. The Outback is aimed at the "outdoors" set, with 2-tone paint, a roof rack, white-lettered tires, and mud guards. Impreza is intended to be a more mainstream offering than the quirky Loyale it has replaced, but that makes it just another small car in an already crowded field. Impreza's only real distinction is AWD, which is unique among subcompact cars. An AWD wagon we tested with the 5-speed felt sluggish off the line and an AWD sedan with the automatic was downright slow. The new 2.2-liter engine gives the AWD versions adequate acceleration. Impreza has sufficient interior space for four adults. Entry/exit isn't easy to the rear because the doors are narrow at the bottom on the sedan and wagon, and the coupe has little space for squeezing into the rear. Because this car hasn't sold well, Subaru dealers should be offering big discounts.

Subaru Impreza prices are on page 429.

CONSUMER GUIDE®

SUBARU IMPREZA LX

Rating Guide	1	2	3	4	5
Performance					
Acceleration	▓▓▓▓▓▓▓▓▓▓▓ (3)				
Economy	▓▓▓▓▓▓▓▓▓▓▓ (3)				
Driveability	▓▓▓▓▓▓▓▓▓▓▓ (3)				
Ride	▓▓▓▓▓▓▓▓▓▓▓ (3)				
Steering/handling	▓▓▓▓▓▓▓▓▓▓▓▓▓▓ (4)				
Braking	▓▓▓▓▓▓▓▓▓▓▓▓▓▓▓▓▓ (5)				
Noise	▓▓▓▓▓▓▓▓▓▓▓ (3)				
Accommodations					
Driver seating	▓▓▓▓▓▓▓▓▓▓▓▓▓▓ (4)				
Instruments/controls	▓▓▓▓▓▓▓▓▓▓▓▓▓▓ (4)				
Visibility	▓▓▓▓▓▓▓▓▓▓▓▓▓▓ (4)				
Room/comfort	▓▓▓▓▓▓▓▓▓▓▓ (3)				
Entry/exit	▓▓▓▓▓▓▓▓▓▓▓ (3)				
Cargo room	▓▓▓▓▓▓▓▓▓▓▓ (3)				
Workmanship					
Exterior	▓▓▓▓▓▓▓▓▓▓▓▓▓▓ (4)				
Interior	▓▓▓▓▓▓▓▓▓▓▓ (3)				
Value	▓▓▓▓▓▓▓▓▓▓▓ (3)				

Total Points...56

Specifications

Body type ....2-door notchback
Wheelbase (in.) 99.2
Overall length (in.) 172.2
Overall width (in.) 67.1
Overall height (in.) 55.5
Curb weight (lbs.) 2840
Seating capacity...........................5
Front head room (in.) 39.2
Max. front leg room (in.) 43.1
Rear head room (in.) 36.7
Min. rear leg room (in.) 32.5
Cargo volume (cu. ft.).............11.1

Engine type ....ohc flat-4
Engine size (l/cu. in.)..........2.2/135
Horsepower @ rpm ...135 @ 5400
Torque @ rpm ....140 @ 4400
Transmission.................auto/4-sp.
Drive wheels ....all
Brakes, F/R..........disc/disc (ABS)
Tire size 195/60HR15
Fuel tank capacity (gal.) 13.2
EPA city/highway mpg 22/29
Test mileage (mpg) ....NA

Warranties The entire car is covered for 3 years/36,000 miles. Body perforation rust is covered for 5 years/unlimited miles.

Rating scale 5=Exceptional; 4=Above average; 3=Average; 2=Below average; 1=Poor

SUBARU LEGACY

Built in Lafayette, Ind.

Subaru Legacy LS wagon

COMPACT

Subaru's compact sedan and wagon have been redesigned and wear new sheetmetal wrapped around a chassis that's about two inches longer in wheelbase. Overall length has grown about two inches as well. Both body styles are offered with front-wheel drive or permanently engaged all-wheel drive (AWD). The sedan comes in base, L, LS, and LSi versions and the wagon in base, L, LS, LSi, Brighton, and Outback models. The base and L have standard front-wheel drive. All others come with AWD, which is optional on the L. Traction control is a new option for front-drive L models. All Legacys have a 2.2-liter horizontally opposed 4-cylinder engine that produces 135 horsepower. All but the LS and LSi come with a standard 5-speed manual transmission. The LS and LSi come with a 4-speed automatic, which is optional on all others except the base models. Dual air bags are standard across the board. Anti-lock brakes are standard on the LS, LSi, and Outback, and optional on the L. The new Brighton wagon is a "value-priced" AWD model, while the new Outback is two inches higher than other Legacy wagons. Legacy's 2.2-liter engine is adequate for most chores, but it throbs and feels strained in hard acceleration. The automatic transmission shifts smoothly and downshifts promptly. Legacy's suspension strikes an admirable balance between ride and handling, with ride taking precedent. A low dashboard and narrow roof pillars allow clear visibility to all directions. Space in front is ample. In back, people under 6-feet tall should have adequate room. Legacy is a competitive entry in the compact class, though its trump card remains all-wheel drive.

Subaru Legacy prices are on page 430.

SUBARU LEGACY LS

Rating Guide	1	2	3	4	5
Performance					
Acceleration	▮▮▮▮▮▮▮				
Economy	▮▮▮▮▮				
Driveability	▮▮▮▮▮▮▮				
Ride	▮▮▮▮▮▮▮				
Steering/handling	▮▮▮▮▮▮▮				
Braking	▮▮▮▮▮▮▮▮				
Noise	▮▮▮▮▮▮▮▮				
Accommodations					
Driver seating	▮▮▮▮▮▮▮▮				
Instruments/controls	▮▮▮▮▮▮▮▮				
Visibility	▮▮▮▮▮▮▮▮▮				
Room/comfort	▮▮▮▮▮▮▮▮▮				
Entry/exit	▮▮▮▮▮▮▮▮				
Cargo room	▮▮▮▮▮▮▮▮				
Workmanship					
Exterior	▮▮▮▮▮▮▮▮				
Interior	▮▮▮▮▮▮▮▮				
Value	▮▮▮▮▮▮▮▮				

Total Points...59

Specifications

Body type	5-door wagon	Engine type	ohc flat-4
Wheelbase (in.)	103.5	Engine size (l/cu. in.)	2.2/135
Overall length (in.)	183.9	Horsepower @ rpm	135 @ 5400
Overall width (in.)	67.5	Torque @ rpm	140 @ 4400
Overall height (in.)	57.1	Transmission	auto/4-sp.
Curb weight (lbs.)	3120	Drive wheels	all
Seating capacity	5	Brakes, F/R	disc/disc (ABS)
Front head room (in.)	38.1	Tire size	190/60HR15
Max. front leg room (in.)	43.3	Fuel tank capacity (gal.)	15.9
Rear head room (in.)	37.7	EPA city/highway mpg	22/28
Min. rear leg room (in.)	34.6	Test mileage (mpg)	NA
Cargo volume (cu. ft.)	73.0		

Warranties The entire car is covered for 3 years/36,000 miles. Body perforation rust is covered for 5 years/unlimited miles.

Rating scale 5=Exceptional; 4=Above average; 3=Average; 2=Below average; 1=Poor

TOYOTA AVALON

Built in Georgetown, Ky.

Toyota Avalon XL

FULL-SIZE

Built on an extended version of the compact, front-drive Camry platform, Avalon is billed as the roomiest Japanese-brand sedan ever sold in the U.S. In exterior dimensions, Avalon matches mid-size domestic cars like the Ford Taurus. The interior volume of 120.9 cubic feet, however, is full-size territory. A power split front bench seat and column-mounted transmission shift lever are optional to give Avalon 6-passenger seating. Both the base XL and upscale XLS models come with standard front bucket seats, a center console, and a floor-mounted shift lever. Most mechanical components are borrowed from the Camry. They include a 3.0-liter V-6, with 192 horsepower versus Camry's 188, an electronic 4-speed automatic transmission, and 4-wheel disc brakes with optional anti-lock control. Both models come with standard dual air bags, air conditioning, power windows, mirrors, and locks. Compared to the Camry, Avalon has more body lean on twisting roads. However, it's nearly as agile and the soft suspension provides a supple, absorbent ride. Toyota's silky 3.0-liter V-6 provides spirited acceleration but requires premium gas. It's complemented by a responsive 4-speed automatic transmission. The interior has ample room for four adults. Six can tolerate shorter trips on models with the front bench seat, but everyone will be squeezed and the front center passenger won't have much leg room. Avalon's dashboard is conveniently laid out. We also are impressed with the car's solid feel, good workmanship, and low noise levels. If you crave a larger Camry, Avalon might be just the ticket. However, a loaded XLS runs about $29,000.

Toyota Avalon prices are on page 433.

TOYOTA AVALON XL

Rating Guide	1	2	3	4	5
Performance					
Acceleration	▓▓▓▓▓▓▓▓▓▓▓▓▓▓▓▓▓				
Economy	▓▓▓▓▓▓				
Driveability	▓▓▓▓▓▓▓▓▓▓▓▓▓▓				
Ride	▓▓▓▓▓▓▓▓▓▓▓▓▓▓				
Steering/handling	▓▓▓▓▓▓▓▓▓▓▓				
Braking	▓▓▓▓▓▓▓▓▓▓▓▓▓▓▓▓▓▓				
Noise	▓▓▓▓▓▓▓▓▓▓▓▓▓				
Accommodations					
Driver seating	▓▓▓▓▓▓▓▓▓▓▓▓▓				
Instruments/controls	▓▓▓▓▓▓▓▓▓▓▓▓▓				
Visibility	▓▓▓▓▓▓▓▓▓▓▓▓▓				
Room/comfort	▓▓▓▓▓▓▓▓▓▓▓▓▓▓▓▓▓				
Entry/exit	▓▓▓▓▓▓▓▓▓▓▓▓▓				
Cargo room	▓▓▓▓▓▓▓▓▓▓▓				
Workmanship					
Exterior	▓▓▓▓▓▓▓▓▓▓▓▓▓				
Interior	▓▓▓▓▓▓▓▓▓▓▓▓▓				
Value	▓▓▓▓▓▓▓▓▓▓▓▓▓				

Total Points...**62**

Specifications

Body type	4-door notchback	Engine type	dohc V-6
Wheelbase (in.)	107.1	Engine size (l/cu. in.)	3.0/180
Overall length (in.)	190.2	Horsepower @ rpm	192 @ 5200
Overall width (in.)	70.3	Torque @ rpm	210 @ 4400
Overall height (in.)	56.1	Transmission	auto/4-sp.
Curb weight (lbs.)	3263	Drive wheels	front
Seating capacity	6	Brakes, F/R	disc/disc (ABS)
Front head room (in.)	39.1	Tire size	205/65HR15
Max. front leg room (in.)	44.1	Fuel tank capacity (gal.)	18.5
Rear head room (in.)	37.8	EPA city/highway mpg	20/28
Min. rear leg room (in.)	38.3	Test mileage (mpg)	18.2
Cargo volume (cu. ft.)	15.4		

Warranties The entire car is covered for 3 years/36,000 miles. Major powertrain components are covered for 5 years/60,000 miles. Body perforation rust is covered for 5 years/unlimited miles.

Rating scale 5=Exceptional; 4=Above average; 3=Average; 2=Below average; 1=Poor

TOYOTA CAMRY

Built in Georgetown, Ky., and Japan.

Toyota Camry XLE

COMPACT

Toyota's popular front-drive Camry gets a mild facelift, with a new grille and headlamps and minor rear appearance changes. Anti-lock brakes are now standard on the top-line XLE sedan (they remain optional elsewhere) and all Camrys now meet the government's 1997 side-impact requirements. The DX 5-door wagon has been dropped, but the rest of last year's lineup returns. That includes base DX and LE 2-door coupes and 4-door sedans, an LE wagon, a sporty SE coupe and sedan, and the XLE sedan. A 125-horsepower 4-cylinder engine is standard on all models except the SE. A 188-horsepower 3.0-liter V-6 is standard on both SE models and optional on the LE and XLE. An electronic 4-speed automatic transmission is standard on all Camrys except the DX coupe and sedan, which come with a 5-speed manual. Camry sets the standard for refinement among mid-size and compact family cars. It's quiet, refined, and has excellent assembly quality. The 4-cylinder engine is smooth, responsive, and provides adequate acceleration. The silky V-6 is perhaps the smoothest in this class, and though it makes the Camry much quicker, it also uses more gas—and requires premium. Camry has a soft, absorbent ride that soaks up most bumps and ruts easily, and it corners with confidence. Camry has more interior room than some mid-size cars, though the rear seatback is stiff and too reclined, making it uncomfortable for some people. The dashboard has a modern, convenient design, and all models have a split rear seatback that folds down for more cargo space. Camry is one of the more expensive compacts, but it should be high on your shopping list.

Toyota Camry prices are on page 434.

TOYOTA CAMRY XLE

Rating Guide	1	2	3	4	5
Performance					
Acceleration					
Economy					
Driveability					
Ride					
Steering/handling					
Braking					
Noise					
Accommodations					
Driver seating					
Instruments/controls					
Visibility					
Room/comfort					
Entry/exit					
Cargo room					
Workmanship					
Exterior					
Interior					
Value					

Total Points...63

Specifications

Body type ....4-door notchback	Engine type ....dohc I-4
Wheelbase (in.) 103.1	Engine size (l/cu. in.).........2.2/132
Overall length (in.)...............187.8	Horsepower @ rpm ...125 @ 5400
Overall width (in.) 69.7	Torque @ rpm ....145 @ 4400
Overall height (in.) 55.1	Transmission..................auto/4-sp.
Curb weight (lbs.) 2932	Drive wheels ....front
Seating capacity.........................5	Brakes, F/R..........disc/disc (ABS)
Front head room (in.) 38.4	Tire size 195/70HR14
Max. front leg room (in.) 43.5	Fuel tank capacity (gal.) 18.5
Rear head room (in.) 37.1	EPA city/highway mpg 21/28
Min. rear leg room (in.) 35.0	Test mileage (mpg) 20.9
Cargo volume (cu. ft.).............14.9	

Warranties The entire car is covered for 3 years/36,000 miles. Major powertrain components are covered for 5 years/60,000 miles. Body perforation rust is covered for 5 years/unlimited miles.

Rating scale 5=Exceptional; 4=Above average; 3=Average; 2=Below average; 1=Poor

TOYOTA CELICA

Built in Japan.

Toyota Celica GT 3-door

SPORTS COUPE

A convertible joins the Celica lineup for 1995. It has a standard power top with a glass rear window and electric defroster and power rear side windows. The Celica coupes return with no major changes. The base ST uses a 1.8-liter 4-cylinder engine with 110 horsepower. The GT coupes and the convertible use a 2.2-liter 4-cylinder with 130 horsepower. Both team with a standard 5-speed manual or optional 4-speed automatic transmission. Dual air bags are standard on all Celicas and anti-lock brakes are optional. Celica comes in two versions that aren't created equal. For instance, the 1.8-liter engine in the ST is smooth and fairly quiet except when worked hard. However, it's weak on low-end torque, so it can't pull with any gusto with the optional automatic transmission. The GT's 2.2-liter packs a pretty good punch with the automatic, but it's unpleasantly loud in hard acceleration. Regardless of model, tire noise is high. We have tested a GT hatchback for more than 10,000 miles and have experienced no problems. All models handle well. The firmer suspension included in the optional Sport Packages delivers extra cornering precision in exchange for a stiffer ride. The optional anti-lock brakes are far more worthwhile. Celica's interior is typical of small coupes, with little room in the rear seat for adults and, with the optional sunroof, marginal head room for 6-footers. The dashboard design is modern and convenient. Though the Celica GT performs well and has an impressive reliability record, it's more expensive than V-6 rivals like the Ford Probe GT and Mazda MX-6 LS.

Toyota Celica prices are on page 435.

CONSUMER GUIDE®

TOYOTA CELICA GT

Rating Guide	1	2	3	4	5
Performance					
Acceleration				�▓	
Economy			▓		
Driveability			▓		
Ride			▓		
Steering/handling			▓		
Braking					▓
Noise		▓			
Accommodations					
Driver seating				▓	
Instruments/controls				▓	
Visibility			▓		
Room/comfort		▓			
Entry/exit		▓			
Cargo room			▓		
Workmanship					
Exterior					▓
Interior				▓	
Value		▓			
Total Points					**54**

Specifications

Body type	3-door hatchback
Wheelbase (in.)	99.9
Overall length (in.)	174.0
Overall width (in.)	68.9
Overall height (in.)	50.8
Curb weight (lbs.)	2560
Seating capacity	4
Front head room (in.)	34.3
Max. front leg room (in.)	44.2
Rear head room (in.)	29.2
Min. rear leg room (in.)	26.6
Cargo volume (cu. ft.)	16.2
Engine type	dohc I-4
Engine size (l/cu. in.)	2.2/132
Horsepower @ rpm	130 @ 5400
Torque @ rpm	145 @ 4400
Transmission	auto/4-sp.
Drive wheels	front
Brakes, F/R	disc/disc (ABS)
Tire size	205/55VR15
Fuel tank capacity (gal.)	15.9
EPA city/highway mpg	23/30
Test mileage (mpg)	23.7

Warranties The entire car is covered for 3 years/36,000 miles. Major powertrain components are covered for 5 years/60,000 miles. Body perforation rust is covered for 5 years/unlimited miles.

Rating scale 5=Exceptional; 4=Above average; 3=Average; 2=Below average; 1=Poor

TOYOTA COROLLA/ GEO PRIZM

✓ BEST BUY

Built in Fremont, Calif., Canada, and Japan.

Toyota Corolla LE

SUBCOMPACT

The front-drive Toyota Corolla and similar Geo Prizm are built side-by-side and share most mechanical components. Both come with standard dual air bags. Neither sees any major changes for 1995. Corolla comes as a 4-door notchback sedan in base, DX, and LE versions, and as a wagon in DX trim. Prizm comes only as a sedan in base and LSi models. The base Corolla has a 1.6-liter 4-cylinder engine rated at 105 horsepower and 100 pounds/feet of torque. Other Corollas come with a 1.8-liter four that loses 10 horsepower this year (to 105) but gains two pounds/feet of torque (now 117). A 5-speed manual transmission is standard on the base and DX models. A 3-speed automatic is optional on the base sedan and a 4-speed automatic is optional on the DX. The 4-speed automatic is standard on the LE. The only other change for 1995 is new interior fabric for the DX 4-door notchback sedan and 5-door wagon. The 1.6-liter engine is standard on both Prizms and the 1.8-liter engine is optional on the LSi. On the Prizm, the 5-speed manual is standard with both engines. The 3-speed automatic is optional with the 1.6-liter and the 4-speed automatic is optional with the 1.8-liter. Leather upholstery is a new option for the LSi. Prizm models carry lower base prices than similar Corollas, but the Toyotas are a half-step ahead in terms of refinement because Toyota uses more sound insulation. Both are top choices in the subcompact field because they have good fuel economy, good assembly quality, and strong reputations for reliability and durability.

Toyota Corolla prices are on page 437.
Geo Prizm prices are on page 331.

TOYOTA COROLLA LE

Rating Guide	1	2	3	4	5
Performance					
Acceleration			▮		
Economy			▮		
Driveability			▮		
Ride			▮		
Steering/handling			▮		
Braking					▮
Noise			▮		
Accommodations					
Driver seating			▮		
Instruments/controls			▮		
Visibility			▮		
Room/comfort			▮		
Entry/exit			▮		
Cargo room			▮		
Workmanship					
Exterior					▮
Interior				▮	
Value			▮		

Total Points 60

Specifications

Body type	4-door notchback	Engine type	dohc I-4
Wheelbase (in.)	97.4	Engine size (l/cu. in.)	1.8/110
Overall length (in.)	172.0	Horsepower @ rpm	105 @ 5200
Overall width (in.)	66.3	Torque @ rpm	117 @ 2800
Overall height (in.)	53.5	Transmission	auto/4-sp.
Curb weight (lbs.)	2447	Drive wheels	front
Seating capacity	5	Brakes, F/R	disc/disc (ABS)
Front head room (in.)	38.8	Tire size	185/65R14
Max. front leg room (in.)	42.4	Fuel tank capacity (gal.)	13.2
Rear head room (in.)	37.1	EPA city/highway mpg	27/34
Min. rear leg room (in.)	33.0	Test mileage (mpg)	30.1
Cargo volume (cu. ft.)	12.7		

Warranties The entire car is covered for 3 years/36,000 miles. Major powertrain components are covered for 5 years/60,000 miles. Body perforation rust is covered for 5 years/unlimited miles.

Rating scale 5=Exceptional; 4=Above average; 3=Average; 2=Below average; 1=Poor

TOYOTA PREVIA

Built in Japan.

Toyota Previa LE

MINIVAN

Toyota offers a supercharged engine on the lower-priced DX model for 1995. The supercharged engine debuted last year as an option for the top-of-the-line LE model. This increases Previa offerings from six to eight, the variations being naturally aspirated or supercharged engines with either rear drive or "All-Trac" all-wheel drive in both the DX and LE price levels. All-Trac is a permanently engaged 4-wheel-drive system. All models come with dual air bags and meet all current passenger-car safety standards. Anti-lock brakes are optional across the board. The base engine is a 2.4-liter 4-cylinder with 138 horsepower. The supercharged variant produces 161. Models with the supercharged engine are badged S/C. A 4-speed automatic transmission is standard on all Previas. Models with the base engine have adequate acceleration from low speeds, but there's not enough power for quick passing. The supercharged models are more responsive off the line and feel much stronger in passing situations. Previa has a roomy interior with adequate cargo space at the rear with all seats in place. The center seat is removable and the rear seat is split so that both halves can fold outward against the sides of the vehicle. That's a clever alternative to removable seats, though it blocks the driver's view over the right shoulder when deployed for maximum cargo space. Previa is an impressive family vehicle, but it is one of the most expensive minivans. Chrysler Corporation's minivans and the Ford Windstar offer comparable safety features, just as much versatility, and stronger V-6 engines at lower prices.

Toyota Previa prices are on page 438.

TOYOTA PREVIA LE

Rating Guide	1	2	3	4	5
Performance					
Acceleration	▮▮▮▮▮▮▮				
Economy	▮▮▮▮				
Driveability	▮▮▮▮▮▮▮▮				
Ride	▮▮▮▮▮▮▮▮				
Steering/handling	▮▮▮▮▮▮▮				
Braking	▮▮▮▮▮▮▮				
Noise	▮▮▮▮▮▮▮				
Accommodations					
Driver seating	▮▮▮▮▮▮▮				
Instruments/controls	▮▮▮▮▮▮▮				
Visibility	▮▮▮▮▮▮▮				
Room/comfort	▮▮▮▮▮▮▮▮▮▮				
Entry/exit	▮▮▮▮▮▮▮▮				
Cargo room	▮▮▮▮▮▮▮▮▮▮				
Workmanship					
Exterior	▮▮▮▮▮▮▮▮				
Interior	▮▮▮▮▮▮▮▮				
Value	▮▮▮▮▮▮▮				

Total Points..57

Specifications

Body type	4-door van	Engine type	dohc I-4
Wheelbase (in.)	112.8	Engine size (l/cu. in.)	2.4/149
Overall length (in.)	187.0	Horsepower @ rpm	138 @ 5000
Overall width (in.)	70.8	Torque @ rpm	154 @ 4000
Overall height (in.)	68.7	Transmission	auto/4-sp.
Curb weight (lbs.)	3580	Drive wheels	rear
Seating capacity	7	Brakes, F/R	disc/disc
Front head room (in.)	39.4	Tire size	215/65R15
Max. front leg room (in.)	40.1	Fuel tank capacity (gal.)	19.8
Rear head room (in.)	38.5	EPA city/highway mpg	17/22
Min. rear leg room (in.)	36.6	Test mileage (mpg)	18.5
Cargo volume (cu. ft.)	157.8		

Warranties The entire vehicle is covered for 3 years/36,000 miles. Major powertrain components are covered for 5 years/60,000 miles. Body perforation rust is covered for 5 years/unlimited miles.

Rating scale 5=Exceptional; 4=Above average; 3=Average; 2=Below average; 1=Poor

TOYOTA TERCEL

Built in Japan.

Toyota Tercel DX 2-door

SUBCOMPACT

It's touted as "all-new" by Toyota, but the 1995 Tercel rides the same 93.7-inch wheelbase as last year and is the same size and weight. The front-drive Tercel is sold in three notchback sedan models—a Standard 2-door and better-equipped DX 2-door and 4-door. Dual air bags are now standard, both front seats have new height-adjustable manual seatbelts, and all models meet the more stringent 1997 side-impact standards. Anti-lock brakes are again optional on all models. Under the hood, Tercel exchanges a 1.5-liter 4-cylinder with a single overhead camshaft and 82 horsepower for a more potent dual-camshaft version with 93 horsepower. The Standard 2-door comes with a 4-speed manual transmission and for the first time is available with an optional 3-speed automatic. The DX models have a standard 5-speed manual and an optional 4-speed automatic. The new engine is little if any quieter than last year's, but its greater power shows up in quicker acceleration with the automatic transmissions. Acceleration is still far from lively even with a manual transmission. The suspension allows a lot of bouncing on wavy roads and the ride becomes choppy on rough surfaces. In addition, there's still lots of road noise. Handling ability is hampered by narrow tires that run out of grip early in hard cornering. Since interior dimensions are unchanged, the rear seat remains tight for anyone over 5-foot-10. The new dashboard is functional and looks more "uptown" than the previous design. The new Tercel doesn't match class leaders like the Toyota Corolla and Geo Prizm, but it's a well-made subcompact that should be thrifty and reliable.

Toyota Tercel prices are on page 440.

TOYOTA TERCEL DX

Rating Guide	1	2	3	4	5
Performance					
Acceleration	▮▮▮▮▮▮▮		(≈3)		
Economy	▮▮▮▮▮▮▮			(≈4)	
Driveability	▮▮▮▮▮▮▮			(≈4)	
Ride	▮▮▮▮▮▮▮		(≈3.5)		
Steering/handling	▮▮▮▮▮▮▮		(≈3.5)		
Braking	▮▮▮▮▮▮▮		(≈3.5)		
Noise	▮▮▮▮▮	(≈2.5)			
Accommodations					
Driver seating	▮▮▮▮▮▮▮		(≈3.5)		
Instruments/controls	▮▮▮▮▮▮▮			(≈4)	
Visibility	▮▮▮▮▮▮▮▮				(≈5)
Room/comfort	▮▮▮▮▮▮▮		(≈3.5)		
Entry/exit	▮▮▮▮▮▮▮		(≈3.5)		
Cargo room	▮▮▮▮▮▮		(≈3)		
Workmanship					
Exterior	▮▮▮▮▮▮▮			(≈4)	
Interior	▮▮▮▮▮▮▮			(≈4)	
Value	▮▮▮▮▮▮▮		(≈3.5)		
Total Points					**55**

Specifications

Body type	2-door notchback	Engine type	dohc I-4
Wheelbase (in.)	93.7	Engine size (l/cu. in.)	1.5/89
Overall length (in.)	161.8	Horsepower @ rpm	93 @ 5400
Overall width (in.)	64.8	Torque @ rpm	100 @ 4400
Overall height (in.)	53.2	Transmission	auto/4-sp.
Curb weight (lbs.)	2025	Drive wheels	front
Seating capacity	5	Brakes, F/R	disc/drum
Front head room (in.)	38.6	Tire size	155/80SR13
Max. front leg room (in.)	41.2	Fuel tank capacity (gal.)	11.9
Rear head room (in.)	36.5	EPA city/highway mpg	30/39
Min. rear leg room (in.)	31.9	Test mileage (mpg)	29.9
Cargo volume (cu. ft.)	9.3		

Warranties The entire car is covered for 3 years/36,000 miles. Major powertrain components are covered for 5 years/60,000 miles. Body perforation rust is covered for 5 years/unlimited miles.

Rating scale 5=Exceptional; 4=Above average; 3=Average; 2=Below average; 1=Poor

TOYOTA 4RUNNER

Built in Japan.

Toyota 4Runner 4WD

SPORT-UTILITY VEHICLE

The 4Runner gets only minor changes for 1995. Last year, 4Runner gained a center high-mounted stoplamp, side-guard door beams, CFC-free air conditioning and, on V-6 models, optional 4-wheel anti-lock brakes. It comes only as a 5-door wagon with a drop-down tailgate and power rear window. The lineup again consists of a V-6 rear-drive model and 4-cylinder and V-6 versions with 4-wheel drive. The 4-cylinder is a 2.4-liter with 116 horsepower and the V-6 is a 3.0-liter with 150 horsepower. The 4-cylinder teams exclusively with a 5-speed manual transmission, while the V-6 2WD model comes only with a 4-speed electronic automatic. The 4WD V-6 is available with either transmission. Toyota's 4WDemand is standard on the 4x4s. It's a part-time setup (for use only on slick surfaces) that permits "shift-on-the-fly" between 2WD and 4WD High at speeds up to 50 mph. Rear anti-lock brakes are standard on V-6 models and optional on the 4-cylinder 4x4. A 4-wheel anti-lock system is optional on V-6 models. An air bag isn't available. The 4Runner's chief attractions are tight, thorough assembly quality and a commendable reputation for reliability. However, 4Runner is much smaller inside than domestic sport-utilities, with barely adequate space for four. Entry/exit is hurt by a higher than usual stance. Fuel economy is mediocre at best, and acceleration is nothing special either. We prefer the Ford Explorer, Jeep Grand Cherokee, and Chevrolet Blazer/GMC Jimmy, which have more room, full-time 4WD, a driver-side air bag (dual air bags on the Explorer), and better all-around performance for less money.

Toyota 4Runner prices are on page 441.

TOYOTA 4RUNNER

Rating Guide	1	2	3	4	5
Performance					
Acceleration	▮▮▮				
Economy	▮				
Driveability	▮▮▮				
Ride	▮▮▮				
Steering/handling	▮▮▮				
Braking	▮▮▮				
Noise	▮▮				
Accommodations					
Driver seating	▮▮▮				
Instruments/controls	▮▮▮				
Visibility	▮▮▮				
Room/comfort	▮▮▮				
Entry/exit	▮▮				
Cargo room	▮▮▮▮▮				
Workmanship					
Exterior	▮▮▮				
Interior	▮▮▮				
Value	▮▮▮				

Total Points...53

Specifications

Body type	5-door wagon	Engine type	ohc V-6
Wheelbase (in.)	103.3	Engine size (l/cu. in.)	3.0/180
Overall length (in.)	176.0	Horsepower @ rpm	150 @ 4800
Overall width (in.)	66.5	Torque @ rpm	180 @ 3400
Overall height (in.)	67.3	Transmission	auto/4-sp.
Curb weight (lbs.)	4105	Drive wheels	rear/all
Seating capacity	5	Brakes, F/R	disc/drum (ABS)
Front head room (in.)	38.7	Tire size	31x10.5R15
Max. front leg room (in.)	41.5	Fuel tank capacity (gal.)	17.2
Rear head room (in.)	38.3	EPA city/highway mpg	14/16
Min. rear leg room (in.)	31.6	Test mileage (mpg)	13.8
Cargo volume (cu. ft.)	78.3		

Warranties The entire vehicle is covered for 3 years/36,000 miles. Major powertrain components are covered for 5 years/60,000 miles. Body perforation rust is covered for 5 years/unlimited miles.

Rating scale 5=Exceptional; 4=Above average; 3=Average; 2=Below average; 1=Poor

VOLKSWAGEN CABRIO

Built in Germany.

Volkswagen Cabrio

SPORTS COUPE

The 1995 Cabrio, which debuted early in 1994, is based on the new front-drive Golf/Jetta III and is larger inside and outside than the old Cabriolet it replaces. Cabrio comes with standard dual air bags, anti-lock brakes, a manual convertible top, power windows and locks, cruise control, a cassette player, and other amenities. Among the few options are leather upholstery, air conditioning, alloy wheels, and a trunk-mounted CD changer. The only engine is a 115-horsepower 2.0-liter 4-cylinder. A 5-speed manual transmission is standard and a 4-speed automatic is optional. Cabrio has a fixed roll bar over the interior that adds structural rigidity and provides mounting points for the height-adjustable manual front seatbelts. The rear seat has two belts, making this car a 4-seater. Cabrio has adequate get-up-and-go from a stop and reasonable highway passing power with either transmission. Road noise is moderate and with the top up, wind noise is surprisingly low for a convertible. The body feels more solid than most convertibles. The ride is firm but absorbent enough to soak up most bumps, and the Cabrio has sprightly handling and firm, precise steering. The front seats are firm and supportive, but aren't wide enough to be comfortable for larger people. Rear-seat room is adequate for two. Cabrio's top folds flatter than before, so it doesn't interfere as much with rear visibility. However, with the top raised, there are large blind spots at both rear corners. Trunk capacity is meager, and though the folding rear seat expands the cargo area, it isn't easy to load bulky items because the trunk opening is small.

Volkswagen Cabrio prices are on page 443.

VOLKSWAGEN CABRIO

Rating Guide	1	2	3	4	5
Performance					
Acceleration	▓▓▓▓▓▓▓▓▓				
Economy	▓▓▓▓▓▓▓				
Driveability	▓▓▓▓▓▓▓▓▓▓				
Ride	▓▓▓▓▓▓▓▓				
Steering/handling	▓▓▓▓▓▓▓▓				
Braking	▓▓▓▓▓▓▓▓▓▓▓				
Noise	▓▓▓▓▓▓				
Accommodations					
Driver seating	▓▓▓▓▓▓▓▓				
Instruments/controls	▓▓▓▓▓▓▓▓				
Visibility	▓▓▓▓▓▓▓▓				
Room/comfort	▓▓▓▓▓▓▓				
Entry/exit	▓▓▓▓▓▓▓				
Cargo room	▓▓▓▓▓▓				
Workmanship					
Exterior	▓▓▓▓▓▓▓▓				
Interior	▓▓▓▓▓▓▓▓				
Value	▓▓▓▓▓▓▓				
Total Points					**54**

Specifications

Body type	2-door convertible	Engine type	dohc I-4
Wheelbase (in.)	97.2	Engine size (l/cu. in.)	2.0/121
Overall length (in.)	160.4	Horsepower @ rpm	115 @ 5400
Overall width (in.)	66.7	Torque @ rpm	122 @ 3200
Overall height (in.)	56.0	Transmission	manual/5-sp.
Curb weight (lbs.)	2701	Drive wheels	front
Seating capacity	4	Brakes, F/R	disc/drum (ABS)
Front head room (in.)	38.7	Tire size	195/60HR14
Max. front leg room (in.)	42.3	Fuel tank capacity (gal.)	14.5
Rear head room (in.)	36.6	EPA city/highway mpg	24/31
Min. rear leg room (in.)	31.1	Test mileage (mpg)	20.8
Cargo volume (cu. ft.)	7.8		

Warranties The entire car is covered for 2 years/24,000 miles. Major powertrain components are covered for 10 years/100,000 miles. Body perforation rust is covered for 6 years/unlimited miles.

Rating scale 5=Exceptional; 4=Above average; 3=Average; 2=Below average; 1=Poor

VOLKSWAGEN GOLF/JETTA −

Built in Mexico.

Volkswagen Jetta GL

SUBCOMPACT

The front-drive Golf hatchback and Jetta sedan received standard dual air bags during the 1994 model year. For 1995, all Golfs and Jettas get height adjustable manual front seatbelts with emergency tensioners, side-impact beams that meet 1997 federal standards, and daytime running lights. Golf comes as a 3-door hatchback in Sport and new GTI price levels and as a 5-door hatchback in base and GL price levels. Jetta comes in base, GL, GLS, and GLX versions. Standard engine in the Golf Sport and all Jettas except the GLX is a 115-horsepower 2.0-liter 4-cylinder. The GTI and GLX come with Volkswagen's 172-horsepower 2.8-liter V-6. Both engines team with a standard 5-speed manual transmission or optional 4-speed automatic. Anti-lock brakes are standard on the GTI and GLX and optional on the Jetta GL and GLS and Golf Sport. The 2.0-liter engine delivers adequate acceleration from a standing start and surprisingly strong passing power with the 4-speed automatic, though the transmission often shifts harshly. Acceleration is better with the 5-speed. We've driven the V-6 GTI and GLX models briefly and were impressed with their stronger acceleration. Golf and Jetta have sporty handling and no longer suffer from constant bumping and thumping from the suspension and tires, which was the case with the previous generation. Road and exhaust noise are still prominent at highway speeds. Front-seat room is ample and rear leg room is adequate. Both body styles have ample cargo space and the Jetta's trunk is huge for the car's exterior size. Golf and Jetta are conservatively styled but fun to drive, and they are worthwhile alternatives to Japanese and domestic subcompacts.

Volkswagen Golf/Jetta prices are on page 443.

VOLKSWAGEN JETTA GL

Rating Guide	1	2	3	4	5
Performance					
Acceleration					
Economy					
Driveability					
Ride					
Steering/handling					
Braking					
Noise					
Accommodations					
Driver seating					
Instruments/controls					
Visibility					
Room/comfort					
Entry/exit					
Cargo room					
Workmanship					
Exterior					
Interior					
Value					

Total Points..**57**

Specifications

Body type	4-door notchback	Engine type	ohc I-4
Wheelbase (in.)	97.4	Engine size (l/cu. in.)	2.0/121
Overall length (in.)	173.4	Horsepower @ rpm	115 @ 5400
Overall width (in.)	66.7	Torque @ rpm	122 @ 3200
Overall height (in.)	56.2	Transmission	auto/4-sp.
Curb weight (lbs.)	2735	Drive wheels	front
Seating capacity	5	Brakes, F/R	disc/drum (ABS)
Front head room (in.)	39.2	Tire size	195/60R14
Max. front leg room (in.)	42.3	Fuel tank capacity (gal.)	14.5
Rear head room (in.)	37.3	EPA city/highway mpg	23/29
Min. rear leg room (in.)	31.6	Test mileage (mpg)	22.7
Cargo volume (cu. ft.)	15.0		

Warranties The entire car is covered for 2 years/24,000 miles. Major powertrain components are covered for 10 years/100,000 miles. Body perforation rust is covered for 6 years/unlimited miles.

Rating scale 5=Exceptional; 4=Above average; 3=Average; 2=Below average; 1=Poor

VOLKSWAGEN PASSAT

Built in Germany.

Volkswagen Passat GLX 4-door

COMPACT

Volkswagen has extensively revamped its front-drive compact for 1995. Though it is little changed mechanically, the new Passat gets revised sheetmetal along with dual air bags, manual 3-point seatbelts with emergency tensioners, and side-impact beams that meet 1997 federal standards. A redesigned interior has a new dashboard, cup holders, and a dust and pollen filter for the climate control system. A 4-door sedan and 5-door wagon are offered only in a GLX trim level. Both are powered by Volkswagen's 172-horsepower narrow-angle 2.8-liter V-6 that uses a single cylinder head for both banks. It comes standard with a 5-speed manual transmission; an electronic 4-speed automatic is optional. Other standard equipment includes anti-lock 4-wheel disc brakes, traction control, power steering, 8-speaker stereo, power windows and locks, and a theft alarm. The only major options are the automatic transmission, power glass sunroof, leather upholstery, and a trunk-mounted CD changer. Passat's V-6 delivers more than adequate power over a broad range of speeds. The 5-speed's clutch and shifter work smoothly, while the 4-speed automatic provides smooth, timely shifts. Volkswagen has softened Passat's suspension and ride quality has improved, but it still provides sporty handling. Controls for the radio and climate system are easy to see and reach, though the heater and defroster still can't be operated simultaneously. The interior is exceptionally roomy, especially in back, and there's ample cargo room in both body styles. Passat's price is around $2000 less than last year, making it a roomy, sporty, well-equipped car that offers good value.

Volkswagen Passat prices are on page 445.

CONSUMER GUIDE®

VOLKSWAGEN PASSAT (Preliminary)

Rating Guide	1	2	3	4	5
Performance					
Acceleration	▮▮▮▮▮▮▮▮▮▮▮▮▮▮▮ (≈4)				
Economy	▮▮▮▮▮▮▮▮ (≈2.5)				
Driveability	▮▮▮▮▮▮▮▮▮▮▮▮▮ (≈4)				
Ride	▮▮▮▮▮▮▮▮▮▮▮▮▮ (≈4)				
Steering/handling	▮▮▮▮▮▮▮▮▮▮▮▮▮ (≈4)				
Braking	▮▮▮▮▮▮▮▮▮▮▮▮▮▮▮▮ (≈5)				
Noise	▮▮▮▮▮▮▮▮▮▮ (≈3)				
Accommodations					
Driver seating	▮▮▮▮▮▮▮▮▮▮▮▮▮ (≈4)				
Instruments/controls	▮▮▮▮▮▮▮▮▮▮▮▮ (≈4)				
Visibility	▮▮▮▮▮▮▮▮▮▮ (≈3)				
Room/comfort	▮▮▮▮▮▮▮▮▮▮▮▮ (≈4)				
Entry/exit	▮▮▮▮▮▮▮▮▮▮▮▮ (≈4)				
Cargo room	▮▮▮▮▮▮▮▮▮▮▮▮ (≈4)				
Workmanship					
Exterior	▮▮▮▮▮▮▮▮▮▮▮▮ (≈4)				
Interior	▮▮▮▮▮▮▮▮▮▮▮▮ (≈4)				
Value	▮▮▮▮▮▮▮▮▮▮▮▮ (≈4)				

Total Points...61

Specifications

Body type	4-door notchback	Engine type	ohc V-6
Wheelbase (in.)	103.3	Engine size (l/cu. in.)	2.8/170
Overall length (in.)	180.0	Horsepower @ rpm	172 @ 5800
Overall width (in.)	67.5	Torque @ rpm	177 @ 4200
Overall height (in.)	56.4	Transmission	auto/4-sp.
Curb weight (lbs.)	3140	Drive wheels	front
Seating capacity	5	Brakes, F/R	disc/disc (ABS)
Front head room (in.)	39.3	Tire size	215/50HR15
Max. front leg room (in.)	41.5	Fuel tank capacity (gal.)	18.5
Rear head room (in.)	36.6	EPA city/highway mpg	18/25
Min. rear leg room (in.)	37.0	Test mileage (mpg)	NA
Cargo volume (cu. ft.)	14.4		

Warranties The entire car is covered for 2 years/24,000 miles. Major powertrain components are covered for 10 years/100,000 miles. Body perforation rust is covered for 6 years/unlimited miles.

Rating scale 5=Exceptional; 4=Above average; 3=Average; 2=Below average; 1=Poor

VOLVO 850

Built in Belgium.

Volvo 850 Turbo wagon

PREMIUM SEDAN

Volvo's front-drive 850 is the first car to offer side air bags as a supplement to front air bags. The side bags, which deploy in a lateral impact, are standard on this year's 850 Turbo sedan and wagon and a $500 option on non-turbo models. All models also come with dual front air bags and anti-lock brakes. The sedan and wagon come in base, GLT, and Turbo versions. Base models are simply badged as 850s and are equipped like last year's "Level I" cars. The GLT name has been revived to replace "Level II" on the upscale versions. All 850s have a 5-cylinder engine. Base and GLT models have a 2.4-liter with 168 horsepower. This engine comes with a standard 5-speed manual or optional 4-speed automatic. The Turbo has a 2.3-liter engine with 222 horsepower and comes only with the automatic. Traction control is optional on all models. The suspension on the non-turbo models provides a stable highway ride with little bouncing and is absorbent enough to soak up most bumps without breaking stride. Turbo versions, however, are too stiff, resulting in constant bumping and thumping. While the base engine doesn't have enough low-speed torque to accelerate quickly from a stop, the turbo engine makes the 850 a rocket. The automatic transmission is slow to downshift for passing and sometimes shifts with a jolt in hard acceleration. Inside, there's plenty of head and leg room for four adults, but a middle passenger in back will be squeezed. The wagon can be equipped with a rear-facing third seat that gives it 7-passenger capacity. The 850 has an impressive array of safety features and has more going for it than some similarly priced rivals.

Volvo 850 prices are on page 446.

VOLVO 850 TURBO

Rating Guide	1	2	3	4	5
Performance					
Acceleration	▮▮▮▮▮▮▮▮▮				
Economy	▮▮▮▮				
Driveability	▮▮▮▮▮▮▮				
Ride	▮▮▮▮▮▮▮				
Steering/handling	▮▮▮▮▮▮▮▮				
Braking	▮▮▮▮▮▮▮▮▮▮				
Noise	▮▮▮▮▮▮▮				
Accommodations					
Driver seating	▮▮▮▮▮▮▮▮				
Instruments/controls	▮▮▮▮▮▮▮▮				
Visibility	▮▮▮▮▮▮▮▮				
Room/comfort	▮▮▮▮▮▮▮▮				
Entry/exit	▮▮▮▮▮▮▮▮				
Cargo room	▮▮▮▮▮▮▮▮				
Workmanship					
Exterior	▮▮▮▮▮▮▮▮				
Interior	▮▮▮▮▮▮▮▮				
Value	▮▮▮▮▮▮				

Total Points...60

Specifications

Body type	5-door wagon	Engine type	Turbo dohc I-5
Wheelbase (in.)	104.9	Engine size (l/cu. in.)	2.3/141
Overall length (in.)	185.4	Horsepower @ rpm	222 @ 5200
Overall width (in.)	69.3	Torque @ rpm	221 @ 2100
Overall height (in.)	56.9	Transmission	auto/4-sp.
Curb weight (lbs.)	3342	Drive wheels	front
Seating capacity	7	Brakes, F/R	disc/disc (ABS)
Front head room (in.)	39.1	Tire size	205/50ZR16
Max. front leg room (in.)	41.4	Fuel tank capacity (gal.)	19.3
Rear head room (in.)	37.8	EPA city/highway mpg	19/26
Min. rear leg room (in.)	35.3	Test mileage (mpg)	21.7
Cargo volume (cu. ft.)	67.0		

Warranties The entire car is covered for 4 years/50,000 miles. Body perforation rust is covered for 5 years/unlimited miles.

Rating scale 5=Exceptional; 4=Above average; 3=Average; 2=Below average; 1=Poor

VOLVO 940/960

Built in Sweden and Canada.

Volvo 960

PREMIUM SEDAN

The 6-cylinder 960 sedan and wagon have been updated as this
year's main news among the rear-drive Volvos. The 2.3-liter 4-
cylinder 940s are basically unchanged except for daytime running
lights, which also appear on the 960. Volvo has scrapped its con-
fusing "Level I" and "Level II" labels for simple 940, 960, and 940
Turbo nomenclature. All 900s have standard anti-lock brakes and
dual air bags and come only with a 4-speed automatic transmission. An integrated child-booster seat is standard on both the 940
and 960 wagons. The 960 retains a 2.9-liter inline 6-cylinder
engine, but it loses 20 horsepower this year, to 181. Styling
changes include a slimmer grille and headlamps and rounded corners. Inside are a more contoured dashboard, cup holders, new
door panels, and wood accents. The base 940 has a 2.3-liter 4-
cylinder with 114 horsepower, while the Turbo version produces
162 horsepower. The 940s are solid but stolid near-luxury cars with
ample passenger and cargo room. There's too little power in the
base 940 for a car of this size and weight, so acceleration is pokey,
and road and wind noise are on the high side. The 940 Turbo has
much stronger performance and more standard features, but
there's also "turbo lag" before power arrives in a rush and occa-
sional jerky shifts from the automatic transmission. The revamped
960 sedan handles better this year, but its harsher ride makes the
wagon a clear choice for comfort seekers. The best news may be
that Volvo hasn't raised the 960 sedan's prices and has cut the 960
wagon's by $4050, despite adding several standard features.

Volvo 940/960 prices are on page 447.

CONSUMER GUIDE®

VOLVO 960 (Preliminary)

Rating Guide	1	2	3	4	5
Performance					
Acceleration	▮▮▮▮▮▮▮▮			▮	
Economy	▮▮▮▮	▮			
Driveability	▮▮▮▮▮▮▮▮			▮	
Ride	▮▮▮▮▮▮		▮		
Steering/handling	▮▮▮▮▮▮		▮		
Braking	▮▮▮▮▮▮▮▮▮▮				▮
Noise	▮▮▮▮▮▮▮		▮		
Accommodations					
Driver seating	▮▮▮▮▮▮▮▮			▮	
Instruments/controls	▮▮▮▮▮▮▮▮			▮	
Visibility	▮▮▮▮▮▮▮▮			▮	
Room/comfort	▮▮▮▮▮▮▮▮			▮	
Entry/exit	▮▮▮▮▮▮▮▮			▮	
Cargo room	▮▮▮▮▮▮▮▮			▮	
Workmanship					
Exterior	▮▮▮▮▮▮▮▮			▮	
Interior	▮▮▮▮▮▮▮▮			▮	
Value	▮▮▮▮▮▮		▮		

Total Points...60

Specifications

Body type	4-door notchback	Engine type	dohc I-6
Wheelbase (in.)	109.1	Engine size (l/cu. in.)	2.9/178
Overall length (in.)	191.8	Horsepower @ rpm	181 @ 5200
Overall width (in.)	68.9	Torque @ rpm	199 @ 4100
Overall height (in.)	55.5	Transmission	auto/4-sp.
Curb weight (lbs.)	3205	Drive wheels	rear
Seating capacity	5	Brakes, F/R	disc/disc (ABS)
Front head room (in.)	38.6	Tire size	205/55VR16
Max. front leg room (in.)	41.0	Fuel tank capacity (gal.)	19.8
Rear head room (in.)	37.1	EPA city/highway mpg	17/25
Min. rear leg room (in.)	34.7	Test mileage (mpg)	NA
Cargo volume (cu. ft.)	16.6		

Warranties The entire car is covered for 4 years/50,000 miles. Body perforation rust is covered for 5 years/unlimited miles.

Rating scale 5=Exceptional; 4=Above average; 3=Average; 2=Below average; 1=Poor

PRICES

ACURA

Acura Integra	Retail Price	Dealer Invoice	Fair Price
RS 3-door hatchback, 5-speed	$15460	$13272	$14072
RS 3-door hatchback, automatic	16210	13916	14716
LS 3-door hatchback, 5-speed	18140	15573	16373
LS 3-door hatchback, automatic	18890	16217	17017
LS Special Edition 3-door hatchback, 5-speed ..	19890	17076	17876
LS Special Edition 3-door hatchback, automatic	20640	17719	18519
GS-R 3-door hatchback, 5-speed	20350	17470	18270
GS-R 3-door hatchback w/leather, 5-speed	21150	18157	18957
RS 4-door notchback, 5-speed	16220	13925	14725
RS 4-door notchback, automatic	16970	14569	15369
LS 4-door notchback, 5-speed	18940	16260	17060
LS 4-door notchback, automatic	19690	16904	17704
LS Special Edition 4-door notchback, 5-speed ..	20440	17548	18348
LS Special Edition 4-door notchback, automatic	21190	18192	18992
GS-R 4-door notchback, 5-speed	20680	17754	18554
GS-R 4-door notchback w/leather, 5-speed	21480	18441	19241
Destination charge	420	420	420

Standard Equipment:

RS: 1.8-liter DOHC 4-cylinder engine, 5-speed manual or 4-speed automatic transmission, 4-wheel disc brakes, driver- and passenger-side air bags, variable-assist power steering, cloth reclining front bucket seats with driver-side lumbar support adjustment, center console with armrest, 50/50 split folding rear seat (hatchback), one-piece folding rear seat (notchback), power windows and mirrors, power door locks (notchback), AM/FM/cassette player with four speakers, power antenna, tinted glass, remote fuel door and decklid/hatch releases, fog lamps, rear defogger, rear wiper/washer (hatchback), tachometer, coolant temperature gauge, tilt steering column, intermittent wipers, door pockets, cargo cover (hatchback), 195/60HR14 tires, wheel covers. **LS** adds: anti-lock brakes, air conditioning, power door locks (hatchback), power moonroof, cruise control, map lights (hatchback), Michelin 195/60HR14 all-season tires. **LS Special Edition** adds: leather upholstery, rear spoiler (hatchback), wood-pattern console trim (notchback), color-keyed bodyside moldings, Michelin 195/55VR15 tires, alloy wheels. **GS-R** adds to LS: 1.8-liter DOHC VTEC engine, rear spoiler (hatchback), AM/FM/cassette with six speakers, map lights (notchback), Michelin 195/55VR15 all-season tires, alloy wheels.

Options are available as dealer-installed accessories.

Acura Legend	Retail Price	Dealer Invoice	Fair Price
L 4-door notchback, 5-speed	$35500	$29760	$31260
L 4-door notchback, automatic	36300	30430	31930
L 4-door w/leather interior, 5-speed	37000	31017	32517
L 4-door w/leather interior, automatic	37800	31688	33188
LS 4-door notchback, automatic	39700	33281	34781
GS 4-door notchback, 6-speed	42000	35209	36709
GS 4-door notchback, automatic	42000	35209	36709
L 2-door coupe, 6-speed	39400	33029	34529
L 2-door coupe, automatic	39400	33029	34529
LS 2-door coupe, 6-speed	43200	36215	37715
LS 2-door coupe, automatic	43200	36215	37715
Destination charge	420	420	420

Standard Equipment:

L: 3.2-liter V-6, 5-speed manual or 4-speed automatic transmission, anti-lock 4-wheel disc brakes, driver- and passenger-side air bags, variable-assist power steering, air conditioning, front bucket seats, 8-way power driver's seat, 4-way power passenger seat, power windows and locks, cruise control, power tilt/telescopic steering column, steering wheel memory system, power moonroof with sunshade, tinted glass, heated power mirrors, Acura/Bose music system, steering wheel-mounted radio controls, theft-deterrent system, intermittent wipers, bodyside moldings, rear defogger, remote fuel door and decklid releases, lighted visor mirrors, front door pockets, center console with armrest, digital clock, 205/60VR15 tires, alloy wheels. **L Coupe** adds: 6-speed manual transmission, leather upholstery, leather-wrapped steering wheel, rear headrests. **LS** adds: leather upholstery and leather-wrapped steering wheel (sedan), walnut interior trim, heated front seats, automatic climate control, AM/FM cassette with diversity antenna and anti-theft feature, illuminated entry system. **LS Coupe** adds; traction control, 215/55VR16 tires. **GS** adds to LS sedan: 6-speed manual or 4-speed automatic transmission, traction control, sport suspension, body-color grille, 215/55VR16 tires.

Options are available as dealer-installed accessories.

AUDI

Audi A6/S6

	Retail Price	Dealer Invoice	Fair Price
A6 4-door notchback	$30600	$26867	—
A6 5-door wagon	33170	29170	—
S6 4-door notchback	45270	39630	—
Destination charge	445	445	445

Fair price not available at time of publication.

Standard Equipment:

A6: 2.8-liter V-6 engine, 5-speed manual transmission, anti-lock 4-wheel disc brakes, driver- and passenger-side air bags, automatic climate control, speed-sensitive power steering, tilt and telescoping steering column, engine oil cooler, velour reclining front bucket seats with height and lumbar adjustments, 8-way power driver's seat, front folding storage armrest, rear folding armrest with ski sack, center storage console with cup holders, exterior temperature gauge, tachometer, oil temperature and pressure gauges, coolant temperature gauge, trip odometer, Active Auto Check System, power windows and door locks, cruise control, heated power mirrors, power sunroof, remote fuel door and decklid releases, AM/FM/cassette with diversity antenna, seatback pockets, leather-wrapped steering wheel, leather-wrapped manual shift knob, reading lamps, lighted visor mirrors, anti-theft alarm, tinted glass, rear defogger, intermittent wipers, analog clock, front and rear fog lights, floormats, burled walnut trim, color-keyed bumpers and bodyside moldings, 195/65HR15 all-season tires, alloy wheels. **Wagon** deletes diversity antenna and remote decklid release, and adds: 4-speed automatic transmission, transmission oil cooler, 60/40 split folding seat, 2-place rear child seat, roof-mounted antenna, rear wiper/washer, retractable rear window sunshade, roof rails, cargo area cover. **S6** adds to A6 sedan: 2.2-liter turbocharged 5-cylinder engine, Quattro permanent all-wheel drive, voice-activated cellular telephone, voltmeter, leather upholstery, heated front and rear seats, power passenger's seat, 4-way memory driver's seat, Audi/Bose audio system, remote keyless entry, power glass moonroof, heated windshield washer nozzles, headlight washers, fender flares, 225/50ZR16 tires.

Optional Equipment:

4-speed automatic transmission, A6 notchback	900	850	—
Quattro all-wheel drive system, A6	1500	1500	1500
Comfort and Convenience Pkg., A6	1000	870	—

Power front passenger's seat, memory driver's seat, remote keyless entry, power glass moonroof.

	Retail Price	Dealer Invoice	Fair Price
All-Weather Pkg., A6	$490	$426	—
Heated front seats, windshield washer nozzles, and front door locks, headlight washers.			
Leather seats, A6	1460	1270	—
Cellular telephone, A6	990	861	—
10-disc CD changer	790	687	—
Requires Audi/Bose audio system.			
Audi/Bose audio system, A6	620	539	—
Pearlescent metallic paint	530	461	—
215/60VR15 all-season tires, S6	NC	NC	NC

Audi 90/Cabriolet

	Retail Price	Dealer Invoice	Fair Price
90 4-door notchback	$25670	$22578	—
Sport90 4-door notchback	26070	22926	—
Cabriolet 2-door convertible	35900	31545	—
Destination charge	445	445	445

Fair price not available at time of publication.

Standard Equipment:

90: 2.8-liter V-6 engine, 5-speed manual transmission, driver- and passenger-side air bags, anti-lock 4-wheel disc brakes, engine oil cooler, air conditioning, power steering, leather-wrapped steering wheel, AM/FM/cassette, dual diversity antenna, velour reclining front seats with height adjustment, 60/40 split folding rear seat, front and rear fold-down armrests, power windows and door locks, cruise control, tinted glass, headlight washers, alarm system, front and rear fog lights, rear defogger, digital clock, center console, remote decklid and fuel door releases, heated power mirrors, exterior temperature gauge, front seatback map pockets, intermittent wipers, tachometer, coolant temperature gauge, trip odometer, reading lights, lighted visor mirrors, burled walnut trim, floormats, fender flares, 195/65HR15 all-season tires, alloy wheels. **Sport90** deletes front seatback map pockets and adds: sport suspension, cloth sport seats, voltmeter, oil temperature and pressure gauges, leather-wrapped manual shift knob. **Cabriolet** adds to 90: 4-speed automatic transmission, transmission oil cooler, leather upholstery, leather shift knob, color-keyed bodyside moldings, expandable ski/storage sack, power antenna, power top and boot system.

Optional Equipment:

4-speed automatic transmission, 90, Sport90 ..	900	850	—
NA with Quattro all-wheel drive system.			
Quattro all-wheel drive system, 90, Sport90	1500	1500	1500
NA with 4-speed automatic transmission.			

	Retail Price	Dealer Invoice	Fair Price
Comfort and Convenience Pkg., 90, Sport90	$1780	$1549	—

Automatic climate control, power sunroof, 8-way power driver's seats, remote keyless entry. Sport90 requires Quattro all-wheel drive system.

	Retail Price	Dealer Invoice	Fair Price
All-Weather Package	440	383	—
90, Sport90 with Comfort and Convenience Pkg.	340	296	—

Includes heated front door locks (NA with Comfort and Convenience Pkg.), heated front seats, heated windshield washer nozzles. Sport90 with Comfort and Convenience Pkg. requires Quattro all-wheel drive system.

	Retail Price	Dealer Invoice	Fair Price
Leather upholstery, 90, Sport90	1240	1079	—

Sport90 requires Quattro all-wheel drive system and Comfort and Convenience Pkg.

	Retail Price	Dealer Invoice	Fair Price
Pearlescent metallic paint	530	461	—

Sport90 requires Quattro all-wheel drive system and Comfort and Convenience Pkg.

	Retail Price	Dealer Invoice	Fair Price
Interior windscreen, Cabriolet	380	331	—
Power sunroof, 90, Sport90	960	835	—
Expandable ski/storage sack, 90, Sport90	155	135	—

BMW

BMW 3-Series	Retail Price	Dealer Invoice	Fair Price
318i 4-door notchback	$24975	$21010	$22010
318is 2-door notchback	26675	22440	23440
318i 2-door convertible	31050	26120	—
325i 4-door notchback	31450	26455	28455
325is 2-door notchback	32850	27635	29635
325i 2-door convertible	39600	33310	—
M3 2-door notchback	36800	30955	—
Destination charge	470	470	470

Convertible and M3 fair prices not available at time of publication.

Standard Equipment:

318 models: 1.8-liter DOHC 4-cylinder engine, 5-speed manual transmission, variable-assist power steering, anti-lock 4-wheel disc brakes, driver- and passenger-side air bags, dual control air conditioning, cruise control, cloth or leatherette reclining bucket seats with height/tilt adjustments, split folding rear seat, front and rear center armrests (318i convertible), front seatback storage nets, power windows and locks, power mirrors, power sunroof (318i 4-door, 318is), manual folding top (318i convertible), tilt steering wheel (318i convertible), AM/FM/cassette, diversity antenna, tachometer, trip odometer, digital clock, outside temperature display, theft-deterrent system, tinted glass, speed-sensitive intermittent wipers, rear defogger, Service Interval Indicator, map lights, fog lights (318is, 318i convertible), tool kit, 185/65TR15 tires and wheel covers (318i 4-door), 205/60HR15 tires and alloy wheels (318is, 318i convertible), full-size spare tire. **325 models** add: 2.5-liter DOHC 6-cylinder engine, Active Check Control system, fog lights, rear reading lights (325i 4-door, 325is), 8-way power front seats, leatherette upholstery, front center armrest, premium sound system, 205/60HR15 tires. **325is and 325i convertible** add: leather upholstery, tilt steering wheel (325i convertible), power folding top (325i convertible), rear center armrest (325i convertible). **M3** adds to 325: 3.0-liter DOHC 6-cylinder engine, limited-slip differential, sport suspension, front and lower rear spoilers, lower bodyside cladding, heated mirrors, driver-side door lock, and windshield washer jets, leatherette-wrapped steering wheel, leather sport seats with thigh/shoulder adjustments, leather shift knob and handbrake trim, 235/40ZR17 tires, alloy wheels. M3 deletes 8-way power front seats, front center armrest, and cruise control.

Optional Equipment:

	Retail Price	Dealer Invoice	Fair Price
4-speed automatic transmission, 318, 325	$900	$740	$819
Limited-slip differential, 318	530	430	482
Cruise control, M3	455	375	—
Split folding rear seat, 4-doors	275	225	250
Leather upholstery, 4-doors	1300	1070	1183
Rollover Protection System, convertibles	1390	1140	—
ASC + T traction control, 325	995	815	905
318 Premium Pkg., 318i 4-door	2445	2010	2225
318is	1645	1350	1497
318i convertible	1545	1270	—

Leather upholstery, premium sound system, fog lights (4-door), tilt steering wheel (4-door), 205/60R15 tires (4-door), alloy wheels (4-door). NA with Sports Pkg.

325 Premium Pkg, 325i 4-door	1895	1560	1724
325is, 325i convertible	695	570	632

On-board computer, wood interior trim, leather upholstery (4-door), tilt steering wheel (4-door). NA with Sports Pkg.

318 Sports Pkg., 318i 4-door	1695	1390	1542
318is	745	610	678

Limited-slip differential, sport suspension, tilt steering wheel, 205/60R15 tires (4-door), alloy wheels (4-door). NA with Premium Pkg.

325 Sports Pkg, notchbacks	1395	1145	1269
convertible	1295	1065	—

Sport suspension (notchbacks), sport seats, on-board computer, 225/50ZR16 tires, 16-inch alloy wheels. NA with Premium Pkg.

BMW

	Retail Price	Dealer Invoice	Fair Price
Heated front seats and heated mirrors, 318, 325	$450	$370	$410
Heated front seats, M3	370	305	—
Premium sound system, 318	500	410	455
Fog lights, 318i 4-door	240	200	218
On-board computer, 325, M3	430	355	391
Metallic paint (std. M3)	475	390	432
Cloth upholstery, M3	NC	NC	NC
Power sunroof, M3	1120	920	—
Alloy wheels, 318i 4-door	800	655	728
Includes 205/60R15 tires.			

BMW 5-Series

	Retail Price	Dealer Invoice	Fair Price
525i 4-door notchback	$35300	$29585	—
525i Touring 5-door wagon	37700	31595	—
530i 4-door notchback	42750	35825	—
530i Touring 5-door wagon	47050	39430	—
540i 4-door notchback, automatic	47950	40185	—
540i 4-door notchback, 6-speed	48600	40730	—
Destination charge	470	470	470
Gas Guzzler Tax, 530i with manual transmission	1000	1000	1000
540i with manual transmission	1300	1300	1300

Fair price not available at time of publication.

Standard Equipment:

525i: 2.5-liter DOHC 6-cylinder engine, 5-speed manual transmission, variable-assist power steering, anti-lock 4-wheel disc brakes, driver- and passenger-side air bags, cruise control, air conditioning with dual climate controls, 10-way power front seats with power lumbar support adjusters, leather-wrapped steering wheel, folding center armrests, rear center storage armrest, anti-theft AM/FM stereo cassette, diversity antenna, telescopic steering column, power windows and locks, heated power mirrors, fog lights, tinted glass, tachometer, map lights, intermittent wipers, heated windshield-washer jets, heated driver-side door lock, rear defogger, seatback pockets, trip odometer, power sunroof, Service Interval Indicator, Active Check Control system, fuel economy indicator, lighted visor mirrors, tool kit, 205/65HR15 tires, alloy wheels. **525i Touring** deletes diversity antenna and power sunroof and adds: 4-speed automatic transmission, split folding rear seat, rear wiper/washer, cargo area tiedowns and cover, 225/60HR15 tires. **530i** adds to 525i: 3.0-liter DOHC V-8 engine, outside temperature display, automatic ventilation system, onboard computer, remote keyless entry, leather seats, 225/60HR15 tires. **530i Touring** adds to 525i Touring: 3.0-liter DOHC V-8 engine, 5-speed automatic transmission, ASC+T traction control, automatic ventilation system, twin-panel power sunroof, onboard computer, remote keyless entry, leather seats. **540i** adds to 530i: 4.0-liter DOHC V-8 engine, 5-speed automatic transmission, power telescopic steering wheel, 3-position driver's-seat memory. **540i 6-speed** adds: 6-speed manual transmission, sport suspension, 12-way power front seats.

Optional Equipment:

	Retail Price	Dealer Invoice	Fair Price
4-speed automatic transmission, 525i	$900	$740	—
5-speed automatic transmission, 530i	1100	900	—
Premium Package, 525i	3525	2890	—
On board computer, leather seats and door handles, wood interior trim, remote keyless entry and alarm, cross-spoke alloy wheels.			
Premium Package, 525i Touring	4625	3795	—
On board computer, leather seats and door handles, wood interior trim, power sunroof, remote keyless entry and alarm, cross-spoke alloy wheels.			
ASC+T traction control,			
525i and 525i Touring	995	815	—
530i and 540i automatic	1350	1110	—
Twin-panel power sunroof, 525i Touring	1325	1090	—
Heated front seats	370	305	—
Luggage net, Touring models	260	215	—
Metallic paint	NC	NC	NC

BMW 7-Series

	Retail Price	Dealer Invoice	Fair Price
740i 4-door notchback	$57900	—	—
Destination charge	470	470	470
Gas Guzzler Tax, 740i	1000	1000	1000

740i dealer invoice and fair price and 740iL and 750iL prices not available at time of publication.

Standard Equipment:

740i: 4.0-liter DOHC V-8 engine, 5-speed automatic transmission, anti-lock 4-wheel disc brakes, variable-assist power steering, driver- and passenger-side air bags, automatic climate control system with dual controls, 14-way power front seats with driver-side memory system, 4-way driver-seat lumbar support adjustment, power tilt/telescopic steering wheel with memory, leather and walnut interior trim, door pockets, power windows and door locks, heated power mirrors with 3-position memory, remote keyless entry, variable intermittent wipers, heated windshield-washer jets, heated driver-side door lock, cruise control, rear head rests, rear armrest with storage, automatic dimming mirror, front and rear reading lamps, tinted glass, lighted visor mirrors, tachometer, trip odometer, Service Interval Indicator, Active Check Control system, on board computer, rear defogger, interior air filtration system, power sunroof, fog lamps, 10-speaker AM/FM/cassette with diversity antenna and steering wheel controls, luggage net, toolkit, 235/60HR16 tires, alloy wheels, full-size spare tire. **740iL** adds: self-leveling rear suspension. **750iL** adds: 5.4-liter V-12 engine, traction control, Electronic Damping Control, heated seats, 2-way power upper backrest adjustment, power rear seats with power lumbar adjustment, power rear headrests, cellular telephone, 14-speaker audio system, 6-disc CD changer, power rear sunshade, headlight washers, ski sack.

Optional Equipment:

	Retail Price	Dealer Invoice	Fair Price
Cold Weather Pkg., 740i	$1000	—	—
Heated front seats, headlight washers, ski sack.			
14-speaker audio system w/6-disc CD changer, 740i	2000	—	—
Traction control, 740i	1350	—	—
Power upper backrest adjusters, 740i	1000	—	—

BUICK

Buick Century

	Retail Price	Dealer Invoice	Fair Price
Special 4-door notchback	$16360	$14642	$14942
Select Series 4-door notchback, 4-cylinder	15695	14907	—
Select Series 4-door notchback, V-6	16695	15855	—
Limited Select Series 4-door notchback	17995	17035	—
Special 5-door wagon	17080	15287	15587
Special Select Series 5-door wagon, 4-cylinder	16695	15855	—
Special Select Series 5-door wagon, V-6	17695	16803	—
Custom 4-door notchback	17965	16079	16379
Destination charge	535	535	535

Select Series fair prices not available at time of publication. Select Series models include destination charge and are available with limited optional equipment. Additional "value-priced" models may be available in California.

Standard Equipment:

Special: 2.2-liter 4-cylinder engine, 3-speed automatic transmission, anti-lock brakes, driver-side air bag, door-mounted automatic front seatbelts, power steering, air conditioning, automatic power door locks, tilt steering wheel, intermittent wipers, left remote and right manual mirrors, tinted glass, engine temperature gauge, trip odometer, map lights, instrument panel courtesy lights, 55/45 cloth seats with armrest, power front seatback recliners, AM/FM

radio with digital clock with seek and scan, body-color bodyside molding,
185/75R14 tires, wheel covers. **Wagon** has: remote tailgate release, split folding rear seatback, cargo area light, cargo area storage compartments, black
bodyside moldings. **Select Series 4-cylinder** models add: cruise control,
power windows, rear defogger, rear-facing third seat (wagon), front storage
armrest, front reading lights, remote decklid release (notchback), roof luggage carrier (wagon), air deflector (wagon), cargo area cover (wagon),
swingout rear vent windows (wagon), visor mirrors, floormats, 185/75R14
whitewall tires. **Select Series V-6** models add: 3.1-liter V-6 engine, 4-speed
automatic transmission, cassette player. **Limited Select Series** adds to Select
Series V-6: leather upholstery, 6-way power driver's seat, remote keyless
entry, power mirrors, trunk net, wire wheel covers. **Custom** adds to Special:
3.1-liter V-6 engine, 4-speed automatic transmission, rear defogger, front
storage armrest with cup holders, covered visor mirrors, power door locks
and windows, front reading lights, bright wheel opening moldings, body striping, door courtesy lights, 195/75R14 whitewall tires, styled wheel covers.

Optional Equipment:

	Retail Price	Dealer Invoice	Fair Price
3.1-liter V-6 engine, Special	$610	$525	$555
Requires option pkg. and 4-speed automatic transmission.			
4-speed automatic transmission, Special	200	172	182
Requires 3.1-liter V-6 engine.			
Premium Pkg. SC, Special notchback	598	514	544
Special wagon	638	549	581
Front storage armrest, rear defogger, front reading lights, covered visor mirrors, power windows. Wagon also includes air deflector.			
Luxury Pkg. SD, Special notchback	1068	918	972
Special wagon	1126	968	1025
Pkg. SC plus cruise control, remote decklid release (4-door), cassette player, front and rear floormats. Wagon also includes power mirrors.			
Prestige Pkg. SE, Special 4-door	1701	1463	1548
Special wagon	1525	1312	1388
Pkg. SD plus power mirrors (notchback), automatic power antenna (notchback), remote keyless entry (notchback), 6-way power driver's seat (notchback), trunk net (notchback). Wagon also includes rear-facing third seat and swing-out vent window, cargo area security cover, roof luggage carrier.			
Luxury Pkg. SD, Custom	748	643	681
Includes cruise control, power mirrors, cassette player, automatic power antenna, remote decklid release, trunk net, front and rear floormats.			
Prestige Pkg. SE, Custom	1258	1082	1145
Custom Pkg. SD plus 6-way power driver's seat, remote keyless entry, premium speaker system.			
Remote keyless entry	135	116	123
Special notchback requires remote decklid release. NA Select Series 4-cylinder models.			

Prices are accurate at time of publication; subject to manufacturer's change.

BUICK

	Retail Price	Dealer Invoice	Fair Price
Cruise control, Special	$225	$194	$205
Decklid luggage rack, notchbacks	115	99	105
NA Select Series 4-cylinder.			
Cassette player (std. Select Series V-6 models)	140	120	127
CD player, Special w/Pkg. SC, Custom	416	358	379
Special w/Pkg. SD or SE, Select Series V-6 models (NA Limited), Custom			
w/Pkg. SD or SE	276	237	251
Premium speakers, notchbacks	70	60	64
Wagons	35	30	32
Requires cassette or CD player. NA Select Series 4-cylinder notchback.			
Automatic power antenna	85	73	77
NA Select Series 4-cylinder models.			
Power mirrors	78	67	71
NA Select Series 4-cylinder notchback.			
6-way power driver's seat (std. Limited			
Select Series)	305	262	278
Bodyside stripes (std. Custom)	45	39	41
Bodyside woodgrain trim, wagons	380	327	346
Leather and vinyl 55/45 seat			
w/storage armrest, Custom	500	430	455
Rear wiper, wagons	85	73	77
NA Special with air deflector.			
Trunk net, notchbacks	30	26	27
NA Select Series 4-cylinder.			
Remote decklid release, Special	60	52	55
Door edge guards	25	22	23
NA Select Series 4-cylinder notchback.			
Heavy duty engine and transmission cooling	40	34	36
Requires 3.1-liter V-6 engine.			
Engine block heater	18	15	16
Locking wire wheel covers	240	206	218
NA wagons, Select Series 4-cylinder notchback.			
Styled steel wheels	115	99	105
NA Custom.			
Chrome styled wheels	35	30	32
Alloy wheels	295	254	268
Limited Select Series	55	47	50
NA Select Series 4-cylinder notchback.			
185/75R14 tires, Select Series models (credit)	(68)	(58)	(58)
185/75R14 whitewall tires, Special	68	58	62
195/75R14 tires, Special	40	34	36
195/75R14 tires, Select Series wagons (credit)	(28)	(24)	(24)
Custom (credit)	(72)	(62)	(62)

CONSUMER GUIDE®

	Retail Price	Dealer Invoice	Fair Price
195/75R14 whitewall tires, Special	$108	$93	$98
Select Series wagons	40	34	36
Floormats, Special, Custom notchbacks	45	39	41
Floormats delete, Special (credit)	(45)	(39)	(39)

Buick LeSabre

	Retail Price	Dealer Invoice	Fair Price
Custom 4-door notchback	$21735	$19018	$19518
Custom Select Series 4-door notchback	20995	20077	—
Limited 4-door notchback	25465	22282	22782
Limited Select Series 4-door notchback	24695	23248	—
Destination charge	585	585	585

Select Series fair prices not available at time of publication. Select Series models include destination charge and are available with limited optional equipment. Additional "value-priced" models may be available in California.

Standard Equipment:

Custom: 3.8-liter V-6, 4-speed automatic transmission, anti-lock brakes, driver- and passenger-side air bags, power steering, air conditioning, power door locks, power windows with driver-side express down and passenger lockout, AM/FM radio with clock, tilt steering wheel, intermittent wipers, Pass-Key theft-deterrent system, body-color left remote and right manual mirrors, solar-control tinted glass, instrument panel courtesy lights, trip odometer, 55/45 cloth seats with armrest, manual front seatback recliners, 205/70R15 all-season tires, wheel covers. **Custom Select Series** adds to Custom: front storage armrest, floormats, cruise control, rear defogger, remote keyless entry, power mirrors, remote decklid release, trunk net, 6-way power driver's seat, power antenna, cassette player, striping, 205/70R15 all-season whitewall tires, alloy wheels. **Limited** adds to Custom: variable-assist power steering, cruise control, rear defogger, remote keyless entry, remote decklid release, 6-way power driver's seat, front storage armrest with cup holders, cassette player, Concert Sound II speakers, power mirrors, power antenna, passenger-side lighted visor mirror, front and rear door courtesy lights, front and rear reading lights, floormats, trunk net, 205/70R15 all-season whitewall tires, alloy wheels. **Limited Select Series** adds to Limited: automatic air conditioning, rear-seat air conditioning, cornering lamps, oil pressure and engine coolant temperature gauges, voltmeter, tachometer, steering wheel radio controls, 6-way power passenger's seat.

Optional Equipment:

Prestige Pkg. SE, Limited	725	624	660

Includes 6-way power passenger seat, automatic air conditioning, rear-seat air conditioning, steering wheel radio controls, cornering lamps.

BUICK

	Retail Price	Dealer Invoice	Fair Price
Traction control system, Limited	$175	$151	$159
Requires gauge cluster.			
Luxury Pkg. SD, Custom	1161	998	1057
Includes cruise control, rear defogger, cassette player, front seat storage armrest, trunk net, floormats, striping, 205/70R15 all-season whitewall tires, alloy wheels.			
Prestige Pkg. SE, Custom	1977	1700	1799
Pkg. SD plus remote keyless entry system, power mirrors, remote decklid release, 6-way power driver's seat, Concert Sound II speakers, power antenna, passenger-side lighted visor mirror, door edge guards.			
Gran Touring Pkg., Custom w/Pkg. SE, Limited	419	360	381
Includes Gran Touring Suspension, 3:06 axle ratio, automatic level control, leather-wrapped steering wheel, 215/60R16 touring tires, alloy wheels.			
Trailer Towing Pkg., Custom and Limited	325	280	296
Custom and Limited w/Gran Touring Pkg.	150	129	137
Engine and transmission oil coolers, automatic level control.			
Leather upholstery, Custom	995	856	905
Limited	550	473	501
Limited Select Series	NC	NC	NC
Gauge cluster, Limited	163	140	148
Includes oil pressure and engine coolant temperature gauges, voltmeter, tachometer.			
6-way power driver's seat, Custom w/Pkg. SD	305	262	278
Requires power mirrors.			
6-way power passenger seat, Custom w/Pkg. SE, Limited w/Pkg. SD	305	262	278
Power mirrors, Custom w/Pkg. SD	78	67	71
Requires 6-way power driver's seat.			
Remote decklid release, Custom w/Pkg. SD	60	52	55
Requires remote keyless entry.			
Remote keyless entry, Custom w/Pkg. SD	135	116	123
Requires remote decklid release.			
UL0 audio system, Custom w/Pkg. SE, Limited	150	129	137
Includes AM/FM cassette player with clock, seek and scan, automatic tone control, and steering wheel radio controls.			
UN0 audio system, Custom w/Pkg. SE, Limited	250	215	228
Limited w/Pkg. SE, Limited Select Series	100	86	91
Includes AM/FM CD player with clock, seek and scan, automatic tone control, and steering wheel radio controls.			

	Retail Price	Dealer Invoice	Fair Price
UPO audio system, Custom w/Pkg. SE, Limited	$350	$301	$319
Limited w/Pkg. SE, Limited Select Series	200	172	182
UNO audio system plus cassette player.			
Power antenna, Custom w/Pkg. SD	85	73	77
Alloy wheels, Custom	325	280	296
Locking wire wheel covers, Custom w/option pkg., Limited, and Select Series models	NC	NC	NC
NA with Gran Touring Pkg.			
205/70R15 whitewall tires, Custom	76	65	69
NA with Gran Touring Pkg.			
205/70R15 tires, Select Series models	NC	NC	NC
205/70R15 tires, Custom w/option pkg., Limited (credit)	(76)	(65)	(65)
NA with Gran Touring Pkg.			
205/70R15 self-sealing whitewall tires, Custom	226	194	206
Custom with option pkg.	150	129	137
NA Select Series models.			

Buick Park Avenue

	Retail Price	Dealer Invoice	Fair Price
4-door notchback	$28244	$24431	$25031
Select Series 4-door notchback	26995	25809	—
Ultra 4-door notchback	33084	28618	29218
Destination charge	635	635	635

Select Series fair price not available at time of publication. Select Series includes destination charge and is available with limited optional equipment. Additional "value-priced" models may be available in California.

Standard Equipment:

3.8-liter V-6 engine, 4-speed automatic transmission, anti-lock brakes, variable-assist power steering, driver- and passenger-side air bags, air conditioning, 55/45 cloth reclining front seat with storage armrest and cup holders, 6-way power driver's seat, automatic level control, power windows with driver-side express down and passenger lockout, power door locks, power mirrors, overhead console, cruise control, rear defogger, tilt steering wheel, AM/FM/cassette player, solar-control tinted glass, Pass-Key theft-deterrent system, remote decklid and fuel door releases, front and rear reading and courtesy lights, passenger-side lighted visor mirror, intermittent wipers, trip odometer, 205/70R15 tires, alloy wheels. **Select Series** model adds to base: automatic air conditioning, rear-seat air conditioning, 6-way power

BUICK

passenger seat with power recliner, remote keyless entry system, Twilight Sentinel headlamp control, analog gauge cluster with tachometer, trip odometer, coolant temperature and oil pressure gauges, power antenna, door edge guard, power decklid pulldown, automatic power door locks, Reminder Pkg. (includes low washer fluid, low coolant, trunk and door ajar indicators), illuminated entry system with retained accessory power, theft-deterrent system with starter interrupt, automatic day/night inside rearview mirror, 4-note horn, Concert Sound II speakers, lighted driver-side visor mirror, trunk net, cornering lights, 205/70R15 whitewall tires. **Ultra** adds to base: supercharged 3.8-liter V-6 engine, automatic climate control with dual temperature controls, rear seat climate controls, 6-way power front seats with power recliners, leather upholstery, leather-wrapped steering wheel, rear head restraints, remote keyless entry system, illuminated entry system with retained accessory power, Twilight Sentinel headlamp control, analog gauge cluster with tachometer, trip odometer, coolant temperature and oil pressure gauges, power antenna, power decklid pulldown, automatic programmable power door locks, Reminder Pkg. (includes low washer fluid, low coolant, and door ajar indicators), theft-deterrent system with starter interrupt, trunk net, cornering lamps, automatic day/night inside rearview mirror, Concert Sound II speakers, lighted driver-side visor mirror, 4-note horn, 215/70R15 all-season tires.

Optional Equipment:

	Retail Price	Dealer Invoice	Fair Price
Luxury Pkg. SD, base	$1846	$1588	$1680

Includes power passenger seat with power recliner, illuminated entry with retained accessory power, remote keyless entry, automatic air conditioning, theft-deterrent system with starter interrupt, automatic programmable door locks, power decklid pulldown, power antenna, automatic day/night inside rearview mirror, driver-side visor mirror, analog gauge cluster, lamp monitors, Twilight Sentinel headlamp control, Concert Sound II speakers, cornering lamps, Reminder Pkg. (includes low washer fluid, low coolant, and door ajar indicators), door edge guards, trunk net, 4-note horn, 215/70R15 whitewall tires.

Prestige Pkg. SE, base	2671	2297	2431

Pkg. SD plus steering wheel radio controls, heated outside mirrors with automatic left day/night mirror, power driver's seat recliner, memory driver's seat and mirrors, rear seat climate controls, rear seat storage armrest, automatic day/night mirror with compass, self-sealing tires, trunk mat.

Luxury Pkg. SD, Ultra	730	628	664

Includes automatic ride control, traction control system, steering wheel radio controls.

Prestige Pkg. SE, Ultra	1385	1191	1260

Pkg. SD plus heated outside mirrors with automatic left day/night mirror, heated front seats, memory driver's seat and mirrors, automatic day/night mirror with compass, self-sealing tires, trunk mat.

	Retail Price	Dealer Invoice	Fair Price

ULO audio system, base w/Pkg. SD, Ultra,
Select Series $150 $129 $137
Includes AM/FM/cassette player with clock, seek and scan, automatic tone control, and steering wheel radio controls.

UNO audio system, base w/Pkg. SD, Ultra,
Select Series 250 215 228
Base w/Pkg. SE, Ultra w/option pkg. 100 86 91
Includes AM/FM/CD player with clock, seek and scan, automatic tone control, and steering wheel radio controls.

UPO audio system, base w/Pkg. SD, Ultra,
Select Series 350 301 319
Base w/Pkg. SE, Ultra w/option pkg. 200 172 182
UNO audio system plus cassette player.

Astroroof, base w/Pkg. SE 918 789 835
Ultra w/Pkg. SD or SE 802 690 730
Base includes driver's side vanity mirror.

Trailering Pkg. 177 152 161
w/Gran Touring Pkg. 150 129 137
Includes auxiliary transmission oil and engine oil cooling, Gran Touring suspension, and 3:06 axle ratio. Requires traction control system. NA with automatic level control. NA Select Series.

Gran Touring Pkg., base w/option pkg.,
Select Series 399 343 363
Includes Gran Touring suspension, traction control system, 215/60R16 touring tires, 3:06 axle ratio, alloy wheels, leather-wrapped steering wheel. NA with automatic level control.
Ultra w/option pkg., (credit) .... (294) (253) (253)

Automatic level control, base w/SE 380 327 346
Requires traction control system. NA with Trailering or Gran Touring Pkgs.

Traction control system, base w/option pkg. 175 151 159

Leather/vinyl 55/45 seat w/storage armrest,
base w/Pkg.SD, Select Series 650 559 592
base w/Pkg.SE 600 516 546

Heated front seats, base w/Pkg. SE,
Ultra w/Pkg. SD 120 103 109

Solid paint color, Ultra .... NC NC NC

205/70R15 self-sealing whitewall tires, base 226 194 206
Ultra 150 129 137

205/70R15 whitewall tires, base 76 65 69

205/70R15 tires, base w/Pkg. SD (credit) .... (76) (65) (65)
Base w/Pkg. SE (credit) .... (226) (194) (194)
Select Series .... NC NC NC
NA with Gran Touring Pkg.

BUICK

	Retail Price	Dealer Invoice	Fair Price
215/70R15 tires, Ultra, Ultra w/Pkg. SD			
(credit)	(80)	(69)	(69)
Ultra w/Pkg. SE (credit)	(230)	(198)	(198)
Wire wheel covers, base, Select Series	NC	NC	NC
NA with Gran Touring Pkg.			

Buick Regal

	Retail Price	Dealer Invoice	Fair Price
Custom 2-door notchback	$19603	$17153	$17653
Custom Select Series 2-door notchback	18495	17597	—
Custom Gran Sport Select Series			
2-door notchback	19995	18983	—
Custom 4-door notchback	19920	17430	17930
Custom Select Series 4-door notchback	19195	18225	—
Limited 4-door notchback	21235	18581	19081
Gran Sport 4-door notchback	21870	19136	19636
Destination charge	535	535	535

Select Series fair prices not available at time of publication. Select Series models include destination charge and are available with limited optional equipment. Additional "value-priced" models may be available in California.

Standard Equipment:

Custom: 3.1-liter V-6 engine, 4-speed automatic transmission, driver- and passenger-side air bags, anti-lock 4-wheel disc brakes, power steering, air conditioning, cruise control, automatic power door locks, power windows with driver-side express down and passenger lockout, tilt steering wheel, tachometer, voltmeter, oil pressure and engine coolant temperature gauges, cloth reclining 55/45 front seat with storage armrest and cup holders, front seatback recliners, tinted glass, intermittent wipers, Pass-Key theft-deterrent system, left remote and right manual mirrors, front overhead courtesy/reading lights, visor mirrors, AM/FM radio with clock, 205/70R15 tires, wheel covers. **Custom Select Series** adds: 3.8-liter V-6 engine (4-door), automatic air conditioning with dual climate controls, 6-way power driver's seat, power mirrors, cassette player, power antenna, overhead console with courtesy lights, power decklid release, rear defogger, remote keyless entry, rear seat courtesy lights (2-door), dome reading light (4-door), trunk net, body-color grille (4-door), front and rear floormats, alloy wheels (4-door). **Custom Gran Sport Select Series** adds to Custom Select Series 2-door: 3.8-liter V-6 engine, Gran Touring suspension, color-keyed grille, variable effort power steering, cloth bucket seats with console, leather-wrapped steering wheel, cassette player with automatic tone control and Concert Sound II speakers, steering wheel radio controls, 225/60R16 tires, alloy wheels. **Limited** adds to Custom: 3.8-liter V-6 engine, 4-way manual

driver's seat and 2-way manual passenger's seat, seatback map pockets.
Gran Sport adds: Gran Touring suspension, variable effort power steering,
leather-wrapped steering wheel, cloth reclining bucket seats, console with
armrest, storage, and cup holders, argent lower body accent paint, body-
color grille, 225/60R16 all-season tires, alloy wheels.

Optional Equipment:	Retail Price	Dealer Invoice	Fair Price
3.8-liter V-6, Custom,			
Custom Select Series 2-door	$395	$340	$359
Luxury Pkg. SD, Custom	403	347	367
Power mirrors, power antenna, cassette player, floormats.			
Prestige Pkg. SE, Custom	928	798	844
Pkg. SD plus remote keyless entry system, overhead console reading lights, dome light with integral reading lights (4-door), rear seat courtesy lights (2-door), 6-way power driver's seat, trunk net.			
Luxury Pkg. SD, Limited	473	407	430
Power mirrors, cassette player with Concert Sound II speakers, power antenna, floormats.			
Prestige Pkg. SE, Limited	1150	989	1047
Pkg. SD plus 6-way power driver's seat, remote keyless entry, cassette player with automatic tone control and steering-wheel-mounted controls, power mirrors, trunk net.			
Luxury Pkg. SD, Gran Sport	473	407	430
Power mirrors, power antenna, cassette player with Concert Sound II speakers, floormats.			
Prestige Pkg. SE, Gran Sport	1150	989	1047
Pkg. SD plus 6-way power driver's seat, remote keyless entry, cassette player with automatic tone control and steering-wheel-mounted controls, power mirrors, trunk net.			
Gran Touring Pkg., Custom and Limited			
4-doors w/option pkg., Custom Select			
Series 4-door	745	641	678
Gran Touring suspension, leather-wrapped steering wheel, variable-effort power steering, 225/60R16 tires, alloy wheels. Requires 3.8-liter V-6 engine.			
UN6 audio system, Custom	195	168	177
Includes cassette player with clock, seek and scan.			
UL0 audio system	25	22	23
Includes cassette player with clock, seek and scan, automatic tone control.			
Remote keyless entry, Limited w/ Pkg. SD,			
Gran Sport w/Pkg. SD	135	116	123
Steering wheel radio controls	125	108	114
Concert Sound II speakers,			
Custom w/Pkg. SD, Custom Select Series	70	60	64

BUICK

	Retail Price	Dealer Invoice	Fair Price
Power antenna, Custom	$85	$73	$77
UNO audio system, Custom w/option pkg., Limited w/Pkg. SD, Gran Sport w/Pkg. SD, Custom Select Series	125	108	114
Limited w/Pkg. SE, Gran Sport w/Pkg. SE, Custom Gran Sport Select Series	100	86	91
Includes CD player with clock, seek and scan, automatic tone control. Custom with Pkg. SE and Custom Select Series require Concert Sound II speakers.			
UP0 audio system, Custom w/option pkg., Limited w/Pkg. SD, Gran Sport w/Pkg. SD, Custom Select Series	225	194	205
Limited w/Pkg. SE, Gran Sport w/Pkg. SE, Custom Gran Sport Select Series	200	172	182
UNO audio system plus cassette player. Custom with Pkg. SE and Custom Select Series require Concert Sound II speakers.			
Remote keyless entry, Limited w/ Pkg. SD, Gran Sport w/Pkg. SD	135	116	123
Power sunroof, Custom 4-door w/Pkg. SE, Limited w/Pkg. SE, Gran Sport w/Pkg. SE. Custom Select Series 2-door, Custom Gran Sport Select Series	695	598	632
Includes mirror reading lights.			
6-way power driver's seat, Custom w/Pkg. SD	305	262	278
Limited w/Pkg. SD, Gran Sport w/Pkg. SD	270	232	246
Dual 6-way power front seats, Limited w/Pkg. SE, Gran Sport w/Pkg. SE, Custom Gran Sport Select Series	305	262	278
Leather 55/45 front seat with armrest, Limited w/option Pkg.	550	473	501
Requires single or dual 6-way power seats.			
Leather bucket seats with console	550	473	501
NA Custom. Requires 6-way power driver's seat with Gran Sport.			
Cloth bucket seats with console, Custom 2-door	NC	NC	NC
Lighted visor mirrors, Custom 4-door w/Pkg. SE, Custom Select Series 4-door, Custom Gran Sport Select Series	92	79	84
Heavy duty cooling	150	129	137
Includes engine oil cooler. Requires 3.8-liter V-6 engine.			
Decklid luggage rack, 4-doors w/Pkg. SE, Custom Gran Sport Select Series	115	99	105
Monotone paint, Gran Sport	NC	NC	NC

	Retail Price	Dealer Invoice	Fair Price
Engine block heater, Custom 4-door, Limited w/option pkg., Gran Sport w/option pkg., Custom Select Series 2-door, Custom Gran Sport Select Series	$18	$15	$16
Floormats, Custom	45	39	41
Floormats, Custom, 4-door (delete)	(45)	(39)	(39)
15-inch alloy wheels, Custom, Limited, Custom Select Series	325	280	296
NA with Gran Touring Pkg.			
205/70R15 whitewall tires, Custom, Limited with option pkg., Custom Select Series 2-door	76	65	69
NA with Gran Touring Pkg.			

Buick Riviera	Retail Price	Dealer Invoice	Fair Price
2-door notchback	$27632	$24454	—
Destination charge	625	625	625

Fair price not available at time of publication.

Standard Equipment:

3.8-liter V-6 engine, 4-speed automatic transmission, anti-lock 4-wheel disc brakes, driver- and passenger-side air bags, variable-assist power steering, automatic air conditioning with dual climate controls, cruise control, cloth 6-way power 55/45 split bench front seat with power recliners, front storage armrest with cup holders, rear seat armrest, power windows and mirrors, automatic power door locks, remote keyless entry system, Pass-Key II theft-deterrent system, automatic level control, tachometer, coolant temperature gauge, trip odometer, lighted passenger-side visor mirror, power remote fuel door and decklid releases, solar-control tinted glass, AM/FM/cassette, automatic power antenna, intermittent wipers, rear defogger, tilt steering wheel, leather-wrapped steering wheel, front reading and courtesy lights, rear door courtesy lights, supplemental and extendable sunshades, trunk convenience net, 225/60R16 all-season tires, alloy wheels.

Optional Equipment:

3.8-liter supercharged V-6 engine	1100	946	—
Includes 225/60R16 touring tires and specific alloy wheels.			
Power astroroof with sunshade	995	856	—
Memory heated driver's seat and outside mirrors	310	267	—
Power leather front bucket seats with operating console	650	559	—

Prices are accurate at time of publication; subject to manufacturer's change.

BUICK

	Retail Price	Dealer Invoice	Fair Price
SD Luxury Pkg.	$472	$406	—

Twilight Sentinel, driver-side lighted visor mirror, programmable automatic door locks, theft-deterrent system, cornering lights, accent striping.

SE Prestige Pkg.	992	853	—

SD Luxury Pkg. plus memory heated driver's seat, memory heated outside mirrors, automatic inside rear view mirror, steering wheel mounted radio and climate comtrols, driver's seat power lumbar adjustment, traction control system.

Leather 55/45 split bench seats	600	516	—
CD player	244	210	—
Cassette and CD players	434	373	—

Requires power front bucket seats.

Engine block heater	18	15	—

Buick Roadmaster

	Retail Price	Dealer Invoice	Fair Price
4-door notchback	$25265	$22107	$22607
Select Series 4-door notchback	24210	22806	—
Estate 5-door wagon	27070	23686	24186
Limited 4-door notchback	27555	24111	24610
Destination charge	585	585	585

Select Series fair price not available at time of publication. Select Series model includes destination charge and is available with limited optional equipment. Additional "value-priced" models may be available in California.

Standard Equipment:

5.7-liter V-8 engine, 4-speed automatic transmission, anti-lock brakes, driver- and passenger-side air bags, power steering, air conditioning, power windows with driver-side express down and passenger lockout, power door locks, Pass-Key theft-deterrent system with starter interrupt, AM/FM/cassette, cloth 55/45 seats with storage armrest and manual seatback recliners, front seatback map pockets, tilt steering wheel, remote decklid release, inside day/night mirror with reading lights, left remote and right manual mirrors, delayed illuminated entry, tinted glass, rear defogger, intermittent wipers, analog gauge cluster with coolant temperature and oil pressure gauges, trip odometer, low fuel warning light, windshield washer fluid, oil, voltage, and coolant level indicators, oil life monitor, visor mirrors, 4-note horn, trunk net, floormats, 235/70R15 all-season whitewall tires, wheel covers. **Estate Wagon** adds: variable-assist steering, luggage rack, solar-control windshield, rear window wiper/washer, vista roof with shade, cargo cover, door edge guards, woodgrain trim, 225/75R15 tires, alloy wheels. **Select Series** adds to base: automatic climate control, remote keyless entry, automatic door locks, front door courtesy and warning lights, power heated mirrors, power antenna, leather upholstery, 6-way power driver's seat, cassette player with automatic tone control and Concert Sound speakers. **Limited** adds to base: variable-assist steering, automatic climate control, power antenna, remote keyless entry, automatic door locks, front door courtesy and warning lights, automatic day/night rearview mirror, lighted visor mirrors, leather-wrapped steering wheel, 6-way power front seats with power recliners and lumbar supports.

Optional Equipment:

	Retail Price	Dealer Invoice	Fair Price
Luxury Pkg. SD, base 4-door	$768	$660	$684

6-way power driver's seat, power heated mirrors, automatic climate control, power antenna, cassette player with automatic tone control, Concert Sound speakers.

Luxury Pkg. SD, wagon	1258	1082	1120

6-way power driver's seat, cruise control, automatic climate control, automatic day/night rearview mirror, power heated mirrors, power antenna, storage armrest, front door courtesy and warning lights, cassette player with automatic tone control and Concert Sound speakers, floormats.

Prestige Pkg. SE, base 4-door	1475	1269	1313

Pkg. SD plus power passenger seat, automatic power door locks, remote keyless entry, door courtesy and warning lights, automatic day/night rearview mirror, lighted visor mirrors.

Prestige Pkg. SE, Limited	690	593	614

Power decklid pull-down, Twilight Sentinel headlamp control, cornering lamps, cassette player with automatic tone control, heated front seats with memory driver's seat, self-sealing tires.

Prestige Pkg. SE, wagon	1935	1664	1722

Pkg. SD plus 6-way power passenger seat, remote keyless entry, automatic door locks, Twilight Sentinel headlamp control, lighted visor mirrors, cornering lamps.

Limited Wagon Pkg.	2395	2060	2132

Includes 6-way power driver's and passenger seat with storage armrest and power recliners and lumbar adjustment, 6-way headrests, exterior Limited badges, floormats, leather-wrapped steering wheel, cruise control, cassette player with automatic tone control and Concert Sound speakers, power antenna, remote keyless entry, power locks, heated power mirrors, automatic climate control, door courtesy lamps, automatic day/night mirror with reading lamps, lighted visor mirrors, Twilight Sentinel headlight control, cornering lamps.

Gran Touring/Trailer Towing Pkg., wagon	325	280	255
Base 4-door, Limited, Select Series	375	323	334
Limited w/Pkg. SE	225	194	200

Includes 2.93 axle ratio, heavy duty engine cooling, automatic level control, engine oil cooler, heavy duty suspension and solar-control windshield (4-doors). NA with Cooling Pkg. Base 4-door, Select Series require limited-slip differential.

Prices are accurate at time of publication; subject to manufacturer's change.

CONSUMER GUIDE®   261

BUICK

	Retail Price	Dealer Invoice	Fair Price
Limited-slip differential	$100	$86	$89
Cooling Pkg., wagon	150	129	134
4-doors	200	172	178

Includes solar control windshield (4-doors), engine oil cooler, higher-output fans, increased capacity air conditioner. NA with GranTouring/Trailer Towing Pkg.

	Retail Price	Dealer Invoice	Fair Price
Automatic level control	175	151	156
Leather 55/45 seats, base, Limited	775	667	690

Includes leather-wrapped steering wheel on base models.

	Retail Price	Dealer Invoice	Fair Price
UP0 audio system, Limited	250	215	223
base 4-door w/option pkg., Wagon, Limited w/Pkg. SE, Select Series	200	172	178

Includes AM/FM/CD player with cassette player and clock, seek and scan, automatic tone control.

	Retail Price	Dealer Invoice	Fair Price
Cellular telephone prewiring, base 4-door, Limited	35	30	31
Heated front seats with memory driver's seat, wagon, Limited	290	249	258

Wagon requires Limited Wagon Pkg.

	Retail Price	Dealer Invoice	Fair Price
6-way power passenger's seat, Select Series	305	262	271
Automatic door locks, base w/Pkg. SD	25	22	23

Requires remote keyless entry.

	Retail Price	Dealer Invoice	Fair Price
Remote keyless entry, base w/Pkg. SD	135	116	120

Requires automatic door locks.

	Retail Price	Dealer Invoice	Fair Price
Lower accent paint, base and Limited 4-doors	150	129	134
Third seat delete (credit), wagon	(215)	(185)	(185)

NA with Pkg. SE.

	Retail Price	Dealer Invoice	Fair Price
Vinyl landau roof, base and Limited 4-doors	695	598	619
Woodgrain trim delete, wagon	NC	NC	NC
Wire wheel covers, 4-doors	240	206	214
Wagon	NC	NC	NC
Alloy wheels, 4-doors	325	280	289
235/70R15 self-sealing whitewall tires, base 4-door, Limited, Select Series	150	129	134

NA with Gran Touring/Trailer Towing Pkg.

	Retail Price	Dealer Invoice	Fair Price
225/75R15 self-sealing whitewall tires, wagon	150	129	134
Full-size spare tire, 4-doors w/o self-sealing tires, wagon w/wire wheel covers	75	65	68
4-doors w/alloy wheels, w/ self-sealing tires, w/self-sealing tires and wire wheel covers, wagon	125	108	111

	Retail Price	Dealer Invoice	Fair Price
4-doors w/self-sealing tires and alloy wheels, wagon w/self-sealing tires	$175	$151	$156

Buick Skylark

	Retail Price	Dealer Invoice	Fair Price
Custom 2-door notchback	$14320	$13389	$13689
Custom Select Series 2-door notchback	14195	13579	—
Custom 4-door notchback	14320	13389	13689
Custom Select Series 4-door notchback	14195	13579	—
Custom Limited Select Series 2-door notchback	15195	14534	—
Custom Limited Select Series 4-door notchback	15195	14534	—
Custom Gran Sport Select Series 2-door notchback	16895	16042	—
Custom Gran Sport Select Series 4-door notchback	16895	16042	—
Destination charge	495	495	495

Select Series models' fair price not available at time of publication. Select Series models include destination charge and are available with limited optional equipment. Additional "value-priced" models may be available in California.

Standard Equipment:

Custom: 2.3-liter DOHC 4-cylinder engine, 3-speed automatic transmission, driver-side air bag, anti-lock brakes, door-mounted automatic front seat-belts, power steering, tilt steering wheel, cloth 55/45 split bench seat with seatback recliners, trip odometer, AM/FM radio, tinted glass, automatic power locks, remote fuel door and decklid releases, left remote and right manual mirrors, overhead console with courtesy lights, bright grille, 195/70R14 tires, wheel covers. **Select Series** models add to Custom: air conditioning, tilt steering wheel, intermittent wipers, front center storage armrest, rear defogger, floormats. **Limited Select Series** adds: cruise control, power mirrors, power windows, cassette player, 4-way manual driver's seat, visor mirrors, trunk net, alloy wheels. **Gran Sport Select Series** deletes front center storage armrest and adds: 3.1-liter V-6 engine, 4-speed automatic transmission, sport suspension, oil pressure and temperature gauges, voltmeter, tachometer, reclining cloth bucket seats with console, body-color grille, two-tone bodyside cladding, 205/55R16 tires.

Optional Equipment:

3.1-liter V-6 engine, Custom, Select Series models (std. Gran Sport)	350	301	319
Requires 4-speed automatic transmission.			

BUICK

	Retail Price	Dealer Invoice	Fair Price
4-speed automatic transmission (std. Gran Sport Select Series)	$200	$172	$182
Air conditioning, Custom	830	714	755
Cruise control	225	194	205
Prestige Pkg. SE, Custom	1255	1079	1142

Air conditioning, rear defogger, tilt steering wheel, intermittent wipers, floormats.

6-way power driver's seat, Limited and Gran Sport Select Series models	270	232	246
Custom Select Series	305	262	278

Requires rear window grid antenna and power windows. Custom Select Series adds power mirrors.

Bucket seats and full console	160	138	146

Requires analog gauge cluster, cruise control and 4-way manual driver's seat or 6-way power driver's seat.

4-way manual driver's seat	35	30	32
Front-seat storage armrest, Custom	108	93	98
Leather trim, Limited Select Series	471	405	429
Gran Sport Select Series	345	297	314

Limited Select Series includes analog gauge cluster.

Analog gauge cluster (std. Gran Sport Select Series)	126	108	115

Includes tachometer, trip odometer, voltmeter, oil pressure and temperature gauges. Requires bucket seats with console, cruise control.

Custom Headliner Pkg., Custom, Custom Select Series	24	21	22

Includes visor vanity mirrors, front and rear courtesty lights.

Deluxe Headliner Pkg., Limted and Gran Sport Select Series models	135	116	123

Includes assist handles, lighted visor vanity mirrors, extendable sunshade, reading lamps. NA with power sunroof.

Power windows, 2-doors	275	237	250
4-doors	340	292	309
Power sunroof	595	512	541

Includes lighted visor mirrors and reading lamps.

Remote keyless entry system, Limited and Gran Sport Select Series models	135	116	123

Requires rear window grid antenna.

Cassette player	165	142	150
CD player, Limited and Gran Sport Select Series models	256	220	233

Requires Concert Sound II speakers.

Concert Sound II speakers, Limited and Gran Sport Select Series models	45	39	41

	Retail Price	Dealer Invoice	Fair Price
Rear window grid antenna	$22	$19	$20
Requires power windows.			
Lower accent paint	195	168	177
NA Gran Sport Select Series.			
Engine block heater	18	15	16
Floormats delete, Custom (credit)	(45)	(39)	(39)
Styled polycast alloy wheels	115	99	105
NA Limited and Gran Sport Select Series models.			
Styled steel wheel covers	28	24	25
Requires 195/65R15 tires. NA Gran Sport Select Series.			
195/65R15 tires	131	113	119
Requires styled steel wheel covers. NA Gran Sport Select Series.			
195/75R14 whitewall tires, Custom	72	62	66

CADILLAC

Cadillac De Ville/Concours	Retail Price	Dealer Invoice	Fair Price
Sedan De Ville 4-door notchback	$34900	$31934	$32734
Concours 4-door notchback	39400	36051	36851
Destination charge	635	635	635

Standard Equipment:

Sedan De Ville: 4.9-liter V-8 engine, 4-speed automatic transmission, anti-lock 4-wheel disc brakes, traction control, driver- and passenger-side air bags, variable-assist power steering, reclining power front seats with storage armrest, automatic climate control, outside temperature readout, power windows, automatic power locks, remote keyless entry system, illuminated entry, heated power mirrors, cruise control, AM/FM/cassette with equalizer, power antenna, power decklid pulldown, automatic parking brake release, Twilight Sentinel, wiper-activated headlights, tinted glass, automatic level control, intermittent wipers, Driver Information Center, electronic gearshift indicator, trip odometer, tilt steering wheel, leather-wrapped steering wheel, power decklid release and pulldown, remote fuel door release, rear defogger, Pass-Key II anti-theft system, automatic day/night inside rear view mirror, Speed Sensitive Suspension, cornering lamps, accent stripe, trunk mat and cargo net, floormats, 215/70R15 whitewall tires, alloy wheels. **Concours** adds: 4.6-liter DOHC V-8 engine, Road-Sensing Suspension, leather seats, Zebrano wood trim, power front seat recliners, driver's seat power lumbar support with memory, rear center storage armrest, Active Audio System with cassette and 11 speakers, programmable garage door opener, automatic day/night driver-side mirror, front and rear lighted visor mirrors and maplights, 225/60HR16 blackwall tires.

CADILLAC

Optional Equipment:	Retail Price	Dealer Invoice	Fair Price
Option Pkg. 1SB, De Ville	$427	$363	$384
Automatic day/night driver side mirror, lighted visor mirrors, power front seat recliners.			
Heated windshield system	309	263	275
De Ville requires Option Pkg. 1SB.			
Heated front seats	120	102	107
De Ville requires Option Pkg. 1SB and leather seats.			
Leather seats, De Ville	785	667	699
Astroroof, Concours, De Ville w/Pkg. 1SB	1550	1318	1380
De Ville	1700	1445	1513
Includes lighted visor mirrors and rear reading lamps on De Ville without Pkg. 1SB.			
Theft-deterrent system	295	251	263
De Ville requires Option Pkg. 1SB.			
Electronic compass	100	85	89
De Ville requires Option Pkg. 1SB.			
Programmable garage door opener, De Ville	107	91	95
Active Audio System with cassette player,			
De Ville	274	233	244
with cassette and CD player, De Ville	670	570	596
with cassette and CD player, Concours	396	337	352
De Ville requires Option Pkg. 1SB.			
Chrome wheels	1195	523	1064
3000-lb. Trailer Towing Pkg., Concours	110	94	98
White diamond or pearl red paint	500	425	445
Accent striping delete	NC	NC	NC

Cadillac Eldorado	Retail Price	Dealer Invoice	Fair Price
2-door notchback	$38220	$33060	$33860
Touring Coupe 2-door notchback	41535	35928	36728
Destination charge	635	635	635

Standard Equipment:

4.6-liter DOHC V-8 engine, 4-speed automatic transmission, anti-lock 4-wheel disc brakes, driver- and passenger-side air bags, speed-sensitive power steering, automatic parking brake release, Road-Sensing Suspension, automatic level control, traction control, automatic climate control, cloth power front bucket seats with power recliners, center console with armrest and storage bins, overhead console, power windows, automatic power locks, remote keyless entry system, cruise control, heated power mirrors, rear defogger, solar-control tinted glass, automatic day/night rearview mirror, Active Audio AM/FM/cassette, power antenna, remote fuel door release, power decklid release and pull-down, electronic gearshift indicator, trip odometer, Driver Information Center, Zebrano wood trim, intermittent wipers, leather-wrapped steering wheel, tilt steering wheel, Pass-Key II theft-deterrent system, Twilight Sentinel, wiper-activated headlights, fog lamps, cornering lamps, illuminated entry, reading lights, lighted visor mirrors, floormats, trunk mat and cargo net, 225/60R16 tires, alloy wheels. **Touring Coupe** adds: high-output 4.6-liter DOHC V-8 engine, touring suspension, tachometer, power lumbar adjusters, leather seats, center rear seat storage armrest, automatic day/night driver-side mirror, theft-deterrent system, programmable garage door opener, 225/60ZR16 tires.

Optional Equipment:

	Retail Price	Dealer Invoice	Fair Price
Sport Interior Pkg., base	$146	$124	$131
Analog instruments, floor console with leather-wrapped shift knob.			
Astroroof	1550	1318	1395
Heated windshield	309	263	278
Leather upholstery, base	650	553	585
Heated front seats	120	102	108
Base requires leather upholstery.			
Power lumbar support, base	292	248	263
Requires leather upholstery.			
Automatic day/night rearview mirror, base	87	74	77
Electronic compass	100	85	89
Base requires automatic day/night rearview mirror.			
Theft-deterrent system, base	295	251	266
Delco/Bose audio system with cassette and CD players	972	826	875
Programmable garage door opener, base	107	91	95
White diamond or red pearl paint	500	425	450
Striping, base	75	64	68
225/60R16 whitewall tires, base	76	65	68
Chrome wheels	1195	523	1064

Cadillac Fleetwood

	Retail Price	Dealer Invoice	Fair Price
4-door notchback	$35595	$32569	$33369
Destination charge	635	635	635

Standard Equipment:

5.7-liter V-8 engine, 4-speed automatic transmission, anti-lock brakes, driver- and passenger-side air bags, variable-assist power steering, traction control, power 55/45 front seat with power recliners and storage armrest, automatic climate control, outside temperature readout, power windows, automatic power locks, illuminated entry, cruise control, heated power mir-

CADILLAC

rors, lighted vanity mirrors, automatic day/night rearview mirror, map lights, remote keyless entry, Pass-Key II anti-theft deterrent system, AM/FM/cassette with equalizer, power antenna, automatic level control, leather-wrapped tilt steering wheel, trip odometer, cornering lamps, automatic parking brake release, tinted glass, intermittent wipers, rear defogger, floormats, door edge guards, Twilight Sentinel, power decklid pulldown and release, trunk mat and cargo net, 235/70R15 whitewall tires, alloy wheels.

Optional Equipment:	Retail Price	Dealer Invoice	Fair Price
Security Pkg.	$360	$306	$324
Remote fuel door release, theft-deterrent system.			
7000-lb. Trailer Towing Pkg.	215	183	193
Performance axle ratio, base	NC	NC	NC
NA with Trailer Towing Pkg.			
Astroroof	1550	1318	1395
Fleetwood Brougham Pkg. with cloth trim	1680	1428	1512
with leather trim	2250	1913	2025
Heated front seats, 2-position driver's seat memory feature, power lumbar adjustment, articulating front headrests, rear seat storage armrest with cup holders, rear lighted vanity mirrors, programmable garage door opener, full padded roof, unique trim and alloy wheels, 2.93:1 rear axle ratio.			
Leather upholstery, base	570	485	513
Sungate windshield	50	43	45
Compact disc and cassette players	396	337	356
Programmable garage door opener, base	107	91	96
Full padded vinyl roof delete, Brougham	NC	NC	NC
Full padded vinyl roof, base	925	786	833
Chrome wheels	1195	523	1076
NA with full size spare tire.			
Full size spare tire	95	81	86
NA with chrome wheels.			

Cadillac Seville	Retail Price	Dealer Invoice	Fair Price
SLS 4-door notchback	$41935	$36274	$37074
STS 4-door notchback	45935	39734	40534
Destination charge	635	635	635

Standard Equipment:

SLS: 4.6-liter DOHC V-8 engine, 4-speed automatic transmission, anti-lock 4-wheel disc brakes, driver- and passenger-side air bags, speed-sensitive power steering, Road-Sensing Suspension, traction control, automatic level control, cloth power front seats with articulating headrests and power recliners, center console with armrest and storage bins, overhead console, dual zone automatic climate control with outside temperature display, electronic gearshift indicator, Zebrano wood trim, power windows, automatic power door locks, cruise control, heated power mirrors, automatic day/night rearview mirror, AM/FM/cassette, power antenna, remote fuel door and decklid releases, power decklid pull-down, Driver Information Center, Pass-Key II theft-deterrent system, remote keyless entry, leather-wrapped tilt steering wheel, intermittent wipers, wiper-activated headlights, rear defogger, solar-control tinted glass, floormats, decklid liner, trunk mat and cargo net, Twilight Sentinel, cornering lamps, reading lights, lighted visor mirrors, illuminated entry, trip odometer, automatic parking brake release, 225/60R16 tires, alloy wheels. **STS** adds: high-output 4.6-liter V-8 engine, touring suspension, leather upholstery, rear seat center storage armrest, front seat power lumbar adjustment, analog instruments with tachometer, full console, driver-side automatic day/night outside mirror, theft-deterrent system, programmable garage door opener, fog lamps, 225/60ZR16 tires.

Optional Equipment:	Retail Price	Dealer Invoice	Fair Price
Sport Interior Pkg., SLS	$146	$124	$131
Analog instruments, full center console, leather-wrapped shift knob.			
Astroroof	1550	1318	1395
Anti-theft alarm, SLS	295	251	266
Heated windshield	309	263	278
Leather upholstery, SLS	650	553	585
Heated front seats	120	102	108
SLS requires leather upholstery.			
Power lumbar adjustment, SLS	292	248	263
Requires leather upholstery.			
Driver-side automatic day/night outside mirror, base	87	74	78
Electronic compass	100	85	90
Base requires driver-side automatic day/night outside mirror.			
Delco/Bose audio system w/cassette and CD player	972	826	875
Programmable garage door opener, SLS	107	91	108
White diamond or red pearl paint	500	425	450
Striping, SLS	75	64	68
Chrome wheels	1195	523	1076

CHEVROLET

Chevrolet Beretta	Retail Price	Dealer Invoice	Fair Price
2-door notchback	$12995	$11760	$12060
Special Value 2-door notchback (Pkg. 1SKX)	12995	12058	—

Prices are accurate at time of publication; subject to manufacturer's change.

CHEVROLET

	Retail Price	Dealer Invoice	Fair Price
Special Value 2-door notchback (Pkg. 1SLX)	$13495	$12520	—
Special Value 2-door notchback (Pkg. 1SMX) ..	13995	12983	—
Z26 2-door notchback	16295	14747	15047
Z26 Special Value 2-door notchback	16995	15758	—
Destination charge	495	495	495

Special Value models' fair price not available at time of publication. Special Value models include destination charge. Additional "value-priced" models may be available in California.

Standard Equipment:

Base: 2.2-liter 4-cylinder engine, 5-speed manual transmission, anti-lock brakes, driver-side air bag, power steering, air conditioning, automatic door locks, cloth reclining front bucket seats with 4-way manual driver's seat, center shift console with armrest and storage compartment, cup holders, dual remote mirrors, door map pockets, passenger-side visor mirror, tinted glass, AM/FM radio, battery rundown protection, door pockets, 195/70R14 tires, wheel covers. **Special Value Pkg. 1SKX** adds: rear defogger, intermittent wipers, day/night rearview mirror with reading lights, driver-side visor mirror, trunk net, floormats. **Special Value Pkg. 1SLX** adds: 3-speed automatic transmission, cassette player. **Special Value Pkg. 1SMX** adds: 3.1-liter V-6 engine, 4-speed automatic transmission, tilt steering wheel. **Z26** adds to base: 3.1-liter V-6 engine, 4-speed automatic transmission, Level II Sport suspension, 4-way manual passenger seat, front seat lumbar supports, body-color grille and mirrors, front and rear spoilers, fog lamps, intermittent wipers, Gauge Pkg. with tachometer and trip odometer, cassette player, day/night rearview mirror with reading lamps, trunk net, 205/60R15 tires. **Z26 Special Value** adds: rear defogger, tilt steering wheel, power windows, power decklid release, cruise contol, floormats, 205/55R16 tires, alloy wheels.

Optional Equipment:

3.1-liter V-6 engine, base	1275	1097	1122
Requires 4-speed automatic transmission.			
4-speed automatic transmission, base	NC	NC	NC
NA with 2.2-liter 4-cylinder engine.			
3-speed automatic transmission, base	555	477	488
NA with 3.1-liter V-6 engine.			
Preferred Equipment Group 1	165	142	145
Intermittent wipers, day/night rearview mirror with reading lamps, visor mirrors, trunk net, floormats.			
Preferred Group 2	745	641	656
Group 1 plus cruise control, tilt steering wheel, power decklid release, split folding rear seat.			

	Retail Price	Dealer Invoice	Fair Price
Preferred Equipment Group 1, Z26	$463	$398	$407
Cruise control, tilt steering wheel, power decklid release, floormats.			
Cassette player (std. Z26)	140	120	123
CD player, base	396	341	348
Z26	256	220	225
Rear defogger	170	146	150
Gauge Pkg., base	111	95	98
Includes tachometer, coolant temperature and oil pressure gauges, voltmeter, trip odometer.			
Rear spoiler, base	110	95	97
Removable sunroof	350	301	308
Power windows	275	237	242
Engine block heater	20	17	18
205/60R15 tires, base	175	151	154
205/55R16 tires, Z26	372	320	327
Requires styled alloy wheels.			
Styled alloy wheels and wheel locks, Z26	NC	NC	NC

Chevrolet Blazer	Retail Price	Dealer Invoice	Fair Price
3-door wagon, 2WD	$18145	$16421	—
3-door wagon, 4WD	19905	18014	—
5-door wagon, 2WD	19851	17965	—
5-door wagon, 4WD	21953	19867	—
Destination charge	485	485	485

Fair price not available at time of publication.

Standard Equipment:

2WD: 4.3-liter V-6 engine, 4-speed automatic transmission, anti-lock brakes, driver-side air bag, power steering, air conditioning, front and rear stabilizer bars, solar-control tinted glass, coolant temperature and oil pressure gauges, voltmeter, AM/FM radio, digital clock, dual outside mirrors, trip odometer, front bucket seats with manual lumbar adjustment and console (3-door), 60/40 reclining cloth front bench seat with storage armrest (5-door), cupholders, door map pockets, floormats, cargo-area tiedown hooks, intermittent wipers, day/night rearview mirror, color-keyed bumpers, 5-lead trailer wiring harness, 205/75R15 tires, full-size spare tire. **4WD** adds: Insta-Trac part-time 4WD with manual transfer case, folding rear bench seat (5-door) tow hooks, dark gray bumpers.

Optional Equipment:

Optional axle ratio	NC	NC	NC
Locking differential	252	217	—

CHEVROLET

	Retail Price	Dealer Invoice	Fair Price
Electronic shift transfer case, 4WD	$123	$106	—
LS Decor Group 2, 3-door	2635	—	—
5-door, 2WD	2899	—	—
5-door, 2WD	2424	—	—

Luggage rack, deep-tinted glass, chrome grille, rear window wiper/washer, cargo net, additional cupholders, power remote tailgate release, rear defogger, map lights, power outlets, upgraded cloth seat and door trim, rear compartment shade (5-door), leather-wrapped steering wheel, lighted visor mirrors, alloy wheels.

Preferred Equipment Group 2, 3-door	1470	1264	—
5-door, 2WD	1645	1415	—
5-door, 4WD	1170	1006	—

ZQ3 convenience group (includes tilt steering wheel, cruise control), ZQ6 convenience group (includes power windows, door locks and mirrors), luggage rack, cassette player, folding rear bench seat, premium (5-door) or touring (3-door) suspension pkg. (includes gas shock absorbers), 235/70R15 tires.

Preferred Equipment Group 3, 3-door	1849	1590	—
5-door, 2WD	2113	1817	—
5-door, 4WD	1638	1409	—

Group 2 plus LS Decor Group.

Preferred Equipment Group 4, 3-door	2396	2061	—
5-door, 2WD	2821	2426	—
5-door, 4WD	2346	2018	—

Group 3 plus overhead console, remote keyless entry, bucket seats with console, 6-way power driver's seat.

Preferred Equipment Group 5, 5-door 2WD	4489	3861	—
4WD	4022	3459	—

LT Decor Group (LS Decor Group plus remote keyless entry, upper body pinstriping, simulated leather door panel trim, leather bucket seats with 4-way adjustable headrest, power lumbar adjuster and console, 6-way power driver's seat), ZQ3 and ZQ6 convenience groups, luggage rack, rear folding bench seat (2WD), premium suspension pkg., overhead console, air dam with fog lamps (2WD), electronic transfer case (4WD), tachometer, 6-speaker cassette player with graphic equalizer, 235/70R15 tires.

Exterior Appearance Pkg., 5-door with LS Decor Group	346	298	—

Front bumper rub strip, composite headlights, bodyside and wheel lip moldings.

Folding cloth rear seat, base 3-door and 5-door 2WD	475	409	—
Cloth highback reclining bucket seats with console, 5-door with Group 3	161	138	—
Overhead console, LS Group 3	147	126	—

	Retail Price	Dealer Invoice	Fair Price
6-way power driver's seat, with LS Decor Group	$240	$206	—
Requires remote keyless entry.			
Driver Convenience Pkg. ZQ3, base	383	329	—
Includes cruise control and tilt steering wheel.			
Driver Convenience Pkg. ZQ6,			
base 3-door	475	409	—
5-door	650	559	—
Includes power windows, door locks and mirrors.			
Driver Convenience Pkg. ZM8,			
base, base with Group 2	322	277	—
Includes rear defogger, remote tailgate release and rear wiper/washer.			
Remote keyless entry system, LS Group 3	135	116	—
Requires 6-way power driver's seat.			
Air dam with fog lamps, 2WD	115	99	—
NA base, base with Group 2.			
Heavy duty battery	56	48	—
Exterior spare wheel and tire carrier,			
3-door 4WD	159	137	—
Cold Climate Pkg.	89	77	—
Includes heavy duty battery, engine block heater.			
Roof rack, base	126	108	—
Tachometer	59	51	—
Radio delete (credit)	(226)	(194)	(194)
NA with LS and LT Decor Groups.			
Cassette player, base	122	105	—
Cassette player with equalizer, base	327	281	—
base with Group 2, LS Decor Group	205	176	—
CD player, with LS Decor Group	284	244	—
with LT Decor Group	124	107	—
Shield Pkg., 4WD	126	108	—
Includes transfer case and front differential skid plates, fuel tank and steering linkage shields.			
Smooth ride suspension, 5-door with option			
group, (credit)	(275)	(237)	(237)
Solid/smooth ride suspension, 3-door with			
option group, (credit)	(275)	(237)	(237)
Touring suspension, base	197	169	—
Includes gas shock absorbers.			
Off-road suspension, 3-door 4WD	555	477	—
3-door 4WD with option group	166	143	—
Includes gas shock absorbers, uprated torsion bar, jounce stabilizer bar.			
Premium ride suspension, base 5-door	197	169	—
Includes gas shock absorbers.			

Prices are accurate at time of publication; subject to manufacturer's change.

CHEVROLET

	Retail Price	Dealer Invoice	Fair Price
Trailering Special Equipment (heavy duty)	$210	$181	—
Includes platform hitch, heavy duty flasher and 7-lead wiring harness. 2WD and 5-door 4WD require touring or premium suspension. 3-door 4WD requires off-road or touring suspension.			
Sport 2-tone paint	172	148	—
Requires LS Decor Group.			
Rear compartment shade, 3-door 4WD with LS Decor Group	69	59	—
Requires exterior spare tire carrier.			
Argent alloy wheels, base 2WD, base 2WD with Group 2	248	213	—
Cast alloy wheels, base 4WD, base 4WD with Group 2	280	241	—
Silver-painted alloy wheels	NC	NC	NC
Requires LS Decor Group.			
205/75R15 all-season white letter tires	121	104	—
235/70R15 all-season white outline letter tires	325	280	—
with option group	133	114	—
235/70R15 all-season tires, base 5-door	192	165	—
235/75R15 on/off road white outline letter tires, 4WD	335	288	—
4WD with option group	143	123	—
Requires off-road or touring suspension. Requires exterior spare tire carrier with 3-door.			

Chevrolet Camaro

	Retail Price	Dealer Invoice	Fair Price
3-door hatchback	$14250	$13039	$13750
2-door convertible	19495	17838	18995
Z28 3-door hatchback	17915	16392	17415
Z28 convertible	23095	21132	22595
Destination charge	500	500	500

Standard Equipment:

3.4-liter V-6 engine, 5-speed manual transmission, anti-lock brakes, driver- and passenger-side air bags, power steering, reclining front bucket seats with 4-way adjustable driver's seat, center console with cup holders and lighted storage compartment, folding rear seatback, solar-control tinted glass, color-keyed left remote and right manual sport mirrors, tilt steering wheel, intermittent wipers, AM/FM cassette, day/night rearview mirror with dual reading lights, Pass-Key theft-deterrent system, tachometer, voltmeter, oil pressure and temperature gauges, trip odometer, low oil level indicator system, covered visor mirrors, door map pockets, rear spoiler, front floormats, 215/60R16 all-season tires. **Z28** adds: 5.7-liter V-8 engine, 6-speed manual transmission, 4-wheel disc brakes, limited-slip differential, performance ride and handling suspension, black roof and mirrors, low coolant indicator system, 235/55R16 all-season tires, alloy wheels. **Base and Z28 convertibles** add: rear defogger, power folding top, 3-piece hard boot with storage bag, color-keyed mirrors (Z28), 4-way adjustable driver's seat (Z28).

Optional Equipment:

	Retail Price	Dealer Invoice	Fair Price
4-speed automatic transmission	$750	$645	$713
Base Preferred Equipment Group 1,			
hatchback and convertible	1240	1066	1178
Air conditioning, cruise control, remote hatch/decklid release, fog lamps.			
Base Preferred Equipment Group 2,			
hatchback and convertible	2036	1751	1934
Group 1 plus power windows with driver-side express down, power locks and mirrors, remote illuminated entry, leather-wrapped steering wheel, transmission shifter and parking brake release.			
Z28 Preferred Equipment Group 1,			
hatchback with manual transmission	1385	1191	1316
hatchback with automatic transmission	1275	1097	1211
convertible with manual transmission	1350	1161	1283
hatchback with automatic transmission	1240	1066	1178
Air conditioning, cruise control, remote hatch/decklid release, fog lamps, engine oil cooler (with 6-speed manual transmission), 4-way manual seat adjuster (hatchback).			
Z28 Preferred Equipment Group 2,			
hatchback with manual transmission	2181	1876	2072
hatchback with automatic transmission	2071	1781	1967
convertible with manual transmission	2146	1846	2039
convertible with automatic transmission	2036	1751	1934
Group 1 plus power windows with driver-side express down, power locks and mirrors, remote illuminated entry, leather-wrapped steering wheel, transmission shifter and parking brake release.			
Performance Pkg., Z28 hatchback	310	267	295
Engine oil cooler, Special Handling Suspension System (includes larger stabilizer bars, stiffer shock absorbers and bushings). Requires 245/50ZR16 tires and Group 1. NA with power seat or removable roof panels.			
6-way power driver's seat	270	232	257
Z28 hatchback requires option group.			
Leather bucket seats	499	429	474
Z28 hatchback without option group	534	459	507
Performance axle ratio, Z28 hatchback			
and convertible	250	215	238
Requires 4-speed automatic transmission and 245/50ZR16 tires.			

Prices are accurate at time of publication; subject to manufacturer's change.

CHEVROLET

	Retail Price	Dealer Invoice	Fair Price
Rear defogger	$170	$146	$162
Power door locks	220	189	209
Requires Preferred Group 1.			
Removable roof panels	970	834	922
Includes locks and storage provisions. Base adds black roof and mirrors.			
Hatch roof sunshades	25	22	24
Color-keyed roof and mirrors, base with removable roof panels, Z28	NC	NC	NC
Delco/Bose AM/FM cassette player, hatchbacks	350	301	333
Requires option group.			
Delco/Bose AM/FM CD player, hatchbacks	606	521	576
Requires option group.			
AM/FM CD player, convertibles	226	194	215
Color-keyed bodyside moldings	60	52	57
Rear floormats	15	13	14
235/55R16 all-season tires, base	132	114	125
Requires alloy wheels.			
245/50ZR16 tires, Z28 hatchback and convertible	225	194	214
Includes 150 mph speedometer.			
245/50ZR16 all-season tires, Z28 hatchback and convertible	225	194	214
Includes 150 mph speedometer.			
Alloy wheels, base	275	237	261

Chevrolet Caprice/Impala SS	Retail Price	Dealer Invoice	Fair Price
Classic 4-door notchback	$20310	$17771	$18271
Classic Special Value 4-door notchback (Pkg. 1SLX)	19495	18266	—
Classic Special Value 4-door notchback (Pkg. 1SMX)	20295	19014	—
Classic Special Value 4-door notchback (Pkg. 1SNX)	21195	19855	—
Classic 5-door wagon	22840	19985	20485
Classic Special Value 5-door wagon	21995	20603	—
Impala SS 4-door notchback	22910	20963	—
Destination charge	585	585	585

Special Value and Impala SS fair prices not available at time of publication. Special Value prices include destination charge. Additional "value-priced" models may be available in California.

Standard Equipment:

Classic: 4.3-liter V-8 engine, 4-speed automatic transmission, anti-lock brakes, driver- and passenger-side air bags, power steering, air conditioning, power door locks, custom 55/45 cloth seats with recliners and seatback pockets, front and rear armrests, tilt steering wheel, AM/FM radio, Pass-Key theft-deterrent system, tinted glass, voltmeter and oil pressure gauge, trip odometer, oil change monitor, intermittent wipers, door pockets, front door courtesy lamps, left remote and right manual mirrors, passenger-side visor mirror, cup holders, floormats, 215/75R15 tires, full wheel covers. **Wagon** has 5.7-liter V-8 engine, rear-facing third seat, cassette player, luggage rack, 2-way tailgate, rear wiper/washer, power tailgate window release, 225/75R15 whitewall tires. **Special Value Pkg. 1SLX** adds to Classic notchback: power windows, rear defogger, power decklid release, cruise control, cassette player, conventional spare tire, 215/75R15 whitewall tires, deluxe wheel covers. **Special Value Pkg. 1SMX** adds: power front seats, premium cassette player, alloy wheels. **Special Value Pkg. 1SNX** adds: power antenna, power mirrors, leather upholstery, Twilight Sentinel, remote keyless entry system, Custom Interior Pkg. **Special Value wagon** adds to Classic Wagon: automatic leveling suspension, power windows, cruise control, power mirrors, cassette player with automatic tone control and premium speakers, power antenna, power front seats, Custom Interior Pkg., automatic day/night mirror, rear defogger, deluxe rear compartment trim, rear reading lamps, wire wheel covers, conventional spare tire. **Impala SS** adds to Classic: 5.7-liter V-8 engine, 4-wheel disc brakes, extra capacity engine cooling, transmission oil cooler, special ride and handling suspension, limited-slip differential, gas shock absorbers, rear spoiler, power windows, cassette player, cruise control, leather-wrapped steering wheel, 45/45 leather seats with recliners, power driver's seat, console, driver-side visor mirror, power trunk release, power mirrors, color-keyed grille and moldings, blackout exterior trim, cargo net, conventional spare tire, 5-spoke alloy wheels, 255/50ZR17 tires.

Optional Equipment:

	Retail Price	Dealer Invoice	Fair Price
5.7-liter V-8 engine, Classic notchback	$550	$473	$490

Includes transmission oil cooler. Requires sport suspension and option group.

Preferred Equipment Group 1,			
Classic notchback	703	605	626

Cruise control, power windows with driver-side express down, power mirrors and decklid release.

Preferred Equipment Group 2,			
Classic notchback	1382	1189	1230
with premium cassette player	1437	1236	1279
with CD player	1537	1322	1368

Group 1 plus 6-way power driver's seat, cassette player, power antenna, passenger-side lighted visor mirror, front and rear reading lamps.

CHEVROLET

	Retail Price	Dealer Invoice	Fair Price
Preferred Equipment Group 3,			
Classic notchback	$2016	$1734	$1794
with premium cassette player	2071	1781	1843
with CD player	2171	1867	1932
Group 2 plus cornering lamps, automatic day/night mirror with reading lamps, remote keyless entry, power passenger's seat, Twilight Sentinel.			
Preferred Equipment Group 1, wagon	948	815	844
Cruise control, power windows with driver-side express down, power mirrors, 6-way power driver's seat.			
Preferred Equipment Group 2,			
wagon	1821	1566	1621
Group 1 plus 6-way power passenger's seat, rear defogger, heated mirrors, power antenna, automatic day/night rearview mirror, passenger-side lighted visor mirror, rear reading lights, deluxe rear compartment decor, rear compartment security cover.			
Preferred Equipment Group 1, Impala SS	890	765	792
Automatic day/night rearview mirror, rear defogger with heated mirrors, power antenna, 6-way power passenger's seat, remote keyless entry and trunk release, Twilight Sentinel.			
Cruise control	225	194	200
Classic notchback requires option group.			
Rear defogger	170	146	151
Impala SS, Classic with option group	205	176	182
Impala SS and Classic with option group include heated outside mirror.			
Custom Interior Pkg., notchback with			
Group 3, wagon with Group 2	130	112	116
Cargo net, front courtesy lamps, driver-side visor mirror, custom door trim.			
Leather 55/45 seat, Classic notchback with			
Group 3	645	555	574
6-way power driver's seat,			
Classic notchback with Group 1	305	262	271
Limited-slip differential,			
Classic notchback with standard engine	250	215	223
wagon	100	86	89
Wagon requires Trailering Pkg.			
Sport suspension,			
notchbacks (except Impala SS)	508	437	452
Limited slip differential, leather-wrapped steering wheel, Trailering Pkg., 235/70R15 tires. Requires 5.7-liter V-8 engine.			
Automatic leveling suspension,			
Classic wagon with Group 2	175	151	156
Ride/handling suspension,			
notchbacks (except Impala SS)	49	42	44

	Retail Price	Dealer Invoice	Fair Price
Trailering Pkg., Classic wagon	$21	$18	$19
Includes heavy duty cooling.			
Cassette player, Classic notchback	200	172	178
Includes AM/FM radio with seek and scan, auto reverse, digital clock.			
Premium cassette player,			
Classic notchback	255	219	227
Classic wagon, Impala SS	55	47	49
Includes AM/FM radio with seek and scan, digital clock, automatic tone control, theft lock, speed-compensated volume and premium speakers.			
CD player, Classic notchback	355	305	316
Classic wagon, Impala SS	155	133	138
Includes AM/FM radio with seek and scan, digital clock, automatic tone control, theft lock, speed-compensated volume and premium speakers.			
Woodgrain exterior trim, wagons	595	512	530
2-tone paint	141	121	125
Pinstriping, Classic notchback	61	52	54
Cargo net (std. Impala SS)	30	26	27
Wire wheel covers, Classic	215	185	191
Deluxe wheel covers, Classic	70	60	62
Alloy wheels, Classic notchback	250	215	223
215/75R15 all-season whitewall tires,			
Classic notchback	80	69	71
225/70R15 all-season whitewall tires,			
Classic notchback	176	151	157
Requires ride/handling suspension.			
235/70R15 all-season whitewall tires,			
Classic notchback	90	77	80
Requires 5.7-liter V-8 engine.			
Full-size spare for above tires	65	56	58
235/70R15 all-season full-size spare tire	60	52	53
Engine block heater	20	17	18

Chevrolet Cavalier

	Retail Price	Dealer Invoice	Fair Price
2-door notchback	$10060	$9507	—
4-door notchback	10265	9700	—
LS 4-door notchback	12465	11530	—
Destination charge	485	485	485

Fair price not available at time of publication. Additional "value-priced" models may be available in California.

Standard Equipment:

2.2-liter 4-cylinder engine, 5-speed manual transmission, anti-lock brakes, driver- and passenger-side air bags, power steering, tinted glass, cloth reclining front bucket seats, fold-down rear seat, battery rundown protection, floor console with armrest, left remote and right manual mirrors, 195/70R14 tires, wheel covers. **LS** adds: 3-speed automatic transmission, air conditioning, AM/FM radio, tachometer, trip odometer, dual reading lamps, visor mirrors, mechanical decklid release, color-keyed fascias and bodyside moldings, front mud guards, trunk net, 195/65R15 tires.

Optional Equipment:	Retail Price	Dealer Invoice	Fair Price
3-speed automatic transmission, base	$495	$441	—
Air conditioning	785	699	—
Preferred Equipment Group 1, base 2-door	210	187	—
base 4-door	193	172	—
Remote decklid release, intermittent wipers, visor mirrors, charcoal bodyside moldings, floormats. 2-door adds easy-entry front passenger seat.			
Preferred Equipment Group 2, base 2-door	580	516	—
base 4-door	563	501	—
Group 1 plus cruise control, tilt steering wheel.			
Preferred Equipment Group 1, LS	435	387	—
Tilt steering wheel, intermittent wipers, cruise control.			
Preferred Equipment Group 2, LS	1101	980	—
Group 1 plus power mirrors, power door locks, power windows.			
Exterior Appearance Pkg.,			
2-door with Group 1 or 2	200	178	—
Color-keyed fascias and bodyside molding, 195/65R15 tires, 15-inch wheel covers.			
Rear defogger	170	151	—
Power sunroof, 2-door with Group 1 or 2	595	530	—
Power door locks, 2-door	210	187	—
4-door	250	223	—
AM/FM radio, base	332	295	—
AM/FM cassette, base	472	420	—
LS	140	125	—
AM/FM CD player, base	728	648	—
LS	396	352	—
Engine block heater	20	18	—
Alloy wheels, LS	259	231	—

Chevrolet Corsica	Retail Price	Dealer Invoice	Fair Price
4-door notchback	$13890	$12570	$12870
Special Value 4-door notchback (Pkg. 1SPX) ...	13595	12613	—
Special Value 4-door notchback (Pkg. 1SQX) ...	14595	13538	—
Destination charge	495	495	495

Special Value models' fair price not available at time of publication. Special Value models include destination charge. Additional "value-priced" models may be available in California.

Standard Equipment:

Base: 2.2-liter 4-cylinder engine, 3-speed automatic transmission, anti-lock brakes, driver-side air bag, door-mounted automatic front seatbelts, power steering, air conditioning, automatic power door locks, cloth reclining front bucket seats, 4-way manual driver's seat, center console with cup holders and storage, AM/FM radio, color-keyed remote manual mirrors, color-keyed grille and bodyside moldings, tinted glass, passenger-side visor mirror, front door pockets, 195/70R14 tires, full wheel covers. **Special Value Pkg. 1SPX** adds: intermittent wipers, rear defogger, day/night rearview mirror with reading lamps, visor mirrors, trunk net, floormats. **Special Value Pkg. 1SQX** adds: 3.1-liter V-6 engine, 4-speed automatic transmission, cassette player, tilt steering wheel.

Optional Equipment:	Retail Price	Dealer Invoice	Fair Price
3.1-liter V-6	$720	$619	$634
Includes 4-speed automatic transmission.			
Preferred Equipment Group 1	165	142	145
Intermittent wipers, reading lights, driver- and passenger-side covered visor mirrors, trunk net, floormats.			
Preferred Equipment Group 2	745	641	656
Group 1 plus cruise control, tilt steering wheel, power decklid release, split folding rear seat with armrest.			
Power windows	340	292	299
Rear defogger	170	146	150
AM/FM cassette player	140	120	123
AM/FM CD player	396	341	348
Styled steel wheels	56	48	49
195/70R14 whitewall tires	68	58	60
Engine block heater	20	17	18

Chevrolet Corvette	Retail Price	Dealer Invoice	Fair Price
3-door hatchback	$36785	$31451	$32451
2-door convertible	43665	37334	38534
Destination charge	560	560	560

Standard Equipment:

5.7-liter V-8, 6-speed manual or 4-speed automatic transmission, heavy duty anti-lock 4-wheel disc brakes, driver- and passenger-side air bags, power steering, Acceleration Slip Regulation traction control, gas shock

CHEVROLET

absorbers, Pass-Key theft-deterrent system, automatic keyless entry with remote hatch release, air conditioning, liquid-crystal gauges with analog and digital display, AM/FM cassette, power antenna, cruise control, rear defogger, reclining leather bucket seats, center console with coin tray and cassette/CD storage, armrest with lockable storage compartment, leather-wrapped tilt steering wheel, solar-control tinted glass, heated power mirrors, power windows with driver-side express down, power door locks, intermittent wipers, removable roof panel (hatchback), day/night rearview mirror with reading lights, fog lamps, lighted visor mirrors, door armrest storage compartment, Goodyear Eagle GS-C tires (255/45ZR17 front, 285/40ZR17 rear), alloy wheels. **Convertible** adds: manual folding top.

Optional Equipment:

	Retail Price	Dealer Invoice	Fair Price
ZR-1 Special Performance Pkg.	$31258	$26257	—
5.7-liter DOHC V-8, Selective Ride and Handling Pkg., 6-way power driver's and passenger's seats, leather adjustable sport bucket seats, automatic climate control, low-tire-pressure warning, Delco/Bose audio system with CD and cassette players, 275/40ZR17 front and 315/35ZR17 rear tires, 5-spoke alloy wheels.			
Preferred Equipment Group 1	1333	1120	1186
Automatic climate control, Delco/Bose audio system, 6-way power driver's seat.			
ZO7 Adjustable Performance Handling Pkg.	2045	1718	1820
Selective Ride and Handling Pkg., Bilstein Adjustable Ride Control System, stiffer springs, stabilizer bars, and bushings, 275/40ZR17 tires. Requires power seats; 4-speed automatic transmission requires performance axle ratio.			
FX3 Selective Ride and Handling Pkg.	1695	1424	1509
Bilstein Adjustable Ride Control System. Requires power seats.			
Leather adjustable sport bucket seats	625	525	556
Requires driver's and passenger's 6-way power seats.			
6-way power seats, each	305	256	271
Power passenger's seat requires power driver's seat.			
Delco/Bose audio system with cassette and CD player with Group 1	396	333	352
Performance axle ratio	50	42	45
Requires 4-speed automatic transmission.			
Low-tire-pressure warning indicator	325	273	289
Transparent blue- or bronze-tint removable roof panel	650	546	579
Roof Pkg.	950	798	846
Standard solid removable roof panel and transparent blue- or bronze-tint roof panel.			
Removable hardtop, convertible	1995	1676	1776
Includes rear defogger.			

	Retail Price	Dealer Invoice	Fair Price
Extended Mobility Tires	$70	$59	$62
Front 255/45ZR17 and rear 285/40ZR17 tires. Requires low-tire-pressure warning indicator. NA with Performance Handling Pkg.			
Spare tire delete (credit)	(100)	(84)	(84)
Requires Extended Mobility Tires and low-tire-pressure warning indicator.			

Chevrolet Lumina Minivan	Retail Price	Dealer Invoice	Fair Price
4-door van	$17595	$15923	$16423
Destination charge	540	540	540

Additional "value-priced" models may be available in California.

Standard Equipment:

3.1-liter V-6, 3-speed automatic transmission, anti-lock brakes, driver-side air bag, power steering, reclining front bucket seats, 4-way manual driver's seat, 3-passenger middle seat, tinted glass with solar-control windshield, lockable center console with cup holders, overhead console, front and rear reading lights, rear auxiliary power outlet, left remote and right manual mirrors, AM/FM radio, intermittent wipers, rear wiper/washer, 205/70R15 tires, wheel covers.

Optional Equipment:

3.8-liter V-6 engine	619	532	551
Requires 4-speed automatic transmission.			
4-speed automatic transmission	200	172	178
Requires 3.8-liter V-6 engine.			
Front air conditioning	830	714	739
Front and rear air conditioning	450	387	401
Requires 3.8-liter V-6 engine and Preferred Equipment Group 2 or 3.			
Preferred Equipment Group 1	778	669	692
Front air conditioning, cruise control, tilt steering wheel, power door/tailgate locks with side door delay, power mirrors.			
Preferred Equipment Group 2	2323	1998	2067
Group 1 plus cassette player, power windows with driver-side express down, rear defogger, remote keyless entry, deep-tinted glass, 7-passenger seating, cargo area net.			
Preferred Equipment Group 3	2843	2445	2530
Group 2 plus LS Trim Pkg. (includes body-color bumpers and rocker panels, upgraded cloth upholstery) and 6-way power driver's seat.			
7-passenger seating, base, base with Group 1	660	568	587
Two front bucket seats and five modular rear seats.			

Prices are accurate at time of publication; subject to manufacturer's change.

CHEVROLET

	Retail Price	Dealer Invoice	Fair Price
Trailering Pkg.	$320	$275	$285
Includes load leveling suspension. Requires 3.8-liter V-6 engine, and Preferred Equipment Group 2 or 3.			
Traction Control	350	301	312
Requires Group 3.			
Manual sunroof (NA base or with Group 1)	300	258	267
Luggage rack (NA base)	145	125	129
Rear defogger	170	146	151
Deep-tinted glass	245	211	218
Power door/tailgate locks	300	258	267
Power windows, Group 1	275	237	245
Includes driver-side express down.			
Power mirrors	78	67	69
6-way power driver's seat, Group 3	270	232	240
Cloth highback bucket seats	182	157	162
Integral child safety seats, dual	225	194	200
single	125	108	111
Requires 7-passenger seating and option group.			
Power sliding side door	350	301	312
Requires Group 2 or 3.			
Load leveling suspension	170	146	151
Requires 205/70R15 tires, alloy wheels and Group 2 or 3.			
Cruise control	225	194	200
Tilt steering wheel	145	125	129
Cassette player	140	120	125
CD player	396	341	352
with Group 2 and 3	256	220	228
Custom 2-tone paint	148	127	132
Cargo area net	30	26	27
205/70R15 touring tires	35	30	31
Requires alloy wheels.			
205/70R15 self-sealing tires	150	129	134
Alloy wheels	275	237	245
Requires 205/70R15 touring tires.			
Engine block heater	20	17	18

Chevrolet Lumina/Monte Carlo	Retail Price	Dealer Invoice	Fair Price
Lumina 4-door notchback	$15470	$14000	$14970
Lumina LS 4-door notchback	16970	15358	16470
Monte Carlo LS 2-door notchback	16770	15177	16270
Monte Carlo Z34 2-door notchback	18970	17168	18470
Destination charge	525	525	525

Standard Equipment:

Lumina: 3.1-liter V-6 engine, 4-speed automatic transmission, driver- and passenger-side air bags, power steering, air conditioning, power door locks, 60/40 cloth reclining front seat with center armrest and 4-way manual driver-side adjustment, seatback storage pocket, cup holder, tilt steering wheel, AM/FM radio with digital clock, visor mirrors, reading lights, Pass Key theft-deterrent system, low oil level sensor, trip odometer, tinted glass, floor-mats, left remote and right manual mirrors, intermittent wipers, body-color grille, bodyside moldings, wheel covers, 205/70R15 tires. **Lumina LS/Monte Carlo LS** add: anti-lock brakes, power windows, custom cloth 60/40 reclining front seat with center armrest and 4-way manual driver-side adjustment, split fold-down rear seat (Monte Carlo LS), tachometer, cassette player, lighted passenger-side visor mirror, body-color mirrors, chrome grille (Monte Carlo LS), lower body accent paint, deluxe wheel covers. **Monte Carlo Z34** adds to Monte Carlo LS: 3.4-liter DOHC V-6 engine, ride and handling suspension, custom cloth front bucket seats with center console, cruise control, power decklid release, power mirrors, remote keyless entry, black lower body molding, trunk net, alloy wheels, 225/60R16 tires.

Optional Equipment:	Retail Price	Dealer Invoice	Fair Price
3.4-liter DOHC V-6 engine, Lumina LS	$960	$854	$912
Requires 225/60R16 tires and alloy wheels.			
Anti-lock brakes, base Lumina	386	344	367
Preferred Equipment Group 1, base Lumina	707	629	672
Power windows and mirrors, cruise control, power decklid release, trunk net.			
Preferred Equipment Group 1, Lumina LS, Monte Carlo LS	500	445	475
Remote keyless entry, power mirrors, cruise control, power decklid release, trunk net.			
Rear defogger	164	146	156
Remote keyless entry, base Lumina	130	116	124
Requires Group 1.			
Cassette player, base Lumina	135	120	128
Premium cassette player, base Lumina	207	184	197
Lumina LS, Monte Carlo	72	64	68
Power driver's seat	260	231	247
Custom cloth front bucket seats w/center console, Lumina LS, Monte Carlo LS	48	43	46
Lumina LS requires Group 1.			
Custom cloth 60/40 seat, Monte Carlo Z34 (credit)	(48)	(43)	(43)
Leather front bucket seats, Monte Carlo LS	600	534	570

Prices are accurate at time of publication; subject to manufacturer's change.

	Retail Price	Dealer Invoice	Fair Price
Monte Carlo Z34	$552	$491	$524
Cruise control (std. Monte Carlo Z34)	217	193	205
Cellular telephone pre-wiring	43	38	41
NA with bucket seats.			
Lower body accent paint,			
Lumina LS (credit)	(37)	(33)	(33)
White wheel covers, base Lumina	NC	NC	NC
Requires white exterior paint.			
Deluxe wheel covers, base Lumina	68	61	65
Alloy wheels (std. Monte Carlo Z34)	251	223	238
Requires 225/60R16 tires.			
White alloy wheels, Monte Carlo	NC	NC	NC
Requires white exterior paint. LS requires alloy wheels and 225/60R16 tires.			
225/60R16 tires, Lumina LS	150	134	143
Requires alloy wheels.			
225/60R16 touring tires			
(NA Monte Carlo Z34)	135	120	128
Requires alloy wheels.			
Engine block heater	19	17	18

CHRYSLER

Chrysler Cirrus	Retail Price	Dealer Invoice	Fair Price
LX 4-door notchback	$17435	15987	—
LXi 4-door notchback	19365	17705	—
Destination charge	535	535	535

Fair price not available at time of publication.

Standard Equipment:

LX: 2.5-liter V-6 engine, 4-speed automatic transmission, anti-lock brakes, driver- and passenger-side air bags, variable-assist power steering, air conditioning, cloth reclining front bucket seats with driver's-side manual height and lumbar adjusters, front seat back map pockets, console, folding rear bench seat, AM/FM/cassette, digital clock, trip odometer, oil pressure and coolant temperature gauges, voltmeter, tachometer, cruise control, tilt steering column, rear defogger, power windows and door locks, tinted glass with solar-control windshield, heated power mirrors, speed-sensitive intermittent wipers, remote keyless entry, security alarm, illuminated entry, remote decklid release, reading lights, auxiliary power outlet, color-keyed bodyside moldings, lighted visor mirrors, fog lights, floormats, trunk net,

195/65R15 tires, wheel covers. **LXi** adds: sport suspension, leather and vinyl upholstery, leather-wrapped steering wheel and shift lever, 8-way power driver's seat, anti-theft alarm, 6-speaker cassette player, power antenna, alloy wheels, 195/65HR15 touring tires.

Optional Equipment:

	Retail Price	Dealer Invoice	Fair Price
Power driver's seat, LX	$377	$336	—
Cloth upholstery, LXi (credit)	(289)	(257)	(257)
Integrated child safety seat	100	89	—
Includes fixed rear seatback. Requires cloth upholstery.			
Premium cassette player, LX	368	328	—
Includes six speakers and power amplifier.			
CD player, LX	491	437	—
LXi	122	109	—
Includes six speakers and power amplifier.			
Anti-theft alarm, LX	149	133	—
Extra-cost paint	97	86	—
Full-size spare tire	95	85	—
Engine block and battery heater	30	27	—

Chrysler Concorde	Retail Price	Dealer Invoice	Fair Price
4-door notchback w/Pkg. 22B	$20550	$18496	$19296
Destination charge	535	535	535

Standard Equipment:

Pkg. 22B: 3.3-liter V-6 engine, 4-speed automatic transmission, anti-lock 4-wheel disc brakes, driver- and passenger-side air bags, touring suspension, power steering, air conditioning, tinted glass with solar-control front and rear windows, cloth front bucket seats, lumbar support adjuster, front console with armrest, power windows and door locks, tachometer, trip odometer, coolant temperature gauge, AM/FM/cassette, rear defogger, intermittent wipers, heated power mirrors, tilt steering wheel, cruise control, remote decklid release, lighted visor mirrors, reading lights, trunk cargo net, floormats, 205/70R15 tires.

Optional Equipment:

Pkg. 22C/26C	630	551	599
Automatic temperature control, power driver's seat, illuminated/remote entry systems. Pkg. 26C requires 3.5-liter engine.			
Pkg. 22D/26D	1755	1536	1667
Pkg. 22C/26C plus variable-assist power steering, Infinity cassette system, overhead console, security alarm, automatic day/night rearview mirror. Pkg. 26D requires 3.5-liter engine.			

Prices are accurate at time of publication; subject to manufacturer's change.

CHRYSLER

	Retail Price	Dealer Invoice	Fair Price
3.5-liter V-6 engine	$725	$634	$689
Requires Pkg. 26C or 26D.			
Traction control	175	153	166
Requires option pkg.			
Integrated child seat	100	88	95
NA with leather seats.			
Cloth 50/50 front bench seat	NC	NC	NC
NA with Pkg. 22D/26D.			
Power driver's seat	377	330	358
Power driver's and front			
passenger's seats	754	660	716
with option pkg.	377	330	358
Leather seats	1069	935	1016
Includes power front seats, leather-wrapped steering wheel and shift knob. Requires option pkg. NA with integrated child seat.			
Power moonroof, w/Pkg. 22C/26C	1094	957	1039
w/Pkg. 22D/26D	716	627	680
Includes mini overhead console. Mini console replaces full overhead console with Pkg. 22D/26D.			
Remote/Illuminated Entry System	221	193	210
Security alarm, w/Pkg. 22C/26C	149	130	142
Full overhead console, w/Pkg. 22C/26C	378	331	359
Includes trip computer, compass, outside temperature readout, automatic day/night mirror, slighted visor mirrors.			
Chrysler/Infinity cassette system,			
w/Pkg. 22C/26C	708	620	673
Includes equalizer, 11 speakers, amplifier, power antenna.			
Chrysler/Infinity CD system,			
w/Pkg. 22C/26C	877	767	833
w/Pkg. 22D/26D	169	148	161
Includes equalizer, 11 speakers, amplifier, power antenna.			
16-inch Wheel and Handling Group	628	550	597
w/Pkg. 22D/26D	524	459	498
Variable-assist power steering, 225/60R16 touring tires, alloy wheels.			
Conventional spare tire	95	83	90
Extra cost paint	97	85	92
Bright platinum metallic paint	200	175	190
Engine block heater.............................	20	18	19

Chrysler LeBaron	Retail Price	Dealer Invoice	Fair Price
GTC 2-door convertible	$17469	$16367	$16867
Destination charge	530	530	530

Standard Equipment:

GTC: 3.0-liter V-6 engine, 4-speed automatic transmission, driver- and passenger side air bags, power steering, power convertible top, air conditioning, cloth reclining front bucket seats, center console with armrest, rear defogger, tinted glass, tachometer, coolant temperature and oil pressure gauges, voltmeter, trip odometer, dual remote mirrors, AM/FM cassette radio, power windows, intermittent wipers, reading lights, 205/60R15 tires, wheel covers.

Optional Equipment:

	Retail Price	Dealer Invoice	Fair Price
Pkg. 26T	$1000	$850	$870
Deluxe Convenience Group, Power Convenience Group, power driver's seat, remote decklid release, floormats.			
Pkg. 26W	2100	1785	1827
Pkg. 26T plus leather seats, leather-wrapped steering wheel, Light Group, alloy wheels.			
Anti-lock disc brakes	699	594	608
Deluxe Convenience Group	372	316	324
Cruise control, tilt steering wheel.			
Power Convenience Group	338	287	294
Automatic power locks, heated power mirrors.			
Bright LX Decor Group	60	51	52
Bright grille, decklid and taillamp moldings, bodyside moldings, exterior badges, deluxe wheel covers.			
Light Group, w/Pkg. 26T	324	275	282
Illuminated entry system, lighted visor mirrors, remote keyless entry system.			
Vinyl seats	102	87	89
NA with Pkg. 26W.			
Leather seats, w/Pkg. 26T	668	568	581
Includes 6-way power driver's seat.			
Trip computer	93	79	81
Requires option pkg.			
Security alarm	149	127	130
Requires option pkg.			
AM/FM cassette w/equalizer and Infinity speakers	524	445	456
Requires option pkg.			
CD player w/equalizer and Infinity speakers	694	590	604
Requires option pkg.			
Extra-cost paint	97	82	84
15-inch alloy wheels	328	279	285
Engine block heater	20	17	18

Prices are accurate at time of publication; subject to manufacturer's change.

CHRYSLER

Chrysler New Yorker/LHS

	Retail Price	Dealer Invoice	Fair Price
New Yorker 4-door notchback	$25596	$23067	$23867
LHS 4-door notchback	29595	26646	27445
Destination charge	595	595	595

Standard Equipment:

New Yorker: 3.5-liter V-6 engine, 4-speed automatic transmission, anti-lock 4-wheel disc brakes, driver- and passenger-side air bags, variable-assist power steering, air conditioning, 50/50 cloth front seat with center armrests, 8-way power driver's seat with manual lumbar adjustment, tilt steering wheel, cruise control, power windows and locks, heated power mirrors, speed-sensitive intermittent wipers, rear defogger, solar control tinted glass, tachometer, trip odometer, coolant temperature gauge, AM/FM/cassette, power decklid release, automatic headlights, lighted visor mirrors, reading lights, floormats, trunk cargo net, touring suspension, 225/60R16 touring tires, wheel covers. **LHS** adds: traction control, automatic temperature control, leather upholstery, 8-way power passenger seat, front bucket seats with power recliners, center console with cup holders and storage bin, overhead console with compass and thermometer, trip computer, leather-wrapped steering wheel and shift knob, power antenna, automatic day/night rearview mirror, remote keyless illuminated entry system, Chrysler/Infinity cassette system with equalizer and 11 speakers, theft security alarm, fog lamps, alloy wheels, conventional spare tire.

Optional Equipment:

New Yorker Pkg. 26B	1338	1171	1271

Automatic temperature control, mini overhead console with compass and outside temperature readout, trip computer, Remote/Illuminated Entry Group, Chrysler/Infinity AM/FM/cassette system with equalizer and 11 speakers, power antenna, automatic day/night rearview mirror, time-delay headlamp system, security alarm, lighted visor mirrors.

New Yorker Pkg. 26C	2743	2400	2606

Pkg. 26B plus traction control, 8-way power passenger seat, leather upholstery, leather-wrapped steering wheel, alloy wheels, conventional spare tire.

8-way power front passenger seat, New Yorker	377	330	358
Leather seats, New Yorker	1075	941	1021

Includes power front passenger seat and leather-wrapped steering wheel. Requires option pkg.

Alloy wheels, New Yorker	328	287	312
Traction control, New Yorker	175	153	166
Power moonroof	792	693	752

New Yorker requires option pkg.

CHRYSLER

	Retail Price	Dealer Invoice	Fair Price
Chrysler/Infinity CD System, New Yorker with option pkg., LHS	$169	$148	$161
Includes equalizer, power antenna, and 11 speakers.			
Extra cost paint	97	85	92
Bright platinum metallic paint	200	175	190
Conventional spare tire, New Yorker	95	83	90
Engine block heater	20	18	19

Chrysler Sebring

Prices not available at time of publication.

Standard Equipment:

LX: 2.0-liter DOHC 4-cylinder engine, 5-speed manual transmission, driver- and passenger-side air bags, variable-assist power steering, air conditioning, cloth front bucket seats, console with storage armrest and auxiliary power outlet, split folding rear seat, rear headrests, tinted glass, rear defogger, tilt steering column, AM/FM radio, trip odometer, oil pressure and coolant temperature gauges, tachometer, variable intermittent wipers, remote fuel door and decklid releases, dual remote mirrors, map lights, color-keyed front and rear fascias, visor mirrors, 189/60HR14 tires, wheel covers. **LXi** adds: 2.5-liter V-6 engine, 4-speed automatic transmission, anti-lock 4-wheel disc brakes, power windows and door locks, power mirrors, upgraded cloth upholstery and driver's seat lumbar support adjuster, leather-wrapped steering wheel, 8-speaker Infinity audio system with equalizer, cruise control, lighted visor mirrors, trunk net, remote keyless entry, security alarm, floormats, 205/55HR16 tires, alloy wheels.

Chrysler Town & Country

	Retail Price	Dealer Invoice	Fair Price
4-door van	$27680	$25048	$25848
AWD 4-door van	29775	26892	27692
Destination charge	560	560	560

Standard Equipment:

3.8-liter V-6, 4-speed automatic transmission, anti-lock brakes, power steering, driver- and passenger-side air bags, front and rear air conditioning, 7-passenger seating (bucket seats in front and middle rows and 3-passenger rear bench seat), power driver's seat, leather upholstery, power front door and rear quarter vent windows, programmable power locks, forward storage console, overhead console (with compass, outside temperature readout, front and rear reading lights, and trip computer), rear defogger, intermittent wipers, rear wiper/washer, cruise control, leather-wrapped tilt steering wheel, illuminated remote keyless entry system, remote fuel door and decklid releases, tinted windshield and front door glass, sunscreen glass (other windows), electronic instruments (tachometer, coolant temperature and oil pressure gauges, trip odometer), floormats, luggage rack, heated power mirrors, lighted visor mirrors, AM/FM/cassette with graphic equalizer and 6 Infinity speakers, fog lamps, 205/70R15 tires, gold painted alloy wheels. **AWD** has permanent all-wheel drive.

Optional Equipment:

	Retail Price	Dealer Invoice	Fair Price
Leather seat trim	NC	NC	NC
7-passenger bench seating	NC	NC	NC
Front bucket seats, reclining 2-passenger middle and folding 3-passenger rear bench seats. Includes integrated child seats.			
Tinted side and rear glass	NC	NC	NC
Replaces standard sunscreen glass.			
Heavy Duty Trailer Towing Group	$270	$230	$236
AWD	200	170	175
Heavy duty brakes, flasher, suspension and radiator, trailer wiring harness, transmission oil cooler.			
CD player	170	145	149
Extra cost paint	100	85	88
Alloy wheels, white painted	NC	NC	NC
Engine block heater	35	30	31

DODGE

Dodge Avenger	Retail Price	Dealer Invoice	Fair Price
2-door notchback	$13341	$12293	—
ES 2-door notchback	17191	15720	—
Destination charge	430	430	430

Fair price not available at time of publication.

Standard Equipment:

Base: 2.0-liter DOHC 4-cylinder engine, 5-speed manual transmission, driver- and passenger-side air bags, variable-assist power steering, cloth front bucket seats, console with storage armrest and auxiliary power outlet, split folding rear seat, rear headrests, tinted glass, rear defogger, tilt steering column, AM/FM radio, trip odometer, oil pressure and coolant temperature gauges, tachometer, intermittent wipers, remote fuel door and decklid releases, dual remote mirrors, map lights, color-keyed front and rear fascias, visor mirrors, 189/60HR14 tires, wheel covers. **ES adds:** 2.5-liter V-6 engine, 4-speed automatic transmission, anti-lock 4-wheel disc brakes, air conditioning, upgraded cloth upholstery and driver's seat lumbar support adjuster, cassette player, cruise control, handling suspension, trunk net, decklid spoiler, fog lights, floormats, 205/55HR16 tires, alloy wheels.

Optional Equipment:	Retail Price	Dealer Invoice	Fair Price
4-speed automatic transmission, base	$683	$608	—
Pkg. 21B/22B, base	1216	1082	—
Air conditioning, cruise control, cassette player, floormats. Pkg. 22B requires 4-speed automatic transmission.			
Pkg. 21C/22C, base	1750	1558	—
Pkg. 21B/22B plus power windows and door locks, power mirrors, trunk net. Pkg. 22C requires 4-speed automatic transmission.			
Pkg. 24E, ES	534	475	—
Power windows and door locks, power mirrors, lighted visor mirrors.			
Pkg. 24F, ES	2199	1957	—
Pkg. 24E plus cassette player with equalizer and Infinity speakers, power driver's seat, security alarm, remote keyless entry system, power sunroof.			
Anti-lock brakes, base	599	533	—
Leather upholstery, ES	423	376	—
Requires option pkg. and power driver's seat.			
Power driver's seat, base w/Pkg. 21C/22C, ES w/Pkg.24E	203	181	—
Cassette player, base	174	155	—
Cassette player with Infinity speakers and equalizer	550	490	—
Base requires option pkg.			
CD player with Infinity speakers and equalizer	707	629	—
Base requires option pkg.			
Security alarm, base w/Pkg. 21C/22C, ES w/Pkg. 24E	272	242	—
Includes remote keyless entry system.			

Dodge Caravan	Retail Price	Dealer Invoice	Fair Price
Base SWB	$16160	$14721	$15221
Base Grand	18605	16897	17697
SE SWB	18855	17092	17592
Grand SE	19595	17769	18569
Grand SE AWD	22270	20123	20923
LE SWB	23380	21074	21574
Grand LE	23680	21363	22163
Grand LE AWD	25755	23189	23989
ES SWB	23890	21523	22023
Grand ES	24190	21812	22612

Prices are accurate at time of publication; subject to manufacturer's change.

DODGE

	Retail Price	Dealer Invoice	Fair Price
Grand ES AWD	$26265	$23638	$24438
Destination charge	560	560	560

SWB denotes standard wheelbase; AWD denotes All-Wheel Drive.

Standard Equipment:

Base: 2.5-liter 4-cylinder engine, 3-speed automatic transmission, driver- and passenger-side air bags, power steering, cloth front bucket seats, 3-passenger middle bench seat, tinted glass, trip odometer, coolant temperature gauge, dual outside mirrors, visor mirrors, AM/FM radio, automatic day/night mirror, intermittent wipers, rear wiper/washer, 195/75R14 tires, wheel covers. **Base Grand** adds: 3.0-liter V-6 engine, 4-speed automatic transmission, 7-passenger seating (front bucket seats, 2-place middle bench and 3-place rear bench seats), rear trim panel storage and cup holders, 205/70R15 tires. **SE** adds to Base: 3.0-liter V-6 engine, 7-passenger seating (front bucket seats, 2-place middle bench and 3-place rear bench seats), cruise control, power mirrors, 6-speaker cassette player, power remote tailgate release, tilt steering wheel, front passenger lockable underseat storage drawer, striping, dual note horn. **Grand SE** adds to Base Grand: 3.3-liter V-6 engine, cruise control, power mirrors, 6-speaker cassette player, power remote tailgate release, tilt steering wheel, front passenger lockable underseat storage drawer, striping, dual note horn. **LE** adds to SE: 4-speed automatic transmission, anti-lock brakes, front air conditioning, front storage console, overhead console with trip computer, rear defogger, power rear quarter vent windows, power door locks, remote keyless entry system, tachometer, oil pressure gauge, voltmeter, heated power mirrors, lighted visor mirrors, illuminated entry system, headlamp time delay, floormats, 205/70R15 tires. **Grand LE** adds to Grand SE: anti-lock brakes, front air conditioning, front storage console, overhead console with trip computer, rear defogger, power rear quarter vent windows, power door locks, remote keyless entry system, tachometer, oil pressure gauge, voltmeter, heated power mirrors, lighted visor mirrors, illuminated entry system, headlamp time delay, floormats. **ES** adds to LE and Grand LE: ES Decor Group. AWD models have permanently engaged all-wheel drive.

Quick Order Packages:

Pkg. 22T/24T Base SWB, Pkg. 26T Base SWB, Base Grand, ...	225	191	207

Front air conditioning, map and cargo lights, power remote liftgate release, front passenger underseat lockable storage drawer, bodyside molding, dual horns. Pkg. 24T requires 3.0-liter engine; Pkg. 26T requires 3.0-liter engine and 4-speed transmission.

Pkg. 27T Base SWB	5210	4428	4793

Pkg. 22T/24T/26T plus 3.3-liter compressed natural gas V-6 engine. Requires 4-speed automatic transmission.

	Retail Price	Dealer Invoice	Fair Price
Pkg. 24B/26B SE SWB, Pkg. 26B Grand SE,			
Pkg. 28B SE SWB, Grand SE	$220	$187	$202

Pkg. 24B/26B/28B adds to SE standard equipment: front air conditioning, map and cargo lights, rear defogger. SE SWB Pkg. 26B requires 4-speed automatic transmission; Grand SE Pkg. 26B requires 3.0-liter engine; SE SWB Pkg. 28B requires 3.3-liter engine and 4-speed automatic transmission.

Pkg. 27B SE SWB	5205	4424	4789

Pkg. 24B/26B/28B plus 3.3-liter compressed natural gas V-6 engine. Requires 4-speed automatic transmission.

Pkg. 24D/26D/28D SE SWB, Pkg. 28D			
Grand SE AWD, ...	1080	918	994
Pkg. 26D/28D Grand SE	1580	1343	1454

Pkg. 24D/26D/28D adds to Pkg. 24B/26B/28B: anti-lock brakes (Grand SE), forward and overhead consoles, oil pressure and voltage gauges, tachometer, lighted visor mirrors, Light Group, power door locks and rear quarter vent windows, floormats. SE SWB Pkg. 26D requires 4-speed automatic transmission; Grand SE Pkg. 26D requires 3.0-liter engine; SE SWB Pkg. 28D requires 3.3-liter engine and 4-speed automatic transmission.

Pkg. 27D SE SWB	5226	5064	4808

Pkg. 24D/26D/28D plus 3.3-liter compressed natural gas V-6 engine. Requires 4-speed automatic transmission.

Pkg. 24E/26E/28E SE SWB, Pkg. 28E			
Grand SE AWD	1960	1666	1803
Pkg. 26E/28E Grand SE	2460	2091	2263

Pkg. 24E/26E/28E adds to Pkg. 24D/26D/28D: trip computer, remote keyless entry, power driver's seat, passenger assist handle, power windows. SE SWB Pkg. 26E requires 4-speed automatic transmission; Grand SE Pkg. 26E requires 3.0-liter engine; SE SWB Pkg. 28E requires 3.3-liter engine and 4-speed automatic transmission.

Pkg. 27E SE SWB	6838	5812	6291

Pkg. 24E/26E/28E plus 3.3-liter compressed natural gas V-6 engine. Requires 4-speed automatic transmission.

Pkg. 26K/28K LE SWB, Pkg. 28K/29K			
Grand LE AWD	315	268	290
Pkg. 28K/29K Grand LE	215	183	198

Pkg. 26K/28K/29K adds to LE standard equipment: power driver's seat, power windows, AM/FM radio with cassette player, equalizer and six Infinity speakers, sunscreen glass. LE SWB Pkg. 28K requires 3.3-liter engine; Grand LE and Grand LE AWD Pkg. 29K require 3.8-liter engine.

Pkg. 26M/28M ES SWB	445	378	409
Pkg. 28M/29M Grand ES	345	293	317

DODGE

	Retail Price	Dealer Invoice	Fair Price
Pkg. 28M/29M Grand ES AWD	$315	$268	$290

Pkg. 26M/28M/29M adds to Pkg. 26K/28K/29K ES SWB, Grand ES: ES Decor Group (body-color fascia, cladding, and grille, fog lamps, alloy wheels), Sport Handling Group (heavy duty brakes, firmer front and rear sway bars, upgraded front struts and rear shocks, 205/70R15 tires, alloy wheels). Pkg. 28M/29M adds to Pkg. 28K/29K Grand ES AWD: ES Decor Pkg. 205/70R15 tires, alloy wheels. (Sport Handling Group not available with AWD); deletes 2-tone paint. ES SWB Pkg. 28M requires 3.3-liter engine; Grand ES and Grand ES AWD Pkg. 29M require 3.8-liter engine.

Individual Options:

	Retail	Dealer	Fair
3.0-liter V-6, Base SWB			
w/Pkgs. 24T/26T	770	655	708
Grand SE (credit)	(105)	(89)	(89)
3.3-liter compressed natural gas V-6,			
Base SWB	875	744	805
SE SWB	105	89	97
Requires 4-speed automatic transmission.			
3.3-liter V-6, SE SWB w/Pkgs. 28B/28D/28E,			
LE SWB w/Pkg. 28K, ES SWB w/Pkg. 28M,			
Grand SE	105	89	97
SWB models require 4-speed automatic transmission.			
3.8-liter V-6, Grand LE and Grand LE AWD			
w/Pkg. 29K, Grand ES and			
Grand ES AWD w/Pkg. 29M	305	259	281
Includes 4-speed transmission.			
4-speed automatic transmission, Base and			
SE SWB, Base Grand w/Pkg. 26T	200	170	184
Anti-lock brakes:			
SE SWB w/Pkgs. 24B/26B/28B,			
24D/26D/28D or 24E/26E/28E	690	587	635
SE SWB w/Pkgs. 24D/26B/28B,			
24D/26D/28D or 24E/26E/28E and Sport			
Handling, Sport Decor or SE Decor			
Groups	600	510	552
Front air conditioning, Base SWB and			
Base Grand	860	731	791
Front air conditioning with sunscreen glass,			
Base SWB w/option pkg., SE SWB			
w/option pkg, Base Grand w/option pkg.,			
Grand SE w/option pkg.	415	353	382
Sunscreen glass, Grand SE	415	353	382

	Retail Price	Dealer Invoice	Fair Price
Rear air conditioning with rear heater and sunscreen glass, Base Grand w/option pkg., Grand SE w/option pkg.	$850	$752	$782

Pkg. 24T/26T requires rear window defogger.

	Retail Price	Dealer Invoice	Fair Price
Grand SE w/Pkgs. 26D/28D or 26E/28E and Sport or SE Decor Groups, Grand LE and Grand ES w/option pkg., Grand SE AWD w/Sport or SE Decor Groups	470	400	432
Grand LE and Grand ES w/option pkg. and Trailer Towing Group, AWD w/Trailer Towing Group	405	344	373
Rear bench seat, Base SWB	350	298	322
7-passenger seating w/integrated child seat, Base SWB	575	489	529
SE, LE and ES SWB, Grand, Grand AWD	225	191	207
Quad Command Seating, SE, LE and ES	600	510	552

Two front and two middle bucket seats, 3-passenger rear bench seat.

	Retail Price	Dealer Invoice	Fair Price
Leather trim, Grand SE w/Pkg.28K/29K, Grand ES, Grand SE AWD, Grand ES AWD	865	735	796

NA with integrated child seat.

	Retail Price	Dealer Invoice	Fair Price
Heavy Duty Trailer Towing Group, Grand LE w/Pkg. 28K/29K	445	378	409
Grand LE w/Pkg. 28K/29K and Sport Handling Group, Grand ES w/Pkg. 26M/28M	410	349	377
Grand LE AWD w/Pkg. 28K/29K, Grand ES AWD w/Pkg. 28M/29M	375	319	345

Heavy duty battery, load suspension and radiator, transmission oil cooler, trailer towing wiring harness, conventional spare tire.

	Retail Price	Dealer Invoice	Fair Price
Sport Handling Group, SWB LE and Grand LE w/Pkg. 26K/28K	505	429	465

Front and rear sway bars, 205/70R15 touring tires, alloy wheels.

	Retail Price	Dealer Invoice	Fair Price
LE SWB w/Pkg. 26K/28K, Grand LE w/Pkg. 28K/29K	488	415	449

Heavy duty brakes, front and rear sway bars, 205/70R15 tires, alloy wheels.

	Retail Price	Dealer Invoice	Fair Price
Sport Decor Group, SWB SE with Pkgs. 24B/26B/28B, 24D/26D/28D or 24E/26E/28E, Grand SE and Grand SE AWD w/option pkg.	800	680	736

Luggage rack, sunscreen glass, Sport Handling Group, exterior Sport decals, white-painted alloy wheels, 205/70R15 touring tires (Grand SE AWD). NA with SE Decor Group. NA Grand SE AWD with sunscreen glass.

Prices are accurate at time of publication; subject to manufacturer's change.

DODGE

	Retail Price	Dealer Invoice	Fair Price
SE Decor Group, SWB SE with Pkgs. 24B/26B/28B, 24D/26D/28D or 24E/26E/28E, Grand SE and Grand SE AWD w/option pkg.	$750	$638	$690
Heavy duty brakes (SWB SE), dark quartz front and rear fascias, sunscreen glass, two-tone paint, exterior SE decals, alloy wheels, 205/70R15 tires (SWB SE). NA with Sport Decor Group. NA Grand SE AWD with sunscreen glass.			
Convenience Group I, Base SWB and Base Grand w/option pkg.	375	319	345
Cruise control, tilt steering wheel.			
Convenience Group II, Base SWB and Base Grand w/option pkg.	700	595	644
SE SWB w/Pkg. 24/26B/27B/28B, Grand SE w/Pkg. 26B/28B	265	225	244
Convenience Group I plus power mirrors and door locks.			
Convenience Group III, SE SWB w/Pkg. 24B/26B/27B/28B, Grand SE w/Pkg. 26B/28B	675	574	621
SE SWB w/Pkg. 26D/28D, Grand SE w/Pkg. 26D/28D	410	349	377
Convenience Group II plus power windows and remote keyless entry system.			
AWD Convenience Group II, Grand SE AWD with Pkg. 28D	410	349	377
Power windows and remote keyless entry system.			
Rear defogger	170	145	156
Power door locks, Base w/option pkg.	265	225	244
Luggage rack	143	122	132
Base requires option pkg.			
Cassette player, Base	170	145	156
AM and FM stereo with CD player, equalizer and six Infinity speakers LE SWB w/Pkg. 26K/28K, Grand LE w/Pkg. 28K/29K, Grand LE AWD w/Pkg. 28K/29K, ES SWB w/Pkg. 28M/29M, Grand ES w/ Pkg. 28M/29M, Grand ES AWD w/Pkg. 28M/29M	170	145	156
Infinity speaker system, SE w/Pkgs. 24D/26D/27D/28D or 24E/26E/27E/28E	205	174	189
Conventional spare tire	110	94	101
NA with 3.3-liter compressed natural gas V-6.			
Extra-cost paint	100	85	92

	Retail Price	Dealer Invoice	Fair Price
15-inch alloy wheels, LE SWB w/Pkg. 26K/28K, Grand LE w/Pkg. 28K/29K, Grand LE AWD w/Pkg. 28K/29K	$375	$319	$345
Engine block heater	35	30	32

Dodge Intrepid

	Retail Price	Dealer Invoice	Fair Price
4-door notchback	$17974	$16227	$17027
ES 4-door notchback	20844	18739	19539
Destination charge	535	535	535

Standard Equipment:

3.3-liter V-6 engine, 4-speed automatic transmission, driver- and passenger-side air bags, power steering, air conditioning, cloth front bucket seats, console with armrest and cupholders, solar control glass, heated power mirrors, rear defogger, tilt steering wheel, intermittent wipers, AM/FM cassette with six speakers, tachometer, coolant temperature gauge, headlamp shut-off delay, trip odometer, AM/FM radio, reading lights, visor mirrors, touring suspension, 205/70R15 tires, wheel covers. **ES** adds: anti-lock 4-wheel disc brakes, variable-assist power steering, cruise control, power windows and door locks, premium cloth front bucket seats with lumbar support adjustment, remote decklid release, fog lamps, Message Center, floormats, trunk cargo net, 225/60R16 touring tires, alloy wheels.

Optional Equipment:

Pkg. 22C/24C, base	723	633	687

Power windows and locks, cruise control, floormats. Pkg. 24C requires 3.3-liter "Flex Fuel" V-6 engine.

Pkg. 22D/26D, base	1407	1231	1337

Pkg. 22C/24C plus 4-wheel disc brakes, power driver's seat, remote decklid release, Message Center, lighted visor mirrors. Pkg. 26D requires 3.5-liter V-6 engine.

Pkg. 22L/26L, ES	693	606	658

Power driver's seat, Remote/Illuminated Entry Group, leather-wrapped steering wheel, lighted visor mirrors, passenger assist handles. Pkg. 26L requires 3.5-liter engine.

Pkg. 22M/26M, ES	2085	1824	1955

Traction control, power driver's seat, Remote/Illuminated Entry Group, leather-wrapped steering wheel, automatic temperature control, overhead console with compass and thermometer, Chrysler/Infinity cassette system, security alarm, conventional spare tire. Pkg. 26M requires 3.5-liter engine.

3.3-liter "Flex Fuel" V-6 engine, base	150	131	143

Prices are accurate at time of publication; subject to manufacturer's change.

DODGE

	Retail Price	Dealer Invoice	Fair Price
3.5-liter V-6 engine	$725	$634	$689
Anti-lock 4-wheel disc brakes, base	624	546	593
base w/Pkg. 22D/26D	599	524	569
Traction control, ES	175	153	166
Automatic temperature control,			
ES w/Pkg. 22L/26L	152	133	144
Overhead console,			
base w/option pkg.	296	259	281
ES w/Pkg. 22L/26L	378	331	359
Compass/temperature/traveler displays, front and rear reading lamps, storage compartment, automatic day/night mirror (ES). NA with power sunroof. Base requires bucket seats.			
Chrysler/Infinity Spatial Imaging Cassette Sound System, base w/Pkg. 22D/26D,			
ES w/Pkg. 22L/26L	708	620	673
AM/FM cassette with equalizer, amplifier, 11 Infinity speakers, power antenna.			
Chrysler/Infinity Spatial Imaging Compact Disc Sound System,			
ES w/Pkg. 22L/26L	877	767	833
ES w/Pkg. 22M/26M	169	148	161
AM/FM stereo, compact disc player, equalizer, amplifier, power antenna.			
Power moonroof, base w/Pkg. 22D/26D	1012	886	961
ES w/Pkg. 22L/26L	1094	957	1039
ES w/Pkg. 22M/26M	716	627	680
Includes mini overhead console.			
Power door locks, base	250	219	238
Power decklid release,			
base w/Pkg. 22C/24C	61	53	58
Integrated child seat	100	88	95
Not available with leather seats.			
Cloth 50/50 front bench seat, base	NC	NC	NC
Power driver's and passenger's seats,			
ES w/option pkg.	377	330	358
Leather front bucket seats,			
ES w/option pkg.	1009	883	959
Includes power front seats, leather-wrapped shift knob. NA with integrated child seat.			
Cruise control, base	224	196	213
Remote/ Illuminated Entry Group,			
base w/Pkg. 22D/26D	221	193	210
Keyless remote and illuminated entry systems.			
Security alarm, ES w/Pkg. 22L/26L	149	130	142
Requires automatic temperature control.			

CONSUMER GUIDE®

DODGE

	Retail Price	Dealer Invoice	Fair Price
Performance Handling Group, ES w/Pkgs. 26L, 26M	$217	$190	$206

Performance suspension, 225/60R16 performance tires. Requires traction control, conventional spare tire.

| 16-inch Wheel and Handling Group, base w/Pkgs. 22C/24C, 22D/26D | 404 | 354 | 384 |

Variable-assist power steering, 16-inch polycast wheels, 225/60R16 touring tires.

Conventional spare tire	95	83	90
Floormats	46	40	44
Extra-cost paint	97	85	92
Bright platinum metallic paint, ES	200	175	190
Engine block heater	20	18	19

Dodge Neon

	Retail Price	Dealer Invoice	Fair Price
Base 4-door notchback	$9500	$8815	$9300
Highline 4-door notchback	11240	10416	10940
Highline 2-door notchback	11240	10416	10940
Sport 4-door notchback	13267	12015	12767
Sport 2-door notchback	13567	12285	13067
Destination charge	500	500	500

Standard Equipment:

Base: 2.0-liter 4-cylinder engine, 5-speed manual transmission, driver- and passenger-side air bags, cloth reclining bucket seats, floor storage console with dual cup holders and coin holder, left remote outside rearview mirror, passenger-side visor mirror, 165/80R13 all-season tires. **Highline** adds: power steering, 60/40 split folding rear seat, tinted glass, intermittent wipers, dual manual remote mirrors, driver-side visor mirror, AM/FM radio with four speakers, touring suspension, bodyside moldings, 185/70R13 all-season tires, wheel covers. **Sport 4-door** adds: anti-lock brakes, power mirrors and door locks, padded covered floor storage console with tissue pack holder, dual cup holders, and cassette/CD holders, rear defogger, remote decklid release, tilt steering wheel, tachometer, low fuel light, fog lights, 185/65R14 all-season touring tires, alloy wheels. **Sport 2-door** adds: DOHC engine, 16:1 ratio power steering, performance-tuned suspension, rear spoiler, 185/65R14 all-season performance tires.

Optional Equipment:

	Retail Price	Dealer Invoice	Fair Price
2.0-liter 4-cylinder engine, Sport 2-door (credit)	(100)	(89)	(89)
Anti-lock brakes, Base and Highline w/13-inch wheels	565	503	537

Prices are accurate at time of publication; subject to manufacturer's change.

DODGE

	Retail Price	Dealer Invoice	Fair Price
Highline w/14-inch wheels	$565	$503	$537

Models with 14-inch wheels require Wheel Dress-Up Pkg. and option pkg.

| DOHC engine, Highline 2-door w/ Competition Pkg. .... | 150 | 138 | 143 |

Required with Competition Pkg.

| 3-speed automatic transmission .... | 557 | 496 | 529 |
| Base Pkg. 21B/22B .... | 1861 | 1712 | 1675 |

Air conditioning, power steering, rear defogger, intermittent wipers, AM/FM radio, dual manual remote mirrors, touring suspension, bodyside moldings, tinted glass. Pkg. 22B requires 3-speed automatic transmission.

| Base Pkg. 25B .... | 2981 | 2687 | 2832 |

Competition Pkg. plus air conditioning, rear defogger, intermittent wipers, dual manual remote mirrors.

| Highline Pkg. 21D/22D .... | 703 | 626 | 668 |

Air conditioning, rear defogger, floor storage console, remote decklid release. Pkg. 22D requires 3-speed automatic transmission.

| Highline Pkg. 23D, 2-door .... | 1693 | 1536 | 1608 |

Competition Pkg. plus air conditioning, rear defogger, floor storage console, remote decklid release. Deletes AM/FM radio.

| Highline Pkg. 21F/22F, 4-door .... | 1371 | 1220 | 1302 |
| 2-door .... | 1330 | 1184 | 1264 |

Pkg 21D/22D plus 14-inch front disc/rear drum brakes, power mirrors and door locks, tilt steering wheel, tachometer with low fuel light, 14-inch Wheel Dress-Up Pkg., Light Pkg. (lighted visor mirrors, lighted ignition key cylinder, ashtray and glove box lights, trunk and underhood lamps), and rear floormats. Pkg. 22F requires 3-speed automatic transmission.

| Sport Pkg. 21K/22K (4-door), 23K/24K (2-door) .... | 626 | 557 | 595 |

Air conditioning, Light Pkg., AM/FM cassette player, front and rear floor mats. Pkg. 22K/24K requires 3-speed automatic transmission.

| Sport Pkg. 21K/22K (2-door) .... | 526 | 468 | 500 |

4-door Pkg. 21K/22K plus credit for 2.0-liter 4-cylinder engine. Pkg. 22K requires 3-speed automatic transmission.

| Competition Pkg., Base .... | 1575 | 1449 | 1496 |
| Highline 2-door .... | 990 | 911 | 941 |

4-wheel disc brakes, color-keyed grille bar (4-door), tinted glass (4-door), heavy duty radiator, 16:1 ratio power steering, competition suspension, tachometer with low fuel light, 175/65HR14 tires (4-door) or 185/60HR 14 tires (2-door), alloy wheels. Highline requires DOHC engine.

| Convenience Group, Highline 4-door .... | 297 | 264 | 282 |
| Highline 2-door .... | 256 | 228 | 243 |

Power mirrors and door locks. Requires Pkg. 21D/22D.

	Retail Price	Dealer Invoice	Fair Price
Rear defogger, Base and Highline	$173	$154	$164
Bodyside moldings, Base	30	27	29
14-inch Wheel Dress-Up Pkg., Highline w/Pkg. 21D/22D	80	71	76
185/65R14 all-season touring tires, wheel covers, 14-inch front disc/rear drum brakes.			
Dual manual remote mirrors, Base	70	62	67
AM/FM radio with four speakers, Base	334	297	317
AM/FM cassette player with six speakers	250	223	238
Base requires Pkg. 21B/22B.			
AM/FM CD player with six speakers	488	434	464
Sport with option pkg.	238	212	226
Base requires Pkg. 21B/22B.			
Roof rack	100	89	95
Integrated child seat	100	89	95
Cruise control, Highline and Sport	224	199	213
Highline requires option pkg.			
Tilt steering wheel	148	132	141
Base requires Pkg. 21B/22B.			
Power front door windows, Sport 4-door	210	187	200
Tachometer with low fuel light, Highline	93	83	88
Intermittent wipers, Base	66	59	63
Front and rear floormats	46	40	44
Extra-cost paint, Base and Highline	97	86	92

Dodge Spirit

	Retail Price	Dealer Invoice	Fair Price
4-door notchback	$14323	$12969	$13169
Destination charge	505	505	505

Standard Equipment:

2.5-liter 4-cylinder engine, 3-speed automatic transmission, power steering, driver-side air bag, air conditioning, cruise control, motorized front passenger shoulder belt, cloth 50/50 front bench seat, coolant temperature gauge, voltmeter, trip odometer, center console, tilt steering wheel, rear defogger, tinted glass, dual remote mirrors, visor mirrors, bodyside moldings, AM/FM/cassette with four speakers, intermittent wipers, floormats, striping, 185/70R14 tires, wheel covers.

Optional Equipment:

3.0-liter V-6 engine	798	678	702
Includes 195/70R14 tires.			
Power driver's seat, w/Pkg. 26E	306	260	269

Prices are accurate at time of publication; subject to manufacturer's change.

DODGE

	Retail Price	Dealer Invoice	Fair Price
Power locks	$250	$213	$220
Pkg. 26E	735	625	647

Power windows and locks, heated power mirrors, remote decklid release. Requires 3.0-liter V-6 engine.

Gold Decor Special Equipment Group	200	170	176

Luggage rack, gold badging and trim, 195/70R14 tires, alloy wheels with gold accents.

Conventional spare tire	95	81	84
Extra-cost paint	97	82	85
Engine block heater	20	17	18

Dodge Stealth	Retail Price	Dealer Invoice	Fair Price
3-door hatchback	$23236	$21063	$21563
R/T 3-door hatchback	26795	24195	25195
R/T Turbo 3-door hatchback	37905	33972	35472
Destination charge	430	430	430

Standard Equipment:

3.0-liter V-6 engine, 5-speed manual transmission, 4-wheel disc brakes, power steering, driver- and passenger-side air bags, air conditioning, cloth reclining front bucket seats, 10-way power driver's seat with lumbar adjustment, front seat height adjusters, split folding rear seat, console with armrest, tachometer, coolant temperature and oil pressure gauges, trip odometer, tinted glass, rear defogger, intermittent wipers, remote fuel door and hatch releases, power mirrors, auto-off headlights, AM/FM/cassette with equalizer and 6 speakers, tilt steering column, leather-wrapped steering wheel, fog lamps, rear spoiler, tonneau cover, visor mirrors, 205/65HR15 tires, wheel covers. **R/T** adds: DOHC engine, cruise control, floormats, security alarm, rear wiper/washer, 225/55VR16 tires, alloy wheels. **R/T Turbo** adds: turbocharged engine, 6-speed manual transmission, permanent 4-wheel drive, anti-lock brakes, turbo boost gauge, heated power mirrors, power windows and locks, power driver's seat with power lumbar adjustment, black painted roof, remote keyless entry system, 245/45ZR17 tires.

Optional Equipment:

Pkg. 21C/22C, base	906	779	815

Power windows and door locks, cruise control, remote keyless entry system, rear wiper/washer, floormats. Pkg. 22C requires automatic transmission.

Pkg. 23H/24H, R/T	531	457	478

Power windows and door locks, remote keyless entry system. Pkg. 24H requires automatic transmission.

	Retail Price	Dealer Invoice	Fair Price
Pkg. 23M/24M, R/T	$2394	$2059	$2155

Pkg. 23H/24H plus anti-lock brakes, security alarm, trunk-mounted CD changer, cassette player with equalizer and eight Infinity speakers. Pkg. 24M requires automatic transmission.

	Retail Price	Dealer Invoice	Fair Price
Pkg. 25W, R/T			
Turbo AWD	1746	1502	1571

Trunk-mounted CD changer, eight Infinity speakers, leather upholstery.

	Retail Price	Dealer Invoice	Fair Price
Pkg. 25Y, R/T			
Turbo AWD	3019	2596	2717

Pkg. 25W plus sunroof, 245/40ZR18 tires, chrome wheels.

	Retail Price	Dealer Invoice	Fair Price
4-speed automatic transmission, base, R/T	883	759	795
Anti-lock brakes, base, R/T	799	687	719
Leather seats, R/T and R/T			
Turbo AWD	843	725	759
Trunk-mounted CD changer	542	466	488
Sunroof	361	310	325

Base, R/T require option pkg.

	Retail Price	Dealer Invoice	Fair Price
Wheel Group, R/T Turbo AWD	912	784	821

245/40ZR18 tires, chrome wheels.

	Retail Price	Dealer Invoice	Fair Price
Extra-cost paint	205	176	185

NA base.

Dodge Stratus

Prices not available at time of publication.

Standard Equipment:

Base: 2.0-liter DOHC 4-cylinder engine, 5-speed manual transmission, driver- and passenger-side air bags, power steering, air conditioning, cloth reclining front bucket seats with driver's-side manual height and lumbar adjusters, front seat back map pockets, console, folding rear bench seat, AM/FM/cassette, digital clock, trip odometer, oil pressure and coolant temperature gauges, voltmeter, tachometer, cruise control, tilt steering column, rear defogger, tinted glass with solar-control windshield, speed-sensitive intermittent wipers, illuminated entry, remote decklid release, reading lights, auxiliary power outlet, color-keyed bodyside moldings, lighted visor mirrors, floormats, trunk net, 195/70R14 tires, wheel covers. **ES** adds: 2.5-liter DOHC V-6 engine, 4-speed automatic transmission, anti-lock brakes, sport suspension, variable-assist power steering, leather and vinyl upholstery, leather-wrapped steering wheel and shift lever, 8-way power driver's seat, power windows and door locks, heated power mirrors, remote keyless entry, anti-theft alarm, fog lights, alloy wheels, 195/65R15 tires.

EAGLE

Eagle Summit	Retail Price	Dealer Invoice	Fair Price
DL 2-door notchback	$9836	$9387	$9587
ESi 2-door notchback	10859	10320	10520
LX 4-door notchback	12221	11593	11793
ESi 4-door notchback	13025	12263	12463
Destination charge	430	430	430

Standard Equipment:

DL 2-door: 1.5-liter 4-cylinder engine, 5-speed manual transmission, driver- and passenger-side air bags, cloth/vinyl reclining front bucket seats, engine temperature gauge, automatic day/night mirror, left manual mirror, 145/80R13 tires; **ESi 2-door** adds: cloth seats, dual remote mirrors, trip odometer, passenger visor mirror, color-keyed bumpers and bodyside moldings, rear spoiler, 155/80R13 tires, wheel covers. **LX 4-door** adds to DL 2-door: 1.8-liter 4-cylinder engine, power steering, cloth seats, touring suspension, dual manual mirrors, trip odometer, color-keyed bumpers, 175/70R13 tires, wheel covers. **ESi 4-door** adds: split folding rear seat with armrest, dual remote mirrors, intermittent wipers, remote fuel door release, tachometer (5-speed), visor mirrors, color-keyed bodyside moldings, rear spoiler 185/65R14 tires.

Optional Equipment:

Pkg. 21C/22C, DL	431	371	379

Tinted glass, rear defogger, dual manual mirrors, AM/FM radio. Pkg. 22C requires 3-speed automatic transmission.

Pkg. 21D/22D, DL	1241	1067	1092

Pkg. 21C plus air conditioning. Pkg. 22D requires 3-speed automatic transmission.

Pkg. 21E/22E, DL	1612	1386	1419

Pkg. 21D plus color-keyed bodyside moldings and front and rear fascias, power steering, touring suspension, 175/70R13 tires, wheel covers. Pkg. 22E requires 3-speed automatic transmission.

Pkg. 23K/24K, ESi 2-door	1968	1692	1732

1.8-liter 4-cylinder engine, ESi Group (touring suspension, front disc brakes, dual-tip exhaust, 185/65R14 tires, alloy wheels; 5-speed adds tachometer), air conditioning, Convenience Group 1 (power mirrors, dual-note horn, variable-intermittent wipers, remote fuel door and decklid release, split folding rear seat, tilt steering column, trunk trim, trunk light), rear defogger, power steering, tinted glass, AM/FM cassette player. Pkg. 24K requires 4-speed automatic transmission.

	Retail Price	Dealer Invoice	Fair Price
Pkg. 23C/24C, LX	$92	$79	$81

Tinted glass, rear defogger, AM/FM radio, bodyside moldings, front floor-mats, Convenience Group 2 (dual remote mirrors, remote fuel door and decklid releases, intermittent wipers, passenger visor mirror, cigarette lighter, trunk trim, trunk light). Pkg. 24C requires 4-speed automatic transmission.

Pkg. 23D/24D, LX	902	775	794

Pkg. 23C plus air conditioning. Pkg. 24D requires 4-speed automatic transmission.

Pkg. 23L/24L, ESi 4-door	2042	1756	1797

Air conditioning, tinted glass, rear defogger, AM/FM cassette, front floor-mats, power windows and door locks, Convenience Group 3 (tilt steering column, cruise control, variable-intermittent wipers, power mirrors), alloy wheels. Pkg. 24L requries 4-speed automatic transmission.

3-speed automatic transmission, DL	528	454	465
4-speed automatic transmission, ESi	654	562	576
LX	716	616	630

Requires 1.8-liter engine.

Anti-lock brakes,			
ESi 4-door with Pkg. 23L/24L	699	601	615
Rear defogger	66	57	58
AM/FM radio, LX	283	243	249
AM/FM/cassette, DL, LX	181	156	159

Requires option pkg.

Bodyside moldings, DL	54	46	48

Requires option pkg.

Eagle Talon

	Retail Price	Dealer Invoice	Fair Price
ESi 3-door hatchback	$14362	$13346	—
TSi 3-door hatchback	17266	15989	—
TSi AWD 3-door hatchback	19448	17973	—
Destination charge	430	430	430

Fair price not available at time of publication.

Standard Equipment:

ESi: 2.0-liter DOHC 4-cylinder engine, 5-speed manual transmission, 4-wheel disc brakes, driver- and passenger-side air bags, power steering, cloth reclining front bucket seats, folding rear seat, front console with storage and armrest, tinted glass, tachometer, coolant temperature gauge, trip odometer, map lights, dual remote mirrors, visor mirrors, AM/FM radio, digital clock, remote fuel door and hatch releases, tilt steering column, intermittent wipers, rear wiper/washer, rear spoiler, color-keyed bodyside moldings, 195/70R14 tires, wheel covers. **TSi** adds: turbocharged engine, sport-tuned exhaust system, upgraded suspension, driver's seat lumbar support adjustment, split folding rear seat, leather-wrapped steering wheel and manual gearshift handle, power mirrors, turbo boost and oil pressure gauges, cassette player, lighted visor mirrors, rear defogger, cargo area cover, cargo net, lower bodyside cladding, fog lamps, 205/55R16 tires, alloy wheels. **TSi AWD** adds: permanent 4-wheel drive, cruise control, power locks and windows, 215/55VR16 tires.

Optional Equipment:

	Retail Price	Dealer Invoice	Fair Price
Pkg. 21B/22B, ESi	$1601	$1361	—
Air conditioning, cruise control, rear defogger, power mirrors, cassette player, cargo area cover, front floormats. Pkg. 22B requires 4-speed automatic transmission.			
Pkg. 21C/22C, ESi	2135	1815	—
Pkg. 21B/22B plus power windows and locks, cargo net, upgraded interior trim. Pkg. 22C requires 4-speed automatic transmission.			
Pkg. 23P/24P, TSi	1574	1338	—
Air conditioning, cruise control, power windows and locks, front floormats. Pkg. 24P requires automatic transmission.			
Pkg. 25S/26S, TSi AWD	880	748	—
Air conditioning, front floor mats. Pkg. 26S requires automatic transmission.			
Pkg. 25H/26H, TSi AWD	2983	2536	—
Pkg. 25S/26S plus power driver's seat, cassette player with equalizer, power sunroof, remote keyless entry with security alarm. Pkg. 26H requires automatic transmission.			
4-speed automatic transmission, ESi	738	627	—
TSi	883	751	—
TSi AWD	852	724	—
TSi AWD includes 205/55VR16 tires.			
Anti-lock brakes	649	552	—
Limited-slip differential, TSi AWD	266	226	—
Remote keyless entry with security alarm	332	282	—
Requires option pkg.			
Rear defogger, ESi	162	138	—
AM/FM cassette with CD player	634	539	—
Requires option pkg.			
AM/FM cassette with graphic equalizer, TSi, TSi AWD	709	603	—
Requires option pkg.			
Power sunroof	730	621	—
Requires option pkg.			
Leather upholstery, TSi, TSi AWD	457	338	—
Requires power driver's seat and option pkg.			
Power driver's seat, TSi, TSi AWD	332	282	—

Eagle Vision

	Retail Price	Dealer Invoice	Fair Price
ESi 4-door notchback	$19697	$17750	$18350
TSi 4-door notchback	22871	20562	21162
Destination charge	535	535	535

Standard Equipment:

ESi: 3.3-liter V-6 engine, 4-speed automatic transmission, 4-wheel disc brakes, driver- and passenger-side air bags, power steering, air conditioning, reclining front bucket seats with lumbar support adjustment, console with armrest and cup holders, remote decklid release, rear defogger, tinted glass with solar-control windshield and rear window, speed-sensitive intermittent wipers, tachometer, trip odometer, coolant temperature gauge, power windows and door locks, power mirrors, AM/FM/cassette, tilt steering wheel, cruise control, touring suspension, dual visor mirrors, reading lights, 2-tone front and rear fascias, floormats, 205/70R15 tires, wheel covers. **TSi** adds: 3.5-liter V-6 engine, anti-lock brakes, variable-assist power steering, automatic temperature control, power driver's seat, overhead console with compass and thermometer, illuminated/remote keyless entry system, trip computer, leather-wrapped steering wheel and shift knob, lighted visor mirrors, trunk cargo net, fog lamps, 225/60R16 tires, alloy wheels.

Optional Equipment:

Pkg. 22C, ESi	601	526	571
Power driver's seat, illuminated/remote keyless entry sytem, lighted visor mirrors.			
Pkg. 22D, ESi	1767	1546	1679
Pkg. 22C plus automatic temperature control, automatic day/night rearview mirror, Chrysler/Infinity cassette system, security alarm, overhead console with compass and thermometer, trip computer.			
Pkg. 26L, TSi	1127	986	1071
Traction control, power front passenger's seat, automatic day/night rearview mirror, Chrysler/Infinity cassette system.			
Pkg. 26M, TSi	1853	1621	1760
Pkg. 26L plus leather seats, security alarm, conventional spare tire.			
Anti-lock brakes, ESi	599	524	569
Traction control, TSi w/Pkg. 26L, 26M	175	149	166
Power moonroof, ESi w/Pkg. 22C	1012	886	961
ESi w/Pkg. 22D, TSi w/option pkg.	716	627	680
Mini overhead console replaces full console in Pkg 22D and TSi.			
Power passenger seat, TSi	377	330	358
Power driver's seat, ESi	377	330	358
Integrated child seat	100	88	95
Not available with leather seats.			
Leather seats, TSi w/Pkg. 26L	620	543	589

Prices are accurate at time of publication; subject to manufacturer's change.

	Retail Price	Dealer Invoice	Fair Price
Performance Handling Group, TSi w/option pkg.	$217	$190	$206
Performance suspension, 225/60VR16 performance tires. Requires conventional spare tire.			
Chrysler/Infinity cassette system	708	620	673
Includes equalizer, 11 speakers, power antenna.			
Chrysler/Infinity CD system, ESi w/Pkg. 22D, TSi w/option pkg.	169	148	161
Includes equalizer, 11 speakers, power antenna.			
Security alarm, TSi w/Pkg. 26L	149	130	142
Alloy Wheel and Touring Tire Group, ESi (std. TSi)	374	327	355
225/65R16 tires, alloy wheels, variable-assist power steering.			
Conventional spare tire	95	83	90
Extra-cost paint	97	85	92
Bright platinum metallic paint	200	175	190
Engine block heater	20	18	19

FORD

Ford Aspire	Retail Price	Dealer Invoice	Fair Price
3-door hatchback	$8440	$7805	$8105
5-door hatchback	9055	8365	8665
SE 3-door hatchback	9415	8692	8992
Destination charge	295	295	295

Standard Equipment:

1.3-liter 4-cylinder engine, 5-speed manual transmission, driver- and passenger-side air bags, reclining front seats, folding rear bench seat, cloth and vinyl upholstery, trip odometer, Radio Prep Pkg., body-color bumpers and grille, dual outside mirrors, floor console with cup holders, 165/70R13 all-season tires. **SE** adds: fog lamps, rear liftgate spoiler, split folding rear seat, AM/FM radio, tachometer, cargo area light, intermittent wipers, remote mirrors, upgraded upholstery and door trim panels, cargo cover, door map pockets.

Optional Equipment:

3-speed automatic transmission, base	580	516	522
5-door requires power steering.			
Rear defogger	160	143	144
Anti-lock brakes	565	503	509

	Retail Price	Dealer Invoice	Fair Price
Air conditioning	$825	$735	$743
Includes tinted glass.			
Power steering, base 5-door	250	223	225
Requires 3-speed automatic transmission.			
Interior Decor and Convenience Group, base	265	236	239
Intermittent wipers, manual remote mirrors, upgraded upholstery and door trim, split folding rear seat, cargo area cover, door map pockets.			
AM/FM radio, base	300	267	270
AM/FM cassette, base	465	414	419
SE	165	147	149
Premium AM/FM cassette, base	525	468	473
SE	225	201	203
Premium AM/FM CD player, base	625	557	563
SE	325	290	293
Alloy wheels	355	316	320
NA base 3-door.			

Ford Contour

	Retail Price	Dealer Invoice	Fair Price
GL 4-door notchback	$13310	$12036	—
LX 4-door notchback	13995	12646	—
SE 4-door notchback	15695	14159	—
Destination charge	495	495	495

Fair price not available at time of publication.

Standard Equipment:

GL: 2.0-liter DOHC 4-cylinder engine, 5-speed manual transmission, driver- and passenger-side air bags, power steering, solar-control tinted glass, cloth reclining front bucket seats, console, dual remote mirrors, digital clock, trip odometer, coolant temperature gauge, tilt steering column, variable intermittent wipers, visor mirrors, AM/FM radio, remote fuel door and decklid release, passenger compartment air filtration system, color-keyed bodyside moldings, 185/70R14 tires, wheel covers. **LX** adds: fog lamps, heated power mirrors, console with armrest and cupholders, lumbar support adjusters, split folding rear seat, tachometer, lighted visor mirrors, cassette player. **SE** adds: 2.5-liter DOHC V-6 engine, 4-wheel disc brakes, sport suspension, leather-wrapped steering wheel, rear spoiler, 205/60R15 tires, alloy wheels.

Optional Equipment:

2.5-liter V-6 engine, GL	1080	961	—
LX	1045	930	—
Includes 4-wheel disc brakes, tachometer (GL), sport suspension, 195/65R14 tires. Requires Groups 1 and 2 on GL, Groups 2 and 3 on LX.			

Prices are accurate at time of publication; subject to manufacturer's change.

FORD

	Retail Price	Dealer Invoice	Fair Price
4-speed automatic transmission	$815	$725	—
Requires option group.			
Traction control	800	712	—
Includes anti-lock brakes.			
Anti-lock brakes	565	503	—
Air conditioning	780	694	—
Preferred Pkg. 235A, GL	850	757	—
Console with armrest and cupholders, cassette player, air conditioning, rear defogger, heated power mirrors.			
Preferred Pkg. 236A, GL	1310	1166	—
Pkg. 235A plus light group (lighted visor mirrors, illuminated entry, courtesy and map lights), power door locks.			
Preferred Pkg. 240A, GL	2530	2252	—
Pkg. 236A plus 2.5-liter V-6 engine, power windows.			
Preferred Pkg. 237A, LX	1350	1202	—
Air conditioning, rear defogger, light group, power door locks and windows.			
Preferred Pkg. 238A, LX	2245	1998	—
Pkg. 237A plus 2.5-liter V-6 engine.			
Preferred Pkg. 239A, SE	1350	1202	—
Air conditioning, rear defogger, light group, power door locks and windows.			
Option Group 1, GL	220	196	—
Console with armrest and cupholders, cassette player.			
Option Group 2, GL	1030	917	—
LX, SE	950	846	—
Heated power mirrors (GL), air conditioning, rear defogger.			
Option Group 3	345	307	—
Light group (lighted visor mirrors, illuminated entry, courtesy and map lights), power door locks.			
Power door locks and light group,			
GL with Pkg. 235A	345	307	—
Leather upholstery, LX	645	574	—
SE	595	530	—
LX includes leather-wrapped steering wheel and requires power windows and power driver's seat. SE requires power windows.			
Power driver's seat, LX	330	294	—
SE	290	258	—
Requires Group 3. LX seat includes 10-way adjustment; SE seat includes 6-way adjustment.			
Rear defogger	160	143	—
Premium cassette player, GL	295	263	—
GL with Group 1, LX, SE	130	116	—
Includes upgraded speakers and amplifier.			

	Retail Price	Dealer Invoice	Fair Price
CD player and premium sound system, GL	$435	$387	—
GL with Group 1, LX, SE	270	240	—
Cruise control	215	191	—
Remote keyless entry	160	143	—
Requires power locks and light group, power windows, Group 1.			
Alloy wheels, GL, LX	265	236	—
Requires option group.			
Power windows, GL with Pkg. 236A	340	302	—
Requires power locks and light group, rear defogger.			
Power sunroof	595	530	—
Requires power locks and light group.			
Floormats	45	40	—
Engine block heater	20	18	—

Ford Crown Victoria	Retail Price	Dealer Invoice	Fair Price
4-door notchback	$20160	$18601	$19101
Special Value 4-door notchback	19990	17919	—
LX 4-door notchback	21970	20248	20748
LX Special Value 4-door notchback, with Pkg. 113A	22225	19944	—
LX Special Value 4-door notchback, with Pkg. 114A	24845	22275	—
Destination charge	575	575	575

Special Value models' fair price not available at time of publication. Special Value models include destination charge.

Standard Equipment:

4.6-liter V-8, 4-speed automatic transmission, 4-wheel disc brakes, variable-assist power steering, driver- and passenger-side air bags, air conditioning, cloth reclining split bench seat, map pockets, digital clock, power windows and mirrors, voltmeter, oil pressure and coolant temperature gauges, trip odometer, tilt steering wheel, solar-control tinted glass, automatic parking brake release, rear defogger, intermittent wipers, AM/FM radio, utility power outlet, 215/70R15 all-season tires, wheel covers. **Special Value** adds: Preferred Equipment Pkg. 111A. **LX** adds: upgraded interior trim, power driver's seat with power recliner, power front seat lumbar support adjusters, remote fuel door release, power driver's seat, carpeted spare tire cover. **LX Special Value** adds: Preferred Equipment Pkg. 113A or 114A.

Optional Equipment:

Anti-lock brakes with Traction Assist	665	592	599

Prices are accurate at time of publication; subject to manufacturer's change.

FORD

	Retail Price	Dealer Invoice	Fair Price
Automatic air conditioning	$175	$156	$158
Preferred Equipment Pkg. 111A, base	395	352	356
Group 1 plus front and rear floormats, radial-spoke wheel covers.			
Preferred Equipment Pkg. 113A, LX	820	730	738
Pkg. 111A plus Group 2.			
Pkg. 114A, LX	3440	3061	3096
Pkg. 113A plus Group 3.			
Group 1, base	660	587	594
LX	600	534	540
Power Lock Group, remote fuel door release (base), cruise control, illuminated entry, spare tire cover (base).			
Group 2, LX	985	877	887
AM/FM cassette player, Light/Decor Group, leather-wrapped steering wheel, cornering lamps, alloy wheels.			
Group 3, LX	2765	2462	2350
Automatic air conditioning, anti-lock brakes with Traction Assist, high-level audio system, electronic instruments, automatic day/night mirror, rear air suspension, remote keyless entry, 6-way power passenger seat, driver memory seat.			
Keyless remote entry, LX	215	191	194
Requires Group 1.			
Rear air suspension, LX	270	240	243
Leather upholstery, LX	645	574	581
Requires power front passenger seat.			
Power front seats, each	360	321	324
Power passenger seat NA with base.			
Power memory driver's seat, LX	175	156	158
Requires remote keyless entry, Group 1, power passenger seat.			
Heavy Duty Trailer Towing Pkg.	795	708	716
with Pkg. 114A	500	445	450
Includes rear air suspension, heavy duty battery and flasher system, heavy duty U-joint, extra cooling, dual exhaust, wiring harness, power steering and transmission oil coolers, engine oil cooler, full-size spare tire, Traction-Lok axle (except with anti-lock brakes). Not available with Handling and Performance Package.			
Light/Decor Group	225	201	203
Includes illuminated visor mirrors, map and dome lights, engine compartment lights, bodyside paint stripes, secondary visors.			
AM/FM cassette	185	165	167
High-level audio system, LX	545	485	491
with Group 2 or Pkg. 113A	360	321	324
AM/FM cassette, upgraded amplifier and speakers.			
JBL audio system, LX			
with Group 3 or Pkg. 114A	500	445	448

	Retail Price	Dealer Invoice	Fair Price
with Group 2 or Pkg. 113A	$860	$766	$774
Handling and Performance Pkg.	1100	979	990
LX with Group 2	680	605	612
LX with Group 3	830	739	747
LX with Pkg. 114A	410	365	369

Includes performance springs, shocks and stabilizer bars, alloy wheels, anti-lock brakes with Traction Assist, dual exhaust, 3.27 axle ratio, power steering cooler, rear air suspension, 225/60R15 tires. NA with Trailer Towing Pkg.

	Retail Price	Dealer Invoice	Fair Price
215/70R15 whitewall tires	80	71	72
Full-size spare tire	80	71	72
with Handling and Performance Pkg.	260	232	234
Floormats, front	25	23	24
Floormats, front with preferred equipment pkg. (credit)	(25)	(23)	(23)
Floormats, rear	20	18	19
Floormats, rear with preferred equipment pkg. (credit)	(20)	(18)	(18)
Engine block heater	25	23	24

Ford Escort

	Retail Price	Dealer Invoice	Fair Price
3-door hatchback	$9580	$8867	$9067
LX 3-door hatchback	10435	9646	9846
LX 4-door notchback	11040	10196	10396
LX 5-door hatchback	10870	10042	10242
LX 5-door wagon	11425	10547	10747
GT 3-door hatchback	12720	11726	11926
Destination charge	375	375	375

Standard Equipment:

Std.: 1.9-liter 4-cylinder engine, 5-speed manual transmission, driver- and passenger-side air bags, motorized front shoulder belts, cloth and vinyl reclining bucket seats, folding rear seat, center console with cup holders, tinted glass, trip odometer, variable intermittent wipers, flip-out quarter window (3-door), cargo cover, door pockets, right visor mirror, 175/70R13 all-season tires. **LX** adds: upgraded upholstery and door trim panels, 60/40 split rear seatback, AM/FM radio, digital clock, bodyside molding, full wheel covers, 175/65R14 all-season tires. **GT** adds: 1.8-liter DOHC engine, power steering, 4-wheel disc brakes, sport suspension, tachometer, cloth sport seats, cassette player, Light Group, lighted visor mirrors, removable cup holder tray, remote fuel door release, power mirrors, lighted visor mirrors, fog lamps, rear spoiler, rocker panel cladding, 185/60HR15 all-season tires, alloy wheels.

Prices are accurate at time of publication; subject to manufacturer's change.

FORD

Optional Equipment:	Retail Price	Dealer Invoice	Fair Price
4-speed automatic transmission	$815	$725	$734
LX requires power steering.			
Anti-lock brakes, GT	565	503	509
Air conditioning, LX and GT	785	699	707
LX requires power steering.			
Power steering, LX	250	223	225
Comfort Group, base	860	766	774
Air conditioning, power steering.			
Preferred Pkg. 320M, LX	190	170	171
Power steering, Light/Convenience Group, Sport Appearance Group (3-door), rear defogger.			
Preferred Pkg. 330A, GT	435	387	392
Rear defogger, air conditioning.			
One Price Pkg. 321M (5-speed) and 322M (automatic):			
LX 3-door, 5-speed	1185	1055	—
LX 3-door, automatic	2000	1781	—
LX 4-door, 5-speed	580	517	—
LX 4-door, automatic	1395	1242	—
LX 5-door, 5-speed	750	669	—
LX 5-door, automatic	1565	1394	—
LX wagon, 5-speed	195	174	—
LX wagon, automatic	1010	899	—
Air conditioning, power steering, Light/Convenience Group, rear defogger. Pkg 322A includes 4-speed automatic transmission. Wagon adds Wagon Group; 3-door adds Sport Appearance Group.			
Ultra Violet Decor Group, GT	400	356	360
Ultraviolet clearcoat paint, color-keyed wheels, grey cloth upholstery, front floormats with "GT" embroidered in violet, leather-wrapped steering wheel.			
Sport Appearance Group, LX 3-door	720	641	648
Alloy wheels, tachometer, liftgate spoiler, rear cladding.			
Rear defogger	160	143	144
Light/Convenience Group, LX	160	143	144
Light Group, power mirrors, removable cup holder tray.			
Light Group, LX	65	58	59
Removable cup holder tray, dual map lights, cargo area and engine compartment lights, headlights-on warning chime, lighted visor mirrors.			
Power mirrors, LX	95	85	86
Luxury Convenience Group, LX 3-door, LX 4-door, LX 5-door	465	414	419
LX wagon, LX 3-door with Sport Appearance Group	410	365	369

	Retail Price	Dealer Invoice	Fair Price
GT	$460	$410	$414

Tilt steering column, cruise control, tachometer, remote decklid release (except wagon), leather-wrapped steering wheel (GT). Requires Light/Convenience Group.

Power Equipment Group,			
LX 5-door and wagon	575	512	518
LX 4-door, 5-door and wagon with Luxury			
Convenience Group	520	463	468
LX 3-door	515	458	464
GT, LX 3-door with Luxury Convenience			
Group	460	410	414

Power windows and door locks, tachometer.

Integrated child seat	135	120	122
Power moonroof, LX, GT	525	468	473

LX requires Light/Convenience Group, power steering. NA wagon.

AM/FM radio, base	300	267	270
AM/FM/cassette, base	465	414	419
LX	165	147	149
CD player, base	625	557	563
LX	325	290	293
GT	160	143	144
Premium sound system	60	54	55

Requires AM/FM/cassette.

Radio delete (credit), LX	(300)	(267)	(267)
GT (credit)	(465)	(414)	(414)
Wagon Group	240	213	216

Luggage rack, rear wiper/washer. Requires Light/Convenience Group.

Clearcoat paint	85	76	77
with preferred equipment group, Sport			
Appearance Group	NC	NC	NC
Engine block heater	20	18	19

1994 Ford Explorer	Retail Price	Dealer Invoice	Fair Price
XL 3-door wagon, 2WD	$17970	$16004	$16504
XL 3-door wagon, 4WD	19720	17544	18044
Sport 3-door wagon, 2WD	18945	16862	17362
Sport 3-door wagon, 4WD	20655	18366	18866
Eddie Bauer 3-door wagon, 2WD	21905	19466	19966
Eddie Bauer 3-door wagon, 4WD	23605	20962	21462
XL 5-door wagon, 2WD	18860	16787	17487
XL 5-door wagon, 4WD	20630	18344	19044
XLT 5-door wagon, 2WD	21280	18916	19616
XLT 5-door wagon, 4WD	23080	20500	21200

Prices are accurate at time of publication; subject to manufacturer's change.

FORD

	Retail Price	Dealer Invoice	Fair Price
Eddie Bauer 5-door wagon, 2WD	$23750	$21090	$21790
Eddie Bauer 5-door wagon, 4WD	25555	22678	23378
Limited 5-door wagon, 2WD	27110	24047	24947
Limited 5-door wagon, 4WD	28910	25631	26531
Destination charge	485	485	485

Standard Equipment:

XL: 4.0-liter V-6, 5-speed manual transmission, anti-lock brakes, power steering, knitted vinyl front bucket seats, split folding rear seat, tinted glass, Light Group, intermittent wipers, dual outside mirrors, carpet, load floor tiedown hooks, rear seat heat duct, tachometer, coolant temperature gauge, tachometer, trip odometer, AM/FM radio, digital clock, 225/70R15 all-season tires, full-size spare tire. **Sport** adds: rear quarter and rear window privacy glass, rear wiper/washer, rear defogger, map light, load floor tiedown net, cargo area cover, leather-wrapped steering wheel, lighted visor mirrors, alloy wheels. **XLT** adds: cloth captain's chairs, floor console, power mirrors, upgraded door panels with pockets, power windows and locks, cruise control, tilt steering wheel, privacy glass rear door, rear quarter and liftgate, map pockets, floormats. **Eddie Bauer** adds to Sport: power driver's seat with lumbar support, power passenger seat (5-door), duffle and garment bags, luggage rack, privacy glass on rear quarter and liftgate windows (5-door includes rear door windows), 235/75R15 OWL tires. **Limited** adds: air conditioning, power luxury leather bucket seats with 3-position driver's-side memory, matching split/folding rear seat, floor console, color-keyed overhead console with compass, temperature gauge, reading lamps and storage compartment, Electronic Group (remote keyless entry with theft-deterrent system, and electrochromic mirror with autolamp), color-keyed front bumper, front fascia with fog lamps, grille, bodyside moldings, striping, color-keyed leather-wrapped steering wheel, and spoke interior trim, heated mirrors, spoke alloy wheels. 4WD models have Touch Drive part-time 4WD.

Optional Equipment:

4-speed automatic transmission	890	757	845
Limited-slip rear axle	255	217	242
Optional axle ratio (upgrade)	45	38	42
Optional axle ratio (upgrade) with trailer tow	360	306	342
Air conditioning	805	684	765
with manual transmission	NC	NC	NC
Super engine cooling	55	47	52
Electronics Group, XLT and Eddie Bauer 5-doors	485	413	460

Remote keyless entry with theft-deterrent system, electrochromatic mirror with autolamp feature.

	Retail Price	Dealer Invoice	Fair Price
Preferred Pkg. 931A, Sport 3-door	$25	$21	$24

Air conditioning, Power Equipment Group, cloth captain's chairs with console, 235/75R15 outlined white letter tires.

	Retail Price	Dealer Invoice	Fair Price
Preferred Pkg. 932A, Eddie Bauer 3-door	125	106	119

Air conditioning, JBL audio system with cassette, leather seats.

	Retail Price	Dealer Invoice	Fair Price
Preferred Pkg. 941A,			
XLT with automatic	470	399	447
XLT with 5-speed	25	21	24

Air conditioning, striping, premium cassette player.

	Retail Price	Dealer Invoice	Fair Price
Preferred Pkg. 942A, Eddie Bauer 5-door	275	235	262

Air conditioning, premium cassette player, leather seats.

	Retail Price	Dealer Invoice	Fair Price
Preferred Pkg. 943A, Limited	395	336	375

JBL Audio System with cassette, running boards (5-door), step bars (3-door).

	Retail Price	Dealer Invoice	Fair Price
Cloth captain's chairs,			
XL and Sport	280	238	266
Cloth 60/40 split bench seat,			
XL 5-door	255	216	242
XLT (credit)	(20)	(17)	(17)
Power cloth sport bucket seats, Sport	1020	867	969
upgrade from captain's chairs	750	637	712
XLT	955	812	907
Power leather sport bucket seats,			
Sport	1600	1360	1520
upgrade from captain's chairs	1326	1127	1259
XLT	1530	1301	1453
Eddie Bauer	NC	NC	NC
Privacy glass	220	187	209
Floor-mounted transfer case w/manual locking hubs,			
4WD (credit)	(105)	(89)	(89)
Bodyside molding	120	102	114
Power Equipment Group, XL 3-door	900	765	855
XL 5-door	1235	1050	1173

Power windows, locks and mirrors, rear defogger, rear wiper/washer, upgraded door trim panels.

	Retail Price	Dealer Invoice	Fair Price
Luggage rack	140	119	133
with manual transmission and Pkg. 941A	NC	NC	NC
Power Equipment Group delete,			
Sport with Pkg. 931A (credit)	(190)	(162)	(162)

Power Equipment Group deleted without loss of Pkg. discount.

	Retail Price	Dealer Invoice	Fair Price
Tilt-up sunroof	280	238	266

Prices are accurate at time of publication; subject to manufacturer's change.

FORD

	Retail Price	Dealer Invoice	Fair Price
Cruise control and tilt steering wheel	$385	$328	$365
Sport with manual transmission and Pkg. 931A	NC	NC	NC
Alloy wheels, Sport	NC	NC	NC
Deep dish alloy wheels,			
XL and Sport	250	212	237
XLT and Eddie Bauer	NC	NC	NC
Trailer Towing Pkg.	105	89	99
Rear defogger and wiper/washer, XL	280	238	266
Premium AM/FM cassette	210	178	199
Sport with manual transmission and Pkg. 931A	NC	NC	NC
Ford JBL Audio System	700	595	665
Upgrade from premium cassette	490	416	465
Ford JBL Audio System			
with CD player	1000	850	950
Upgrade from premium cassette	790	672	750
Limited	300	255	285
Consolette, XL 5-door and XLT	30	26	28
Running boards, 5-door	395	336	375
Delete for credit, Limited	(395)	(336)	(336)
Step bars, 3-doors	245	208	232
Engine block heater	35	30	33
Deluxe tape stripe, 5-doors	55	47	52
Special Appearance Pkg.	285	243	270
Fog lamps, black bodyside molding, tape stripes.			
Deluxe 2-tone paint	120	102	114
Fog lamps, XL and Sport	185	158	175
235/75R15 outline white letter			
all-terrain tires	230	196	218
Floormats	45	38	42

Ford Mustang

	Retail Price	Dealer Invoice	Fair Price
2-door notchback	$14330	$12984	$13830
2-door convertible	20795	18738	20295
GT 2-door notchback	17905	16165	17405
GT 2-door convertible	22595	20340	22095
Cobra 2-door notchback	—	—	—
Cobra 2-door convertible	—	—	—
Destination charge	475	475	475

Cobra prices not available at time of publication.

Standard Equipment:

3.8-liter V-6 engine, 5-speed manual transmission, driver- and passenger-side air bags, 4-wheel disc brakes, variable-effort power steering, reclining cloth bucket seats, split folding rear seat, armrest storage console with cup holder and CD/cassette storage, power mirrors, AM/FM radio, visor mirrors, tachometer, trip odometer, coolant temperature and oil pressure gauges, tilt steering wheel, intermittent wipers, tinted glass, 205/65R15 all-season tires, wheel covers. **Convertible** adds: power convertible top, power mirrors, power door locks and decklid release, power windows. **GT** adds to convertible: 5.0-liter V-8 engine, 4-way head restraint and power lumbar support for front seats, GT Suspension Pkg., Traction-Lok Axle, fog lamps, rear decklid spoiler, leather-wrapped steering wheel, 225/55ZR16 all-season tires, alloy wheels. **Cobra** adds: high-output 5.0-liter V-8 engine, anti-lock brakes, firmer suspension, 4-way power driver's seat, front air dam with fog lamps, Cobra-unique decklid spoiler, Cobra interior trim and exterior badging, 80-watt cassette player (notchback), 245/45ZR17 all-season tires, 17-inch alloy wheels.

Optional Equipment:	Retail Price	Dealer Invoice	Fair Price
4-speed automatic transmission	$790	$703	$751
Includes leather-wrapped shifter knob.			
Anti-lock brakes	565	503	537
Air conditioning	780	694	741
Preferred Pkg. 241A, base	565	503	537
Air conditioning, cassette player.			
Preferred Pkg. 243A,			
base notchback	1955	1741	1857
base convertible	1550	1381	1473
Air conditioning, Groups 1, 2, and 3.			
Preferred Pkg. 249A, GT	1540	1372	1463
Anti-lock brakes, air conditioning, Group 2, power driver's seat.			
Group 1, base notchback	505	449	480
Power windows and door locks, power remote decklid release.			
Group 2, base notchback	870	775	827
base convertible	775	690	736
GT	510	454	485
Cruise control, AM/FM/cassette with premium sound, lighted visor mirrors (base notchback), alloy wheels (std. GT).			
Group 3	310	276	295
Illuminated remote keyless entry system, cargo net. Requires Group 1.			
Power driver's seat	175	156	166
Leather upholstery,			
base convertible with Pkg. 243A, GT	500	445	475
Rear defogger	160	143	152

Prices are accurate at time of publication; subject to manufacturer's change.

FORD

	Retail Price	Dealer Invoice	Fair Price
AM/FM/cassette with premium sound	$165	$147	$157
Mach 460 AM/FM/cassette	670	596	637
with Group 2	375	333	356
Includes 460 watts peak power, AM stereo, 60-watt equalizer, CD changer compatibility, soft touch tape controls, 10 speakers. Requires Group 1.			
CD player	375	334	356
Requires cassette player.			
Optional axle ratio, GT	45	40	43
Alloy wheels, base	265	236	252
17-inch alloy wheels			
and 245/45ZR17 tires, GT	380	338	361
Bodyside moldings	50	45	48
Front floormats	30	27	29
Engine block heater	20	18	19

Ford Probe	Retail Price	Dealer Invoice	Fair Price
3-door hatchback	$14180	$12825	$13325
GT 3-door hatchback	16545	14930	15730
Destination charge	360	360	360

Standard Equipment:

Base: 2.0-liter DOHC 4-cylinder engine, 5-speed manual transmission, power steering, driver- and passenger-side air bags, cloth reclining front bucket seats with memory, split folding rear seat, tachometer, coolant temperature and oil pressure gauges, voltmeter, trip odometer, tinted rear and quarter windows, right visor mirror, center console, dual remote mirrors, AM/FM radio, 195/65R14 all-season tires, wheel covers. **GT** adds: 2.5-liter DOHC V-6 engine, 4-wheel disc brakes, full console with armrest and storage, door pockets, multi-adjustable power seats with driver-side lumbar support and side bolsters, leather-wrapped steering wheel and manual transmission shift knob, cargo net, fog lights, lower bodyside cladding, 225/50VR16 tires, alloy wheels.

Optional Equipment:

4-speed automatic transmission	790	703	711
Requires option pkg.			
Preferred Pkg. 251A, Base	560	499	504
Air conditioning, cassette player.			
SE Preferred Pkg. 253A, Base	2545	2267	2291
Air conditioning, AM/FM cassette with premium sound, Groups 1, 2 and 3, SE Appearance Group (GT front fascia without fog lights, SE badging, alloy wheels, 205/55R15 tires), color-keyed bodyside moldings.			

FORD

	Retail Price	Dealer Invoice	Fair Price
Preferred Pkg. 261A, GT	$1790	$1595	$1611
Air conditioning, cassette player with premium sound, Groups 1 and 2, color-keyed bodyside moldings, front floormats.			
Preferred Pkg. 263A, GT	3495	3113	3146
Pkg. 261A plus Group 4, rear wiper/washer, power driver's seat, rear spoiler, anti-lock brakes.			
Group 1, Base	260	232	234
Rear defogger, power mirrors.			
Group 2, Base	570	508	513
Console with storage armrest (Base), cruise control, intermittent wipers, tilt steering column, remote fuel door and rear hatch release.			
Group 3, GT	485	432	437
Power windows and door locks. Requires Group 1.			
Group 4, SE, GT	485	432	437
Illuminated entry, lighted visor vanity mirrors, map lights, remote keyless entry, convenience lights, battery saver, headlight-on warning chime. Requires Group 3.			
Anti-lock brakes, Base	735	654	662
GT	565	503	509
Includes 4-wheel disc brakes.			
Rear wiper/washer, GT	130	116	117
6-way power driver's seat, GT	290	258	261
Leather seats, GT	500	445	450
Includes 6-way power driver's seat. Requires Groups 1 and 3.			
CD player, Base with Pkg. 251A	430	383	387
Base with 253A, GT with 261A or 263A	270	240	243
Anti-theft system, GT	190	169	171
Requires Groups 1 and 3.			
Rear spoiler	235	209	212
Color-keyed bodyside moldings	50	45	46
Sliding power roof	615	547	554
Includes dome light with map lights.			
Alloy wheels and 205/55R15 tires, Base	430	383	387
Includes sport suspension.			
Chrome wheels, GT	390	347	351
Floormats	30	27	28
Engine block heater	20	18	19

Ford Taurus

	Retail Price	Dealer Invoice	Fair Price
GL 4-door notchback	$17585	$15887	$16387
SE 4-door notchback, 3.0-liter	18630	16817	17317
SE 4-door notchback, 3.8-liter	19760	17813	18313
LX 4-door notchback	19400	17486	17986

Prices are accurate at time of publication; subject to manufacturer's change.

FORD

	Retail Price	Dealer Invoice	Fair Price
SHO 4-door notchback	$25140	$22594	$23094
GL 5-door wagon	18680	16845	17345
LX 5-door wagon	21010	18919	19419
Destination charge	535	535	535

Standard Equipment:

GL: 3.0-liter V-6, 4-speed automatic transmission, air conditioning, power steering, driver- and passenger-side air bags, cloth reclining split bench seat with dual center armrests, tilt steering wheel, power mirrors, tinted glass, intermittent wipers, rear defogger, door pockets, AM/FM radio, digital clock, coolant temperature gauge, trip odometer, wheel covers, luggage rack (wagon), 205/65R15 tires. **SE** adds: Preferred Pkg. 205A (Groups 2A, 3 and 3A, floormats). **LX** adds to GL: 3.8-liter V-6 on wagon, variable-assist power steering, upgraded cloth reclining front bucket seats with power lumbar support (notchback), console with armrest and storage (notchback), 6-way power driver's seat, power windows and door locks, illuminated entry, remote fuel door and decklid/liftgate releases, tachometer, diagnostic alert lights, automatic parking brake release, automatic on/off clear-lens headlights, cornering lamps, bodyside cladding, Light Group, illuminated entry, lighted visor mirrors, cargo tiedown net, alloy wheels. **SHO** deletes automatic parking brake release and clear-lens headlights and adds: 3.0-liter DOHC V-6 with dual exhaust, 5-speed manual transmission, anti-lock 4-wheel disc brakes, speed-sensitive variable effort power steering, automatic air conditioning, cruise control, fog lamps, cloth and leather front bucket seats, rear spoiler, handling suspension, extended range fuel tank, cornering lights, high-level audio system, power antenna, leather-wrapped steering wheel, floormats, 215/60ZR16 tires.

Optional Equipment:

3.8-liter V-6 engine	630	561	567
Standard LX wagon. NA GL with Pkg. 203A or SHO.			
Cellular telephone with storage armrest	500	445	450
Requires split bench seat.			
Anti-lock 4-wheel disc brakes (std. SHO)	565	503	509
4-speed automatic transmission, SHO	790	703	711
Includes 3.2-liter DOHC V-6 engine and 215/60HR16 tires.			
Automatic air conditioning, LX	175	156	158
Preferred Pkg. 204A, GL	775	690	698
with 3.8-liter V-6 engine	1275	1135	1148
Groups 2 and 3, floormats, GL Equipment Group.			
Preferred Pkg. 208A, LX notchback	355	316	320
LX wagon	545	485	491
Groups 2 and 4, floormats. Wagons add: Group 5, load floor extension.			

	Retail Price	Dealer Invoice	Fair Price
Group 2, GL with Pkg. 204A	$1115	$992	$1004
LX	380	338	342

Cruise control, cassette player, power windows and door locks, Light Group (GL, includes engine compartment light, under-dash courtesy lights, map and reading lights, headlights-on chime), remote fuel door and decklid/liftgate releases.

Group 2A, SE	NC	NC	NC

Power door locks and windows, cassette player.

Group 2B	270	240	243

Light Group, cruise control. Requires option group.

Group 3, GL with Pkg. 204A, SE	NC	NC	NC

Power driver's seat, deluxe wheel covers (GL).

Group 3A, SE	NC	NC	NC

Cloth and leather bucket seats, console with floor-mounted shifter, clear-lens headlights, alloy wheels.

Group 4	405	360	365

Remote keyless entry system, leather-wrapped steering wheel, power antenna.

Group 5, wagon	195	174	176

Rear wiper/washer, cargo area cover.

Luxury Convenience Group, SHO	1555	1384	1400

Power front seats, power moonroof, Ford JBL audio system, remote keyless entry system.

LX Convenience Group	1030	917	927

Power front seats, power moonroof.

GL Equipment Group, SE	245	218	221

Variable-assist power steering, visor mirrors, dual driver-side visor, striping.

Bucket seats and console, GL	NC	NC	NC
Split bench seat, LX notchback	NC	NC	NC
Leather bucket seats and console,			
GL with Pkg. 204A	595	530	536
LX	495	441	446
Leather bucket seats, SE, SHO	495	441	446
Leather split bench seat, LX	495	441	446
6-way power driver's seat, GL	290	258	261
Power front passenger seat, LX, SHO	290	258	261
Rear facing third seat, wagons	150	134	135
Cassette player	165	147	149
High-level audio system, LX	480	427	432
LX with Group 2	315	280	284
CD player, LX, SHO	375	334	338
Ford JBL audio system,	500	445	450
NA GL and wagons.			

FORD

	Retail Price	Dealer Invoice	Fair Price
Cruise control	$215	$191	$194
Remote keyless entry, GL	390	347	351
GL with Group 2	295	263	266
LX, SHO	215	191	194

Requires power door locks and windows. Includes illuminated entry with Group 2. Includes illuminated entry and remote fuel door and decklid/lift-gate releases without Group 2.

	Retail Price	Dealer Invoice	Fair Price
Power windows, GL, SE	340	302	306
Power door locks, GL	245	218	231

Requires power windows.

	Retail Price	Dealer Invoice	Fair Price
Remote fuel door and decklid releases, SE	95	85	86
Rear spoiler, SE	270	240	243
Alloy wheels, GL with Pkg. 204A	230	205	207
Deluxe wheel covers, GL	80	71	72
Full-size spare tire	70	62	63
NA SHO.			
Heavy duty suspension	25	23	24
NA SHO.			
Heavy duty battery	30	27	28
NA SHO.			
Engine block heater	20	18	19
NA SHO.			
Floormats	45	40	41

Ford Thunderbird

	Retail Price	Dealer Invoice	Fair Price
LX 2-door notchback	$17400	$15696	$16196
Super Coupe 2-door notchback	22910	20600	21100
Destination charge	495	495	495

Standard Equipment:

LX: 3.8-liter V-6, 4-speed automatic transmission, driver- and passenger-side air bags, power steering, air conditioning, cruise control, cloth reclining front bucket seats with power driver's seat, center console with dual cup holders, rear seat center armrest, dual power mirrors, visor mirrors, solar-control tinted glass, coolant temperature gauge, tachometer, voltmeter, tilt steering wheel, trip odometer, AM/FM cassette, power windows and door locks, leather-wrapped steering wheel and shift knob, illuminated entry system, remote fuel door and decklid release, body-color side moldings, intermittent wipers, 205/70R15 tires, wheel covers. **Super Coupe** deletes cruise control, voltmeter, power door locks, power driver's seat, remote fuel door and decklid releases, and adds: 3.8-liter supercharged V-6 with dual exhaust, 5-speed manual transmission, anti-lock 4-wheel disc brakes, vari-

FORD

able-assist power steering, adjustable sport suspension, semi-automatic temperature control, Traction-Lok axle, articulated cloth/leather/vinyl sport seats with power lumbar and side bolsters, seatback pockets, leather-wrapped parking brake handle, tachometer, boost gauge, fog lights, lower bodyside cladding, 225/60ZR16 tires, locking alloy wheels.

Optional Equipment:

	Retail Price	Dealer Invoice	Fair Price
4.6-liter V-8, LX	$1130	$1006	$1017
Includes variable-assist power steering and heavy duty battery.			
4-speed automatic transmission, SC	790	703	711
Includes heavy duty battery.			
Anti-lock 4-wheel disc brakes, LX	565	503	509
Preferred Pkg. 155A, LX	NC	NC	NC
Groups 2 and 3.			
Preferred Pkg. 157A, SC	NC	NC	NC
Groups 1 and 2.			
Group 1, SC	800	712	720
Power door locks, remote fuel door and decklid releases, cruise control, power driver's seat.			
Group 2, LX	315	280	284
SC	160	143	144
Semi-automatic temperature control (LX), rear defogger.			
Group 3, LX	210	187	189
215/70R15 tires, alloy wheels.			
Luxury/Lighting Group, LX	350	313	315
SC	325	290	293
Autolamp system, power antenna, illuminated entry (SC), Light Group (LX), integrated warning lamp (LX), illuminated visor mirrors. Requires Groups 1, 2 and 3.			
Cellular Phone Group	530	472	477
Includes voice-activated cellular telephone, cassette player with premium sound system.			
Leather seat trim, LX	490	436	441
SC	615	547	554
6-way power passenger's seat	290	258	261
Requires Group 1.			
Traction-Assist, LX	210	187	189
Requires anti-lock brakes and Luxury/Lighting Group.			
Traction-Lok axle, LX,			
SC with 4-speed automatic transmission	95	85	86
Tri-coat paint	225	201	203
Premium cassette player	290	258	261
Premium CD player	430	383	387
Remote keyless entry, LX and SC			
with Luxury/Lighting Group	215	191	194

Prices are accurate at time of publication; subject to manufacturer's change.

CONSUMER GUIDE®   327

FORD

	Retail Price	Dealer Invoice	Fair Price
SC	$295	$263	$266
Requires Groups 1, 2 and 3.			
Power moonroof	740	658	666
Requires Groups 1, 2 and 3, and Luxury/Lighting Group.			
Front floormats	30	27	28
225/60ZR16 all-season performance tires, SC	70	62	63
Heavy duty battery	25	23	24
Engine block heater	20	18	19

Ford Windstar

	Retail Price	Dealer Invoice	Fair Price
GL 4-door van	$19590	$17495	$19090
LX 4-door van	23760	21164	23260
Destination charge	540	540	540

Standard Equipment:

GL: 3.8-liter V-6 engine, 4-speed automatic transmission, driver- and passenger-side air bags, height-adjustable front shoulder belts, anti-lock brakes, power steering, 7-passenger seating (high-back front buckets, 2-place middle and 3-place rear bench seats), solar tinted windshield and front door glass, dual outside mirrors, AM/FM radio with digital clock, intermittent wipers, rear wiper/washer, cup holders, front-door map pockets, tachometer, coolant temperature gauge, color-keyed bodyside moldings, 205/70R15 tires, full wheel covers. **LX** adds: front air conditioning, power mirrors, power front windows with 30-second delay feature, power rear quarter vent windows, power locks, premium cassette player, Light Group, illuminated entry, illuminated visor vanity mirrors, tilt steering wheel, low-back bucket seats with power lumbar adjustment, 6-way power driver's seat, map pockets on front seatbacks, 7-inch rear seat travel, storage drawer under front passenger seat, cargo net, 25-gallon fuel tank, 215/70R15 tires, alloy wheels.

Optional Equipment:

Preferred Pkg. 470C, GL	640	544	608
Includes air conditioning and 7-inch rear seat travel.			
Preferred Pkg. 471C, GL	1265	1076	1139
Pkg. 470C plus Light Group, Power Convenience Group, rear window defroster.			
Preferred Pkg. 472C, GL	1635	1391	1472
Pkg. 471C plus premium cassette player, cruise control, and tilt steering wheel.			
Preferred Pkg. 476C, LX	320	272	288
Rear window defroster, cruise control, tilt steering wheel, front and rear floormats, luggage rack, 2-tone paint.			

	Retail Price	Dealer Invoice	Fair Price
Preferred Pkg. 477C, LX	$1270	$1080	$1143
Pkg. 476C plus quad bucket seats, privacy glass, remote entry.			
Front and rear air conditioning			
(NA GL w/Pkg. 470C)	465	395	442
Includes rear heater. Requires privacy glass. GL also requires cruise control, tilt steering wheel, and Light Group.			
Load-levelling air suspension, LX	290	247	261
Requires Power Convenience Group.			
Rear defogger, GL w/Pkg. 470C	170	144	162
Cruise control and tilt steering wheel,			
GL w/Pkg. 471C	370	314	352
Electronic instrument cluster, LX	490	417	466
Includes autolamp feature and electrochromatic mirror. Requires rear defroster.			
Floor console, LX, GL w/Pkg. 472C	140	119	133
Includes cup holders and covered storage bin. Requires rear air conditioning.			
Privacy glass (NA GL w/Pkg. 470C)	415	352	394
Light Group, GL w/Pkg. 470C (std. LX)	50	43	48
Front map/dome light and glove box, instrument panel and engine compartment lights.			
Interior Convenience Group,			
GL w/Pkgs. 471C or 472C	80	67	72
Left rear storage bin, covered center bin, underseat storage drawer, cargo net.			
Power Convenience Group,			
GL w/Pkg. 470C	80	67	72
Power front windows with 30-second delay feature, power rear quarter vent windows, power door locks and mirrors.			
Trailer Towing Pkg.	375	319	338
Fog lamps, LX	110	93	105
Requires electronic instrument cluster.			
Luggage rack, GL w/Pkg. 472C	175	149	158
Remote entry, GL w/Pkgs. 471C or 472C,			
LX w/Pkg. 476C	145	123	131
Remote entry system and illuminated entry. Requires Power Convenience Group.			
Keyless entry pkg., LX	340	289	323
Keyless entry system, anti-theft system, and heated mirrors. Requires remote entry and rear defroster.			
Premium cassette player, GL	325	276	309
Premium AM/FM CD player, GL w/Pkg. 471C ...	535	455	482
GL w/Pkg. 472C, LX	170	144	162
Requires cruise control and tilt steering wheel, Light Group.			

Prices are accurate at time of publication; subject to manufacturer's change.

FORD • GEO

	Retail Price	Dealer Invoice	Fair Price
JBL audio system, LX w/Pkg. 477C	$510	$433	$485
Requires premium cassette or CD player.			
Seat bed, GL w/Pkg. 472C	615	522	566
Quad bucket seats, LX	600	510	570
Leather upholstery, LX	865	735	779
Requires quad bucket seats.			
Integrated child seats	225	192	214
Requires adjustable third seat track. NA with quad buckets.			
Floor mats, GL	90	76	81
2-tone paint, LX w/Pkg. 476C or 477C (credit) .	(135)	(115)	(115)
25-gallon fuel tank, GL (std. LX)	30	26	27
NA with Pkg. 470C.			
Engine block heater	35	30	33
Alloy wheels, GL w/Pkg. 472C (std. LX)	415	353	374
Includes 215/70R15 tires.			
Conventional spare tire	110	93	105

GEO

Geo Metro

	Retail Price	Dealer Invoice	Fair Price
Base 3-door hatchback	$8085	$7616	—
Base 4-door notchback	9085	8467	—
LSi 3-door hatchback	8385	7815	—
LSi 4-door notchback	9485	8840	—
Destination charge	310	310	310

Fair price not available at time of publication.

Standard Equipment:

Base 3-door: 1.0-liter 3-cylinder engine, 5-speed manual transmission, driver- and passenger-side air bags, daytime running lights, cloth and vinyl reclining front bucket seats, one-piece folding rear seatback, day/night rearview mirror, temperature gauge, console with cup holders and storage tray, door pockets, 155/80R13 tires. **LSi 3-door** adds: remote hatch release, dual manual mirrors, intermittent wipers, trip odometer, passenger visor mirror, bodyside moldings, wheel covers. **Base 4-door** adds to base 3-door: 1.3-liter 4-cylinder engine, dual manual mirrors, trip odometer, intermittent wipers, passenger visor mirror, bodyside moldings, wheel covers. **LSi 4-door** adds: color-keyed bumpers, remote fuel door and decklid release, remote mirrors, cloth door trim, seatback pockets, split folding rear seat, tinted band windshield.

Optional Equipment:

	Retail Price	Dealer Invoice	Fair Price
1.3-liter 4-cylinder engine, LSi 3-door	$360	$320	—
Requires 3-speed automatic transmission.			
3-speed automatic transmission	500	445	—
Requires 1.3-liter 4-cylinder engine.			
Air conditioning	785	699	—
Anti-lock brakes	565	503	—
Power steering, 4-doors	260	231	—
AM/FM radio	301	268	—
Includes seek and scan, digital clock, and four speakers.			
AM/FM cassette player	521	464	—
Includes seek and scan, theft deterrent, tone select, digital clock, and four speakers.			
AM/FM cassette and CD players	721	642	—
Includes seek and scan, theft deterrent, tone select, digital clock, and four speakers. NA base 3-door.			
Preferred Equipment Group 2, 4-doors	1045	930	—
Air conditioning, power steering.			
Expressions exterior appearance pkg., LSi 3-door	199	177	—
Includes color-keyed bumpers and bodyside moldings, 7-spoke wheel covers.			
Power door locks, 4-doors	220	196	—
Rear defogger	160	142	—
Rear wiper/washer, LSi 3-door	125	111	—
Requires rear defogger.			
Tachometer	55	49	—
base 3-door	70	62	—
Includes trip odometer with base 3-door.			
Dual manual mirrors, base 3-door	20	18	—
Dual remote mirrors, LSi 3-door, base 4-door	20	18	—
Front and rear floormats	35	31	—
Bodyside moldings, base 3-door	50	45	—
Cargo security cover, LSi 3-door	50	45	—

Geo Prizm	Retail Price	Dealer Invoice	Fair Price
4-door notchback	$11675	$11115	$11415
LSi 4-door notchback	12340	11377	11877
Destination charge	375	375	375

Standard Equipment:

1.6-liter DOHC 4-cylinder engine, 5-speed manual transmission, driver- and

GEO

passenger-side air bags, left remote and right manual mirrors, reclining front bucket seats, cloth/vinyl upholstery, center console with storage tray and cup holders, remote fuel door release, tinted glass, rear-seat heating ducts, bodyside molding, 175/65R14 tires. **LSi** adds: tilt steering wheel, upgraded full-cloth upholstery, center console with storage box, dual front storage pockets, split-folding rear seat, visor mirrors, wheel covers.

Optional Equipment:

	Retail Price	Dealer Invoice	Fair Price
1.8-liter 4-cylinder engine, LSi	$352	$303	$308
Includes rear stabilizer bar and 185/65R14 tires. Requires option group.			
3-speed automatic transmission	495	426	433
Requires 1.6-liter engine and option group.			
4-speed automatic transmission, LSi	800	688	700
Requires 1.8-liter engine.			
Anti-lock brakes	595	512	521
Air conditioning, base with Group 2	795	684	696
Cruise control, LSi w/Preferred Equipment Group 2	175	151	153
Leather upholstery, LSi with Group 3	595	512	521
Rear defogger	170	146	149
Power door locks	220	189	193
Power sunroof, LSi	660	568	578
Includes map light.			
Intermittent wipers	40	34	35
Tachometer	60	52	53
AM/FM radio	330	284	289
Includes seek and scan, digital clock, and four speakers.			
AM/FM cassette player	550	473	481
with option group	220	189	193
Includes seek and scan, theft deterrent, tone select, digital clock, and four speakers.			
AM/FM radio with CD and cassette players, LSi with option group	420	361	368
Includes seek and scan, theft deterrent, tone select, digital clock, and six speakers.			
Base Preferred Equipment Group 2	590	507	516
Power steering and AM/FM radio with digital clock.			
LSi Preferred Equipment Group 2	1545	1329	1352
Air conditioning, AM/FM radio with digital clock, dual power mirrors, power steering, remote decklid release, intermittent wipers.			
LSi Preferred Equipment Group 3	2240	1926	1960
LSi Preferred Equipment Group 2 plus power windows and door locks, cruise control.			
Alloy wheels, LSi	335	288	293
Requires option group.			

	Retail Price	Dealer Invoice	Fair Price
Wheel covers, base	$52	$45	$46
Front and rear floormats	40	34	35

Geo Tracker

	Retail Price	Dealer Invoice	Fair Price
2-door convertible, 2WD	$11670	$11110	$11310
2-door convertible, 4WD	12935	12314	12514
2-door wagon, 4WD	13015	12390	12590
LSi 2-door convertible, 4WD	14305	13618	13818
LSi 2-door wagon, 4WD	14485	13790	13990
Destination charge	310	310	310

Standard Equipment:

1.6-liter 4-cylinder engine, 5-speed manual transmission, anti-lock rear brakes, rear defogger (wagon), cloth/vinyl reclining front bucket seats, folding rear bench seat (4WD), center console with storage tray and cup holders, tachometer (4WD), trip odometer, dual mirrors, intermittent wipers, full-size lockable spare tire, spare tire cover, front and rear tow hooks, 195/75R15 tires, (205/75R15 tires 4WD). **LSi** adds: automatic locking front hubs, power steering, AM/FM radio, floormats, tinted glass, upgraded cloth/vinyl upholstery and door trim, adjustable rear bucket seats, rear wiper/washer (wagon), bodyside moldings, styled steel wheels.

Optional Equipment:

3-speed automatic transmission	595	530	538
Air conditioning	745	663	674
Tilt steering wheel	115	102	104
AM/FM radio (std. LSi)	306	272	277
Includes seek and scan, digital clock, and four speakers.			
AM/FM cassette player	526	468	476
LSi	220	196	199
Includes seek and scan, theft deterrent, tone select, digital clock, and four speakers.			
AM/FM radio with CD and cassette player	726	646	657
LSi	420	374	380
Includes seek and scan, theft deterrent, tone select, digital clock, and four speakers.			
Preferred Group 2, base	581	517	526
AM/FM radio, power steering.			
With AM/FM cassette, add	220	196	199
With AM/FM radio, CD, and cassette player, add	420	374	380
Preferred Group 2, LSi	965	859	873
Air conditioning, cassette player.			

Prices are accurate at time of publication; subject to manufacturer's change.

	Retail Price	Dealer Invoice	Fair Price
With CD player, add	$200	$178	$181
Rear seat delete, 2WD	NC	NC	NC
Folding rear bench seat, 2WD	445	396	403
Transfer case shield, 4WD	75	67	68
Alloy wheels	335	298	303
NA with accent pkgs.			
Floormats, base	28	25	26
Bodyside moldings, base wagon	59	53	54
Convertibles	85	76	77
Blue Accent Package,			
base convertibles	499	444	452
LSi convertible	425	378	385
Green Accent Package,			
base convertibles	499	444	452
LSi convertible	425	378	385
Tan Accent Package,			
LSi convertible	425	378	385

GMC

GMC Jimmy

	Retail Price	Dealer Invoice	Fair Price
3-door wagon, 2WD	$18274	$16538	—
3-door wagon, 4WD	19980	18082	—
5-door wagon, 2WD	20157	18242	—
5-door wagon, 4WD	22205	20096	—
Destination charge	485	485	485

Fair price not available at time of publication.

Standard Equipment:

3-door: 4.3-liter V-6 engine, 4-speed automatic transmission, part-time 4WD with electronic transfer case (4WD), anti-lock brakes, driver-side air bag, air conditioning, power steering, tinted glass, coolant temperature and oil pressure gauges, tachometer, voltmeter, trip odometer, AM/FM radio, digital clock, dual outside manual mirrors, illuminated entry, front reclining cloth bucket seats with manual lumbar support adjusters, console with storage and cupholders, intermittent wipers, door map pockets, passenger-side visor mirror, floormats, 205/75R15 tires, full-size spare tire, trailering harness, front tow hooks (4WD), wheel trim rings. **5-door** adds: cloth 60/40 front bench seat with storage armrest, folding rear 3-passenger bench seat.

Option Pkgs., 3-door:

	Retail Price	Dealer Invoice	Fair Price
SL Pkg. 2	$1470	$1264	—

Base plus cassette player, power windows, door locks and mirrors, cruise control, tilt steering wheel, split folding rear 3-passenger bench seat, Euro-Ride Suspension Pkg., roof rack, 235/70R15 tires.

SLS Pkg. 3	1901	1635	—

SL Pkg. 2 contents plus SLS Sport Decor Pkg.

Option Pkgs., 5-door:

SL Pkg. 5, 2WD	1645	1415	—
4WD	1170	1006	—

Base plus cassette player, power windows, door locks and mirrors, cruise control, tilt steering wheel, split folding rear 3-passenger bench seat, Luxury Ride Suspension Pkg., roof rack, 235/70R15 tires.

SLS Pkg. 6, 2WD	2326	2000	—
4WD	1851	1592	—

SL Pkg. 5 contents plus SLS Sport Decor Pkg.

SLE Pkg. 6, 2WD	2416	2078	—
4WD	1941	1669	—

SL Pkg. 5 contents plus SLE Comfort Decor Pkg.

SLT Pkg. 7, 2WD	4227	3635	—
4WD	3752	3227	—

SL Pkg. 5 contents plus SLT Touring Decor Pkg., cassette player with equalizer.

Individual Options:

Optional axle ratio	NC	NC	NC
Locking differential	252	217	—
Manual transfer case, 4WD (credit)	(123)	(106)	(106)

Replaces standard electronic push button shift with manual floor mounted shift.

SLS Sport Decor Pkg., 3-door	2712	2332	—
5-door 2WD	3137	2698	—
5-door 4WD	2662	2289	—

Adds to standard SL Decor Pkg.: cargo net, cloth door trim panels, reading lamps, dual auxiliary power outlets, power windows and door locks, power mirrors, cassette player, cargo cover (5-door), front reclining cloth bucket seats with manual lumbar support adjusters (5-door), split folding rear seat, leather-wrapped steering wheel, lighted visor mirrors, power remote tailgate release, rear defogger, intermittent rear wiper/washer, tilt steering wheel, cruise control, roof rack, striping, deep-tinted glass on rear doors (5-door) and rear quarter windows, alloy wheels.

SLE Comfort Decor Pkg., 5-door 2WD	3227	2775	—
5-door 4WD	2752	2367	—

	Retail Price	Dealer Invoice	Fair Price
5-door 2WD with 2-tone paint	$3399	$2923	—
5-door 4WD with 2-tone paint	2924	2515	—

Adds to standard SL Decor Pkg.: cargo net, cloth door trim panels, reading lamps, dual auxiliary power outlets, power windows and door locks, power mirrors, cassette player, cargo cover, split folding rear seat, leather-wrapped steering wheel, lighted visor mirrors, power remote tailgate release, rear defogger, intermittent rear wiper/washer, tilt steering wheel, cruise control, roof rack, lower body moldings, deep-tinted glass on rear doors and rear quarter windows, alloy wheels.

SLT Touring Decor Pkg., 5-door 2WD	4833	4156	—
5-door 4WD	4358	3748	—
5-door 2WD with 2-tone paint	5005	4304	—
5-door 4WD with 2-tone paint	4530	3896	—

Adds to standard SL Decor Pkg.: cargo net, console with storage and cupholders, overhead console with reading lamps, outside temperature gauge and compass, simulated leather door trim panels, remote keyless entry system, dual auxiliary power outlets, power windows and door locks, power mirrors, cassette player, cargo cover, leather front bucket seats with power lumbar support adjusters, 6-way power seat, leather split folding rear seat, leather-wrapped steering wheel, lighted visor mirrors, power remote tailgate release, rear defogger, intermittent rear wiper/washer, tilt steering wheel, cruise control, roof rack, lower body moldings, deep-tinted glass on rear doors and rear quarter windows, alloy wheels.

Split folding rear seat, 3-door	475	409	—
Rear seat delete, SL	NC	NC	NC
NA 5-door 4WD.			
Cloth bucket seats with SLE Decor Pkg.	161	138	—
Cloth 60/40 front bench seat			
with storage armrest, 5-door (credit)	(161)	(138)	(138)
NA with SLT Decor Pkg.			
6-way power driver's seat and remote keyless			
entry, SLS, SLE	375	323	—
Overhead console	147	126	—
Includes reading lights, outside temperature gauge, and compass. Requires SLS or SLE decor pkgs., bucket seats.			
Heavy duty battery	56	48	—
Cold Climate Pkg.	89	77	—
Heavy duty battery, engine block heater.			
Convenience Pkg. ZQ3	383	329	—
Cruise control, tilt steering wheel.			
Convenience Pkg. ZM8	322	277	—
Power remote tailgate release, rear defogger, rear wiper/washer.			
Convenience Pkg. ZQ6, 3-door	475	409	—

	Retail Price	Dealer Invoice	Fair Price
5-door	$650	$559	—
Power windows, mirrors, and door locks.			
Air deflector with fog lamps, 2WD	115	99	—
Requires option pkg.			
Roof rack	126	108	—
Cassette player	122	105	—
Cassette player with equalizer	327	281	—
with SLS, SLE, or SLT Decor Pkgs.	205	176	—
CD player with SLS, SLE, or SLT Decor Pkgs.	329	283	—
Radio delete, SL (credit)	(226)	(194)	(194)
Shield Pkg., 4WD	126	108	—
Front differential skid plates, transfer case, steering linkage and fuel tank shields.			
Smooth Ride Suspension Pkg., 5-door with option pkg.	114	98	—
Gas shock absorbers, front and rear stabilizer bars. Requires 205/75R15 tires.			
Luxury Ride Suspension Pkg., 5-door	197	169	—
Gas shock absorbers, urethane jounce bumpers, front and rear stabilizer bars. Requires 235/75R15 tires.			
Solid Smooth Ride Suspension Pkg., 3-door with Pkg. 2 or 3	114	98	—
Gas shock absorbers, urethane jounce bumpers, front and rear stabilizer bars, upgraded rear springs. Requires 205/75R15 tires.			
Euro-Ride Suspension Pkg.	197	169	—
Gas shock absorbers, front and rear stabilizer bars, heavy duty springs.			
Off-road Suspension Pkg., 3-door 4WD	220	189	—
Gas shock absorbers, urethane jounce bumpers, front and rear stabilizer bars, upgraded torsion bars.			
Heavy duty trailering equipment	210	181	—
Weight distributing hitch platform, 7-lead wiring harness, heavy duty flasher.			
205/75R15 all-season white letter tires	121	104	—
235/70R15 all-season tires	192	165	—
235/70R15 all-season white letter tires	325	280	—
235/75R15 on/off-road white letter tires, 4WD .	335	288	—
Requires exterior spare tire carrier with 3-door.			
Exterior spare tire carrier, 3-door 4WD	159	137	—
Alloy wheels, 2WD	248	213	—
4WD	280	241	—
Cargo cover, 3-door 4WD with SLS Decor Pkg.	69	59	—
Requires exterior spare tire carrier.			

Prices are accurate at time of publication; subject to manufacturer's change.

HONDA

Honda Accord

	Retail Price	Dealer Invoice	Fair Price
LX 2-door notchback, 5-speed	$17550	$15508	$16008
LX 2-door notchback, automatic	18300	16171	16671
LX 2-door notchback, 5-speed w/ABS	18500	16347	16847
LX 2-door notchback, automatic w/ABS	19250	17010	17510
EX 2-door notchback, 5-speed	20110	17770	18570
EX 2-door notchback, automatic	20860	18432	19232
EX 2-door notchback, 5-speed w/leather	21160	18697	19497
EX 2-door notchback, automatic w/leather	21910	19360	20160
DX 4-door notchback, 5-speed	14800	13078	13578
DX 4-door notchback, automatic	15550	13741	14241
LX 4-door notchback, 5-speed	17750	15685	16185
LX 4-door notchback, automatic	18500	16347	16847
LX 4-door notchback w/ABS, 5-speed	18700	16524	17024
LX 4-door notchback w/ABS, automatic	19450	17187	17687
LX 4-door notchback V-6, automatic	22300	19705	—
EX 4-door notchback, 5-speed	20310	17946	18746
EX 4-door notchback, automatic	21060	18609	19409
EX 4-door notchback w/leather, 5-speed	21360	18874	19674
EX 4-door notchback w/leather, automatic	22110	19537	20337
EX 4-door notchback V-6, automatic	24950	22047	—
LX 5-door wagon, 5-speed	18710	16533	17033
LX 5-door wagon, automatic	19460	17195	17695
EX 5-door wagon, automatic	22090	19520	20020
Destination charge	380	380	380

V-6 fair price not available at time of publication.

Standard Equipment:

DX: 2.2-liter 4-cylinder engine, 5-speed manual or 4-speed automatic transmission, variable-assist power steering, driver- and passenger-side air bags, cloth reclining front bucket seats, folding rear seatback, front console with armrest, tachometer, coolant temperature gauge, trip odometer, digital clock, tinted glass, tilt steering column, intermittent wipers, rear defogger, dual remote mirrors, remote fuel door and decklid releases, door pockets, maintenance interval indicator, passenger-side visor mirror, 185/70R14 tires, wheel covers. **Models with ABS** add anti-lock 4-wheel disc brakes. **LX** adds: air conditioning, cruise control, power windows and door locks, power mirrors, AM/FM/cassette, power antenna (4-door notchback, wagon), rear armrest, lighted visor mirrors, beverage holder; wagon has rear wiper/washer, split folding rear seatback, cargo cover, 195/60HR15 tires, full-size spare tire. **LX V-6** adds to LX: 2.7-liter V-6 engine, 4-speed automatic transmission, anti-lock

4-wheel disc brakes, variable intermittent wipers, 205/60R15 tires. **EX** adds to LX: 145-horsepower VTEC engine, anti-lock 4-wheel disc brakes, driver's seat lumbar support and power height adjusters, power moonroof, upgraded audio system, color-keyed bodyside moldings, 195/60HR15 tires, alloy wheels; wagon adds remote keyless entry. **EX V-6** adds to EX: 2.7-liter V-6 engine, 4-speed automatic transmission, leather upholstery, 8-way power driver's seat, variable intermittent wipers, 205/60R15 tires.

Options are available as dealer-installed accessories.

Honda Civic

	Retail Price	Dealer Invoice	Fair Price
CX 3-door hatchback, 5-speed	$9750	$9146	$9646
DX 3-door hatchback, 5-speed	11100	9959	10859
DX 3-door hatchback, automatic	12080	10839	11739
VX 3-door hatchback, 5-speed	11800	10587	11487
Si 3-door hatchback, 5-speed	13540	12148	13048
DX 2-door notchback, 5-speed	11590	10399	11299
DX 2-door notchback, automatic	12570	11277	12177
EX 2-door notchback, 5-speed	14030	12588	13488
EX 2-door notchback, automatic	14780	13261	14161
EX 2-door notchback w/ABS, 5-speed	14880	13351	14251
EX 2-door notchback w/ABS, automatic	15630	14024	14924
DX 4-door notchback, 5-speed	11980	10749	11649
DX 4-door notchback, automatic	12730	11422	12322
LX 4-door notchback, 5-speed	13320	11950	12850
LX 4-door notchback, automatic	14070	12623	13523
LX 4-door notchback w/ABS, 5-speed	14170	12713	13613
LX 4-door notchback w/ABS, automatic	14920	13386	14286
EX 4-door notchback, 5-speed	16200	14535	15435
EX 4-door notchback, automatic	16950	15208	16108
Destination charge	380	380	380

Standard Equipment:

CX: 1.5-liter (70 horsepower) 4-cylinder engine, 5-speed manual transmission, driver- and passenger-side air bags, reclining cloth front bucket seats, split folding rear seatback, remote fuel door and hatch releases, tinted glass, rear defogger, dual remote mirrors, 165/70R13 tires. **DX** adds: 1.5-liter (102 horsepower) engine, 5-speed manual or 4-speed automatic transmission, power steering (4-door; hatchback and 2-door with automatic transmission only), rear wiper/washer (hatchback), tilt steering column, remote decklid release (notchbacks), cargo cover (hatchback), intermittent wipers, bodyside moldings, front spoiler (2-door), 175/70R13 tires. **VX** adds to CX: 1.5-liter (92 horsepower) engine, tachometer, front spoiler, alloy wheels. **Si** adds to DX: 1.6-liter engine, 4-wheel disc brakes, power steering, power mirrors, power moonroof, digital clock, tachometer, sport seats, cruise control, rear wiper/washer, right visor mirror, wheel covers,

HONDA

185/60HR14 tires. **LX 4-door** adds to DX 4-door: power mirrors, power windows and door locks, cruise control, AM/FM/cassette, digital clock, tachometer, front console with storage armrest, lockable folding rear seat, right visor mirror, 175/65R14 tires, wheel covers. **Models with ABS** add anti-lock 4-wheel disc brakes. **EX 4-door** adds to LX 4-door: 1.6-liter engine, anti-lock 4-wheel disc brakes, air conditioning, power moonroof, upgraded audio system and interior trim. **EX 2-door** adds to DX 2-door: 1.6-liter engine, power steering (with manual transmission), power windows and door locks, power mirrors, power moonroof, tachometer, cruise control, lockable folding rear seat, AM/FM/cassette, digital clock, right visor mirror, wheel covers, 185/60HR14 tires.

Options are available as dealer-installed accessories.

Honda del Sol

	Retail Price	Dealer Invoice	Fair Price
S 2-door notchback, 5-speed	$14780	$13261	$14061
S 2-door notchback, automatic	15760	14140	14940
Si 2-door notchback, 5-speed	16950	15208	16008
Si 2-door notchback, automatic	17700	15880	16680
VTEC 2-door notchback, 5-speed	19200	17226	18026
Destination charge	380	380	380

Standard Equipment:

S:1.5-liter 4-cylinder engine, 5-speed manual or 4-speed automatic transmission, driver- and pasenger-side air bags, power steering (with automatic transmission), reclining bucket seats, center armrest with storage, lockable rear storage compartments, removable roof panel, power windows, rear defogger, intermittent wipers, tilt steering column, tachometer, digital clock, manual exterior mirrors, passenger-side visor mirror, remote fuel door and decklid releases, 175/70R13 tires, wheel covers. **Si** adds: 1.6-liter 4-cylinder engine, power steering, 4-wheel disc brakes, cruise control, AM/FM/cassette, power mirrors and door locks, 185/60HR14 tires, alloy wheels. **VTEC** adds: 1.6-liter DOHC VTEC engine, 5-speed manual transmission, anti-lock brakes, front and rear stabilizer bars, 195/60VR14 tires.

Options are available as dealer-installed accessories.

Honda Odyssey

Prices not available at time of publication.

Standard Equipment:

LX: 2.2-liter 4-cylinder engine, 4-speed automatic transmission, anti-lock 4-wheel disc brakes, driver- and passenger-side air bags, variable-assist power steering, front and rear air conditioning, cloth front bucket seats, split folding middle bench seat (7-passenger seating) or removable captain's chairs (6-passenger seating), folding third bench seat, AM/FM cassette, digital clock, power windows and door locks, power mirrors, cruise control, tilt steering column, tinted glass, cupholders, rear wiper/washer, wheel covers, 205/65R15 tires. **EX** adds: power sunroof, 6-passenger seating, remote keyless entry system, 6-speaker sound system, map lights, color-keyed bodyside moldings, alloy wheels.

Options are available as dealer-installed accessories.

Honda Passport

	Retail Price	Dealer Invoice	Fair Price
DX 2WD 5-door wagon, 5-speed	$16230	$14396	$15196
LX 2WD 5-door wagon, 5-speed	19635	17417	18217
LX 2WD 5-door wagon, automatic	20555	18232	19032
LX 4WD 5-door wagon, 5-speed	22300	19780	20580
LX 4WD 5-door wagon with 16-inch Wheel Pkg., 5-speed	22900	20312	21112
LX 4WD 5-door wagon, automatic	23450	20800	21600
LX 4WD 5-door wagon with 16-inch Wheel Pkg., automatic	24050	21322	22122
EX 4WD 5-door wagon, 5-speed	25400	22530	23330
EX 4WD 5-door wagon, automatic	26550	23550	24350
Destination charge	380	380	380

Standard Equipment:

DX: 2.6-liter 4-cylinder engine, 5-speed manual transmission, anti-lock rear brakes, variable-assist power steering, front bench seat with folding center armrest, folding rear seatback, tinted glass, rear defogger, cargo area light, dual exterior mirrors, fuel tank skid plate, full-size spare tire, outside mounted spare tire carrier, 225/75R15 mud and snow tires, styled steel wheels. **LX 2WD** adds: 3.2-liter V-6 engine, 5-speed manual or 4-speed automatic transmission, 4-wheel disc brakes, cruise control, power windows and door locks, reclining front bucket seats, center storage console, tilt steering column, remote tailgate release, tachometer, upgraded door trim panels, door courtesy lights, AM/FM/cassette player. **LX 4WD** adds to LX 2WD: part-time 4-wheel drive, automatic locking front hubs, air conditioning, 2-speed transfer case, transfer case skid plate, alloy wheels. 16-inch Wheel Pkg. adds: limited-slip differential, flared wheel opening moldings, splash guards, 245/70R16 tires, 16-inch alloy wheels. **EX** adds to LX 4WD: removable tilt-up moonroof, heated power mirrors, 60/40 split folding rear bench seat, chrome bumpers, rear privacy glass, rear wiper/washer, leather-wrapped steering wheel, intermittent wipers, cargo net, visor mirrors, map lights, 16-inch Wheel Pkg.

Options are available as dealer-installed accessories.

Prices are accurate at time of publication; subject to manufacturer's change.

Honda Prelude

	Retail Price	Dealer Invoice	Fair Price
S 2-door notchback, 5-speed	$19550	$16950	$17950
S 2-door notchback, automatic	20300	17600	18600
Si 2-door notchback, 5-speed	22200	19247	20247
Si 2-door notchback, automatic	22950	19898	20898
VTEC 2-door notchback, 5-speed	25350	21978	22978
Destination charge	380	380	380

Standard Equipment:

S: 2.2-liter 4-cylinder engine, 5-speed manual or 4-speed automatic transmission, 4-wheel disc brakes, variable-assist power steering, driver- and passenger-side air bags, air conditioning, cloth reclining front bucket seats, console with storage armrest, split folding rear seat, power moonroof, AM/FM/cassette with power antenna, digital clock, remote fuel door and decklid releases, rear defogger, intermittent wipers, power windows, power mirrors, cruise control, tilt steering column, tachometer, visor mirrors, color-keyed bumpers, front and rear stabilizer bars, 185/70HR14 tires, wheel covers. **Si** adds: 2.3-liter DOHC 4-cylinder engine, anti-lock brakes, power door locks, driver-seat height and lumbar support adjusters, 6-speaker sound system, 205/55VR15 tires, alloy wheels. **VTEC** adds: 2.2-liter DOHC VTEC engine, 5-speed manual transmission, leather seats, leather-wrapped steering wheel, 7-speaker sound system, rear spoiler, map lights.

Options are available as dealer-installed accessories.

HYUNDAI

Hyundai Accent

Prices not available at time of publication.

Standard Equipment:

L: 1.5-liter 4-cylinder engine, 5-speed manual transmission, driver- and passenger-side air bags, cloth reclining front bucket seats, folding rear seat, console with cup holder, coolant temperature gauge, trip odometer, dual exterior remote mirrors, intermittent wipers, rear defogger, remote fuel door release, front door map pockets, passenger-side visor mirror, cargo area cover, color-keyed bumpers, 155/80R13 tires. **Base** adds: digital clock, remote hatch (3-door) or decklid (4-door) release, bodyside moldings, 175/70R13 tires, wheel covers. 4-door deletes cargo area cover and rear seat folding feature.

Hyundai Elantra	Retail Price	Dealer Invoice	Fair Price
4-door notchback, 5-speed	$10199	$9207	$9407
4-door notchback, automatic	11499	10376	10576
GLS 4-door notchback, 5-speed	11599	10234	10634
GLS 4-door notchback, automatic	12324	10885	11285
Destination charge	405	405	405

Standard Equipment:

1.6-liter DOHC 4-cylinder engine, 5-speed manual transmission, power steering, driver-side air bag, cloth reclining front bucket seats, center console, digital clock, remote fuel door and decklid releases, rear defogger, variable-intermittent wipers, coolant temperature gauge, trip odometer, tinted glass, lighted visor mirrors, dual remote outside mirrors, color-keyed grille, 175/65R14 tires, wheel covers. **Automatic** adds: 4-speed automatic transmission, 1.8-liter DOHC engine. **GLS** adds: 1.8-liter DOHC engine, 6-way adjustable driver's seat, split folding rear seat, upgraded upholstery, power mirrors, front map pockets, tachometer, power windows and door locks, tilt steering column, map lights, AM/FM/cassette, 185/60R14 tires.

Optional Equipment:

Option Pkg. 2, base	350	268	305
AM/FM/cassette.			
Option Pkg. 3, base	1245	998	1108
Pkg. 2 plus air conditioning.			
Option Pkg. 4, base	1465	1178	1305
Pkg. 3 plus cruise control.			
Option Pkg. 10, GLS	1303	1053	1163
Air conditioning, uplevel AM/FM/cassette, cruise control.			
Option Pkg. 11, GLS	1643	1330	1468
Pkg. 10 plus alloy wheels.			
Option Pkg. 12, GLS	1813	1469	1621
Pkg. 10 plus sunroof.			
Option Pkg. 13, GLS	2078	1764	1899
Pkg. 10 plus anti-lock brakes.			
Option Pkg. 14, GLS	3120	2605	2827
Pkg. 13 plus high level AM/FM/cassette, alloy wheels, sunroof.			
Option Pkg. 15, GLS	2345	1894	2093
Deletes anti-lock brakes from Pkg. 14.			
CD player	395	290	338
Front console armrest	108	70	88
Door edge guards	36	23	29
Mud guards, front and rear	78	47	62
Sunroof wind deflector	52	30	40
Floormats	58	38	47

Prices are accurate at time of publication; subject to manufacturer's change.

HYUNDAI

Hyundai Sonata	Retail Price	Dealer Invoice	Fair Price
4-door notchback, 5-speed	$13399	$12027	$12527
4-door notchback, automatic	14209	12820	13320
GL 4-door notchback, automatic	14929	13248	13748
GL 4-door notchback, V-6 automatic	15919	14016	14516
GLS 4-door notchback, V-6 automatic	17399	15085	15585
Destination charge	405	405	405

Standard Equipment:

2.0-liter DOHC 4-cylinder engine, 5-speed manual or 4-speed automatic transmission, air conditioning, power steering, driver- and passenger-side air bags, cloth reclining front bucket seats with 4-way adjustable driver's seat, center console, tachometer, coolant temperature gauge, trip odometer, AM/FM/cassette, tilt steering column, digital clock, remote fuel door and decklid releases, rear defogger, door pockets, remote outside mirrors, body-side molding, tinted glass, intermittent wipers, visor mirrors, 195/70R14 tires. **GL** adds: 2.0-liter DOHC 4-cylinder or 3.0-liter V-6 engine, 4-speed automatic transmission, power windows and door locks, power mirrors. **GLS** adds to GL: 3.0-liter V-6 engine, 6-way adjustable driver's seat, 60/40 split folding rear seat with center armrest, dual map lights, power antenna, upgraded cloth upholstery and door trim, upgraded cassette player, lighted passenger-side visor mirror, front seatback pockets, 205/60R15 tires, alloy wheels.

Optional Equipment:

Option Pkg. 5, GL and GL V-6	230	188	219
Cruise control.			
Option Pkg. 6, GL and GL V-6	830	678	789
Cruise control, sunroof.			
Option Pkg. 8, GL V-6	1110	1014	1055
Anti-lock brakes, cruise control.			
Option Pkg. 10, GLS	600	490	570
Sunroof.			
Option Pkg. 11, GLS	1400	1214	1330
Leather Pkg. (leather upholstery, leather-wrapped steering wheel), CD player.			
Option Pkg. 13, GLS	2880	2530	2736
Anti-lock brakes, Leather Pkg., CD player, sunroof.			
Option Pkg. 14, GLS	2000	1704	1900
Leather Pkg., CD player, sunroof.			
Option Pkg. 15, GLS	1350	1102	1283
Leather Pkg., sunroof.			
Sunroof wind deflector	55	32	52
Front console armrest	135	84	128
Mud guards	75	43	71
Floormats	72	42	68

INFINITI

Infiniti G20	Retail Price	Dealer Invoice	Fair Price
4-door notchback, 5-speed	$22875	$19215	$20015
4-door notchback, automatic	23875	20055	20855
G20t with Touring Package, 5-speed	25975	21819	22619
G20t with Touring Package, automatic	26975	22659	23459
Destination charge	450	450	450

Standard Equipment:

2.0-liter DOHC 4-cylinder engine, 5-speed manual or 4-speed automatic transmission, anti-lock 4-wheel disc brakes, power steering, driver- and passenger-side air bags, automatic climate control, cloth reclining front bucket seats, tachometer, coolant temperature gauge, trip odometer, power windows and locks, power mirrors, AM/FM radio with CD player, power antenna, leather-wrapped steering wheel, remote fuel door and decklid releases, tinted glass, anti-theft device, 195/65HR14 all-season tires, alloy wheels. **G20t** adds: Touring Package (limited-slip differential, rear spoiler, fog lamps, Leather Appointment Group, folding rear seat).

Optional Equipment:

Power glass sunroof, base	1000	840	—
Leather Appointment Group, base	2300	1932	—

Includes leather seats, 4-way power front seats, padded leather center console armrest, remote keyless entry system, power glass sunroof.

Infiniti J30	Retail Price	Dealer Invoice	Fair Price
4-door notchback	$38550	$31997	$34997
J30t with Touring Package	40550	33657	36657
Destination charge	450	450	450

Standard Equipment:

3.0-liter DOHC V-6 engine, 4-speed automatic transmission, anti-lock 4-wheel disc brakes, variable-assist power steering, limited-slip differential, driver- and passenger-side air bags, 8-way heated power front bucket seats, driver's seat power lumbar adjuster, leather upholstery, walnut inlays, automatic climate control, cruise control, tilt steering column, AM/FM/cassette and CD player with six speakers, power sunroof, tinted glass, power windows and locks, heated power mirrors, remote fuel door and decklid releases, remote keyless entry and anti-theft alarm systems, intermittent wipers, tachometer, trip odometer, leather-wrapped steering wheel, automatic day/night mirror, rear folding armrest, floormats, 215/60HR15 all-season tires, cast alloy wheels. **J30t** adds: Touring Pkg. (rear spoiler, firmer suspension, larger stabilizer bars, forged alloy wheels).

Infiniti Q45	Retail Price	Dealer Invoice	Fair Price
4-door notchback	$52400	$43672	—
Q45t with Touring Pkg.	55850	46536	—
Q45a with Full-Active Suspension	59350	50089	—
Destination charge	450	450	450

Fair price not available at time of publication. Prices include Gas Guzzler Tax.

Standard Equipment:

4.5-liter DOHC V-8, 4-speed automatic transmission, anti-lock 4-wheel disc brakes, power steering, limited-slip differential, driver- and passenger-side air bags, cruise control, automatic climate control, leather reclining front bucket seats (wool is available at no charge), wood interior trim, Nissan/Bose AM/FM/cassette, power antenna, power sunroof, tinted glass, power windows and locks, remote keyless entry system, power driver's seat with 2-position memory (memory includes tilt/telescopic steering column), power passenger seat, heated power mirrors, fog lights, remote fuel door and decklid releases, intermittent wipers, front and rear folding armrests, theft deterrent system, 215/65VR15 tires, alloy wheels. **Q45t** adds to base: Touring Pkg. (Includes rear spoiler, forged alloy wheels, larger front stabilizer bar, rear stabilizer bar, performance tires, trunk-mounted CD changer, heated front seats). **Q45a** adds to base: Full-Active Suspension, heated front seats, traction control, trunk-mounted CD changer, larger front stabilizer bar, rear stabilizer bar, all-season tires.

Optional Equipment:

Traction control, base	1950	1619	—
with Touring Pkg.	1850	1536	—
Includes all-season tires, heated front seats.			

ISUZU

Isuzu Rodeo	Retail Price	Dealer Invoice	Fair Price
S 4-cylinder 2WD 5-door wagon, 5-speed	$15840	$14256	$15056
S V-6 2WD 5-door wagon, 5-speed	18500	16188	16988
S V-6 2WD 5-door wagon, automatic	19420	16993	17793
LS V-6 2WD 5-door wagon, automatic	23990	20991	21791

	Retail Price	Dealer Invoice	Fair Price
S V-6 4WD 5-door wagon, 5-speed	$20340	$17698	$18498
S V-6 4WD 5-door wagon, automatic	21490	18698	19498
LS V-6 4WD 5-door wagon, 5-speed	25110	21848	22648
LS V-6 4WD 5-door wagon, automatic	26260	22849	23649
Destination charge	410	410	410

Standard Equipment:

S: 2.6-liter 4-cylinder engine, 5-speed manual transmission, anti-lock rear brakes, power steering, cloth front bench seat with folding armrest, folding rear seat with headrests, rear defogger, tinted glass, day/night mirror, oil pressure and coolant temperature gauges, voltmeter, trip odometer, cargo rope hooks, carpet, 225/75R15 all-season tires, styled steel wheels with bright center caps. **S V-6** adds: 3.2-liter V-6, 5-speed manual or 4-speed automatic transmission, 4-wheel disc brakes, reclining front bucket seats, center console, tachometer, intermittent rear wiper/washer, outside spare tire, wheel trim rings. **LS** adds: air conditioning, tilt steering column, split folding rear seat, power windows and door locks, cruise control, AM/FM/cassette, velour upholstery, front door map pockets, map and courtesy lights, intermittent wipers, visor mirrors, leather-wrapped steering wheel, roof rack, privacy rear quarter and rear side glass, cargo net, carpeted floormats, alloy wheels. **4WD** adds: part-time 4WD, automatic locking hubs, tow hooks, skid plates, 245/70R16 tires all-season tires, alloy wheels.

Optional Equipment:

Air conditioning, S	850	722	786
Preferred Equipment Pkg., S V-6	2350	1998	2174

Air conditioning, tilt steering column, power windows and door locks, power mirrors, cruise control, intermittent rear wiper/washer, visor mirrors, roof rack, AM/FM/cassette, cargo net, courtesy lamp, map pocket.

Bright Pkg., S V-6 2WD	950	808	879
S V-6 4WD	1510	1273	1397

Chrome door handle, rear lamp, exterior mirror, wheel arch and bumper trim, alloy wheels, limited slip differential (4WD). Requires Preferred Equipment Pkg.

Alloy Wheel Pkg., S 4WD	990	847	919

16-inch alloy wheels, 245/70R16 tires, limited-slip differential, fender flares, mud flaps.

Exterior Appearance Pkg., S 4-cylinder	349	269	323

Bodyside moldings, striping, roof rack, wheel trim rings.

Limited-slip differential, LS 4WD	260	210	235
Sunroof, LS	300	255	278
Remote keyless entry	350	245	324

S requires Preferred Equipment Pkg.

ISUZU

	Retail Price	Dealer Invoice	Fair Price
Rear wiper/washer, S 4-cylinder	$185	$158	$172
Outside spare tire carrier, S 4-cylinder	275	234	255
Brush/grille guard	305	216	261
AM/FM/cassette, S	585	410	498
CD player, LS	550	385	468
Aero roof rack, S	195	137	166
Sport side step, 4WD	345	245	319
Running boards, 2WD V-6	270	190	250
Splash guards, 2WD	40	28	37
Carpeted floormats, S 4-cylinder	55	39	51

1994 Isuzu Trooper

	Retail Price	Dealer Invoice	Fair Price
S 4-door 4WD wagon, 5-speed	$22300	$19290	$20090
S 4-door 4WD wagon, automatic	23450	20285	21085
LS 4-door 4WD wagon, 5-speed	27550	23425	24225
LS 4-door 4WD wagon, automatic	28700	24400	25200
RS 2-door 4WD wagon, 5-speed	24700	21740	22540
RS 2-door 4WD wagon, automatic	25850	22755	23555
SE 4-door 4WD wagon, automatic	33650	28440	29240
Destination charge	420	420	420

Standard Equipment:

S: 3.2-liter V-6 engine, 5-speed manual transmission, power steering, 4-wheel disc brakes, anti-lock rear brakes, part-time 4WD system with automatic locking front hubs, cloth reclining front bucket seats, folding rear seat, full door trim, AM/FM cassette, center console, dual outside mirrors, rear defogger, tilt steering column, intermittent wipers, rear wiper/washer, skid plates, tachometer, voltmeter, oil pressure gauge, visor mirrors, tinted glass, rear step pad, rear air deflector, 245/70R16 tires, wheel trim rings. **LS** adds: 3.2-liter DOHC engine, 4-wheel anti-lock brakes, limited-slip differential, air conditioning, power windows and locks, cruise control, multi-adjustable driver's seat, split folding rear seat, bright exterior trim, color-keyed bumpers, variable intermittent wipers, headlamp wiper/washer, leather-wrapped steering wheel, heated power mirrors, privacy glass, premium cassette system with six speakers, power antenna, anti-theft alarm, visor mirrors, fog lamps, cargo floor rails, retractable cargo cover, cargo net, alloy wheels. **RS** deletes 4-wheel anti-lock brakes, bright exterior trim and adds: anti-lock rear brakes, sport cloth interior, one-piece folding and reclining rear seat, flip-out quarter windows, color-keyed grille, 2-tone paint, gas shocks. **SE** adds to LS: engine oil cooler, heated leather power seats, CD player, 2-tone paint.

Optional Equipment:

	Retail Price	Dealer Invoice	Fair Price
4-wheel anti-lock brakes, S and RS	$1100	$880	$990
Limited-slip differential, S	260	210	235
Requires Preferred Equipment Pkg.			
Air conditioning, S	900	720	810
Preferred Equipment Pkg., S	1880	1600	1740
Air conditioning, power windows and locks, 6-speaker radio, split-folding rear seat, power mirrors, cruise control, retractable cargo cover, cargo net.			
Appearance Pkg., S	750	600	675
Alloy wheels with locks, bright radiator grille and mirrors, color-keyed bumpers. Requires Preferred Equipment Pkg.			
Remote keyless entry	250	175	225
NA S.			
Security system, S	350	245	315
Power sunroof, LS	1100	880	990
Heated leather power seats, LS	2250	1915	2083
Split folding rear seat, S	250	200	225
CD player, S with Preferred Equipment Pkg., RS and LS	550	385	468
2-tone paint, LS	280	225	253
Retractable cargo cover, S	120	84	102
Cargo net, S	30	21	26

JAGUAR

Jaguar XJ Sedan	Retail Price	Dealer Invoice	Fair Price
XJ6 4-door notchback	$53450	$43615	—
Vanden Plas 4-door notchback	62200	50755	—
XJR 4-door notchback	65000	53040	—
XJ12 4-door notchback	77250	63036	—
Destination charge	580	580	580

Fair price not available at time of publication.

Standard Equipment:

XJ6: 4.0-liter DOHC 6-cylinder engine, driver- and passenger-side side air bags, 4-speed automatic transmission, anti-lock 4-wheel disc brakes, variable-assist power steering, 12-way power front bucket seats with power lumbar support adjusters, leather upholstery, automatic climate control, power windows and door locks, cruise control, heated power mirrors, heated door locks and windshield washer nozzles, intermittent wipers, trip computer, tilt steering column, fog lamps, remote entry and alarm system, remote fuel door and decklid releases, rear defogger, AM/FM/cassette, folding rear armrest, lighted visor mirrors, automatic day/night rearview mirror, seatback pockets, console with storage, overhead console, map lights, cellular phone pre-wiring, cup holders, walnut trim, rear headrests, color-keyed bodyside moldings, 225/60ZR16 tires, alloy wheels. **Vanden Plas** adds: footwell rugs, wood- and leather-rimmed steering wheel, driver's seat memory system, power tilt steering column, power sunroof, folding burl walnut picnic tables on front seatbacks, storage in rear armrest, rear reading lights. **XJR** deletes seatback picnic tables, walnut trim, and footwell rugs and adds: supercharged engine, traction control, limited-slip differential, sport suspension, Harman/Kardon audio system with CD changer, heated front seats, maple interior trim and shifter knob, mesh grille with color-keyed frame, 255/45ZR17 tires. **XJ12** adds to Vanden Plas: 6.0-liter V-12 engine, traction control, Harman/Kardon audio system with CD changer, heated front seats, upgraded leather upholstery, upgraded suspension, walnut shifter knob.

Optional Equipment:

	Retail Price	Dealer Invoice	Fair Price
Luxury Pkg., XJ6	$2900	$2320	—
Driver's seat memory system, power tilt steering column, power sunroof.			
All-weather Pkg., XJ6, Vanden Plas	2000	1600	—
Traction control, heated front seats. XJ6 requires Luxury Pkg.			
CD changer, XJ6, Vanden Plas	800	640	—
Harman/Kardon audio system w/CD changer, XJ6, Vanden Plas	1800	1440	—
Wood- and leather-trimmed steering wheel, XJ6	—	—	—
Upgraded leather upholstery, Vanden Plas	250	200	—
Chrome hood ornament	200	160	—
Non-standard color/trim option	2000	1600	—
Chrome wheels	1500	1200	—
NA XJR.			
Full-size spare tire	100	80	—
Engine block heater	100	80	—

JEEP

Jeep Cherokee

	Retail Price	Dealer Invoice	Fair Price
SE 3-door 2WD	$13639	$12866	$13116
SE 3-door 4WD	15154	14265	14515
SE 5-door 2WD	14677	13831	14281
SE 5-door 4WD	16188	15226	15676
Sport 3-door 2WD	16060	14588	14838

	Retail Price	Dealer Invoice	Fair Price
Sport 3-door 4WD	$17572	$15938	$16188
Sport 5-door 2WD	17094	15518	15968
Sport 5-door 4WD	18606	16868	17318
Country 5-door 2WD	18656	16892	17342
Country 5-door 4WD	20170	18245	18695
Destination charge	495	495	495

Standard Equipment:

SE: 2.5-liter 4-cylinder engine, 5-speed manual transmission, driver-side air bag, power steering, vinyl front bucket seats, front armrest, folding rear seat, mini console, AM/FM radio with two speakers, tinted glass, dual remote mirrors, 215/75R15 tires; 4WD system is Command-Trac part-time. **Sport** adds: 4.0-liter 6-cylinder engine, cloth reclining front bucket seats, AM/FM stereo with four speakers and sound bar, tachometer, trip odometer, oil pressure and coolant temperature gauges, voltmeter, intermittent wipers, Sport Decor Group, spare tire cover, cargo tiedown hooks, 2-tone paint, 225/75R15 outlined white letter all-terrain tires. **Country** adds: front console with armrest and storage, rear seat heater ducts, Light Group, leather-wrapped steering wheel, roof rack, rear wiper/washer, dual remote break-away mirrors, Country Decor Group, Extra-Quiet Insulation Pkg., front floormats, bodyside cladding, 225/70R15 tires, lattice-design alloy wheels.

Optional Equipment:

Pkg. 23B/25B/26B, SE	216	184	189

Cloth reclining bucket seats, floor console with armrest, Visibility Group. Pkg. 25B requires 4.0-liter 6-cylinder engine. Pkg. 26B requies 4.0-liter 6-cylinder engine and automatic transmission.

Pkg. 25E/26E, Sport	969	824	848

Air conditioning, floor console, roof rack, leather-wrapped tilt steering wheel, rear wiper/washer, floormats. Pkg. 26E requires 4-speed automatic transmission.

Pkg. 25H/26H, Country	624	530	546

Air conditioning, cruise control, cassette player with four speakers, tilt steering wheel. Pkg. 26H requires automatic transmission.

4.0-liter 6-cylinder engine	812	690	711
4-speed automatic transmission	897	762	785

Requires 4.0-liter 6-cylinder engine.

3-speed automatic transmission, SE 4WD	648	551	567

NA with 4.0-liter 6-cylinder engine.

Selec-Trac full-time 4WD, Sport, Country	394	335	345

Requires automatic transmission.

Trac-Lok rear differential	285	242	249

Requires conventional spare tire.

JEEP

	Retail Price	Dealer Invoice	Fair Price
Anti-lock brakes	$599	$509	$524
Requires 4.0-liter 6-cylinder engine, Visibility Group.			
Heavy Duty Alternator/Battery Group	135	115	118
with rear defogger	63	54	55
Air conditioning	836	711	732
Includes Heavy Duty Alternator/Battery Group.			
Rear defogger	161	137	141
Requires air conditioning or Heavy Duty Alternator/Battery Group.			
Visibility Group, SE	208	177	182
Intermittent wipers, rear wiper/washer.			
Fog lamps, Sport, Country	110	94	96
Requires air conditioning or Heavy Duty Alternator/Battery Group.			
Rear wiper/washer, Sport	147	125	129
Deep-tinted glass,			
Sport 3-door	305	259	267
Sport and Country 5-doors	144	122	126
Power Windows and Door Locks Group,			
Sport 3-door	437	371	382
Sport and Country 5-doors	582	495	509
Power windows and locks, remote keyless entry.			
Dual remote break-away mirrors, SE, Sport	22	19	20
Power mirrors, Country	100	85	88
Sport	122	104	107
Requires floor console (Sport), and Power Windows and Door Locks Group.			
Tilt steering wheel	132	112	116
SE requires Visibility Group.			
Cruise control	230	196	201
SE requires Visibility Group.			
Leather-wrapped steering wheel, SE, Sport	48	41	42
Cassette player with four speakers,			
SE	291	247	255
Sport, Country	201	171	176
Premium speakers (six), Sport, Country	128	109	112
Requires Power Windows and Door Locks Group.			
Rear sound bar, SE	140	119	123
Cloth seats, SE	61	52	53
Power driver's seat, Country	296	252	259
Leather seats, Country 5-door	831	706	727
Includes power driver's seat.			
Floor console with armrest, SE, Sport	147	125	129
Overhead console, Sport, Country	203	173	178
Includes compass and thermometer, reading lights. Requires Power Windows and Door Locks Group.			

	Retail Price	Dealer Invoice	Fair Price
Cargo area cover	$72	$61	$63
Roof rack, SE, Sport	139	118	122
Light Group, SE, Sport	195	166	171
with cassette player or rear sound bar	156	133	137

Headlamp-off delay system, lighted visor mirrors, misc. lights. Rear sound bar NA with Sport.

	Retail Price	Dealer Invoice	Fair Price
Bright Group, Country	202	172	177

Bright dual power remote mirrors, front and rear bumpers, grille and headlamp bezels, door handles and escutcheons. Requires Power Windows and Door Locks Group.

	Retail Price	Dealer Invoice	Fair Price
Trailer Tow Group	358	304	313
4WD models with			
Off-Road Suspension	242	206	212

Requires 4.0-liter engine, automatic transmission, Heavy Duty Alternator/Battery Group or air conditioning, conventional spare tire.

	Retail Price	Dealer Invoice	Fair Price
Off-Road Suspension, 4WD, SE	761	647	666
Sport	448	381	392
Country	360	306	315

Gas shock absorbers, heavy duty springs, tow hooks, skid plates, auxiliary fan (with 4.0-liter 6-cylinder engine), heavy duty engine cooling, transmission oil cooler (with automatic transmission and 4.0-liter 6-cylinder engine), 225/75R15 outline white letter tires, conventional spare tire. Requires Heavy Duty Alternator/Battery Group or air conditioning, dual remote break-away mirrors.

	Retail Price	Dealer Invoice	Fair Price
Skid Plates Group,			
4WD models	144	122	126
225/75R15 outline white letter tires			
(four), SE	313	266	274

Requires conventional spare tire.

	Retail Price	Dealer Invoice	Fair Price
225/75R15 outline white letter conventional			
spare tire, SE, Sport	116	99	102
215/75R15 conventional			
spare tire, SE	71	60	62
Conventional (225/70R15) spare tire,			
Country	140	119	123
10-hole alloy wheels, SE	435	370	381
Sport	332	282	291
Country	87	74	76

Requires conventional spare tire.

	Retail Price	Dealer Invoice	Fair Price
Matching fifth alloy wheel, Sport	26	22	23
Country	87	74	76

Requires conventional spare tire.

	Retail Price	Dealer Invoice	Fair Price
Front floormats, SE, Sport	20	17	18
Engine block heater	31	26	27

JEEP

Jeep Grand Cherokee	Retail Price	Dealer Invoice	Fair Price
SE 5-door 2WD	$22643	$20571	$21371
SE 5-door 4WD	24580	22315	23115
Limited 5-door 2WD	28260	25514	26314
Limited 5-door 4WD	30687	27690	28490
Destination charge	495	495	495

Standard Equipment:

SE: 4.0-liter 6-cylinder engine, 4-speed automatic transmission, driver-side air bag, anti-lock 4-wheel disc brakes, power steering, cloth reclining front bucket seats, split folding rear seat, air conditioning, power windows and door locks, leather-wrapped tilt steering wheel, cruise control, tachometer, voltage and temperature gauges, illuminated entry system, console with armrest and cupholders, AM/FM cassette, tinted glass, rear defogger, intermittent rear wiper/washer, remote keyless entry system, dual outside mirrors, remote fuel door release, trip odometer, map lights, roof rack, striping, 215/75R15 tires, wheel covers. 4WD system is Command-Trac part-time. **Limited** adds: automatic temperature control, leather power front seats, automatic day/night rearview mirror, automatic headlamp system, anti-theft alarm, overhead console with compass and temperature display, trip computer, heated power mirrors, fog lamps, deep tinted side and rear glass, 8-speaker Infinity Gold AM/FM cassette with equalizer and amplifier, power antenna, lighted visor mirrors, cargo tiedown hooks, 225/70R15 outlined white letter tires, alloy wheels, full-size spare tire. 4WD system is Quadra-Trac permanent 4WD.

Optional Equipment:

Laredo Pkg. 26E/28E, SE	631	536	599

Power mirrors, lighted visor mirrors, Laredo Decor Group, Protection Group, cargo area tie-down hooks and skid strips, 225/75R15 outline white letter tires, alloy wheels. Pkg. 28E requires 5.2-liter V-8 engine. Pkg. 28E NA with 2WD.

Laredo Pkg. 26F, 2WD SE	2367	2012	2249
Laredo Pkg. 26F/28F, 4WD SE	2838	2412	2696

Package 26E plus Luxury Group, security alarm, overhead console, deep-tinted glass, cassette player with equalizer and six speakers, Selec-Trac full-time 4WD (with base engine). Pkg. 28F requires 5.2-liter V-8 engine.

Orvis Pkg. 26L/28L, 4WD Limited	663	564	630

Orvis Decor Group, Up Country Suspension Group, Trailer Tow Prep Group.

5.2-liter V-8 engine, 4WD SE and Laredo	1177	1000	1118
Laredo Pkg. 28F	783	666	744
4WD Limited	733	623	696
Orvis Pkg. 28L	616	524	585

Includes Quadra-Trac permanent 4WD, Trailer Tow Prep Group.

	Retail Price	Dealer Invoice	Fair Price
Selec-Trac full-time 4WD, SE, Laredo	$394	$335	$374
Limited	NC	NC	NC
Not available with 5.2-liter V-8.			
Quadra-Trac permanent 4WD, SE, Laredo	444	377	422
with 4WD Laredo Pkg. 26F	50	43	48
Trac-Lok rear differential	285	242	271
Luxury Group, Laredo	667	567	634
Power front seats, automatic day/night rearview mirror, automatic head-lamp system.			
Protection Group, SE	118	100	112
Cargo area cover and net, floormats.			
Trailer Tow Prep Group	101	86	96
Trailer Tow Group III	359	305	341
NA with 5.2-liter V-8.			
Trailer Tow Group IV	242	206	230
Requires 5.2-liter V-8.			
Fog lamps, 2WD SE and Laredo	110	94	105
Fog Lamp/Skid Plate Group (4WD),			
SE, Laredo	254	216	241
with Up Country Suspension Group	110	94	105
4WD Limited with 4.0-liter engine	144	122	137
Up Country Suspension Group, SE 4WD	794	675	754
Laredo 4WD	578	491	549
Limited 4WD	423	360	402
Skid Plate Group, tow hooks, high-pressure gas shocks, 245/70R15 out-lined white letter all-terrain tires, conventional spare tire, matching fifth wheel.			
Security alarm, SE, Laredo	149	127	142
Power sunroof, SE, Laredo	1073	912	1019
Limited	759	645	721
Limited includes mini overhead console.			
Overhead console, Laredo	232	197	220
Includes compass, thermometer, and trip computer.			
Leather seats, Laredo	576	490	547
Requires Luxury Group.			
Luxury leather seats, Limited	300	255	285
Integrated child safety seat	150	128	143
Deletes split folding rear seat. NA with Orvis Pkg. 26L/28L.			
Power mirrors, SE	95	81	90
Heated power mirrors, SE	140	119	133
Laredo	45	38	43
Deep tinted glass, SE, Laredo	226	192	215
Flip-up liftgate glass	90	77	86
AM/FM cassette with equalizer,			

Prices are accurate at time of publication; subject to manufacturer's change.

JEEP

	Retail Price	Dealer Invoice	Fair Price
SE, Laredo	$617	$524	$586
Includes eight speakers, amplifier, power antenna.			
AM/FM with CD and equalizer, SE, Laredo	787	669	748
Laredo Pkg. 26F, 28F, Limited	170	145	162
Includes eight speakers, amplifier, power antenna.			
Conventional spare tire, SE	130	111	124
Laredo, Limited	160	136	152
225/75R15 outlined white letter tires, SE	246	209	234
225/75R15 outlined white letter all-terrain			
tires, SE	313	266	297
Laredo	67	57	64
Limited	NC	NC	NC
Engine block heater	31	26	29

Jeep Wrangler	Retail Price	Dealer Invoice	Fair Price
S soft top	$11818	$11391	$11691
SE soft top	15437	13985	14285
Destination charge	495	495	495

Standard Equipment:

S: 2.5-liter 4-cylinder engine, 5-speed manual transmission, vinyl front bucket seats, tachometer, coolant temperature and oil pressure gauges, voltmeter, trip odometer, tinted windshield, fuel tank skid plate, swingaway outside spare tire carrier, 205/75R15 tires. **SE** adds: 4.0-liter 6-cylinder engine, power steering, reclining front seats, fold-and-tumble rear seat, carpeting, right outside mirror, rear bumperettes, AM/FM radio, 215/75R15 all-terrain tires, 6-spoke steel wheels.

Optional Equipment:

3-speed automatic transmission	624	530	543
Requires tilt steering wheel.			
Pkg. 23B/22B, S	1030	876	896
Power steering, vinyl reclining front bucket seats, rear seat, right outside mirror, carpeting, rear bumperettes. Pkg. 22B requires automatic transmission and tilt steering wheel.			
Rio Grande Pkg. 23X/22X, S	1947	1655	1752
Pkg. 23B/22B plus AM/FM/cassette, sound bar, cloth upholstery, exterior graphics, 215/75R15 all-terrain tires, 5-spoke steel wheels. Pkg. 22X requires automatic transmission and tilt steering wheel.			
Pkg. 25D/24D, SE	536	456	482
Tilt steering wheel, Convenience Group, 20-gallon fuel tank, conventional spare tire. Pkg. 24 D requires automatic transmission.			

	Retail Price	Dealer Invoice	Fair Price
Sport Pkg. 25F/24F, SE	$1242	$1056	$1118

Pkg. 25D/24D plus sound bar, sport striping, color-keyed fender flares, bodyside steps, 215/75R15 outline white letter all-terrain tires, 5-spoke steel wheels. Pkg. 24F requires automatic transmission.

Sahara Pkg. 25H/24H, SE	2025	1721	1823

Sahara Decor Group (black exterior trim, fog lights, vinyl spare tire cover, exterior graphics, color-keyed fender flares and bodyside steps, cloth upholstery, map pockets, leather-wrapped steering wheel, carpeting, front floormats, Convenience Group, power steering, 20-gallon fuel tank, front tow hooks, off-road gas shocks, full face steel wheels), tilt steering wheel, cassette player, sound bar, conventional spare tire. Pkg. 24H requires automatic transmission.

Anti-lock brakes, SE	599	509	521
Trac-Lok rear differential	278	236	242

Requires conventional spare tire.

Air conditioning, SE	878	746	764

Includes Heavy Duty Alternator/Battery Group.

Power steering, S	300	255	261
Vinyl reclining front seats, S	75	64	66

Requires rear seat and carpeting.

Cloth reclining front bucket seats with rear bench seat, SE	107	91	93
Rear seat, S	455	387	396

Requires carpeting and reclining front seats.

Add-A-Trunk lockable storage	125	106	109

Requires carpeting.

Carpeting, S	137	116	119

Requires reclining front seats and rear seat.

Hardtop	755	642	657
SE with Sahara Pkg.	923	785	803

Includes rear wiper/washer, tinted glass (deep-tinted on Sahara), full doors with vent windows, cargo light. S (except with Rio Grande Pkg.) requires right outside mirror.

Rear quarter window sunscreen glass	168	143	151

Requires hardtop.

Bright Exterior Group, SE	197	167	171

Includes bright bumpers, grille overlay, and headlamp bezels. NA with Sahara Pkg.

Bodyside steps, SE	73	62	64
Convenience Group	233	198	203
with tilt steering column	170	145	148

Intermittent wipers, center console with cup holders, misc. lights, glove box lock.

Heavy Duty Alternator/Battery Group	135	115	117

Prices are accurate at time of publication; subject to manufacturer's change.

JEEP

	Retail Price	Dealer Invoice	Fair Price
with hardtop and rear defogger	NC	NC	NC
Right outside mirror, S	$27	$23	$24
Rear defogger for hardtop	164	139	143
Requires Heavy Duty Alternator/Battery Group or air conditioning.			
Off-Road Pkg., SE	129	110	112
Heavy duty shock absorbers, draw bar, tow hooks.			
Sound bar with 2 rear speakers, SE	243	207	219
AM/FM radio with 2 speakers, S	270	230	235
AM/FM/cassette with			
2 speakers, S	534	454	465
S with Sound Group,			
SE	264	224	230
Sound Group, S	494	420	430
AM/FM stereo, Sound Bar, sport bar padding.			
Tilt steering wheel	193	164	168
Includes intermittent wipers.			
Leather-wrapped steering wheel	48	41	42
Five 215/75R15 outline white letter all-terrain			
tires, S	272	231	237
S w/Rio Grande Pkg., SE	228	194	198
SE w/Pkg. 25D/24D	117	99	102
Requires 5-spoke steel or alloy wheels.			
Five 225/75R15 outline white letter all-terrain			
tires, S	463	394	403
S w/Rio Grande Pkg., SE	419	356	365
SE w/Pkg. 25D/24D	308	262	268
SE w/Sport Pkg.	191	162	166
Requires 5-spoke steel or alloy wheels.			
Conventional spare tire	111	94	97
Four 5-spoke steel wheels, S	230	196	207
SE	102	87	89
S requires 215/75R15 or 225/75R15 outline white letter tires.			
Five 5-spoke steel wheels, SE	128	109	111
Requires conventional spare tire.			
15x7 alloy wheels, S	441	375	397
S w/Rio Grande Pkg.,			
SE w/Sahara Pkg.	237	201	206
SE	339	288	295
SE w/Sport Pkg.	211	179	184
Requires conventional spare and 215/75R15 or 225/75R15 outline white letter tires.			
Rear bumperettes, S	36	31	32
20-gallon fuel tank	62	53	54
Engine block heater	31	26	27

LEXUS

Lexus ES 300	Retail Price	Dealer Invoice	Fair Price
4-door notchback	$31500	$26145	—
Destination charge	480	480	480

Fair price not available at time of publication.

Standard Equipment:

3.0-liter DOHC V-6, 4-speed automatic transmission, anti-lock 4-wheel disc brakes, variable-assist power steering, driver- and passenger-side air bags, tilt steering column, automatic climate control, cruise control, power windows and locks, AM/FM cassette, cloth multi-adjustable power front bucket seats, split folding rear seatback, rear defogger, variable intermittent wipers, lighted visor mirrors, outside temperature indicator, automatic on/off headlamps, remote fuel door and decklid releases, tool kit, first aid kit, cellular phone pre-wiring, remote keyless entry system, theft deterrent system, fog lamps, 205/65VR15 tires, alloy wheels.

Optional Equipment:

Leather Trim Pkg.	1300	1040	1235
Heated front seats	400	320	380
Power moonroof with sunshade	900	720	855
Remote 6-CD auto changer	1000	750	950
205/65VR15 all-season tires	NC	NC	NC

Lexus GS 300	Retail Price	Dealer Invoice	Fair Price
4-door notchback	$42700	$35441	$37441
Destination charge	480	480	480

Standard Equipment:

3.0-liter DOHC 6-cylinder engine, 4-speed automatic transmission, anti-lock 4-wheel disc brakes, driver- and passenger-side air bags, variable-assist power steering, dual power/heated outside mirrors, electronic analog instruments, power tilt/telescopic steering column, cloth power driver and front passenger seats, power windows and door locks, walnut wood trim, automatic climate control, automatic on/off headlamps, remote entry system, illuminated entry system, rear defogger, variable intermittent wipers, theft-deterrent system, illuminated visor mirrors, remote electric trunk and fuel-filler door releases, Lexus Premium Audio System with AM/FM cassette and seven speakers, power diversity antenna, cellular phone pre-wiring, outside temperature indicator, illuminated entry system, tool kit, first aid kit, 215/60VR16 tires, alloy wheels.

LEXUS

Optional Equipment:	Retail Price	Dealer Invoice	Fair Price
Traction Control System	$1800	$1440	$1710
Includes heated front seats. Requires Leather Trim Package and all-season tires.			
Leather Trim Package	1300	1040	1235
Lexus/Nakamichi Premium Audio System	1100	825	1045
Requires Leather Trim Package and remote 12-CD auto changer.			
Remote 12-CD auto changer	1000	750	950
Power tilt and slide moonroof with sunshade ...	900	720	855
All-season tires	NC	NC	NC
Wheel locks	50	30	48
Floormats	115	69	109
Carpeted trunk mat	68	41	65

Lexus LS 400	Retail Price	Dealer Invoice	Fair Price
4-door notchback	$51200	$41984	—
Destination charge	480	480	480

Fair price not available at time of publication.

Standard Equipment:

4.0-liter DOHC V-8 engine, 4-speed automatic transmission, anti-lock 4-wheel disc brakes, driver- and passenger-side air bags, variable-assist power steering, seatbelt pretensioners, air conditioning with automatic climate control, leather upholstery, reclining front bucket seats with 10-way power adjustment, power windows and locks, cruise control, remote entry system, walnut wood trim, heated power mirrors, tachometer, trip odometer, coolant temperature gauge, outside temperature indicator, remote fuel door and decklid releases, lighted visor mirrors, theft-deterrent system, automatic on/off headlamps, power tilt/telescopic steering column, AM/FM cassette with seven speakers and power diversity antenna, intermittent wipers, cellular phone pre-wiring, tool kit, first aid kit, 225/60VR16 tires, alloy wheels.

Optional Equipment:

Power moonroof with sunshade	1000	800	—
Traction control with heated front seats	1900	1520	—
Requires memory seats and all-season tires.			
Electronic air suspension	1700	1360	—
Requires Lexus/Nakamichi Premium Audio System and traction control.			
Seat memory system	750	600	—
Lexus/Nakamichi Premium Audio System	1100	825	—
Requires 6-CD auto changer.			
6-CD auto changer	1000	750	—

	Retail Price	Dealer Invoice	Fair Price
Wheel locks	$50	$30	—
Floormats	115	69	—
Carpeted trunk mat	68	41	—
Chrome wheels	1100	880	—
All-season tires	NC	NC	NC

Lexus SC 300/400	Retail Price	Dealer Invoice	Fair Price
300 2-door notchback, 5-speed	$40900	$33947	—
300 2-door notchback, automatic	41800	34694	—
400 2-door notchback	48400	39688	—
Destination charge	480	480	480

Fair price not available at time of publication.

Standard Equipment:

300: 3.0-liter DOHC 6-cylinder engine, 5-speed manual or 4-speed automatic transmission, anti-lock 4-wheel disc brakes, variable-assist power steering, driver- and passenger-side air bags, air conditioning with automatic climate control, tinted glass, power front seats, tilt/telescoping steering column, rear defogger, heated power mirrors, power windows and door locks, remote entry system, illuminated entry system, cruise control, tachometer, AM/FM/cassette with seven speakers and automatic power diversity antenna, automatic on/off headlamps, lighted visor mirrors, remote fuel door and decklid releases, variable intermittent wipers, theft-deterrent system, cellular phone pre-wiring, tool kit, first aid kit, 225/55VR16 tires, alloy wheels. **400** adds: 4.0-liter DOHC V-8 engine, 4-speed automatic transmission, power tilt/telescoping steering column, leather upholstery, driver-side seat memory system.

Optional Equipment:

Traction control system with heated front seats	1800	1440	1710
Requires automatic transmission.			
Remote 12-CD auto changer	1000	750	950
Lexus/Nakamichi Premium Sound System	1100	825	1045
Requires remote CD changer; 300 also requires Leather Trim Pkg. with seat memory system.			
Leather Trim Pkg. with seat memory system, 300	1800	1440	1710
Power moonroof with sunshade	900	720	855
Heated front seats, 300 with manual transmission	400	320	380
Rear spoiler, 400	400	320	380

Prices are accurate at time of publication; subject to manufacturer's change.

	Retail Price	Dealer Invoice	Fair Price
Floormats	$115	$69	$109
Trunk mats	68	41	65
Wheel locks	50	30	48
All-season tires	NC	NC	NC

LINCOLN

Lincoln Continental

Prices not available at time of publication.

Standard Equipment:

4.6-liter DOHC V-8 engine, 4-speed automatic transmission, anti-lock 4-wheel disc brakes, driver- and passenger-side air bags, programmable variable-assist power steering, air conditioning, reclining front bucket seats with power lumbar adjusters, 6-way power driver's seat, center console, power windows and mirrors, automatic power door locks, Road Calibrated Suspension system, 2-driver memory system for seat, mirror, radio station, and steering effort/ride settings, automatic load leveling, solar-control tinted glass, AM/FM/cassette, theft-deterrent system, remote keyless entry, overhead console, systems message center, interior air filtration system, burl walnut interior trim, reading lights, automatic day/night rearview mirror, 225/60R16 tires, alloy wheels.

Lincoln Mark VIII

	Retail Price	Dealer Invoice	Fair Price
2-door notchback	$38800	$33793	$34593
Destination charge	625	625	625

Standard Equipment:

4.6-liter DOHC V-8 engine, 4-speed automatic transmission, anti-lock 4-wheel disc brakes, driver- and passenger-side air bags, automatic air conditioning, variable-assist power steering, tilt steering wheel, analog instrumentation with message center and programmable trip functions, tachometer, service interval reminder, console with cup holder and storage bin, leather seat trim, Autoglide dual reclining 6-way power front seats with power lumbar supports and remote driver-side memory, leather-wrapped steering wheel, automatic headlamps, door map pockets, solar-control tinted glass, anti-theft alarm system, cruise control, dual exhaust, power windows and locks, heated power mirrors with remote 3-position memory, programmable garage door opener, lighted visor mirrors, rear defogger, remote decklid and fuel door releases, illuminated and remote keyless entry systems, AM/FM cassette stereo with premium sound system, automatic power antenna, intermittent wipers, cargo net, floormats, 225/60VR16 tires, alloy wheels.

Optional Equipment:

	Retail Price	Dealer Invoice	Fair Price
Traction Assist	$215	$184	$204
Power moonroof	1515	1302	1439
Voice-activated celluar telephone	690	594	656
Requires JBL Audio System.			
Electrochromatic auto dimming inside/outside mirrors	215	184	204
JBL Audio System	565	486	537
Trunk-mounted CD changer	815	700	774
Requires JBL Audio System.			
Tri-coat paint	300	258	285
Cast alloy wheels	50	44	48
Chrome wheels	845	726	803
Engine block heater	60	52	57

Lincoln Town Car

	Retail Price	Dealer Invoice	Fair Price
Executive 4-door notchback	$36400	$31699	$32499
Signature Series 4-door notchback	38500	33505	34305
Cartier Designer Series 4-door notchback	41200	35827	36627
Destination charge	625	625	625

Standard Equipment:

Executive: 4.6-liter V-8, 4-speed automatic transmission, anti-lock 4-wheel disc brakes, adjustable variable-assist power steering, driver- and passenger-side air bags, automatic climate control, 6-way power twin-comfort lounge seats with 2-way front head restraints, front and rear folding armrests, power windows and door locks, tilt steering wheel, leather-wrapped steering wheel, cruise control, automatic parking brake release, heated power mirrors, rear defogger, AM/FM cassette with premium sound, diversity antenna, coolant temperature gauge, solar-control tinted glass, remote fuel door and decklid release, power decklid pulldown, illuminated and remote keyless entry systems, automatic headlights, anti-theft alarm system, cornering lamps, intermittent wipers, electronic instruments, digital clock, map pockets on front doors, lighted visor mirrors, front and rear floormats, dual exhaust, trunk net, 215/70R15 whitewall tires, alloy wheels. **Signature Series** adds: dual shade paint, driver's seat position memory and power lumbar support, power front recliners, memory mirrors, dual footwell lights, front seat storage with cup holders, steering wheel radio and climate controls, programmable garage door opener, map pockets on front seatbacks, striping. **Cartier Designer Series** adds: Traction Assist, leather

LINCOLN • MAZDA

upholstery, heated seats, 4-way front seat headrests, Ford JBL audio system, compass, automatic day/night mirror, upgraded door trim panels, 225/60R16 tires.

Optional Equipment:	Retail Price	Dealer Invoice	Fair Price
Traction Assist (std. Cartier)	$215	$184	$194
Leather seat trim (std. Cartier)	570	490	513
Heated front seats, Signature	290	250	261
Requires leather seat trim.			
Automatic day/night mirror (std. Cartier)	110	94	99
Power moonroof	1515	1302	1364
NA Executive.			
Ford JBL audio system (std. Cartier)	565	486	509
Trunk-mounted CD changer	815	700	734
Requires Ford JBL audio system.			
Ride Control Pkg., Signature	300	258	270
Cartier	100	86	90
Auxiliary power steering fluid cooler, 3.27 rear axle ratio, 225/60R16 whitewall tires (Signature), 16-inch alloy wheels (Signature). NA with Livery/Heavy Duty Trailer Towing Pkg.			
Livery/Heavy Duty Trailer Towing Pkg.	575	494	518
Wiring harness, heavy duty engine cooling, auxiliary power steering and transmission fluid coolers, 3.27 rear axle ratio, heavy duty U-joints and shock absorbers, larger front stabilizer bar, full-size spare tire, heavy duty battery, 5000-lb. towing capacity, heavy duty flasher and turn signals, Y-spoke alloy wheels. NA with Ride Control Pkg.			
Voice activated cellular telephone	690	594	621
NA Executive.			
Tri-coat paint	300	258	270
Monotone paint, Signature	NC	NC	NC
Engine block heater	60	52	54
Full-size spare tire	220	190	198

MAZDA

Mazda Miata	Retail Price	Dealer Invoice	Fair Price
2-door convertible	$17500	$15768	$17000
Destination charge	440	440	440

Prices are for vehicles distributed by Mazda Motor of America, Inc. Prices may be higher in areas served by independent distributors.

Standard Equipment:

1.8-liter DOHC 4-cylinder engine, 5-speed manual transmission, 4-wheel disc brakes, driver- and passenger-side air bags, cloth reclining bucket seats, tachometer, oil pressure and coolant temperature gauges, trip odometer, intermittent wipers, AM/FM cassette, digital clock, passenger visor mirror, dual outside mirrors, center console, dual courtesy lights, tinted glass, remote fuel door and decklid releases, 185/60HR14 tires, styled steel wheels.

Optional Equipment:	Retail Price	Dealer Invoice	Fair Price
4-speed automatic transmission	$850	$739	$765
Requires Popular Equipment Group or Leather Pkg.			
Anti-lock brakes	900	765	810
Requires Popular Equipment Group or Leather Pkg.			
Air conditioning	900	720	828
Power Steering Pkg.	300	252	270
Includes wheel trim rings.			
Detachable hardtop	1500	1215	1350
Requires Popular Equipment Group or Leather Pkg.			
Sensory Sound System	875	700	788
Requires Leather Pkg.			
Popular Equipment Group, with 5-speed	2090	1756	1881
with automatic	1700	1428	1530
Power steering, power mirrors, leather-wrapped steering wheel, headrest speakers, limited-slip differential (5-speed), power windows, cruise control, power antenna, alloy wheels.			
Leather Pkg., with 5-speed	2985	2507	2687
with automatic	2595	2180	2336
Popular Equipment Group plus tan interior with leather seating surfaces, tan vinyl top.			
Option Pkg. R	1500	1260	1350
Limited-slip differential, sport suspension, front and rear spoilers, locking alloy wheels. Not available with Popular Equipment Group or Leather Pkg.			
Floormats	80	56	72

Mazda Millenia	Retail Price	Dealer Invoice	Fair Price
4-door notchback	$25995	$23279	—
4-door notchback w/Leather Pkg.	28895	25563	—
S 4-door notchback	31995	27960	—
Destination charge	440	440	440

Fair price not available at time of publication. Prices are for vehicles distributed by Mazda Motor America, Inc. Prices may be higher in areas served by independent distributors.

Prices are accurate at time of publication; subject to manufacturer's change.

MAZDA

Standard Equipment:

2.5-liter DOHC V-6 engine, 4-speed automatic transmission, anti-lock 4-wheel disc brakes, driver- and passenger-side air bags, automatic climate control, power steering, 8-way power driver's seat, power tilt steering column, power windows and locks, heated power mirrors, anti-theft alarm, AM/FM/cassette, illuminated entry system, projector low-beam headlamps, integrated projector fog lamps, wood console trim, 205/65HR15 tires, alloy wheels. **Leather Pkg.** adds: leather upholstery, 4-way power front passenger seat, remote keyless entry, power glass moonroof. **S** adds: 2.3-liter DOHC Miller-cycle V-6 engine, traction control, Leather Package, 215/55VR16 tires.

Optional Equipment:	Retail Price	Dealer Invoice	Fair Price
4-Seasons Package, base	$600	$504	—
S	300	252	—
Traction control (base), heated front seats, heavy-duty wipers, heavy-duty starter, extra capacity windshield washer tank.			
CD changer	900	720	—
Base model requires Leather Pkg.			
Bose audio system with CD changer	1200	960	—
Base model requires Leather Pkg.			
Protection Package	125	87	—
Carpeted floor mats and wheel locks.			
White Pearl metallic paint,			
base with Leather Pkg., S	350	294	—
Deep Sea metallic paint,			
base with Leather Pkg., S	175	147	—

Mazda MPV	Retail Price	Dealer Invoice	Fair Price
L 4-door van	$21135	$19042	$19542
LX 4-door van	21985	19809	20309
LXE 4-door van	24375	21963	22463
LX 4WD 4-door van	25380	22868	23368
LXE 4WD 4-door van	27670	24930	25430
Destination charge	470	470	470

Prices are for vehicles distributed by Mazda Motor of America, Inc. Prices may be higher in areas served by independent distributors.

Standard Equipment:

L: 3.0-liter V-6 engine, 4-speed automatic transmission, 4-wheel disc brakes, anti-lock rear brakes, driver-side air bag, variable-assist power steering, cloth reclining front bucket seats, removable reclining 2-passenger middle seat, folding 3-passenger rear seat, tachometer, map pockets, remote fuel door release, tinted glass, 195/75R15 tires, wheel covers. **LX** adds: power mirrors, tilt steering column, cruise control, rear defogger, 6-speaker AM/FM/cassette, digital clock, power windows and door locks, variable intermittent wipers, intermittent rear wiper/washer, color-keyed grille. **LXE** adds: leather upholstery, leather-wrapped steering wheel, 2-tone paint, Towing Pkg., 215/65R15 tires, alloy wheels. **4WD models** add: part-time 4-wheel drive, 4-Seasons Pkg., heavy duty cooling fan, conventional spare tire, 215/65R15 tires (LX), alloy wheels (LX).

Optional Equipment:

	Retail Price	Dealer Invoice	Fair Price
Single air conditioning, L	$900	$738	$828
LX Preferred Equipment Group 1LX	700	595	644
Air conditioning, privacy glass, floormats.			
LX Preferred Equipment Group 2LX	1400	1190	1288
Replaces air conditioning in Group 1LX with front and rear air conditioning.			
LXE Preferred Equipment Group, 2WD	2000	1700	1853
4WD	1550	1318	1436
Front and rear air conditioning, remote keyless entry, privacy glass, floormats, special alloy wheels, 215/65R15 tires (2WD).			
Power glass moonroof, LX, LXE	1200	1020	1106
Towing Pkg., LX 2WD	595	506	560
LX 4WD	495	421	467
Transmission oil cooler, automatic load leveling, heavy duty cooling fan (2WD), conventional spare (2WD).			
4-Seasons Pkg., 2WD	350	298	330
Rear heater, large-capacity windshield washer tank, heavy duty battery.			
Alloy Wheel Pkg., LX 2WD	495	421	467
215/65R15 tires, alloy wheels.			
Extra cost paint, LX	350	298	330
Floormats, L	100	70	88

Mazda MX-6

	Retail Price	Dealer Invoice	Fair Price
2-door notchback	$18573	$16546	$17046
Destination charge	440	440	440

Prices are for vehicles distributed by Mazda Motor of America, Inc. Prices may be higher in areas served by independent distributors.

Standard Equipment:

2.0-liter DOHC 4-cylinder engine, 5-speed manual transmission, power steering, driver- and passenger-side air bags, cloth reclining front bucket seats, driver's-seat thigh support adjustment, 60/40 folding rear seat with

MAZDA

armrest, console with storage, power windows and door locks, cruise control, power mirrors, visor mirrors, AM/FM/cassette with power antenna, tachometer, coolant temperature gauge, trip odometer, tilt steering column, power mirrors, door pockets, tinted glass, remote fuel door and decklid releases, rear defogger, 195/65R14 tires, full wheel covers.

Optional Equipment:

	Retail Price	Dealer Invoice	Fair Price
4-speed automatic transmission	$800	$696	$760
Anti-lock brakes	950	808	903
with LS Equipment Group	800	680	760

Base includes 4-wheel disc brakes and requires Popular Equipment Group.

Air conditioning	900	720	854
Popular Equipment Group	1000	840	950

Power sunroof, anti-theft alarm, variable intermittent wipers, 6-speaker audio system, alloy wheels.

LS Equipment Group	3075	2583	2921

Popular Equipment Group plus 2.5-liter DOHC V-6 engine, 4-wheel disc brakes, air conditioning, power sunroof, leather-wrapped steering wheel and manual shift knob, fog lamps, front mudguards, floormats, 205/55VR15 tires.

Leather Pkg.	1100	880	1045

Leather seats, power driver's seat, keyless remote entry system, heated outside mirrrors. Requires LS Equipment Group.

Rear spoiler	375	300	356
Floormats	80	56	75

Mazda Protege

	Retail Price	Dealer Invoice	Fair Price
DX 4-door notchback	$11995	$11174	—
LX 4-door notchback	13395	12341	—
ES 4-door notchback	16145	14710	—
Destination charge	440	440	440

Fair price not available at time of publication. Prices are for vehicles distributed by Mazda Motor of America, Inc. Prices may be higher in areas served by independent distributors.

Standard Equipment:

DX: 1.5-liter DOHC 4-cylinder engine, 5-speed manual transmission, driver- and passenger-side air bags, variable-assist power steering, cloth reclining front bucket seats, rear seat headrests, tilt steering column, driver footrest, remote control mirrors, tinted glass, rear defogger, remote fuel door release, trip odometer, color-keyed bumpers and grille, child safety rear door locks, 175/70R13 tires. **LX** adds: cruise control, AM/FM/cassette, velour upholstery, split folding rear seat, remote decklid release, tachometer, digital clock, power windows and door locks, power mirrors, map lights, passenger-side vanity mirror, front side storage trays, full wheel covers. **ES** adds: 1.8-liter DOHC 4-cylinder engine, anti-lock 4-wheel disc brakes, air conditioning, upgraded cloth upholstery, 185/65HR14 tires.

Optional Equipment:

	Retail Price	Dealer Invoice	Fair Price
4-speed automatic transmission	$800	$720	—
Anti-lock brakes, LX	800	680	—
Convenience Pkg., DX	1575	1292	—
Air conditioning, AM/FM/cassette, floormats.			
Luxury Pkg., LX	1145	939	—
Air conditioning, raised console armrest (automatic transmission-equipped models), floormats.			
Premium Pkg., ES	1195	956	—
Alloy wheels with locks, power sunroof.			
Touring Pkg., ES	105	84	—
Floormats, raised console armrest. Requires automatic transmission.			
Power sunroof, LX	700	560	—
Floormats	80	64	—
NA ES with automatic transmission.			

Mazda 626

	Retail Price	Dealer Invoice	Fair Price
DX 4-door notchback	$14795	$13632	$14232
LX 4-door notchback	17395	15673	16273
LX V-6, 4-door notchback	19595	17656	18256
ES V-6, 4-door notchback	22695	20219	20819
Destination charge	440	440	440

Prices are for vehicles distributed by Mazda Motor of America, Inc. Prices may be higher in areas served by independent distributors.

Standard Equipment:

DX: 2.0-liter DOHC 4-cylinder engine, 5-speed manual transmission, power steering, driver- and passenger-side air bags, cloth reclining front bucket seats, driver's-seat thigh support adjustment, 60/40 folding rear seat with armrest, console with armrest and storage, tachometer, coolant temperature gauge, trip odometer, tilt steering column, intermittent wipers, dual remote mirrors, door pockets, tinted glass, remote fuel door and decklid releases, rear defogger, 195/65R14 tires, full wheel covers. **LX** adds: air conditioning, power windows and locks, cruise control, power mirrors, AM/FM/cassette with power antenna, map lights. **LX V-6** adds: 2.5-liter DOHC V-6 engine, 4-wheel disc brakes, 205/55VR15 tires, alloy wheels. **ES**

MAZDA

adds: anti-lock brakes, anti-theft alarm, remote keyless entry, power moon-roof, leather seats, heated power mirrors, fog lamps.

Optional Equipment:	Retail Price	Dealer Invoice	Fair Price
4-speed automatic transmission	$800	$696	$760
Anti-lock brakes, LX	950	808	903
LX V-6	800	680	760
LX includes rear disc brakes.			
Convenience Pkg., DX	1595	1276	1515
Air conditioning, AM/FM/cassette, floormats.			
Luxury Pkg., LX	1595	1276	1515
Power moonroof, heated power mirrors, anti-theft alarm, 6-speaker sound system, remote keyless entry, floormats, alloy wheels.			
Premium Pkg., LX V-6	1995	1596	1895
Anti-lock brakes, power driver's seat, power moonroof, heated power mirrors, anti-theft alarm, 6-speaker sound system, remote keyless entry, floormats.			
Floormats	80	58	76

Mazda 929	Retail Price	Dealer Invoice	Fair Price
4-door notchback	$35795	$30802	$31602
Destination charge	440	440	440

Prices are for vehicles distributed by Mazda Motor of America, Inc. Prices may be higher in areas served by independent distributors.

Standard Equipment:

3.0-liter DOHC V-6 engine, 4-speed automatic transmission, anti-lock 4-wheel disc brakes, variable-assist power steering, driver- and passenger-side air bags, automatic climate control, leather reclining power front bucket seats, console with storage and wood trim, rear seat storage armrest, power windows and door locks, remote keyless entry, tachometer, coolant temperature gauge, voltmeter, trip odometer, heated power mirrors, analog clock, variable intermittent wipers, cruise control, illuminated entry, AM/FM/cassette, diversity antenna system, theft-deterrent alarm, power sunroof, tinted glass, rear defogger, remote fuel door and decklid releases, automatic headlights, leather-wrapped steering wheel with integral cruise control and radio controls, leather-wrapped shifter knob, front seatback storage pockets, front door map pockets, map lights, fog lights, lighted visor mirrors, rear defogger, 205/65HR15 tires, alloy wheels.

Optional Equipment:

Solar Ventilation System	650	533	592
Floormats	125	87	108

	Retail Price	Dealer Invoice	Fair Price
Four Seasons Pkg.	$650	$540	$595

Heated front seats, limited-slip differential, heavy duty wiper motor, larger washer reservoir, heavy duty battery, low windshield washer fluid level warning light, all-season tires.

MERCEDES-BENZ

Mercedes-Benz C-Class	Retail Price	Dealer Invoice	Fair Price
C220 4-door notchback	$30950	$26330	—
C280 4-door notchback	36300	30880	—
Destination charge	475	475	475

Fair price not available at time of publication.

Standard Equipment:

C220: 2.2-liter DOHC 4-cylinder engine, 4-speed automatic transmission, anti-lock 4-wheel disc brakes, driver- and passenger-side air bags, power steering, air conditioning, automatic climate control, cruise control, power windows, heated power mirrors, 10-way power driver's seat, 10-way manual adjustable passenger seat, center console with armrest and bi-level storage, folding rear armrest, cellular phone and CD pre-wiring, tinted glass, fog lamps, AM/FM cassette, automatic power antenna, power steel sunroof, lighted visor mirrors, rear defogger, first aid kit, 195/65HR15 all-season tires, alloy wheels. **C280** adds: 2.8-liter DOHC 6-cylinder engine, Bose sound system, power passenger seat.

Optional Equipment:

C1 Option Pkg., C220	1605	1332	—
C280	2835	2353	—
ETS electronic traction system (C220), ASR automatic slip control (C280), headlamp washer/wipers, heated front seats.			
C2 Option Pkg.	330	274	—
Split folding rear seat, trunk pass-through with ski sack.			
C3 Option Pkg., C280	1760	1461	—
Leather upholstery, power glass sunroof, retractable rear head restraints.			
Leather upholstery, C280	1625	1349	—
Anti-theft alarm system	590	490	—
Headlamp washer/wipers	320	266	—
Bose sound system, C220	500	415	—
Rear head restraints	340	282	—
Power glass sunroof	225	187	—
Power passenger seat, C220	575	477	—

Prices are accurate at time of publication; subject to manufacturer's change.

MERCEDES-BENZ

	Retail Price	Dealer Invoice	Fair Price
Power front seat orthopedic backrests (each) ...	$365	$303	—
Metallic paint	580	481	—

Mercedes-Benz E-Class

	Retail Price	Dealer Invoice	Fair Price
E300 Diesel 4-door notchback	$41000	$34880	—
E320 4-door notchback	43500	37010	—
E320 2-door notchback	63000	52290	—
E320 2-door convertible	79000	65570	—
E320 5-door wagon	47500	40410	—
E420 4-door notchback	52500	43580	—
Destination charge	475	475	475

Fair price not available at time of publication.

Standard Equipment:

E300 Diesel/E320: 3.0-liter DOHC 6-cylinder diesel engine (E300 Diesel), 3.2-liter DOHC 6-cylinder engine (E320), 4-speed automatic transmisssion, driver- and passenger-side air bags, anti-lock 4-wheel disc brakes, power steering, cruise control, automatic climate control, cloth power front seats, rear head rests, seat pockets, anti-theft alarm system, power windows and door locks, AM/FM/cassette, automatic power antenna, tinted glass, rear defogger, visor mirrors, leather-wrapped steering wheel, cellular phone and CD pre-wiring, power steel sunroof, first aid kit, fog lamps, outside temperature indicator, 195/65R15 all-season tires, alloy wheels. **E320 4-door** adds to E300 Diesel: leather upholstery. **E320 2-door** adds to E320 4-door: high performance sound system, headlamp washers/wipers, rear console storage box, adjustable steering column with memory, memory driver's seat. **E320 convertible** adds to E320 2-door: wind deflector, power convertible top, heated front seats; deletes rear console storage box. **E320 wagon** adds to E320 4-door: cloth upholstery, luggage rack, rear facing third seat, luggage cover. **E420 4-door** adds to E320 4-door: 4.2-liter DOHC V-8 engine, headlamp washers/wipers, high performance sound system, adjustable steering column with memory, memory driver's seat.

Optional Equipment:

E1 Option Pkg. , E300 Diesel	1605	1332	—
E320 4-door and E320 wagon	2835	2353	—
E320 2-door, E420 4-door	2575	2137	—

ETS electronic traction system (E300 Diesel), ASR automatic slip control (NA E300 Diesel), headlamp washers/wipers (std. E320 2-door and Cabriolet, E420), heated front seats.

E2 Option Pkg., E300 Diesel and E320 4-door ...	1080	896	—

Memory driver's seat, adjustable steering column with memory, high performance sound system.

	Retail Price	Dealer Invoice	Fair Price
E3 Option Pkg., E320 wagon	$665	$552	—
Memory driver's seat, adjustable steering column with memory.			
Sportline Pkg., E320 4-door	1905	1581	—
E320 2-door	1090	905	—
4-place sport seats (4-door), sport suspension and steering.			
Leather upholstery, E300 Diesel and			
E320 wagon	1625	1349	—
ASR automatic slip control	2150	1785	—
NA E300 Diesel.			
Headlamp washers/wipers	320	266	—
Power adjustable steering column	365	303	—
Power front seat orthopedic backrests (each) ...	365	303	—
NA with Sportline Pkg.			
Power rear window sunshade	410	340	—
NA wagon, Cabriolet.			
Rear reading lamps	90	75	—
Metallic paint	665	552	—
E320 2-door, Cabriolet and E420 4-door	NC	NC	NC

Mercedes-Benz S-Class

	Retail Price	Dealer Invoice	Fair Price
S350 Turbodiesel 4-door notchback			
(NA California and New York)	$65900	$54700	—
S320 4-door notchback	65900	54700	—
S420 4-door notchback	73900	61340	—
S500 4-door notchback	87500	72630	—
S500 2-door notchback	91900	76280	—
S600 4-door notchback	130300	108150	—
S600 2-door notchback	133300	110640	—
Destination charge	475	475	475
Gas Guzzler Tax, S420, S500	1700	1700	1700
S600	3000	3000	3000

Fair price not available at time of publication.

Standard Equipment:

S350 Turbodiesel: 3.5-liter 6-cylinder turbodiesel engine, 4-speed automatic transmission, power steering, anti-lock 4-wheel disc brakes, driver- and passenger-side air bags, ETS electronic traction system, anti-theft alarm, power windows and locks, automatic climate control, tinted glass, AM/FM/cassette, CD and cellular phone pre-wiring, automatic power antenna, power leather front seats with 3-position memory, power telescopic steering column with memory, leather-wrapped steering wheel and shift knob, rear defogger, cruise control, headlamp wipers/washers, speed-sensi-

tive intermittent wipers, heated windshield washer jets, power sunroof, fog
lights, heated power memory mirrors, automatic day/night memory
rearview mirror, outside temperature indicator, tachometer, coolant temperature and oil pressure gauges, trip odometer, remote trunk release, front
and rear center armrests with cupholders, remote retractable rear-seat head
restraints, front and rear reading lights, first aid kit, lighted visor mirrors,
225/60HR16 tires, alloy wheels. **S320** adds: 3.2-liter DOHC 6-cylinder
engine, 5-speed automatic transmission. **S420** adds: 4.2-liter DOHC V-8
engine, 4-speed automatic transmission, ASR electronic traction control,
235/60HR16 tires. **S500** adds: 5.0-liter DOHC V-8 engine, rear axle level
control, heated front and rear seats (sedan), power rear seat (sedan), active
charcoal ventilation filter, rear storage console (coupe). **S600** adds to S500:
6.0-liter DOHC V-12 engine, ADS Adaptive Damping System, rear air conditioner, 10-disc CD changer, integrated cellular telephone, power rear window sunshade, upgraded leather interior, orthopedic front backrests,
235/60ZR16 tires.

Optional Equipment:

	Retail Price	Dealer Invoice	Fair Price
Rear air conditioner (std. 600)	$1895	$1573	—
ADS (Adaptive Damping System),			
350, 320, and 420	2835	2353	—
500	2100	1743	—
ASR traction control, 320	1650	1370	—
Power rear window sunshade (std. 600)	410	340	—
Orthopedic front backrests, each (std. 600)	365	303	—
4-place power seating, 500 4-door	5375	4461	—
600 4-door	4100	3403	—
Heated front seats, 350, 320, and 420	590	490	—
Active charcoal filter, 350, 320, and 420	515	427	—
Rear axle level control, 350, 320, and 420	885	735	—
Power glass sunroof	395	328	—
Portable cellular telephone	900	747	—
Metallic paint	NC	NC	NC

MERCURY

Mercury Cougar

	Retail Price	Dealer Invoice	Fair Price
XR7 2-door notchback	$16860	$15216	$15716
Destination charge	495	495	495

Standard Equipment:

3.8-liter V-6, 4-speed automatic transmission, power steering, driver- and passenger-side air bags, air conditioning, reclining front bucket seats with power lumbar support, cloth and leather upholstery, floor storage console with cup holders, tilt steering wheel, intermittent wipers, tinted glass, power windows, AM/FM/cassette, oil pressure and coolant temperature gauges, voltmeter, tachometer, center console with storage, power windows and mirrors, rear armrest, door map pockets, color-keyed bodyside moldings, bumpers and door trim panels, rear heater ducts, visor mirrors, 205/70R15 tires, wheel covers.

Optional Equipment:

	Retail Price	Dealer Invoice	Fair Price
4.6-liter V-8 engine	$1130	$1006	$1017
Includes variable-assist power steering, heavy duty battery. Requires Pkg. 260A.			
Traction-Lok axle	95	85	86
NA with Traction Assist. Requires Pkg. 260A.			
Anti-lock 4-wheel disc brakes	565	503	509
Requires Pkg. 260A.			
Automatic air conditioning	155	138	140
Requires automatic headlamp on/off delay and Pkg. 260A.			
Preferred Pkg. 260A	990	882	891
with 4.6-liter V-8 engine	475	424	428
Cruise control, rear defogger, power driver's seat, AM/FM/cassette, Power Lock Group (includes power locks, remote fuel door and decklid releases), illuminated entry, leather-wrapped steering wheel, 215/70R15 tires, alloy wheels, front floormats.			
Group 1	270	241	243
Rear defogger, illuminated entry, front floor mats.			
Group 2	515	458	464
Cruise control, leather-wrapped steering wheel, alloy wheels, 215/70R15 tires.			
Group 3	585	521	527
Power Lock Group, power driver's seat.			
Luxury Light Group	140	124	126
Interior courtesy lights, engine compartment light, lighted visor mirrors. Requires Pkg. 260A.			
Sport Appearance Group	115	102	104
BBS alloy wheels, non-functional luggage rack. Requires Pkg. 260A.			
Automatic headlamp on/off delay	70	62	63
Requires automatic air conditioning and Pkg. 260A.			
Keyless entry system	215	191	194
Requires Pkg. 260A.			
Power moonroof	740	658	666
Includes dual reading lights, pop-up air deflector, sunshade, rear tilt-up. Requires Pkg. 260A.			
Premium electronic AM/FM/cassette	290	258	261
Includes amplifier and premium speakers. Requires Pkg. 260A.			

Prices are accurate at time of publication; subject to manufacturer's change.

MERCURY

	Retail Price	Dealer Invoice	Fair Price
Premium electronic AM/FM/CD player	$430	$383	$387
Includes amplifier and premium speakers. Requires Pkg. 260A.			
Tri-coat paint	225	201	203
Power antenna	80	71	72
Requires Pkg. 260A.			
Dual power seats	290	258	232
Requires Pkg. 260A.			
Individual leather seats	490	436	441
Requires dual power seats and Pkg. 260A.			
Heavy duty battery	25	23	24
Requires Pkg. 260A.			
Traction Assist	210	187	189
Requires anti-lock brakes and Pkg. 260A.			
Engine block heater	20	18	19
Requires Pkg. 260A.			

Mercury Grand Marquis

	Retail Price	Dealer Invoice	Fair Price
GS 4-door notchback	$21270	$19626	$20126
GS Special Value 4-door notchback	20990	19422	—
LS 4-door notchback	22690	20918	21418
LS Special Value 4-door notchback	23195	21412	—
Destination charge	575	575	575

Special Value fair price not available at time of publication. Special Value prices include destination charge.

Standard Equipment:

GS: 4.6-liter V-8, 4-speed automatic transmission, 4-wheel disc brakes, power steering, driver- and passenger-side air bags, air conditioning, cloth twin comfort lounge seats with power recliners, 6-way power driver's seat, dual front and rear folding armrests, power windows and mirrors, solar-control tinted glass, AM/FM cassette, right visor mirror, intermittent wipers, rear defogger, digital clock, tilt steering wheel, oil pressure and coolant temperature gauges, voltmeter, trip odometer, Luxury Sound Insulation Pkg., remote fuel door release, auxiliary power outlet, automatic parking brake release, 215/70R15 all season whitewall tires, wheel covers. **GS Special Value** adds: Preferred Equipment Pkg. 157A. **LS** adds: upgraded upholstery and door trim, rear seat headrests, driver's seat power lumbar adjuster. **LS Special Value** adds: Preferred Equipment Pkg. 172A.

Optional Equipment:

Anti-lock brakes w/Traction-Assist	665	592	599
Automatic climate control, LS	175	156	158

	Retail Price	Dealer Invoice	Fair Price
Preferred Pkg. 157A, GS	$285	$255	$257
Cruise control, Power Lock Group, illuminated entry, floormats, radial-spoke wheel covers.			
Preferred Pkg. 172A, LS	1070	953	963
Pkg. 157A plus bodyside paint stripe, leather-wrapped steering wheel, Luxury Light Group (includes underhood light, dual dome/map lights, rear reading lights, dual secondary sun visors, lighted visor mirrors), alloy wheels, remote keyless entry, cornering lights.			
Group 1, GS	555	495	500
LS	260	232	234
Cruise control, floormats, radial-spoke wheel covers (GS).			
Group 2	385	343	347
Power Lock Group (includes power locks, remote fuel door and decklid releases), illuminated entry.			
Group 3, LS	1040	925	936
Luxury Light Group, bodyside paint stripe, leather-wrapped steering wheel, cornering lights.			
Luxury Light Group	190	169	171
Includes underhood light, dual dome/map lights, rear reading lights, dual secondary sun visors, lighted visor mirrors.			
Electronic Group, LS	455	405	410
Digital instrumentation, tripminder computer. Requires Automatic climate control, premium cassette player.			
Keyless entry system	215	191	194
Requires Group 2.			
Handling Pkg., LS	1020	908	918
with Pkg. 172A	600	534	540
Includes rear air suspension, tuned suspension, larger stabilizer bars, dual exhaust, 3.27 axle ratio, 225/60R16 whitewall tires, alloy wheels. NA with Trailer Tow III.			
Rear air suspension, LS	270	240	243
Trailer Tow III Pkg., LS	900	801	810
Includes rear air suspension, heavy duty battery, dual exhaust, trailer towing wiring harness, power steering and transmission oil coolers, conventional spare tire, 3.27 Traction-Lok axle. Requires alloy wheels. NA with Handling Pkg.			
Power front passenger's seat, LS	360	321	324
Includes power lumbar support and recliners for both front seats.			
Leather seat trim, LS	645	574	581
Requires power front passenger's seat.			
Premium electronic AM/FM cassette, LS	360	321	324
Requires automatic climate control.			
Conventional spare tire, LS	185	165	167

Prices are accurate at time of publication; subject to manufacturer's change.

MERCURY

	Retail Price	Dealer Invoice	Fair Price
with Handling Pkg.	$240	$213	$216
Includes alloy wheel.			
Cast alloy wheels, LS	NC	NC	NC
Requires Group 3.			
Bodyside paint stripe	60	54	55
Engine block heater	25	23	24

Mercury Mystique

	Retail Price	Dealer Invoice	Fair Price
GS 4-door notchback	$13855	$12531	—
LS 4-door notchback	15230	13755	—
Destination charge	495	495	495

Fair price not available at time of publication.

Standard Equipment:

GS: 2.0-liter DOHC 4-cylinder engine, 5-speed manual transmission, driver- and passenger-side air bags, power steering, front and rear stabilizer bars, solar-control tinted glass, cloth reclining front bucket seats with 4-way adjustable headrests, console, split folding rear seat, tilt steering column, coolant temperature gauge, tachometer, trip odometer, day/night rearview mirror, color-keyed bumpers and bodyside moldings, AM/FM radio, power mirrors, intermittent wipers, remote fuel filler door and decklid release, front seatback and door map pockets, passenger assist handles, passenger compartment air filtration system, visor mirrors, 185/70R14 tires. **LS** adds: 10-way power driver's seat, cassette player, rear defogger, heated mirrors, power antenna, fog lights, leather-wrapped steering wheel, floormats, 205/60R15 tires, alloy wheels.

Optional Equipment:

4-speed automatic transmission	815	725	—
Traction control	800	712	—
Includes anti-lock brakes.			
Anti-lock brakes	565	503	—
Air conditioning	780	694	—
Leather upholstery, LS	595	530	—
Preferred Pkg. 370A, GS	895	797	—
Air conditioning, rear defogger, cassette player, heated mirrors, power antenna.			
Preferred Pkg. 371A, GS	1485	1323	—
Pkg. 370A plus power door locks and windows, cruise control, light group.			
Preferred Pkg. 372A, GS	2430	2164	—
Pkg. 371A plus 2.5-liter V-6 engine. Includes 4-wheel disc brakes, sport suspension, low-profile tires.			

	Retail Price	Dealer Invoice	Fair Price
Preferred Pkg. 380A, LS	$1380	$1228	—
Air conditioning, power door locks and windows, cruise control, light group, remote keyless entry.			
Preferred Pkg. 381A, LS	2220	1976	—
Pkg. 380A plus 2.5-liter V-6 engine. Includes 4-wheel disc brakes, sport suspension, low-profile tires.			
Comfort/Convenience Group 1, GS	250	223	—
Rear defogger, heated mirrors, power antenna.			
Comfort/Convenience Group 2, GS	945	841	—
LS	780	694	—
Cassette player (GS), air conditioning.			
Comfort/Convenience Group 3, GS	675	601	—
LS	835	743	—
Remote keyless entry (LS), power door locks and windows, light group.			
Power door locks and light group, GS with Pkg. 370A	335	299	—
10-way power driver's seat, GS with Pkgs. 371A or 372A	330	294	—
Power sunroof	595	530	—
NA GS with Pkg. 370A.			
Cruise control	215	191	—
Remote keyless entry	160	143	—
NA GS with Pkg. 370A.			
Premium cassette player	130	116	—
CD player, GS	435	387	—
GS with Group 2, LS	270	240	—
Rear defogger, GS	160	143	—
Floormats, GS	45	40	—
Alloy wheels, GS	265	236	—
Engine block heater	20	18	—

Mercury Sable	Retail Price	Dealer Invoice	Fair Price
GS 4-door notchback	$18210	$16432	$16932
LS 4-door notchback	20470	18443	18943
LTS 4-door notchback	21715	19526	20026
GS 5-door wagon	19360	17456	17956
LS 5-door wagon	21570	19422	19922
Destination charge	535	535	535

Standard Equipment:

GS: 3.0-liter V-6, 4-speed automatic transmission, power steering, driver- and passenger-side air bags, air conditioning, cloth reclining 50/50 front seat with armrests, rear center armrest, tinted glass (solar-control on wind-

MERCURY

shield and 4-door rear window), intermittent wipers, rear defogger, tachometer, coolant temperature gauge, trip odometer, low fuel light, power mirrors, tilt steering wheel, AM/FM radio, Sound Insulation Pkg., dual visor mirrors, front door and seatback map pockets, 205/65R15 tires; **wagon** has 60/40 folding rear seat, tiedown hooks, luggage rack, rear wiper, lockable under-floor storage. **LS** adds: anti-lock 4-wheel disc brakes, reclining bucket seats with power lumbar support (4-door) and 4-way adjustable headrests, power driver's seat (4-door), cassette player, power windows, automatic parking brake release, remote fuel door and decklid releases, Light Group, bodyside cladding, 50/50 reclining front seats with power driver's seat (wagon), console with armrest (4-door), cargo net, lighted visor mirrors, alloy wheels. **LTS** adds: Preferred Pkg. 470A (LTS Decor Group [6-way power leather bucket seats, bodyside cladding, leather-wrapped shift handle, upgraded carpeting, LTS floormats, upgraded alloy wheels], Groups 1, 2 and 4).

Optional Equipment:	Retail Price	Dealer Invoice	Fair Price
3.8-liter V-6	$630	$561	$567
Includes heavy duty battery.			
Anti-lock 4-wheel disc brakes, GS	565	503	509
Automatic climate control	175	156	158
NA GS.			
Preferred Pkg. 450A, GS	800	712	720
Power Lock Group (includes power locks, remote fuel door and decklid/liftgate releases), power windows, cruise control, Light Group (includes underhood light, courtesy lights, lighted visor mirrors), floormats, striping.			
Preferred Pkg. 451A, GS	765	680	689
with 3.8-liter V-6 engine	1265	1125	1139
Pkg. 450A plus power driver's seat, cassette player, alloy wheels.			
Preferred Pkg. 461A, LS	445	397	401
Leather-wrapped steering wheel, cruise control, Premium AM/FM cassette, power antenna, keyless entry system, Power Lock Group, Light Group, striping, floormats.			
Preferred Pkg. 462A, LS	780	695	702
Pkg. 461A plus electronic instruments, autolamp system, air conditioning with automatic climate control.			
Group 1, GS	160	143	144
LS, LTS	105	93	95
Light Group (GS), floormats, striping.			
Group 2, GS	885	787	797
LS, LTS	460	410	414
Power windows (GS), power door locks, cruise control.			
Group 3, GS	710	632	639
6-way power driver's seat, AM/FM/cassette, alloy wheels.			

	Retail Price	Dealer Invoice	Fair Price
Group 4, LS, LTS	$800	$712	$720
Leather-wrapped steering wheel, high-level cassette, power antenna, remote keyless entry. Requires Group 2.			
Group 5, LS	535	476	482
LTS	335	298	302
Automatic climate control, autolamp system, electronic instrument cluster.			
Cargo area cover, wagons	65	58	59
Extended-range fuel tank	45	40	41
Not available with Group 5.			
Remote keyless entry	295	263	266
Includes illuminated entry; requires Group 2.			
Power moonroof	740	658	666
NA GS.			
Cassette player, GS	165	147	149
CD player	375	334	338
Requires Group 4.			
Rear-facing third seat, wagons	150	134	135
Not available with conventional spare tire.			
Power driver's seat, GS	290	258	261
Dual power seats, GS with Pkgs. 450A or 451A without Group 3	580	516	522
GS with Pkg. 451A and Group 3, LS with Pkgs. 461A or 462A	290	258	261
Leather Twin Comfort Lounge seats, LS	495	441	446
Leather individual seats, LS	495	441	446
Cloth individual seats, GS	NC	NC	NC
Cellular telephone	500	445	450
Requires Twin Comfort Lounge seats.			
Heavy duty suspension	25	23	24
Full-size spare tire	70	62	63
Not available on wagons with rear facing third seat.			
Alloy wheels, GS	255	227	230
Chrome wheels, LTS	580	516	522
Heavy duty battery	30	27	28
Engine block heater	20	18	19

Mercury Tracer	Retail Price	Dealer Invoice	Fair Price
4-door notchback	$11280	$10424	$10624
5-door wagon	11800	10898	11098
LTS 4-door notchback	13140	12117	12417
Destination charge	375	375	375

Prices are accurate at time of publication; subject to manufacturer's change.

MERCURY

Standard Equipment:

1.9-liter 4-cylinder engine, 5-speed manual transmission, driver- and passenger-side air bags, motorized front shoulder belts, power steering, cloth reclining front bucket seats, 60/40 split rear seatback, AM/FM radio, tachometer, trip odometer, digital clock, console, coolant temperature gauge, low fuel warning light, door map pockets, variable intermittent wipers, visor mirrors, tinted glass, 175/65R14 tires, wheel covers. **Wagon** adds: power mirrors, cargo cover, rear defogger, rear wiper/washer. **LTS** adds: 1.8-liter DOHC engine, 4-wheel disc brakes, sport suspension, tilt steering column, cassette player, Light Group (includes dual map lights, trunk and engine compartment lights, rear door courtesy light), remote decklid release, cruise control, leather-wrapped steering wheel, front air dam, rear spoiler, 185/60HR14 tires, alloy wheels.

Optional Equipment:	Retail Price	Dealer Invoice	Fair Price
Preferred Pkg. 540A, base 4-door	$385	$343	$347
wagon	135	121	122
Remote decklid release (4-door), rear defogger (4-door), Light Group, power mirrors (4-door), air conditioning.			
Preferred Pkg. 541A, base 4-door	1115	992	1004
wagon	860	765	774
Pkg. 540A plus AM/FM/cassette, Convenience Group, Power Group.			
Preferred Pkg. 555A, LTS	930	827	837
Air conditioning, Power Group.			
4-speed automatic transmission	815	725	734
Anti-lock brakes, LTS	565	503	509
Power Group, base	520	463	468
Power door locks and windows.			
Convenience Group	355	316	320
Tilt steering wheel, cruise control.			
Trio Pkg., base 4-door	310	276	279
wagon	210	187	189
Leather-wrapped steering wheel, decklid spoiler (4-door), alloy wheels. Requires Pkg. 540A or 541A.			
Power moonroof, LTS	525	468	473
Integrated child seat	135	120	122
NA LTS.			
Cassette player, base	165	147	149
Premium sound system	60	54	55
Requires cassette or CD player.			
CD player, base	325	290	293
LTS	160	143	144
Luggage rack, wagon	110	98	99
Engine block heater	20	18	19

Mercury Villager

	Retail Price	Dealer Invoice	Fair Price
GS 4-door van	$19045	$17014	$18245
LS 4-door van	23825	21221	23025
Nautica 4-door van	25305	22523	24505
Destination charge	540	540	540

Standard Equipment:

GS: 3.0-liter V-6 engine, 4-speed automatic transmission, driver-side air bag, motorized front shoulder belts, anti-lock brakes, power steering, cloth reclining front bucket seats, 3-passenger bench seat, cloth upholstery, AM/FM/cassette, tachometer, coolant temperature gauge, trip odometer, dual outside mirrors, visor mirrors, tinted glass, variable-intermittent wipers, rear wiper/washer, remote fuel door release, black bodyside moldings, color-keyed bumpers, cornering lamps, front door map pockets, floormats, 205/75R15 all-season tires, wheel covers. **LS** adds: front air conditioning, 2-passenger middle and 3-passenger rear bench seats, tilt steering column, cruise control, power windows and locks, Light Group, privacy glass, rear defogger, lighted visor mirrors, luggage rack, lighted visor mirrors, leather-wrapped steering wheel, seatback map pockets, rear cargo net, lockable underseat storage bin, 2-tone paint, color-keyed bodyside molding, striping. **Nautica** adds to LS: two middle bucket seats, leather upholstery, unique exterior paint, yellow striping, white alloy wheels, duffle bag.

Optional Equipment:

Front air conditioning, GS	855	727	787
Power windows and locks, GS	530	451	488
Requires 7-passenger seating.			
Auxiliary rear air conditioning with rear heater, GS	465	395	428
Includes rear seat fan and temperature controls. Requires Preferred Equipment Pkg. 692A.			
Preferred Equipment Pkg. 691A, GS	1505	1279	1385
Front air conditioning, 7-passenger seating, power windows and door locks, tilt steering column, cruise control, rear defogger, power mirrors.			
Preferred Equipment Pkg. 692A, GS	2310	1964	2125
Pkg. 691A plus power driver's seat, cassette player, luggage rack, underseat storage bin, alloy wheels.			
Preferred Equipment Pkg. 695A, LS	285	244	262
Power driver's seat, rear air conditioning with rear heater, premium cassette player, flip open liftgate window, alloy wheels.			
Preferred Equipment Pkg. 696A, LS	1690	1437	1555
Pkg. 695A plus power passenger seat, quad bucket seats, keyless entry system, headlamp delay system, electronic instrumentation. Requires auxiliary rear air conditioning and rear heater.			

MERCURY

	Retail Price	Dealer Invoice	Fair Price
Preferred Equipment Pkg. 697A, Nautica	$1690	$1437	$1555

Power driver's seat, power passenger seat, rear air conditioning with rear heater, premium cassette player, flip open liftgate window, keyless entry system, headlamp delay system, electronic instrumentation, locking alloy wheels.

Light Group, GS	155	132	143

Overhead dual map lights, dual liftgate lights, front door step lights, power rear vent windows, under instrument panel lights with time delay. Requires rear defogger.

Handling Suspension, LS	85	73	79

Includes 215/70R15 performance tires, firm ride suspension, rear stabilizer bar. Requires alloy wheels.

Trailer Towing Pkg.	250	213	230

Includes heavy duty battery, conventional spare tire, 3500-pound trailer rating.

Power mirrors, GS	100	85	92
Power moonroof, LS and Nautica	775	659	714
7-passenger seating, GS	330	281	304
Quad captain's chairs, LS	600	510	552

Requires auxiliary rear air conditioning and rear heater.

8-way power driver's seat	395	336	363
4-way power front passenger's seat	195	166	179

Requires 8-way power driver seat.

Leather upholstery, LS	865	735	796

Requires quad captain's chairs, power driver and passenger seats.

Electronic instrumentation, LS	245	208	225
Keyless entry and headlamp delay systems, LS	300	255	276
Tilt steering column and cruise control, GS	370	314	340
Rear defogger, GS	170	144	156
Flip open liftgate window	90	77	83

Requires rear defogger.

Privacy glass, GS	415	352	382

Requires rear defogger.

Premium cassette player, LS	270	229	248

Includes rear radio controls with front seat lockout, dual mini headphone jacks, cassette/CD storage console, diversity antenna. GS requires Preferred Equipment Pkg. 629A.

Premium cassette and CD players, GS with Pkg. 629A	560	477	515
LS with Pkg. 695A or 696A, and Nautica with Pkg. 697A	295	251	271

Includes rear radio controls with front seat lockout, dual mini headphone jacks, cassette/CD storage console, diversity antenna.

	Retail Price	Dealer Invoice	Fair Price
Premium cassette and CD players, LS and Nautica	$865	$735	$796

Includes rear radio controls with front seat lockout, dual mini headphone jacks, cassette/CD storage console, power diversity antenna, subwoofer speaker.

Luggage rack, GS	145	123	133
Underseat storage bin, GS	35	30	32
Bodyside striping, GS	45	38	41
Locking alloy wheels	380	323	350

MITSUBISHI

Mitsubishi Diamante	Retail Price	Dealer Invoice	Fair Price
LS 4-door notchback	$35250	$28208	$28708
5-door wagon	—	—	—
Destination charge	470	470	470

Wagon prices not available at time of publication.

Standard Equipment:

LS: 3.0-liter DOHC V-6, 4-speed automatic transmission, anti-lock 4-wheel disc brakes, speed-sensitive power steering, driver- and passenger-side air bags, 7-way adjustable front bucket seats, power memory driver's seat, leather upholstery, automatic climate control, power windows and door locks, heated power mirrors, cruise control, alarm system, remote keyless entry system, automatic shut-off headlamps, rear defogger, console with armrest, tilt steering column, folding rear armrest, dual cup holders, tinted glass, automatic day-night mirror, front and rear map lights, remote fuel door and decklid releases, tachometer, coolant temperature gauge, trip odometer, variable intermittent wipers, Mitsubishi/Infinity audio system with equalizer and eight speakers, power diversity antenna and steering wheel-mounted radio controls, analog clock, woodgrain interior accents, floormats, 205/65VR15 tires, alloy wheels, full-size spare tire. **Wagon** deletes double overhead camshafts, anti-lock brakes, speed-sensitive power steering, leather upholstery, driver's seat memory, automatic day-night mirror, Mitsubishi/Infinity audio system, heated mirrors, and remote keyless entry and adds: power steering, 6-way adjustable velour front bucket seats, 7-speaker AM/FM/cassette with equalizer, rear wiper/washer, 60/40 split folding rear seatback, digital clock, luggage tiedown hooks, 205/65HR15 tires.

Optional Equipment:

Anti-lock brakes, wagon	—	—	—

MITSUBISHI

	Retail Price	Dealer Invoice	Fair Price
CD auto changer, LS	$739	$517	$612
CD player, wagon	—	—	—
Power sunroof, LS	954	763	837
wagon	—	—	—
Wagon w/sunroof deletes standard front map lights.			
Leather Seat Pkg., wagon	—	—	—
Includes power memory driver's seat, leather seat and console trim.			
Traction control, LS	718	589	636
Power passenger seat with memory, LS	490	392	429
Remote keyless entry system, wagon	—	—	—
Sunroof wind deflector	60	39	47
Cargo net, wagon	—	—	—

Mitsubishi Eclipse

	Retail Price	Dealer Invoice	Fair Price
RS 3-door hatchback, 5-speed	$14359	$12497	—
RS 3-door hatchback, automatic	15059	13102	—
GS 3-door hatchback, 5-speed	16329	14204	—
GS 3-door hatchback, automatic	17019	14809	—
GS-T 3-door hatchback, 5-speed	19999	17397	—
GS-T 3-door hatchback, automatic	20829	18121	—
GSX 3-door hatchback, 5-speed	22929	19717	—
GSX 3-door hatchback, automatic	23739	20416	—
Destination charge	420	420	420

Fair price not available at time of publication.

Standard Equipment:

RS: 2.0-liter DOHC 4-cylinder engine, 5-speed manual or 4-speed automatic transmission, driver- and passenger-side air bags, power steering, cloth reclining front bucket seats, center console, folding rear seat, tilt steering column, map lights, remote fuel door and rear hatch releases, tachometer, coolant temperature gauge, trip odometer, low fluid warning lights, AM/FM radio, digital clock, on-board diagnostic system, tinted glass, rear defogger, dual manual mirrors, color-keyed bumpers, full wheel covers, 195/70HR14 tires. **GS** adds: 4-wheel disc brakes, 7-way adjustable driver's seat, split folding rear seat, cassette player, color-keyed power mirrors, color-keyed front air dam and rear spoiler, lower bodyside cladding, 205/55HR16 tires. **GS-T** adds: turbocharged and intercooled engine, engine oil cooler, leather-wrapped steering wheel and manual shift knob, cruise control, rear window wiper/washer, fog lamps, turbo boost gauge, oil pressure gauge, Infinity 8-speaker AM/FM/cassette with equalizer, bright dual exhaust outlets, sport-tuned shock absorbers, alloy wheels. **GSX** adds: permanent all-wheel drive, limited-slip differential, power windows and door locks, Leather Pkg., 215/55VR16 tires (manual transmission), 205/55VR16 tires (automatic transmission).

Optional Equipment:	Retail Price	Dealer Invoice	Fair Price
Air conditioning, RS	$891	$731	—
Anti-lock brakes	716	587	—
RS includes rear disc brakes.			
Cruise control, GS	213	175	—
Preferred Equipment Pkg. PM, RS	1148	941	—
Air conditioning, cassette player, cargo cover.			
Preferred Equipment Pkg. PH, GS	1582	1298	—
Air conditioning, full-logic cassette player, rear wiper/washer, power windows and door locks.			
Alarm system	332	272	—
Includes remote keyless entry. NA RS.			
Remote keyless entry	136	88	—
GS requires PH Pkg. NA RS.			
Leather Pkg., GS-T	789	647	—
Leather front seats, power driver's seat.			
Cassette player, RS	221	181	—
Infinity 8-speaker AM/FM/cassette with equalizer, GS	660	541	—
Requires PH Pkg.			
CD player, RS and GS	599	399	—
RS requires cassette player or PM Pkg.			
6-disc CD changer (NA RS)	899	598	—
GS requires Infinity AM/FM cassette with equalizer.			
Power sunroof with sunshade	731	599	—
Cargo cover, RS	77	63	—
Cargo net, RS	26	17	—
Floormats	49	32	—
Mud guards	123	80	—
Alloy wheels, RS, GS	337	276	—
Wheel locks, RS, GS	32	21	—

Mitsubishi Galant	Retail Price	Dealer Invoice	Fair Price
S 4-door notchback, 5-speed	$14349	$12771	—
S 4-door notchback, automatic	15249	13572	—
ES 4-door notchback, automatic	18669	15867	—
LS 4-door notchback, automatic	20269	17233	—
Destination charge	420	420	420

Fair price not available at time of publication.

Prices are accurate at time of publication; subject to manufacturer's change.

MITSUBISHI

Standard Equipment:

S: 2.4-liter 4-cylinder engine, 5-speed manual or 4-speed automatic transmission, driver- and passenger-side air bags, power steering, 5-way adjustable driver's seat, tinted glass, cloth and vinyl upholstery, rear defogger, tilt steering column, center console armrest with storage, driver-side door map pocket, cup holders, remote fuel door and decklid releases, driver-side visor mirror, intermittent wipers, tachometer, coolant temperature gauge, color-keyed bumpers and bodyside moldings, manual remote outside mirrors, digital clock, 185/70HR14 all-season tires, full wheel covers. **ES** adds: 4-speed automatic transmission, air conditioning, cruise control, power windows and door locks, AM/FM/cassette with six speakers, automatic power diversity antenna, color-keyed power mirrors, folding rear seat with center armrest, full cloth upholstery and door trim, passenger-side visor mirror, door map pockets. **LS** adds: power glass sunroof with sun shade, variable intermittent wipers, 6-way adjustable front seats, fog lamps, ETACS-IV (includes ignition key illumination, seat belt warning timer/chime, headlight on warning chime, rear defogger timer, fade out dome light), lighted visor mirrors, front seatback map pockets, center sunvisor, floormats, 195/60HR15 all-season tires, alloy wheels.

Optional Equipment:	Retail Price	Dealer Invoice	Fair Price
Anti-lock brakes, ES, LS	$952	$781	—
Air conditioning, S	891	731	—
Preferred Equipment Pkg., S with			
automatic transmission	2250	—	—
Power windows and door locks, AM/FM/cassette, trunk mat and trim, door storage pockets.			
Luxury Group Pkg., LS	2222	—	—
Leather seats, power driver's seat, Mitsubishi/Infinity audio system, theft-deterrent system, remote keyless entry.			
AM/FM/cassette, S	457	297	—
CD player	641	449	—
S requires AM/FM/cassette.			
Remote keyless entry system, ES, LS	223	145	—
Mud guards	117	76	—
Floormats, S	73	47	—
Trunk net	23	19	—

Mitsubishi Mirage	Retail Price	Dealer Invoice	Fair Price
S 2-door notchback, 5-speed	$9799	$9012	$9212
LS 2-door notchback, 5-speed	12569	11315	11515
LS 2-door notchback, 4-speed automatic	13229	11903	12103
Destination charge	420	420	420

Standard Equipment:

S: 1.5-liter 4-cylinder engine, 5-speed manual transmission, driver- and passenger-side air bags, vinyl front bucket seats, locking fuel-filler door, color-keyed bumpers and grille, rear defogger, center console with storage, coolant temperature gauge, dual exterior mirrors, remote decklid release, front door map pockets, radio accommodation package, 145/80R13 tires.
LS adds: 1.8-liter engine, 5-speed manual or 4-speed automatic transmission, power steering, height-adjustable driver's seat, split folding rear seat, cloth upholstery, leather-wrapped manual shift knob, tachometer (with manual transmission), intermittent wipers, tilt steering column, full trunk trim, digital clock, trunk light, AM/FM/cassette, rear spoiler, power mirrors, day/night rearview mirror, remote fuel door release, trip odometer, tinted glass, color-keyed bodyside molding, passenger-side visor mirror, 185/65R14 all-season tires, alloy wheels.

Optional Equipment:	Retail Price	Dealer Invoice	Fair Price
Air conditioning	$854	$700	$769
Value Pkg., LS	853	853	853
Includes air conditioning, CD player, floormats, trunk net, wheel locks.			
CD player	615	407	554
S requires AM/FM cassette player.			
AM/FM/cassette, S	490	312	441
Wheel locks, LS	33	21	30
Wheel trim rings, S	68	44	61
Mudguards	99	70	89
Floormats	64	41	58
Trunk net	37	25	33

Mitsubishi Montero	Retail Price	Dealer Invoice	Fair Price
LS 5-door wagon, 5-speed	$27625	$23620	$24120
LS 5-door wagon, automatic	28475	24348	24848
SR 5-door 4WD wagon, automatic	34625	28912	29612
Destination charge	445	445	445

Standard Equipment:

LS: 3.0-liter V-6, 5-speed manual transmission or 4-speed automatic transmission, full-time 4-wheel drive, 4-wheel disc brakes, driver-side air bag, air conditioning, power steering, engine oil cooler, tilt steering column, digital clock, trip odometer, cloth reclining front bucket seats with armrests, folding middle seat with headrests, dual folding rear seats, tachometer, coolant temperature and oil pressure gauges, voltmeter, inclinometer, LCD compass, exterior thermometer, trip odometer, AM/FM/cassette, front and rear tow hooks, remote fuel door release, front and rear mud guards, storage

MITSUBISHI

console with cup holders, leather-wrapped steering wheel, power mirrors, power windows and door locks, cruise control, rear defogger, intermittent wipers, intermittent rear wiper/washer, tinted glass, skid plates, map lights, cargo tie-down hooks, rear door-mounted tool kit, rear seat heater ducts, passenger-side visor mirrors, front and rear stabilizer bars, 235/75R15 tires, alloy wheels. **SR** adds: 3.5-liter DOHC V-6 engine, 4-speed automatic transmission, anti-lock brakes, remote keyless entry, heated power mirrors, Multi-Meter, cassette with equalizer, power diversity antenna, headlamp washers, power sunroof, lighted driver-side visor mirror, wide body fender flares, spare tire cover, 265/70R15 all-weather tires.

Optional Equipment:

	Retail Price	Dealer Invoice	Fair Price
Anti-lock brakes, LS	$1425	$1140	$1283
CD auto changer	966	676	869
Includes cargo mat and net.			
CD player, LS	686	446	617
Cassette player with equalizer, LS	384	269	346
Leather and Wood Pkg., SR	2163	1730	1947
Includes leather seats, leather-wrapped assist grip, burled wood instrument panel accents, power driver's seat, adjustable shock absorbers.			
Power sunroof, LS	900	720	810
Fog lights	230	152	207
Cargo mat, net and cover	235	153	212
Side step	335	218	302
Roof rack	246	160	221
Remote keyless entry, LS	216	150	194
Chrome wheels, SR	938	750	844
Spare tire cover, LS	78	51	70

Mitsubishi 3000GT

	Retail Price	Dealer Invoice	Fair Price
3-door hatchback, 5-speed	$28450	$23317	$23817
3-door hatchback, automatic	29325	24043	24543
SL 3-door hatchback, 5-speed	33750	27664	28664
SL 3-door hatchback, automatic	34625	28390	29390
SL Spyder 2-door convertible, automatic	—	—	—
VR-4 3-door hatchback, 6-speed	43050	35302	36802
VR-4 Spyder 2-door convertible, 6-speed	—	—	—
Destination charge	470	470	470

Spyder prices not available at time of publication.

Standard Equipment:

3.0-liter DOHC V-6, 5-speed manual or 4-speed automatic transmission, 4-wheel disc brakes, power steering, driver- and passenger-side air bags, air conditioning, power windows, door locks and mirrors, ETACS alarm control system, cruise control, rear spoiler, 6-way adjustable cloth front bucket seats, split folding rear seat, center storage console with coin and cup holders, tachometer, coolant temperature and oil pressure gauges, voltmeter, trip odometer, remote fuel door and hatch releases, Mitsubishi/Infinity audio system with external amp and eight speakers, power antenna, tilt steering column, leather-wrapped steering wheel, manual shifter knob, and parking brake handle, fog lamps, variable intermittent wipers, rear intermittent wiper, visor mirrors, rear defogger, digital clock, tinted glass, cargo area cover, 225/55VR16 tires, alloy wheels. **SL** adds: anti-lock brakes, electronically controlled suspension, automatic climate control, leather seats, 7-way adjustable driver's seat with 5-way power adjustments, rear wiper/washer, remote keyless entry with anti-theft system, steering-wheel mounted radio controls, heated power mirrors, auxiliary power outlet. **VR-4** adds: turbocharged intercooled engine, 6-speed manual transmission, permanent 4-wheel drive, 4-wheel steering, limited-slip rear differential, automatic climate control, Active Aero with retractable front air dam extension and motorized rear spoiler, turbo boost gauge, engine oil cooler, lighted visor mirrors, 245/40ZR18 tires, chrome wheels. **Spyder** models add to SL and VR-4: power folding hardtop, automatic day/night mirror, fixed rear spoiler, CD changer, 245/45ZR17 tires, chrome wheels.

Optional Equipment:

	Retail Price	Dealer Invoice	Fair Price
CD auto changer, hatchbacks	$699	$488	$601
Manual sunroof, SL and VR-4	375	300	322
Power sunroof, SL	900	720	774
VR-4	525	420	452
Deletes electronically controlled suspension from VR-4.			
Chrome wheels, SL	600	480	516
Yellow pearl paint	313	250	269
Mud guards	130	85	112

NISSAN

Nissan Altima

	Retail Price	Dealer Invoice	Fair Price
XE 4-door notchback, 5-speed	$14799	$13185	$13785
XE 4-door notchback, automatic	15629	13924	14524
GXE 4-door notchback, 5-speed	15799	13913	14513
GXE 4-door notchback, automatic	16629	14644	15244
SE 4-door notchback, 5-speed	18869	16520	17120
SE 4-door notchback, automatic	19699	17246	17846
GLE 4-door notchback, automatic	19889	17413	18013

Prices are accurate at time of publication; subject to manufacturer's change.

NISSAN

	Retail Price	Dealer Invoice	Fair Price
Destination charge	$390	$390	$390

Standard Equipment:

XE: 2.4-liter DOHC 4-cylinder engine, 5-speed manual or 4-speed automatic transmission, driver- and passenger-side air bags, power steering, tilt steering column, rear defogger, dual cup holders, remote fuel door and decklid releases, cloth reclining bucket seats, center front console, tachometer, coolant temperature gauge, trip odometer, low fuel warning light, child safety rear door locks, tinted glass, power mirrors, front map pockets, visor mirrors, 205/60R15 tires, wheel covers. **GXE** adds: power windows with auto down driver's window, power locks, front seat console with armrest, rear seat center armrest with trunk pass-through. **SE** adds: 4-wheel disc brakes, sport-tuned suspension, air conditioning, cruise control, front sport seats, AM/FM cassette, power diversity antenna, digital clock, variable intermittent wipers, fog lights, front cornering lights, bodyside cladding and rear spoiler, power sunroof, front sport seats, leather-wrapped steering wheel and manual shift knob, alloy wheels. **GLE** adds to GXE: 4-speed automatic transmission, automatic temperature control, cruise control, upgraded velour upholstery, variable intermittent wipers, front cornering lights, theft deterrent system, AM/FM cassette and CD player, power diversity antenna, digital clock, power sunroof, adjustable lumbar support, lighted visor mirrors, alloy wheels.

Optional Equipment:

Anti-lock brakes	999	854	899
Requires option pkg. with XE and GXE.			
Cruise control, XE	229	196	206
Requires automatic transmission.			
Leather Trim Pkg., SE and GLE	1049	897	944
Includes leather-wrapped steering wheel on GLE.			
XE Opt. Pkg.	1829	1563	1646
Air conditioning, AM/FM cassette with digital clock, cruise control.			
Power sunroof, GXE	829	709	746
Requires GXE Value Option Pkg.			
GXE Value Opt. Pkg.	1199	1025	1079
AM/FM cassette with digital clock, air conditioning, cruise control, power antenna.			

Nissan Maxima	Retail Price	Dealer Invoice	Fair Price
GXE 4-door notchback, 5-speed	$19999	$17818	—
GXE 4-door notchback, automatic	21599	19021	—
SE 4-door notchback, 5-speed	21599	18910	—
SE 4-door notchback, automatic	22599	19785	—

	Retail Price	Dealer Invoice	Fair Price
GLE 4-door notchback, automatic	$24819	$21729	—
Destination charge	390	390	390

Fair price not available at time of publication.

Standard Equipment:

GXE: 3.0-liter DOHC V-6 engine, 5-speed manual transmission, driver- and passenger-side air bags, 4-wheel disc brakes, air conditioning, power steering, power windows with auto-down driver's window, power locks, cruise control, tilt steering column, velour cloth reclining bucket seats, multi-adjustable driver's seat with cushion tilt adjustment, center console, fold-down rear armrest, front door map pockets, rear defogger, power mirrors, illuminated entry, child-safety rear door locks, remote trunk and fuel filler releases, tinted glass, tachometer, coolant temperature gauge, trip odometer, digital clock, AM/FM cassette audio system with power diversity antenna, visor vanity mirrors, map light, color-keyed bodyside moldings, full wheel covers, 205/65R15 tires. **SE** adds: sport-tuned suspension, fog lamps, body-colored rear spoiler, leather-wrapped steering wheel and shift knob, black-out exterior trim, alloy wheels, 215/60R15 tires. **GLE** adds to GXE: 4-speed automatic transmission, automatic air conditioning, 8-way power driver's seat, leather seating surfaces, leather-wrapped steering wheel and shift knob, simulated wood trim on console and around power window/lock buttons, automatic temperature control, remote keyless entry, dual illuminated visor vanity mirrors, variable intermittent wipers, remote keyless entry system with trunk release, security system, Bose 6-speaker cassette/CD audio system, 205/60HR15 tires, alloy wheels.

Optional Equipment:

Anti-lock brakes	999	854	—
NA GXE with 5-speed manual transmission.			
Leather Trim Pkg., SE	1099	939	—
Includes leather seats, automatic temperature control, passenger-side seatback pocket. Requires Security and Convenience Pkg., power sunroof and Bose six-speaker audio system.			
Cold Weather Pkg.	199	174	—
Includes heated front seats, heated outside mirrors, heavy-duty battery, low windshield washer fluid warning light. GLE requires anti-lock brakes. SE and GXE require anti-lock brakes and Security and Convenience Pkg. NA GXE with 5-speed manual transmission.			
Security and Convenience Pkg., SE, GXE	699	612	—
Includes 8-way power driver's seat, remote keyless entry system, power trunk release, security system, illuminated visor vanity mirrors, variable intermittent wipers, chrome tailpipe tip (GXE), 205/60HR15 tires (GXE). SE requires power sunroof. NA GXE with 5-speed manual transmission.			

NISSAN

	Retail Price	Dealer Invoice	Fair Price
Bose six-speaker cassette/CD audio system	$799	$700	—

Requires Security and Convenience Pkg. NA GXE with 5-speed manual transmission.

Power sunroof	899	768	—

NA GXE with 5-speed manual transmission.

Nissan Pathfinder

	Retail Price	Dealer Invoice	Fair Price
XE 2WD 5-door wagon, 5-speed	$20589	$18238	$18738
XE 2WD 5-door wagon, automatic	21779	19292	19792
XE 4WD 5-door wagon, 5-speed	22229	19690	20190
XE 4WD 5-door wagon, automatic	23599	20904	21404
SE 4WD 5-door wagon, 5-speed	26539	23508	24008
SE 4WD 5-door wagon, automatic	27639	24483	24983
LE 2WD 5-door wagon, automatic	28059	24855	25355
LE 4WD 5-door wagon, automatic	30359	26892	27392
Destination charge	390	390	390

Standard Equipment:

XE: 3.0-liter V-6, 5-speed manual or 4-speed automatic transmission, anti-lock rear brakes, power steering, part-time 4WD with automatic locking front hubs, cloth reclining front bucket seats, split folding and reclining rear seat, tachometer, coolant temperature gauge, trip odometer, digital clock, rear wiper/washer, tinted glass, dual outside mirrors, AM/FM cassette with diversity antenna, tilt steering column, rear defogger, front door map pockets, remote fuel door release, cargo tiedown hooks, skid plates, fender flares and mud guards (4WD), 235/75R15 tires, chrome wheels. **SE** adds: power windows and locks, cruise control, variable-intermittent wipers, heated power mirrors, remote rear window release, voltmeter, rear quarter, passenger door and liftgate window privacy glass, upgraded upholstery, flip-up removable sunroof with sunshade, roof rack, lighted visor mirrors, map lights, driver's seat height and lumbar support adjustments, folding rear armrests, step rail, fog lamps, rear wind deflector, alloy wheels, remote security system, outside spare tire carrier, 31 x 10.5 tires. **LE** adds: 4-speed automatic transmission, 4-wheel disc brakes (4WD), air conditioning, limited-slip differential (4WD), front tow hook, running board and splash guards, heated front seats, leather upholstery, leather-wrapped steering wheel, CD player, floormats.

Optional Equipment:

SE Off-Road Pkg.	579	496	550

Limited-slip rear differential, dual-rate adjustable shock absorbers, rear disc brakes, black exterior trim, front tow hook. Requires air conditioning.

NISSAN

	Retail Price	Dealer Invoice	Fair Price
Air conditioning, XE and SE	$999	$854	$949
XE Convenience Pkg.	1550	1326	1473

Cruise control, power windows and door locks, heated power mirrors, map lights, variable intermittent wipers, remote entry and vehicle security system. Requires air conditioning.

XE Sport Pkg.	860	735	817

Includes outside spare tire carrier, spare tire cover, fender flares (2WD), fog lights, limited-slip differential (4WD), cargo net, front tow hook. Requires XE Convenience Pkg.

Leather Trim Pkg., SE	1259	1076	1196

Includes leather seats, leather-wrapped steering wheel, shift knob and parking brake handle, heated front seats with individual controls. Requires air conditioning.

Nissan Quest

	Retail Price	Dealer Invoice	Fair Price
XE 7-passenger	$19839	$17369	$19039
GXE 7-passenger	24609	21545	23809
Destination charge	390	390	390

Standard Equipment:

XE: 3.0-liter V-6 engine, 4-speed automatic transmission, driver-side air bag, motorized front shoulder belts, front air conditioning, power steering, cloth reclining front bucket seats, 2-passenger middle bench seat and 3-passenger rear bench seat, Quest Trac flexible seating, remote fuel door release, rear defogger, tilt steering column, dual mirrors, tachometer, coolant temperature gauge, trip odometer, variable intermittent wipers, rear intermittent wiper/washer, color-keyed bodyside moldings, visor mirrors, cornering lamps, door map pockets, AM/FM cassette, diversity antenna, digital clock, tinted glass, carpeted front and rear floormats, console with cassette/CD storage, tilt-out middle and rear quarter windows, cargo area net, cargo area mat, full wheel covers, 205/75R15 all-season tires. **GXE** adds: anti-lock brakes, rear air conditioning, rear heater controls, cruise control, power driver's seat, dual middle row captain's chairs, power locks and windows, power rear quarter windows, automatic headlight control, upgraded upholstery and door trim panels, power mirrors, illuminated visor mirrors, upgraded radio with rear controls, leather-wrapped steering wheel, dual liftgate with opening window, side and rear privacy glass, map light, lockable underseat storage, alloy wheels.

Optional Equipment:

Anti-lock brakes, XE	700	599	644

Requires Convenience Pkg.

Prices are accurate at time of publication; subject to manufacturer's change.

NISSAN

	Retail Price	Dealer Invoice	Fair Price
Handling Pkg., XE	$979	$837	$901
GXE	479	410	441

Tuned springs and shock absorbers, rear stabilizer bar, leather-wrapped steering wheel (XE), wiring harness, full-size spare tire, 215/70R15 tires, alloy wheels (XE). XE requires rear air conditioning.

Power and Privacy Glass Pkg., XE	1240	1060	1141

Power windows, locks, and mirrors, side and rear privacy glass.

Convenience Pkg., XE	529	452	487

Cruise control, cargo net, lighted right visor mirror, roof rack, lockable underseat storage. Requires Power and Privacy Glass Pkg.

Rear air conditioning, XE	629	537	579

Requires Convenience Pkg.

2-tone paint, GXE	300	256	276
Middle row bench seat, GXE	NC	NC	NC
Leather Trim Pkg., GXE	1200	1026	1104

Leather uphostery, 4-way power passenger seat. Requires Luxury Pkg.

Luxury Pkg., GXE	1279	1094	1177

Iluminated entry, CD player, power sunroof.

Nissan Sentra

Prices not available at time of publication.

Standard Equipment:

Base: 1.6-liter DOHC 4-cylinder engine, 5-speed manual transmission, driver- and passenger-side air bags, cloth reclining front bucket seats, console, tinted glass, tilt steering column, coolant temperature gauge, trip odometer, rear defogger, front door map pockets, color-keyed grille, auxiliary power outlet, 155/80R13 tires. **XE** adds: power steering, air conditioning, AM/FM/cassette, digital clock, intermittent wipers, remote trunk and fuel door releases, dual exterior mirrors, color-keyed bumpers, 175/70R13 tires, wheel covers. **GXE** adds: split folding rear seat, upgraded interior trim, power windows and door locks, power mirrors, passenger-side visor mirror. **GLE** adds: power glass sunroof, velour seat trim, remote keyless entry, security alarm, tachometer, color-keyed bodyside moldings, 175/65R14 tires, alloy wheels.

Nissan 240SX	Retail Price	Dealer Invoice	Fair Price
2-door notchback, 5-speed	$17499	$15500	—
2-door notchback, automatic	18369	16271	—
SE 2-door notchback, 5-speed	21219	18795	—
SE 2-door notchback, automatic	22049	19531	—
Destination charge	390	390	390

Fair price not available at time of publication.

Standard Equipment:

2.4-liter DOHC 4-cylinder engine, 5-speed manual or 4-speed automatic transmission, 4-wheel disc brakes, driver- and passenger-side air bags, power steering, cloth reclining front bucket seats, folding rear seat, power windows with auto-down driver's window, body-color power mirrors, rear defogger, AM/FM/cassette, tachometer, coolant temperature gauge, trip odometer, digital clock, tilt steering column, variable intermittent wipers, remote fuel door and decklid releases, center console with storage, door pockets, visor vanity mirror, body-color bumpers, day/night mirror, tinted glass, 195/60HR15 all-season tires, wheel covers. **SE** adds: air conditioning, power locks, cruise control, front and rear spoilers, keyless remote entry with security system, fog lamps, driver-adjustable seat lumbar support, CD player with six speakers and power diversity-type antenna, sport-tuned suspension, rear stabilizer bar, alloy wheels, 205/55VR16 all-season tires.

Optional Equipment:	Retail Price	Dealer Invoice	Fair Price
Convenience Pkg., base	$949	$831	—
Power locks, cruise control, CD player with six speakers. Requires air conditioning.			
Leather Pkg.	1199	1025	—
Leather seats, leather-wrapped steering wheel and manual shift lever knob, map lights. Base requires alloy wheels and sunroof. SE requires anti-lock brakes.			
Air conditioning, base	999	854	—
Anti-lock brakes and limited-slip differential	1199	1025	—
Power sunroof	899	768	—
Pearlglow paint	350	300	—
Alloy wheels, base	399	341	—

Nissan 300ZX	Retail Price	Dealer Invoice	Fair Price
3-door hatchback w/o T-roof, 5-speed	$35009	—	—
3-door hatchback, 5-speed	36489	—	—
3-door hatchback, automatic	37439	—	—.
Turbo 3-door hatchback, 5-speed	41409	—	—
Turbo 3-door hatchback, automatic	42359	—	—
2+2 3-door hatchback, 5-speed	37799	—	—
2+2 3-door hatchback, automatic	38749	—	—
2-door convertible, 5-speed	42189	—	—
2-door convertible, automatic	43189	—	—
Destination charge	390	390	390

Dealer invoice and fair price not available at time of publication.

Prices are accurate at time of publication; subject to manufacturer's change.

NISSAN • OLDSMOBILE

Standard Equipment:

3.0-liter DOHC V-6 engine, 5-speed manual or 4-speed automatic transmission, anti-lock 4-wheel disc brakes, driver- and passenger-side air bags, limited-slip differential, power steering, cloth reclining front bucket seats, 7-way adjustable driver's seat, power driver's seat (except 3-door w/o T-roof), power passenger seat (convertible), folding rear seat (2+2), leather upholstery (convertible), air conditioning, automatic temperature control, power windows and door locks, cruise control, heated power mirrors, theft-deterrent system, remote keyless entry, AM/FM cassette with two speakers (convertible; all others have Nissan Bose system with four speakers), power diversity antenna, tachometer, coolant temperature and oil pressure gauges, trip odometer, digital clock, variable intermittent wipers, rear defogger, rear wiper/washer (except convertible), remote fuel door and hatch releases, illuminated entry, cargo area cover (except convertible), dual overhead map lights, leather-wrapped steering wheel and gear shift knob, seatback pockets, tinted glass, fog lights, 225/50VR16 tires, alloy wheels. **Turbo** adds: turbocharged, intercooled engine, Super HICAS 4-wheel steering, adjustable shock absorbers, rear spoiler, 225/50ZR16 front and 245/45ZR16 rear tires, 5-spoke alloy wheels.

Optional Equipment:	Retail Price	Dealer Invoice	Fair Price
Leather Pkg., 2-seater with T-roof	$1079	—	—
2+2	1279	—	—
Pearlglow paint, with T-roof and convertible with leather	350	—	—

OLDSMOBILE

Oldsmobile Achieva	Retail Price	Dealer Invoice	Fair Price
S 2-door notchback (Series I)	$13500	$12623	—
S 4-door notchback (Series I)	13500	12623	—
S 2-door notchback (Series II)	15200	14212	—
S 4-door notchback (Series II)	15200	14212	—
Destination charge	495	495	495

Fair price not available at time of publication.

Standard Equipment:

S 4-door (Series I): 2.3-liter DOHC 4-cylinder engine, 5-speed manual transmission, anti-lock brakes, driver-side air bag, power steering, air conditioning, cloth reclining front bucket seats, left remote and right manual mirrors, console with storage armrest, tilt steering wheel, intermittent wipers, tachometer, voltmeter, coolant temperature and oil pressure gauges, trip odometer, AM/FM radio, tinted glass, rear defogger, automatic power locks, remote fuel door and decklid releases, illuminated entry, reading and map lights, visor mirrors, map pockets, color-keyed bodyside moldings, floormats, 195/70R14 tires, wheel covers. **2-door** adds: power mirrors, rear window grid antenna, rear spoiler. **S 4-door (Series II)** adds to Series I 4-door: 4-speed automatic transmission, cruise control, power mirrors and windows, cassette player, gauge cluster with low fluid warning lights. **2-door** adds: rear window grid antenna, rear spoiler.

Optional Equipment:

	Retail Price	Dealer Invoice	Fair Price
3.1-liter V-6	$412	$354	—
Includes variable effort power steering. Requires 4-speed automatic transmission. Series I requires gauge cluster and cruise control.			
5-speed manual transmission, Series II (credit)	(755)	(649)	(649)
4-speed automatic transmission, Series I	755	649	—
Cruise control, Series I	225	194	—
Requires 3.1-liter V-6 engine.			
Gauge cluster with low fluid warning lights, Series I	126	108	—
Requires 3.1-liter V-6 engine.			
Rear spoiler and rear window grid antenna, Series I 4-door	224	193	—
Series II 4-door	147	126	—
Remote keyless entry, Series II	125	108	—
Cassette player, Series I	165	142	—
Requires 4-speed automatic transmission.			
CD player, Series II	256	220	—
Alloy wheels, Series II	391	336	—
Includes 195/65R15 touring tires.			
Engine block heater	18	15	—

Oldsmobile Aurora

	Retail Price	Dealer Invoice	Fair Price
4-door notchback	$31370	$29017	—
Destination charge	625	625	625

Fair price not available at time of publication.

Standard Equipment:

4.0-liter DOHC V-8 engine, 4-speed automatic transmission, anti-lock 4-wheel disc brakes, driver- and passenger-side air bags, traction control, variable-assist power steering, automatic climate control system, solar-control tinted glass, cruise control, AM/FM/cassette with CD player, power

OLDSMOBILE

antenna, steering wheel climate and radio touch controls, leather-wrapped steering wheel, leather upholstery, center storage console, power front bucket seats with 2-position memory for driver's side, power windows, automatic programmable door locks, power memory mirrors, intermittent wipers, fog lamps, tilt steering wheel, Pass-Key theft deterrent system, Twilight Sentinel automatic headlamp control, remote keyless illuminated entry system, tachometer, temperature, voltage, and oil pressure gauges, trip odometer, oil level sensor, rear defogger, folding rear armrest with trunk pass-through, front and rear floormats, 235/60R16 tires, alloy wheels.

Optional Equipment:

	Retail Price	Dealer Invoice	Fair Price
Power sunroof	$995	$856	—
Bose Acoustimass Sound System	671	577	—
Heated driver and front passenger seats	295	254	—
235/60VR16 tires	395	340	—
Includes 3.71 axle ratio.			
Engine block heater	18	15	—
Cloth upholstery	NC	NC	NC

Oldsmobile Cutlass Ciera

	Retail Price	Dealer Invoice	Fair Price
SL 4-door notchback (Series I)	$14460	$13665	—
SL 4-door notchback (Series II)	16060	15177	—
SL 5-door wagon	17060	16122	—
Destination charge	535	535	535

Fair price not available at time of publication.

Standard Equipment:

SL (Series I): 2.2-liter 4-cylinder engine, 3-speed automatic transmission, anti-lock brakes, driver-side air bag, power steering, air conditioning, 55/45 bench seat with armrest and power seatback recliners, automatic power locks, tilt steering wheel, AM/FM/cassette, digital clock, tinted glass, left remote and right manual mirrors, rear defogger, intermittent wipers, illuminated entry system, reading lights, map pockets, color-keyed bodyside moldings, visor mirrors, floormats, 185/75R14 whitewall tires, wheel covers. **SL (Series II)** adds: 3.1-liter V-6 engine, 4-speed automatic transmission, power windows, cruise control, power mirrors. **SL wagon** adds: rear air deflector, roof rack, split folding rear seat, rear-facing third seat, locking rear storage compartment.

Optional Equipment:

3.1-liter V-6 engine, Series I	810	697	—
Includes 4-speed automatic transmission.			
Power driver's seat, Series II, wagon	305	262	—

	Retail Price	Dealer Invoice	Fair Price
Remote keyless entry, Series II	$185	$159	—
Wagon	125	108	—
Engine block heater	18	15	—
195/75R14 tires	NC	NC	NC

Oldsmobile Cutlass Supreme

	Retail Price	Dealer Invoice	Fair Price
SL 2-door notchback (Series I)	$17460	$16500	—
SL 4-door notchback (Series I)	17460	16500	—
SL 2-door notchback (Series II)	18460	17445	—
SL 4-door notchback (Series II)	18460	17445	—
2-door convertible	25460	23041	—
Destination charge	535	535	535

Fair price not available at time of publication.

Standard Equipment:

SL (Series I): 3.1-liter V-6 engine, 4-speed automatic transmission, anti-lock brakes, driver- and passenger-side air bags, power steering, air conditioning, cruise control, cloth reclining front bucket seats, tilt steering wheel, tachometer, engine temperature gauge, center console with storage armrest and cup holder, leather-wrapped steering wheel, automatic power door locks, AM/FM/cassette, digital clock, power windows, power mirrors, tinted glass, rear defogger, intermittent wipers, illuminated entry system, reading lights, Pass-Key theft-deterrent system, fog lamps, map pockets, visor mirrors, floormats, 215/60R16 tires, alloy wheels. **SL (Series II)** adds: variable effort power steering, leather upholstery, 6-way power driver's seat, split folding rear seat, 6-speaker audio system, power antenna, remote keyless entry system, lighted visor mirrors. **Convertible** deletes 6-speaker audio system, lighted visor mirrors and adds: touring suspension, power top, color-keyed bumpers, gauge cluster with low fluid warning lights, power decklid release, 225/60R16 tires.

Optional Equipment:

55/45 front seats, Series I	NC	NC	NC
3.4-liter DOHC V-6, Series I, Series II	1223	1052	—
convertible	1255	1079	—
convertible with option pkg.	1185	1019	—

Includes oil level monitor, variable-effort power steering (Series I and II), sport suspension, rear spoiler (2-door notchback and convertible), dual exhausts, 225/60R16 tires (Series I and II).

Option Pkg. 1SB, convertible	216	186	—

Lighted visor mirrors, variable-effort power steering, 6-speaker audio system.

Prices are accurate at time of publication; subject to manufacturer's change.

OLDSMOBILE

	Retail Price	Dealer Invoice	Fair Price
Option Pkg. 1SC, convertible	$536	$461	—
Pkg. 1SB plus automatic air conditioning, steering wheel controls for radio and air conditioner.			
CD player, convertible	100	86	—
Cassette and CD players	200	172	—
Series I includes 6-speaker audio system. Convertible requires option pkg.			
Steering wheel controls for radio and air conditioner, Series II	320	275	—
Includes automatic air conditioning.			
Bodyside moldings, convertible	60	52	—
Engine block heater	18	15	—
Trunk cargo net, convertible	30	26	—

Oldsmobile Eighty Eight

	Retail Price	Dealer Invoice	Fair Price
Royale 4-door notchback	$20410	$19492	—
Royale LS 4-door notchback	22710	21688	—
LSS 4-door notchback	24010	22930	—
Destination charge	585	585	585

Fair price not available at time of publication.

Standard Equipment:

Royale: 3.8-liter V-6, 4-speed automatic transmission, driver- and passenger-side air bags, anti-lock brakes, power steering, high capacity engine cooling, air conditioning, cruise control, 55/45 cloth front seat with armrest and reclining seatback, 6-way power driver's seat, power windows, power mirrors, tinted glass with solar-control windshield and rear window, rear defogger, intermittent wipers, AM/FM/cassette with six speakers, power antenna, leather-wrapped steering wheel, tilt steering wheel, Pass-Key theft-deterrent system, power decklid release, power door locks, remote keyless entry system, coolant temperature gauge, trip odometer, reading lights, lighted visor mirrors, front door map pockets, floormats, trunk net, 205/70R15 tires, alloy wheels. **Royale LS** adds: automatic air conditioning, overhead console, steering wheel controls for radio and air conditioner, velour upholstery, rear seat storage armrest with cup holders, automatic day/night mirror with compass, cornering lamps. **LSS** adds: variable-effort power steering, traction control, automatic load-leveling touring suspension, leather front bucket seats, 6-way power driver's seat with power recliner, console with storage armrest, cup holders and dual auxiliary power outlets, tachometer, 225/60R16 tires.

Optional Equipment:

	Retail Price	Dealer Invoice	Fair Price
Supercharged 3.8-liter V-6 engine, LSS	$1022	$879	—
Traction control system (std. LSS)	175	151	—
Leather seats, Royale	610	525	—
Royale LS	515	443	—
Wire wheel covers	NC	NC	NC
Includes 205/70R15 whitewall tires. NA LSS.			
Cassette and CD players	200	172	—
Engine block heater	18	15	—

Oldsmobile Ninety Eight

	Retail Price	Dealer Invoice	Fair Price
Regency Elite 4-door notchback (Series I)	$26060	$24887	—
Regency Elite 4-door notchback (Series II)	27160	25938	—
Destination charge	635	635	635

Fair price not available at time of publication.

Standard Equipment:

Regency Elite (Series I): 3.8-liter V-6, 4-speed automatic transmission, anti-lock brakes, driver- and passenger-side air bags, power steering, dual zone air conditioner, high capacity engine cooling, leather 55/45 reclining front seat with storage armrest, 6-way power front seats with power recliners and lumbar support adjusters, rear seat storage armrest, cruise control, power windows and door locks, power mirrors, AM/FM/cassette with eight speakers, power antenna, steering wheel controls for radio and air conditioner, power remote fuel door and decklid releases, remote keyless entry system, coolant temperature gauge, trip odometer, tilt steering wheel, automatic leveling suspension, tinted glass with solar control windshield and rear window, intermittent wipers, rear defogger, Pass-Key theft deterrent system, lighted visor mirrors, reading lights, front door map pockets, trunk net, floormats, 205/70R15 whitewall tires, alloy wheels. **Regency Elite (Series II)** adds: traction control, electronic instrument cluster, cornering lamps, driver's seat and outside mirror memory controls, heated mirrors, automatic day/night mirror with compass, Twilight Sentinel headlight control, power decklid pulldown.

Optional Equipment:

Supercharged 3.8-liter V-6 engine,			
Series II	1022	879	—
Includes touring suspension, analog tachometer, variable-effort power steering, leather-wrapped steering wheel, 225/60R16 tires.			
Traction control, Series I	175	151	—
Astroroof, Series II	995	856	—
Wire wheel covers, Series I	NC	NC	NC

Prices are accurate at time of publication; subject to manufacturer's change.

OLDSMOBILE

	Retail Price	Dealer Invoice	Fair Price
Cassette and CD players	$200	$172	—
Cloth seat trim	NC	NC	NC
Engine block heater	18	15	—

Oldsmobile Silhouette

	Retail Price	Dealer Invoice	Fair Price
4-door van (Series I)	$20255	$19344	—
4-door van (Series II)	21755	20776	—
Destination charge	540	540	540

Fair price not available at time of publication.

Standard Equipment:

Series I: 3.8-liter V-6, 4-speed automatic transmission, anti-lock brakes, driver-side air bag, power steering, front air conditioning, cruise control, power windows and door locks, 4-way adjustable driver's seat, 7-passenger seating (front bucket seats, three middle and two rear modular seats), center console with locking storage, overhead console, power mirrors, tachometer, coolant temperature and oil pressure gauges, voltmeter, trip odometer, remote keyless entry system, AM/FM cassette, digital clock, tilt steering wheel, tinted glass with solar control windshield, intermittent wipers, rear wiper/washer, rear defogger, fog lamps, reading lights, roof rack, black roof paint, color-keyed bodyside moldings, visor mirrors, front door map pockets, floormats, cargo area auxiliary power outlet, cargo net, 205/70R15 tires, alloy wheels. **Series II** adds: power sliding door, 6-way power driver's seat, leather upholstery, leather-wrapped steering wheel with auxiliary radio controls.

Optional Equipment:

Traction control system, Series II	555	477	—
Includes FE3 touring suspension.			
Integrated child seat	125	108	—
Integrated dual child seats	225	194	—
Rear air conditioning	450	387	—
Power driver's seat, Series I	270	232	—
Power sliding door, Series I	350	301	—
Towing Pkg., Series II	705	606	—
Includes FE3 touring suspension, traction control system, engine and transmission oil coolers, 5-lead wiring harness.			
CD player, Series I	256	220	—
Series II	226	194	—
Engine block heater	18	15	—
Black roof delete	NC	NC	NC

CONSUMER GUIDE®

PLYMOUTH

Plymouth Acclaim	Retail Price	Dealer Invoice	Fair Price
4-door notchback	$14323	$12969	$13169
Destination charge	505	505	505

Standard Equipment:

2.5-liter 4-cylinder engine, 3-speed automatic transmission, power steering, driver-side air bag, air conditioning, cruise control, motorized front passenger shoulder belt, cloth 50/50 front bench seat, coolant temperature gauge, voltmeter, trip odometer, center console, tilt steering wheel, rear defogger, tinted glass, dual remote mirrors, visor mirrors, bodyside moldings, AM/FM/cassette with four speakers, intermittent wipers, floormats, striping, 185/70R14 tires, wheel covers.

Optional Equipment:

3.0-liter V-6 engine	798	678	702
Includes 195/70R14 tires.			
Pkg. 26E	735	625	647
Power windows and door locks, heated power mirrors, remote decklid release. Requires 3.0-liter V-6 engine.			
Gold Decor Special Equipment Group	200	170	176
Luggage rack, gold badging and trim, 195/70R14 tires, alloy wheels with gold accents.			
Power driver's seat, w/Pkg. 26E	306	260	269
Power locks	250	213	220
Conventional spare tire	95	81	84
Extra-cost paint	97	82	85
Engine block heater	20	17	18

Plymouth Neon	Retail Price	Dealer Invoice	Fair Price
Base 4-door notchback	$9500	$8815	$9300
Highline 4-door notchback	11240	10416	10940
Highline 2-door notchback	11240	10416	10940
Sport 4-door notchback	13267	12015	12767
Sport 2-door notchback	13567	12285	13067
Destination charge	500	500	500

Standard Equipment:

Base: 2.0-liter 4-cylinder engine, 5-speed manual transmission, driver- and passenger-side air bags, cloth reclining bucket seats, floor storage console

PLYMOUTH

with dual cup holders and coin holder, left remote outside rearview mirror, passenger-side visor mirror, 165/80R13 all-season tires. **Highline** adds: power steering, 60/40 split folding rear seat, tinted glass, intermittent wipers, dual manual remote mirrors, driver-side visor mirror, AM/FM radio with four speakers, touring suspension, bodyside moldings, 185/70R13 all-season tires, wheel covers. **Sport 4-door** adds: anti-lock brakes, power mirrors and door locks, padded covered floor storage console with tissue pack holder, dual cup holders, and cassette/CD holders, rear defogger, remote decklid release, tilt steering wheel, tachometer, low fuel light, fog lights, 185/65R14 all-season touring tires, alloy wheels. **Sport 2-door** adds: DOHC engine, 16:1 ratio power steering, performance-tuned suspension, rear spoiler, 185/65R14 all-season performance tires.

Optional Equipment:	Retail Price	Dealer Invoice	Fair Price
2.0-liter 4-cylinder engine, Sport 2-door (credit)	($100)	($89)	($89)
DOHC engine, Highline 2-door w/ Competition Pkg.	150	138	143
Required with Competition Pkg.			
3-speed automatic transmission	557	496	529
Anti-lock brakes,			
Base and Highline w/13-inch wheels	565	503	537
Highline w/14-inch wheels	565	503	537
Models with 14-inch wheels require Wheel Dress-Up Pkg. and option pkg.			
Base Pkg. 21B/22B	1861	1712	1675
Air conditioning, power steering, rear defogger, intermittent wipers, AM/FM radio, dual manual remote mirrors, touring suspension, bodyside moldings, tinted glass. Pkg. 22B requires 3-speed automatic transmission.			
Base Pkg. 25B	2981	2687	2832
Competition Pkg. plus air conditioning, rear defogger, intermittent wipers, dual manual remote mirrors.			
Highline Pkg. 21D/22D	703	626	668
Air conditioning, rear defogger, floor storage console, remote decklid release. Pkg. 22D requires 3-speed automatic transmission.			
Highline Pkg. 23D, 2-door	1693	1536	1608
Competition Pkg. plus air conditioning, rear defogger, floor storage console, remote decklid release. Deletes AM/FM radio.			
Highline Pkg. 21F/22F, 4-door	1371	1220	1302
2-door	1330	1184	1264
Pkg 21D/22D plus 14-inch front disc/rear drum brakes, power mirrors and door locks, tilt steering wheel, tachometer with low fuel light, 14-inch Wheel Dress-Up Pkg., Light Pkg. (lighted visor mirrors, lighted ignition key cylinder, ashtray and glove box lights, trunk and underhood lamps), and rear floormats. Pkg. 22F requires 3-speed automatic transmission.			

CONSUMER GUIDE®

	Retail Price	Dealer Invoice	Fair Price
Sport Pkg. 21K/22K (4-door), 23K/24K (2-door)	$626	$557	$595
Air conditioning, Light Pkg., AM/FM/cassette, front and rear floor mats. Pkg. 22K/24K requires 3-speed automatic transmission.			
Sport Pkg. 21K/22K (2-door)	526	468	500
4-door Pkg. 21K/22K plus credit for 2.0-liter 4-cylinder engine. Pkg. 22K requires 3-speed automatic transmission.			
Competition Pkg., Base	1575	1449	1496
Highline 2-door	990	911	941
4-wheel disc brakes, color-keyed grille bar (4-door), tinted glass (4-door), heavy duty radiator, 16:1 ratio power steering, competition suspension, tachometer with low fuel light, 175/65HR14 tires (4-door) or 185/60HR14 tires (2-door), alloy wheels. Highline requires DOHC engine.			
Convenience Group, Highline 4-door	297	264	282
Highline 2-door	256	228	243
Power mirrors and door locks. Requires Pkg. 21D/22D.			
Rear defogger, Base and Highline	173	154	164
Bodyside moldings, Base	30	27	29
14-inch Wheel Dress-Up Pkg., Highline w/Pkg. 21D/22D	80	71	76
185/65R14 all-season touring tires, wheel covers, 14-inch front disc/rear drum brakes.			
Dual manual remote mirrors, Base	70	62	67
AM/FM radio with four speakers, Base	334	297	317
AM/FM/cassette with six speakers	250	223	238
Base requires Pkg. 21B/22B.			
AM/FM/CD player with six speakers	488	434	464
Sport with option pkg.	238	212	226
Base requires Pkg. 21B/22B.			
Roof rack	100	89	95
Integrated child seat	100	89	95
Cruise control, Highline and Sport	224	199	213
Highline requires option pkg.			
Tilt steering wheel	148	132	141
Base requires Pkg. 21B/22B.			
Power front door windows, Sport 4-door	210	187	200
Tachometer with low fuel light, Highline	93	83	88
Intermittent wipers, Base	66	59	63
Front and rear floormats	46	40	44
Extra-cost paint, Base and Highline	97	86	92

Prices are accurate at time of publication; subject to manufacturer's change.

PLYMOUTH

Plymouth Voyager

	Retail Price	Dealer Invoice	Fair Price
Base SWB	$16160	$14721	$15221
Base Grand	18605	16897	17697
SE SWB	18855	17092	17592
Grand SE	19595	17769	18569
Grand SE AWD	22270	20123	20923
LE SWB	23380	21074	21574
Grand LE	23680	21363	22163
Grand LE AWD	25755	23189	23989
Destination charge	560	560	560

SWB denotes standard wheelbase; AWD denotes All Wheel Drive.

Standard Equipment:

Base: 2.5-liter 4-cylinder engine, 3-speed automatic transmission, driver- and passenger-side air bags, power steering, cloth front bucket seats, 3-passenger middle bench seat, tinted glass, trip odometer, coolant temperature gauge, automatic day/night mirror, dual outside mirrors, visor mirrors, AM/FM radio, variable intermittent wipers, rear wiper/washer, 195/75R14 tires, wheel covers. **Base Grand** adds: 3.0-liter V-6 engine, 7-passenger seating (front bucket seats and 2-place middle and 3-place rear bench seats), rear trim panel storage and cup holders, 205/70R15 tires. **SE** adds to Base: 3.0-liter V-6 engine, cruise control, power mirrors, 6-speaker cassette player, power remote tailgate release, tilt steering wheel, front passenger lockable underseat storage drawer, striping, dual note horn. **Grand SE** adds to Base Grand: 3.3-liter V-6 engine, 4-speed automatic transmission, cruise control, power mirrors, 6-speaker cassette player, power remote tailgate release, tilt steering wheel, front passenger lockable underseat storage drawer, striping, dual note horn. **LE** adds to SE: 4-speed automatic transmission, anti-lock brakes, front air conditioning, front storage console, overhead console with trip computer, rear defogger, power rear quarter vent windows, power door locks, remote keyless entry system, tachometer, oil pressure gauge, voltmeter, heated power mirrors, lighted visor mirrors, illuminated entry system, headlamp time delay, floormats, 205/70R15 tires. **Grand LE** adds to Grand SE: anti-lock brakes, front air conditioning, front storage console, overhead console with trip computer, rear defogger, power rear quarter vent windows, power door locks, remote keyless entry system, tachometer, oil pressure gauge, voltmeter, heated power mirrors, lighted visor mirrors, illuminated entry system, headlamp time delay, floormats. AWD models have permanently engaged all-wheel drive.

Quick Order Packages:

Pkg. 22T/24T/26TBase SWB and Pkg.26T Base Grand	225	191	207

	Retail Price	Dealer Invoice	Fair Price

Air conditioning, map and cargo lights, power remote liftgate release, front passenger underseat lockable storage drawer, bodyside molding, dual horns. Pkg. 24T requires 3.0-liter engine; Pkg. 26T requires 3.0-liter engine and 4-speed transmission (Base SWB).

Pkg. 24B/26B/28B SE SWB and Pkg. 26B/28B

Grand SE	$220	$187	$202

Pkg. 24B/26B/28B adds to SE standard equipment: front air conditioning, map and cargo lights, rear defogger. SE SWB Pkg. 26B requires 4-speed automatic transmission; SE SWB Pkg. 28B requires 3.3-liter engine and 4-speed automatic transmission. Grand SE Pkg. 26B requires 3.0-liter V-6 engine.

Pkg. 24D/26D/28D SE SWB,

Pkg. 28D Grand SE AWD	1080	918	994
Pkg. 26D/28D Grand SE	1580	1343	1454

Pkg. 24D/26D/28D adds to Pkg. 24B/26B/28B: anti-lock brakes (Grand SE), forward and overhead consoles, oil pressure and voltage gauges, tachometer, lighted visor mirrors, Light Group, power door locks and rear quarter vent windows, floormats. SE SWB Pkg. 26D requires 4-speed automatic transmission; SE SWB Pkg. 28D requires 3.3-liter engine and 4-speed automatic transmission. Grand SE Pkg. 26D requires 3.0-liter V-6 engine.

Pkg. 24E/26E/28E SE SWB,

Pkg. 28E Grand SE AWD	1960	1666	1803
Pkg. 26E/28E Grand SE	2460	2091	2263

Pkg. 24E/26E/28E adds to Pkg. 24D/26D/28D: computerized compass, thermometer and trip odometer, remote keyless entry system, power driver's seat, passenger assist handle, power windows. SE SWB Pkg. 26E requires 4-speed automatic transmission; SE SWB Pkg. 28E requires 3.3-liter engine and 4-speed automatic transmission. Grand SE Pkg. 26E requires 3.0-liter V-6 engine.

Pkg. 26K/28K LE SWB and Pkg.28K/29K

Grand LE AWD	315	268	290
Pkg. 28K/29K Grand LE	215	183	198

Pkg. 26K/28K/29K adds to LE standard equipment: power driver's seat, power windows, AM/FM radio with cassette player, equalizer and six Infinity speakers, sunscreen glass. LE SWB Pkg. 28K requires 3.3-liter engine. Grand LE and Grand LE AWD Pkg. 29K require 3.8-liter engine.

Individual Options:

3.0-liter V-6, Base SWB	770	655	708
Grand SE w/Pkgs. 26A/26B/26D/26E (credit)	(105)	(89)	(89)
3.3-liter V-6, SE and LE SWB	105	89	97

Requires 4-speed automatic transmission.

PLYMOUTH

	Retail Price	Dealer Invoice	Fair Price
3.8-liter V-6, Grand LE, Grand LE AWD	$305	$259	$281
4-speed automatic transmission	200	170	184
Anti-lock brakes:			
SE SWB with Pkgs. 24B/26B/28B, 24D/26D/28D, or 24E/26E/28E	690	587	635
SE SWB with Pkgs. 24B/26B/28B, 24D/26D/28D, or 24E/26E/28E and Rallye Decor or Sport Wagon Groups; Grand SE with Pkg. 26B/28B	600	510	552
Front air conditioning, Base SWB and Base Grand	860	731	791
Front air conditioning with sunscreen glass, Base SWB w/Pkg. 22T/24T/26T/27T, SE SWB w/Pkgs. 24B/26B/27B/28B, 24D/26D/27D/28D, and 24E/26E/27E/28E, Base Grand w/Pkg. 26T, SE Grand w/Pkgs. 26B/28B, 26D/28D, and 26E/28E	415	353	382
Sunscreen glass, Grand SE AWD	415	353	382
Rear air conditioning with rear heater and sunscreen glass, Base Grand with Pkg. 26T, Grand SE with option pkg., Grand SE AWD	885	752	814
Grand SE with option pkg. and Sport Wagon Decor or Rallye Decor Groups, Grand LE with Pkg. 28K/29K, Grand SE AWD with Sport Wagon or Rallye Decor Groups, Grand LE AWD	470	400	432
Grand LE with Pkg. 28K/29K and Trailer Tow Group, Grand LE AWD with Trailer Tow Group	405	344	373
Requires rear defogger.			
Rear bench seat, Base SWB	350	298	322
7-passenger seating with integrated child seat, Base SWB	575	489	529
SE and LE SWB, Grand, Grand AWD	225	191	207
Quad Command Seating, SE, LE	600	510	552
Two front and two middle bucket seats, 3-passenger rear bench seat.			
Leather trim, Grand LE w/Pkg. 28K/29K, Grand LE AWD	865	735	796
NA with integrated child seat.			
Heavy Duty Trailer Towing Group, Grand LE w/Pkg. 28K/29K	445	378	409
Grand LE w/Pkg. 28K/29K and Sport Handling Group	410	349	377

CONSUMER GUIDE®

PLYMOUTH

	Retail Price	Dealer Invoice	Fair Price
Grand LE AWD w/Pkgs. 28K/29K	$375	$319	$345
Heavy duty battery, load suspension and radiator, transmission oil cooler, heavy duty flasher, trailer towing wiring harness, conventional spare tire.			
Sport Handling Group, LE SWB w/Pkg. 26K/28K, Grand LE w/Pkg. 28K/29K	505	429	465
Heavy duty brakes, front and rear sway bars, 205/70R15 tires, alloy wheels.			
Convenience Group I, Base SWB and Base Grand	375	319	345
Cruise control, tilt steering wheel. Requires option pkg.			
Convenience Group II, Base SWB and Base Grand	700	595	544
SE SWB w/Pkg. 24B/26B/28B, Grand SE w/Pkg. 26B/28B	265	225	244
Convenience Group I plus power mirrors and door locks. Base SWB and Base Grand require option pkg.			
Convenience Group III, SE SWB w/Pkg. 24B/26B/28B and Grand SE w/Pkg. 26B/28B	675	574	621
SE SWB w/Pkg. 24D/26D/28D, Grand SE w/Pkg. 26D/28D	410	349	377
Convenience Group II plus power windows and remote keyless entry system.			
AWD Convenience Group II, Grand SE AWD with Pkg. 28D	410	349	377
Power windows and remote keyless entry system.			
Sport Wagon Decor Group, SE w/Pkgs. 24B/26B/28B, 24D/26D/28D, or 24E/26E/28E	750	638	690
Sunscreen glass, front and rear fascias, leather-wrapped steering wheel, fog lamps, Sport Handling Group, bodyside moldings, alloy wheels. NA with Rallye Decor Group.			
Rallye Decor Group, SE	750	638	690
Driftwood lower body and fascia paint, badging, sunscreen glass, 15-inch front disc/rear drum brakes, 205/70R15 tires, alloy wheels. Requires option pkg. NA with Sport Wagon Decor Group.			
Rear defogger	170	145	156
Power door locks, Base with option pkg.	265	225	244
Luggage rack	145	123	133
Base requires option pkg.			
Cassette player, Base	170	145	156

Prices are accurate at time of publication; subject to manufacturer's change.

	Retail Price	Dealer Invoice	Fair Price
AM/FM stereo with CD player, equalizer and six Infinity speakers, LE SWB w/Pkg. 26K/28K, Grand LE w/Pkg. 28K/29K, Grand LE AWD w/Pkg. 28K/29K	$170	$145	$156
Infinity speaker system, SE w/Pkgs. 24D/26D/28D and 24E/26E/28E	205	174	189

PONTIAC

Pontiac Bonneville

	Retail Price	Dealer Invoice	Fair Price
SE 4-door notchback sedan	$20804	$18828	$19328
SSE 4-door notchback sedan	25804	23353	23853
Destination charge	585	585	585

Standard Equipment:

SE: 3.8-liter V-6, 4-speed automatic transmission, anti-lock brakes, power steering, driver- and passenger-side air bags, cruise control, air conditioning, cloth 45/55 reclining front seats, tilt steering wheel, power windows with driver-side express down, power door locks, AM/FM radio, tinted glass, left remote and right manual mirrors, fog lamps, coolant temperature and oil pressure gauges, voltmeter, tachometer, trip odometer, Lamp Group (includes rear courtesy lights, rear assist handles, headlamp-on warning, engine compartment light), intermittent wipers, Pass-Key theft-deterrent system, visor mirrors, floormats, 215/65R15 tires, wheel covers. **SSE** adds: dual exhaust, variable-assist power steering, Computer Command ride and handling suspension with electronic load leveling, 45/45 cloth bucket seats with center storage console and rear air conditioning vents, overhead console with power outlet, 6-way power driver's seat, rear center armrest with cup holders, rear defogger, heated power mirrors, 6-speaker cassette player with equalizer and steering wheel controls, leather-wrapped steering wheel, power antenna, Driver Information Center, remote decklid release, Twilight Sentinel, rear spoiler, accessory emergency road kit (includes spot light, first aid kit, air hose, windshield scraper, gloves), illuminated entry, lighted visor mirrors, deluxe floormats, trunk net, 225/60R16 tires, alloy wheels.

Optional Equipment:

Supercharged 3.8-liter V-6 engine, SE	1187	1056	1068
SSE	1167	1039	1050

SE requires SLE Pkg. SSE includes SSEi Pkg. (engine plus boost gauge, driver-selectable shift controls, 2.97 axle ratio, upgraded carpet, SSEi badging and floormats, 225/60HR16 tires).

	Retail Price	Dealer Invoice	Fair Price
Automatic climate control, SE	$150	$134	$135
Requires Group 1SC or 1SD.			
Option Group 1SB, SE	270	240	243
Illuminated entry, cassette player.			
Option Group 1SC, SE	923	821	831
Group 1SB plus variable-assist steering, 6-way power driver's seat, power mirrors, rear defogger, remote decklid release.			
Option Group 1SD, SE	1584	1410	1426
Group 1SC plus remote keyless entry system, 45/55 cloth front seat with storage armrest and cup holders, lighted visor mirrors, Twilight Sentinel, leather-wrapped steering wheel, power antenna, trunk net.			
Sport Luxury Edition (SLE), SE			
with Group 1SC	2635	2360	2372
with Group 1SD	2830	2534	2547
Group 1SC or 1SD plus 45/45 leather bucket seats with center storage console and rear air conditioning vents, leather-wrapped steeing wheel and shift knob, Monotone Appearance Pkg., power antenna, rear decklid spoiler, 225/60R16 tires, silver crosslace alloy wheels.			
Option Group 1SB, SSE	1440	1282	1296
6-way power seat, head-up display, automatic climate control, remote keyless entry system, automatic day/night rearview mirror, traction control, 8-speaker sound system, theft-deterrent system.			
Enhancement Group, SE with			
Group 1SC	206	183	185
with Group 1SC and cloth bucket seats	110	98	99
with Group 1SC and leather bucket seats or			
SLE Pkg.	60	53	54
Lighted visor mirrors, leather-wrapped steering wheel, Twilight Sentinel.			
Performance and Handling Pkg., SE	1183	1053	1065
with SLE Pkg.	775	690	698
Computer Command Ride, traction control, electronic load leveling, 225/60R16 touring tires, 5-blade alloy wheels. Requires bucket seats and Group 1SD.			
Monotone Appearance Pkg., SE	200	178	180
Monotone bodyside and rocker moldings. Requires option group.			
Rear decklid spoiler, SE	110	98	99
Rear decklid spoiler delete (credit)	(110)	(98)	(98)
SE requires SLE Pkg.			
Traction control	175	154	158
SE requires Group 1SC or 1SD, bucket seats and alloy wheels.			
Rear defogger, SE	170	151	153
Power glass sunroof, SE	995	886	896
SE with custom interior, SSE	981	873	883
SE requires alloy wheels and Group 1SC (with SLE Pkg.) or 1SD.			

Prices are accurate at time of publication; subject to manufacturer's change.

PONTIAC

	Retail Price	Dealer Invoice	Fair Price
Custom interior, SE	$235	$209	$212

45/55 reclining front bench seat with storage armrest and cup holders, upgraded cloth upholstery, trunk net, deluxe floormats. Requires option group.

	Retail Price	Dealer Invoice	Fair Price
Custom bucket seat interior, SE	505	449	455
with Group 1SD	174	155	157

45/45 cloth bucket seats with center storage console and rear air conditioning vents, lighted visor mirrors, overhead console with power outlet, trunk net, deluxe floormats. Requires option group.

Custom leather interior, SE	1409	1254	1268
with Group 1SD	1028	915	925

45/45 leather bucket seats with center storage console, leather-wrapped steering wheel, overhead console with power outlet, trunk net, deluxe floormats. Requires Option Group 1SC or 1SD .

45/45 leather bucket seats, SSE	854	760	769
45/45 articulating leather bucket seats, SSE	1404	1250	1264
with Group 1SB	1099	978	989
6-way power driver's seat,			
SE with Group 1SB	305	271	275
6-way power passenger seat	305	271	275

SE requires Group 1SC or 1SD and custom interior.

Remote keyless entry system	135	120	122

SE requires Group 1SC.

Cassette player, SE	195	174	176
CD player, SE	295	263	266
with option group	100	89	90
Cassette player with equalizer, SE	385	343	347
with Enhancement Group or			
leather bucket seats	335	298	302
with SLE Pkg. or Group 1SD	250	223	225

Requires option group.

CD player with equalizer, SE	485	432	437
with Enhancement Group or			
leather bucket seats	435	387	392
with SLE Pkg. or Group 1SD	350	312	315
SSE	100	89	90

SE requires option group.

6-speaker sound system, SE	100	89	90

Requires option group.

Steering wheel radio controls,			
SE with cassette or CD player	125	111	113

Requires option group.

Power antenna, SE	85	76	77

Requires Group 1SB or 1SC.

	Retail Price	Dealer Invoice	Fair Price
Computer Command Ride, SSE with Group 1SB	$380	$338	$342
16-inch 5-blade alloy wheels, SE	324	288	292
Requires option group and 225/60R16 tires. NA with SLE Pkg.			
16-inch gold or silver crosslace alloy wheels, SE with SLE Pkg., SSE	NC	NC	NC
225/60R16 blackwall touring tires, SE	84	75	76
Engine block heater	18	16	17

Pontiac Firebird	Retail Price	Dealer Invoice	Fair Price
3-door hatchback	$14859	$13596	$14359
2-door convertible	21939	20074	21439
Formula 3-door hatchback	19099	17476	18599
Formula 2-door convertible	25129	22993	24629
Trans Am 3-door hatchback	21069	19278	20569
Trans Am 2-door convertible	27139	24832	26639
Destination charge	500	500	500

Standard Equipment:

Base: 3.4-liter V-6, 5-speed manual transmission, anti-lock brakes, power steering, driver- and passenger-side air bags, cloth reclining front bucket seats, folding rear bench seat, tilt steering wheel, center console with storage, lamp and cup holder, remote hatch release, AM/FM cassette, intermittent wipers, solar-control tinted glass, front air dam, rear decklid spoiler, left remote and right manual mirrors, coolant temperature and oil pressure gauges, tachometer, voltmeter, trip odometer, Pass-Key theft-deterrent system, day/night rearview mirror with dual reading lamps, visor mirrors, front floormats, 215/60R16 tires, alloy wheels. **Convertible** adds: air conditioning, cruise control, automatic power door locks, power windows, remote keyless entry, 4-way manually adjustable driver's seat, power mirrors, power top with glass rear window and defogger, 3-piece tonneau cover, color-keyed bodyside molding, rear floormats. **Formula** adds to base hatchback: 5.7-liter V-8 engine, 6-speed manual transmission, 4-wheel disc brakes, air conditioning, performance suspension, 3.42 axle ratio, limited-slip differential, 235/55R16 touring tires, bright silver alloy wheels. **Formula convertible** adds: power mirrors, power windows, automatic power door locks, remote keyless entry, 4-way manually adjustable driver's seat, color-keyed bodyside molding, rear floormats, 235/55R16 touring tires. **Trans Am** adds to Formula hatchback: cruise control, power windows with driver-side express down, leather-wrapped steering wheel and shift knob, steering wheel radio controls, power mirrors, automatic power door locks, rear defogger, color-keyed bodyside molding, fog lamps, rear floormats,

PONTIAC

245/50ZR16 tires. **Trans Am convertible** adds: cassette with equalizer, 6-speaker sound system and power antenna, 4-way manually adjustable driver's seat, remote keyless entry system.

Optional Equipment:

	Retail Price	Dealer Invoice	Fair Price
4-speed automatic transmission	$775	$667	$736
Traction control, Formula, Trans Am	450	387	405
Air conditioning delete, Formula hatchback (credit)	(895)	(770)	(770)

NA with option group.

Option Group 1SB, base hatchback	1005	864	955

Air conditioning, manual 4-way adjustable driver's seat, color-keyed bodyside moldings, rear floormats.

Option Group 1SB, base convertible	508	437	483

Remote keyless entry, cassette player with equalizer, 6-speaker sound system and power antenna, leather-wrapped steering wheel with radio controls.

Option Group 1SC, base hatchback	2614	2248	2483

Group 1SB plus power windows with driver-side express down, automatic power door locks, power mirrors, cruise control, remote keyless illuminated entry, cassette player with equalizer, 10-speaker sound system and power antenna, leather-wrapped steering wheel with radio controls, rear defogger.

Option Group 1SB, Formula hatchback	1076	925	1022

Cruise control, power windows with driver-side express down, automatic power door locks, power mirrors, rear defogger, color-keyed bodyside moldings, rear floormats.

Option Group 1SB, Formula convertible	508	437	483

Remote keyless entry, cassette player with equalizer, 6-speaker sound system and power antenna, leather-wrapped steering wheel with radio controls.

Option Group 1SC, Formula hatchback	1684	1448	1600

Group 1SB plus remote keyless illuminated entry, cassette player with equalizer, 10-speaker sound system and power antenna, leather-wrapped steering wheel with radio controls,

Cruise control, base hatchback with Group 1SB	225	194	214
Rear defogger, base and Formula hatchbacks ..	170	146	162
Removable locking hatch roof	970	834	922

Requires option group with base and Formula.

Hatch roof sunshades	25	22	24
Rear performance axle, Formula, Trans Am hatchback	175	151	166

Includes 3.23 axle ratio. Requires 4-speed automatic transmission, 245/50ZR16 tires. Formula hatchback requires option group. Std. Trans Am convertible with automatic transmission.

CONSUMER GUIDE®

	Retail Price	Dealer Invoice	Fair Price
Upgraded decklid spoiler, Trans Am	$350	$301	$333
Color-keyed bodyside moldings,			
Base and Formula hatchbacks	60	52	57
Power mirrors,			
base and Formula hatchbacks	96	83	91

Requires power door locks and windows. Base requires option group.

Automatic power door locks,			
base and Formula hatchbacks	220	189	209

Base requires option group.

Power windows, base and Formula hatchbacks	290	249	276

Includes driver-side express down. Base requires option group.

Cassette player w/equalizer,			
Base and Formula hatchbacks	473	407	449
Trans Am hatchback	398	342	378
Base and Formula convertibles	373	321	354

Includes power antenna, leather-wrapped steering wheel with radio controls (base and Formula models), 6- (convertibles) or 10-speaker (hatchbacks) sound system. Base and Formula hatchbacks require option group and power windows, door locks, and mirrors.

CD player, base and Formula hatchbacks	100	86	95
CD player with equalizer, hatchbacks			
Base and Formula with Group 1SB	573	493	544
Base and Formula with Group 1SC	100	86	95
Trans Am	498	428	473

Includes power antenna, leather-wrapped steering wheel with radio controls (base and Formula), 10-speaker sound system. Requires power windows, mirrors, and door locks.

Cloth articulating bucket seats, Trans Am	330	284	314
Leather articulating bucket seats,			
base and Formula hatchbacks with			
Option Group 1SC	804	691	764
convertibles, Trans Am hatchback	829	713	788
4-way manual driver's seat, hatchbacks	35	30	33

NA Formula.

6-way power driver's seat, hatchbacks	305	262	290
convertibles, base hatchback with option			
group	270	232	257

NA with articulating seats.

Remote keyless entry system			
(std. Trans Am convertible)	135	116	128

Requires power windows, power door locks and power mirrors. Base hatchback requires option pkg.

235/55R16 touring tires, base	132	114	125
245/50ZR16 tires, Formula	144	124	137

Prices are accurate at time of publication; subject to manufacturer's change.

PONTIAC

	Retail Price	Dealer Invoice	Fair Price
245/50ZR16 performance tires, Formula	$225	$194	$214
Trans Am	91	78	86
NA with traction control.			
Rear floormats, base and Formula hatchbacks .	15	13	14

Pontiac Grand Am

	Retail Price	Dealer Invoice	Fair Price
SE 2-door notchback	$12904	$11807	$12207
SE 4-door notchback	13004	11899	12299
GT 2-door notchback	14854	13591	13991
GT 4-door notchback	14954	13683	14083
Destination charge	495	495	495

Standard Equipment:

SE: 2.3-liter DOHC 4-cylinder engine, 5-speed manual transmission, anti-lock brakes, driver-side air bag, power steering, cloth reclining front bucket seats, center console with armrest, storage and coin holder, overhead compartment, left remote and right manual mirrors, front door map pockets, AM/FM radio, tinted glass, automatic power locks, remote decklid release, fog lamps, coolant temperature gauge, trip odometer, illuminated entry, visor mirrors, rear seat headrests, floormats, 195/70R14 tires, wheel covers. **GT** adds: air conditioning, tachometer, voltmeter, oil pressure gauge, 6-way power driver's seat, tilt steering wheel, intermittent wipers, rear decklid spoiler, 205/55R16 tires, alloy wheels.

Optional Equipment:

3.1-liter V-6 engine	350	312	315
Requires 4-speed automatic transmission. SE also requires air conditioning and 15- or 16-inch tires.			
3-speed automatic transmission, SE	555	494	505
NA with Group 1SC.			
4-speed automatic transmission	755	672	687
Air conditioning, SE	830	739	755
Option Group 1SB, SE	1575	1402	1433
Air conditioning, cruise control, cassette player, intermittent wipers, rear defroster, tilt steering wheel.			
Option Group 1SC, SE 2-door	2221	1977	1999
SE 4-door..	2286	2035	2057
Group 1SB plus power windows with driver-side express down, power mirrors, split folding rear seat, remote keyless entry.			
Option Group 1SB, GT	597	531	537
Cruise control, cassette player, rear defroster, variable-effort power steering.			

	Retail Price	Dealer Invoice	Fair Price
Option Group 1SC, GT 2-door	$1243	$1106	$1119
GT 4-door	1308	1164	1177

Group 1SB plus power windows with driver-side express down, power mirrors, split folding rear seat, remote keyless entry.

	Retail Price	Dealer Invoice	Fair Price
Sport Interior Group, SE and GT			
with cloth upholstery and Group 1SB	432	384	393
cloth with Group 1SC	282	251	257
with leather upholstery and Group 1SB	907	807	825
leather with Group 1SC	757	674	689

Driver-seat lumbar adjuster, articulated front headrests, 4-way manual seat adjuster, leather-wrapped steering wheel and shift knob, reading and courtesy lamps, sunvisor extensions, split folding rear seat.

	Retail Price	Dealer Invoice	Fair Price
Rally gauge cluster, SE	111	99	101

Includes tachometer, coolant temperature and oil pressure gauges, voltmeter. Requires option group.

	Retail Price	Dealer Invoice	Fair Price
Cruise control	225	200	205
Rear defogger	170	151	155
Power driver's seat	340	303	309
with Sport Interior Group	305	271	278

Requires Group 1SC with SE and GT.

	Retail Price	Dealer Invoice	Fair Price
Power windows with driver-side express			
down, SE and GT with Group 1SB 2-door	275	245	250
4-door	340	303	309
Power sunroof	595	530	536

Requires option group.

	Retail Price	Dealer Invoice	Fair Price
Split folding rear seat	150	134	137
Tilt steering wheel, SE	145	129	132
Intermittent wipers, SE	65	58	59
Remote keyless entry system,			
SE and GT with Group 1SB	135	120	123

Requires power windows.

	Retail Price	Dealer Invoice	Fair Price
Cassette player	140	125	127
Cassette player with equalizer	375	334	341
with option group	235	209	214
CD player with equalizer	580	516	528
with option group	440	392	400
Rear decklid spoiler, SE	110	98	99
Rear decklid spoiler delete,			
GT (credit)	(110)	(98)	(98)
195/65R15 tires, SE	131	117	119
205/55R16 tires, SE	223	198	203
15-inch alloy wheels, SE	259	231	233
16-inch alloy wheels, SE	284	253	256
Engine block heater	18	16	17

Prices are accurate at time of publication; subject to manufacturer's change.

PONTIAC

Pontiac Grand Prix

	Retail Price	Dealer Invoice	Fair Price
SE 4-door notchback	$16634	$15220	$15720
SE 2-door notchback	17384	15906	16406
Destination charge	535	535	535

Standard Equipment:

4-door: 3.1-liter V-6 engine, 4-speed automatic transmission, 4-wheel disc brakes, driver- and passenger-side air bags, power steering, air conditioning, power windows with driver-side express down, automatic power door locks, 45/55 cloth reclining front seat with folding armrest, integrated rear seat headrests, AM/FM radio, Pass-Key theft-deterrent system, tachometer, trip odometer, coolant temperature gauge, tilt steering wheel, left remote and right manual mirrors, tinted glass, intermittent wipers, fog lamps, day/night rearview mirror, door map pockets, 205/70R15 tires, wheel covers. **2-door** adds: cruise control, cloth reclining bucket seats with storage console, cassette player, leather-wrapped steering wheel with radio controls, power mirrors, rear defogger, remote decklid release, visor mirrors, front and rear floormats, 215/60R16 tires, alloy wheels.

Optional Equipment:

Anti-lock brakes	450	401	404
Option Group 1SB, 4-door	742	660	668
Cruise control, rear defogger, power mirrors, cassette player, remote decklid release, visor mirrors.			
Option Group 1SC, 4-door	1937	1724	1743
Group 1SB plus anti-lock brakes, 6-way power driver's seat, leather-wrapped steering wheel with radio controls, remote keyless entry, power antenna, floormats.			
Special Edition Coupe Pkg., 2-door	621	553	559
Front and rear fascias, lower aero skirting, wheel flares, dual exhaust, sport suspension, 225/60R16 performance tires, 16-inch alloy wheels.			
GT Performance Pkg., 4-door with Group 1SB .	2275	2025	2048
with Group 1SC	1825	1624	1643
3.4-liter DOHC V-6 engine, anti-lock brakes, sport suspension, dual exhaust, variable-effort power steering, bucket seats, hood louvers, GT nameplates, 225/60R16 tires, alloy wheels.			
GTP Performance Pkg., 2-door	2256	2008	2030
Special Edition Coupe Pkg. plus 3.4-liter DOHC V-6 engine, anti-lock brakes, variable-effort power steering, hood louvers, GTP nameplates.			
White Special Edition Pkg., 2-door	295	263	266
Decklid spoiler, white 5-spoke alloy wheels, striping. Requires white exterior paint and Special Edition Coupe or GTP Performance Pkg.			
6-way power driver's seat	305	271	274
Cruise control, 4-door	225	200	202

	Retail Price	Dealer Invoice	Fair Price
Remote decklid release, 4-door	$60	$53	$54
Rear defogger, 4-door	170	151	153
Power glass sunroof	646	575	581
Requires custom interior.			
Trip computer	199	177	179
Requires anti-lock brakes. 4-door requires option group.			
Head-up instrument display	250	223	225
Requires anti-lock brakes. 4-door requires option group.			
Remote keyless entry	135	120	121
4-door requires option group and remote decklid release.			
Cassette player, 4-door	195	174	176
Cassette player with equalizer,			
4-door with Group 1SB	325	289	293
4-door with Group 1SB and custom interior	275	245	248
4-door with Group 1SC	150	134	135
2-door	175	156	158
Includes leather-wrapped steering wheel with radio controls (4-door), 8-speaker sound system. 4-door requires option group.			
CD player, 4-door	295	263	266
4-door with option group	100	89	90
2-door	125	111	113
CD player with equalizer,			
4-door with Group 1SB	425	378	383
4-door with Group 1SB and custom interior	375	334	376
4-door with Group 1SC	250	223	225
2-door	275	245	248
Includes leather-wrapped steering wheel with radio controls (4-door), 8-speaker sound system. 4-door requires option group.			
Steering wheel radio controls, 4-door	175	156	157
4-door with custom interior	125	111	112
Requires radio with cassette or CD player and option group.			
Power antenna	85	76	77
Rear decklid spoiler, 2-door	175	156	158
Dual exhausts	90	80	81
4-door requires option group.			
Alloy wheels, 4-door	259	231	233
215/60R16 touring tires, 4-door	112	100	101
Requires alloy wheels.			
Cellular phone provisions	35	31	32

Pontiac Sunfire	Retail Price	Dealer Invoice	Fair Price
SE 2-door notchback	$11074	$10243	—
SE 4-door notchback	11224	10382	—

Prices are accurate at time of publication; subject to manufacturer's change.

PONTIAC

	Retail Price	Dealer Invoice	Fair Price
Destination charge	$485	$485	$485

Fair price not available at time of publication.

Standard Equipment:

SE: 2.2-liter 4-cylinder engine, 5-speed manual transmission, driver- and passenger-side air bags, anti-lock brakes, power steering, cloth reclining front bucket seats, center console, folding rear seat, tinted glass, tachometer, trip odometer, dual exterior mirrors, 195/70R14 tires, wheel covers.

Optional Equipment:

3-speed automatic transmission	495	441	—
Air conditioning	785	699	—
Option Group 1SB	1295	1153	—
Air conditioning, AM/FM cassette player, tilt steering wheel, rear defogger.			
Option Group 1SC	1665	1482	—
Group 1SB plus cruise control, intermittent wipers, Convenience Pkg.			
Option Group 1SD, 2-door	2226	1981	—
4-door	2331	2075	—
Group 1SC plus power mirrors, windows and door locks.			
Convenience Pkg., with Group 1SB	80	71	—
Remote decklid release, trunk net, reading lamps, overhead console.			
Sport Interior Pkg.	80	71	—
Leather seat side bolsters and seatback map pockets, leather-wrapped steering wheel, parking brake handle and shifter. Requires option group 1SC or 1SD.			
Cruise control, with Group 1SB	225	200	—
Rear defogger	170	151	—
Power door locks, 2-door	210	187	—
4-door	250	223	—
Requires option group.			
Power windows, 2-door	265	236	—
4-door	330	294	—
Requires option group and power door locks.			
AM/FM/cassette	195	174	—
AM/FM/cassette with equalizer	230	205	—
with option group	35	31	—
AM/FM/cassette/CD player with equalizer	330	294	—
with option group	135	120	—
Decklid spoiler, 2-door	70	62	—
Tilt steering wheel	145	129	—
Power sunroof, 2-door	556	495	—
Replaces overhead console when ordered with Convenience Pkg. Requires Group 1SC or 1SD.			

	Retail Price	Dealer Invoice	Fair Price
195/65R15 touring tires	$131	$117	—
Alloy wheels	259	231	—
Engine block heater	18	16	—

Pontiac Trans Sport

	Retail Price	Dealer Invoice	Fair Price
SE 4-door van	$17889	$16190	$16690
Destination charge	540	540	540

Standard Equipment:

SE: 3.1-liter V-6 engine, 3-speed automatic transmission, anti-lock brakes, driver-side air bag, power steering, 4-way adjustable driver's seat, front reclining bucket seats, 3-passenger middle seat, cloth upholstery, power windows, tinted glass with solar-control windshield, tachometer, coolant temperature and oil pressure gauges, voltmeter, trip odometer, AM/FM radio, Lamp Group (includes overhead console map lights, rear reading lights, cargo area lights, underhood light), left remote and right manual mirrors, door and seatback pockets, intermittent wipers, fog lamps, rear wiper/washer, black roof paint, visor mirrors, floormats, 205/70R15 tires, wheel covers.

Optional Equipment:

3.8-liter V-6 engine	819	729	734

Includes 4-speed automatic transmission. Requires option group.

Front air conditioning	830	739	744
Front and rear air conditioning with rear heater	1280	1139	1147
with Group 1SC, 1SD, or 1SE	450	401	403

Requires 3.8-liter V-6 engine, 7-passenger seating, deep-tint glass.

Automatic level control, with Group 1SC	200	178	179
with Group 1SD	170	151	152

Includes rear saddle bags. Requires 3.8-liter V-6 engine and 205/70R15 touring tires.

Option Group 1SB	1418	1262	1276

Front air conditioning, cruise control, cassette player, power mirrors, tilt steering wheel.

Option Group 1SC	2513	2255	2262

Group 1SB plus automatic power door locks, power windows with driver-side express down, rear defogger, 7-passenger seating, deep-tint glass.

Option Pkg. 1SD	3093	2771	2784

Group 1SC plus 6-way power driver's seat, remote keyless entry system, roof rack.

Option Pkg. 1SE	4197	3753	3777

Group 1SD plus automatic level control, cassette player with equalizer, overhead console, self-sealing touring tires, alloy wheels.

PONTIAC

	Retail Price	Dealer Invoice	Fair Price
Rear defogger	$170	$151	$152
Deep-tint glass, with Group 1SB	245	218	220
Pop-up glass sunroof, with Group 1SC, 1SD or 1SE	300	267	269
NA with overhead console.			
Roof rack	175	156	157
Includes rear saddle bags.			
Automatic power door locks, with Group 1SB ..	300	267	269
6-way power driver's seat, with Group 1SC	270	240	242
Power windows with driver-side express down, with Group 1SB	275	245	246
Requires automatic power door locks.			
Power sliding side door, with Groups 1SC, 1SD or 1SE	350	312	314
Requires remote keyless entry.			
Remote keyless entry system, with Group 1SC .	135	120	121
Cassette player	140	125	126
NA with Group 1SE.			
Cassette player with equalizer, with Group 1SD	315	280	284
Includes steering wheel radio controls and leather-wrapped steering wheel.			
CD player with equalizer, with Group 1SD	541	481	485
with Group 1SE	206	183	185
Includes steering wheel radio controls and leather-wrapped steering wheel.			
Overhead console, with Group 1SC or 1SD	175	156	157
Requires remote keyless entry. NA with sunroof.			
7-passenger seating	705	627	632
with leather upholstery	870	774	780
Three second row and two third row modular seats, cargo area net. Leather upholstery requires Group 1SD or 1SE.			
Integral child seat	125	111	112
Requires 7-passenger seating.			
Two integral child seats	225	200	202
Requires 7-passenger seating.			
Traction control, with Group 1SC, 1SD or 1SE .	350	312	314
Requires 3.8-liter V-6 engine.			
Trailer towing provisions, with Group 1SC, 1SD or 1SE	150	134	135
Includes wiring harness and heavy duty cooling. Requires 3.8-liter V-6 engine and automatic level control.			
2-tone paint	125	111	112
Requires 205/70R15 touring tires and alloy wheels.			

CONSUMER GUIDE®

SAAB

Saab 900

	Retail Price	Dealer Invoice	Fair Price
S 3-door hatchback	$23695	$20970	—
S 5-door hatchback	23375	20687	—
S 2-door convertible	32995	29201	—
SE 3-door hatchback	28990	25656	—
SE 5-door hatchback	28680	25381	—
SE 2-door convertible	39520	34383	—
SE 2-door convertible, V-6	40070	34850	—
Destination charge	470	470	470

Convertible dealer invoice and fair prices not available at time of publication.

Standard Equipment:

S: 2.3-liter 4-cylinder engine, 5-speed manual transmission, anti-lock 4-wheel disc brakes, driver- and passenger-side air bags, front seatbelt pretensioners, daytime running lights, power steering, air conditioning, cruise control, power door and trunk locks, theft alarm system, power windows, automatic power antenna, power top and boot cover (convertible), telescopic steering wheel, front fog lamps, rear fog lamp, heated power mirrors, rear defogger, intermittent wipers, solar-control tinted glass, AM/FM cassette, trip computer, cellular phone pre-wiring (hatchbacks), CD changer pre-wiring, cloth (hatchbacks) or leather (convertible) heated reclining front bucket seats, folding rear seat, front console with storage, removable cup and coin holder, headlamp wipers/washers, rear wiper/washer (hatchbacks), tachometer, analog clock, front spoiler, front and rear stabilizer bars (hatchbacks), tool kit, bodyside moldings, floormats, 195/60VR15 tires, full wheel covers (hatchbacks) or alloy wheels (convertible). **SE 3-door and convertible** add: 2.0-liter turbocharged 4-cylinder engine, leather upholstery (3-door), power front seats, automatic air conditioning, power glass sunroof (3-door), premium sound system, CD changer (convertible), Saab Car Computer, sport suspension, 205/50ZR16 tires, alloy wheels (3-door). **SE 5-door and V-6 convertible** add: 2.5-liter V-6, traction control, 195/60VR15 tires.

Optional Equipment:

4-speed automatic transmission	995	843	—
NA SE 3-door.			
Power glass sunroof, S hatchbacks	995	843	—
Alloy wheels, S hatchbacks	380	322	—

SAAB

Saab 9000

	Retail Price	Dealer Invoice	Fair Price
CS 5-door hatchback	$29845	$26338	—
CSE Turbo 5-door hatchback	36510	31581	—
CSE V-6 5-door hatchback	38650	33433	—
CDE 4-door notchback	38995	33731	—
Aero 5-door notchback	41300	35105	—
Destination charge	470	470	470

Fair price not available at time of publication.

Standard Equipment:

CS: 2.3-liter turbocharged 4-cylinder engine, 5-speed manual transmission, anti-lock 4-wheel disc brakes, driver- and passenger-side air bags, daytime running lights, power steering, automatic climate control, removable AM/FM cassette player, cruise control, telescopic steering wheel, cloth reclining heated bucket seats, folding rear seat, power door locks and windows, anti-theft alarm system, dual heated power mirrors, automatic power antenna, remote decklid release, tachometer, trip odometer, intermittent wipers, headlamp wipers/washers, rear wiper/washer, solar-control tinted glass, dual visor mirrors, rear defogger, locking center console with storage, overhead console with swivel map light, front and rear fog lamps, courtesy lights, dual rear reading lights, lighted visor mirrors, front spoiler, analog clock, floormats, 195/65TR15 tires, alloy wheels. **CSE Turbo** adds: 200-horsepower 2.3-liter turbocharged engine with intercooler, turbo boost gauge, power glass sunroof, power front seats with driver-side memory, leather upholstery, leather-wrapped steering wheel and shift boot cover, Saab Car Computer with digital clock, Harmon/Kardon audio system with CD player, 195/65VR15 tires. **CSE V-6** adds to CSE: 3.0-liter V-6 engine, 4-speed automatic transmission, traction control. **CDE** deletes rear fog lamp, adds to CSE V-6: wood interior trim, rear seat pass-through, 205/60ZR15 tires. **Aero** deletes traction control and adds: 225-horsepower 2.3-liter turbocharged 4-cylinder engine, 5-speed manual or 4-speed automatic transmission, aerodynamic body trim, sport suspension, rear spoiler, 205/55ZR16 tires.

Optional Equipment:

4-speed automatic transmission, CS,		
CSE Turbo,	1045	885	—
Power glass sunroof,		
CS	1115	945	—
Leather Pkg., CS	1335	1131	—
Leather upholstery, leather-wrapped steering wheel and shift boot cover.		
Traction control,		
Aero	450	383	—

SATURN

Saturn SC1/SC2	Retail Price	Dealer Invoice	Fair Price
SC1 2-door notchback, 5-speed	$11895	$10349	—
SC1 2-door notchback, automatic	12715	11062	—
SC2 2-door notchback, 5-speed	12995	11306	—
SC2 2-door notchback, automatic	13815	12019	—
Destination charge	360	360	360

Fair price not available at time of publication.

Standard Equipment:

SC1: 1.9-liter 4-cylinder engine, 5-speed manual or 4-speed automatic transmission, driver- and passenger-side air bags, power steering, cloth reclining front bucket seats, 60/40 folding rear seatback, coolant temperature gauge, tachometer, trip odometer, tilt steering column, tinted glass, intermittent wipers, rear defogger, AM/FM radio, remote fuel door and deck-lid releases, door pockets, digital clock, right visor mirror, front and rear consoles, dual remote outside mirrors, color-keyed bumpers, wheel covers, 175/70R14 tires. **SC2** adds: 1.9-liter DOHC engine, variable-assist power steering, driver's seat height and lumbar support adjustments, sport suspension, upgraded upholstery, leather-wrapped steering wheel, retractable headlamps, 195/60R15 tires.

Optional Equipment:

Anti-lock brakes, with manual transmission	725	631	—
with automatic transmission	780	679	—
Includes traction control (with automatic transmission), rear disc brakes.			
Air conditioning	905	787	—
Option Pkg. 1, SC1	1680	1462	—
Air conditioning, cruise control, power windows and door locks, power right outside mirror.			
Option Pkg. 2, SC2	1885	1640	—
Option Pkg. 1 plus teardrop alloy wheels.			
Power sunroof	675	587	—
Cassette player	200	174	—
Cassette player with equalizer	365	318	—
12-disc CD changer	—	—	—
Coaxial speakers	75	65	—
Cruise control	250	218	—
Fog lights	155	135	—
Leather upholstery, SC2	675	587	—
Rear spoiler	180	157	—

Prices are accurate at time of publication; subject to manufacturer's change.

SATURN

	Retail Price	Dealer Invoice	Fair Price
Sawtooth alloy wheels, SC1	$405	$352	—
Includes 195/60R15 tires.			
Teardrop alloy wheels, SC2	205	178	—

Saturn Sedan/Wagon

	Retail Price	Dealer Invoice	Fair Price
SL 4-door notchback, 5-speed	$9995	$8696	—
SL1 4-door notchback, 5-speed	10995	9566	—
SL1 4-door notchback, automatic	11815	10279	—
SL2 4-door notchback, 5-speed	11995	10436	—
SL2 4-door notchback, automatic	12815	11149	—
SW1 5-door wagon, 5-speed	11695	10175	—
SW1 5-door wagon, automatic	12515	10888	—
SW2 5-door wagon, 5-speed	12695	11045	—
SW2 5-door wagon, automatic	13515	11758	—
Destination charge	360	360	360

Fair price not available at time of publication.

Standard Equipment:

SL: 1.9-liter 4-cylinder engine, 5-speed manual transmission, driver- and passenger-side air bags, cloth reclining front bucket seats, 60/40 folding rear seatback, tachometer, coolant temperature gauge, trip odometer, tilt steering column, tinted glass, intermittent wipers, rear defogger, AM/FM radio, remote fuel door and decklid releases, door pockets, digital clock, right visor mirror, front console, child-safety rear door locks, wheel covers, 175/70R14 tires. **SL1** adds: 5-speed manual or 4-speed automatic transmission, power steering, dual outside mirrors, upgraded interior trim. **SL2** adds: 1.9-liter DOHC engine, variable-assist power steering, driver's seat height and lumbar support adjustments, sport suspension, upgraded upholstery, color-keyed bumpers, 195/60R15 tires. **SW1** adds to SL1: rear wiper/washer, cargo area net. **SW2** adds to SW1: 1.9-liter DOHC engine, variable-assist power steering, color-keyed bumpers, driver's seat height and lumbar support adjustments, sport suspension, upgraded upholstery, 195/60R15 tires.

Optional Equipment:

Anti-lock brakes, with manual transmission	725	631	—
with automatic transmission	780	679	—
Includes traction control (with automatic transmission), rear disc brakes.			
Air conditioning	905	787	—
Option Pkg. 1, SL1, SW1, SW2	1805	1570	—
Air conditioning, cruise control, power windows and door locks, power right outside mirror.			

	Retail Price	Dealer Invoice	Fair Price
Option Pkg. 2, SL2	$2110	$1836	—
Option Pkg. 1 plus sawtooth alloy wheels.			
Power sunroof, SL1, SL2	675	587	—
Cassette player	200	174	—
Cassette player with equalizer	365	318	—
12-disc CD changer, notchbacks	—	—	—
Coaxial speakers	75	65	—
Power door locks	250	218	—
NA on SL.			
Cruise control	250	218	—
NA on SL.			
Right outside mirror, SL	35	30	—
Fog lamps, SL2, SW2	155	135	—
Leather upholstery, SL2, SW2	675	587	—
Rear spoiler, SL2	180	157	—
Sawtooth alloy wheels, SL2, SW2	305	265	—

SUBARU

Subaru Impreza	Retail Price	Dealer Invoice	Fair Price
Base 2-door notchback	$11850	$11061	$11461
Base 4-door notchback	11850	11061	11461
L 2-door notchback	13750	12565	12965
L 4-door notchback	13750	12565	12965
L AWD 5-door Sport Wagon	15150	13728	14128
Outback AWD 5-door Sport Wagon	15750	14271	14671
LX AWD 2-door notchback	17295	15658	16058
LX AWD 4-door notchback	16995	15385	15785
LX AWD 5-door Sport Wagon	17395	15747	16147
Destination charge	475	475	475

Prices are for vehicles distributed by Subaru of America. Prices may be higher in areas served by independent distributors.

Standard Equipment:

Base: 1.8-liter 4-cylinder engine, 5-speed manual transmission, driver- and passenger-side air bags, power steering, reclining front bucket seats, rear defogger, dual manual outside mirrors, tinted glass, tilt steering column, intermittent wipers, cup holders, center console, remote fuel door release, 165/80R13 tires. **L** adds: air conditioning, power mirrors, split folding rear seat, remote trunk release (notchbacks), tachometer, AM/FM/cassette, digital clock, 175/70HR14 tires (wagon). **Outback** adds: roof rack, splash

SUBARU

guards, upgraded cloth interior, cargo mat, two-tone paint, striping, 185/70HR14 white letter tires. **LX** adds to L: 2.2-liter 4-cylinder engine, 4-speed automatic transmission, anti-lock 4-wheel disc brakes, power windows and door locks, decklid spoiler (notchbacks), roof spoiler (wagon), cruise control, upgraded cloth interior, trunk/cargo area light, power antenna, map lights, rear stablizer bar, 195/60HR15 tires.

Optional Equipment:	Retail Price	Dealer Invoice	Fair Price
4-speed automatic transmission, L 2WD	$800	$716	$720
2.2-liter 4-cylinder engine, L, Outback	1000	895	920
Includes 4-speed automatic transmission, rear stabilizer bar, decklid spoiler (notchbacks), 195/60HR15 tires. Requires all-wheel drive.			
All-wheel drive, Base, L notchbacks	1000	801	900
Includes 175/70HR14 tires with L.			
Active safety Group, L 2-door	1800	1517	1620
L 4-door	1500	1249	1350
L wagon	500	448	474
All-wheel drive, anti-lock brakes with rear discs, cruise control.			

Subaru Legacy	Retail Price	Dealer Invoice	Fair Price
4-door notchback $14364		$13271	$13771
Brighton 5-door wagon, AWD	15999	14905	15405
L 4-door notchback	16620	15062	15562
L 5-door wagon	17320	15680	16180
Outback 5-door wagon, AWD	19820	17760	18260
LS 4-door notchback, AWD	21120	18907	19407
LS 5-door wagon, AWD	21820	19525	20025
LSi 4-door notchback, AWD	23620	21130	21630
LSi 5-door wagon, AWD	24320	21748	22248
Destination charge	475	475	475

Prices are for vehicles distributed by Subaru of America. Prices may be higher in areas served by independent distributors.

Standard Equipment:

Base: 2.2-liter 4-cylinder engine, 5-speed manual transmission, driver- and passenger-side air bags, cloth reclining front bucket seats, console with storage, variable-assist power steering, tilt steering column, tinted glass, rear defogger, remote fuel door and decklid releases, child safety rear door locks, 185/70SR14 all-season tires, wheel covers. **Brighton** adds: full-time all-wheel drive, air conditioning, AM/FM/cassette. **L** adds to base: air conditioning, split folding rear seat, rear headrests, tachometer, power windows and door locks, power mirrors, 4-speaker AM/FM/cassette, digital clock, right visor mirror. **Wagon** deletes rear headrests and adds: rear wiper/washer, power tailgate lock, cargo area divided storage box, cargo cover. **Outback** adds to L wagon: full-time all-wheel drive, anti-lock 4-wheel disc brakes, cruise control, roof rack, fog lights, 2-tone paint, upgraded cloth interior, cargo hooks, cargo area power outlet, 195/60HR15 all-season tires, alloy wheels. **LS** adds to L: 4-speed automatic transmission, full-time all-wheel drive, anti-lock 4-wheel disc brakes, manual 4-way adjustable driver's seat, velour upholstery, cruise control, power moonroof with sunshade, power antenna, variable intermittent wipers, leather-wrapped steering wheel, shift knob and parking brake handle, folding rear center armrest (notchback), color-keyed bodyside moldings, lighted visor mirrors, 195/60HR15 all-season tires, alloy wheels. **Wagon** adds: rear headrests. **LSi** adds: 6-speaker compact disc player, leather upholstery, security system.

Optional Equipment:

	Retail Price	Dealer Invoice	Fair Price
4-speed automatic transmission, Brighton, L, Outback	$800	$715	$720
All-wheel drive, L	1000	748	900
Moonroof Group, L	1300	1157	1170
Power moonroof with sunshade, cruise control, power antenna. Requires automatic transmission. NA with Active Safety Group.			
Active Safety Group, L notchback	1500	1335	1400
L wagon	1500	1342	1400
L with AWD	1500	1190	1300
Anti-lock brakes (includes rear disc brakes), traction control or all-wheel drive, cruise control. Notchbacks and front-wheel drive wagon require automatic transmission. NA with Moonroof Group.			
Metallic paint	NC	NC	NC

SUZUKI

Suzuki Sidekick	Retail Price	Dealer Invoice	Fair Price
JS 2WD 2-door conv., 5-speed	$11699	$10997	$11197
JS 2WD 2-door conv., 5-speed (Massachusetts and California)	11999	11279	11479
JS 2WD 2-door conv., automatic	12299	11561	11761
JS 2WD 2-door conv., automatic (Massachusetts and California)	12599	11843	12043
JX 4WD 2-door conv., 5-speed	13499	12419	12619
JX 4WD 2-door conv., automatic	14099	12971	13171
JS 2WD 5-door, 5-speed	13499	12284	12684
JS 2WD 5-door, automatic	14609	13294	13694
JX 4WD 5-door, 5-speed	14809	13180	13580

Prices are accurate at time of publication; subject to manufacturer's change.

SUZUKI

	Retail Price	Dealer Invoice	Fair Price
JX 4WD 5-door, automatic	$15759	$14025	$14425
JLX 4WD 5-door, 5-speed	16319	14524	14924
JLX 4WD 5-door, automatic	17269	15369	15769
Destination charge, 2-door	345	345	345
5-door	370	370	370

Standard Equipment:

JS 2-door: 1.6-liter 4-cylinder engine, 5-speed manual or 3-speed automatic transmission, rear-wheel drive, anti-lock rear brakes, cloth reclining front bucket seats and folding rear seat, center console, tilt steering column, front door map pockets, fuel tank skid plate, folding canvas top, tinted glass, dual outside mirrors, intermittent wipers, security alarm, trip odometer, carpeting, 195/75R15 tires. **JX 2-door** adds: part-time 4WD, automatic locking front hubs, 2-speed transfer case, power steering, power mirrors, tachometer, 205/75R15 tires. **JS 5-door** adds to JS 2-door: 5-speed manual or 4-speed automatic transmission, power steering, power mirrors, rear defogger, child-safety rear door locks, carpeting, locking fuel door, AM/FM cassette, split folding rear seat, tachometer. **JX 5-door** adds to JX 2-door: 5-speed manual or 4-speed automatic transmission, sport steering wheel, split folding rear seat, AM/FM cassette, map lights. **JLX 5-door** adds: power windows and door locks, cruise control, rear wiper/washer, remote fuel door release, deluxe upholstery, locking spare tire case, 205/75R15 outline white letter mud and snow tires, alloy wheels.

Options are available as dealer-installed accessories.

Suzuki Swift	Retail Price	Dealer Invoice	Fair Price
3-door hatchback, 5-speed	$8699	$8003	—
3-door hatchback, 5-speed w/anti-lock brakes	9259	8518	—
3-door hatchback, automatic	9349	8601	—
3-door hatchback, automatic w/anti-lock brakes	9909	9116	—
Destination charge	330	330	330

Fair price not available at time of publication.

Standard Equipment:

1.3-liter 4-cylinder engine, 5-speed manual or 3-speed automatic transmission, driver- and passenger-side air bags, cloth reclining front bucket seats, folding rear seat, tinted glass, intermittent wipers, rear defogger, trip odometer, front console, dual outside mirrors, wheel covers, 155/80R13 tires. ABS-equipped models add four-wheel anti-lock brakes.

Options are available as dealer-installed accessories.

TOYOTA

Toyota Avalon	Retail Price	Dealer Invoice	Fair Price
XL 4-door notchback, front bucket seats	$22758	$19730	—
XL 4-door notchback, front bench seat	23548	20416	—
XLS 4-door notchback	26688	22866	—
Destination charge	385	385	385

Fair price not available at time of publication. Prices are for vehicles distributed by Toyota Motor Sales, U.S.A., Inc. The dealer invoice, fair price, and destination charge may be higher in areas served by independent distributors.

Standard Equipment:

XL: 3.0-liter DOHC V-6 engine, 4-speed automatic transmission, 4-wheel disc brakes, driver- and passenger-side air bags, power steering, air conditioning, cruise control, cloth 6-way adjustable front bucket seats or power split bench seat with storage armrest, rear headrests, AM/FM cassette, power windows and door locks, power mirrors, tinted glass, tilt steering column, auto-off headlamps, rear defogger, front door pockets, cup holders, 205/65HR15 all-season tires, full-size spare tire. **XLS** adds: anti-lock brakes, automatic temperature control, 7-way power driver-side bucket seat, premium cassette player with six speakers and equalizer, theft-deterrent system, remote keyless entry, illuminated entry, variable intermittent wipers, leather-wrapped steering wheel and shift knob, alloy wheels.

Optional Equipment:

Anti-lock brakes, XL	950	779	—
Theft-deterrent system, XL	200	170	—
Includes remote keyless entry.			
Leather Trim Pkg., XL with bucket seats	1810	1487	—
XL with bench seat	1030	824	—
XLS	975	780	—
Leather seat and simulated leather door trim. XL adds leather-wrapped steering wheel and shift knob. XL requries alloy wheels.			
7-way power driver's seat,			
XL with bucket seats	780	663	—
Power moonroof, XL	970	776	—
XLS	950	760	—
Includes map light.			
Premium cassette player, XL	240	180	—
Includes six speakers and equalizer.			
Premium cassette player and CD changer, XL ..	1425	1069	—

TOYOTA

	Retail Price	Dealer Invoice	Fair Price
Diamond white pearlescent paint	$190	$161	—
Includes bronze-tint glass.			
Mud guards	50	40	—
Alloy wheels, XL	420	336	—

Toyota Camry

	Retail Price	Dealer Invoice	Fair Price
DX 2-door notchback, 5-speed	$16128	$14147	$14628
DX 2-door notchback, automatic	16928	14849	15428
LE 2-door notchback, automatic	19268	16705	17768
LE V-6 2-door notchback, automatic	21588	18717	20088
SE V-6 2-door notchback, automatic	23208	20121	21708
DX 4-door notchback, 5-speed	16418	14401	14918
DX 4-door notchback, automatic	17218	15103	15718
LE 4-door notchback, automatic	19558	16956	18058
LE 5-door wagon, automatic	20968	18179	19468
XLE 4-door notchback, automatic	21618	18742	20118
SE V-6 4-door notchback, automatic	23498	20372	21998
LE V-6 4-door notchback, automatic	21878	18967	20378
LE V-6 5-door wagon, automatic	23308	20208	21808
XLE V-6 4-door notchback, automatic	24398	21152	22898
Destination charge	385	385	385

Prices are for vehicles distributed by Toyota Motor Sales, U.S.A., Inc. The dealer invoice, fair price, and destination charge may be higher in areas served by independent distributors.

Standard Equipment:

DX: 2.2-liter DOHC 4-cylinder engine, 5-speed manual or 4-speed automatic transmission, driver- and passenger-side air bags, power steering, tachometer, coolant temperature gauge, trip odometer, cloth reclining front bucket seats, split folding rear seat with armrest, remote fuel door and trunk releases, rear defogger, dual remote outside mirrors, front door pockets, tilt steering column, cup holders, auto-off headlamps, intermittent wipers, AM/FM radio, tinted glass, 195/70HR14 all-season tires. **LE** adds: 2.2-liter DOHC 4-cylinder or 3.0-liter DOHC V-6 engine, 4-speed automatic transmission, 6-way manual driver's seat, air conditioning, cruise control, power windows, door locks, and mirrors, cassette player, power antenna, upgraded interior trim, cargo cover (wagon), rear wiper (wagon), door courtesy lights (2-door), 205/65HR15 all-season tires (V-6). **SE** adds to DX: 3.0-liter DOHC V-6 engine, 4-speed automatic transmission, air conditioning, cruise control, cassette player, power antenna, power windows, door locks, and mirrors, sport suspension, rear spoiler, leather-wrapped steering wheel, shift knob, and parking brake handle, passenger-side visor mirror, illuminated entry, 205/65VR15 all-season tires, alloy wheels. **XLE** adds to LE: anti-lock brakes, 7-way power driver's seat, illuminated entry, lighted visor mirrors, variable intermittent wipers, alloy wheels. V-6 models have 4-wheel disc brakes.

Optional Equipment:

	Retail Price	Dealer Invoice	Fair Price
Anti-lock brakes, 4-cylinder models	$1100	$902	$1045
Includes rear disc brakes.			
LE V-6, SE V-6	950	779	903
Air conditioning, DX	975	780	926
Power Pkg., DX 4-door	740	592	703
DX 2-door	645	516	613
Power windows, door locks, and mirrors, courtesy lamp (2-door).			
Power driver's seat, LE 2-door	230	184	219
Folding third seat, 4-cylinder wagon	465	375	442
V-6 wagon	315	252	299
Includes cargo area cover.			
Leather Trim Pkg., LE 2-door	1260	1008	1197
XLE	1250	1000	1188
SE	975	780	926
Leather seat and door trim, power driver's seat (LE 2-door), power passenger seat (XLE), leather-wrapped steering wheel (LE 2-door, XLE), adjustable headrest, leather-wrapped parking brake handle (4-cylinder models).			
Cruise control, DX	265	212	252
Power moonroof	970	776	922
Includes map lights and sunshade. NA DX.			
Cassette player, DX	220	165	209
Premium AM/FM/cassette	240	180	228
NA DX.			
Premium cassette player and CD changer	1155	866	1097
NA DX.			
Mud guards	50	40	48
Alloy wheels, LE	400	320	380
LE V-6	420	336	399

Toyota Celica

	Retail Price	Dealer Invoice	Fair Price
ST 2-door notchback, 5-speed	$16888	$14727	$15327
ST 2-door notchback, automatic	17688	15425	16025
GT 2-door notchback, 5-speed	19288	16722	17322
GT 2-door notchback, automatic	20088	17416	18016
ST 3-door hatchback, 5-speed	17238	15032	15632
ST 3-door hatchback, automatic	18038	15730	16330
GT 3-door hatchback, 5-speed	19778	17147	17747

TOYOTA

	Retail Price	Dealer Invoice	Fair Price
GT 3-door hatchback, automatic	$20578	$17840	$18440
GT 2-door convertible, 5-speed	23998	21046	21646
GT 2-door convertible, automatic	24798	21740	22340
Destination charge	385	385	385

Prices are for vehicles distributed by Toyota Motor Sales, U.S.A., Inc. The dealer invoice, fair price, and destination charge may be higher in areas served by independent distributors.

Standard Equipment:

ST: 1.8-liter DOHC 4-cylinder engine, 5-speed manual or 4-speed automatic transmission, driver- and passenger-side air bags, power steering, cloth 4-way adjustable front sport seats, center console with armrest, split folding rear seat, dual cup holders, digital clock, rear defogger, remote fuel door and trunk/hatch releases, map lights, coolant temperature gauge, tachometer, trip odometer, intermittent wipers, auto-off headlamps, tinted glass, dual outside mirrors, AM/FM radio with four speakers, visor mirrors, cargo area cover (hatchback), 185/70R14 all-season tires, wheel covers. **GT** adds: 2.2-liter DOHC 4-cylinder engine, 4-wheel disc brakes, AM/FM cassette with six speakers, power antenna, power windows and door locks, tilt steering column, intermittent rear wiper (hatchback), upgraded door and interior trim, engine oil cooler (5-speed), 205/55VR15 all-season tires. **Convertible** adds: power top, glass rear window.

Optional Equipment:

Anti-lock brakes	825	676	784
Requires cruise control.			
Air conditioning	975	780	926
Power Pkg., ST	510	408	485
Power windows and door locks. Requires cruise control.			
Leather Trim Pkg., GT notchback and convertible	1045	836	993
Leather sport seats, leather-wrapped steering wheel and manual shift knob, leather door trim.			
Sport Pkg., GT 3-door hatchback	905	724	860
Cloth sport seats, leather-wrapped steering wheel and manual shift knob, front sport suspension, alloy wheels. Requires cruise control.			
Sport Pkg. w/leather, GT 3-door hatchback	1565	1252	1487
Adds Leather Pkg. seats to Sport Pkg. Requires cruise control.			
Rear spoiler, hatchbacks	375	300	356
ST requires intermittent rear wiper.			
Intermittent rear wiper, ST hatchback	155	127	147
Tilt steering column, ST	155	133	147
Power sunroof	740	592	703

	Retail Price	Dealer Invoice	Fair Price
Cruise control	$265	$212	$252
Cassette player, ST	220	165	209
Premium cassette player, GT			
notchback, hatchback	200	149	190
convertible	150	112	135
Includes graphic equalizer and six speakers.			
Cassette and CD player, GT			
notchback, hatchback	1255	941	1192
convertible	1205	904	1145
Includes graphic equalizer and eight speakers.			
Alloy wheels, GT	420	336	399

Toyota Corolla	Retail Price	Dealer Invoice	Fair Price
4-door notchback, 5-speed	$12378	$11236	$11736
4-door notchback, automatic	12878	11690	12190
DX 4-door notchback, 5-speed	13488	11829	12329
DX 4-door notchback, automatic	14288	12531	13031
LE 4-door notchback, automatic	16678	14578	15078
DX 5-door wagon, 5-speed	14618	12821	13321
DX 5-door wagon, automatic	15418	13524	14024
Destination charge	385	385	385

Prices are for vehicles distributed by Toyota Motor Sales, U.S.A., Inc. The dealer invoice, fair price, and destination charge may be higher in areas served by independent distributors.

Standard Equipment:

1.6-liter DOHC 4-cylinder engine, 5-speed manual or 3-speed automatic transmission, driver- and passenger-side air bags, cloth reclining front bucket seats, console with storage, coolant temperature gauge, trip odometer, remote decklid and fuel door releases, auto-off headlights, cup holders, color-keyed bumpers, wheel covers, tinted glass, 175/65R14 all-season tires. **DX** adds: 1.8-liter DOHC 4-cylinder engine, 5-speed manual or 4-speed automatic transmission, power steering, passenger visor mirror, cloth door trim with map pockets, full cloth seats with headrests, rear seat headrests, 60/40 split folding rear seat, dual remote mirrors, bodyside moldings, rear luggage lamp, digital clock, intermittent wipers, rear defogger, rear cargo cover and power hatch lock (wagon), 185/65R14 all-season tires. **LE** adds: 4-speed automatic transmission, air conditioning, power windows and door locks, cruise control, 4-way adjustable driver's seat, power mirrors, dual visor mirrors, tachometer, variable intermittent wipers, AM/FM radio with four speakers, tilt steering column, All Weather Guard Pkg.

Prices are accurate at time of publication; subject to manufacturer's change.

TOYOTA

Optional Equipment:	Retail Price	Dealer Invoice	Fair Price
Anti-lock brakes	$825	$676	$743
Air conditioning, base and DX	920	736	828
Power steering, base	260	222	234
Alloy wheels, LE	400	320	360
Value Pkg., base	847	762	803
Air conditioning, power steering, floormats.			
Value Pkg., DX 4-door	1667	1500	1584
wagon	1512	1361	1436
Air conditioning, tilt steering column (4-door), Power Pkg., deluxe AM/FM cassette player with four speakers, floormats.			
Value Pkg., LE	1692	1523	1607
Anti-lock brakes, sunroof, deluxe AM/FM cassette player with four speakers, alloy wheels, floormats.			
Convenience Pkg., base	1180	958	1062
Includes power steering, air conditioning.			
Tilt steering column, DX	155	133	140
Power sunroof, DX 4-door, LE	580	464	522
Includes map light.			
Rear wiper, wagon	175	143	158
Radio Prep Pkg., base and DX	100	75	90
Includes two speakers, wiring harness, antenna.			
AM/FM radio with four speakers, base and DX	385	289	347
AM/FM cassette with four speakers, base and DX	605	454	545
LE	220	165	198
Power Pkg., DX	620	496	558
Power windows and door locks.			
Tachometer, DX with 5-speed	65	52	59
Cruise control, DX	265	212	239
Includes variable intermittent wipers.			
All Weather Guard Pkg., base, 5-speed	235	191	212
base, automatic	245	199	221
DX	65	55	59
Heavy duty rear defogger, battery, heater and wiper motor, 4.5-liter windshield washer tank. Base with automatic includes rear defogger with timer.			
Rear window defogger, base	170	136	153
Mudguards, DX and LE	50	40	48

Toyota Previa	Retail Price	Dealer Invoice	Fair Price
DX 2WD	$22318	$19463	$20163
DX S/C 2WD	22818	19899	20599

	Retail Price	Dealer Invoice	Fair Price
LE 2WD	$26578	$23042	$23742
LE S/C 2WD	27078	23476	24176
DX All-Trac	25648	22237	22937
DX S/C All-Trac	26148	22670	23370
LE All-Trac	29718	25765	26465
LE S/C All-Trac	30218	26198	26898
Destination charge	385	385	385

Prices are for vehicles distributed by Toyota Motor Sales, U.S.A., Inc. The dealer invoice, fair price, and destination charge may be higher in areas served by independent distributors.

Standard Equipment:

DX: 2.4-liter DOHC 4-cylinder engine, 4-speed automatic transmission, driver- and passenger-side air bags, power steering, tilt steering column, cloth reclining front bucket seats, console with storage, 2-passenger center seat, 3-passenger split-folding rear seat, AM/FM radio, rear defogger, variable intermittent wipers, rear intermittent wiper/washer, auto-off headlamps, tinted glass, digital clock, dual outside mirrors, tilt-out rear quarter windows, wheel covers, 215/65R15 all-season tires, full-size spare tire. **LE** adds: dual air conditioners, 4-wheel disc brakes, cruise control, power windows and door locks, power mirrors, cassette player, upgraded upholstery and interior trim, passenger-side lighted visor mirror. **All-Trac** adds: permanently engaged 4-wheel drive. **S/C** adds: 2.4-liter supercharged 4-cylinder engine.

Optional Equipment:

Anti-lock brakes, DX	1100	899	1000
LE	950	779	865
DX includes 4-wheel disc brakes and requires Value Pkg. 1.			
Dual air conditioners, DX	1685	1348	1517
Value Pkg. 1, DX	1425	1282	1318
LE	385	346	356
Air conditioning (DX), cruise control (DX), Power Pkg. (DX), cassette player (DX), privacy glass (LE), anti-lock brakes (LE).			
Value Pkg. 2, LE	625	562	578
Pkg. 1 plus captain's chairs.			
Value Pkg. 3, LE	1125	1012	1041
Pkg. 1 plus leather captain's chairs.			
Power Pkg., DX	745	596	671
Power windows and door locks, power mirrors.			
Privacy glass, LE	385	308	347
Cruise control, DX	275	220	248
Cassette player, DX 2WD	220	165	198
DX All-Trac	170	127	149

Prices are accurate at time of publication; subject to manufacturer's change.

TOYOTA

	Retail Price	Dealer Invoice	Fair Price
Premium cassette player, LE 2WD	$270	$202	$243
LE All-Trac	435	326	381
Includes seven speakers and programmable equalizer. Requires Value Pkg. 1, 2, or 3.			
Premium cassette and CD players, LE 2WD	1225	919	1072
LE All-Trac	1275	956	1116
Includes nine speakers and programmable equalizer. Requires Value Pkg. 1, 2, or 3.			
Dual moonroofs, LE 2WD	1550	1240	1395
Includes sunshade and rear spoiler.			
Captain's chairs with armrests, LE	790	632	711
Leather Trim Package, LE	1790	1432	1611
Security Pkg., DX	945	756	851
LE	200	160	180
Anti-theft system, Power Pkg. (DX).			
Alloy wheels, LE	420	336	378

Toyota Tercel

	Retail Price	Dealer Invoice	Fair Price
Standard 2-door notchback, 4-speed	$9998	$9329	—
Standard 2-door notchback, automatic	10698	9983	—
DX 2-door notchback, 5-speed	11028	10123	—
DX 2-door notchback, automatic	11738	10775	—
DX 4-door notchback, 5-speed	11328	10398	—
DX 4-door notchback, automatic	12038	11050	—
Destination charge	385	385	385

Fair price not available at time of publication. Prices are for vehicles distributed by Toyota Motor Sales, U.S.A., Inc. The dealer invoice, fair price, and destination charge may be higher in areas served by independent distributors.

Standard Equipment:

Standard: 1.5-liter 4-cylinder engine, 4-speed manual or 3-speed automatic transmission, driver- and passenger-side air bags, vinyl reclining front bucket seats, coolant temperature gauge, left outside mirror, center console, color-keyed grille, 155/80SR13 tires. **DX** adds: 5-speed manual or 4-speed automatic transmission, cloth reclining seats, cloth door trim, dual outside mirrors, trip odometer, tinted glass, cup holders, full wheel covers.

Optional Equipment:

Anti-lock brakes	825	676	—
Air conditioning	900	720	—
Rear defogger	170	144	—
Power steering, DX	260	222	—

	Retail Price	Dealer Invoice	Fair Price
Power Pkg., DX 4-door	$620	$496	—
Power windows and door locks.			
Value Equipment Pkg., DX 2-door	1260	1033	—
Air conditioning, power steering, AM/FM radio with two speakers.			
Convenience Pkg., DX	330	264	—
Intermittent wipers, digital clock, remote mirrors, 60/40 folding rear seatback, remote fuel door and decklid releases.			
AM/FM radio with two speakers	240	180	—
with four speakers, DX	385	289	—
AM/FM/cassette with four speakers, DX	605	454	—
All Weather Guard Pkg.	235	201	—
Heavy duty battery, heater, starter, and rear defogger.			
Color-keyed bumpers, DX	85	68	—

Toyota 4Runner

	Retail Price	Dealer Invoice	Fair Price
2WD 5-door wagon, V-6, automatic	$21748	$18744	$19344
4WD 5-door wagon, 5-speed	21098	18291	18891
4WD 5-door wagon, V-6, 5-speed	23148	19951	20551
4WD 5-door wagon, V-6, automatic	24198	20855	21455
Destination charge	385	385	385

Prices are for vehicles distributed by Toyota Motor Sales, U.S.A., Inc. The dealer invoice, fair price, and destination charge may be higher in areas served by independent distributors.

Standard Equipment:

2.4-liter 4-cylinder engine, 5-speed manual transmission, 4WDemand part-time 4WD (4WD models), power steering, cloth reclining front bucket seats with center console, split folding rear seat, tachometer, coolant temperature and oil pressure gauges, voltmeter, trip odometer, remote fuel door release, dual outside mirrors, tinted glass, power tailgate window, rear wiper/washer, digital clock, front and rear mudguards, 225/75R15 all-season tires. **V-6** models add: 3.0-liter V-6, 5-speed manual or 4-speed automatic transmission, anti-lock rear brakes, variable intermittent wipers, rear defogger, AM/FM radio, tilt steering column, passenger-side visor mirror.

Optional Equipment:

Anti-lock rear brakes, 4-cylinder	300	255	278
4-wheel anti-lock brakes, V-6	660	541	601
Includes auto-off headlights.			
Air conditioning	955	764	860
Tilt steering column, 4-cylinder	215	183	199
Includes variable intermittent wipers.			

Prices are accurate at time of publication; subject to manufacturer's change.

TOYOTA

	Retail Price	Dealer Invoice	Fair Price
Rear heater	$160	$128	$144
Value Pkg. 1, 4-cylinder	2043	1839	1890
V-6	1438	1294	1330

Air conditioning, Chrome Pkg., courtesy lights, Power Pkg., cruise control, variable intermittent wipers (4-cylinder), leather-wrapped steering wheel (4-cylinder), AM/FM/cassette, 4-speaker system (4-cylinder), floormats.

Value Pkg. 2, 4WD V-6	2283	2055	2112
2WD V-6	1908	1717	1765

Pkg 1 plus alloy wheels, modified rear bumper, 31-inch tires (4WD).

Limited Pkg., 4WD V-6	3588	3229	3319

Value Pkg. 2 plus Leather Trim Pkg., Limited badging, monogrammed floormats.

Chrome Pkg.	245	196	221

Chrome grille, bumpers, and trim.

Cruise Control	375	300	338

Includes variable intermittent wipers (4-cylinder), ignition key and glovebox lights, headlights-on warning buzzer (V-6). Requires Power Pkg. and tilt steering wheel.

Power Pkg.	790	632	711

Power windows and door locks, chrome power mirrors. Requires Chrome Pkg. and either cruise control, alloy wheels with 31-inch tires or Leather Trim Pkg.

Sports Pkg.	450	360	405

7-way adjustable cloth sport seats, rear privacy glass. Requires Chrome Pkg., Value Pkg. 1 or 2, or alloy wheels with 31-inch tires.

Leather Trim Pkg., 4WD V-6	1680	1344	1512

Leather upholstery, privacy glass, leather-wrapped steering wheel, courtesy lights, cruise control, variable intermittent wipers (4-cylinder). Requires Power Pkg.

All Weather Guard Pkg.,			
4-cylinder	235	191	213
V-6	65	55	60

Rear defogger (4-cylinder), heavy duty battery (V-6), wiper motor, and heavy duty starter motor, distributor cover.

Bronze rear privacy glass	NC	NC	NC
Power moonroof, V-6	810	648	729
AM/FM/cassette, 4-cylinder	605	454	545
V-6	320	245	288

V-6 includes power antenna.

Premium cassette player, V-6	560	420	504

Includes power antenna, diversity antenna, six speakers.

Cassette and CD players, V-6	1475	1106	1291

Includes power antenna, diversity antenna, six speakers.

	Retail Price	Dealer Invoice	Fair Price
Alloy wheels and 31-inch tires, 4WD V-6	$1090	$872	$981
Includes Chrome Pkg.			
Alloy wheels, V-6	470	376	423
Requires Chrome Pkg. or Value Pkg. 1.			
Metallic paint	NC	NC	NC

VOLKSWAGEN

Volkswagen Cabrio	Retail Price	Dealer Invoice	Fair Price
2-door convertible	$19975	$18161	—
Destination charge	390	390	390

Fair price not available at time of publication.

Standard Equipment:

2.0-liter 4-cylinder engine, 5-speed manual transmission, anti-lock brakes, driver- and passenger-side air bags, power steering, cloth reclining front sport seats with driver's side height adjustment, folding rear seat, anti-theft alarm, central locking system with illuminated key, tinted glass, cruise control, tilt steering column, digital clock, trip odometer, tachometer, coolant temperature gauge, service indicator, power windows, console, cupholders, leather shift boot and parking brake handle, front door storage pockets, driver- and passenger-side lighted visor mirrors, AM/FM/cassette with theft deterrent system, glass rear window with defogger, variable-speed intermittent wipers, body-color power mirrors, body-color grille and bumpers, black rocker panel and bumper bottom extensions, integral roll bar, manual folding top, bodyside moldings, 195/60HR14 all-season tires, full wheel covers.

Optional Equipment:

4-speed automatic transmission	875	856	—
Air conditioning	850	742	—
CD changer	495	412	—
Metallic paint	175	153	—
Leather seats	1275	1113	—
7-spoke alloy wheels with wheel locks	585	511	—

Volkswagen Golf/Jetta	Retail Price	Dealer Invoice	Fair Price
Golf 5-door hatchback	$12500	$11941	$12441
Golf GL 5-door hatchback	14200	13096	13596
Golf Sport 3-door hatchback	15250	14050	14550
Golf GTI VR6 3-door hatchback	18875	17458	17958

Prices are accurate at time of publication; subject to manufacturer's change.

VOLKSWAGEN

	Retail Price	Dealer Invoice	Fair Price
Jetta 4-door notchback	$13475	$12850	$13350
Jetta GL 4-door notchback	15675	14207	14707
Jetta GLS 4-door notchback	17025	15413	15913
Jetta GLX 4-door notchback	19975	18441	18941
Destination charge	390	390	390

Standard Equipment:

Golf: 2.0-liter 4-cylinder engine, 5-speed manual transmission, driver- and passenger-side air bags, power steering, cloth reclining bucket seats, driver's seat height adjustment, 60/40 split folding rear seat, anti-theft alarm, central power locking system with remote hatch and fuel door releases, tachometer, coolant temperature gauge, trip odometer, digital clock, center console with storage, cup holders, daytime running lights, dual manual remote mirrors, tinted glass, variable intermittent wipers, heated headlight washers, rear defogger and wiper/washer, front door map pockets, passenger-side visor mirror, color-keyed bumpers, grille and bodyside molding, front and rear spoilers, front floormats, 185/60HR14 all-season tires, full wheel covers. **Golf GL** adds: 8-speaker AM/FM/cassette, air conditioning. **Golf Sport** adds: cloth sport seats, fog lights, color-keyed mirrors, black roof-mounted antenna and rocker panel molding, power glass sunroof, dark-tinted tail light lenses, 195/60HR14 all-season tires, 7-spoke alloy wheels. **Golf GTI VR6** adds: 2.8-liter V-6 engine, close-ratio 5-speed manual transmission, anti-lock 4-wheel disc brakes, sport suspension, traction control, power windows and mirrors, cruise control, trip computer, leather-wrapped steering wheel, shift knob and parking brake handle, heated front seats, 215/50HR15 tires, lattice-style alloy wheels. **Jetta** adds to Golf: air conditioning, cruise control, heated power mirrors, tilt steering column, rear center armrest, lighted visor mirrors. Deletes rear wiper/washer and spoiler. **Jetta GL** adds: 8-speaker AM/FM/cassette with theft-deterrent system. **Jetta GLS** adds: power windows, rear reading lights, heated front seats, height adjustable front passenger seat, adjustable front seat lumbar supports, power glass sunroof, folding rear armrest, color-keyed mirrors, 7-spoke alloy wheels. **Jetta GLX** deletes front seat lumbar supports and adds: 2.8-liter V-6 engine, close-ratio 5-speed manual transmission, anti-lock 4-wheel disc brakes, sport suspension, traction control, sport seats with leather trim, leather-wrapped steering wheel, shift knob and parking brake handle, heated front door locks, fog lamps, trip computer, brake wear indicator, rear spoiler, black roof-mounted antenna and rocker panel molding, 215/50HR15 tires, lattice-style alloy wheels.

Optional Equipment:

4-speed automatic transmission	875	856	866
NA with base Golf, base Jetta, GTI.			
Leather upholstery, Jetta GLX	800	698	720

	Retail Price	Dealer Invoice	Fair Price
Anti-lock brakes, Golf Sport, Jetta GL and GLS	$775	$727	$751
Power glass sunroof, GL models	585	511	527
Downgraded cassette player, GL models (credit)	(125)	(105)	(105)
CD changer	495	412	446
NA with base Golf, base Jetta. NA with downgraded cassette player.			
Clearcoat metallic paint	175	153	158
NA with base Golf, base Jetta.			

Volkswagen Passat

	Retail Price	Dealer Invoice	Fair Price
GLX 4-door notchback	$20890	$18801	—
GLX 5-door wagon	21320	19185	—
Destination charge	390	390	390

Fair price not available at time of publication.

Standard Equipment:

2.8-liter V-6 engine, 5-speed manual transmission, anti-lock 4-wheel disc brakes, driver- and passenger-side air bags, air conditioning, traction control, power steering, power windows and locks, heated power mirrors, cruise control, 8-speaker AM/FM cassette with theft-deterrent system, remote fuel door release, power decklid release (4-door), leather-wrapped steering wheel, shift knob and parking brake handle, rear reading lights, child-safety rear door locks, cloth reclining front bucket seats with adjusable height, thigh and lumbar supports, 60/40 folding rear seatback, rear armrest, center storage console, tachometer, coolant temperature gauge, trip odometer, digital clock, trip computer, interior pollen filter, rear defogger, tinted glass, variable-speed intermittent wipers, front door and seatback pockets, tilt steering column, lighted visor mirrors, color-keyed bumpers and bodyside moldings, fog lamps, rear spoiler (4-door), alarm system, 215/50HR15 all-season tires, 8-spoke alloy wheels. **Wagon** adds cargo cover, rear wiper/washer, remote tailgate release, black roof rails.

Optional Equipment:

4-speed automatic transmission	800	777	—
Leather upholstery	850	742	—
6-disc CD changer	495	412	—
Power glass sunroof	850	742	—
All-Weather Package	300	262	—

Includes heated front seats and windshield washer nozzles. Requires leather upholstery.

VOLVO

Volvo 850	Retail Price	Dealer Invoice	Fair Price
4-door notchback, 5-speed	$24680	$22480	—
4-door notchback, automatic	25580	23380	—
5-door wagon, 5-speed	25980	23780	—
5-door wagon, automatic	26880	24680	—
GLT 4-door notchback, 5-speed	27110	24710	—
GLT 4-door notchback, automatic	28010	25610	—
GLT 5-door wagon, 5-speed	28410	26010	—
GLT 5-door wagon, automatic	29310	26910	—
Turbo 4-door notchback, automatic	31045	28095	—
Turbo 5-door wagon, automatic	32345	29395	—
Destination charge	460	460	460

Fair price not available at time of publication.

Standard Equipment:

Base: 2.4-liter DOHC 5-cylinder engine, 5-speed manual or 4-speed automatic transmission, driver- and passenger-side air bags, seat-belt tensioners, anti-lock 4-wheel disc brakes, air conditioning, power steering, tilt/telescoping steering wheel, tinted glass, rear-window defroster, digital clock, intermittent wipers, cloth reclining front bucket seats, fold-down rear seat with armrest, integrated child booster seat (wagon), power windows and door locks, heated power mirrors, cruise control, AM/FM/cassette with anti-theft circuitry, power antenna (4-doors), integrated window antenna (wagons), heated front seats, daytime running lights, 195/60R15 tires. **GLT** adds: power glass sunroof, remote entry/security system, cargo net (wagons), 24-spoke alloy wheels. **Turbo** adds: turbocharged 2.3-liter 5-cylinder engine, 4-speed automatic transmission, side air bags, automatic climate control, 8-way power driver's seat with 3-position driver's seat memory, Alpine AM/FM/cassette with anti-theft circuitry, wood instrument panel trim, trip computer, rear head restraints, leather-wrapped steering wheel, leather upholstery, 205/50ZR16 tires, 5-spoke alloy wheels.

Optional Equipment:

Side air bags, base, GLT	500	500	—
Traction control	385	305	—
Grand Lux Pkg., base	1145	915	—

Power memory driver's seat, remote keyless entry system, 24-spoke alloy wheels.

	Retail Price	Dealer Invoice	Fair Price
Touring Pkg., GLT	$650	$520	—
Automatic climate control, trip computer, leather-wrapped steering wheel.			
Traction Control and Cold Weather Pkg.	750	600	—
Traction control, heated front seats, headlamp wiper/washer, ambient temperature gauge.			
Cold Weather Pkg.	450	360	—
Heated front seats, headlamp wiper/washer, ambient temperature gauge.			
Leather upholstery, base, GLT	995	795	—
Power driver's seat, base, GLT	495	395	—
Power front passenger seat, GLT, Turbo	495	395	—
Decklid spoiler, notchbacks	325	260	—
Trip computer, GLT	275	220	—
Automatic climate control, base, GLT	350	280	—
Sport suspension, notchbacks	150	120	—
Wood instrument panel trim, base, GLT	600	480	—
24-spoke alloy wheels, base	400	320	—
195/60R15 all-season tires, Turbo	NC	NC	NC
Includes 6-spoke alloy wheels.			

Volvo 940/960

	Retail Price	Dealer Invoice	Fair Price
940 4-door notchback	$23360	$22160	—
940 5-door wagon	24460	23460	—
940 Turbo 4-door notchback	24360	23160	—
940 Turbo 5-door wagon	25660	24460	—
960 4-door notchback	29900	27700	—
960 5-door wagon	31200	29000	—
Destination charge	460	460	460

Fair price not available at time of publication.

Standard Equipment:

940: 2.3-liter 4-cylinder engine, 4-speed automatic transmission, anti-lock 4-wheel disc brakes, automatic locking differential, power steering, driver- and passenger-side air bags, cloth reclining front bucket seats, integrated child booster seat (wagon), air conditioning, power windows and locks, cruise control, power mirrors, 6-speaker AM/FM/cassette, power antenna (4-door), integrated window antenna (wagon), clock, tachometer, coolant temperature gauge, trip odometer, tinted glass, rear defogger, intermittent wipers, daytime running lights, remote decklid release, wheel covers, 185/65R15 tires. **940 Turbo** adds: 2.3-liter turbocharged engine, upgraded AM/FM/cassette, 195/65VR15 tires, 10-spoke alloy wheels. **960** adds to 940: 2.9-liter 6-cylinder engine, 4-speed automatic transmission, rear self-

VOLVO

leveling shock absorbers and stabilizer bar, power driver's seat with 3-position memory, power front passenger seat, power glass sunroof, automatic climate control, upgraded AM/FM/cassette, remote keyless entry and alarm system, leather upholstery, leather-wrapped tilt steering wheel, headlight wiper/washers, front fog lamps, 195/65HR15 tires (wagon), 205/55VR16 tires (notchback), alloy wheels.

Optional Equipment:	Retail Price	Dealer Invoice	Fair Price
Power driver's seat, 940	$610	$395	—
CD changer, 960	750	485	—
Leather upholstery, 940	1225	795	—
Cold Weather Pkg., 960	350	225	—
940	435	280	—
Heated front seats, heated power mirrors (940), ambient temperature gauge.			
Roof rails, wagons	300	195	—
Power sunroof, 940	980	635	—
15-inch 20-spoke alloy wheels, 940	495	320	—
15-inch 10-spoke alloy wheels, 940	495	320	—